www.wadsworth.com

www.wadsworth.com is the World Wide Web site
for Wadsworth and is your direct source to dozens
of online resources.

At *www.wadsworth.com* you can find out about
supplements, demonstration software, and student
resources. You can also send email to many of our
authors and preview new publications and exciting
new technologies.

www.wadsworth.com
Changing the way the world learns®

From the Wadsworth Series in Speech Communication

Communication Between Cultures

Fifth Edition

Larry A. Samovar
San Diego State University

Richard E. Porter
California State University, Long Beach, Emeritus

THOMSON
WADSWORTH

Australia • Canada • Mexico • Singapore • Spain
United Kingdom • United States

THOMSON

WADSWORTH

™

Publisher: Holly J. Allen
Editor: Annie Mitchell
Assistant Editor: Breanna Gilbert
Technology Project Manager: Jeanette Wiseman
Marketing Manager: Kimberly Russell
Marketing Assistant: Alanna Kelly
Advertising Project Manager: Shemika Britt
Project Manager, Editorial Production:
  Cathy Linberg
Print/Media Buyer: Doreen Suruki
Permissions Editor: Sommy Ko

Production Service: Graphic World
  Publishing Services
Text Designer: Ellen Petengell
Photo Researcher: Roberta Broyer
Copyeditor: Mike O'Neal
Cover Designer: Roy Neuhaus
Cover Image: © José Ortega/SIS
Compositor: Graphic World, Inc.
Printer: Webcom
Photo Credits: 1: © Thomas Nebbia/Woodfin Camp Associates;
  137: © George Roger/Magnum Photos, Inc.; **201:** © ABBAS/
  Magnum Photos, Inc.; **279:** © Gloria Thomas.

Printed in Canada
2 3 4 5 6 7 07 06 05 04

For more information about our products, contact us at:
Thomson Learning Academic Resource Center
1-800-423-0563
For permission to use material from this text, contact us by:
Phone: 1-800-730-2214   **Fax:** 1-800-730-2215
Web: http://www.thomsonrights.com

Library of Congress Control Number: 2003105187

Student Edition ISBN: 0-534-56929-3

Instructor's Edition ISBN: 0-534-56931-5

Wadsworth/Thomson Learning
10 Davis Drive
Belmont, CA 94002-3098
USA

Asia
Thomson Learning
5 Shenton Way #01-01
UIC Building
Singapore 068808

Australia/New Zealand
Thomson Learning
102 Dodds Street
Southbank, Victoria 3006
Australia

Canada
Nelson
1120 Birchmount Road
Toronto, Ontario M1K 5G4
Canada

Europe/Middle East/Africa
Thomson Learning
High Holborn House
50/51 Bedford Row
London WC1R 4LR
United Kingdom

Latin America
Thomson Learning
Seneca, 53
Colonia Polanco
11560 Mexico D.F.
Mexico

Spain/Portugal
Paraninfo
Calle/Magallanes, 25
28015 Madrid, Spain

Contents

PREFACE

We approached the occasion of a fifth edition with three very different responses: gratification, excitement, and caution. Our pride and egos were delighted that our previous efforts were successful enough to warrant this new edition. We were also excited over the prospects of tinkering with what we had done in the four earlier editions. We knew we had to be prudent when advancing additional perspectives and material so that we did not abandon the orientation that contributed to the popularity of the earlier editions. We believe that in this new edition we have been able to balance the past, present, and future of intercultural communication. We have retained the core of the field, added current thinking and research, and staked out some new territory.

This book is still about the unique relationship between communication and culture. More specifically, it is about what happens when people from different cultures come together to share ideas, feelings, and information. Because communication and culture work in tandem, we have tried to incorporate the basic principles from both topics throughout this book.

This text is intended for those whose professional or private life is likely to include encounters with people from cultures or co-cultures different from their own. We, therefore, deal with both communication among international cultures and communication among co-cultures in the United States.

RATIONALE

Worldwide interest in intercultural communication grows out of two assumptions. First, you live in an age when changes in technology, travel, economic and political systems, immigration patterns, and population density have created a world in which you increasingly interact with people from different cultures. And whether you like it or not, those interactions will continue to grow in both frequency and intensity. Huston Smith said much the same thing when he wrote: "When historians look back on our century they may remember it most, not for space travel or the release of nuclear energy, but as the time when the peoples of the world first came to take one another seriously."[1]

---

[1]Huston Smith, *The World's Religions* (New York: HarperCollins, 1991), 7.

Second, people now know that culture affects communication in subtle and profound ways. Your cultural backgrounds and experiences help determine how the world looks to you and how you interact in that world.

APPROACH

Fundamental to our approach to intercultural communication is the belief that all forms of human communication involve action. Put in slightly different terms, communication is an activity that affects you as well as other people. Whether you are generating or receiving words or movements, you are creating and producing action. Any study of communication, therefore, must include information about the choices that you make in selecting your messages, as well as a discussion of the consequences of those choices. Hence, this book takes the view that engaging in intercultural communication is pragmatic, philosophical, and ethical. We have attempted throughout to translate ideas and concepts into practices that can improve your communication and help you attain your communication goals. We also continue to remind you in each chapter about the consequences of your choices.

PHILOSOPHY

A dual philosophy has guided us in the preparation of this book. First, it is to the advantage of all six and a half billion of us who share the planet to improve our interpersonal and intercultural communication abilities. The world has grown so small that we all depend on each other now. What happens in one place in the world affects other places. Second, most of the obstacles to understanding can be overcome with motivation, knowledge, and appreciation of cultural diversity. We hope to supply you with all three.

Culture and communication, we have come to believe, involve personal matters, and we have therefore developed our own philosophy about intercultural interaction that can be summarized by the notion that the First Commandment of any civilized society must be: Let people be different. At times, as you read this book, you will observe that we have openly stated our own positions, and we make no apologies for them. We have also made a conscious effort to keep our own ethnocentrism in check, but for those instances in which it has accidentally emerged, we apologize.

ORGANIZATION

We have organized the book in manageable increments that build on one another. What you learn in one chapter, you will carry into the next. The book is divided into four interrelated parts. Part 1 introduces you to the study of communication and culture. In Chapter 1 we point out the importance of intercultural communication and its link to human communication. Chapter 2 examines culture and how it shapes and modifies your view of reality and alters your perceptions. In this chapter we also identify some specific cultural patterns that are reflected during human interaction. In Chapter 3, we consider the sources of those perceptions, behaviors, and patterns by looking at cultural differences in world view, family experiences, and history.

Part 2 puts the theory of intercultural communication into practice. Chapters 4 and 5 explore differences between verbal and nonverbal messages and how those differences can impact the intercultural encounter.

The goal of Part 3 is to demonstrate how diversity is acted out in three specific settings: The business (Chapter 6), educational (Chapter 7), and health care (Chapter 8) settings.

In Part 4, we extend what you have learned throughout the preceding chapters by converting knowledge into action. In Chapter 9, we present a discussion of some potential problems that can plague any intercultural exchange. In Chapter 10, we offer guidelines for improvement, advance an intercultural ethic, and conclude with statements regarding the future of intercultural communication.

NEW FEATURES

The fifth edition of *Communication Between Cultures* brings a number of significant changes and new features. Our addition of new content has been guided by the excellent feedback provided by our readers and reviewers. We have, of course, infused a great deal of current material that reflects our own interpretation and vision of the field of intercultural communication. Although some of the new features will be obvious to users of the fourth edition, many other changes are less visible. Let us mention a few of the alterations from both categories.

- One of the major new additions to the fifth edition is a chapter on intercultural competence—Chapter 10. Reviewing the work of others, and infusing our own views into this chapter, we present material that is intended to improve the manner in which you interact with members of cultures different than your own. This chapter contains new material on interpersonal and intercultural conflict, listening, empathy, and cultural adaptation.
- In Chapter 2, in addition to updating the traditional cultural taxonomies advanced by Kluckhohn, Hall, and Hofstede, we have included some new taxonomies that will assist you in examining the values and cultural patterns found in most cultures.
- Based on our strong belief that culture should be at the core of any study of human interaction, we have greatly expanded three important sections to our discussion of the deep structure of culture. First, cultural identity, while treated throughout the book, is developed in much more detail in this new edition. Second, because of the events of September 11, 2001, and the lack of understanding regarding the Islamic faith, we have significantly expanded out discussion of Islam in Chapter 3.
- Due to the increased racial tensions in the United States and abroad, we have expanded a number of sections of the book that deal with racism, stereotyping, prejudice, discrimination, and ethnocentrism.
- In addition to adding new material to the fifth edition, we have expanded numerous portions of the book. For example, new material has been added to our critique of culture shock, ethics, social perception, the future of intercultural communication, cultural adaptation, the role of world view in health care, intercultural management, and the social contexts in which intercultural communication occurs.
- This edition also offers an increased focus on the role of co-cultures in North America. As with prior editions, we have integrated fresh examples throughout the book. We have also added hundreds of new references to this current volume.

ACKNOWLEDGMENTS

No book is the sole domain of the authors. Many people contributed to this new edition, and we would like to thank them. We begin by thanking our publisher, Wadsworth Publishing Company. In this day of fads and short-lived friendships, we greatly appreciate an association that spans thirty-three years and includes sixteen books. The staff and editors at Wadsworth and Graphic World have offered us support, sound advice, and the freedom to advance new ideas. We especially acknowledge the editorial production direction provided by Cathy Linberg and Mike Ederer.

We thank Connie Ruzich of Robert Morris College in Pittsburgh, Pennsylvania, for writing the InfoTrac College Edition questions that appear at the end of each chapter.

We are grateful to our manuscript reviewers for their many helpful suggestions:

Carlos Galvan Aleman, James Madison University

Rex L. Crawley, Robert Morris University

Laura E. Drake, University of Maryland

Jane Elvins, University of Colorado, Boulder

Antonio C. La Pastina, Texas A&M University

Richard L. Wiseman, California State University, Fullerton

Finally, we express our appreciation to the thousands of students who have read past editions. They have allowed us to "talk to them" about intercultural communication and, by finding something useful in our exchange, have justified yet another edition of *Communication Between Cultures*.

Larry A. Samovar

Richard E. Porter

part 1
Communication and Culture

chapter 1

The Challenge of Intercultural Communication: Interaction in a Diverse World

Human beings draw close to one another by their common nature, but habits and customs keep them apart.

CONFUCIUS

All people have the right to be equal and the equal right to be different.

SHIMON PEREZ

I have made a ceaseless effort not to ridicule, not to bewail, not to scorn human actions, but to understand them.

SPINOZA

THE CHALLENGE OF INTERCULTURAL COMMUNICATION

You are about to embark on an important and challenging venture. Important because you now live in an age when all the inhabitants of earth are interconnected. The undertaking is challenging because learning to understand people whose background is different from your own is not an easy assignment. That challenge, put in slightly different terms, is to become an effective and successful intercultural communicator as you interact with neighbors who might speak a "strange" language or a business partner who stops and prays in the middle of a meeting. For you to be successful in both these interactions, and the thousands of others you will face in this new world, you must be able to communicate with people whose entire backgrounds, whose very way of viewing the world and doing things, may be completely different from yours. In short, functioning in this new world means that you understand the theories, principles, and dynamics of intercultural communication.

Intercultural communication is the circumstance in which people from diverse cultural backgrounds interact with one another. You rightly might wonder what is significant or unique about this kind of interaction. The answer is found in the sometimes extreme cultural diversity of backgrounds, experiences, and assumptions resident in communicators. Cultural diversity has the potential to make intercultural communication very difficult—and in some instances utterly impossible.

The crucial element in this form of communication is culture and the impact it has on your communicative behavior. Culture strongly influences your beliefs, values, and world views; it is reflected in your use of language, your nonverbal behavior, and how you relate to others. It shapes your relationships with your family and friends; it teaches you how to raise your children, and provides you with prescriptions for forms of communication appropriate to a variety of social situations. As you can see, culture is elaborate, multidimensional, and quite pervasive; it constitutes a complete pattern of living. Various aspects of cultural influence are acted out each time members of different cultures come together to share ideas and information. In Chapter 2, we will consider culture in depth and show you how it impacts the intercultural communication process.

Intercultural communication, as you might suspect, is not a new human endeavor. Since the dim beginnings of civilization when the first humans formed tribal groups, intercultural contact occurred whenever people from one tribe encountered others and discovered that they were different. Later, as civilization developed, traders, religious missionaries, and invading warriors all encountered alien people different from themselves. Alien differences have long been recognized, but in the absence of accompanying cultural knowledge, this recognition most often elicited the human propensity to respond malevolently to those differences. This reaction to aliens—to those who are physically or socially different—was well expressed over two thousand years ago by the Greek playwright Aeschylus, who wrote, "Everyone is quick to blame the alien." This penchant to blame the alien is still a powerful element in today's social and political rhetoric. For instance, it is not uncommon in the United States and elsewhere to hear charges that immigrants are responsible for all of the perceived social and economic problems affecting society.

From a historical perspective, successful intercultural communication has been the exception rather than the rule. The history of humankind details an ongoing antipathy and hostility toward those who are different. The twentieth century, for instance, suffered two world wars and witnessed the introduction and use of chemical, biological, and nuclear weapons with the potential to destroy humankind. The world also endured the Holocaust and various smaller-scale conflicts such as those in Korea, Vietnam, Kuwait, Iraq, Chechnya, and Afghanistan. Now, the world is faced with the aftermath of the destruction of the World Trade Center in New York City and the ensuing war on terrorism. In addition, there are numerous ongoing religious, ethnic, and tribal clashes that seem beyond resolution. The on-going clash between primarily Hindu India and predominately Muslim Pakistan over Kashmir, which occasionally leads them to the brink of nuclear war, is a case in point. In Indonesia, one of the most populous countries in the world, a bomb goes off outside a Bali disco and a new wave of ethnic violence engulfs the country.

The world, people, and societies are always in a state of change. This ongoing process continually produces new sets of social dynamics with which you must deal. Intercultural communication is about that change—changes in the world's fabric of social relationships that challenge us to keep pace with the changing world order. These changes at both the international and domestic levels have brought us into direct and indirect contact with people who, because of their cultural diversity, often behave in ways that we do not understand. With or without our consent, the last four decades have thrust us into social and professional situations with people who often appear alien, exotic, and perhaps even wondrous. These people may live thousands of miles away or right next door.

Reduced air fares make the tourist industry one of the largest producers of revenue in the world.

This book, in many respects, is about those changes and the challenges they present. In this chapter, we explore these changes. Many of you will be able to verify the examples we offer to document these alterations in intercultural contact, for some of you have had firsthand experiences with people whose cultures are different from your own.

Our rationale for looking at these changes is threefold. First, as the familiar gives way to a new and different world, the entire human race is affected. Second, many of the events that have brought diverse groups together have been too subtle to detect and have taken place over a long period. Hence, we believe that many of them may have been overlooked. Finally, by learning about these changes, you will learn to understand the role and impact of culture on communication and rise to meet the intercultural communication challenges posed in the twenty-first century. We begin our inquiry by examining the places and circumstances under which you may find yourself engaging in communication with people from diverse cultural backgrounds.

INTERCULTURAL CONTACT

Your intercultural interaction will have two distinct points of contact: *international* and *domestic*. International contacts are those between people from different countries and cultures. Cultural differences between Chinese and Israelis, for instance, are easy to discern. It is also at the international level that perhaps the greatest cultural diversity will be found. Imagine, if you will, the vast diversity in backgrounds and experiences between an Aleut villager of northeastern Canada and a Tutsi villager living in Uganda. Try to imagine how this diversity leads to different perceptions of the world, different ideas about how people ought to lead and live their lives, and what constitutes effective and appropriate communicative behavior.

Also, it is important for you to understand that within each culture there are numerous co-cultures and specialized cultures. These provide the opportunity for domestic points of intercultural contact. In this situation we are referring to communication between people of diverse cultural backgrounds that live within an overarching societal group. This includes communication involving such diverse co-cultures as African Americans, Asian Americans, Native Americans, and Latinos as well as women, gays and lesbians, and the disabled. We will investigate domestic contacts in greater depth later in this chapter.

International Interaction

Because of international contacts, it is becoming obvious that a symbiotic relationship ties all people together. No nation, group, or culture can remain aloof or autonomous. If you touch one part of the world, you touch all parts. Three international developments have made intercultural contact more axiomatic and pervasive: (1) *new technology and information systems*, (2) *changes in the world's population*, and (3) *rapid movement toward a global economy*.

New Technology and Information Systems

Technology, while giving you the obvious "toys" such as handheld computers and cell phones that transmit pictures, has also accelerated intercultural contact. This contact has been spurred on by developments in two areas: *transportation systems* and *information systems*. You can now board a plane and fly anywhere in the world in a matter of hours. You can now attend a breakfast meeting in San Francisco and a dinner conference in Paris on the same day. Reduced airfares now make the tourist industry one of the largest producers of revenue in the world. One result of these expanded travel opportunities is that you may routinely encounter cultures that sometimes seem bizarre or even mysterious. Sources of diversity now go far beyond eating utensils, traditional attire, and modes of travel. You can be exposed to cultural idiosyncrasies in the perception of time and space, the treatment of women and the elderly, the ways and means of conducting business, and even the discovery and meaning of truth.

Other developments in transportation technology are on the horizon—developments that will further increase cultural contact. Aerospace companies such as Boeing have experimental vehicles designed to power themselves vertically into Earth's orbit and then return to land in another part of the world. This means that travel time measured in hours today may soon be measured in minutes: Instead of taking twelve or more hours to fly from Boston to Beijing, you may be able to do so in ninety minutes. With this increased level of mobility, you will surely encounter new cultures at a greater rate than before.

New and advanced information systems continue to encourage and facilitate cultural interaction. Communication satellites, sophisticated television transmission equipment, and fiber-optic or wireless connection systems permit people throughout the world to share information and ideas instantaneously. The growth in wireless

For the first time in history, people are beginning to realize that population growth is a serious problem.

© Gloria Thomas

telephone systems, for example, is expanding rapidly with well over fifty thousand new subscribers each day. And, of course, the impact of Internet on communication exchanges is phenomenal. You can now, with the simple click of mouse, "talk" to anyone almost anywhere in the world. It has also permitted what Microsoft's Bill Gates has referred to as "the ability to conduct business at the speed of thought."

Evolving Populations

The second impetus to international communication is a rapid increase in and redistribution of the world's population. The world's population increases at a rate of approximately 85 million every year. In 2000, the world population was estimated to be 6.1 billion with projections of it reaching 9.3 billion by 2050.[1]

Not only is the world's population growing rapidly, it is also on the move. As many as 100 million people are living outside the country of their birth, and millions more latter-generation immigrants maintain their ethnic identities. Noncitizens now typically constitute more than 5 percent of the population in industrialized societies.

It should not surprise you that with increases in the world's population, numerous problems have arisen that make successful international contact more important than ever before. Let us touch on some of the problems.

Finite Natural Resources. The world must come to realize that the resources necessary to life and survival are finite. For instance, over the next half century, it is predicted that water, our most precious natural resource, will replace oil as the prime trigger for international conflict. Swomley believes that

> A worldwide water crisis looming on the horizon is expected to reach dire proportions within the next ten to thirty years. . . . It takes 1,000 tons of water to raise one ton of grain. At this rate, the 2.4 billion people projected to be added to the world's population over the next thirty years would require a quantity of water equal to twenty Nile Rivers or ninety-seven Colorado Rivers.[2]

Some Middle Eastern countries as well as parts of Asia and Africa are already experiencing water shortages and threats of water wars. These conflicts may be an early sign of the approaching water crisis.[3]

Water is just one of many resources that is being affected by a massive growth in the world's population. A decrease in food sources, both from the ground and the sea, is another example of how limited resources can produce intercultural friction. Shortages of productive land to grow crops and disputes over fishing rights have generated serious armed clashes. And, of course, there is the human cost of these shortages. For example, the United Nations estimates that each year over forty thousand children die of malnutrition.

Negotiating the limits on natural resources and avoiding strife and disorder are among the goals of intercultural communication. When we consider that well over a billion people worldwide lack sufficient food to meet energy and protein requirements for a productive and healthy life, it is easy to see how food insecurities could pit nation against nation. Finite natural resources provide yet another reason for people to come together for international understanding.

The Environment. Environmental problems do not observe geographic or cultural boundaries and thus affect all cultures. Hence, the importance of a healthy environment to the well-being of all people provides yet another important reason to develop facility as an intercultural communicator. From China to Central America, weather-related flooding events have resulted from deforestation that left many hillsides bare, causing rainfall to run quickly into rivers rather than being absorbed, thus leading to devastating landslides and floods. In addition, as Schmidt has suggested, an African drought may be partly responsible for a decline in Caribbean Sea coral because of coral-damaging fungi found in the dust blown across the ocean.[4]

Although nations are beginning to realize that they must work together to solve environmental problems, progress is slow and serious problems numerous. The environmental crisis produces a long and somber list of problems that touch all cultures. Destruction of the rain forests, famine, the pollution of air and water, the growing list of endangered plants and animals, toxic dumping, and the greenhouse effect are just a few of the many conundrums we all face as we try to balance population and the health of the planet.

Yet while almost everyone agrees that dire problems are looming on the horizon, few want to be the first to relinquish their living standards. Nature, however, may in the long run have the upper hand. Recent predictions, for instance, suggest that the western portion of the United States may soon face a severe water shortage because global warming could result in more rain and less snow, causing a depletion of the snowpacks that provide water during the hot, rainless summer months.

International Conflict. Conflict among nations and peoples provides yet another reason to encourage effective intercultural communication. A recent *Time* magazine reports that more than twenty-seven armed conflicts are taking place around the world.[5] Additionally, Mattern emphasizes the seriousness of the potential for conflict when he reports that "the year 2000 began with over 30,000 nuclear weapons stockpiled around the world."[6] But, Specter and Robbins spell out the most devastating news:

> Simply stated, nuclear, biological, and chemical weapons of mass destruction pose the greatest single threat to the United States and the world. Some twenty-five nations today have such weapons. North Korea has developed long-range missiles that could reach Alaska and Hawaii. Some weapons capable of decimating continents can cross international borders in a suitcase. The knowledge needed to turn common industrial materials into a death cloud is no longer the province of just a few scientists. Even the Internet carries how-to guides.[7]

Since ineffective communication can lead to increased tensions and violence, it should be obvious to you that effective intercultural communication is the superior means of reducing international conflict.

Recent events have given credence to the axiom that hostility anywhere has the potential to become hostility everywhere. Distance no longer matters. The terrorist attack against the World Trade Center has shown that the United States, although thousands of miles away, is not immune to conflict. Continued tensions between Israel and Palestine, between China and Taiwan, between India and Pakistan, and between Islamic militants and the West pose serious concerns. Again, the need for effective intercultural communication is apparent.

Tension, conflict, and hostility are not new to humankind. As Schlesinger has pointed out: "The hostility of one tribe for another is among the most instinctive human reactions."[8] When people of different nationalities and ethnic origins, who frequently speak different languages and hold different convictions, attempt to work and live together, conflicts can easily arise. "Unless a common purpose binds them together," Schlesinger said, "tribal hostilities will drive them apart. Ethnic and racial conflict, it seems evident, will now replace the conflict of ideologies as the explosive issue of our times."[9]

The increasing levels of terrorism and the spread of nuclear weapons sorely indicate the need for effective intercultural communication. People must discover that the resolution of conflict by communication is superior to the use of force. Unfortunately, such issues as ethnic pride, religious fervor, famine, and economic concerns often act as barricades to effective communication. And, when communication fails, other political means invariably follow. In numerous attempts to dissuade terrorism or the pursuit of nuclear weapons, the United States has imposed economic sanctions. In the past eighty years, economic sanctions have been imposed about 120 times. But sanctions seldom work and usually only increase the suffering of the poor.

The Global Economy

A Russian proverb states, "Boris has one custom and Sergei another." This saying can easily be extended to the global economy, where people from diverse cultures come together to engage in commerce and, of course, communicate. The extent of the global economy is aptly stated by Cowin: "The world economy is 'borderless' and markets are becoming essentially one. Corporations are looking at the free flow of goods and services, capital and human resources as well as information as the pathway to growth."[10] And, as Goldsmith, Walt, and Doucet indicate, "The trend toward globally connected markets is likely to become even stronger in the future."[11]

Globalization will have a major impact on the business and political leaders of the future. "In the past a major company could focus on its own region (or even its own country) and still prosper. Those days are soon going to be over."[12] China, for instance, is now faced with the problem of trying to reconcile capitalism amid communism. "Together, those twin motifs will define the next decade of Chinese communism as the party wrestles to maintain its rule over a civilization many millennia old." [13] In the arena of business, for instance, as Gibbs points out,

> Crossing the border between Mexico and the United States on a daily basis are 1 million barrels of crude oil, 432 tons of bell peppers, 238,000 light bulbs, 166 brand-new Volkswagen Beetles, 16,250 toasters, $51 million worth of auto parts, everything from the little plastic knob on the air conditioner to your cell-phone charger.[14]

These and countless other economic ties mean that it would not be unusual for you to work for an organization that does business in many countries or for you to conduct business in remote parts of the world. In Chapter 6, we have more to say more about your possible role in the culturally diverse business setting.

Domestic Interaction

The second major point of contact for intercultural interaction is at home in the domestic arena. Before we begin looking at the intercultural contacts you may make with members of co-cultures in the United States, we want to pause and look briefly at the dominant American culture. While demographic studies tell us that most of you belong to this culture, it is important for you to appreciate what constitutes membership in the cultures and how that membership might influence the manner in which you approach, perceive, and interact with other cultures. An understanding of this culture is so important that in every chapter that follows we will discuss the dominant culture as a reference point for cultural comparisons on such things as world views, values, verbal and nonverbal communication, and interaction patterns in settings such as business, education, and health care.

The "Dominant" Culture

Within each society you will find a dominant or national culture. Before we define this culture, we should point out that this culture is not monolithic. That is to say, within the dominant culture you will find numerous co-cultures and specialized cultures. As Victor suggests, "A national culture is never a homogeneous thing of one piece. In every culture there are internal contradictions or polarities. U.S. culture is no exception." [15]

When we use *culture* throughout this book, we are applying the term to the dominant culture found in most societies. In discussions of the United States, many terms have been employed to represent this group. In the past, words such as *umbrella culture, mainstream culture, U.S. Americans,* or *European Americans* have been applied when speaking of this collection of people. We prefer the term *dominant culture* because it clearly indicates that the group we are talking about is the one in power. And whether the co-cultures within a society like it or not, this power allows this segment of the population to speak for the whole while setting the tone for the culture. The people in power are those who historically have controlled, and who still control, the major institutions within the culture: church, government, education, military, mass media, monetary systems, and the like. As McLemore notes:

> The dominant group in American society was created as people of English ethnicity settled along the Atlantic seacoast and gradually extended their political, economic, and religious control over the territory. This group's structure, values, customs, and beliefs may be traced to (a) the English system of law, (b) the organization of commerce during the sixteenth century, and (c) English Protestant religious ideas and practices.[16]

In the United States, white males generally meet the requirements of dominance—and have since the establishment of this country. Although white males constitute only 34 percent of the U.S. population, it is their positions of power, not their numbers, that foster this degree of control. White males are at the center of the dominant culture because their positions of power enable them to determine and manipulate the content and flow of the messages produced by those institutions. By controlling most of the cultural messages, they are thus able to control the images presented to the majority of the population. Whether it is the church, mass media, or the government, the dominant culture sets goals, perpetuates customs, establishes values, and makes the major decisions affecting the bulk of the population. Their power allows them to influence what people think, what they aspire to be, and what they talk about. As Folb has noted, "Power is often defined as the ability to get others to do what you want."[17] It should be noted that a dominant group that greatly influences perceptions, communication patterns, beliefs, and values marks all cultures. What these groups use as the bases for their power may differ, but they all lead the way. Folb made the same point when she wrote:

> High status and attendant power may be accorded those who are seen or believed to be great warriors or hunters; those invested with magical, divine, or special powers; those who are deemed wise; or those who are in possession of important, valued and/or vital societal resources and goods.[18]

Regardless of the source of power, certain people within every culture have a disproportionate amount of influence, and that influence gets translated into how those people, and those around them, behave.

Co-Cultures

Having identified what constitutes the dominant culture, we are now ready to look at some of the co-cultures within the United States that interact with the dominant culture.

As changes have taken place throughout the world during the last few decades, so too has the cultural landscape of the United States been altered. Within our own boundaries, people are redefining and rethinking the meaning of being a member of the U.S. population. What once was considered a homogeneous group has changed. Recognition that the U.S. population comes in different colors and from diverse cultural backgrounds has had a profound effect on national identity. From all over the world, people from a large variety of cultures are now calling the United States their home. Simultaneously, groups that, for a host of reasons, remained silent for years, now ask—and at times demand—to be heard. The members of these groups, like the members of the dominant culture, share perceptions, values, modes of communication, and lifestyles that make them unique.

We believe that the best way to identify these groups is through the use of the term *co-cultures*. The key to defining co-cultures is twofold. First, it should be obvious that people often hold dual or multiple cultural memberships, and that these affiliations create behaviors and perceptions that are learned. We will, therefore, use the word *co-culture* when discussing groups or social communities exhibiting communication characteristics, perceptions, values, beliefs, and practices that are significantly different enough to distinguish them from the other groups, communities, and the dominant culture. Before we move on, however, we need to stress that members of co-cultures, because they live within the dominant culture, often share many patterns and perceptions found within the larger dominant culture.

While most co-cultures share many of the patterns and perception found within the larger dominant culture, they also have distinct and unique patterns of communication that they have learned as part of their membership in the co-culture. As you will see in Chapter 2 when we discuss culture in detail, most of the co-cultures in the United States meet many of the criteria and characteristics that we will apply to describe culture. For example, as Lane notes, "Deaf culture provides its members with traditions, values, and rules for behavior that are handed down from generation to generation."[19] Gays as well, Goodwin points out, have their own language, traditions, and behavioral codes.[20] What is important about all co-cultures is that being gay, disabled, Latino, African American, Asian American, or female exposes a person to a specialized set of messages that helps determine how he or she perceives some aspects of the external world. It also significantly influences how members of that co-culture communicate those perceptions. As we already noted, these co-cultural affiliations can be based on race, ethnic background, gender, age, sexual preference, and so forth.[21] For example, the African American co-culture has evolved language and behavior characteristics that constitute a co-culture. And, as Hecht, Ribeau, and Sedano suggest, we could offer the same conclusions with regard to the Mexican American co-culture.[22]

All of the co-cultures we mentioned, as is the case with the dominant culture, have numerous "carriers" (such as media, churches, schools, parents, religion) that transmit the experiences that are learned by each new set of members—be they children or adults. In the next paragraph, we try to explain this important point by looking at one American co-culture—women. We have selected the issue of gender for our extended example because, as Wood tells us, "we know more about it than other co-cultures."[23] It is important, however, to keep in mind that we could do much of the same analysis for any co-culture composed of individuals who had shared common messages and experiences over a long period.

If, as Bate states, culture is "a relatively organized set of beliefs and expectations about how people should talk, think, and organize their lives,"[24] we can understand how women and men grow up in two distinct communication cultures. Although at first glance it may appear that they share common environments and experiences, such as judicial systems, homes, schools, churches, and media, the messages they receive from these institutions are often quite different.

Think for just a moment about what is being "taught" to women in the United States by the following messages. A woman usually gives up her name once she gets married. Schools, according to the research reported by Wood, "tend to encourage dependence, quietness, and deference and frown on assertiveness in female students" and "reward independence, self-assertion, and activity in boys."[25] Girls are expected to do indoor chores and boys outdoor chores. Girls have to stay near the house while boys can go exploring. Boys and girls grow up playing very different games.[26] Girls' games are calm and restrictive; boys engage in games that are active, aggressive, combative, and competitive.[27] And think of the messages embedded in the selection of toys: dolls for girls, and cars and guns for boys. Books, magazines, movies, and television offer stories and images that encourage gender-specific views of what is important and even who is important. These messages, and thousands of others, produce two groups of people who perceive themselves differently (women have lower self-esteem than do men), see the world differently (women view the world with more anxiety and hostility), act differently (92 percent of all people in prison are men), relate to people differently (women are more empathetic than men), talk differently (women use more tag lines and interrupt less), and make different use of nonverbal cues (women smile more, engage in more eye contact, and use smaller gestures). Our list of distinctions could fill this book, but that is not our point. What needs to be remembered is the idea that unique experiences generate unique modes of behavior that influence communication.

Interacting with Co-Cultures

Through your own life experiences, you should recognize that there are many diverse co-cultures within the United States. They include people who may look quite like members of the dominant culture but have a different sexual preference, people who have a physical disability such as deafness, and people who appear physically different and speak a primary language other than English. As Guerrière points out, "America is the most successful poly-racial, poly-ethnic, and poly-religious society in history."[28] And, for the most part, co-cultures are recognized and accepted to varying degrees. Yet, there are those who have an aversion to some or all co-cultures, and that leads to cultural conflict.

To foster cohesive relationships between the dominant culture and the myriad simultaneously existing co-cultures, you must accept Grant's notion of human rights:

> Human rights are not legal fictions conferred by governments but are inherent features of our nature as human beings. And while it is clear that our knowledge and understanding of human rights are relatively modern, human rights themselves are as old as humanity.[29]

To better understand the dynamics of communication with co-cultures, we first look at the impact of immigration on the United States. Then we will examine some of the major co-cultures resident in the United States.

Immigration. Historically, the United States has made it relatively easy for people from other countries to move here. The United States permits more legal immigration than the rest of the world combined. As a consequence, the U.S. population contains a higher proportion of foreign-born individuals than at any time in the past hundred years, increasing from approximately 8 million in 1900 to around 70 million in 2000. Previous immigrants came mainly from Europe. Most of today's immigrants are non-European and come from Asian, Caribbean, and Central and Latin American countries.[30] Many observers believe that immigration to America will continue to increase because the rest of the world does not welcome foreigners to the degree the United States does. Data from the 2000 census reveals that "One out of every four Americans is a minority, with minority defined as anyone who is not a non-Hispanic white."[31] This data also indicates that there are probably more than 8.5 million illegal immigrants in the United States, more than half of whom entered legally but overstayed their visa expiration date.[32] When you consider immigrants' American-born children, "births are becoming the most important source of population growth."[33]

This change in the ethnic face of the United States has altered intercultural contacts among members of the U.S. population. Thus, immigration has not only brought us into contact with more and varied cultures, it has also increased the number of interactions with people who do not speak English as a first language

Co-cultures, as we have already mentioned, are those groups within a society that share many common cultural attributes—world views, beliefs, values, language, nonverbal behaviors, and identity—yet do not share power with the dominant culture. In the United States there are numerous co-cultures that have become increasingly prominent because of their numbers and partly because many of their members do not subscribe to nor conform to many of the dominant cultural beliefs, values, and attitudes. America has been successful in attempting to integrate these co-cultures into mainstream society because immigrants have been permitted to retain their native culture. As Guerrière notes, they are be able to "speak their native tongues, have their own newspapers, settle in common areas, build their churches, maintain their cuisine, enjoy their music, do their preferential work—almost anything they wanted to keep, they could."[34]

To help you understand the cultural dynamics of co-cultures and their prominence in the United States, we will examine four co-cultures: *Latinos, African Americans, Asian Americans,* and *Muslim Americans.*

Latinos are the fastest growing population in the United States. In 2000 nearly 32.8 million people, or 12 percent of the American population, considered themselves of Latino origin, with over 66 percent having their roots in Mexico.[35] Two years later that number had grown to over 36 million. Although Latinos in the United States come from a wide variety of national origins, two prominent issues common to this co-culture create turbulence in the quality of their interactions in American society: (1) illegal immigration and (2) English as a national language.

First, many members of the dominant culture resent the hundreds of thousands of Latinos that enter the United States—either legally or illegally each year. This large number of immigrants from a single location have created calls for everything from walling off the border with Mexico to a more rigid immigration policy with Mexico. The Latino population has also heard the anti-Latino views being espoused by both lay people and political leaders.

Second, many Latinos have retained their native language rather than adopting English. Only Mexico and Colombia exceed the United States in the number of people who speak Spanish.[36] This large segment of Spanish speakers has led to a rapid increase in the number of Spanish-language approaches to this population. Spanish-language broadcast and print media have proliferated in recent years in both major and minor markets. The realm of politics has also recognized the importance of the Spanish-speaking population. Gamboa has reported that "candidates for Congress and governor aired more than 16,000 Spanish-language television spots during the 2002 campaign, and politicians seeking federal, statewide or legislative office spent at least $16 million on such advertisements."[37]

Many North Americans believe that lack of a shared national language is detrimental to a unified society. As we see in later chapters, businesses, schools, and health care organizations are struggling to find an equitable solution to the issue of language diversity. Intercultural communication will be a crucial part of orchestrating a solution.

African Americans numbered over 34.6 million in 2000 and accounted for some 12 percent of the total U.S. population.[38] Prior to the Civil Rights Act of 1964,

African Americans and members of the dominant culture had only limited contact. Since that time, both groups have interacted with much greater regularity. As is often the case, however, when two diverse cultures come into contact, not all the encounters are successful. Two important perceptual issues are at the heart of many of these problems. The first issue is racism. Many African Americans believe that racism causes the economic disparity between themselves and members of the dominant culture. This view does have some merit because, as Estrin explains, "Race continues to play a powerful role in the chances for success in the United States from job opportunities to education to housing, at least in the metropolitan areas of Boston, Atlanta, Detroit and Los Angeles."[39]

Secondly, whites and African Americans continue to argue over the role racism plays in both the legal and educational institutions of the United States. When the results of legal trials bring riots and deep-seated ill feelings, we know that racism influences perception and communication. Hence, it is a topic that demands our attention. We return to this topic throughout the book and suggest ways to deal with this intercultural problem.

Asian Americans—particularly those of Chinese and Japanese ancestry—have been present in the United States since the late 1800s. Recent census data indicates there are over 10.2 million residents who claim Asian only ancestry.[40] It is recent arrivals, however, who pose the most perplexing communication problems. Imagine, if you will, the adjustment problems faced by a refugee from Thailand who immigrated to the United States at the age of four. In a cultural sense, she is not quite Asian, and she is not quite American. She speaks the Mien language at home, English with her friends, and a blend of the two languages to her children.

Not only are these people finding it difficult to cope with living in the United States so far away from both their homelands and their cultures, but they also can create difficult and unique communication problems for those who must relate to them.

Muslim Americans number an estimated 6 to 7 million[41] and are increasing steadily. The American Muslim community constitutes what Ostling calls "a growing and maturing community that worships at over 1200 mosques across the United States."[42] The rapid growth of this co-culture is not the only reason we have included this group in our discussion of co-cultures. They have also been incorporated into our discussion because of the all the news and false information surrounding this group since the events surrounding the involvement of the United States in Iraq.

The children of Muslim immigrants who came to the United States in the 1960s are coming of age. As Ostling reports, their "mosques seem to be less bound by ethnic and racial divisions than in the past and are adapting to American culture, even though some leaders are ambivalent about the United States."[43] Both pious and modern, they are the future of the Islamic faith in the United States. These children, however, are emerging as a co-culture: young Islamic Americans who are a blend of traditional Muslim and American institutions. These children might know it is time to pray, not by a muezzin's call from a mosque minaret, but because his or her PowerMac has chimed.

There are many additional co-cultures in the United States: women, gays and lesbians, the deaf, incarcerated, gangs, the homeless, prostitutes, the disabled, and the elderly. Many members of these groups do not subscribe to all of the mainstream beliefs, values, and attitudes shared by the dominant culture.

DEFINITION OF INTERCULTURAL COMMUNICATION

Because we have been using the term *intercultural communication* from the beginning, it only seems appropriate that we pause at this time and give meaning to those two words. For us, intercultural communication occurs when a member of one culture produces a message for consumption by a member of another culture. *More precisely, intercultural communication involves interaction between people whose cultural perceptions and symbol systems are distinct enough to alter the communication event.*

Before we apply the above definition to a systematic study of intercultural communication, we need to pause and talk about human communication. Our rationale for beginning with communication is a simple one. Let us explain. While this book is about the role of culture in communication, it is also about what the phrase *intercultural communication* implies, about human interaction. By understanding some principles inherent in communication, you will be able to observe how these principles get acted out in the intercultural setting. We should add that what we are about to do for communication we will do for culture in the next chapter. That is, we will discuss the pertinent dynamics of culture and how by understanding them you are furnished with a solid foundation for understanding intercultural communication.

ESSENTIALS OF HUMAN COMMUNICATION

Communication—your ability to share your beliefs, values, ideas, and feelings—is the basis of all human contact. Whether you live in a city in Canada, a village in India, a commune in Israel, or the Amazon jungles of Brazil, you participate in the same activity when you communicate. The results and the methods might be different, but the process is the same. The more than 6 billion people that inhabit this planet engage in communication so that they can share their realities with other human beings.

Communication Defined

There was good reason for the English statesman Benjamin Disraeli to say "I hate definitions." While definitions are necessary, they can also be troublesome. For example, it is nearly impossible to find a single definition of *human communication*. Over thirty years ago, Dance and Larson canvassed the literature on communication and found 126 definitions of communication;[44] since then, countless others have been added to their list. Isolating the commonalities of those definitions, and being concerned with the intercultural dimensions of communication, we hold to the definition advanced by Ruben and Stewart: "*Human communication is the process through which individuals—in relationships, groups, organizations, and societies—respond to and create messages to adapt to the environment and one another.*[45]

Principles of Communication

For you to better understand Ruben and Stewart's definition and the process of communication itself, we will examine some of the basic principles of communication that are in operation whenever you attempt to share your internal states with someone else.

There are a few points to keep in mind before we catalog some of the basic principles of communication. First, communication has more characteristics than we can discuss in the next few pages. Just as a description of a forest that mentions only the trees and flowers but omits the lakes and streams does not do justice to the entire setting, our inventory is not exhaustive. We, too, are forced to leave out some of the landscape. Second, while the linear nature of language forces us to discuss one principle at a time, you need to keep in mine that in reality the elements of communication work in combination with one another.

Communication Is a Dynamic Process

Communication Is Ongoing. Notice that very early in their definition, Rubin and Stewart refer to communication as a process. We would simply now add that it is a dynamic process. The statement *communication is a dynamic process* carries more than one meaning. First, it means that communication is an ongoing activity. It is not fixed. Communication is like a motion picture, not a single snapshot. A word or action does not stay frozen when you communicate; it is immediately replaced with yet another word or action. As participants in communication, you too experience its dynamic nature. You are constantly affected by other people's messages and, as a consequence, are always changing. From the moment of conception through the instant of death (and some cultures believe even after death), you experience an almost endless variety of physical and psychological changes, some too subtle to notice, others too profound to ignore. As you shall see later in Chapter 2, culture too is dynamic. It is no wonder that twenty-five hundred years ago the Greek philosopher Heraclitus wrote, "There is nothing permanent except change."

Communication Is Transitory. Communication is dynamic because once a word or an action is employed, it cannot be retracted. T. S. Eliot might well have been referring to this transitory aspect of communication when he wrote, "In the life of one person, never the same time returns." Once an event takes place, you cannot have it again—perhaps you can experience a similar event, but not an identical one. The judge who advises the jury to "disregard the testimony just given" knows full well that this is impossible. The words were spoken, and they cannot be unspoken. An Asian proverb makes much the same point: "Once the arrow has been shot it cannot be recalled."

Inattention Brings Change. Communication is also dynamic because inattention pervades your communication behavior. Briefly survey your own actions and you will realize that your mind often does not like what it is doing and hence dashes from idea to idea, seeking something it does like. People often shift topics in the middle of a sentence, and research shows that when they listen, their attention span is brief. This trait of communication is so common that in the writings of the Buddha it is said, "The mind is fickle and flighty, it flies after fancies wherever it likes: it is difficult indeed to restrain."[46]

Communication Is Symbolic

Inherent in our definition of communication is the fact that humans are symbol-making creatures. It is this symbol-making ability that allows for everyday interaction. It also enables culture to be passed on from generation to generation. You employ symbols to share your internal states. Other animals may participate in the communication process, but none of them has the unique communication capabilities of people. Through millions of years of physical evolution, and thousands of years of cultural evolution, you are now able to generate, receive, store, and manipulate symbols. This sophisticated system allows you to use a symbol—be it a sound, a mark on paper, a statue, Braille, a movement, or a painting—to represent something else. Reflect for a moment on the wonderful gift you have that allows you to hear the words "The kittens look like little cotton balls" and, like magic, have an image in your head. Or what about the joy you experience when you see the smile of your dearest friend? These two sets of symbols—words and actions—help you let other human beings know how you experience the world and what you think or feel about that world.

In terms of intercultural communication, it is important for you to keep in mind the fact that the symbols you use are discretionary and subjective. As Gudykunst and Kim remind us, "The important thing to remember is that symbols are symbols only because a group of people agree to consider them as such. There is not a natural connection between symbols and their referents: the relationships are arbitrary and vary from culture to culture."[47] What is being said here is that although all cultures use symbols, they usually assign their own meanings to the symbols. Not only do Mexicans say *perro* for dog, but also the image they form when they hear the sound is probably quite different from the one Americans may form. Even when the word is the same, you can observe cultural differences in the meaning of the word. While the dominant culture might have a common meaning for the word "time," the meaning for this word, as Chapter 5 points out, is very different for Native Americans. In addition to having different meanings for symbols, cultures also use these symbols for different purposes. In America and much of Europe, the prevalent view is that communication is used to get things done. Or as Trenholm and Jensen note, "Communication is a powerful way of regulating and controlling our world."[48] In contrast, people in Japan, Taiwan, and China believe that most members of the culture internalize information, so not much needs to be coded. Because symbols are at the core of communication, we return to them throughout the book. For now, we remind you that symbols, by virtue of their standing for something else, give you an opportunity to share your personal realities.

Communication Is Systemic

We use the word *systemic* here to define the idea that communication does not occur in isolation or in a vacuum, but rather is part of a larger system.

Setting. You send and receive messages not in isolation but in a specific setting. According to Littlejohn, "Communication always occurs in context, and the nature of communication depends in large measure on this context."[49] Put more simply, setting and environment help determine the words and actions you generate and the meanings you give the symbols produced by other people. Context provides what Shimanoff calls a "prescription that indicates what behavior is obligated, preferred, or prohibited."[50] Dress, language, topic selection, and the like are all adapted to context. For example, under most circumstances, males would not, even in hot weather, attend a university lecture without wearing a shirt. The rules for each context, be it boardroom, classroom, or courtroom, are culturally based and therefore relative. Many of these contextual rules are directly related to your culture. For example, in the business setting, all cultures have stated and unstated rules regarding who takes part in the decision-making process during meetings. In the United States, the rule tells us it is the "boss." The simple American proverb "The buck stops here" gives us a clue as to the operational rule regarding decision making in the United States. In Japan, nearly everyone is consulted as part of the decision-making process. The Japanese proverb "Consult everyone, even your knees" demonstrates the Japanese approach to decision making.

When we speak of communication being systemic, we are referring to much more than the setting of the interaction. Other elements associated with the systemic nature of communication are *location, occasion, time,* and *number of participants.* Even though these are found in all communication encounters, culture influences how we respond to them.

Location. People do not act the same way in every environment. Whether in an auditorium, restaurant, or office, the location of your interaction provides guidelines for your behavior. Either consciously or unconsciously, you know the prevailing rules, many of which are rooted in your culture. Nearly all cultures, for example, have religious buildings, but the rules of behavior in those buildings are culturally based. In Mexico, men and women go to church together and remain quiet. In Iran, men and women do not worship together, and chanting instead of silence is the rule.

Occasion. The occasion of a communication encounter also controls the behavior of the participants. You know from your own experience that an auditorium can be the occasion for a graduation ceremony, pep rally, convocation, play, dance, or memorial service. Each of these occasions calls for distinctly different forms of behavior, and each culture has its own specifications for these behaviors. For example, in one culture the occasion of a wedding calls for solitude and silence (as would be the case of a royal wedding in Japan), yet in the Jewish culture the same occasion calls for vociferous music, dancing, and a great deal of merriment.

Time. The influence of time on communication is so subtle that its impact is often overlooked. To understand this concept, you must answer these questions: How do you feel when someone keeps you waiting for a long time? Do you respond to a phone call at 2:00 A.M. the same way you do to one at 2 P.M.? Do you find yourself rushing the conversation when you know you have very little time to spend with someone? Your answers to these questions reveal how the clock often controls your actions. Every communication event takes place on a time–space continuum, and the amount of time allotted, whether it is for social conversation or a formal speech, affects that event. Cultures as well as people use time to communicate. In the United States, schedules and time constraints are ever present. As Hall and Hall note, "For Americans, the use of appointment-schedule time reveals how people feel about each other, how significant their business is, and where they rank in the status system."[51] Because time influences communication and the use of it is culture-bound, we treat the topic in greater detail in Chapter 5 that deals with nonverbal communication.

Number of People. The number of people with whom you communicate also affects the flow of communication. You know from personal experience that you feel and act differently if you are speaking with one person, in a group, or before a great many people. Cultures also respond to changes in number. For example, people in Japan find group interaction much to their liking, yet they often feel extremely uncomfortable when they have to give a formal public speech.

Cultural Setting.   A still more general part of the communication event is the cultural setting. Wood notes, "The largest system affecting communication is your culture, which is the context within which all your interactions take place."[52] The rules, values, norms, traditions, taboos, and customs of a culture all affect the other areas of the communication system.

Communication Involves Making Inferences

Because there is no direct mind-to-mind contact between people, you cannot access the thoughts and feelings of other human beings but can only infer what they are experiencing. You make these inferences from a single word, from silence, from long speeches, from simple head nods, and from glances in your direction or away from you.

This characteristic of communication has always frustrated human beings, because, in a very real sense, everyone is isolated from one another by the enclosure of their skin. What you know and feel remains inside of you unless you communicate. It is as if you lived in a house with doors and windows that never opened. Perhaps the day will come when one of the futuristic devices from *Star Trek* becomes a reality and another human being can have direct access to what you are experiencing, but for now you must live in a kind of solitary confinement. An African proverb makes this point figuratively: "The earth is a beehive; we all enter by the same door but live in different cells."

Although the inability to have direct mind-to-mind contact is universal, the methods used to adjust to this limitation are culturally based. Some cultures believe that because they share a common pool of history and many similar experiences, they do indeed know what their partners are feeling and thinking. Yet in many Western cultures, the lack of direct access to another's mind places great demands on such communication behaviors as asking questions, engaging in self-disclosure, and ooververbalizing. You can well imagine some of the problems that might arise when people from these two orientations come together. We will discuss some of these problems throughout the book.

Communication Is Self-Reflective

The American philosopher Emerson once wrote, "Wherever we go, whatever we do, self is the sole subject we study and learn." Emerson, whether he employed communication terminology or not, was referring to the idea that human beings think about themselves, watch how they define the world, and reflect on their past, present, and future.

The importance of this focus on the self is clearly manifest in the following explanation offered by Wood:

> Just as we use symbols to reflect on what goes on outside of us, we also use them to reflect on ourselves. Humans don't simply exist and act. Instead, we think about our existence and reflect on our actions. Self-reflection is a basis for human identity. If we weren't able to reflect on ourselves and our activities civilized society would be impossible.[53]

As you can tell from Wood's description, this unique endowment lets you be participant and observer simultaneously: You can watch, evaluate, and alter your "performance" as a communicator at the very instant you are engaged in the act. Humans are the only species that can simultaneously be at both ends of the camera.

There is, as you have learned by now, an intercultural dimension to your capacity to be self-reflective, though this capacity may not always be manifest. Some cultures are much more concerned with the self than are others and therefore devote a great deal of energy to watching and even worrying about the self. The "I" is at the heart of

Western religion and psychology. For example, from Locke, who said rationality meant you could know the answer to all questions, to modern self-help "experts" who speak of "personal power," Americans grow up believing the individual is at the center of the universe. Cultures that are more group oriented focus on other people, so although they can engage in self-reflective activity during communication, their main concern is with the other not with the self.

Communication Has a Consequence

As has been the case with all of the characteristics we have examined to this point, the next characteristic is woven throughout every chapter. It implies that when you receive a message, something happens to you. Also, all of your messages—to one degree or another—affect someone else. This is not a philosophical or metaphysical theory but a biological fact. It is impossible not to respond to the sounds and actions of others.

The responses you have to messages vary in degree and kind. It might help you to visualize your potential responses as forming a continuum (see Figure 1-1). At one end of the continuum lie responses to messages that are overt and easy to understand. Someone sends you a message by asking directions to the library. Your response is to say, "It's on your right." You might even point to the library. The message from the other person has thus produced an overt observable response.

A little farther across the continuum are those messages that produce only a mental response. If someone says to you, "The United States doesn't spend enough money on higher education," and you only think about this statement, you are still responding, but your response does not have to be an observable action.

As you proceed across the continuum, you come to responses that are harder to detect. These are responses to messages you receive by imitating, observing, and interacting with others. Generally, you are not even aware that you are receiving these messages. Your parents act out their gender roles, and you receive messages about your gender role. People greet you by shaking hands instead of hugging, and without being aware of it, you are receiving messages about forms of address.

At the far end of the continuum are the responses to messages that are received unconsciously. That is, your body responds even if your cognitive processes are kept to a minimum. Messages that come into you can alter your chemical secretions, your heart rate, or the temperature of your skin, modify pupil size, and trigger a host of other internal responses. These chemical and biological responses are covert, and they are the most difficult to classify. They do, however, give credence to our assertion that communication has a consequence. If your internal reactions produce chaos to your system, as is the case with severe stress, you can become ill. So regardless of the content of the message, it should be clear that the act of communication produces change in people.

All of you receive and respond to messages, yet the nature of your responses is rooted in your culture. The grief associated with the death of a loved one is as natural

Figure 1-1 *Communication Responses*

1————————25————————50————————75————————100
Overt   Covert   Unconscious   Biological

as breathing; each culture, however, determines ways of coping with and sharing that grief. These responses to the outside world can range from wailing loudly to maintaining a stoic exterior.

The response you make to someone's message does not have to be immediate. You can respond minutes, days, or even years later. For example, your second-grade teacher may have asked you to stop throwing rocks at a group of birds. Perhaps the teacher added that the birds were part of a family and were gathering food for their babies. She might also have indicated that birds feel pain just like people. Perhaps twenty years later, as you think about eating an animal, you remember those words from your teacher and decide to become a vegetarian. It is important to remember the power of your messages and to consider the ethical consequences of your communication actions. For whether or not you want to grant those consequences, you are changing people each time you exchange messages with them. In Chapter 10, we offer some guidelines that you can employ as you evaluate your ethical responsibilities.

Communication Is Complex

One point should be obvious by now: Communication is complex. Think for a moment of all the bodily and mental activity that accompanies even the simple act of saying "hello" to a friend. From the stimulation of your nerve endings, to the secretion of chemicals in your brain, to the moving of your lips and tongue to produce sound, thousands of components are in operation (and most of them at the same time). Notice how the notion of complexity is clearly captured in the following observation advanced by Smith: "Human communication is a subtle and ingenious set of processes. It is always thick with a thousand ingredients—signals, codes, meanings—no matter how simple the message or transaction."[54] Communication becomes even more complex when cultural dimensions are added. Although all cultures use symbols to share their realities, the specific realities and the symbols employed are often quite different. In one culture you smile in a casual manner as a form of greeting, whereas in another you bow formally in silence, and in yet another you acknowledge your friend with a full embrace.

Another often overlooked reason why communication is complex is that people are both alike and different. As you would suspect, this notion is difficult to explain. You need only reread the last sentence to begin appreciating our difficulty: We have to explain a statement that, at first glance, contains two contradictory ideas. We solve this problem by treating this apparent contradiction as a statement of two ideas that are both true.

People Are Alike. Let us start by talking about the premise that in many ways we are like every other human being. If you reflect for a moment, this entire section has focused on how people are alike: Each of you communicates by employing the same basic communication components—you construct and transmit symbols to represent your internal states, and other people receive and respond to those symbols. Your commonalities as a species, however, go far beyond the ways in which you share ideas and information. Because people are more alike than they are different, any inventory of these common qualities will be incomplete. Nevertheless, let us highlight a few commonalities so that you can better appreciate our starting premise

People are identical in numerous physiological and chemical ways. We all have a heart, lungs, brain, and the like. You are also literally made of the same "stuff": water, salt, and so on. In fact, as Recer reports, "An analysis of the Y chromosome taken from 1,007 men from 25 different locations in Europe found a pattern that suggests that four out of five of the men shared a common male ancestor about 40,000 years ago."[55] It would seem, therefore, that both your genes and culture cause you to seek pleasure and avoid pain. That is, every human being—and all of the other animals with which we share this planet—devotes a great deal of energy to trying to avoid physical discomfort. Should you experience pain, you will suffer in much the same way as everyone else. Although the medical treatment might be different, a wound to the arm in Peru is much like a wound to the arm in Beverly Hills.

People also seek emotional pleasure and dislike injury to their feelings. Although the word *ego* may be very Western, the concepts behind it (self-respect, admiration, vanity, and the like) are common to all cultures. Ego may be called face-saving in China, macho in Mexico, and pride in Jordan, but the feelings evoked are very much the same.

You are also alike because *all of you*, regardless of your culture, must, at some point in life, face and attempt to resolve four fundamental truths. First, everyone realizes at some point *that life is finite*: You will not go on, at least in your present form, forever. As Shakespeare wrote in the *Tempest*: "We are such stuff / As dreams are made on, and our little life / Is rounded with a sleep." Second, everyone discovers early in life that they are *isolated from all other human beings*. As we noted earlier, the envelope of your skin separates you so that no one knows your exact internal states. Third, all of you, regardless of your culture, are thrown into a world that forces you to *make choices*. In the face of peer pressure as well as cultural and legal constraints, you make choices every instant of your life. Finally, the world has no built-in scheme that gives it meaning. It is, at the moment of birth, a meaningless world. Everyone must give it meaning.

We should add that cultures as well as individuals contribute to the pool of similarities. For example, every culture has a language, rules and norms about age and gender, a system of government, religions, economic systems, recreational and play activity, art, music, and the like.

There are, of course, numerous other commonalities, even those that relate to perception. People find the act of childbirth a dazzling and near mystical event. Nearly everyone belongs to a family, enjoys play and laughter, desires a mate, and wants someone to love and care for them. These and other universal experiences support the notion that people are very much alike. Having said that, we now look at how they are different.

People Are Different. The English statesman Lord Chesterfield once wrote, "There never were, since the creation of the world, two cases exactly parallel." He might have also said that there have never been two people exactly alike. This belief is predicated on the simple fact that your experience of the world is both internal and unique. When you hear a word, or someone touches you, your body reacts from the inside out. The significance of this is apparent if you think about just two of the many actions in which people engage when they receive messages. First, the external world impinges on your nerve endings, causing something to happen within you. Second, you think about what is happening by employing symbols from your past (although you might have similar backgrounds, you have experienced each event in a unique way). We admit that this explanation is rather elementary, but it is nevertheless accurate. We have already noted that symbols, for example, do not mean the same thing to everyone—their interpretations are subjective. If you write the simple phrase "I like going to the racetrack," it can elicit a wide variety of responses depending on the listeners' background. One person might believe horse racing is "an evil form of gambling" and believe that you are foolish, yet another, reading the same words, could respond by saying, "I also like the races." Subjectivity is always the rule. A common beginning, anatomy, gender, age, culture, and the like may bind you, but your isolated minds and unique experiences keep you apart. The English essayist George Gissing captured the impossibility of knowing exactly what another person is experiencing: "It is the mind which creates the world about us, and even though we stand side by side in the same meadow, my eyes will never see what is beheld by yours, my heart will never stir to the emotions by which yours is touched."

Cultural, as well as individual, differences keep people apart. Although the philosophical issues of death, isolation, free choice, and meaning confront everyone, our resolutions for each issue have their roots deep in culture. For example, Hinduism tells its members that they will be reincarnated when they die. In Islam, death moves people into heaven or hell, depending on how they lived. Everyone thus deals with death in a personal way, but the options employed are cultural. Sitaram and Cogdell summarize this point:

> Members of different cultures look differently at the world around them. Some believe that the physical world is real. Others believe that it is just an illusion. Some believe everything around them is permanent while others say it is transient. Reality is not the same for all people.[56]

This notion of different realities, combined with the idea of cultural similarities, is at the heart of this book. That is why we repeatedly return to the theme that a *successful intercultural communicator appreciates similarities and accepts differences.*

From our discussion, you should now have an understanding of the concept of intercultural communication, the dynamic nature of communication, and the role it plays in normal everyday interaction. With this background in mind, we now want to turn your attention to the study of intercultural communication. In the section below, we will provide you with some of the problems inherent in the study of intercultural communication.

STUDYING INTERCULTURAL COMMUNICATION

If we have been successful in our endeavors thus far, you have been convinced that learning to become successful in intercultural interactions is a necessary and worthwhile pursuit. We now want to alert you to some of the problems you will face in meeting the challenge of intercultural communication.

Understanding the characteristics of diverse cultures and co-cultures as well as your own culture is the first step toward meeting the challenge of successful intercultural communication. The need to understand such significant differences as social relations, concepts of the universe, and views of suffering is a major theme of this book. We ask you to remain open-minded throughout your intercultural inquiry and consider the following Arab proverb: "The eyes are of little use if the mind is blind."

Although many intercultural interactions are synchronous and harmonious, friction, conflict, and numerous misunderstandings complicate others. Differences in language, food, dress, attitudes toward time, work habits, social behavior, and the like can cause many of our intercultural contacts to be frustrating or even unsuccessful. These issues, however, account for only some of the problems associated with intercultural communication; most misunderstandings go beyond these superficial differences. The deep structure of a culture primarily determines how a person responds to events and other people. What members of a particular culture value and how they perceive the universe are usually far more important than whether they eat with chopsticks, their hands, or metal utensils. The deep structures of culture will cause you the greatest problems in being an effective intercultural communicator. Most of these problems, however, stem from two factors: (1) the failure to recognize the uniqueness of the individual and (2) the inability to be objective. We will discuss each of these briefly in order to give you an insight into the work that lies ahead.

Individual Uniqueness

Although it is not very profound, it is nevertheless true that all human beings, regardless of their culture, share common universal experiences. Each of you is a member of the human species sharing universal needs, a member of a specific culture sharing common cultural patterns, and at the same time a distinct person with an individual psychology following a unique script. Regardless of your culture, you all share such common emotions as fear, love, anger, hostility, shame, envy, guilt, grief, and joy. Each culture has its forms of ethnocentrism, face-saving, ego defense, pride, and forms of play. And in every culture people stress manners and civility to one another, practice sexual taboos, adhere to mating practices, and follow specific gender roles. But, *you are much more than your culture.*

Although this book focuses on the cultural influences that moderate human interaction, you must keep in mind that at your basic core you are not captives of your culture. You are, instead, thinking individuals with the rationality and potential to engage in free choice. Consequently, the values and behaviors of a particular culture may not be the values and behaviors of all the individuals within that culture. Each human being is unique and shaped by countless factors, culture being but one. At any given moment, your behavior is the product of millions of years of evolution; your genetic makeup; the social groups you have been in; your gender, age, individual and family history, political affiliation, perceptions of others, and current circumstances; and many other factors. As the Roman playwright Terence noted over two thousand years ago, "As many men, so many minds; every one his own way." Because every person has "their own way" you must be cautious and prudent when making cultural generalizations. What we said at the end of the last paragraph is worth repeating—as you study intercultural communication, always keep on mind that *people are more than their culture.*

Objectivity

The inability to be truly objective in intercultural encounters is a problem impossible to overcome completely. In this instance, you are the problem. The issue is simply this: You study other cultures from the perspective of your own culture, so your observations and your conclusions are tainted by your personal and cultural orientations. It is difficult, if not impossible, to see and to give meaning to words and behaviors with which you are not familiar. How, for example, do you make sense of someone's silence if you come from a culture that does not value silence? You might make the mistake of thinking "How could someone be so insensitive as to be silent at a time like this?" Your ethnocentrism not only impedes intercultural communication, but also is often difficult to identify because it is unconscious. We encourage you to be aware of your ethnocentrism so that it does not limit your perceptions.

Objectivity requires the elimination of both overt and subtle hostility or ambivalence by members of one culture against members of another culture or co-culture. This negative behavior not only is contrary to the ideals of most cultures but cripples both the perpetrators of the behavior and the target. To discriminate against someone simply because he or she has skin of a different color, lives in a different country, prays to a different god, has a dissimilar world view, or speaks a different language diminishes everyone. Our view about appreciating and accepting differences is clearly expressed by Joseph when he writes, "…diversity need not divide; that the fear of difference is a fear of the future; that inclusiveness rightly understood and rightly practiced is a benefit and not a burden." [57] To achieve those benefits it will take all the people of the world working together to achieve a truly multicultural society, a world in which you endeavor to follow the advice of Weinberg when he exhorts you to learn to value discrete groups of people regardless of race, ethnicity, religion, country of origin, gender, or sexual preference. [58]

PREVIEW OF THE BOOK

We have divided this book into four interrelated parts. Part 1, called Communication and Culture, has three chapters. In Chapter 1 we attempted to introduce you to the challenges facing anyone who seeks to study intercultural communication. We also demonstrated the various contact points people from diverse cultures would be experiencing. This first chapter also introduced you to the topic of human communication and alerted you to some problems inherent in learning about intercultural communication. In Chapter 2 we will define culture and discuss its salient characteristics, and relate it directly to communication. Chapter 2 also examines the cultural patterns of behavior that people depend on to define their identity and their reality. Chapter 3 explores the deep structures at the root of cultural behavior: perception and behaviors revealed in a culture's world view, interaction patterns within the family, and cultural history.

Part 2, Exchanging Cultural Messages, moves us from the theoretical to the practical by analyzing the mechanisms of intercultural interaction. Chapter 4 looks at the people involved in intercultural communication and their attempts to communicate through verbal messages. Examining the kinds of messages that are exchanged will help us appreciate the responses those messages produce. Chapter 5 canvasses the effect of cultural diversity on nonverbal communication and the ways in which nonverbal messages support verbal communication in a variety of cultures.

Part 3 is called The Role of Context in Intercultural Communication. The three chapters in this part acknowledge the importance of two communication principles: first, that communication is rule governed; and second, that those rules are often tied to a particular cultural context. Our investigation looks at cultural variations in the business (Chapter 6), education (Chapter 7), and health care (Chapter 8) settings.

Part 4, Knowledge into Action, is concerned with the improvement of intercultural communication skills. In a sense, our entire study focuses on the issue of improvement, but in Chapters 9 and 10 specific advice and recommendations are set forth. Chapter 9 focuses on problems that can plague any encounter when people from different cultures or co-cultures come together. Chapter 10 attempts to offer some solutions that we hope will remedy many of the problems highlight in Chapter 9. In addition, the final chapter suggests new philosophical and ethical ways to think about the topic of intercultural communication.

SUMMARY

- Intercultural communication presents you with a challenge you must meet if you are to become an effective communicator in today's world.
- New and improved technology, growth in the world's population, and shifts in the global economic arena have contributed to increased international contacts.
- Everyone worldwide will be affected by and need to communicate about finite natural resources and the environment to help reduce and avoid international conflict.
- Domestic contacts are increasing because new immigrants and co-cultures are growing in numbers.
- All cultures have a dominant or national culture.
- Co-cultural communication is communication between members who hold two or more cultural experiences that might influence the communication process.
- Co-cultural interaction is necessary to foster cohesive relationships between the dominant culture and the myriad existing co-cultures.
- Intercultural communication is communication between people whose cultural perceptions and symbol systems are distinct enough to alter the communication event.
- Human communication is the process through which individuals—in relationships, groups, organizations, and societies—respond to and create messages and adapt to the environment and one another.
- Communication is dynamic; it is ongoing and ever changing.
- Communication is transitory; once a word is spoken or an action taken, it cannot be retracted.
- Inattention brings change; inattention pervades your communication behavior causing you to shift your attention from idea to idea.
- Communication is symbolic.
- Communication is systemic and is therefore influenced by setting, location, occasion, time, number of participants, and cultural setting.
- We can only infer what another is experiencing, and we do this by using the symbols that we and other people have produced.
- Communication is self-reflective: We can watch ourselves and evaluate how we are communicating while we are doing it.
- Your communication behavior has consequences.
- Communication is complex.
- One of the hazards of studying intercultural communication is forgetting that each individual is unique and that culture is just one of many factors that influence human behavior.
- A lack of objectivity can impede successful intercultural communication.

INFOTRAC® COLLEGE EDITION EXERCISES

1. Your text is accompanied by a valuable research and learning tool, the *InfoTrac College Edition* research database. Take time to explore the *InfoTrac College Edition* web site and investigate the ways in which *InfoTrac College Edition* can make your learning and research more meaningful and productive. Access the *InfoTrac College Edition* web page at http://www. infotrac-college.com and type in the password from the free subscription card that you received with your textbook. After registering, you will automatically be directed to the EasyTrac search page and asked to enter a keyword search term. Type "intercultural communication" and click on the "Search" icon. Read the titles of the articles listed to gain a sense of the variety

of issues and themes that are related to intercultural communication. Select an article that interests you and write a one-paragraph summary of the article to share with the class.

2. Want to know more about America's dominant culture? Locate and read the article "Surrounding Ourselves with Difference" by Leny Mendoza Strobel. (Hint: use key words from the title and/or the author's name to find articles.) According to Strobel, why do students need to explore what it means to be White? What are *Whiteness* and *White privilege,* and how are they relevant to the ways in which Americans experience the American Dream? With your classmates, discuss the ways in which your own experiences either affirm or contradict Strobel's views.

3. Want to know more about America's changing views on race? Locate and read Tamar Jacoby's article on the 2000 U.S. census, "An End to Counting by Race?" According to Jacoby, what is the significance of allowing people to identify themselves as multiracial? Why do you think this identification option has been so hotly debated? (For more on the 2000 census, locate and read Kenneth Prewitt's article, "Demography, diversity, and democracy: the 2000 census story" or use the key word search term "2000 census").

ACTIVITIES

1. Explain the following statement: "In studying other cultures we do so very often from the perspective of our own culture."

2. Give some examples of how men and women in the United States might experience communication difficulties.

3. Explain how changes in technology, the new global economy, and increases in the world's population might affect you.

4. Explain how and why communication and culture are linked.

5. Attend a meeting of social function of a culture or co-culture different from your own. Try to notice the various ways that you can see specific cultural characteristics of that culture being acted out.

DISCUSSION IDEAS

1. In small groups, discuss national or domestic news stories from the past week to determine under what circumstances cultures coming in contact with one another display communication problems. Cite both the cultures and the problems.

2. In small groups, identify your culture or co-culture. Discuss with other members of the group the types of communication problems that have occurred when you have interacted with people from cultures different than your own. Explain how these difficulties have made you feel.

3. In small groups, discuss the various ways in which the dominant culture influences and controls the values, attitudes and behavior of co-cultures.

4. In a small group, discuss the following topic: "We are alike and we are different." Have the group produce list for both concepts.

5. In a small group, discuss how changes in the demographics of the United States have affected you. How do you believe these changes will ultimately affect society?

chapter 2

Understanding Culture: Alternative Views of Reality

How shall I talk of the sea to the frog, if he has never left his pond? How shall I talk of the frost to the bird of the summer land if he has never left the land of his birth? And how shall I talk of life with the sage if he is a prisoner of his doctrine?

CHUNG TZU

There never were, in the world, two opinions alike, no more than two hairs, or two grains; the most universal quality is diversity.

MONTAIGNE

No object is mysterious. The mystery is in your eye.

ELIZABETH BOWEN

UNDERSTANDING CULTURE

In the last chapter we talked about communication. We now move from that topic to culture. The transition should be a smooth one, for as Hall reminds us, "Culture is communication and communication is culture."[1] Put into slightly different terms—when looking at communication and culture, it is hard to decide which is the voice and which is the echo.

Some people in Korea and China put dogs in their ovens, but people in the United States put them on their couches and beds. Why? People in Tabriz or Tehran sit on the floor and pray five times each day, but people in Las Vegas sit up all night in front of video poker machines. Why? Some people speak Tagalog; others speak English. Why? Some people paint and decorate their entire bodies, but others spend millions of dollars painting and decorating only their faces. Why? Some people talk to God, but others have God talk to them. And still others say there is no God. Why? The general answer to these questions is the same. People learn to think, feel, believe, and act as they do because of the messages that have been communicated to them—messages that bear the stamp of culture. This omnipresent quality of culture leads Hall to conclude, "There is not one aspect of human life that is not touched and altered by culture."[2] Hall is correct: Culture is important because it is everything and everywhere. In a very real sense your culture is part of who you are. What makes culture so unique is that you share your

People are not born knowing what clothes to wear, what games to play, what foods to eat, or which gods to worship.

© Robert Fonseca

culture with other people who have been exposed to similar experiences. Hofstede clearly underscored this point when he noted, "Culture is to a human collective what personality is to an individual."[3] Nolan reaffirms this idea when he suggests that culture is a group worldview, the way of organizing the world that a particular society has created over time. This framework or web of meaning allows the members of that society to make sense of themselves, their world, and their experiences in that world.[4]

Notice that Nolan talks about making sense of the world. This is important, for as we noted in Chapter 1, you are born into a world without meaning. You do not arrive in this world knowing how to dress, what toys to play with, what to eat, which gods to worship, what to strive for, or how to spend your money and your time. Culture is both teacher and textbook. From how much eye contact you employ in conversations to explanations of why you get sick, culture plays a dominant role in your life. As we have already noted, this book is about how different cultures produce different lives. In short, when cultures differ, communication practices also differ, as Smith pointed out:

In modern society different people communicate in different ways, as do people in different societies around the world; and the way people communicate is the way they live. It is their culture. Who talks with whom? How? And about what? These are questions of communication and culture. A Japanese geisha and a New England librarian send and receive different messages on different channels and in different networks. When the elements of communication differ or change, the elements of culture differ or change. Communication and culture are inseparable.[5]

Because culture conditions you toward one particular mode of communication over another, it is imperative that you understand how culture operates as a first step toward improving intercultural communication. Although we will try to convince you that culture is a powerful force in how you see the world and interact in that world, we need to once again remind you that a combination of elements contribute to the manner in which you communicate. Hanson offered a similar point of view when she wrote:

> Behavior is governed by many factors—socioeconomic status, sex, age, length of residence in a locale, education—each of which will have an impact on cultural practices as well. Finally, individuals may differ by the degree to which they choose to adhere to a set of cultural patterns. Some individuals identify strongly with a particular group; others combine practices from several groups.[6]

In this chapter, we (1) explain why cultures develop, (2) highlight the essential features of culture, (3) define culture, (4) discuss the major components of culture, and (5) examine numerous culture patterns that influence intercultural communication.

The Basic Functions of Culture

The anthropologist Haviland suggests that "people maintain cultures to deal with problems or matters that concern them."[7] Triandis offers a more specific function when referring to culture: "It functions to improve the adaptation of members of the culture to a particular ecology, and it includes the knowledge that people need to have in order to function effectively in their social environment."[8]

Culture serves the basic need of laying out a predictable world in which each of you is firmly grounded and thus enables you to make sense of your surroundings. As Haviland notes, "In humans, it is culture that sets the limits on behavior and guides it along predictable paths."[9] The English writer Fuller echoed the same idea in rather simple terms when he wrote two hundred years ago, "Culture makes all things easy." It makes "things easy" for two reasons. First, culture helps facilitate the transition from the womb to this new life by providing meaning to events, objects, and people—thus making the world a less mysterious and frightening place. Second, culture makes life less confusing because, as we shall see later, most of culture is automatic and subconscious. Shapiro explains this idea:

> Thus, the influence of culture becomes habitual and subconscious and makes life easier, just as breathing, walking and other functions of the body are relegated to subconscious controls, freeing the conscious parts of the brain of this burden and releasing it for other activities.[10]

Culture, using the family as its first of many conduits, teaches the child how to behave in a manner that is acceptable to adults and that garners them rewards. There is no need for members of a culture to expend energy deciding what each event means or how to respond to it; usually, all those who share a common culture can be expected to behave correctly, automatically, and predictably. Hence, culture shields people from the unknown by offering them a blueprint for all of life's activities. While people in all cultures might deviate from this blueprint, they at least know what their culture expects from them. Try to imagine a single day in your life without having the guidelines of your culture. From how to earn a living, to a systematic economic system, to how to greet strangers, to explanations of illness, to how to find a mate, culture provides you with structure. We might even go so far as to agree with Harris that "our primary mode of biological adaptation is culture, not anatomy."[11]

In addition to making the world a less perplexing place, cultures have now evolved to the point where they are people's primary means of satisfying three types of needs: basic needs (food, shelter, physical protection), derived needs (organization of work, distribution of food, defense, social control), and integrative needs (psychological security, social harmony, purpose in life).[12]

The Elements of Culture

Before we define culture, it might be helpful if we paused and attempted to answer the following question: What elements mark a collection of people as a culture?[13] We will answer this question by looking at five features that all cultures possess. Understanding these elements will enable you to appreciate the notion that while all cultures share a common core of elements, these elements often distinguish one culture from another.

History

All cultures seem to believe in the idea that history is a kind of chart that guides its members into the future. What is interesting about a culture's history is that, like most of the important elements of culture, it gets passed on from generation to generation. These stories of the past offer the members of a culture part of their identity while highlighting the culture's origins, what is deemed important, and what accomplishments it can be proud of. As you shall see in the next chapter, while all cultures pass on a history that helps shape their members, each history is unique to a particular culture and carries a specific cultural message. The "lessons" of the Spanish conquest of Mexico tell a different tale than the building of the Great Wall of China, or the American Revolution.

Religion

Another feature of all cultures is their religion. More specifically, according to Parkes, Laungani, and Young, all cultures possess "A dominant, organized religion within which salient beliefs and activities (rites, rituals, taboos and ceremonies) can be given meaning and legitimacy."[14] The influence of religion can be seen in the entire fabric of a culture. Both consciously and unconsciously, and in vary degrees, religion impacts everything from business practices (the Protestant work ethic) to politics (the link between Islam and government) to individual behavior (a code of ethics). Because religion is so powerful and pervasive we shall examine it in great deal in the next chapter.

Values

Values are another feature of every culture. The connection between values and culture is so strong that it is hard to talk about one without the other. As Macionis notes, values are "culturally defined standards of desirability, goodness, and beauty that serve as broad guidelines for social living."[15] The key word in any discussion of cultural values is "guidelines." In other words, values help determine how people ought to behave. To the extent that cultural values differ, and we will demonstrate later in the chapter that they do, you can expect that intercultural communication participants will tend to exhibit and to anticipate different behaviors under similar circumstances. For example, while all cultures have a value toward the elderly, it is often very different as you move from culture to culture. In the Korean and Native American cultures, the elderly are highly respected and revered. They are even sought out for advice and counsel. This is, of course in stark contrast to the United States, where the emphasis is on youth.

Social Organization

Another feature found in all cultures is what we call "social organizations." These organizations (sometimes referred to as social systems or social structures) represent the various social units contained within in the culture. These units and institutions—such as the family, government, schools, and tribes—help the members of the culture organize their lives. These social systems establish communication networks and regulate norms of personal, familial and social conduct.[16] How these organizations function and the norms they advance are unique to each culture. Nolan underscores the nature of these organizations in the following illustration:

> Social structures reflect our culture, for example, whether we have kings and queens, or presidents and prime ministers. Within our social structure, furthermore, culture assigns roles to the various players – expectations about how individuals will behave, what they will stand for, and even how they will dress.[17]

Language

Language is another feature that is common to all cultures and that allows the members of the culture to communication with one another. As we shall see later in this chapter, and again in Chapter 4, not only does language allow the members of the culture to share ideas, feelings, and information, but it is also one of chief methods for the transmission of the culture. Whether it be English, Swahili, Chinese, or French, most words, meanings, grammar, and syntax bear the identification mark of a specific culture.

Definitions of Culture

The preceding discussion of the functions and features of culture should enable you so see how culture is ubiquitous, multidimensional, complex, all-pervasive, and difficult to define. As Harrison and Huntington note, "The term 'culture,' of course, has had multiple meanings in different disciplines and different contexts."[18] The elusive nature of the term is perhaps best reflected in the fact that as early as 1952, Kroeber and Kluckhohn listed 164 definitions of culture that they found in the anthropology literature.[19] Definitions of culture range from those that are all-encompassing ("it is everything") to those that are narrow ("it is opera, art, and ballet"). For our purposes, we are concerned with a definition that contains the recurring theme of how culture and communication are linked together. A definition that meets our needs is one advanced by Marsella:

> Culture is shared learned behavior which is transmitted from one generation to another for purposes of promoting individual and social survival, adaptation, and growth and development. Culture has both external (e.g., artifacts, roles, institutions) and internal representations (e.g., values, attitudes, beliefs, cognitive/affective/sensory styles, consciousness patterns, and epistemologies).[20]

We like Marsella's definition because it includes what Harrison and Huntington call the "subjective" elements of culture—the elements such as "values, attitudes, beliefs, orientations, and underlying assumptions prevalent among people in a society."[21] These are the elements that shape and control perception and interaction. Think for just a moment of all the subjective cultural beliefs and values you hold that influence your interpretation of the world and interactions in it. How you feel about the notion of a soul to how you respond to the American flag is all part of your cultural membership. Your views on work, immigration, freedom, age, cleanliness and hygiene, ethics, dress, property rights, etiquette, healing and health, death and mourning, play, law, magic and superstition, modesty, sex, status differentiation, courtship, formality and informality, bodily adornment, and the like are all part of your cultural membership.

Characteristics of Culture

Regardless of how many features or definitions we could have examined, there would have been a great deal of agreement concerning the major characteristics of culture. Examining these characteristics will help you become a better communicator for two reasons. First, as we move through these characteristics, the strong connection between culture and communication will become apparent. You will discover that culture deals with matters of substance that influence communication. As Huntington notes, "The heart of culture involves language, religion, values, traditions, and customs."[22] Second, this might be the first time you have been asked to examine your own culture or been exposed to the theory of culture. As Brislin points out, "People do not frequently talk about their own culture or the influence that culture has on their behavior."[23] Remember, most of culture is in the taken-for-granted realm and below the conscious level. Learning about culture can therefore be a stimulating awakening as you give meaning to your actions and the actions of others. Shapiro offered much the same "pep-talk" when he wrote: "The discovery of culture, the awareness that it shapes and molds our behavior, our values and even our ideas, the recognition that it contains some element of the arbitrary, can be a startling or an illuminating experience."[24]

Culture Is Learned

We begin with perhaps that most important characteristic of culture—it is learned. From the moment of birth to the end of your life, you seek to define the world that impinges on your senses. This idea is often difficult to comprehend, for most of you cannot remember a world without definitions and meanings. Yet perhaps you can imagine what a confusing place this world must be to a newborn infant. After living in a peaceful environment, the child, with but a brief transition, confronts sights, sounds, tastes, and other sensations that, at this stage of life, have no meanings. It must be, as the psychologist William James noted, a bubbling, babbling mass of confusion that greets the newborn. But from that first moment on, the search for meaning becomes a lifelong endeavor. As you move from word to word, event to event, and person to person, you seek meaning in everything. The meanings you give to these experiences are learned and culturally based. In some ways, this entire book is about how different cultures "teach" their members to define the circumstances and people that confront them. The notion of learning is the single most important characteristic of culture. Without the advantages of learning from those who lived before, you would not have culture. In fact, "the group's knowledge stored up (in memories, books and objects) for future use" is at the core of the concept of culture.[25] All of you are born with basic needs—needs that create and shape behavior—but how you go about meeting those needs and developing behaviors to cope with them is learned. As Bates and Plog note:

> Whether we feed ourselves by growing yams or hunting wild game or by herding camels and raising wheat, whether we explain a thunderstorm by attributing it to meteorological conditions or to a fight among the gods—such things are determined by what we learn as part of our enculturation.[26]

The term *enculturation* denotes the total activity of learning one's culture. More specifically, enculturation is, as Hoebel and Frost say, "conscious or unconscious conditioning occurring within that process whereby the individual, as child and adult, achieves competence in a particular culture."[27] In social psychology and sociology, the term socialization is often used synonymously with enculturation. Regardless of which word is applied, the idea is the same. From infancy, members of a culture learn their patterns of behavior and ways of thinking until most of them become internalized and habitual. Enculturation usually takes place through interaction (your parents kiss you and you learn about kissing—whom, when, and where to kiss), observation (you watch your father do most of the driving of the family car and you learn about gender roles—what a man does, what a woman does), and imitation (you laugh at the same jokes your parents laugh at and you learn about humor).

The words conscious and unconscious used in Hoebel and Frost's definition help us make our next point about learning. When you look at the word learned as it applies to culture, you find it has numerous meanings. Just as the word pain is used to denote the discomfort caused by a small splinter in the finger or the anguish felt by a burn victim, so too the word learned is asked to represent a host of variations. You learn your culture in many ways and from a variety of sources. From parents to play to peers, culture is always "teaching." A little boy in the United States whose grandfather tells him to shake hands when he is introduced to a friend of the family is learning good manners. An Arab baby who is read the Koran when he or she is one day old is learning about God. An Indian child who lives in a home where the women eat after the men is learning gender roles. A Jewish child who helps conduct the Passover ceremony is learning about traditions. An Egyptian child who is told by his uncle that his behavior brings shame to his family is learning cultural values. A Japanese girl who attends tea ceremony classes is learning about patience. A fourth-grade student sees a film on saving the Alamo and is learning about patriotism and fortitude. In these examples, people are learning their culture.

Because culture influences you from the instant you are born, you are rarely aware of many of the messages that it sends. As Keesing says, "It is a tenet of cultural anthropology that culture tends to be unconscious."[28] This unconscious or hidden dimension of culture leads many researchers to claim that culture is invisible. Ruben, for example, writes that "the presence of culture is so subtle and pervasive that it simply goes unnoticed. It's there now, it's been there as long as anyone can remember, and few of us have reason to think much about it."[29] Most of you would have a difficult time pointing to a specific event or experience that taught you about such things as direct eye contact, your use of silence and space, the importance of attractiveness, your view of aging, your ability to speak one language instead of another, and your preference for activity over meditation or for one mode of dealing with conflict over another. In short, while you would readily recognize that you had to learn how to solve a mathematics problem, you are apt to overlook the fact that you also had to learn how to worry and what to worry about, who to love and who not to love, who to touch and who not to touch.

A number of points should be clear by now. First, learning cultural perceptions, rules, and behaviors usually goes on without your being aware of it. Second, the essential messages of a culture get reinforced and repeated. And third, you learn your culture from a large variety of sources. Family, church, and state, as the three most powerful "teaching" forces, are examined in the next chapter. In Chapter 7 we discuss how schools are also a conduit for culture. But for now, let us touch on some of the more invisible "instructors" and "instructions" that often supplement family, church, and state.

Learning Culture Through Proverbs. In nearly every culture, proverbs, communicated in colorful and vivid language, offer an important set of instructions for members to follow. Proverbs are learned easily and repeated with great regularity. Because they are so brief (a line or two), their power as a "teacher" is often overlooked. Yet the great Chinese philosophers such as Confucius, Mencius, Chung Tzu, and Lao-tzu used proverbs and maxims to express their thoughts to their disciples—thoughts that still endure in the Chinese culture. These "words of wisdom" survive, so that each generation learns about what a culture deems significant. As Sellers tells us, "Proverbs reunite the listener with his or her ancestors."[30] Seidensticker notes that "They say things that people think important in ways that people remember. They express common concerns."[31] Hence, "proverbs are a compact treatise on the values of culture."[32]

Because all people, regardless of their culture, share common experiences, many of the same proverbs appear throughout the world. For example, in nearly every culture some degree of thrift and hard work is stressed. Hence, in Germany the proverb states, "One that does not honor the penny is not worthy of the dollar." In the United States people are told, "A penny saved is a penny earned." However, in spite of numerous universal proverbs, there are also thousands of proverbs that cultures use to teach important lessons that are unique to that particular culture. The importance of proverbs as a reflection of a culture is underscored by the fact that "interpreters at the United Nations prepare themselves for their extremely sensitive job by learning proverbs of the foreign language" they will be translating.[33] As Mieder notes, "Studying proverbs can offer insights into a culture's world view regarding such matters as education, law, business, and marriage."[34] They are, as Mieder adds, "the true voice of the people."[35]

Below are a few proverbs and sayings from the United States, each of which attempts to teach an important value held by the dominant culture.

Strike while the iron is hot. He who hesitates is lost. Both of these proverbs underscored the idea that in the United States people who take quick action are highly valued.

Actions speak louder than words. As we note later in this chapter, Americans are a "doing" culture; hence, activity and "getting things done" are important to the dominant culture.

God helps those who help themselves. Pull yourself up by your bootstraps. These sayings call attention to the strong belief in America that people should show individual initiative.

A man's home is his castle. This expression not only tells us about the value of privacy, but it also demonstrates the male orientation in the United States by implying the home belongs to the man.

The squeaky wheel gets the grease. In the United States, people are encouraged to be direct, "speak up," and make sure their views are heard.

Below are some proverbs from places other than the United States. You may see some of these proverbs again elsewhere in this book as we use them to explain the beliefs, values, and communication behavior of the cultures from which they are drawn.

One does not make the wind but is blown by it. This saying, found in many Asian cultures, suggests that people are guided by fate rather than by their own devices.

The ill-mannered child finds a father wherever he goes. This African proverb demonstrates the value of the extended family, for it is saying that everyone takes a hand in raising the child.

Sweep only the front of your own door. This German proverb reflects the very private nature of the Germans and their strong dislike of gossip. There is a somewhat similar proverb found in the Swedish culture. *He who stirs another's porridge often burns his own.*

Nothing done with intelligence is done without speech. This Greek saying emphasizes the importance of talk as a means of communication.

Wisdom is an unfinished symphony. The merchandise of wisdom is better than that of silver. These Jewish proverbs express the importance of learning and education.

A zebra does not despise its stripes. From the Maasai of Africa, this saying expresses the value of accepting things as they are. There is a similar proverb found in the Mexican culture: *I dance to the tune that is played.*

A man's tongue is his sword. With this saying, Arabs are taught to value words and use them in a powerful and forceful manner.

Those who know do not speak and those who speak do not know. This famous doctrine, in the *Analects* of Confucius, stressing silence over talk, is very different from the advice give in the above Arab proverb.

Conversation is the food for the soul. In this Mexican proverb we see yet another view toward talking. The Mexican culture has a long tradition of valuing interaction among friends and family.

When spider webs unite they can tie up a lion. This Ethiopian proverb teaches the importance of collectivism and group solidarity. In the Japanese culture the same idea is expressed with the following proverb: *A single arrow is easily broken, but not in a bunch.* And for the Yoruba of Africa, the same lesson is taught with the proverb that notes, *A single hand cannot lift the calabash to the head.*

The spit aimed at the sky comes back to one. This Japanese proverb attempts to teach the importance of controlling anger. The Koreans, who also believe that anger should be kept in check, offer the following proverb: *Kick a stone in anger and you harm your own foot.*

Learning Culture Through Folktales, Legends, and Myths. While folktales, legends, and myths are slightly different, we use the three words interchangeably because they all tell stories that are intended to transmit the important aspects of the culture from person to person and from generation to generation. Anthropologists Nanda and Warms highlight the importance of this form of cultural learning as follows:

> Folktales and storytelling usually have an important moral, revealing which cultural values are approved and which are condemned. The audience for folktales is always let, through the ways the tale is told, to know which characters and attributes are a cause for ridicule or scorn and which characters and attributes are to be admired.[36]

Haviland confirms that the subject matter of these cultural stories concern "the fundamentals of human existence: where we and everything in our world came from, why we are here, and where we are going."[37] Whether it be Pinocchio's nose growing larger because of his lies, Columbus being glorified because he was daring, Captain Ahab's heroics as he seeks to overcome the power of nature, Abraham Lincoln learning to read by drawing letters on a shovel by the fireside, folklore constantly reinforces our fundamental values. A case in point is the popular folktale "Cinderella." Although nearly every culture has its own version of this story, the emphasis varies. In the American version, Cinderella's attractiveness is crucial; she is also rather passive and weak. In the Algonquin Indian tale, the virtues of truthfulness and honesty are the basis of Cinderella's character. The Japanese story accentuates intellectual ability and gentleness. In one Japanese version, there are only two sisters and they wish to go to a Kabuki play. In place of the famous slipper test is the challenge of having to compose a song extemporaneously. One sister manages only a simple, unimaginative song, which she sings in "a loud harsh voice." But Cinderella composes a song that has both meter and metaphor, and she sings it in "sweet gentle tones." Traits that are important to the specific culture are reflected in each version of the tale.

Every culture has hundreds of tales, each stressing a fundamental value. Americans revere the tough, independent, fast-shooting cowboy of the Old West; the English admiration of good manners, courtly behavior, and dignity is reflected in The Canterbury Tales; the Japanese learn about the importance of duty, obligation, and loyalty in the ancient story of "The Tale of the Forty-Seven Ronin"; and the Sioux Indians use the legend of "Pushing Up the Sky" to teach what people can accomplish if they work together. For Superhuman heroes, the Greeks learn about Hercules, the Jews about Samson, and Americans learn about Superman. In Zaire, children are told the Myth of Invincibility. In this story young boys learn that if they wrap green vines around their head, the enemies' weapons cannot hurt them.[38]

Legends, folktales, and myths do more than accent cultural values: "They confront cosmic questions about the world as a whole."[39] In addition, they can tell you about specific details of life that might be important to a group of people. Writing about Native American myths and legends, Erdoes and Ortiz make the following point concerning what stories can tell us about what was, and is, important to the Native American culture:

> They are also magic lenses through which we can glimpse social orders and daily life: How families were organized, how political structures operated, how men caught fish, how religious ceremonies felt to the people who took part, how power was divided between men and women, how food was prepared, how honor in war was celebrated.[40]

As you have seen, myths, folktales and legends are found is every culture and are useful tools for teaching some of the major values of the culture. Perhaps their most significant contribution is that they deal with the ideas that matter most to a culture—ideas about life, death, relationships, nature, and the like. Campbell maintains that, "Myths are stories of our search through the ages for truth, for meaning, for significance. We all

In Western art the emphasis has been on the individual.

© Gloria Thomas

need to tell our story and to understand our story."[41] Because myths offer clues into culture, Campbell urges us not only to understand our story but also to "read other people's myths."[42] We strongly concur with Campbell—when you study the myths of a culture, you are studying what is important to that culture.

Learning Culture Through Art. A trip to any museum in the world quickly reveals how the art of a culture is yet another method of passing on culture. According to the art historian Gombrich, the Chinese have long "thought of art as a means of reminding people of the great examples of virtue in the golden ages of the past."[43] Nanda points out that the link between art and culture can be found in every culture:

> Art is a symbolic way of communicating. One of the most important functions of art is to communicate, display, and reinforce important cultural themes and values. The arts thus have an integrative function in society.[44]

One of the functions that Nanda is referring to is how the individual, through art, learns about himself or herself. Cultural differences in what art teaches are clearly seen in what is the subject matter of the painting or artwork. In Asian cultures, most art depicts objects, animals, and landscapes, seldom focusing on people. It even attempts to highlight spiritual concerns. According to Hunter and Sexton, Chinese art often represents "Buddhist and Taoist concerns with the mind in meditation, with the relative insignificance of human striving in the great cosmos, and with the beauty of nature."[45]

American and European art, however, often emphasizes people. This difference reflects a difference in views: Asians believe that nature is more powerful and important than a single individual, whereas Americans and Europeans consider people as the center of the universe. In addition, in Western art, the artist tries to create a personal message. This is not the case with most Asian artists. As Campbell notes, "Such ego-oriented thinking is alien completely to the Eastern life, thought, and religiosity."[46] The rule of the Asian artist is not to "innovate or invent."[47]

As we already indicated, art is a relevant symbol, a forceful teacher, and an avenue for cultural values. Two more examples will further illustrate this point. We need only look at the art on totem poles to see what matters to Native Americans. The carvings on these poles tell us the story of a people who are concerned about their lineage and their identity. Hence, we see carvings that show relationships "between humans and animals, plants, and inanimate objects."[48] For many African cultures, art is used to call attention to the importance of such things as animals and "ancestor worship and reverence of royalty."[49]

Learning Culture Through Mass Media. It is common knowledge that the mass media do much more than supply entertainment. As Thompson notes:

> Few people would deny that the nature of cultural experience in modern societies has been profoundly affected by the development of mass communication. Books, magazines and newspapers, radio, television and cinema, records, tapes and videos: These and other forms of mass communication occupy a central role in our lives.[50]

As Thompson points out, the term mass media applies to a variety of sources, each helping to shape your perceptions of the world. While granting the importance of printed media, it is television, at least in the United States, that is most influential. Television contributes to what Williams calls "mass social learning," which has us "taking on the values of the images" we are exposed to on television.[51] Because exposure is five to six hours a day for the average American, it is easy to see how these images affect our attitudes toward sex, leisure time, and people of different ethnic, gender, and/or age groups. Mass media can even shape our views toward violence. In the United States, films, police stories, and many documentaries glorify violence. The language we use in sports mirrors and sanctions violence. Sitting in front of a television set, one hears words and statements such as "kill," "head-hunter," "It's a war," and "They destroyed the offense."

Delgado offers an excellent summary of the power of mass media by noting that they "help constitute our daily lives by shaping our experiences and providing the content for much of what we talk about (and how we talk) at the interpersonal level."[52]

As we have said elsewhere, the messages that are strategic for any culture are repeated, are reinforced, and come from various sources. Think for a moment of the thousands of ways you have been told the importance of being popular and well liked, or the many messages you have received concerning competition and winning. Our games, sports, toys, movies, and so on all fortify the need to win. A famous tennis player tells us that he "feels like dying when he comes in second." And the president of a major car company concludes his television pitch by announcing, "We want to be number one—what else is there?" Although the carriers of culture are nearly the same for all people, the messages they transmit, as we point out throughout this book, are specific to each culture.

As discussed in Chapter 1, in the twenty-first century, because of the rapid growth of information technology, we now have a situation where cultures, willingly or unwillingly, are being exposed to the "messages" from cultures other than their own. The sources of these messages are as diverse as the messages themselves. Whether it is CNN News, television programs, films, videocassettes, or high-powered radio stations, mass media is now characterized by what Gross calls "a global flow of information."[53] While this information moves in every direction, it is the United States that is currently dominating information technology. This command of the technology means that it influences the socialization process in cultures other than its own. Kim offers an excellent example of this influence when she notes:

> Indeed, I have experienced the power of American culture wherever I have gone. *Titanic*, CNN, *Friends*, Oprah, and the Backstreet Boys have followed me to Japan, Korea, Thailand, Australia, France, and Italy. U.S. entertainment is the second largest export industry. American films, music and books fascinate both young and old around the globe.[54]

Whether it is Iranian objections to America's media reflecting immoral messages, or the French complaining about American commercialism, not everyone welcomes American media thrusting its values on their culture; it is nevertheless a truism that the media is an important component of how people learn.

We conclude our description of the first characteristic of culture by reminding you of three key points. First, most of the behaviors we label as cultural are not only automatic and invisible but also engaged in without your being aware of them. For example, in American culture, women smile more often than men,[55] a behavior learned unconsciously and performed almost habitually. And to this day, Jews, while reading from the Torah, sway backward and forward like camel riders, having inherited this behavior unconsciously from centuries ago. Because Jews then were prohibited from riding camels, this imitation of riding was developed as a form of compensation.[56] Although the motive for the behavior is gone, the action has been passed on to each new generation by

Culture is transmitted from generation to generation.

© Barbara Alper/Stock Boston

means of the silent, invisible power of culture. Such cultural behaviors, and there are thousands of them, tend to be unconscious in both acquisition and expression.

Second, it is important that we remind you that we have only mentioned some of the many ways we learn our culture. Space constraints have forced us to leave out many subtle yet powerful "teachers." For example, in every culture sports is much more than simple play. As Nanda and Warms tell us, "Football in America and bull fighting in Spain are both popular because they illustrate important themes of the respective cultures. They are exciting in part because they tell stories loaded with cultural meaning."[57] According to Gannon we can see these stories and their cultural meanings in everything from the Japanese gardens, to the Brazilian samba, to the German symphony, to the Italian opera.[58] These "cultural metaphors" represent and teach, according to Gannon "the underlying values expressive of the culture itself."[59] We will return to some very important cultural influences when we look at family, state, and religion in Chapter 3.

Finally, it should be remembered that one of key elements of culture is that common experiences contribute to common behaviors. The sharing of experience and behavior binds members and makes a culture unique. The Polish poet Stanislaw said it far more eloquently: "All of our separate fictions add up to a joint reality." Discovering those realities is what this book is all about.

Culture Is Transmitted from Generation to Generation

The American philosopher Thoreau once wrote, "All the past is here." As it regards culture, Thoreau is correct. For, if a culture is to endure, it must make certain that its crucial messages and elements are passed on. In this way the past become the present and helps prepare for the future. As Brislin said, "If there are values considered central to a society that have existed for many years, these must be transmitted from one generation to another."[60] According to Charon, this process of transmitting culture can be seen as a kind of "social inheritance."[61] Charon elaborates on this idea when he writes:

> Culture is a social inheritance; it consists of ideas that may have developed long before we were born. Our society, for example, has a history reaching beyond any individual's life, the ideas developed over time are taught to each generation and "truth" is anchored in interaction by people long before dead.[62]

As you saw in our first characteristic, the means of transmitting the culture can take a variety of forms (proverbs, stories, art, etc.) and can have numerous "carriers" (family, peers, media, church, etc.), but the key elements of culture must be shared with each new generation. This idea supports our assertion that culture and communication are linked: Communication makes culture a continuous process, for once cultural habits, principles, values, attitudes, and the like are "formulated," they are communicated to each member of the culture. So strong is the need for a culture to bind each generation to past and future generations that, Keesing tells us, "Any break in the learning chain would lead to a culture's disappearance."[63]

Culture Is Based on Symbols

When you talk about symbols, you are also talking about culture. Notice the link between symbols and culture in the definition of the word symbol advanced by Macionis: "A symbol is anything that carries a particular meaning recognized by people who share culture."[64] So important are symbols to a culture that the anthropologist Kluckhohn once wrote, "Human culture without language is unthinkable."[65] The emergence of language was the giant step that made possible the remarkable and intricate system we call culture.

Your cerebral cortex and all the neurological structures associated with it have developed in a way that enables you to use symbols at a level of sophistication not shared by any other creature. Not only can you transmit knowledge from person to person, you also can pass ideas from generation to generation—a characteristic of culture we just examined. At our disposal are the speculations, observations, facts, experiments, and wisdom accumulated over thousands of years—what the linguist Weinberg called "the grand insights of geniuses which, transmitted through symbols, enable us to span the learning of centuries."[66] Through language—be it verbal, nonverbal, or iconic—it is, as Goodenough says, "possible to learn from cumulative, shared experience."[67] Bates and Plog offer an excellent summary of the importance of language to culture:

> Language thus enables people to communicate what they would do if such-and-such happened, to organize their experiences into abstract categories ("a happy occasion," for instance, or an "evil omen"), and to express thoughts never spoken before. Morality, religion, philosophy, literature, science, economics, technology, and numerous other areas of human knowledge and belief—along with the ability to learn about and manipulate them—all depend on this type of higher-level communication.[68]

The symbols any culture employs take a variety of forms. Cultures can use the spoken word as a symbol and tell people about the importance of freedom. They can use the written word as a symbol and let others read about the War of Independence. They can use nonverbal actions, such as shaking hands or bowing, as symbols to greet one another. They can use flags as symbols to claim territory or demonstrate loyalty. They have the means to use automobiles or jewelry as symbols of success and status. They can use a cross, crescent, or six-pointed star to show the love of God. And even a man dressed in the colors of the American flag, who is named Uncle Sam, can symbolize an entire country.

The portability of symbols allows you to package and store them as well as transmit them. The mind, books, pictures, films, videos, computer disks, and the like enable a culture to preserve what it deems to be important and worthy of transmission. This makes each individual, regardless of his or her generation, heir to a massive repository of information that has been gathered and maintained in anticipation of his or her entry into the culture. Culture is therefore accumulative, historical, and perceivable.

The important elements of culture get transmitted through a variety of symbols.

© Gloria Thomas

Culture Is Subject to Change

The Greek philosopher Heraclitus might well have been talking about culture, when, over two thousand years ago, he observed: "You cannot step twice into the same river, for other waters are continually flowing in." What he was telling us then is true even today—cultures do not exist in a vacuum; they, because of "other waters continually flowing in," are subject to change. As Ethington notes, they are in a never-ending "process of reinvention."[69] Part of that reinvention stems from cultures coming in contact with one another. From the wandering nomad of thousands of years ago to millions of people all watching the same news event on CNN, cultures are constantly being confronted with ideas and information from outside sources. As we demonstrated earlier, today, because of the spread of Western capitalism and the advancement of information technology systems, cultures are being bombarded with new ideas that are often being presented by a host of "strangers." These "foreigners" may live next door or across the globe, but contact and change, whether in small increments or dramatic bursts, are now inevitable.

The point we are trying to make is that cultures are subject to fluctuations and seldom remain constant. Luckmann makes this point in the following manner:

> Although culture provides strength and stability, it is never static. Cultural groups face continual challenges from such powerful forces as environmental upheavals, plagues, wars, migration, the influx of immigrants, and the growth of new technologies. As a result, cultures change and evolve over time.[70]

Having used Luckmann's observation to speak about change in general terms, let us examine three mechanisms that are usually associated with change: (1) innovation, (2) diffusion, and (3) acculturation.

Innovation. Innovation refers to the discovery of new practices, tools, or concepts that many members of the culture eventually accept and that may produce slight changes in social habits and behaviors.[71] In the United States, television, the computer, and wireless phones are good examples of products that reshaped culture.

Diffusion. Another mechanism of change is called diffusion. It is the borrowing by one culture from another. Historically, diffusion has been part of cultural contact for as long as cultures have existed. Whether it be the sugar from a plant of Middle Eastern origin taken to the New World, missionaries taking God everywhere, or the McDonald's hamburger now being sold throughout the world, diffusion is universal way of life. As we have stressed elsewhere, technology has greatly influenced the notion of diffusion. As Macionis notes: "With new information technology sending words, sounds, and images around the world instantly, the level of cultural diffusion has never been greater than it is today."[72]

Because cultures want to endure, they usually adopt only those elements that are compatible with their values and beliefs or that can be modified without causing major disruption. The assimilation of what is borrowed accelerates when cultures come into direct regular contact with each other. For example, as Japan and the United States have more commerce, we see Americans assimilating Japanese business practices and the Japanese using American marketing tactics.

Acculturation. Acculturation is yet another type of cultural change. According to Haviland, "Acculturation occurs when groups having different cultures come into intensive first hand contact, with subsequent massive changes in the original cultural patterns of one or both groups."[73] In most instances that change take places in the culture that has come under the influence of a more dominant culture.[74] This type of change is common to international immigrants, who for a variety of reasons find themselves in another culture. These people, as part of the acculturation process, need to cope with a considerable amount of cultural change. In most instances, they "begin to detect new patterns of thinking and behavior and to structure a personality relevant to adaptation to the host society."[75] Inherent in acculturation is the idea that most people, as they are adapting, are also holding on to many of the values, customs, and communication patterns found in their primary culture.

We will return to the topic of acculturation in Chapter 10 when we offer some concrete advice as to how the transition from one culture to another can be made less stressful.

We conclude by pointing out a major consideration when analyzing cultural changes: Although many aspects of culture are subject to change, the deep structure of a culture resists major alterations. That is, changes in dress, food, transportation, housing, and the like are compatible with the existing value system. However, values associated with such things as ethics and morals, work and leisure, definitions of freedom, the importance of the past, religious practices, the pace of life, and attitudes toward gender and age are so deeply embedded in a culture that they persist generation after generation—a point Barnlund makes when he writes, "The spread of Buddhism, Islam, Christianity, and Confucianism did not homogenize the societies they enveloped. It was usually the other way around: Societies insisted on adapting the religions to their own cultural traditions."[76] In the United States, studies conducted on American values show that most contemporary core values are similar to the values of the last two hundred years. In short, when assessing the degree of change within a culture, you must always consider what is changing. Do not be fooled because downtown Tokyo looks much like Paris or New York. Most of what you call culture is below the surface, or like the moon: You observe the front, which appears flat and one-dimensional, but there are other dimensions that we cannot see.

Culture Is an Integrated System

Throughout this chapter, we have broken down and isolated various pieces of culture and talked about them as if they were discrete units. The nature of language makes it impossible to do otherwise; yet in reality, culture functions as an integrated whole—it is, like communication, systemic. That is, culture "is composed of parts that are related to each other."[77] The interrelationship of these various parts is so important that Haviland states, "All aspects of culture must be reasonably well integrated in order to function."[78] Think of all the important ingredients of culture that are functioning when families take children to church where they learn some of the key cultural values that they act out at school and even outside in the playground. As Hall said, "You touch a culture in one place and everything else is affected."[79] Values toward materialism will influence family size, the work ethic, spiritual pursuits, and the like. A complex example of the interconnectedness of cultural elements is the civil rights movement in the United States. This movement has brought about changes in housing patterns, discrimination practices, educational opportunities, the legal system, career opportunities, and even communication. This one aspect of culture has altered American attitudes, values, and behaviors.

We conclude this section on the characteristics of culture by reminding you that the pull of culture is so strong because teaching begins at birth and continues throughout life. Using the standard language of her time (sexist by today's standards), anthropologist Ruth Benedict offered an excellent explanation of why culture is such a puissant influence on all our lives:

> The life history of the individual is first and foremost an accommodation to the patterns and standards traditionally handed down in his community. From the moment of his birth the customs into which he is born shape his experience and behavior. By the time he can talk, he is the little creature of his culture, and by the time he is grown and able to take part in its activities, its habits are his habits, its beliefs his beliefs, its impossibilities his impossibilities. Every child that is born into his group will share them with him, and no child born into the opposite side of the globe can ever achieve the thousandth part.[80]

The important point to take away from our entire discussion of culture is beautifully expressed in the following sentence: "God gave to every people a cup, a cup of clay, and from this cup they drank life. . . . They all dipped in the water, but their cups were different."[81] Let us now spend the reminder of this chapter discussing how those "different cups" influence how people perceive the world and behave in that world.

PERCEPTION

We now open our discussion of perception with a few questions that are intended to direct you toward the topic of perception. The moon is a rocky physical sphere that orbits the Earth; yet when looking at this object, many Americans often see a man in the moon, many Native Americans perceive a rabbit, the Chinese claim a lady is fleeing her husband, and Samoans report a woman weaving—why? In Japan and China people fear the number four, in the United States it is the number thirteen. For Americans, a "V" sign made with two fingers usually represents victory. Australians equate this gesture with a rude American gesture usually made with the middle finger— why? Most Asians respond negatively to white flowers because white is associated with death. For Peruvians, Iranians, and Mexicans, yellow flowers often invoke the same reaction—why?[82] In all these examples, the external objects (moon, hands, flowers) were the same, yet the responses were different. The reason is perception, and that is what we are about to discuss—more specifically, how distinct cultures have "taught" their members to look differently at the world around them. To this end we will (1) define perception; (2) link perception to culture; (3) briefly discuss beliefs and values; and (4) look at differences in cultural perception that influence intercultural communication.

Defining Perception

Perception is the means by which you make sense of your physical and social world. As the German novelist Hermann Hesse states, "There is no reality except the one contained within us"—and it has been placed in us, in part, by our culture. The world inside of us, says Singer, "includes symbols, things, people, ideas, events, ideologies, and even faith."[83] Your perceptions give meaning to external forces. As Gamble and Gamble state, "Perception is the process of selecting, organizing, and interpreting sensory data in a way that enables us to make sense of our world."[84] In other words, perception is the process whereby people convert the physical energy of the world outside of them into meaningful internal experiences. Because that outside world embraces everything, we can never completely know it. As Singer notes, "We experience everything in the world not as it is—but only as the world comes to us through our sensory receptors."[85] Although the physical dimension is an important phase of perception, you must realize it is the psychological aspects of perception that help you understand intercultural communication.

Perception and Culture

Whether you feel delighted or ill at the thought of eating the flesh of a cow, fish, dog, or snake depends on what your culture has taught you about food. Whether you are repulsed at the sight of a bull being jabbed with sharp swords and long steel spears or believe it is a poetic sport depends on culture. By exposing a large group of people to similar experiences (such as foods or sports), culture generates similar meanings and similar behaviors. This does not mean, of course, that everyone in a particular culture is exactly the same. Because this is a book about culture, we offer a serious example of how culture affects perception and communication. In a classic study by Bagby, Mexican children from a rural area and children from the dominant culture in the United States viewed, for a split second, stereograms in which one eye was exposed to a baseball game while the other was exposed to a bullfight. In the main, the children reported seeing the scene according to their culture; Mexican children tended to report seeing the bullfight and American children tended to report the baseball game.[86] What should be obvious is that the children made selections based on their cultural background; they tended to see and to report what was most familiar. This study would, of course, yield different results with Mexican children from a large city, for they are familiar with baseball.

In yet another experiment demonstrating how culture influences perception, Caucasian mothers tended to interpret as positive those aspects of their children's speech and behavior that reflected assertiveness, excitement, and interest. Navajo mothers who observed the same behavior in their children reported them as being mischievous and lacking discipline. To the Navajo mothers, assertive speech and behavior reflected discourtesy, restlessness, self-centeredness, and lack of discipline; to the Caucasian mothers, the same behaviors reflected self-discipline and were, therefore, beneficial for the child.[87]

Personal credibility is another perceptual trait that is touched by culture. People who are credible inspire trust, know what they are talking about, and have good intentions. Americans usually hold that expressing one's opinion as openly and forcefully as possible is an admirable trait. Hence, someone is perceived as being highly credible if he or she is articulate and outspoken. For the Japanese, a person who is quiet and spends more time listening than speaking is more credible because they regard constant talking as a sign of shallowness. Among Americans, credible people seem direct, rational, decisive, unyielding, and confident. Among the Japanese, credible persons are perceived as being indirect, sympathetic, prudent, flexible, and humble.[88] In Japan, social status is a major indicator of credibility, but in the United States it has only modest import. Even the perception of something as simple as the blinking of one's eyes is affected by culture, as Adler and Rodman note: "The same principle causes people from different cultures to interpret the same event in different ways. Blinking while another person talks may be hardly noticeable to North Americans, but the same behavior is considered impolite in Taiwan."[89]

How we perceive the elderly is also affected by culture. In the United States, we find a culture that "teaches" the value of youth and rejects growing old. In fact, "young people view elderly people as less desirable interaction partners than other young people or middle-aged people."[90] This disapproving view of the elderly is not found in all cultures. For example, in the Arab, Asian, Latin American, and Native American cultures, old people are perceived in a very positive light. And notice what Harris and Moran tell us about the elderly in Africa: "It is believed that the older one gets, the wiser one becomes—life has seasoned the individual with varied experiences. Hence, in Africa age is an asset. The older the person, the more respect the person receives from the community, and especially from the young."[91] It is clear from these few examples that culture strongly influences our subjective reality and that there are direct links among culture, perception, and behavior. As Triandis noted, "cultural factors provide some of the meaning involved in perception and are, therefore, intimately implicated with the process."[92]

We are now ready to summarize how culture is "implicated with the process" of perception in two ways. First, perception is selective. This simply means that because there are too many stimuli impinging on your senses at the same time, you "allow only selected information through [y]our perceptual screen to our conscious mind."[93] What is allowed in, as discussed earlier, is in part determined by culture. Second, your perceptual patterns are learned. As we have pointed out on a number of occasions, everyone is born into a world without meaning, and it is culture that gives meaning to most of our experiences. As Adler points out, "perception is culturally determined. We learn to see the world in a certain way based on our cultural background."[94] As is the

© Owen Franken/Stock Boston

What makes belief systems important is that they are learned, endure, and are subject to cultural interpretations.

case with all of culture, perceptions are stored within each human being in the form of beliefs and values. These two, working in combination, form what are called cultural patterns.

BELIEFS

The Spanish poet Antonio Machado once noted that "Under all that we think, lives all we believe, like the ultimate veil of our spirits." Although not directly saying so, he was, of course, talking about our belief systems. According to Rogers and Steinfatt, "Beliefs serve as the storage system for the content of our past experiences, including thoughts, memories, and interpretations of events. Beliefs are shaped by the individual's culture."[95] Beliefs are important, as noted by Purnell and Paulanka, because they are "something that is accepted as truths."[96] Beliefs are usually reflected in your actions and communication behavior. If, for instance, you believe that snakes are slimy, you avoid them. On the other hand, if you believe that only through the handling of snakes can you find God (as do some religious sects), you handle them and believe your faith will protect you from venomous bites. You might embrace the New York Times or the CBS Evening News as arbiter of the truth because you respect them. If you value the Islamic tradition, you will believe that the Koran is an infallible source of knowledge and thus accept the miracles and promises that it offers. Whether you trust as sources of truth and knowledge the Times, the Bible, the Koran, the entrails of a goat, tea leaves, Madonna, the Dalai Lama, the visions induced by peyote, or the changes specified in the Taoist I Ching depends on your cultural background and experiences. If someone believes that sitting quietly for long periods of time can guide him or her along the proper path, you cannot throw up your hands and declare the belief wrong. You must be able to recognize the fact that cultures have different realities and belief systems. People who grow up in cultures where Christianity is the predominant religion usually believe that salvation is attainable only through Christ. People who are Jewish, Islamic, Buddhist, Shinto, or Hindu do not subscribe to that belief. They hold their own beliefs about salvation or what happens to the human spirit when the body dies. What is enthralling about beliefs is that they are so much a part of culture that in most instances we do not demand proof or question them. We simply accept them because we "know they are true."

VALUES

One of the most important functions of beliefs is that they are the basis of your values. Values are, according to Rokeach, "a learned organization of rules for making choices and for resolving conflicts."[97] As Nanda and Warms point out, "Values are shared ideas about what is true, right, and beautiful that underlie cultural patterns and guide society in response to the physical and social environment."[98] Because this is a book about culture, it is essential that you note that Nanda and Warms used the word shared in their description, for values are not only held by individuals, they are also the domain of the collective.[99] Albert highlights the significance of values when he notes that "a value system represents what is expected or hoped for, required or forbidden. It is not a report of actual conduct but is the system of criteria by which conduct is judged and sanctions applied."[100] While any list of "conduct" would be incomplete, Hofstede offers a short list of some of things with which values deal:[101]

- Evil versus good
- Dirty versus clean
- Dangerous versus safe
- Decent versus indecent
- Ugly versus beautiful
- Unnatural versus natural
- Abnormal versus normal
- Paradoxical versus logical
- Irrational versus rational
- Moral versus immoral

Your cognitive structure consists of many values. These values are highly organized and, as Rokeach says, "exist along a continuum of relative importance."[102] Values can be classified as primary, secondary, and tertiary. Primary values are the most important: They specify what is worth the sacrifice of human life. In the United States, democracy and the protection of oneself and close family are primary values. Secondary values are also quite important. In the United States, the relief of the pain and suffering of others is a secondary value. The securing of material possessions is also a secondary value for most Americans. We care about such values, but we do not hold the same intense feeling toward them as we do with primary values. Tertiary values are at the bottom of our hierarchy. Examples of tertiary values in the United States are hospitality to guests and cleanliness. Although we strive to carry out these values, they are not as profound or consequential as values in the other two categories.

As you saw earlier in this chapter, values are transmitted by a variety of sources (family, proverbs, media, school, church, state, etc.) and therefore tend to be broad based, enduring, and relatively stable. In addition, as is the case with most aspects of culture, Hofstede reminds us that "values are programmed early in our lives" and therefore are often nonrational."[103]

As you saw from the list of sample values offered by Hofstede, values generally are normative and evaluative in that they inform a member of a culture what is good and bad, and right and wrong. Cultural values define what is worthwhile to die for, what is worth protecting, what frightens people, and what are proper subjects to study and which deserve ridicule. As already indicated, values are learned within a cultural context. For example, the outlook of a culture toward the expression of emotion is one of the many values that differ among cultures. In the United States, people are encouraged to express their feelings outwardly and taught not to be timid about letting people know they are upset. Think for a moment about what is being said by the proverb we cited earlier in the chapter: "The squeaky wheel gets the grease." This positive value toward the expression of emotion is very different from the one found in China. As Gao and Ting-Toomey note, "Chinese are socialized not to openly express their own personal emotions, especially strong negative ones."[104] There is even a Chinese proverb that states, "A harsh word dropped from the tongue cannot be brought back by a coach and six horses." What is important about values is that they get translated into action. And knowing those actions can help you as a communicator. For instance, being aware that the Japanese value detail and politeness might cause you to examine carefully a proffered Japanese business card, as the Japanese do, rather than immediately relegate it to a coat pocket or purse. Attentiveness to cultural values might also offer partial insight into a culture's approach to business. Oppenheimer, citing the work of Huntington, Harrison, and Fukuyama, offers an excellent example linking values to cultural characteristics when he notes, "South Koreans are prospering because they value thrift, investment, hard work, education, organization and discipline."[105]

STUDYING CULTURAL PATTERNS

People and cultures are extremely complex and consist of numerous interrelated cultural orientations in addition to beliefs and values. A useful umbrella term that allows us to talk about these and other orientations collectively instead of separately is cultural patterns. You should think of cultural patterns as a system of beliefs and values that work in combination to provide a coherent, if not always consistent, model for perceiving the world. These patterns contribute not only to the way a people perceive and think about the world, but just as importantly for our purposes, the manner in which they live in that world. As you would suspect, these cultural patterns are useful in the study of intercultural communication because they are systematic and repetitive instead of random and irregular.[106] Because of this systematic and recurring characteristic of cultural patterns, and because they are widely shared by most members of the culture, they can be isolated and investigated.

Obstacles in Studying Cultural Patterns

Before we open our discussion of cultural patterns, we need to offer a few cautionary remarks that will enable you to better use the cultural patterns that we present in the remainder of this chapter.

We Are More Than Our Culture

We begin with an important point we made elsewhere. Simply stated, the value of the culture may not be the value of all individuals within the culture. Factors as divergent as "socioeconomic status, educational level, occupation, personal experience,"[107] age, gender, and co-culture affiliations also shape your view of your environment. Although we grant the complex nature of human behavior, we suggest, however, that culture has the strongest influence on your communication behavior because all of your other experiences take place within a cultural context. In addition, as we noted earlier in this chapter, cultural learning occurs very early in life. As Lynch and Hanson point out, "Lessons learned at such early ages become in integral part of thinking and behavior."[108]

Cultural Patterns Are Interrelated

Although we will be forced by the liner nature of language to speak of but one cultural pattern at a time, it is important to keep in mind that patterns are interrelated and do not operate in isolation. It might be helpful to visualize these patterns as a large stone being cast into a pond that creates ripples. For example, a pattern that stresses a spiritual life over materialism (a large stone) also directs values toward age, status, social relationships, and the use of time (the ripples). Another example of patterns being linked could be found in a culture's view of formality (large stone). Values toward dress, language, greeting behavior, the use of space, and age (ripples) would grow out of the key pattern.

Heterogeneity Influences Cultural Patterns

Any attempt to delineate a national culture or typical cultural patterns for any culture is extremely hazardous because of the heterogencity of many societies. For example, it is estimated that together the United States and Russia contain over 125 ethnic groups. The Encyclopedia of American Religions identifies nearly 1,200 different religions in the United States. And, of course, the United States is home to numerous co-cultures that do not share many of the values associated with the dominant culture. Lynch and Hanson make this point rather clear in the following paragraph:

> In the United States, competition is highly prized; however, the reverse is true in many Native American, Hispanic/Latino, Asian, Pacific Island, and Southeast Asian cultures. Competition is viewed as self-serving; and the emphasis is on cooperation and teamwork. Because competition is a negative trait in these cultures, being viewed as competitive rather than cooperative would bring shame rather than pride.[109]

Because of the cultural diversity found in the United States, you might believe that the United States is the only country with ethnic variety, but we can assure you that this is not the case. For example, Romania has Hungarians, Germans, Serbs, Croats, and Turks; Peru has Indians, whites, blacks, Japanese, and Chinese. And in Afghanistan, Goodson notes, "Islam is divided by hundreds of variations," regional politics, and "tribal social groupings" based on communal loyalties that make it difficult to speak of a single nation or culture.[110] Hence, common cultural patterns that could be said to hold for the whole country must be limited to the dominant culture in each country.

Cultural Patterns Change

As we noted earlier in this chapter, cultures change and therefore so do the values of the culture. The "women's movement," for example, has greatly altered social organizations and some value systems in the United States. With more women than men now getting college degrees, we can see how the workplace and classrooms have changed in the United States during the last twenty years.[111] As industrialization and Western capitalism and culture move throughout the world, we see young people in some traditional countries now wearing Levi's and dancing to American pop music. However, even granting the dynamic nature of culture and value systems, we again remind you that regardless of the culture, the deep structure of a culture resists change.

Cultural Patterns Are Often Contradictory

In many instances, we find contradictory values in a particular culture. In the United States, we speak of "all people being created equal," yet we observe pervasive racial prejudice and violence directed against gays. Individualism is at the heart of American culture, yet the United States is the most humanitarian country in the world. Americans claim to be a moral and honorable group of people, yet the United States is one of the world's most violent societies. These sorts of contradictions are found in all cultures. In China, where Confucianism and Buddhism stress interpersonal harmony, you will witness human rights violations. The Koran teaches brotherhood among all people, yet in many Arab cultures there is a vast gulf between the very rich and the very poor. Even with the reservations we have just offered, it is our contention that study of cultural patterns is a worthwhile pursuit.

Selecting Cultural Patterns

Deciding on what cultural patterns to examine is not an easy assignment. We have already mentioned the idea that culture is composed of countless elements. This fact influenced our decision regarding what patterns to examine and which to exclude from our analysis. We are not the first writers who have faced this problem of what in include and what to exclude. Leading scholars in the area of intercultural communication have advanced numerous classifications and typologies. While there is obviously a great deal of overlap in these systems, it might help you appreciate the problems associated with isolating the key patterns if we pause for a moment and simply listed some of the topics suggested by four different scholars. At the conclusion of this initial, and somewhat brief catalog, we will offer a detailed analysis of the taxonomies we have selected for further development.

Gannon's Four-Stage Model of Cross-Cultural Understanding[112]

For Gannon, cross-cultural understanding can best be achieved if you examine the topics contained in his four-stage model. The first stage, called emotional expressive, is concerned with "the degree to which a culture fosters and encourages open emotional expression."[113]

Stage two suggests that to know another culture you need to discover how it values collectivism or individualism—two concepts that we will discuss in great detail later in the chapter. Stage three revolves around some general dimensions on which cultures often differ. More specifically, Gannon suggests that to understand another culture you need to investigate "dimensions such as achievement, motivation . . . uncertainty avoidance, time horizon, and femininity or assertiveness."[114] In the fourth stage, "cultural metaphors are employed for understanding a culture."[115] This is Gannon's most detailed stage in that topics such as competitiveness, pride, being self-sufficient, and the like are explored.

Trompenaars and Hampden-Turner's Basis of Cultural Differences[116]

Trompenaars and Hampden-Turner believe that if you are to appreciate and know another culture you must examine and compare cultures along the following eight categories:

- Relationship with people
- Universalism versus particularism
- Individualism versus communitarianism
- Neutral versus emotional
- Specific versus diffuse
- Achievement versus ascription
- Attitudes to time
- Attitudes to the environment

Grondona's Cultural Typology[117]

Although Grondona is writing about economic development, he nevertheless presents an excellent typology of seventeen cultural patterns (which he calls *values systems*) that can offer significant insight into a culture. These patterns are religion, trust in the individual, morality, the value of work, the role of heresy, education, the importance of utility, virtues, time focus, rationality, authority, worldview, life view, salvation, views toward utopias, the nature of optimism, and visions of democracy.

Weaver's Contrast Culture Continuum[118]

Weaver maintains that cultures can be studied and compared along eight cultural dimensions. As is the case with all discussions of cultural patterns, the eight general categories of Weaver's typology can be divided into numerous subsets. To help clarify his groupings we will mention a few specific examples for each of the main headings.

- Characteristic culture (urban vs. rural, heterogeneous vs. homogeneous)
- Social structure (individualist vs. collective, flexible roles vs. rigid roles)
- Philosophic outlook (objective vs. subjective, melodramatic/escapist vs. tragic/realistic)
- Psychological orientation (need for achievement vs. need for affiliation, schizoid or fragmented vs. comprehensive or holistic)
- Thought patterns (dichotomous/divisions vs. holistic/joining together, linear separation vs. nonlinear comprehensive)
- Basic values (change/action vs. stability/harmony, self-reliance vs. reliance upon others)
- Perception (mind/body dichotomy vs. mind/body unity, future orientation vs. past or present orientation)
- Interaction (competition vs cooperation, verbal emphasis vs. nonverbal emphasis)

Two points should emerge from our brief listing of the four typologies. First, for most scholars of intercultural communication, cultural patterns are points lying on a continuum. The rationale is a simple one—cultural differences are usually matters of degree. Second, there is a great deal of duplication and overlap in any discussion of cultural patterns. In fact, as we develop the patterns we have selected to discuss in detail, you will see many of the patterns we just alluded to in our review of Gannon, Trompenaars and Hampden, Grondona, and Weaver.

DOMINANT AMERICAN CULTURAL PATTERNS

We have already alluded to many of the difficulties in allowing a specific cultural pattern to apply to an entire culture. This problem is, of course, even more transparent when dealing with the United States and its diverse multiracial and ethnic culture. As Charon notes, "Listing American values is a difficult task because there are so many exceptions and contradictions."[119] However, Charon adds, "On a general level, Americans do share a value system."[120] Kim echoes this same notion when she writes, "There are similar characteristics that all Americans share, regardless of their age, race, gender, or ethnicity."[121]

Although this textbook is used in many foreign countries, we nevertheless believe that a section on American cultural patterns would be helpful for all of our readers. For people who are not members of the dominant culture, we trust that our discussion of cultural patterns would offer insights into that culture. For those who are members of the dominant culture, we offer our analysis of cultural patterns for three reasons. First, as we have said throughout this book, people carry their culture wherever they go, and that culture influences how they respond to the people they meet. To understand the communication event in which you find yourself, you must appreciate your role in that event. Second, examining one's own cultural patterns can reveal information about culture that is often overlooked. As the anthropologist Hall notes, "Culture hides more than it reveals, and strangely enough what it hides, it hides most effectively from its own participants." Finally, one's cultural patterns can serve as reference point by which comparisons can be made.

We limit our discussion of American cultural patterns to the dominant culture as defined in Chapter 1. You will recall we said that the dominant culture is that part of the population, regardless of the culture being studied, that controls and dominates the major institutions and determines the flow and content of information. In the United States, that group has been, and continues to be, white, male, and of European heritage.[122]

Individualism

The single most important pattern in the United States is individualism. Broadly speaking, individualism refers to the doctrine, spelled out in detail by the seventeenth-century English philosopher John Locke, that each individual is unique, special,

The importance of individualism can be seen in how Americans use space.

© Larry Samovar

completely different from all other individuals, and "the basic unit of nature."[123] Locke's view is a simple one: The interests of the individual are or ought to be paramount, and that all values, rights, and duties originate in individuals. The value of individualism is so commanding that other imperative American values spring from individualism. Gannon underscores the link between individualism and other values when he writes:

> Equality of opportunity, independence, initiative, and self-reliance are some of the values that have remained as basic American ideals throughout history. All of these values are expressive of a high degree of individualism.[124]

As Gannon noted, this emphasis on the individual, while found elsewhere in the world, has emerged as the cornerstone of American culture. Huntington points out, that this "sense of individualism and a tradition of individual rights and liberties is unique among civilized societies."[125] The origin of this value has had a long history and a variety of champions. Benjamin Franklin told Americans that "God helps those who help themselves" and Herbert Hoover reminded them that "the American system was based on rugged individualism." Whether it is in sexual, social, or ethical matters, the self for Americans holds the pivotal position. So strong is this notion that some Americans believe that there is something wrong with someone who fails to demonstrate individualism. Think of the power of the concept in the words of former Supreme Court justice Felix Frankfurter: "Anybody who is any good is different than anybody else." Whether it is literature, art, or American history, the message is the same: Individual achievement, sovereignty, and freedom are the virtues most glorified and canonized. American role models, be they the cowboys of the Old West or action heroes in today's movies, videos, or computer games, are all portrayed as independent agents who accomplish their goals with little or no assistance. The result of these and countless other messages is that most Americans believe that each person has his or her own separate identity, which should be recognized and reinforced. As Kim points out, "In America, what counts is who you are, not who others around you are. A person tends to be judged on his or her own merit."[126]

Equality

Closely related to individualism is the American value of equality. As Hanson observes, "The United States was founded on the principle that 'all men are created equal.'"[127] You can see examples of equality being emphasized in everything from government (everyone has the right to vote) to social relationships ("Just call me by my first name"). Americans believe that all people have a right to succeed in life and that the state, through laws and educational opportunities, should ensure that right. The value of equality is prevalent in both primary and secondary social relationships: For instance, most of the primary social relationships within a family tend to advance equality rather than hierarchy. Formality is not important, and children are often treated as adults. In secondary relationships, you find that most friendships and coworkers are also treated as equals. People from cultures that have rigid, hierarchical social structures often find it disconcerting to work with Americans, who they believe negate the value of hierarchical structures within a society.

We would be remiss if, when describing the dominant culture in the United States, we did not once again remind you of some of the contradictions that often exist when we speak of individualism and equality. As Macionis points out, "Despite prevailing ideas about individualism and freedom, many people in the United States still evaluate others according to their sex, race, ethnicity, and social class."[128] He adds, "Although we describe ourselves as a nation of equals, there is little doubt that some of us rank as 'more equal than others.'"[129] While granting that many Americans have experienced periods of inequality, Hanson is correct when she writes, "Not all citizens have had equal rights throughout the course of the country's history, but Americans nevertheless value the notion highly and strive toward this ideal."[130]

Materialism

For most Americans, materialism has always been an integral part of life. As Stewart and Bennett note, "Americans consider it almost a right to be materially well off and physically comfortable."[131] Althen endorses the same idea when he notes that for Americans materialism "is natural and proper."[132] A popular bumper sticker proclaims, "The person who dies with the most toys wins." Americans expect to have swift and convenient transportation (preferably controlled by themselves), a large variety of foods at their disposal, clothes for every occasion, and comfortable homes equipped with countless labor-saving devices.

Science and Technology

For most Americans, science and technology, or what Clark calls "the value of know how,"[133] take on the qualities often associated with a god. The following inscription, found on the National Museum of American History in Washington, D.C., expresses the same idea: "Modern civilization depends on science." Clark maintains that Americans think that scientific and technical knowledge are linked to their very survival.[134] This strong belief gives rise to the notion among most Americans that nothing is impossible when scientists, researchers, engineers, and inventors put their minds to a task. From fixing interpersonal relationships to walking on the moon, science has the answer. The American respect for science is based on the assumptions that reality can be rationally ordered by humans and that such an ordering, using the scientific method, allows people to predict and control much of life. Very broadly, this emphasis on science reflects the values of the rationalistic-individualistic tradition that is so deeply embedded in Western civilization. From John Locke to Francis Bacon, René Descartes, Bertrand Russell, and Albert Einstein, Western cultures have long believed that all problems can be solved by science. This emphasis on rationality and science, according to Macionis, helps "explain our cultural tendency (especially among men) to devalue emotion and intuition as sources of knowledge."[135] While Westerners tend to prize rationality, objectivity, empirical evidence, and the scientific method, you will see in the next chapter when we discuss world views that these views often clash with cultures that value and believe in fatalism, subjectivity, mysticism, and intuition.

Progress and Change

In the United States, as Hanson reminds you, "Change, newness, and progress are all highly valued."[136] From changing their personalities with the assistance of self-help gurus, to changing where they live at a faster rate than any other people in the world, they do not value the status quo. Nor have they ever. "Early Americans cleared forests, drained swamps, and altered the course of rivers in order to 'build' the country. Contemporary Americans have gone to the moon in part to prove they could do so."[137] The French writer Alexis de Tocqueville, after visiting the United States over a hundred years ago, reached much the same conclusion when he wrote that the people in the United States "all consider society as a body in a state of improvement, and humanity as a changing scene." From the culture's earliest establishment as a distinct national entity, there has been a diffuse constellation of beliefs and attitudes that may be called the cult of progress. These beliefs and attitudes produce a certain mind-set and a wide range of behavior patterns. Various aspects of this orientation are optimism, receptivity to change, emphasis on the future rather than the past or present, faith in an ability to control all phases of life, and confidence in the perceptual ability of the common person. You can observe this strong conviction in change and progress in how Americans view the environment. Hanson offers a summary of this point when she notes: "This belief also has fostered a use of force in interactions with the environment and other people that is evident in phrases such as 'taming the wilderness,' 'winning the West,' and 'conquering space.'"[138]

A passion for progress fosters not only the acceptance of change but also the conviction, true or false, that changes tend in a definite direction and that the direction is good. Each new generation in the United States wants its opportunity to be part of that change. So strong is the belief in progress and change that Americans seldom fear taking chances. The writer Henry Miller clearly captured this American spirit when he wrote, "Whatever there be in progress in life comes not through adaptation but through daring, through obeying blind urge." As we discuss later in the chapter, many older and more traditional cultures, which have witnessed civilizations rise and fall and believe in fatalism, do not sanctify change, progress, and daring and often have difficulty understanding the way Americans behave. As Althen notes:

> This fundamental American belief in progress and a better future contrasts sharply with the fatalistic (Americans are likely to use that term with a negative or critical connotation) attitude that characterizes people from many other cultures, notably Latin, Asian, and Arab, where there is a pronounced reverence for the past. In those cultures the future is considered to be in the hands of "fate," "God," or at least the few powerful people or families that dominate the society. The idea that they could somehow shape their own futures seems naive or even arrogant.[139]

Work and Leisure

Work, like all major cultural characteristics patterns, has a long history in the United States. McElroy speaks to that history, and to the importance of work in the United States, when he writes:

> The primary American cultural beliefs derive from the initial experience of European settlers in the future United States. They all relate to work, the first necessity for survival in a wilderness. It was the peculiar experiences of work—what kind was done, who did it, how much it was rewarded—that began the process of distinguishing American behavior from European behavior, which led during the next eight generations to the formation of a new American culture.[140]

The value associated with work is so important in the United States that many people who meet each other for the first time ask the common question "What do you do?" Embedded in this simple question is the belief that working (doing something) is important. For most Americans, work represents a cluster of moral and affective conditions of great attractiveness, while at the same time voluntary idleness often constitutes a severely threatening and damaging social condition.

A major reward of hard work, and an important American value, is leisure. Most Americans seem to have embraced the words of the American poet and philosopher George Santayana: "To the art of working well a civilized race would add the art of playing well." For Americans, play is something they have earned. It is relief from the regularity of work; it is in play that we find real joy. This emphasis on recreation and relaxation takes a variety of forms. Each weekend people rush to get away in their recreational vehicles, play golf or tennis, go skiing, ride their mountain bikes, or "relax" at a gambling casino.

Competition

Competition is part of an American's life from early childhood on. Whether it be through the games they play or their striving to be more attractive than the person they are sitting next to in class, a competitive nature is encouraged in the United States. People are ranked, graded, classified, and evaluated so that everyone will know if they are "the best." In sports and at work, we are told the importance of "being number one." Young people are even advised that if they lose and it does not bother them, there is something wrong with them. As Kim points out, "For competitive Americans, who hate losing, everything in life is a game to win."[141] As is the case with all the patterns found in a culture, the origin of a specific pattern has a long history. Notice the call for competition in the following proverb—written at the beginning of the first century by the Roman philosopher Ovid: "A horse never runs so fast as when he has other horses to catch up and outpace." The message was clear then and it is clear now—you need to "outpace" all the other horses. "In its purest form," notes Kim, "competition challenges Americans to become even better."[142]

Competition is yet another pattern that often causes problems for Americans when they interact with people who do not espouse this value. For instance, "Asians believe that it is neither necessary nor beneficial to obsessed with winning.[143] Harris and Moran offer yet another example of differing perceptions of competition as it applies to the French:

> When confronted with individuals with a competitive drive, the French may interpret them as being antagonistic, ruthless, and power-hungry. They may feel threatened, and overreact or withdraw from the discussion.[144]

DIVERSE CULTURAL PATTERNS

So far we have introduced some universal cultural patterns and examined some cultural characteristics as they applied to the dominant American culture. We are now ready to make some cultural comparisons. Many anthropologists, social psychologists, and communication scholars have devised taxonomies that can be used to analyze key behavioral patterns found in every culture. While these patterns are numerous, there are three taxonomies that seem to be at the core of any study of intercultural communication. The first classification, developed by Hofstede, identifies five value dimensions (power distance, uncertainty avoidance, individualism/collectivism, masculinity/femininity, long-term/short-term orientation) that are influenced and modified by culture. The second four orientations grow out of the anthropological work of the Kluckhohns and Strodtbeck (human nature, person-nature, time, activity, social orientation). Hall advanced our third taxonomy, which looks at how high-context and low-context cultures respond to various message systems. Our final classification discusses some cultural patterns that we deem to be important, but that are not directly included in the other taxonomies.

Hofstede's Value Dimensions[145]

Hofstede, in the preface to the second edition of his book, clearly articulates the rationale behind his study:

> This book explores the differences in thinking and social action that exists among embers of more than 50 modern nations. It argues that people carry 'mental programs' that are developed in the family in early childhood and reinforced in schools and organizations, and that these mental programs contain a component of national culture. They are most clearly expressed in the values that predominate among people from different countries.[146]

Hofstede's work was one of the earliest attempts to use extensive statistical data to examine cultural values. In carrying out his research Hofstede, on numerous occasions, surveyed hundreds of thousands of workers in multinational organizations in fifty countries and three regions. After careful analysis, each country and region was assigned a rank of one through fifty in each of the five value dimensions (individualism, uncertainty avoidance, power distance, masculinity-femininity, long-term/short-term orientation) in his study. These rankings not only offer a clear picture of what was valued in each culture, but also help you see comparisons across cultures.

Individualism–Collectivism

Researchers for many years have maintained "self-orientation versus collective orientation is one of the basic pattern variables that determine human action."[147] As Ting-Toomey notes, "Individualistic and collective value tendencies are manifested in everyday family, school, and workplace interactions."[148]

Although Hofstede is often given credit for investigating the concepts of individualism and collectivism, he is not the only scholar who has researched these crucial intercultural dimensions. Triandis, for example, has derived an entire cross-cultural research agenda that focuses on these concepts.[149] While we use Hofstede's work as our basic organizational scheme, we also examine the findings of Triandis and others. Although we speak of individualism and collectivism as if they are separate entities, it is important to keep in mind that all people and cultures have both individual and collective dispositions. Brislin helps clarify this point when he notes, "Although no culture totally ignores individualistic or collective goals, cultures differ significantly on which of these factors they consider more critical."[150]

Individualism. Having already discussed individualism when we looked at American culture, we need only touch on some of its constituents: (1) the individual is the single most important unit in any social setting, (2) independence rather than dependence is stressed, (3) individual achievement is rewarded, and (4) the uniqueness of each individual is of paramount value.[151] According to Hofstede's findings, the United States, Australia, Great Britain, Canada, the Netherlands, and New Zealand tend toward individualism. Goleman highlights some of the characteristics of these and other cultures that value individualism:

> People's personal goals take priority over their allegiance to groups like the family or the employer. The loyalty of individualists to a given group is very weak; they feel they belong to many groups and are apt to change their membership as it suits them, switching churches, for example, or leaving one employer for another.[152]

Table 2.1 *Individualism/Collectivism Values for Fifty Countries and Three Regions*

Rank	Country	Rank	Country
1	United States	28	Turkey
2	Australia	29	Uruguay
3	Great Britain	30	Greece
4/5	Canada/Netherlands	31	Philippines
4/5	Netherlands	32	Mexico
6	New Zealand	33/35	Yugoslavia
7	Italy	33/35	Portugal
8	Belgium	33/35	East Africa
9	Denmark	36	Malaysia
10/11	Sweden	37	Hong Kong
10/11	France	38	Chile
12	Ireland	39/41	Singapore
13	Norway	39/41	Thailand
14	Switzerland	39/41	West Africa
15	Germany	42	Salvador
16	South Africa	43	South Korea
17	Finland	44	Taiwan
18	Austria	45	Peru
19	Israel	46	Costa Rica
20	Spain	47/48	Pakistan
21	India	47/48	Indonesia
22/23	Japan	49	Colombia
22/23	Argentina	50	Venezuela
24	Iran	51	Panama
25	Jamaica	52	Ecuador
26/27	Brazil	53	Guatemala
26/27	Arab countries		

The lower the number the more the country promotes individualism. A higher number means the country can be classified as collective.
Source: Adapted from Geert Hofstede, Cultures Consequences: Comparing Values, Behavior, Institutions and Organizations Across Nations, 2nd ed. (Thousand Oaks, CA: Sage Publications, 2001).

In cultures that tend toward individualism, competition rather than cooperation is encouraged; personal goals take precedence over group goals; people tend not to be emotionally dependent on organizations and institutions; and every individual has the right to his or her private property, thoughts, and opinions. These cultures stress individual initiative and achievement, and they value individual decision making. When thrust into a situation that demands a decision, people from cultures that stress this trait are often at odds with people from collective cultures. This point is made by Foster:

> At the negotiating table, differences in this dimension can clearly cause serious conflict. Individual responsibility for making decisions is easy in individualistic cultures; in group-oriented cultures this can be different. Americans too often expect their Japanese counterparts to make decisions right at the negotiating table, and the Japanese are constantly surprised to find individual members of the American team promoting their own positions, decisions, and ideas, sometimes openly contradicting one another.[153]

Remembering our earlier analogy regarding the stone in the pond that creates ripples, it should be clear by now that the cultural pattern of individualism creates a host of "ripples" that are discernible in a variety of ways. In small groups "individuals are motivated to work for themselves."[154] In the use of space, Andersen notes that "People from individualistic cultures are more remote and distant proximally."[155] Within the family context, Hanson tells us that individualism is stressed through self-determination, self-reliance, and an emphasis on privacy.[156] In the business setting, according to Lewis, individualistic Americans "like going it alone."[157] When moving to the classroom, Hofstede suggests that you find teachers dealing with individual pupils and encouraging pupil initiative.[158]

Collectivism. A rigid social framework that distinguishes between in-groups and out-groups characterizes collectivism. People count on their in-group (relatives, clans, organizations) to look after them, and in exchange for that they believe they owe absolute loyalty to the group. Triandis suggests some of the following behaviors are found in collective cultures:

> Collectivism means greater emphasis on (a) the views, needs, and goals of the in-group rather than oneself; (b) social norms and duty defined by the in-group rather than behavior to get pleasure; (c) beliefs shared with the in-group rather than beliefs that distinguish self from in-group; and (d) great readiness to cooperate with in-group members.[159]

In collective societies, such as those in Pakistan, Colombia, Venezuela, Taiwan, Peru, and much of Africa, people are born into extended families or clans that support and protect them in exchange for their allegiance. Triandis offers an excellent summary of the role and power of the family as a starting point for collective cultures:

> The prototypical collectivist social relationship is the family, where people have strong emotional ties and feel that they "obviously belong together," the link is long term (often for life) and there are many common goals. Cooperation is natural and status is determined by position within the group.[160]

As you can imagine, a "we" consciousness prevails instead of an "I" orientation. This perception of "community" is evident in Africa. As Etounga-Manguelle notes:

> If I had to cite a single characteristic of the African culture, the subordination of the individual by the community would surely be the reference point to remember. African thought rejects any view of the individual as an autonomous and responsible being.[161]

In African and other collective cultures, identity is based on the social system. The individual is emotionally dependent on organizations and institutions, and the culture emphasizes belonging to organizations. Organizations invade private life and the clans to which individuals belong; and individuals trust group decisions even at the expense of individual rights. Regarding China as a collective culture, Meyer notes, "With individual rights severely subordinated, group action has been a distinctive characteristic of Chinese society."[162] Collective behaviors, like so many aspects of culture, have deep historical roots. Look at the message of collectivism in these words from Confucius: "If one wants to establish himself, he should help others to establish themselves at first." You can also notice this view about working as a group in the Chinese proverb, "No matter how stout, one beam cannot support a house."

Collective cultures see the group as the most important social entity.

© Gloria Thomas

We have already suggested that collectivism is found in African societies, where as Richmond and Gestrin point out, "Individual needs and achievement, in contrast to the West, take second place to the needs of the many."[163]

Numerous co-cultures in the United States can be classified as collective. The research of Hecht, Collier, and Ribeau, for example, concludes that African Americans also have the characteristics of collective societies.[164] And, according to Luckman, "Hispanics—including Mexican-Americans, Cubans, Salvadorans, Guatemalans, Puerto Ricans, and others—greatly value the family, and often place the needs of the family members above the needs of individuals."[165]

As is the case with all cultural patterns, collectivism influences a number of communication variables. Kim, Sharkey, and Singles, after studying Korean culture, believe that traits such as indirect communication, saving face, concern for others, and group cooperation are linked to Korea's collective orientation.[166]

Collectivism is also contextual. That is to say, we can observe the collective pattern in various settings and contexts. For example, in collective classrooms, such as those found in Mexico, harmony and cooperation in learning are stressed instead of competition.[167] Think of what is being implied in the Mexican saying, "The more we are the faster we finish." The medical environment also reflects the pattern of individualism and collectivism. Schneider and Silverman offer the following view of the health care context in Egypt: "Even in illness, Egyptians prefer company. A stream of friends and relatives who bring him soda, food, aspirin, and advice will surround a man who has a headache or a fever. Hospitals are crowded with residents and friends visiting patients."[168] And in the business context, Marx maintains that "Negotiations in collective cultures are often attended by a group of people" and that "decision making takes longer."[169]

Table 2.2 *Uncertainty Avoidance Values for Fifty Countries and Three Regions*

Rank	Country	Rank	Country
1	Greece	28	Ecuador
2	Portugal	29	Germany
3	Guatemala	30	Thailand
4	Uruguay	31/32	Iran
5/6	Belgium	31/32	Finland
5/6	Salvador	33	Switzerland
7	Japan	34	West Africa
8	Yugoslavia	35	Netherlands
9	Peru	36	East Africa
10/15	Spain	37	Australia
10/15	Argentina	38	Norway
10/15	Panama	39/40	South Africa
10/15	France	39/40	New Zealand
10/15	Chile	41/42	Indonesia
10/15	Costa Rica	41/42	Canada
16/17	Turkey	43	United States
16/17	South Korea	44	Philppines
18	Mexico	45	India
19	Israel	46	Malaysia
20	Colombia	47/48	Great Britain
21/22	Venezuela	47/48	Ireland
21/22	Brazil	49/50	Hong Kong
23	Italy	49/50	Sweden
24/25	Pakistan	51	Denmark
24/25	Austria	52	Jamaica
26	Taiwan	53	Singapore
27	Arab countries		

The lower the number, the more the country can be classified as one that does not like uncertainty. A higher number is associated with a country that does not feel uncomfortable with uncertainty.
Source: Adapted from Geert Hofstede, Cultures Consequences: Comparing Values, Behavior, Institutions and Organizations Across Nations, 2nd ed. (Thousand Oaks, CA: Sage Publications, 2001).

Uncertainty Avoidance

At the core of uncertainty avoidance is the inescapable truism that the future is unknown. Though you may try, you can never accurately predict the next moment, day, year, or decade. As American playwright Tennessee Williams once noted, "The future is called 'perhaps,' which is the only possible thing to call the future." As the term is used by Hofstede, uncertainty avoidance "defines the extent to which people within a culture are made nervous by situations which they perceive as unstructured, unclear, or unpredictable, situations which they therefore try to avoid by maintaining strict codes of behavior and a belief in absolute truths."[170]

High Uncertainty Avoidance. High-uncertainty-avoidance cultures try to avoid uncertainty and ambiguity by providing stability for their members, establishing more formal rules, not tolerating deviant ideas and behaviors, seeking consensus, and believing in absolute truths and the attainment of expertise. A higher level of anxiety and stress also characterizes them. People with this orientation believe that life has the potential to be a continuous hazard. There is a strong need for written rules, planning, regulations, rituals, and ceremonies, which add structure to life. Nations with a strong uncertainty-avoidance tendency are Portugal, Greece, Peru, Belgium, and Japan.

Low Uncertainty Avoidance. At the other end of the scale, we find countries like Sweden, Denmark, Ireland, Norway, the United States, Finland, and the Netherlands, which have a low-uncertainty-avoidance need. They more easily accept the uncertainty inherent in life and are not as threatened by deviant people and ideas, so they tolerate the unusual. They prize initiative, dislike the structure associated with hierarchy, are more willing to take risks, are more flexible, think that there should be as few rules as possible, and depend not so much on experts as on themselves. As a whole, members of low-uncertainty-avoidance cultures are less tense and more relaxed—traits reflected in the Irish proverb "Life should be a dance, not a race."

As was the case with our first value dimension, differences in uncertainty avoidance affect intercultural communication. In a classroom composed of children from low uncertainty-avoidance cultures, we might expect to see students feeling comfortable in unstructured learning situations and students also being rewarded for innovative approaches to problem solving.[171] As Hofstede points out, the opposite is the case in high-uncertainty-avoidance culture. Here you find "students expect structured learning situations and right answers."[172]

Approaches to uncertainty avoidance would also affect negotiation sessions involving members from both groups. High-uncertainty-avoidance members would most likely want to move at a rather slow pace and ask for a greater amount of detail and planning. Some older members might also feel uncomfortable with young members of the group. There would be differences in the level of formality with which each culture would feel comfortable. In addition, Lewis notes that in high-uncertainty business situations there is a "preference for agendas and sticking to them."[173] The negotiation process would see differences in the level of risk taking on each side. Americans, for example, would be willing to take a risk. Writing about American business practices, Harris and Moran point out, "In light of their history, their perceptions of their rugged individualism, and the rewards of capitalism, Americans have embraced risk and are not risk avoidant."[174]

Power Distance

Another cultural value dimension is power distance, which classifies cultures on a continuum of high and low power distance. Hofstede is talking about the distance between power and the members of a particular culture. He summaries the concept of power distance in the following manner: "Power distance as a characteristic of a culture, defines the extent to which the less powerful person in society accepts inequality in power and considers it as normal."[175] The premise of the dimension deals with the extent to which a society prefers that power in relationships, institutions, and organizations be distributed unequally. Although all cultures have tendencies for both high- and low-power relationships, one orientation seems to dominate. Foster offers a clear and condensed explanation of this dimension:

> What Hofstede discovered was that in some cultures, those who hold power and those who are affected by power are significantly far apart (high power distance) in many ways, while in other cultures, the power holders and those affected by the power holders are significantly closer (low power distance).[176]

High Power Distance. Gudykunst tenders a concise summary of high–power-distance cultures when he writes, "Individuals from high power distance cultures accept power as part of society. As such, superiors consider their subordinates to be different themselves and vice versa."[177] People in high–power-distance countries such as India, Africa, Brazil, Singapore, Greece, Venezuela, Mexico, and the Philippines believe that power and authority are facts of life. Both consciously and unconsciously, these cultures teach their members that people are not equal in this world and that everybody has a rightful place, which is clearly marked by countless vertical arrangements. Social hierarchy is prevalent and institutionalizes inequality. Etounga-Manguelle underscores this point as it applies to Africa when he notes, "In more vertical societies, Africa among them, subordinates consider their superiors to be different having a right to privilege."[178]

In organizations within high–power-distance cultures, you find a greater centralization of power, great importance placed on status and rank, a larger proportion of supervisory personnel, a rigid value system that determines the worth of each job, and the bypassing of subordinates in the decision-making process.[179]

Table 2.3 *Power Distance Values for Fifty Countries and Three Regions*

Rank	Country	Rank	Country
1	Malaysia	27/28	South Korea
2/3	Guatemala	29/30	Iran
2/3	Panama	29/30	Taiwan
4	Philippines	31	Spain
5/6	Mexico	32	Pakistan
5/6	Venezuela	33	Japan
7	Arab countries	34	Italy
8/9	Ecuador	35/36	Argentina
8/9	Indonesia	35/36	South Africa
10/11	India	37	Jamaica
10/11	West Africa	38	United States
12	Yugoslavia	39	Canada
13	Singapore	40	Netherlands
14	Brazil	41	Australia
15/16	France	42/44	Costa Rica
15/16	Hong Kong	42/44	Germany
17	Columbia	42/44	Great Britain
18/19	Salvador	45	Switzerland
18/19	Turkey	46	Finland
20	Belgium	47/48	Norway
21/23	East Africa	47/48	Sweden
21/23	Peru	49	Ireland
21/23	Thailand	50	New Zealand
24/25	Chile	51	Denmark
24/25	Portugal	52	Israel
26	Uruguay	53	Austria
27/28	Greece		

The lower the number, the more the country can be classified as one that has a large power distance. A higher number is associated with a country that demonstrates small power distance.
Source: Adapted from Geert Hofstede, Cultures Consequences: Comparing Values, Behavior, Institutions and Organizations Across Nations, 2nd ed. (Thousand Oaks, CA: Sage Publications, 2001).

Low Power Distance. Low–power-distance countries such as Austria, Finland, Denmark, Norway, United States, New Zealand, and Israel hold that inequality in society should be minimized. Or as Brislin notes, "Cultures referred to as 'low power distance' are guided by laws, norms, and everyday behaviors that make power distinctions as minimal as possible."[180] People in these cultures believe they are close to power and should have access to that power. To them, a hierarchy is an inequality of roles established for convenience. Subordinates consider superiors to be the same kind of people as they are, and superiors perceive their subordinates the same way. People in power, be they supervisors or government officials, often interact with their constituents and try to look less powerful than they really are. The powerful and the powerless try to live in concert.

We can observe signs of this dimension in nearly every communication setting. Within the educational context, Calloway-Thomas, Cooper, and Blake offer the following summary:

> In large power distance societies, the educational process is teacher centered. The teacher initiates all communication, outlines the path of learning students should follow, and is never publicly criticized or contradicted. In large power distance societies, the emphasis is on the personal "wisdom" of the teacher, while in small power distance societies the emphasis is on impersonal "truth" that can be obtained by any competent person.[181]

According to Hofstede, in a business context with low power distance you might observe decisions being shared, subordinates being consulted, "bosses" relying on support teams, and status symbols being kept to a minimum.[182]

Masculinity–Femininity

Hofstede uses the words *masculinity* and *femininity* to refer to the degree to which masculine or feminine traits are valued and revealed. His rationale, and one that is supported by most anthropologists, psychologists, and political scientists, is that many masculine and feminine behaviors are learned and mediated by cultural norms and traditions.

Masculinity. Masculinity is the extent to which the dominant values in a society are male oriented. Hofstede advances an excellent summary of these values when he notes:

> Masculine cultures use the biological existence of two sexes to define very different social roles for men and women. They expect men to be assertive, ambitious, and competitive, and to strive for material success, and to respect whatever is big, strong, and fast.[183]

Ireland, the Philippines, Greece, Venezuela, Austria, Japan, Italy, and Mexico are among countries where you can find many of the masculine values described by Hofstede. For example, in Japan, despite the high level of economic development, the division of labor finds most men in the role of provider; a woman, asserts Meguro, is a "homemaker and breeder."[184]

Femininity. Cultures that value femininity as a trait stress nurturing behaviors. A feminine world view maintains that men need not be assertive and that they can assume nurturing roles; it also promotes sexual equality and holds that people and the environment are important. In addition, in feminine cultures there tend to be "overlapping social roles for the sexes."[185] Interdependence and androgynous behavior are the ideal, and people sympathize with the unfortunate. Nations such as

Table 2.4 *Masculinity Values for Fifty Countries and Three Regions*

RANK	COUNTRY	RANK	COUNTRY
1	Japan	28	Singapore
2/3	Austria	29	Israel
2/3	Venezuela	30/31	Indonesia
4/5	Italy	30/31	West Africa
4/5	Switzerland	32/33	Turkey
6	Mexico	32/33	Taiwan
7/8	Ireland	34	Panama
7/8	Jamaica	35/36	Iran
9/10	Great Britain	35/36	France
9/10	Germany	37/38	Spain
11/12	Philippines	37/38	Peru
11/12	Colombia	39	East Africa
13/14	South Africa	40	Salvador
13/14	Ecuador	41	South Korea
15	United States	42	Uruguay
16	Australia	43	Guatemala
17	New Zealand	44	Thailand
18/19	Greece	45	Portugal
18/19	Hong Kong	46	Chile
20/21	Argentina	47	Finland
20/21	India	48/49	Yugoslavia
22	Belgium	48/49	Costa Rica
23	Arab countries	50	Denmark
24	Canada	51	Netherlands
25/26	Malaysia	52	Norway
25/26	Pakistan	53	Sweden
27	Brazil		

The lower the number, the more the country can be classified as one that favors masculine traits; a higher score is a country that prefers feminine traits.
Source: Adapted from Geert Hofstede, Cultures Consequences: Comparing Values, Behavior, Institutions and Organizations Across Nations, 2nd ed. (Thousand Oaks, CA: Sage Publications, 2001).

Sweden, Norway, Finland, Denmark, and the Netherlands tend toward a feminine world view.

Whether or not a culture stresses one trait over another can be seen in a variety of ways. For instance, placing a greater value on masculine over feminine traits can even be seen in the type of person a culture selects to "lead" them. For example, in Sweden, which had the highest ranking in Hofstede's femininity category, women occupy 41 percent of legislative positions; in Japan, ranked the highest in masculine traits, only 5 percent of legislative offices are held by women.[186]

You can also observe the role of gender in the workplace. As Kim points out:

> In Japan, Germany, and other European and Asian countries, women face serious obstacles to achieving work place equality. They are expected to assist men and are given lower wages, less stable employment, and fewer opportunities for advancement.[187]

Table 2.5 *Long-Term Values for Twenty-Three Countries or Regions*

Rank	Country	Rank	Country
1	China	13	Poland
2	Hong Kong	14	Germany
3	Taiwan	15	Australia
4	Japan	16	New Zealand
5	South Korea	17	United States
6	Brazil	18	Great Britain
7	India	19	Zimbabwe
8	Thailand	20	Canada
9	Singapore	21	Philippines
10	Netherlands	22	Nigeria
11	Bangladesh	23	Pakistan
12	Sweden		

The lower the number, the more the country can be classified as one that favors long planning; a higher score represents a country that has a short-term orientation.

Source: Adapted from Geert Hofstede, Cultures Consequences: Comparing Values, Behavior, Institutions and Organizations Across Nations, 2nd ed. (Thousand Oaks, CA: Sage Publications, 2001).

Long- and Short-Term Orientation

Over the years, there has been some condemnation of Hofstede's work. One major criticism dealt with the Western bias Hofstede used to collect his data.[188] As a means of overcoming this problem, Hofstede offered a new orientation called long- versus short-term orientation. This new survey, involving twenty-three countries, used a form called the Chinese Value Survey (CVS). This was "an instrument developed by Michael Harris Bond in Hong Kong from values suggested by Chinese scholars."[189] This orientation is also known as Confucian dynamism.[190] The link between this fifth orientation and Confucianism is summarized by Hofstede:

> The long-term short-term orientation dimension appears to be based on items reminiscent of the teachings of Confucius, on both poles. It opposes long-term to short-term aspects of Confucian thinking: persistence and thrift to personal stability and respect for tradition.[191]

It is easy to see how these patterns would influence interaction in a variety of settings. For example, in business organizations, cultures that rank high on long-term orientation (China, Hong Kong, Taiwan, Japan, South Korea) would must likely have employees who reflect a strong work ethic and show great respect to their employers. We would also expect individuals who are members of these cultures to value social order and long-range goals. Those cultures that rank low on the long-term orientation index (United States, Great Britain, Canada, Philippines), according to Hofstede, often do not place a high priority on status, try to postpone old age, are concerned with short-term results, and as such seek immediate gratification of their needs.[192]

Kluckhohn and Strodtbeck's Value Orientations

Our next taxonomy is from Kluckhohn and Strodtbeck, who were cultural anthropologists. They based their research on the notion that every individual, regardless of culture, must deal with five universal questions. Although Kluckhohn and Strodtbeck used the phrase "value orientations" to describe these five questions, they were in fact talking about what we have to this point called cultural patterns. These patterns "tell" the members of the culture what is important and also offer guidance for living their life.[193] Since their work was completed, other researchers have added to their findings.[194] As we indicated, after examining numerous cultures, they came to the conclusion that all people turn to their culture to answer the same five basic questions:

1. What is the character of human nature?
2. What is the relation of humankind to nature?
3. What is the orientation toward time?
4. What is the value placed on activity?
5. What is the relationship of people to each other?[195]

Two important points need to be made before we turn to a specific explanation of the five dimensions advanced by Kluckhohn and Strodtbeck. First, as was the case with Hofstede's ranking from one to fifty, Kluckhohn and Strodtbeck's five orientations are best visualized as points on a continuum. Second, as you move through these five orientations, you will undoubtedly notice some of the same characteristics discussed by Hofstede. This is understandable in that both approaches are talking about meaningful values found, with varying degrees, in all cultures. Hence, both sets of researchers were bound to track many of the same patterns.

Human Nature Orientation

Nearly all judgments about human behavior, be they moral or legal, begin with this core question: What is the character of human nature? Was Anne Frank right when she wrote in *The Diary of a Young Girl*, "In spite of everything, I still believe that people are really good at heart"? Or was the philosopher Immanuel Kant correct when he observed, "Out of the crooked timber of humanity no straight thing can ever be made"?

Questions concerning human nature have concerned religious leaders and philosophers for centuries. You can observe the importance of these questions reading Borrowman's brief catalog of some questions related to human nature:

> What are the relative effects of "grace," "will," genetic heredity, geographical conditions, social institutions, and historical accident on the behavior of an individual? Would the "natural" man tend toward love and altruism in his treatment of others, or would he be dominated by greed and brutality? Is reason capable of dominating the behavior of man or merely a tool which he uses to mediate between demands of an insatiable id and an uncompromising super-ego?[196]

Your answers to the questions posed by Borrowman represent a powerful force in how you live your life. As Stevenson and Haberman tell us, "Different conceptions of human nature lead to different views about what we ought to do and how we can do it."[197] Although all people on an individual basis answer questions about human nature, there are also cultural explanations for why people act as they do.

Most discussions of human nature usually deal with divisions of Evil, Good and Evil, and Good. Let us look at each of these issues and how they often differ from culture to culture.

Evil. Some cultures begin with the premise that people are intrinsically evil. In the United States, this orientation, which was inherited from Puritan ancestors, was the prevailing view for many years. In the last hundred years Americans have come to see themselves as a mixture of good and evil. That is, most Americans now believe they are "perfectible." By following certain rules, we can change, improve, and "be saved." According to this view, with constant hard work, control, education, and self-discipline, we can achieve goodness. You can also see this "self-help" approach to life in Christianity. For Christians, God is the "Father" and humans are his children. As is the case with all children, you get guidance but must also make choices. According to Christianity, "We are rational beings, we have self-consciousness, and we have free choice."[198] Through those choices, we can move from being corrupt to being good.

A more restrictive view of the Goodness or Evil of human nature is found in other parts of the Arab world. Here, where Islam is strong, you can find cultures that begin with the notion that people have a penchant for evil and therefore cannot, when left to their own resources, be trusted to make a correct decision. Hence, to help control the actions of their members, numerous institutions, ranging from the religious to the political, are designed to monitor and manage behavior. As we shall see in the next chapter, Islam came to the Middle East at a time when the Bedouin culture was plagued with immorality and hedonism. Allah was needed, the people thought, to save these "sinners."

Good and Evil. People who have the Taoist world view hold that the universe is best seen as an infinite system of elements and forces in balanced dynamic interaction. Further, two of the forces present in this universe are good and evil. And since humanity is part of the universe, these forces are naturally present in humankind. This idea is clearly seen in the notion of yang and yin. Yang and yin are cyclic; they go through natural periods of balanced increase and decrease. Periodic increases in yang are accompanied by corresponding decreases in yin—this followed by an opposite cycle in which yin increases while yang decreases. This view of the good and evil nature of humanity extends the position that people cannot eliminate evil, because it is a natural and necessary part of the universe. That is, good can only be recognized against a background of evil, and evil is only recognizable against a background of good.

We should add that much of Europe, for very different reasons, also have a duality (good/evil) approach to human nature. However, they believe that while we might be born with a propensity for evil, through learning and education people can become "good."

Table 2.6 *Five Value Orientations from Kluckhohn, Kluckhohn, and Strodtbeck*

Orientation	Values and Behavior		
Human nature	Basically evil	Mixture of good and evil	Basically good
Humankind and nature	People subjugated to nature	People in harmony with nature	People the master of nature
Sense of time	Past oriented	Present oriented	Future oriented
Activity	Being	Being in becoming	Doing
Social relationships	Authoritarian	Group oriented	Individualism

Source: F. R. Kluckhohn and F. L. Strodtbeck, Variations in Value Orientations (New York: Row and Peterson), 1960.

Goodness. Perhaps the most extreme view of innate goodness of human nature can be found in the philosophies of Confucianism and Buddhism. Most interpretations of the writings of Confucius maintain that he was "very optimistic" about human nature.[199] Hundreds of years later we see this same view toward the innate goodness of people in the words of the Chinese philosopher Lu Wang: "Human nature is originally good." As we will discuss in Chapter 3, Buddhism also maintains that you are born pure and are closest to what is called "loving kindness" when you enter this world. Hence, people are good, but their culture often makes them evil.

Cutting across the arguments concerning the good and evil of human nature has been the question of the essential rationality of human nature. Throughout history, there has been tension between those who believe in fate or mystic powers and those who believe that the intellect can solve any problem and discover any truth. Imagine for a moment your perceptions of reality if you are French and take the rational approach characteristic of Descartes' philosophy, or if you are Native American and believe that forces outside you control much of your thinking and behavior. And for the Hindu, mysticism, intuition, and spiritual awareness are needed to understand the nature of reality. A belief in fate, as opposed to one that stresses free will, is bound to yield different conclusions.

Person-Nature Orientation

Human Beings Subject to Nature. The differences in conceptions of the relationship between humanity and nature produce distinct frames of reference for human desires, attitudes, and behaviors. At one end of the scale devised by Kluckhohn and Strodtbeck is the view that maintains human beings are subject to nature. Cultures that hold this orientation believe that the most powerful forces of life are outside their control. Whether the force be a god, fate, or magic, a person cannot overcome it and must therefore learn to accept it. This orientation is found in India and parts of South America. For the Hindu, because everything is part of a unified force, "the world of distinct and separate objects and processes is a manifestation of a more fundamental reality that is undivided and unconditional."[200] This "oneness" with the world helps create a perceptual vision of a harmonious world. In Mexico and among Mexican Americans, there is strong tie to Catholicism and the role of fate in controlling life and nature. As Purnell notes, at the heart of this world view is "a stoic acceptance of the ways things are."[201]

"Cooperation" with Nature. The middle or so-called cooperation view is widespread and is associated with East Asians. In Japan and Thailand, there is a perception that nature is part of life and not a hostile force waiting to be subdued. This orientation affirms that people should, in every way possible, live in harmony with nature. The desire to be part of nature and not control it has always been strong among Native Americans. As Joe and Malach note, "Tribal groups continue to teach respect for the land and to forbid desecration of their ancestral lands. These groups also carry out various ceremonies and rituals to ensure harmony with as well as protection of the land (Mother Earth)."[202] Chief Seattle eloquently summarized this orientation when he said: "Humankind has not woven the web of life. We are but one thread within it. Whatever we do to the web we do to ourselves. All things are bound together—all things connect."

Controlling Nature. At the other end of the scale is the view that compels us to conquer and direct the forces of nature to our advantage. This value orientation is characteristic of the Western approach, which, as we noted earlier in the chapter, has a long tradition of valuing technology, change, and science. Americans have historically believed that nature was something that could and had to be mastered. The early immigrants to North America found a harsh and vast wilderness that they needed to "tame." Even today we use terms such as "conquering" space. For people with this orientation there is a clear separation from nature. The American view of nature even has some religious underpinnings. There is a belief that it is God's intention for us to make the earth our private domain. As an article in Newsweek magazine noted, "Environmentalists have long blamed Biblical tradition—specifically God's injunction to man in Genesis to 'subdue the earth'—for providing cultural sanction for the Industrial Revolution and its plundering of nature."[203] We should add that Arabs hold much the same view toward nature because, as Haviland notes, the Koran holds that people have dominion over the earth.[204]

We can often find examples of cultures clashing because of divergent views on how to relate to nature. A case in point is the ongoing controversy between the dominant American culture and some Native American tribes who object to widespread strip mining of coal because it disfigures the earth and displaces spirits worshipped by the tribes. Our cultural orientation of controlling nature can be seen in a host of other instances. Adler highlights some of these:

> Some other examples of the North American dominance orientation include astronauts' conquest (dominance) of space; economists' structuring the market; sales representatives' attempts to influence buyers' decisions; and, perhaps most controversial today, bioengineering and genetic programming.[205]

Time Orientation

As a species, our fixation with time and the power we give it are rather obvious. Over two thousand years ago, the Greek playwright Sophocles observed, "Time is a kindly God." As is the case with most of the issues discussed in this book, cultures vary widely in how much they want to "give in" to that "God." Where they differ is in the value placed on the past, present, and future and how each influences interaction. So important is a culture's use of time that we develop the subject in detail in Chapter 5, but for now let us simply highlight some of the major cultural differences in the perception of time.

Past Orientation. Past-oriented cultures believe strongly in the significance of prior events. History, established religions, and tradition are extremely important to these cultures, so there is a strong belief that the past should be the guide for making decisions and determining truth. You can see this orientation in China, which because of its long and resplendent history continues to respect the past. Even today, Chinese historical dramas lead box-office sales. And, as Adler notes, "Chinese children have no space-age superman to emulate. Even at play they pretend to be the Monkey King, the supernatural hero of a medieval epic."[206] There is even a famous Chinese proverb that states, "The past is as clear as a mirror, the future as dark as lacquer." In Japan, where Shintoism is strong and ancestor worship important, the past still remains paramount. Great Britain, because of its extensive devotion to tradition, including the continuation of a monarchy, resists change as it attempts to cling to the past.

France is yet another culture that can be understood by exploring its view of the past. The French, on many levels, venerate the past. As Curtius notes, "The French live deeply in remembrance and the past."[207] Curtius maintains that you can see admiration for the past in the fact that the French have a feeling that they belong to an ancient civilization and that "true patriotism is the love of the past."[208]

Within the United States, Native Americans—in part because of their strong oral tradition—also value the past. Many Native American stories in fact use the past to set examples and to "provide moral guidelines by which one should live."[209]

As is the case with all the patterns we have looked at in this chapter, a culture's judgment about the past is evident in a variety of situations. For example, when conducting business with a past-oriented culture, Trompenaars and Hampden-Turner suggest you "talk about history" and "show respect for ancestors, predecessors and older people."[210] Lewis adds to the list by telling you that there should be exploration of all issues before decisions are sought."[211]

Present Orientation.   Present-oriented cultures hold that the moment has the most significance. For them, the future is vague, ambiguous, and unknown, and what is real exists in the here and now. For these cultures, enjoyment comes in the present. People of the Philippines, Mexico, and Latin America usually hold these beliefs. Mexican Americans also "prefer to experience life and people around them fully in the present."[212] Luckmann suggests that this view is also characteristic of the African American co-culture.[213]

© Gloria Thomas

Past-orientation cultures place a high value on traditions.

Future Orientation. Future-oriented cultures, such as the one found in the United States, emphasize the future and expect it to be grander than the present. What is going to happen holds the greatest attraction for most Americans because whatever we are doing is not quite as good as what we could be doing. This does not mean that Americans have no regard for the past or no thought of the present, but it is certainly true that most of you, in thought or action, do not want to be "left behind." You all want to wear the most current fashions and to drive a brand-new car.

Like many other orientations, our view of time is related to a host of other values. For example, Americans' view of the future makes them optimistic. This is reflected in the common proverb "If at first you don't succeed, try, try, and try again." This optimistic view of the future also sees Americans believing they can control the future. The power to control the future was clearly spelled out by former president Lyndon Johnson when he told all Americans that "Yesterday is not ours to recover, but tomorrow is ours to win or to lose."

Activity Orientation

Activity orientation is the way a culture views activity. Three common modes of activity expression, as detailed by Kluckhohn and Strodtbeck, are being, being-in-becoming, and doing.

Being Orientation. A being orientation refers to spontaneous expression of the human personality. As Adler and Jelinek point out, "People in being-orientated cultures accept people, events, and ideas as flowing spontaneously. They stress release, indulgence of existing desires, and working for the moment."[214] Most Latin cultures have the view that the current activity is the one that matters the most. In Mexico, for example, people take great delight in the simple act of conversation with family and friends. Mexicans will talk for hours with their companions, for they believe that the act of "being" is one of the main goals and joys of life. Gannon observes that Saudis have much the same approach to life. He points out that "several customers may be helped at the same time, or different business negotiations might be managed at once in the same office. This behavior exemplifies the Being orientation."[215]

Being-in-Becoming. Being-in-becoming orientation stresses the idea of development and growth. It emphasizes the kind of activity that contributes to the development of all aspects of the self as an integral whole. This usually correlates with cultures that value a spiritual life more than a material one. For example, in both Hinduism and Buddhism, people spend a portion of their lives in meditation and contemplation in an attempt to purify and fully advance themselves.

Doing Orientation. Doing orientation describes activity in which accomplishments are measurable by standards external to the individual. The key to this orientation is your trying to visualize a value system that stresses activity and action. It is the doing orientation that most characterizes the dominant American culture. Think of the high value placed on "doing" and "action" in the following two well-known proverbs: "No sooner said than done—so acts your man of worth," and "Idle hands are the Devil's workshop."

Kim offers an excellent synopsis of Americans' attitude toward doing and activity in the following:

> Americans are action oriented; they are go-getters. They get going, get things done, and get ahead. In America, people gather for action—to play basketball, to dance, to go to a concert. When groups gather they play games or watch videos. Many Americans don't have the patience to sit down and talk. . . . Life is in constant motion.[216]

According to Gannon, Israel is also a doing culture. He notes, "Israel is a classic 'doing' society in which action is taken proactively to control situations and overcome environmental problems."[217]

The doing orientation of a culture impinges on many other beliefs and values. Your definition of activity affects your perception of work, efficiency, change, time, and progress. Even the pace at which you live your life—from how fast you walk to the speed at which you reach conclusions—is related to where you land on the being–doing scale. Americans have long admired and rewarded people who can make rapid decisions and "speak up" quickly, and they even become impatient with people who are too reflective. Writing about American education, Newman notes, "The child who speaks when the teacher requests a response is rewarded. The one who ponders is often considered withdrawn, problematic. The educational system appears to favor students who have the immediate answer, not those who take time to consider other questions."[218] This attitude toward activity contrasts with that fostered by the Taoist tradition: The individual is not the active agent; he or she is to remain calm, and truth eventually will make itself apparent. Imagine members of these two cultures sitting down together at a business meeting—or occupying the same classroom.

African Americans are also a "doing" culture. Emotional vitality, activity, openness of feelings, and being expressive, which are part of the African American experience, all involve forms of "doing."[219]

Relational (Social) Orientation

This value orientation is concerned with the ways in which people perceive their relationships with others. Having already discussed, in some detail, the basic ideas behind relational orientations when we examined Hofstede's dimensions of individualism and power distance, our explanations here are rather brief.

Authoritarian Orientation. The value orientations in this category are on a continuum ranging from authoritarianism to individualism. Although most Americans find it difficult to believe, many cultures have had only authoritarian leaders, and therefore believe this type of social relationship to be the norm. In parts of Africa and in much of the Arab world, people believe that there are some individuals who are born to lead while others must follow. In these cultures, authoritarian relationships—from those with the ruling family to those with the leaders of the church—are accepted. The Arab proverb "The eye cannot rise above the eyebrow" demonstrates this accepting attitude.

Collective Orientation. As we noted elsewhere, collective cultures (such as the Chinese, Indian, African, Native American, Mexican, Korean, and Latin American cultures) see the group as the most important of all social entities. Group affiliations take precedence over individual goals. In India, for example, the family influences a person's education, marriage, and occupation choice. So strong is the collective nature of some African tribes that "attempts to get Maasai students to raise their hands and participate in formal classrooms are often futile."[220] The reason is that they do not want to call attention to themselves in a group setting.

Individualism Orientation. Having already spent a number of pages on the topic of individuals, we now simply remind you that cultures that value individualism believe all people should have equal rights and complete control over their destiny. Anything else, as most Americans hold, violates the will of God and the spirit of the Constitution.

Hall's High-Context and Low-Context Orientation

The anthropologist Edward Hall offers us another effective means of examining cultural similarities and differences in both perception and communication. He categorizes cultures as being either high or low context, depending on the degree to which meaning comes from the settings or from the words being exchanged.[221] The assumption underlying Hall's classifications is that "one of the functions of culture is to provide a highly selective screen between man and the outside world. In its many forms, culture therefore designates what we pay attention to and what we ignore."[222]

The word context needs to be understood if you are to appreciate the link between context and communication. Context can be defined as "the information that surrounds an event; it is inextricably bound up with the meaning of the event."[223] Although all cultures contain some characteristics of both high and low variables, most can be placed along a scale showing their ranking on this particular dimension (see Table 2.7). To call your attention to this fact, we have placed various cultures on a continuum rather than only using two rigid categories. The Halls define high and low context in the following manner:

> A high context (HC) communication or message is one in which most of the information is already in the person, while very little is in the coded, explicitly transmitted part of the message. A low context (LC) communication is just the opposite; i.e., the mass of the information is vested in the explicit code.[224]

High Context

In high-context cultures (Native Americans, Latin Americans, Japanese, Arab, Chinese, African American, and Korean), many of the meanings being exchanged during the encounter do not have to be communicated through words. One reason that meanings often do not have to be stated verbally in high-context cultures is that people are very homogeneous. They have similar experiences, information networks, and the like. High-context cultures, because of tradition and history, change very little over time. According to Hofstede, high-context cultures are "more often found in traditional cultures."[225] These are cultures in which consistent messages have produced consistent responses to the environment. "As a result," the Halls say, "for most normal transactions in daily life they do not require, nor do they expect, much in-depth, background information."[226] Because meaning is not necessarily contained in words, in high-context cultures information is provided through gestures and even silence. Space is also used to communicate in high-context cultures. As Gannon points out, "Members of high-context societies tend to have less physical space between them when communicating than do those in low-context societies."[227] High-context cul-

Table 2.7 *Cultures Arranged Along the High-Context and Low-Context Dimension*

High-Context Cultures
|
Japanese
|
Chinese
|
Korean
|
African American
|
Native American
|
Arab
|
Greek
|
Latin
|
Italian
|
English
|
French
|
North American
|
Scandinavian
|
German
|
German/Swiss
|
Lower-Context Cultures

Based on the work of Edward T. Hall. See notes for Chapter 2 at the end of the book.

tures tend to be aware of their surroundings and can express and interpret feelings without stating them. Andersen points out, "High-context cultures are more reliant on and tuned in to nonverbal communication."[228]

Meaning in high-context cultures is also conveyed "through status (age, sex, education, family background, title, and affiliations) and through an individual's informal friends and associates."[229] Because of all the subtle "messages" used by high-context cultures, members of these groups, according to Gudykunst, often "communicate in an indirect fashion."[230]

Low Context

In low-context cultures (German, Swiss, Scandinavian, and North American), the population is less homogeneous and therefore tends to compartmentalize interpersonal contacts. This lack of a large pool of common experiences means that "each time they interact with others they need detailed background information."[231] In low-context cultures, the verbal message contains most of the information and very little is embedded in the context or the participants. This characteristic manifests itself in a host of ways. For example, the Asian mode of communication (high context) is often vague, indirect, and implicit, whereas Western communication (low context) tends to be direct and explicit. In addition, as Lynch notes, "Low-context communicators talk more, speak more rapidly, and often raise their voices."[232] Althen offers an excellent summary of Americans' fascination with language in the following paragraph:

> Americans depend more on spoken words than on nonverbal behavior to convey messages. They think it is important to be able to "speak up" and "say what is on their mind." They admire a person who has a moderately large vocabulary and who can express herself clearly and shrewdly.[233]

Differences in perceived credibility are yet another aspect of communication associated with these two orientations. In high-context cultures, people who rely primarily on verbal messages for information are perceived as less credible. They believe that silence often sends a better message than words, and anyone who needs words does not have the information. As the Indonesian proverb states, "Empty cans clatter the loudest."

Differences in this communication dimension can even alter how conflict is perceived and responded to. As Ting-Toomey has observed, the communication differences between high-context and low-context cultures are also apparent in the manner in which each approaches conflict. For example, because high-context cultures tend to be less open, they hold that conflict is damaging to most communication encounters. For them, Ting-Toomey says, "Conflict should be dealt with discreetly and subtly."[234]

Harris and Moran summarize the low-context dimension as it applies to the business setting in the following manner:

> Unless global leaders are aware of the subtle differences, communication misunderstandings between low- and high-context communicators can result. Japanese communicate by not stating things directly, while Americans usually do the opposite—"spell it out." The former is looking for meaning and understanding in what is not said—in the nonverbal communication or body language, in the silences and pauses, in relationships and empathy. The latter places emphasis on sending and receiving accurate messages directly, usually by being articulate with words.[235]

As we conclude this chapter, we need to urge you to learn about variations in cultural patterns so that you will be able to understand, predict, and even adapt to the behavior of people from cultures different from your own.

SUMMARY

- Culture and communication are so intertwined that it is easy to conceive that culture is communication and communication is culture.
- Culture seeks to tell its member what to expect from life, and therefore it reduces confusion and helps us predict the future
- The basic elements of culture are history, religion, values, social organizations, and language.

- Culture is shared learned behavior that is transmitted from one generation to another for purposes of promoting individual and social survival, adaptation, and growth and development.
- The characteristics of culture that most directly affect communication are that culture is (1) learned, (2) transmitted from generation to generation, (3) based on symbols, (4) dynamic, and (5) an integrated process.
- Perception is best defined as "the process of selecting, organizing, and interpreting sensory data in a way that enables us to make sense of our world."
- Perception is the primary mechanism by which you develop your world view.
- Beliefs are our convictions in the truth of something—with or without proof.
- Values are enduring attitudes about the preferability of one belief over another.
- There are numerous cultural patterns that can be examined: Gannon's Four-Stage Model of Cross-Cultural Understanding, Trompenaas and Hampden-Turner's Basis for Cultural Differences, Groudona's Cultural Typology, and Weaver's Contrast Cultural Continuum.
- Dominant American cultural patterns include individualism, equality, materialism, science and technology, progress and change, work and leisure, and competition.
- The most prominent and diverse culture patterns that explain both perceptual and communication differences are: Hofstede's Values Dimension, which includes (1) individualism and collectivism, (2) uncertainty avoidance, (3) power distance, (4) masculinity and femininity, (5) long-term and short term orientation.
- Kluckhohn and Strodtbeck's Value Orientation includes (1) human nature, (2) the perception of nature, (3) time, (4) activity, and (5) relationships.
- Hall's Context Orientation: (1) high context, (2) low context describe the degree to which individuals rely on internalized information.

INFOTRAC COLLEGE EDITION EXERCISES

1. *InfoTrac* resources can help you to think more about cultural differences. Locate and read the article "Letter from America" by Rob Long. Long's essay is a humorous look at cultural differences, but he raises some serious questions for further consideration. Reflect back upon times when you have found communication difficult due to cultural differences. What kinds of things seem "natural" to you but not to others, or what do you take for granted that others might not view in the same way? In what ways have television, movies or music shaped your perceptions of other cultures? And in what ways have encounters with travelers or tourists shaped your perceptions of other cultures? What can be learned about cultural differences from Long's letter?

2. This chapter discusses the importance of cultural symbols and the ways in which they transmit cultural values. One of the most controversial cultural symbols in America is the Confederate flag. Locate and read the article "The banner that won't stay furled" by John Shelton Reed. According to Reed, what are the various meanings that have been attributed to the Confederate flag? What meanings do you associate with the Confederate flag? How are these meanings reflections of your membership in a co-culture? Compare your own views with those of your classmates and consider ways of resolving differences about this hotly debated symbol.

3. This chapter discusses the ways in which myths, proverbs, folktales, and legends transmit cultural values and give meaning to choices and events. Locate and read the article "The Contents of our Character" by Lindsey Brink et al. (Hint: Use "Personality and Culture" as your subject search terms, or search by author or title.) After reading the article, choose both a book and a movie which you feel most clearly portray the American character and culture to those who are not Americans. Come to class prepared to explain your selections.

ACTIVITIES

1. Ask your partner from another culture to relate a folktale (or a song, a work of art, or something similar) from his or her culture to living in the United States. What cultural values does it convey? Compare it to one from your culture. Do they stand in opposition to each other, or are there similarities?

2. In small groups, list the American cultural values mentioned in this chapter. Try to think of others. Then find examples from American advertising campaigns that illustrate these values. For example, the advertising slogan from an athletic-shoe manufacturer, "Just do it," reflects the American value of accomplishment.

3. Find out as much as you can about the history of your partner's culture. Try to isolate examples of how his or her cultural values have been determined by historical events.

4. In small groups, play a word-association game. Your instructor will compose a list of potentially culture-bound words such as motherhood, freedom, and sex, then say the words one at a time. Write down the first thing that comes into your mind as you hear each word. Compare your reactions. Are there any major differences within the group? Discuss them. Then compare your answers with those of the entire class and discuss.

5. Ask your informant for English translations of sayings and proverbs from his or her culture that reflect important values in that culture. Alternatively, you may want to show the sayings and proverbs in this chapter to your informant and see if he or she has corresponding sayings.

6. In small groups, create an ideal culture and give it a name. Indicate which of the values discussed in this chapter would be primary in the value hierarchy of your culture. Try to accommodate the interests of all group members. Time permitting, describe the outward manifestations of your cultural values (for example, dress, work, play, food preferences, roles).

7. In a small group, conduct a mock business meeting at which half the members are from a high-context culture and the other half from a low-context culture.

8. Ask your friends and/or family members to list ten of the most important characteristics of American culture. Compile these lists to identify the most commonly mentioned American cultural patterns. Compare your list with all the patterns discussed in this chapter and try to identify similarities and differences.

DISCUSSION IDEAS

1. What is meant by the phrase "much of culture is invisible"?

2. Explain American views toward these elements of culture: work, dress, hygiene, courtship, sex, and status.

3. Describe a typical day from morning to night in terms of the cultural values that govern your actions. For example:

Action	Value
Brush teeth	Personal odors are offensive in American culture
Put on jeans and T-shirt	Comfort and informality are acceptable in educational settings.

4. Give additional examples from recent history of cultures that have changed as a result of invention, diffusion, and calamity.

5. Discuss American cultural perceptions of color. What do Americans associate with the colors black, yellow, white, blue, and red? Ask three people from other cultures what they associate with these colors.

6. Find examples of sports and military terms that are used in American business settings. Interview a corporate employee and/or read a weekly business magazine or the business section of your local newspaper. Explain what the terms mean and why you think they are used in this context.

7. How does learning about one's own culture help in understanding other cultures?

8. Why do cultural patterns change over time? What American patterns tend to be relatively stable? Do cultural patterns change faster in America than in some other cultures? Why?

chapter 3

The Deep Structure Of Culture: Roots of Reality

There is only one religion, though there are a hundred versions of it.

GEORGE BERNARD SHAW

The family is the nucleus of civilization.

WILL AND ARIEL DURANT

History is philosophy teaching by example.

HENRY ST. JOHN BOLINGBROKE

One idea should be obvious as you reach this juncture of book—this is book about how your culture helps create and shape your realities. Your "interpretation" of reality determines how you define the world and how you interact in that world. In the last chapter, we emphasized cultural variations in both the patterns and functions of those realities. With that information as a point of reference, we are now ready to discuss the important question of why cultures differ in their perceptions of and responses to reality.

Let us begin with series of questions. Why do members of some cultures seek solitude, whereas those of other cultures feel despondent if they are not continuously in the company of other people? Why do some cultures frantically cling to youth, whereas others welcome old age and even death? Why do some cultures worship the earth, whereas others molest it? Why do some cultures seek material possessions, while others believe they are a hindrance to a peaceful life? These, and countless other such questions, need to be answered if you are to understand how people from different cultures communicate. It is not enough to know that some people bow whereas others shake hands or that some value silence whereas others value talk. Although these behaviors are significant, you also need to know what motivates them. We believe the source of how a culture views the world can be found in its deep structure. It is this deep structure that unifies and makes each culture unique. It is also the focus of this chapter.

THE DEEP STRUCTURE OF CULTURE

Although many intercultural communication problems occur on the interpersonal level, most serious confrontations and misunderstandings can be traced to cultural differences that go to the basic core of what it means to be a member of one culture or another. In the United States when members of the racist sect the Aryan Nations engage in violence against Jews on the Fourth of July,[1] when "a lunchroom fight pitting Arab and non-Arab students turns into an all-out brawl,"[2] and when thousands of Native American Indians protest the use of Indian names for mascots or nicknames,[3] it is the deep structure of culture that is being manifested. Elsewhere we find the same strife because of cultural collisions. News reports abound with stories of "ethnic rioting" in Africa,[4] bloody clashes between Hindus and Muslims in both India and Pakistan,[5] and hundred of people being killed in conflicts between Israelis and Palestinians. We also continue to read where Christians face oppression around the world[6] and that ethnic unrest has come to places such as Indonesia and Fiji. In each of these instances it is the deep structure of culture, not interpersonal communication that is at the heart of these problems. What we are suggesting is that when there are ethnic and cultural confrontations in Boston, Belfast, Beirut, Burundi, and Bombay, the deep structure of culture is being acted out. Although some of our examples are drawn from the past, Huntington speaks to the future of intercultural contact and the potential problems that can arise when cultural beliefs clash: "The great divisions among humankind and the dominating sources of conflict will be cultural."[7] Huntington's reasoning reminds us of the basic theme of this book, as well as the rationale for this chapter:

> The people of different civilizations have different views on the relations between God and man, the individual and the group, the citizen and the state, parents and children, husband and wife, as well as differing views of the relative importance of rights and responsibilities, liberty and authority, equality and hierarchy.[8]

It is important to notice that all the issues Huntington cites penetrate into the very heart of culture. They are what we call in this chapter the deep structure of a culture. Such issues (God, loyalty, family, community, state, allegiance, etc.) have been part of every culture for thousands of years. Hence, our point is a simple one: To better understand any culture, you need to appreciate that culture's deep structure. The deep structure of a culture not only has history on its side, but its roots are deep in the basic institutions of the culture. As Delgado points out, "Culture produces and is reproduced by institutions of society, and we can turn to such sites to help recreate and represent the elements of culture."[9] The aim of this chapter is to look at those "sites" so that we might better understand how and why cultures have different visions of the world.

The how and why behind a culture's collective action can be traced to its (1) world view (religion), (2) family structure, and (3) state (community, government). Since the conception of the world's first culture over forty thousand of years ago, these three social organizations, working in combination, define, create, transmit, maintain, and reinforce the basic elements of every culture. Not only do these three institutions have a long history, but also to Houseknecht and Pankhurst they today remain the "essential components of modern life."[10]

We would suggest four interrelated reasons as to why world view, family, and community hold such a prominent sway over the actions of all cultures. Let us look at these four so that you might be able to appreciate the importance of a culture's deep structure to any study of intercultural communication.

Deep Structure Institutions Carry a Culture's Most Important Beliefs

The three institutions of church, family, and state carry the messages that matter most to people. Your religion, parents, and community are given the task of "teaching" you what is important and what you should strive for. Whether it be a desire to gather material possessions or a life that seeks spiritual fulfillment, the three institutions of church, family, and state help you make those major decisions and choices regarding how to live your life. These institutions tell you how we fit into the grand scheme of things, whether you should believe in fate or the power of free choice, why there is suffering, what to expect from life, where your loyalties should reside, and even how to prepare for death. In short, these and other consequential issues fall under the domain of church, family, and state.

Deep Structure Institutions and Their Messages Endure

These institutions are important because they endure. From the early Cro-Magnon cave drawings in southern France over forty thousand years ago until the present, we can trace the strong pull of religion, family, and community. Generation after generation of children are told about Abraham, Moses, the Buddha, Christ, Muhammad, and the like. Whether it is the Eightfold Path, the Ten Commandments, or the Five Pillars of Islam, the messages of these writings survive. And just as every American knows about the values contained in the story of the Revolutionary War, every Mexican is aware of the consequences of the Treaty of Guadalupe Hidalgo.

The enduring quality of the major institutions of culture, and the messages they carry, is one of the ways in which cultures are preserved. Each generation is given the wisdom, traditions, and customs that make a culture unique. However, as students of intercultural communication you need to be aware of the fact that often deep-seated hatreds that turn one culture against another also endure. We see a vivid example of the longevity of bitterness and revenge in the following *U.S. News & World Report* caption: "For 600 years, violent nationalism has bloodied the Balkans."[11] And in the Middle East we see the enduring nature of culture and conflict reaching back a thousand years. In short, whether it be the clashes in Nazareth on Easter of 1999 that have persisted for two thousand years, or seeing Pakistan name its first nuclear bomb after a sixth-century martyr who fought against India, scorn and distrust also endure.

Deep Structure Institutions and Their Messages Are Deeply Felt

The content generated by these institutions, and the institutions themselves, arouse deep and emotional feelings. Think for a moment about the violent reactions that can be produced by taking God's name in vain, calling someone's mother a dirty name, or burning the American flag. Countries and religious causes have been able to send young men to war, and politicians have attempted to win elections, by arousing people to the importance of God, country, and family. If we would make a hierarchy of the cultural values we discussed in the last chapter, we would find that on the top of every culture's list would be love of family, God (whatever form it might take), and country. In short, regardless of a person's culture, the deep structure of that culture is something people feel intensely about.

Cultural memberships help people define who they are.

© Gloria Thomas

Deep Structure Institutions Supply Much of Our Identity

One of the most important responsibilities of any culture is to assist its member in forming their identities. You are not born with an identity. Through countless interactions you discover who you are. Charon makes much the same point when he notes, "We learn our *identities*—who we are—through socialization."[12] And remember that socialization takes place in the family. As you come in contact with other people, you begin to develop a variety of identities. Even now your identity, who you are, is composed of many facets. As Huntington points out, "Everyone has multiple identities which may compete with or reinforce each other: kinship, occupational, cultural, institutional, territorial, educational, partisan, ideological, and others."[13] These, and countless other "memberships," help define you. However, the identities that mean the most to people are gained through deep structure institutions. That is, at some point in your life you move from identities based on the "I" to identities linked to "We." You begin to see yourself as part of a larger unit. Kakar explains this transition in the following manner:

> At some point of time in early life, the child's "I am!" announces the birth of a sense of community. "I am" differentiates me from other individuals. "We are" makes me aware of the other dominant group (or groups) sharing the physical and cognitive space of my community.[14]

As you can see, this "we" identity connects the individual to cultural groups and the main institutions of the culture. According to Huntington, "People define themselves in terms of ancestry, religion, language, history, values, customs, and institutions."[15] You can observe that Huntington's catalog is the same as our list of family, church, and state. Put in slightly different terms, when you think about yourself, you most likely conclude that you are a member of a family (my name is Jane Smith), that you have a religious orientation (I am a Mormon), and that you live in the United States. Regardless of the culture, each individual identifies himself or herself as a member of these cultural organizations. Those identities are important to the study of intercultural communication in that these identities, according to Guirdham, "can be used to identify similarities and differences in behaviors, interpretations and norms."[16] Lynch and Hanson agree with Guirdham when they point out, "A person's cultural identity exerts a profound influence on his or her lifeways."[17] The remainder of this chapter will look at those "life ways" and their influence on perception and communication.

WORLD VIEW

The importance of world view is clearly imbedded in the following definition advanced by Rapport and Overing, who maintain that world view "is the common English translation of the German word *Weltanschauung*, meaning overarching philosophy or outlook, or conception of the world."[18] It is the phrase "overarching philosophy" that unmistakably marks the significance of world view. Rapport and Overing underscore this importance when they note that world views are "used in constructing, populating and anticipating social worlds."[19] What is unique about these "social worlds" is that they are directly linked to perception and culture. First, as Hoebel and Frost note, world view is an "inside view of the way things are colored, shaped, and arranged according to personal cultural preconceptions."[20] Second, world views, again like culture, are automatic and unconscious. Hall reinforces this key point when he writes:

> Often, worldviews operate at an unconscious level, so that we are not even aware that other ways of seeing the world are either possible or legitimate. Like the air we breathe, worldviews are a vital part of who we are but not a part we usually think much about. [21]

Once more we remind you that world views influence perception, beliefs, and values. Dana offers an excellent summary of the importance of world view:

> Worldview provides some of the unexamined underpinnings for perception and the nature of reality as experienced by individuals who share a common culture. The worldview of a culture functions to make sense of life experiences that might otherwise be construed as chaotic, random, and meaningless. Worldview is imposed by collective wisdom as a basis for sanctioned actions that enable survival and adaptation.[22]

It might be useful to think of a culture's world view as the basic foundation of that culture in that it governs both perception and behavior in large and small ways. As Hoebel writes, "In selecting its customs for day-to-day living, even the little things, the society chooses those ways that accord with its thinking and predilections—ways that fit its basic postulates as to the nature of things and what is desirable and what is not."[23] The pervasive impact of our world view has led Olayiwola to conclude that a culture's world view even influences the social, economic, and political life of a nation.[24]

Because world views deal with the topics that penetrate all phases of human existence, they start with questions about what we commonly call the meaning of life. World view, therefore, is a culture's orientation toward God, humanity, nature, questions of existence, the universe and cosmos, life, moral and ethical reasoning, suffering, sickness, death, and other philosophical issues that influence how its members perceive their world.[25] The importance of examining these crucial issues has been identified by Pennington: "If one understands a culture's world view and cosmology, reasonable accuracy can be attained in predicting behaviors and motivations in other dimensions."[26] For instance, the Islamic world view provides insight into the Islamic culture's perception of women. As Bianquis points out, "Generally speaking woman as an individual was subordinated to man both by the Quran and the Hadith. God created woman from a fragment of man's body that she might serve him."[27]

Knowledge of world view can even help you understand a culture's perception of nature. As we noted in the last chapter, many environmentalists disavow the biblical tradition which tells people that God wants them to be masters over the Earth: "And God said, Let us make man in our image, after our likeness: and let them have domain over the fish of the sea, and over the fowl of the air, and over the cattle, and over all the earth, and over every creeping thing that creepeth upon the earth." Other religious views produce different attitudes. The Shinto religion encourages an aesthetic appreciation of nature in which the focus is on reality and not heaven—a reality that makes nature supreme. Shintoism prescribes an aesthetic love of the land, in whole and in part. Every hill and lake, every mountain and river is dear. Cherry trees, shrines, and scenic resorts are indispensable to a full life. People perceive them as lasting things among which their ancestors lived and died. Here their ancestral spirits look on and their families still abide. People thus preserve nature so that nature can preserve the family.

Another link between world view and behavior can be seen in how a culture perceives the business arena. In two classic textbooks, Weber's *The Protestant Ethic and the Spirit of Capitalism* and Tawney's *Religion and the Rise of Capitalism,* the bond between religion, commerce, and production is examined. Their conclusion—there was a direct link. Bartels reaffirms that link to contemporary times when he tells us, "The foundation of a nation's culture and the most important determinant of social and business conduct are the religious and philosophical beliefs of a people. From them spring role perceptions, behavior patterns, codes of ethics and the institutionalized manner in which economic activities are performed."[28]

Even the manner in which a culture actually conducts its business can be reflected in its world view. For example, if a culture values "out-of-awareness" processes and intuitive problem solving, it might reach conclusions in a manner much different from that of a culture valuing the scientific method. Howell made this same point with a specific example:

> A Japanese manager who is confronted with a perplexing problem studies it thoroughly; once he feels he understands what the problem is, he does not attempt to collect data and develop hypotheses. He waits. He knows that his "center of wisdom" is in his lower abdomen, behind and somewhat below the navel. In due time a message will come from the center, giving him the answer he desires.[29]

What is interesting about Howell's example is that in the Buddhist tradition, where meditation is stressed, a common meditation technique is watching one's breath as it originates in the abdomen. Here again you can see the tie between world view and behavior.

We have attempted to make it very clear that world view, perception, and communication are bound together. Gold clearly illustrates this crucial link between one's spiritual view and how that worldview determines the manner in which people live:

> Ask any Tibetan or Navajo about one's place in the scheme of things and the answer will inevitably be that we must act, speak, and think respectfully and reasonably toward others. Navajos say that we are all people: earth-surface walkers, swimmers, crawlers, flyers, and sky and water people. Tibetans know that we are humans, animals, worldly gods and demi-gods, ghosts and hell beings, and a host of aboriginal earth powers. Regardless of category or description, we're all inextricably connected through a system of actions and their effects, which can go according to cosmic order or fall out of synchrony with it.[30]

RELIGION AS A WORLD VIEW

We have already said that your world view originates in your culture, is transmitted via a multitude of channels, and can take a variety of forms. But what predominant element is found in every culture and has for thousands of years given people their world view? Religion! As Nanda and Warms note, "Religion is a human universal."[31] The human need to confront important issues is so universal that as Haviland points out, "We know of no group of people anywhere on the face of the earth who, at any time over the past 10,000 years, have been without religion."[32] And, as is the case with all deep structure elements, the long history of religion is directly linked to culture. Coogan repeats the same important point when he tells writes, "A belief in the existence of a reality greater than the human has served as a definer and creator of cultures."[33]

Importance of Religion

For some unexplainable reason, the responsibility of generating and preserving the elements of world view has rested with either religious institutions (for example, the Catholic Church) or spiritual leaders (for example, the Buddha). Whether it is the teachings of the Bible, Vedas, Koran, Torah, or I Ching, people have always felt a need to seek outside themselves the values by which they live their lives and guidance on how to view and explain the world. As we already mentioned, in a host of ways, religion has provided the peoples of the world with advice, values, and guidance since antiquity. It appears that for thousands of years billions of people have agreed with the Latin proverb that tells you that "A man devoid of religion is like a horse without a bridle."

Most experts agree that religions have endured because they perform a variety of essential needs. Haviland offers a summary of those needs when he notes:

> All religions serve a number of important psychological and social needs. They reduce anxiety by explaining the unknown and making it understandable, as well as provide comfort with the belief super-natural aid is available in times of crisis. They sanction a wide range of human conduct by providing notions of right and wrong, setting precedents for accepting behavior, and transferring the burden of decision making from individuals to supernatural powers. Through ritual, religion may be used to enhance the learning of oral traditions. Finally, religion plays an important role in maintaining social solidarity.[34]

Nanda presents a more specific listing of what religion provides the individual when she observes that culture "deals with the nature of life and death, the creation of the universe, the origin of society and groups within the society, the relationship of individuals and groups to one another, and the relation of humankind to nature."[35] You will notice that the items highlighted by Nanda offer credence to the basic theme of this chapter: The deep structure of culture deals with issues that matter most to people.

Whether it is conceptions of the first cause of all things, or natural occurrences such as comets, floods, lightning, thunder, drought, famine, disease, or an abundance of food, people rely on religious explanations. Smith eloquently expresses the steadfast importance of religion to the psychological welfare of every individual:

> When religion jumps to life it displays a startling quality. It takes over. All else, while not silenced, becomes subdued and thrown into a supporting role. . . . It calls the soul to the highest adventure it can undertake, a proposed journey across the jungles, peaks, and deserts of the human spirit.[36]

The study of religion not only helps you in your quest for a meaning and purpose to life, but it also gives you clues into the social aspects of a culture. Grondona make the same point when he asserts, "Throughout history, religion has been the richest source of values."[37] Haviland expands on this idea in the following paragraph:

> The social functions of religion are no less important than the psychological functions. A traditional religion reinforces group norms, provides moral sanctions for individual conduct, and furnishes the substratum of common purpose and values upon which the equilibrium of the community depends.[38]

Religion then, be it theology or the everyday practices of a culture, offers you insight into the members of that culture. As Lamb observes, "It is clear that religion and culture are inextricably entwined."[39] Guruge takes much the same stance when he observes "religion and civilization seem to have gone hand in hand in the evolution of human society to an extent that one could conclude that they are co-equal and co-terminus."[40] Studying religious distinctions can be helpful in that they often represent "a set of differences that make a difference."[41] We strongly believe that Paden was correct when he wrote:

> The study of religion . . . prepares us to encounter not only other centers and calendars, and numerous versions of the sacred and profane, but also to decipher and appreciate different modes of language and behavior. Toward that end, knowledge about others plays its indispensable role.[42]

Selecting Religious Traditions for Study

With thousands of religions and world views to choose from, how can we decide which orientations to examine? In the United States alone there are seven hundred to eight hundred religious denominations.[43] So, the question remains—what do we include and what do we exclude in our treatment of world views? Drawing on the research of religious scholars, we have decided to examine Christianity, Judaism, Islam, Hinduism, Buddhism, and Confucianism. And while we grant the importance of other religious traditions and world views, our decision was based on three criteria—numbers, diffusion, and relevance.

First, while statistics of the world's religions are only approximations, most statistical studies reveal that worldwide, Christianity, Islam, and Hinduism each have over a billion followers. And while Buddhists are most difficult to count, Buddhism is practiced in much of Southeast Asian and is one of the many traditions of China and Japan. Hence, regarding our first criteria (*numbers*) Carmody and Carmody note: "When we speak of the great religions we mean the traditions that have lasted for centuries, shaped hundreds of millions of people, and gained respect for their depth and breadth."[44]

Second, by *diffusion* as a criterion we are referring to the notion of dispersion of a religion throughout the world. For example, while the Jewish population is numerically small (14 million worldwide), Jews are spread throughout the world. In fact, only one third of the world's Jews live in Israel. Christianity and Islam, because of their missionary zeal, are also diffused throughout the world.

Finally, the six traditions are worthy of serious study because they are as *relevant today* as they were thousands of years ago. As Smith states, these "are the faiths that every citizen should be acquainted with, simply because hundreds of millions of people live by them."[45] Not only are they important because they have historical significance, but they have a global impact. We need only look at the worldwide reach of Islam to see how information about this religion, and others, can be helpful in understanding other cultures.

Before we treat each of these religions in detail, we need to mention the similarities among these spiritual paths, for as we have said repeatedly; it is often similarities rather than differences that lead to intercultural understanding.

Religious Similarities

It should not be surprising that there are numerous similarities among the world's great religions. Most human beings, from the moment of birth to the time of their death, ask many of the same questions and face many of the same problems. It falls on a religion to supply the answers to these universal questions. Although there are many similarities among all religious traditions, we have selected seven parallel points that illustrate how in many ways cultures, like people, are somewhat alike in their search for a meaning to life and explanations to the experience of death.

Sacred Scriptures

At the heart of all the world's main religious traditions lies a body of sacred wisdom. As Crim points out, "Sacred scriptures express and provide identity, authorization, and ideals for the people of the tradition."[46] Each of these scriptures, whether oral or written, enables a culture to pass on the insights and tradition from generation to generation. As Coogan, notes, "A religion's scriptures are the repository of its essential principles and the touchstone for its formulations of doctrine."[47] We say more about these writings later in the chapter; for now, let us simply touch on the important religious texts for some of the religions we have chosen to discuss.

The Bible, consisting of the thirty-nine books of the Old Testament, written in Hebrew and the twenty-seven books of the New Testament, written in Greek, serves as the written centerpiece of Christianity. For Jews, the Hebrew Bible, or Old Testament, is an important document that has lasted thousands of years and offers guidance to the present and future. The Koran, which Muslims believe was dictated to the prophet Muhammad by Allah, is written in classical Arabic. For Muslims, according to Crystal, "the memorization of the text in childhood acts simultaneously as an introduction to literacy."[48] In Hinduism, the sacred writings are found in the Vedas. These divine wisdoms cover a wide range of texts and are written in Sanskrit. The Pali Canon, based on oral tradition, contains the teaching of the Buddha. "Pali became the canonical language for Buddhists from many countries, but comparable texts came to exist in other languages, such as Chinese and Japanese, as the religion evolved."[49] For the Confucian tradition people will turn to the Analects. This collection has for centuries helped shape the thoughts and actions for billions of people.

Authority

In nearly all cases, religious orientations have one or more individuals who are recognized as having special significance. They are usually authority figures that provide guidance and instruction. Whether the figure is a supreme all-knowing God such as Allah, a philosopher such as the Buddha, Jesus, "the Son of God," recipients of divine revelation such as Moses or Muhammad, or the wise counsel of Confucius, all traditions have someone greater than the individual who can be turned to for emotional and spiritual direction.

Ritual is one of the oldest and persistent symbolic activities associated with religions.

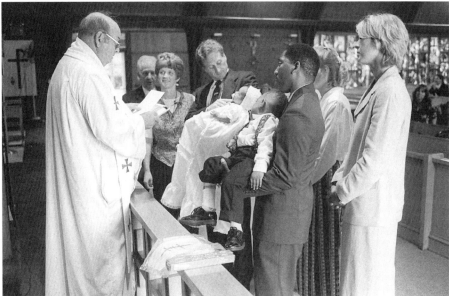

© Michael A. Dwyer/Stock Boston

Traditional Rituals

"Ritual is one of the oldest, most complex, and persistent symbolic activities associated with religions."[50] Rituals, like so many aspects of culture, are not instinctive and, therefore, need to be passed on from generation to generation if they are to endure. Haviland expands on the importance of rituals when he notes, "Not only is ritual a means for reinforcing a group's social bonds and for relieving tensions, but it is also one way many important events are celebrated and crises, such as death, made less socially disruptive and less difficult for individuals to bear."[51] As you can observe, rituals serve an assortment of purposes. In addition to what Haviland notes, rituals also "express the psychic, social, and religious world to its participants" while providing "identity and structure."[52] Rituals take a variety of forms. They range from traditions dealing with rites of passage (Bar Mitzvahs, circumcision, etc.), the lighting of candles or incense, to the wearing of certain attire, to deciding whether to stand, sit, or kneel when you pray. There can be rituals dealing with "space" (Muslims going to Mecca) and others that call attention to "time" (Christians celebrating Christmas and Easter).

Rituals can also be indirect. A good example of an indirect ritual is the Japanese tea ceremony. At first glance, it would appear that the tea ceremony is simply the preparation and drinking of tea, but the importance of the ritual to Buddhism is far greater. As Paden notes:

> Every detailed act, every move and position, embodies humility, restraint, and awareness. This framing of ordinary action in order to reveal some deeper significance—in this example the values are related to the Zen Buddhist idea of imminence of the absolute in the ordinary—is a common element of ritual behavior.[53]

Speculation

Every religion knows that all human beings seek answers to the great mysteries of life. As we noted earlier, each tradition, knowing that people usually are vexed by the great conundrums of life, attempt to address questions about mortality and immortality, suf-

Religion provides its members with a strong sense of identity.

© Lindsay Hebberd/Corbis

fering, the origins of the universe, and countless other events. From Genesis stories to descriptions of reincarnation, death, heaven, and hell, all traditions supply answers to timeless and overpowering questions.

Ethics

Regardless of the tradition, "religion always includes an ethic."[54] It is intriguing that ethical standards are nearly the same for all cultures. In the case of ethics, according to Smith, the message "pretty much tells a cross-cultural story."[55] For example, all religions say you should avoid murder, thieving, lying, and adultery.[56] In addition, they all stress the virtues of "humility, charity, and veracity."[57] According to Coogan, what they all seek to accomplish by the formation of ethical principles is to "enable their adherents to achieve the ultimate objective of the tradition—the attainment of salvation, redemption, enlightenment, and the 'liberation of the soul."[58]

Security

All religions, as we have noted elsewhere, provide their members with a sense of identity and security. Religion unites people by asking them to share symbols, values, and norms. There is a strong feeling of security to know that you are part of a religious family that is feasting on the same day, wearing the same attire when they pray, bowing in one direction or another, or taking Holy Communion.

Part of the similarity of security can be found in the fact that all traditions provide meaning and purpose. Macionis, in the paragraph below, summarizes this sense of refuge and security found in all religious traditions.

> Religious beliefs offer the comforting sense that the vulnerable human condition serves a great purpose. Strengthened by such beliefs, people are less likely to collapse in despair when confronted by life's calamities.[59]

Sacred Time

The acknowledgment of sacred and distinctive times is yet another common experience found in all religious traditions. This recognition of the importance of time may mark important days, months, years, life cycles, and even significant historical events. For some groups sacred times can be "the cosmic rhythms of the sun, moon, planets, and stars."[60]

SIX RELIGIOUS TRADITIONS

As we begin our discussion of the great religions of the world, it is important to keep a few points in mind. First, religion is but one kind of world view, and even the person who says "There is no God" has answers to the large questions about the nature of truth, how the world operates, life, death, suffering, and social relationships. As Ridenour notes, "It is important to realize that everyone has a worldview whether or not he or she can recognize or state it."[61] Second, as Hendry says, "Religion pervades many spheres which we might call secular and it cannot easily be separated from them."[62] It is often difficult to draw a line between religion and a subtle manifestation of religion. What one person might call religion or world view another might call philosophy. For our purposes, the labeling is not nearly as important as the notion that a culture's heritage includes ways of dealing with timeless and fundamental questions. Finally, it is not our intent to offer a course on world religion but rather to isolate those aspects of world view that are most important to the study of intercultural communication. As Coongan notes, "The world's major religious traditions have both reflected and shaped the values of the societies of which they have been an inseparable element."[63] In short, we, like Smith, believe that the locus of religion is in persons and in human interaction.[64]

Christianity

We start with Christianity, a religion of over a billion people scattered throughout the world. Christianity is also the dominant world view found in America. We should begin by pointing out that there are thousands of groups or denominations that can be classified as Christian. For example, the *World Christian Encyclopedia* now lists 33,800 different Christian denominations worldwide.[65] While many of the groups might have specific rituals, beliefs, and traditions that mark them as unique, they are all alike with regard to the basic characteristics and tenets that are called Christianity.

Basic Assumptions

We start our discussion of the basic assumptions behind Christianity with an excellent synopsis advanced by Hale:

> Essentially, Christianity is a monotheistic tradition centered on faith in God (the eternal creator who transcends creation and yet is active in the world) and in Jesus Christ as the savior and redeemer of human kind. Christianity holds that God became incarnate—fully human—as Jesus of Nazareth. Christians believe that Jesus died on a cross and was resurrected, physically rising from the dead. The belief in the Trinity, the sacred mystery of Father, Son, and Holy Spirit as one, triune ('three-in-one') God is central to the Christian tradition.[66]

As you can observe from the above summary, at the heart of Christian faith is the assertion "that the crucified Jesus was resurrected by God and present in the church as 'the body of Christ."[67] Noss and Noss further underscore the importance of Jesus to Christianity when they note, "In the belief that Jesus is the clearest portrayal of the character of God all the rest of Christian doctrine is implied."[68]

Of the thousands of directives that Jesus and his apostles carried to the world, let us select a few of those that have most shaped the Christian tradition. It should be noted that many of the teachings of Jesus, like so many religious doctrines have been modified over time. For example, the Reformation of the sixteenth century, Martin Luther and the Protestant movement have influenced much of modern Christianity. Yet we can still point to numerous characteristics of Christianity that help demonstrate the link between religion, perception, and behavior.

Organized Worship

For Christians the church serves a variety of purposes, ranging from the religious to the social. You can observe the spiritual dimension in the words of Hale when she writes, "Regardless of how humble or lavish, a Christian church is a sacred place of reverence and awe, intended to communicate Christian mysteries and the drama of salvation to its congregants."[69] For our purposes it is the social aspect of Christianity that offers insight into the communication aspects of that tradition. Simply stated, Christian theology believes in organized worship as a means of proclaiming God's message.[70] As Carmody and Carmody note, "Jesus's view of the self was relational. The self was not a monad existing in isolation."[71] Jesus believed, "The closer people drew to God, the closer they could draw to one another."[72] Remember, that even at the Last Supper, Jesus shared his final meal with his twelve leading disciples rather than being alone. Our point is that this notion of organized worship has contributed to the social dimension of Western cultures. Americans are social creatures and belong to numerous clubs, committees, and organizations. The French historian de Tocqueville pointed out over two hundred years ago that Americans had a large series of networks and associations that went well beyond their family unit. Perhaps the stimulus for such behavior can be found in Christianity. In the East, one's spiritual life is conducted in solitude; in the West, God's "message" is shared with others.

Ethics

For the two thousand years of Christian history, starting with Jesus, this religion advanced ethical principles intended to give direction to the followers of the faith. These ethical injunctions are found in the Ten Commandments and scattered throughout the Bible. Perhaps the most powerful ethical teachings are found in the manner in which Jesus lived his life and preached about the importance of love. As Fisher and Luyster note, "The central ethic Jesus taught was love."[73] The word *love* appears with astonishing frequency in the New Testament. We would even suggest that the following ethic regarding love might be the most repeated in history: "Love your neighbor as yourself. What you would like people to do to you do to them."[74] You can clearly observe the manifestations of these ideas of love and compassion reflected in everything from the large amounts of charitable contributions Americans make to their willingness to go to foreign countries to improve the lives of strangers.

Individualism

While membership in a church community is important to Christians, most religious scholars maintain the notion that "Christianity discovered the individual."[75] That is to say, the Western concept of the importance of the individual, which we have discussed throughout this book, can be linked partially to Christianity. For example, salvation, particularly for Protestants, "is achieved by our own efforts alone and there is a tendency for deeds to count more than prayers."[76] Even the Bible carries examples of individualism. As Woodward notes, "The Gospels are replete with scenes in which Jesus works one on one healing this woman's sickness, forgiving that man's sins and calling each to personal conversion."[77] Summarizing this important point, Woodward adds, "Christianity discovers individuality in the sense that it stresses personal conversion."[78] In addition, the Christian theology begins with the assumption that the world is real and meaningful because God created it. Human beings are significant because God created them in his image. God has a special relationship with each person in that God sees and hears, rewards, and punishes. Each person is important to him. The Christian God is a personal God, who desires a relationship with his creation.[79] In a culture that values individualism, Christianity is perhaps the perfect religion.

"Doing"
Much of the Western "doing" orientation (which we discussed in the last chapter) can be found in the life of Jesus. Peter, one of Jesus' disciples, once said, "He went about doing good."[80] This example set by Jesus was translated into action. For instance, the Romans would cast out people into the streets at the first sign of sickness because they were afraid of dying. Christians would take an active role and try to nurse the sick.[81] This is not an isolated instance. Anyone who has studied Christianity and knows the lessons of Jesus is aware that he was an active man and urged his followers to be energetic. As we indicated, the Bible is full of accounts of how he traveled from place to place healing the sick and counseling misfits and ordinary people. In short, activity and Christianity are bound together.

Future
As noted when we discussed attitudes toward "time," Americans are future oriented. Now we are suggesting that one of the "roots" of that reality can be found in Christianity. Put in slightly different terms, in comparison to other religions, one of the "lessons" of Christianity is that the future is important. As Muck points out, for Christians "no matter what happened in the past, it is the future that holds the greatest promise."[82] God forgives mistakes, regret, and remorse. As Blanche and Parkes point out, "Christians hold that those who repent of their sins and turn to Jesus Christ will be forgiven and will join him in heaven after death."[83] In this sense, the individual is to "move on." Hence, even the notion of a heaven places emphasis on the future.

Language
In the last chapter when we talked about high- and low-context cultures, we pointed out that Americans are a low-context culture. One of the reasons for this classification rested on the idea that most Americans placed a high priority on verbal communication—written and spoken. While there are countless reasons for every cultural trait, we are now offering the contention that one of the reasons lies in Christianity—a religion that stresses language.

Much of Christian religion is filtered through language. From the phrase "God as the Word" to the fact that New Testament gospels are a written document, you see that for Christians, language is important. Even the notion of preaching and standing on a pulpit underscores that role of language in Christianity. To be part of a "religious community" you must interact with others. In addition, Christians believe that "God relies on language to reveal himself to humans in the Bible and through godly people."[84] You also see the importance of language revealed in the fact that most of the teachings in the Bible, and the act of "preaching," usually take the form of stories.[85]

Gender

The enduring legacy for women is, of course, the Garden of Eden story. This view of women is perhaps best illustrated when Paul speaks in 1 Timothy:

> I permit no woman to teach or to have authority over men; she is to keep silent. For Adam was formed first, then Eve; and Adam was not deceived, but the woman was deceived and became the transgressor. [86]

While this story is often used to justify placing women in second-class positions, recent events and a more modern interpretation of the Bible reveal a view of women that is more consistent with current perceptions. For example, with the exception of the Catholic Church, the number of women who are becoming priests is growing at a rapid rate. Some biblical scholars are asserting that Jesus might well have been a feminist. They offer some of the following examples to justify their claim. First, prior to the coming of Jesus, Roman society regarded women as inherently inferior to men. Husbands could divorce their wives but wives could not divorce their husbands. Jesus banned all divorce. Men could even marry girls ten or eleven years old. Jesus challenged all of these practices. Wrote one biblical scholar, "The new religion offered women not only greater status and influence within the church, but also more protection as wives and mothers."[87]

Second, "although he called only men to be apostles, Jesus readily accepted women into his circle of friends and disciples."[88] Defying custom, Jesus even invited women to join him at meals. All of this leads Murphy to note, "Women were often prominent in the accounts of his ministry, and he acknowledged the oppression they face."[89]

Finally, Jesus helped define a new role for women by giving them greater responsibility. For example, they "shared with men the cultural responsibility for teaching children, as reflected in the Proverbs: 'My son, keep your father's commandment, and forsake not your mother's teaching.'"[90]

Courage

A strong message in Christianity is courage. As Carmody and Carmody note, "Jesus was courageous."[91] A careful reading of the life of Jesus reveals a man who would not be intimidated by his opponents. On occasion after occasion, we have accounts of Jesus' strong personality emerging. His strength and courage are traits that all Christians are reminded of repeatedly. As you know from your own experience, these are also two powerful values in the American culture. Here again, you can see the link between world view and communication styles.

Judaism

Background

Although Jews represent less than one-half of 1 percent of the world's population (approximately 14 million Jews), and approximately 2 percent of the entire population of the United States,[92] their geographical distribution and their interest in politics, the arts, literature, medicine, finance, and the law have, for thousands of years, made them important and influential. As Smith notes, "It has been estimated that one-third of our Western civilization bears the marks of its Jewish ancestry."[93]

Judaism is the oldest of the religions being practiced today and the smallest of all the major religious traditions. Judaism is believed to have been founded in approximately 1300 B.C. when twelve Israelite tribes came to Canaan from Mesopotamia. Later, many of them settled in Egypt where they were held as slaves until they fled to freedom under the leadership of Moses in about 1200 B.C. As we have indicated, in approximately 3,500 years Judaism has spread throughout the world.

Basic Concepts

Coogan offers an excellent summary of many of the key elements of the Jewish faith in the following paragraph:

> As a religion, Judaism has three essential elements: God, Torah, and Israel. Arguably the oldest monotheistic faith, it believes in one universal and eternal God, the creator and sovereign of all that exists. God has entered into a special relationship, or covenant, with one people, the Jews, or Israel, and given them the task of being a "nation to the nations."[94]

The Jewish faith is unique in that it is both a culture and a religion. It is common, for example, to find nonreligious Jews who identify fully with the culture but not with the theology. Fisher and Luyster elaborate on this point: "Judaism has no single founder, no central leader or group making theological decisions; Judaism is a people, a very old family. This family can be defined either as a religious group or a national group."[95]

"At the heart of the Jewish religion," says Banks, "lies the existence of a covenant between God and his people."[96] Although Jews believe that God's providence extends to all people, they also hold to the notion God entered into this special covenant (solemn agreement) with them. In this agreement God promised to make Israel a great nation; in response the Jewish people were to be obedient to God and to carry God's message by example. From circumcision to the keeping of the Sabbath, signs of the covenant abound in Jewish culture and religion.[97] It is this covenant that is at the heart of why Jews consider themselves God's "chosen people." In Jewish theology this special "consideration never meant advantages for the Jews, only increased responsibilities and hardships."[98]

The Jewish world view is expressed through a number of concepts basic to the faith: (1) God is one, (2) no human ever will be divine, (3) humans are free, (4) humans are the pinnacle of creation, (5) Jews belong to a group or nation whose goal is to serve God, and (6) humans must be obedient to the God-given commandments in the Torah (first five books of the Bible) and assume personal responsibility. These six concepts compose a belief system stressing the secular notion that order must be maintained if Jews are to have a collective life. The Ten Commandments in the Torah therefore give structure to and make possible a social world.[99] Judaism penetrates every area of human existence, providing humankind with a means of communicating with both the secular and transcendental worlds.[100] It is not simply a religion that serves spiritual needs but a guide to worship, ceremonies, justice, friendship, kindness, intellectual pursuits, courtesy, and diet.

Oppression and Persecution

Historically, oppression and persecution have been part of the Jewish religion and view of the world. As Ehrlich notes, "All too often the story of Jews has been presented as a litany of disasters."[101] As Van Doren states, "The history of Judaism and the Jews is a long complicated story, full of blood and tears."[102] Through the belief that God is using them "to introduce insights into history that all people need," suffering, oppression, and persecution seem to be built into the Jewish faith.[103] Prager and Telushkin offer an excellent summary of the long-standing persecution of Jews:

> Only the Jews have had their homeland destroyed (twice), been dispersed wherever they have lived, survived the most systematic attempt in history (aside from that of the Gypsies) to destroy an entire people, and been expelled from nearly every nation among whom they have lived.[104]

Even Moses, as Boorstin says, "felt righteous anger at the oppression of his people."[105] What we have then is a religious group who, for thousands of years, has experienced murder, exile, and discrimination. Even today many Jews have a difficult time trusting non-Jews. Some additional results of religious persecution on the Jewish people is summarized by Van Doren:

> With all that, the Jews are still, essentially the same stubborn, dedicated people, now and forever maybe, affirming the same three things. First, they are a people of the law as given in the only books of Moses. Second, they are the chosen people of God, having a covenant with him. Third, they are a witness that God is and will be forevermore.[106]

Learning

Of additional interest is the importance the Jewish religion places on learning. So strong is this value that the Jewish essayist Elie Wiesel quotes a Jewish saying that "Adam chose knowledge instead of immortality." The attitude helps determine how Jews perceive the world and function in it. For thousands of years Jews have made the study of the Talmud (a holy book that is over five thousand pages long) an important element of Jewish life.[107] Some Hebrew translations of the word *Talmud* actually contain the words "learning, "study," and "teaching."[108] So strong is the value of learning for Jews that the Jewish prayer book speaks of "the love of learning" as one of three principles of faith.[109] References to the importance of education are sprinkled throughout Jewish holy books. "As early as the first century, Jews had a system of compulsory education."[110] Jews have a proverb that states, "Wisdom is better than jewels." Even today, after being in existence for thousands of years, occupations using the mind (teacher, lawyer, doctor, writer, and so on), are popular professions in the Jewish community.

Justice

The Jewish faith also teaches a strong sense of justice. An individual's responsibility and moral commitment to God and other people is clearly spelled out in detail in all Jewish religious writings. Novak notes, "the promotion of justice is a paramount concern" for the Jew.[111] In fact, one of the four categories of Jewish law is actually "To ensure moral treatment of others."[112] You can see this concern for justice in everything from ancient Jewish writings to the active role Jews played during the civil rights movement in the 1960s. So strong is this basic precept that Smith believes much of Western civilization owes a debt to the early Jewish prophets for establishing the notion of justice as a major principle for the maintenance of "social order."[113]

Family

As you shall see later in the chapter, all societies value the family, but for the Jew the family is the locus of worship and devotion. On nearly every occasion, be it in the home or the synagogue, the family is an active participant in the Jewish religion. From circumcisions, to Passover Seders, to Bar or Bas Mitzvahs, to marriage, and death, the family and religion are strongly bond together. Rosten offers a clear digest of this link in the following paragraph:

> For 4,000 years, the Jewish family has been the very core, mortar, and citadel of Judaism's faith and the central reason for the survival of the Jews as a distinct ethnic group. The Jewish home is a temple, according to Judaic law, custom, and tradition.[114]

Islam

We believe Smith is right when he says "Islam is a vital force in the contemporary world."[115] Belt highlights the statistical impact of Islam when he writes, "Some 1.3 billion human beings—one person in five—heed Islam's call in the modern world, embracing the religion at a rate that makes it the fastest growing on Earth, with 80 percent of believers now outside the Arab world."[116] Islam will soon be the second-most-commonly practiced religion in the United States[117] with nearly 7 million members.[118] Yet in spite of these statistics, Islam is, as Belt notes, the "most misunderstood religion on earth."[119] The events of September 11, 2001, seem to have only added to the incomplete or false information many American have about this religion. As Noss and Noss point out:

> The heart of Islam is well hidden from most Westerners, and the outer images of Islamic countries present bewildering contrasts: stern ayatollahs ordering the lash for prostitutes, camel drivers putting down prayer mats in the desert, a sophisticated royal prince discussing international investments, and fiery national liberators proclaiming equality and denouncing Western values.[120]

History

Woodward offers a concise summary of the early history of the Arab people, dating back thousands of years, before the founding of Islam, when he writes:

> The Arabs were mostly polytheists, worshiping tribal deities. They had no sacred history linking them to one universal god, like other Middle Eastern peoples. They had no sacred text to live by, like the Bible; no sacred language, as Hebrew is to Jews and Sanskrit is to Hindus. Above all, they had no prophet sent to them by God, as Jews and Christians could boast.[121]

This early history was greatly altered with the arrival of Muhammad. For Muslims, Muhammad (570–632) was the messenger of God. Muslims believe that their God, Allah, spoke to human beings many times in the past. But it was Muhammad who delivered a religious message and established a social order. Muhammad, believing that community and religion were one and the same, established the city-state that became known as Madinah. This fusion of church and state was unique to Muhammad's time. This and other accomplishments marked him as "one of the most remarkable and charismatic men in history."[122]

Muhammad's message was so powerful that within a few centuries Islamic religion and rule, as Gordon points out, was extended to north Africa, Persia, Jerusalem, Damascus, the Caucasus, central Asia, Europe, Egypt and Turkey.[123] This phenomenal growth and popularity continued unabated until today where Muslims "form the majority in more than fifty countries and a substantial minority in many others."[124]

Pillars of Faith

Islam, like Christianity and Judaism, is monotheistic. It believes in one God, and that God is Allah. The two major forms of Islam—Sunni and Shi'a—both accept that Muhammad was the heir to the religious mantle passed down by the prophets of the Bible. According to Elias, "Muslims are supposed to believe in five cardinal points, which are so central to the religion that they are called the "Pillars of Faith."[125] To better understand how Muslims perceive the world we will now pause and briefly examine these Pillars.

Divine Unity. The first Pillar is called *tawhid*. While this term can have a variety of meanings, it mainly *calls* attention to the fact that Muslims believe in one, unique, incomparable, eternal God.[126] So strong is this commitment to the "one true God" that Muslims believe that every other deity is false and that "it is a grievous sin to worship any other force or being in the universe."[127] You can clearly observe this obligation and commitment to a single God in the word *Islam*, which is the infinitive of the Arab verb meaning "to submit." The word *Muslim* is the present participle of the same verb. A Muslim, then, is one who accepts and submits to the will of Allah. So powerful is this belief in Allah that, according to Fisher and Luyster, "The first sentence chanted in the ear of a traditional Muslim infant is the *Shahadah –'La ilaha illa 'llah.'*"[128] This saying literally means, "There is no god but God." To utter this allegiance to a single God is also one way a person can become a Muslim. You only have to declare, "I testify that there is no god but God, and that Muhammad is the Prophet of God."[129]

As we indicated, God created the universe and called forth a community of beings and charged them with the responsibility to establish righteousness in the world. They also believe that everything, good or evil, proceeds directly from the divine will as it is irrevocably recorded on the Preserved Tablets. This orientation produces fatalism: whatever happens has been willed by Allah. The saying *"in sha'a Allah"* (if God wills it) looms large in the thinking of the average Muslim. The word *inshalle* is also used with great frequency. This word translates as "God willing." This usage is important, for it represents the Islamic theological concept that destiny unfolds according to God's will.

Prophecy. According to Elias, "Muslims are supposed to believe that God wishes to communicate with human beings, and he uses prophets for this purpose."[130] These "messengers of God" included, among others, Adam, Noah, Abraham, Moses, and Jesus. However, Muslims "consider Jesus to have been the second last prophet, who foretold the coming of Muhammad."[131] That is, Muslims believe that his final prophet—Muhammad—revealed God's eternal message.

Revelation. Muslims hold that God revealed scriptures to humanity as guidance for them. According to Elias, "Four such scriptures are recognized: the Torah as revealed to Moses, the Psalms of David, the New Testament of Jesus, and the *Qur'an* of Muhammad."[132] Muslims believe that the all the scriptures before the *Qur'an* were tampered with and corrupted by humans. Hence, they hold that the *Qur'an* is God's final word and "supersedes and over rules all previous writings."[133] Because of the importance of the *Qur'an* to the followers of the Islamic faith, we will expand our discussion of this book a little later in this chapter.

Angelic Agency. Muslims believe in the existence of angels. As Fisher and Luyster note, for Muslims "angels are everywhere; they come to our help in every thought and action."[134] Elias speaks of the two most important angels in Islamic theology and the function they serve:

> The most famous angel is Gabriel, who served as an intermediary between God and Muhammad in the revelation of the Qur'an. Another important figure is Iblis, who used to be the chief of all angles but was punished for disobeying God by being cast out of Heaven. Afer that he turned into Sata and now not only rules Hell but also tries to tempt human beings from the path of goodness. [135]

Last Judgment and Afterlife. The concept of the "final judgment" and the notion of an afterlife are linked because the ending of the earth determines what happens to each person on the Day of Judgment. Let us explain.

Muslims, like Jews and Christians believe in the Day of Judgment (the Day of Resurrection) when all people will be resurrected for God's judgment according to their beliefs and deeds. Put in slightly different terms, "Islam says that what we experience in the after life is a revealing of our tendencies in this life. Our thoughts, actions, and moral qualities are turned into our outer reality."[136] The notion of a moral code, and its tie to an afterlife, is one of the most fundamental and crucial elements of Islamic doctrine. Elias writes, "Judgment, reward, and punishment are central points in Islam and are the foundation upon which its entire system of ethics is based."[137] The result of Allah's judgment determines whether each person will be sent to heaven or hell. The Islamic teaching makes it very clear that these two places are poles apart. Speaking of heaven Elias notes, "The Qur'an paints an extremely vivid picture of Heaven as a garden with streams and fruit trees, where we will live a lavish and comfortable life."[138] The picture of Hell, for those who oppose Allah and his prophet Mohammed, is very different. For example, in Hell, according to Islam "infidels, or unbelievers, will experience the torments of Hell, fire fueled by humans, boiling water, pus, chains, searing winds, food that chokes, and so forth."[139] While many Muslims may only see these two descriptions are metaphors for an afterlife, the two depictions nevertheless underscore the importance of good and evil, and the consequences of each, in Islamic teaching.

Five Pillars of Practice

Having looked at the Five Pillars of Faith, we are now ready to see how these Pillars are put into practice. The acting out of these Pillars is referred to as the Five Pillars of Practice (Statement of Belief, Prayer, Fasting, Alms, and Pilgrimage). Many Muslims follow a sixth Pillar—*Jihad*—which we will include in our analysis. All Muslims are expected to learn and perform these duties and rituals as part of their practice. Referring to these Pillars, Fisher and Luyster maintain that they "outline specific patterns for worship as well as detailed prescriptions for social conduct, to bring remembrance of God into every aspect of daily life and practical ethics into the fabric of society."[140] Here are the Pillars of Practice:

1. Repetition of the creed, often called *Shahada*, literally means uttering of the following creed "There is no God but Allah, and Muhammad is the Prophet of Allah." The first part of this pronouncement expresses the primary principle of monotheism, and the second element reinforces the Muslim belief in Muhammad, thus validating the Koran. These words in Arabic are of course heard everywhere Muslims practice their faith.

2. Prayer (*Salat*), which is a central ritual, performed five times a day: on rising, at noon, in the midafternoon, after sunset, and before retiring. The prayer ritual is very structured: one must face Mecca, recite a prescribed prayer, and be prostrate, with the head to the ground. These prayers can be offered in a mosque, at home or work, or even in a public place. According to tradition "the worshipper concludes each session by uttering the 'Peace,' a phrase known as the *taslim*: 'Peace be on you the mercy and blessing of God'"[141] When observing someone in prayer, you should "avoid staring at, walking in front of, or interrupting" the person.[142]

3. Almsgiving (*Zakat*), which began as a voluntary activity and has since become codified. Muslims are required to give about 2.5 percent of their incomes to support Muslims in need and the Islamic faith. There is, like so much of religious ritual, a deeper meaning behind the act of almsgiving. Schneider and Silverman offer part of the rationale for almsgiving when they write: "Consideration for the needy is part of Islam's traditional emphasis on equality. In the mosque, all are equal; there are no preferred pews for the rich or influential—all kneel together."[143]

4. Fasting (*Sawm*), is a tradition observed during the holy month of Ramadan, which is the ninth month of the Islamic lunar calendar. Ramadan is not only a religious experience for Muslims, but during the period there is "a great emphasis upon social and family ties."[144] During this period, Muslims do not eat, drink, engage in sexual activities, or smoke between sunrise and sunset.[145] The act of fasting is believed to serve a number of purposes. First, it eliminates bodily impurities and initiates a new spiritual awakening. Second, as Nydell, notes, "The purpose of fasting is to experience hunger and deprivation and to perform an act of self-discipline, humility, and faith."[146]

5. The Pilgrimage (*Hajj*) means that once in a lifetime every Muslim, if financially able, is to make a pilgrimage to Mecca (in Saudi Arabia) as evidence of his or her devotion to Allah. During the official three days of Great *Hajj* the individual visits a number of holy sites. The trip involves a series of highly symbolic rituals designed to bring each Muslim closer to Allah. For example, the rituals begin "with the donning of the *ihram*, a white garment; this is a rite of ritual purification that symbolizes a turning away from worldly concerns."[147] The pilgrims also circle the *Kaba* (a simple brick building believed to be built by Abraham) seven times.[148]

6. *Jihad*. The Pillar of *Jihad* is, as Ilias points out, "one of the most misinterpreted concepts in Islam."[149] Gordon speaks to this misinterpretation in the following manner: "*Jihad* is a complex term that has too often been reduced in the Western media and popular imagination to but one of its meanings, namely 'holy war,' the slogan of modern radical Islamic movement."[150] As Gordon indicated, part of the misunderstanding stems of the fact that through the centuries the idea of *Jihad* has come to have two meanings. One deals with the individual (inner *Jihad*) and the other focuses on the entire Islamic tradition (outer *Jihad*). Let us begin with the inner Jihad; what Novak calls "the struggle with oneself."[151] For a more detailed summary of this first interpretation we turn to Sheler when he writes, "Islamic scholars say *Jihad*—literally 'to struggle'—pertains first and foremost to mastering one's passions and leading to a virtuous life."[152] Gordon states the same idea in a slightly different manner when he notes the *Jihad* "is working to achieve a perfect moral order in society as well as in each individual life."[153] What should be clear is that this first view of *Jihad* is concerned with "the battle all individuals wage against their own baser instincts."[154]

The second meaning of the *Jihad*, the one we are referring to as the outer *Jihad*, "covers all activities that either defend Islam or else further its cause."[155] Hence, early wars that Muslims engaged in that brought new lands or people under Islam were known as *Jihad* wars. Muslims often suggest that these wars were much like the Christian crusades. One of the most famous of these wars is discussed by Armstrong when she points out that Arabs, under the name of Islam, "waged a *Jihad* against their imperial masters the Ottoman, believing that Arabs, not Turks, should lead the Muslim peoples."[156] Even today when Arabs believe Muslim lands or the Islamic faith are in danger, "they are bound by Islamic tradition to wage a '*Jihad* of the sword.'"[157] It is easy to see how this orientation, as Gordon points out, contributes to a militant vision of the Islamic tradition.[158] Sheler even indicates that "Some Muslims argue that U.S. support for Israel constitutes a threat that justifies *Jihad*.[159] Regardless of the merits of this line of reasoning, it behooves you to understand the importance of *Jihad* to the Islamic tradition. Perhaps the most vivid example for understanding *Jihad* is found in the words of Ilias: "Political extremists who believe their cause is just often refer to their guerrilla or terrorist wars as *Jihad*."[160]

The *Qu'ran*

We have alluded to the *Qu'ran* on a number of occasions, now let us pause further to explain this important text. When Allah spoke to Muhammad the prophet wrote down, in Arabic, the divine words in the *Qu'ran* (often spelled Koran), the holy book of Islam. To a Muslim, this 114-chapter book represents the unique and exact words of Allah. It is a map, a manual on how to live. A superb capsule of the significance of the *Qu'ran* to all Muslims is put forth by Belt:

> For Muslims the Koran is also a poetic touchstone, a source of the pure Arabic language memorized by Muslim school-children and recited by Muslim adults on very important occasions—weddings, funerals, holidays. In a religion that forbids statuary and icons, this book is the physical manifestation of the faith, and small, tattered copies of it are found tucked into the pockets of every shopkeeper in the Muslim world.[161]

Unlike the Hebrew Bible and the Christian New Testament, the *Qur'an* has very little narrative; instead, it deals with themes "regarding legal and social matters and the general conduct of life."[162] Like so much of Islam, *Qur'an* does not distinguish between religious, social, and political life. Some observers have suggested that the *Qur'an* is the most memorized book in the world. Ilias notes "To this day there is great prestige in memorizing the text, and one who knows it in its entirety is called *hafiz* (literally 'guardian')."[163]

In summary, for Muslims, Allah has spoken completely in the *Qur'an* and he will not speak again. Hence, the book, says Wilson, is "seen as a perfect revelation from God, a faithful reproduction of an original engraved on a tablet in heaven which has existed from all eternity."[164]

A Complete Way of Life

It must be remembered Muhammad, who was Allah's messenger, was both a political and religious prophet. In Islam, religion and social membership are therefore inseparable. In this sense it touches all aspects of the Arab's life. Nydell develops this idea when he notes: "An Arab's religion affects his whole way of life on a daily basis. Religion is taught in school, the language is full of religious expressions, and people practice their religion openly, almost obtrusively, expressing it in numerous ways.[165] Novak said it quite clearly when he wrote, "Contained within its teaching of the path to God is guidance for the entire range of human life—social, political, and economic."[166] Viewed from this perspective, Islam is a codification of all values and ways to behave in every circumstance, from child rearing, to eating, to preparing for bed, to the treatment of homosexuals, to views toward modesty.[167] As Smith noted, Islam is a religion that guides human thought and practice in unparalleled detail.[168]

Like so many world views that are a complete way of life, Islam is taught from infancy. You will recall that we mentioned the fact, the first sentence chanted in the ear of a Muslim infant is "*La ilaha illa 'llah*" (There is no god but God). Lutfiyya summarizes Islam as a philosophy that stresses "(1) a feeling of dependency on God; (2) the fear of God's punishment on earth as well as the hereafter; and (3) a deep-seated respect for tradition and for the past."[169] This religious orientation provides its members with specific guidelines that need to be followed. Says Esler, the Islamic tradition has resulted in "an immense body of requirements and prohibitions concerning religion, personal morality, social conduct, and political behavior. Business and marital relations, criminal law, ritual practices, and much more were covered in this vast system."[170] What Islam did from its beginnings until today is bind "all its millions to a religion, a civilization, and pattern of history."[171]

Gender

The topic of gender differences is a difficult one for a number of reasons. First, as Westerners we are examining this subject as "outsiders." Second, attitudes regarding gender are constantly in a state of flux. And third, broad generalizations regarding gender often overlook regional differences. Even granting these limitations, we agree with Gordon when he notes, "The role of women in Islamic society is a hotly debated topic both within and outside the Islamic world."[172] Contributing to the debate is the fact that the *Qur'an* and other religious teachings offer a variety of interpretations on the subject of women. For example, Islamic scholars point to the *Qur'an* to demonstrate that women must give their consent in marriage, are included in inheritance, and even "teach that men and women have equal religious rights and responsibilities."[173] Yet the *Qur'an* also contains several verses that make it apparent that "men are clearly depicted as superior to women."[174]

The manner in which women dress is also a cultural statement about the role of gender in the Arab culture. For example, the Koran instructs women to "cover their adornments" and to "draw their veils over their bosoms."[175] This attitude is expressed today with the following proverb: "A woman is like a jewel: You don't expose it to thieves."

It must be remembered that when evaluating gender differences, it is important to keep the host culture in mind and not let ethnocentrism color your evaluation. Ilias makes the same point when he writes: "Despite the egalitarian social structure that dominates the majority of Islamic societies, women from all backgrounds usually embrace rather then reject their religious tradition."[176]

Art and Architecture

The tandem relationship that Islam has to all phases of life has helped create a remarkable and brilliant civilization that is "as distinctive in its way as those of China or the Greco-Roman Mediterranean."[177] Part of that civilization is seen in the art and architecture associated with Islam. Many Arab countries are, as Crim notes, "rich in painting, sculpture, and the decorative arts."[178] What is interesting about the artistic magnificence of Arab art is that it reflects Islamic religion. The Koran "teaches that an object and its image are united.[179] This would, in part, help explain why so little Arab art is representational. You will notice that in most Arab art forms the emphasis is on shapes, form, design, style, and image—not people, landscapes, and other representations of reality.

Hinduism

With over a billion followers, Hinduism is perhaps the most difficult of all religious orientations for the Westerner to understand. As Esler notes, "The Hindu religion is extremely ancient, very complicated, and more than a little exotic to Western eyes."[180] Some of the reasons for the differences between Western views and Hinduism are mentioned by Narayanan: "Hinduism is somewhat difficult to define. The religion has no single founder, creed, teacher, or prophet acknowledge by all Hindus as central to the religion, and no single holy book is universally acclaimed as being of primary importance."[181] Boorstin buttresses this view when he writes:

> Western religions begin with a notion that One—One God, One Book, One Son, One Church, One Nation under God—is better than many. The Hindu, dazzled by the wondrous variety of the creation, could not see it that way. For so multiplex a world, the more gods the better! How could any one god account for so varied a creation?[182]

Background

Most historical theories trace the origins of this religion to a time almost four thousand years ago when light-skinned Aryan Indo-European tribes invaded what is now northern India. These conquerors brought their religion with them and combined it with the beliefs of the indigenous people of the Indus Valley.[183] These early stages of Hindu history were "marked not by remarkable personalities (although there must have been many) and great proselytizing movements, but rather by the composition of orally transmitted sacred tests expressing central concepts of what we now call Hinduism."[184]

In many respects, Hinduism is a conglomeration of religious thought, values, and beliefs. As we indicated, not only is there not a single founder, it also does not have an organizational hierarchy, such as that of the Catholic Church. Among the Hindus, one may find magic, nature worship, animal veneration, and an unlimited number of deities. This view of a vast number of deities makes Hindus among the most religious people in the world because they find the divine in everything. As Boorstin notes, "The Hindu is dazzled by a vision of the holy, not merely holy people but places like the Himalayan peaks where the gods live, or the Ganges which flows from Heaven to Earth, or countless inconspicuous sites where gods or goddesses or unsung heroes showed their divine mettle."[185] Rituals are important for showing that God is in everything, and ritual significance can be found in everyday activities such as the lighting of incense, bathing, eating, and marriage ceremonies.

Sacred Texts

Earlier we mentioned that in Hinduism there was not a single text such as the Bible or the *Qur'an*. This does not mean, however, that Hinduism is without some holy books. The oldest, and in some ways most important of these books are the Vedas. The Vedas "transmit the ancient revelations in a series of hymns, ritual texts, and speculations composed over a period of a millennium beginning *ca* 1400 B.C."[186] The most influential of these books is *Upanishads*. Written in Sanskrit, this sacred scripture contains most of the religious and philosophical portion of the Vedas. As Usha notes, "The *Upanishads* teach the knowledge of God and record the spiritual experiences of the sages of ancient India."[187] Prabhavananda and Manchester make the same point with the following description: "The literal meaning of *Upanishad*, 'sitting near devotedly,' brings picturesquely to mind an earnest disciple learning from his teacher."[188] There are more than a hundred *Upanishads*; however, it is the Bhagavad Gita that is the most influential. This eighteen-chapter book "teaches how to achieve union with the supreme Reality through the paths of knowledge, devotion, selfless work, and meditation."[189] One of the most important things the text teaches strikes at the very core of Hinduism. It is that God is an exalted, inspiring, and sublime force within us. Because God is within us, say the Hindus, we can rise above our mortal limitations.

A Complete Way of Life

As is the case with so many religions, Hinduism pervades every part of existence. Radhakrishnan, the former president of India, observed, "Hinduism is more a culture than a creed."[190] This creed "forms the basis of a social system, and thereby governs the types of modalities of interaction even in contemporary society."[191] In this sense, as Venkateswaran points out, "Hinduism is not merely a religion. It encompasses an entire civilization and a way of life, whose roots date back prior to 3000 B.C.E."[192] As Narayana notes, "The boundaries between the sacred and non-sacred spheres do not apply to the Hindu traditions."[193]

Important Teachings

As is the case with all religions, the messages and lessons advanced by the sacred texts, teachers, and prophets are numerous. And, most are beyond the scope of this section this book. However, Hinduism does contain some important teachings that you will find useful when interacting with someone who is a Hindu.

Another Reality. Hinduism is based on the fundamental assumption that the material world, the one we can touch and see, is not the only reality. Instead, they hold that there are other realities that reveal the true nature of life, the mind, and the spirit. According to Hinduism, "What we see as reality is the merest illusion, a game, a dream, or a dance."[194] Hindus are not satisfied with what they see or hear, as reflected in the Hindu saying, "Him the eye does not see, nor the tongue express, nor the mind grasp."

This notion of other realities stems from the Hindu idea of deliverance from the misleading appearances and experiences of the physical world. Hindus believe that finding satisfaction in the material and physical world might gratify us for many lifetimes, but eventually the satisfaction will "wear out." To experience Nirvana, or liberation, one needs to discover the spiritual existence found outside traditional concepts of reality. For Hindus, "Nirvana releases man from the cycle of birth, suffering, death, and all other forms of worldly bondage."[195] Nirvana is, therefore, "a state of spiritual enlightenment."[196] And that "enlightenment" is another reality.

Brahman. In many ways the core of this religion is contained in the following assertion: "Hinduism regards the multiplicity of gods and goddesses in its pantheon as manifestations of the one divine spirit, Brahman."[197] Brahman is the "all-pervading transcendental Reality."[198] Jain and Kussman offer a summary of this importantconcept:

> Brahman is the ultimate level of reality, a philosophical absolute, serenely blissful, beyond all ethical or metaphysical limitations. The basic Hindu view of God involves infinite being, infinite consciousness and infinite bliss.[199]

Discovery of Self. Hindu philosophy, says Hammer, begins with the premise that "the ultimate cause of suffering is people's ignorance of their true nature, the Self, which is omniscient, omnipotent, omnipresent, perfect, and eternal."[200] To help one discover "the Self," Hinduism offers its followers some specific recommendations. Non-Hindus can gain insight into this world view by looking at these historical guidelines.

First, intellect is subordinate to intuition. Truth does not come to the individual; it already resides within each of us. The same point is made in the Bhagavad Gita: "Meditation excels knowledge." Second, dogma is subordinate to experience. One cannot be told about God; one must experience God. Third, outward expression is secondary to inward realization. Communication with God cannot take place through outward expression; it must occur through internal realization of the nature of God. Fourth, the world is an illusion because nothing is permanent. All of nature, including humankind, is in an unending cycle of birth, death, and rebirth or reincarnation. Fifth, it is possible for the human to break the cycle of birth, death, and reincarnation and experience an internal state of bliss called *Nirvana*. One achieves Nirvana by leading a good life and thus achieving higher spiritual status in the next life. Holding materialism in abeyance and practicing introspection and meditation can advance this spiritual status. The path toward Nirvana is also influenced by one's karma, an ethical standard that asserts, "Every act we make and every desire we have, shapes our future experiences" and influences the path toward Nirvana."[201] As Jain and Kussman point out: "The present condition of each individual life is a product of what one did in the previous life, and one's present acts, thoughts, and decisions determine one's future states."[202]

Multiple Paths. Perhaps one of Hinduism's furthermost teachings and appeals through the centuries has been its ability to offer various paths and to adapt to diverse needs. As Smith notes, "Hinduism abounds in directives to persons who would put their shoulders to the collective wheel. It details duties appropriate to age, temperament, and social status."[203] Recognizing four different types of people, Hinduism offers four distinct spiritual paths: (1) *jnana yoga*, the path of knowledge; (2) *bhkti yoga*, the path of devotion; (3) *karma*, the path of work; and (4) *raja yoga*, the path of meditation.[204]

Buddhism

A fifth major religious tradition that can influence intercultural communication is Buddhism. For a variety of reasons many Westerners find it difficult to understand Buddhism because it is very different from Christianity. Thera, quoting the philosopher T. H. Huxley, mentions some of these differences when he writes:

> Buddhism is a system which knows no God in the Western sense, which denies a soul to man, which counts the belief in immortality a blunder, which refuses any efficacy to prayer and sacrifice, which bids men look to nothing but their own efforts for salvation.[205]

The Buddhist view of language represents yet another explanation as to why non-Buddhists have trouble understanding this religious tradition. Part of the dilemma stems from the fact that Buddhism requires abandonment of views generated by the use of ordinary words and scriptures. As Brabant-Smith notes, "Ordinary language tends to deal with physical things and experiences, as understood by ordinary man; whereas Dharma language (Buddha's teaching) deals with the mental world, with the intangible non-physical world."[206] This notion finds expression in two famous Buddhist statements: "Beware of the false illusions created by words," and "Do not accept what you hear by report."[207] These sayings reflect Buddhists' belief that there is a supreme and wonderful truth that words cannot reach or teach—that is transmitted outside of ritual and language. A Buddhist teacher expressed it this way: "A special transmission outside the scriptures; No dependence upon words or letters; Direct pointing at the mind of man; Seeing into one's nature and the attainment of Buddhahood."[208]

History
Buddhism was founded by an Indian prince named Siddhartha Gautama in about 563 B.C. The story of how this man became known as The Enlightened One has two essential parts that are both crucial to the study of Buddhism. First, when Gautama was twenty-nine, he awoke to the recognition that man's fate was to suffer—to grow old and sick, and then die. As Van Doren notes, "Overwhelmed with the sadness, he began to seek some means of allaying the pain of life."[209] Through meditation he found the solution and became known as the Buddha (The Enlightened One). Second, "After this momentous event the Buddha spent the next forty-five years of his life wandering up and down the Ganges Valley preaching the message to ascetic and lay persons alike."[210] In around 230 B.C. Buddhist missionaries were sent into Sri Lanka (previously called Ceylon).[211] In the fourth century Buddhism arrived in Korea, and by the fifth and sixth centuries Buddhism begins to take hold in much of Asia.[212]

Basic Assumptions
At the core of this world view is the idea that Buddha taught that each individual has the potential to seek the "truth" on their own. As Rahula notes, "He taught, encouraged and stimulated each person to develop himself and to work out emancipation, for he has the power to liberate himself from all bondage through his own personal effort and intelligence."[213] Buddha would tell his disciples to "be a refuge to themselves."[214] Fisher and Luyster express the same idea in the following manner: "In its traditional form, it holds that our salvation from suffering lies only in our own efforts. The Buddha taught us that only in understanding how we create suffering for ourselves can we become free."[215] As we have indicated, it is often difficult for Westerners to understand this orientation. While many Western religions stress community and direction from the clergy, Buddhism, to the contrary, challenges each individual to do their own religious seeking. A famous Buddhist saying states, "Be lamps unto yourselves."

The Four Noble Truths
Much of the Buddha's message can be found in the Four Noble Truths. The Four Noble Truths were "formulated by the Buddha as a means of instructing his students into the insights the Buddha gained through meditation."[216] Scholars maintain that from these Truths "we get a fairly good and accurate account of the essential teaching of the Buddha."[217] Simply put, they were the Buddha's answers to the most important ques-

tions about life. As Smith notes, "Together they stand as the axioms of his system, the postulates from which the rest of his teachings logically derive."[218]

The First Noble Truth is that life is *dukka,* usually translated as "suffering." As the Buddha said in his early writings: "Birth is suffering, aging is suffering, illness is suffering, worry, misery, pain, distress and despair are suffering; not attaining what one desires is suffering."[219] The notion of suffering is not as narrow as the word would suggest. For example, "It includes not only acute or manifest states of mental or physical suffering, but also any degree of unpleasantness, discomfort, dissatisfaction, anxiety or unease." [220] The teachers of Buddhism would point out that if your life is not characterized by some degree of suffering, you only need look around the world to see the suffering of others. Contrary to Western interpretation, the Buddha's philosophy is not pessimistic. As Rahula notes, "First of all Buddhism is neither pessimistic nor optimistic. If anything at all, it is realistic, for it takes a realistic view of life and the world.[221] He was, in fact, concerned with the cessation of suffering, so he strove to help others by teaching them to identify the causes of their suffering.

The Second Noble Truth concerns the origin of suffering. The Buddha taught that much of the suffering is caused by self-desire, envy, creed, and craving. Suffering could also come from seeking great wealth and status to "being ignorant to the nature of reality."[222] All these causes of suffering can also keep "the person orientated toward transitory existence rather than Nirvana."[223] The Buddhist view of Nirvana is somewhat different than the orientation we explained during our discussion of Hinduism. For the Buddhist, Nirvana is "described in part as a perfectly peaceful and enlightened state of transformed consciousness in which passions and ignorance are extinguished."[224] In plain language, "Nirvana was simply, directly, and absolutely the end of problems of ordinary human existence."[225]

The Third Noble Truth states that the cessation of suffering is possible. Smith summarized this Third Truth in the following manner:

> The Third Noble Truth follows logically from the Second. If the cause of life's dislocation is selfish craving, its cure lies in the overcoming of *tanha* [desire], such craving. If we could be released from the narrow limits of self-interest into the vast expanse of universal life, we would be relieved of our torment.[226]

The Fourth Noble Truth is often called "the remedy"[227] in that it indicates the way to remove suffering and experience Nirvana. As Eckel states, "The Buddha believed that Nirvana could be attainted through the Noble Eightfold Path."[228] The importance of the these eight concepts is highlighted by Rhula: "Practically the whole of teaching of the Buddha, to which he devoted himself during 45 years, deals in some way or other with this Path."[229] Because of their importance we turn to a brief discussion of the tenets of the Eightfold Path.

The Eightfold Path

We should point out that Buddha made it clear that these eight parts of the path should be learned and practiced simultaneously. As Sole'-Leris notes, "It must be clearly understood that, although the eight factors of the path are enumerated one after the other for purposes of explanation, the idea is not that they should be cultivated successively."[230]

1. *Right view* is achieving a correct understanding and accepting the reality and origins of suffering and the ways leading to the cessation of suffering. Often referred to as

"right knowledge," this first principle obviously implies an awareness of the Four Noble Truths.

2. *Right thought* is being free from ill will, cruelty, and untruthfulness toward the self and others. Buddha believed that we needed to be truthful even about our imperfections.

3. *Right speech* is abstaining from lying, malicious gossip, and harsh and insulting language. Buddha stressed that we should "use communication in the service of truth and harmony."[231]

4. *Right behavior,* some have said, is Buddha's version of the Ten Commandments, for his fourth principle "aims at promoting moral, honourable and peaceful conduct."[232] Among other things this path called for abstaining from the taking of life, from stealing, from sexual misconduct, from lying, and from drinking intoxicants.

5. *Right livelihood,* in the language of today, means not earning ones living by harming any living thing, being free from luxury at the expense of others, and not engaging in any immoral or illegal business practices.

6. *Right efforts* is "summarized in four terms: *avoiding* and *overcoming* unwholesome states of mind while *developing* and *maintaining* wholesome states of mind."[233] Buddha believed this right effort also called for "cultivating mindfulness and concentration."[234]

7. *Right mindfulness* is, as Sole'-Leris notes, "the mindful, unbiased observation of all phenomena in order to perceive them and experience them as they are in actual fact, without emotional or intellectual distortions."[235] This principal calls attention to the crucial Buddhist idea that liberation is said to be through a mind that is aware of the moment.

8. *Right concentrations* is complete concentration on a single object and the achievement of purity of thought, free from all hindrances and distractions. When the mind is still, according to the Buddha, "the true nature of everything is reflected."[236]

Important Teachings

To summarize the Buddhist tradition, we remind you of the following five points. First, *the Buddha believed that to find enlightenment within oneself,* a Buddhist must lead a life that focuses on some of the following behaviors. Through mindfulness, a Buddhist seeks to anchor the mind securely in the present. In achieving right mindfulness through *concentration* and *meditation,* the mind is trained to remain in the present: open, quiet, and alert while contemplating the present event. Says Thich-Thien-An, "If we keep our minds under control, if we can realize the meaning of what we are doing, if we can be what we do, this is meditation."[237]

Second, Buddhism stresses the *impermanent nature of all things*. He taught that everything, both good and bad, were always changing—always in a state of flux. Buddha hoped that this recognition that nothing was permanent would encourage his followers to appreciate the moment and to accept the tentative nature of life. This idea regarding the unpredictable character of life is eloquently stated by the second-century Buddhist philosopher Narajuna: "Life is so fragile, more so than a bubble blown to and fro by the wind. How truly astonishing are those who think that after breathing out, they will surely breathe in again, or that they will awaken after a night's sleep."

Third, *karma* is important because it sets the tone for ethical standards. Karma is concerned with action–reaction and with cause and effect: Good deeds bring good results; corrupt deeds bring corrupt results. As is the case with so much of Buddhism, each individual—not a supernatural power—decides his or her karma. The Buddha stated:

> All beings are the owners of their deeds (Karma), the heirs of their deeds; their deeds are the womb from which they sprang. . . . Whatever deeds they do—good or evil—of such they will be the heirs.[238]

Fourth, as we alluded to earlier, Buddhism is *directed at the individual*. That is to say, each person has the ability to find both truth and peace in this lifetime. A celebrated Buddhist maxim notes: "Betake yourself to no external refuge. Work out your own salvation with diligence." Bodhi develops the same idea in the following manner:

> The Buddha rests his teaching upon the thesis that with the right method man can change and transform himself. He is not doomed to be forever burdened by the weight of his accumulated tendencies, but through his own effort he can cast off all these tendencies and attain a condition of complete purity and freedom.[239]

Finally, in Buddhism we see a world view more concerned *with humanism and the art of living daily life* than supernatural authority or even metaphysical speculation. As Smith noted:

> Buddha preached a religion that skirted speculation. He could have been one of the world's great meta-physicians, but "the thicket of theorizing" was not for him. Whether the world is eternal or not eternal, whether it is finite or infinite, whether the Buddha exists after death or not—on such questions the Buddha maintains a noble silence.[240]

Confucianism

Background

As is the case with all religious traditions, Confucianism, for thousands of years, has had a major role in shaping the culture and history of the people who followed this religion.[241] Even today "many analysts who have studied the East Asian economic miracle over the past three decades have concluded that Confucian values like emphasis on the future, work, achievement, education, merit, and frugality have played a crucial role in their development."[242]

We begin by noting Confucianism is more than a religion. As Crim points out, it is "the system of social, political, ethical, and religious thought based on the teachings of Confucius and his successors."[243] Although Confucianism has had a profound impact on the cultures of Korea, Vietnam, and Japan, its greatest impact for thousands of years has been on the people of China. As Barry, Chen, and Watson note, "If we were to describe in one word the Chinese way of life for the last two thousand years, the word would be 'Confucian.'"[244] The roots of Confucianism are "planted" so very deep in China that even during the antireligious period of Communism the leaders borrowed the Confucian notions of selflessness, allegiance, and deference to help accomplish their purpose of controlling the masses.[245] In some ways this control was made easy by the fact that "Confucianism has no priests, no temples, no religious rituals."[246] It is "a rational, ethical system with strict norms, stressing loyalty to the ruler, obedience toward one's father, and proper behavior."[247]

Basic Assumptions

At the heart of Confucianism you do not find a deep conviction in a God, but rather a commitment and the belief in social harmony. As Yum notes, "Confucianism is a philosophy of human nature that considers proper human relationships as the basis of society."[248] These "proper" relationships involved such things as the protection of "face," dignity, self-respect, reputation, honor, and prestige.

Confucius the Man

As was the case with Buddhism, Confucianism centers around the teachings of a particular man—Confucius. And like Buddha, Confucius was not a ruler, nor did he consider himself a god. In fact, he was not interested in the philosophical and ethereal dimensions of religion. Confucius was born in 551 B.C. in the small feudal state of Lu, which is now Shantung Province in China. Confucius dabbled at various careers early in his life; however, at the age of thirty he turned to teaching. According to McGreal, "People were impressed by his integrity, honesty, and particularly his pleasant personality and his enthusiasm as a teacher. Three thousand people came to study under him and over seventy became well-established scholars."[249] What Confucius taught grew out of his observations about "the human condition" in China during his lifetime. As Crim notes, "Confucius was witness to the political disintegration of the feudal order, an era characterized by the hegemony of various states and almost constant internecine warfare."[250] In response to these observations, "Confucius asserted that government must be founded on virtue, and that all citizens must be attentive to the duties of their position."[251]

The Analects

Confucius did not write down his philosophy. Therefore, the details of his teaching have come to us through his disciples. The most influential and far reaching of these collections is the Analects. This book was not written in a systematic and structured fashion. Instead, what it contains are the aphorisms, sayings, proverbs, and the like that the disciples believed to be the most salient ideas of Confucian philosophy.[252]

Important Teachings

As we have already indicated, Confucianism teaches that the proper and suitable foundation for society is based on respect for human dignity. That respect stressed the proper hierarchy in social relationships between family members, community, and superiors. Confucius set forth five ideals that structured much of his thought about these relationships. (1) *Jen* (humanism) is related to the concept of reciprocity. It is, for Confucius, "the ideal relationship which should pertain between individuals."[253] (2) *Chun tzu* (perfect person) means the kind of person in whom cultivated feeling has maximum development.[254] The trait is often referred to as the "superior man" in that it "is someone fully adequate and poised to accommodate others as much as possible rather than to acquire all that he or she can acquire selfishly."[255] (3) *Li* (rituals, rites, proprieties, conventions) is the outward expression of good manners—the way things should be done. (4) *Te* literally means power. Confucius was concerned with how power was used. He strongly believed that "leaders must be persons of character, sincerely devoted to the common good and possessed of the character that compels respect.[256] (5) *Wen* refers to the arts. Confucius had great reverence for the arts. As Gannon points out, Confucius saw the "arts as a means of peace and as an instrument of moral education."[257] We can further observe that veneration in the following paragraph:

> By poetry the mind is aroused; from music the finish is received. The odes quicken the mind. They induce self-contemplation. They teach the art of sensibility. They help to retrain resentment. They bring home the duty of serving one's parents and one's prince.[258]

Confucianism and Interpersonal Relationships

As is the case with all the world views we have examined, Confucianism influences perception and communication in a variety of ways. First, Confucianism teaches, both directly and indirectly, the notion of *empathy*. For Confucius, *Jen* is "the capacity to measure the feelings of others by one's own."[259] This view toward others would make listening an important element of communication. Second, when communicating, those that follow Confucian philosophy would be concerned with *status relationships*. We can see this in everything from differentiated linguistic codes (words showing respect and rank)[260] to "paternalistic leadership" in business and educational settings.[261] Third, we could also expect great concern for *ritual and protocol* when following Confucian principles. As we noted early, social etiquette was an important part of Confucian teaching. Novak reminds us that "In Confucius's view, attentive performance of social ritual and everyday etiquette shapes human character in accordance with archetypal patterns."[262] Fourth, in Confucian philosophy *interaction within the family* is the model for most social relationships. These relationships have well-defined hierarchical order concerning father and son, husband and wife, and old and young members of the family.[263] Finally, Confucian philosophy would tend to encourage *the use of indirect instead of direct language*. As you learned elsewhere, Americans often ask very direct questions, are blunt, often use the word "no," and like it when people "get to the point" rather quickly. However, Confucian philosophy encourages indirect communication. For example, "In Chinese culture, requests often are implied rather than stated explicitly for the sake of relational harmony and face maintenance."[264] Yum makes much the same point while demonstrating the link between Confucianism and "talk" in the following paragraph:

> The Confucian legacy of consideration for others and concern for proper human relationships has led to the development of communication patterns that preserve one another's face. Indirect communication helps to prevent the embarrassment of rejection by the other person or disagreement among partners.[265]

One of the things we have stressed in this chapter is that we agree with Friedman when he notes "that God speaks multiple languages."[266] Yet because of space constraints we are only able to look at some of the "languages." That is to say, there are numerous world views and religions we have omitted from our analysis. For example, in the West there are millions of people who are Mormons, Jehovah's Witnesses, and Unitarians. There are also people who follow New Age philosophies as a world view or practice Wicca (witchcraft). Turning to Asia and East Asia we did not included Taoism, Daoism, and Shintoism. And in places such as parts of Africa, Australia, the Pacific Islands, and the Indian cultures of North and South America, we omitted primal religions. Should you find the time and opportunity to learn about these religions and world views, you will discover more about the crucial link between world view and communication. You will once again learn one of the central messages of this section—simply that religion, for thousands of years, has had a pronounced impact on the life of every culture. And today, perhaps more than ever before, that impact can't be ignored. The question is clear—can the world's great religions learn to live together? Friedman poses the same question in the following paragraph:

> Can Islam, Christianity and Judaism know that God speaks Arabic on Fridays, Hebrew on Saturday and Latin on Sundays, and that he welcomes different human beings approaching him through their own history, out of their own history, out of their language and cultural heritage?[267]

Religion helps its members cope with both life and death.

© Gloria Thomas

FAMILY

The Chinese say that if you know the family, you do not need to know the individual. There is a Jewish adage that states, "God could not be everywhere and therefore he made mothers." In Africa children learn the proverb "What belongs to me is destroyable by water or fire; what belongs to us is not destroyable by neither water nor fire." And in the United States children are told, "The apple does not fall far from the tree." Although these ideas might differ slightly, they all call attention to the importance of family to every human being's life. The family is among the oldest and most fundamental of all human institutions. It is also a universal experience—found in every culture.[268] Kim endorses these same notions when she notes, "The family is the basic unit of society and it is at the heart of its survival."[269] Although you can constantly see governments change and disappear in places like Africa, Iran, China, and the old Soviet Union "families survive."[270] Because they have survived for thousands the family unit "is a very effective means of providing social regulation and continuity."[271] Nye and Berardo, even suggest that "without the family human society as we know it could not exist."[272]

The Importance of Family

The American author William Thayer offers an excellent introduction to the importance of family when he notes, "As are families, so is society." It is clear what he is saying is that the individual and the culture both need the institution of family. As Galvin and Brommel note, "We are born into a family, mature in a family, form new families, and leave them at our death."[273] Perhaps the importance and power of this union is most manifest in the idea that the family is charged with transforming a biological organism into a human being who must spend the rest of his or her life around other human beings. It is the family that greets you once you leave the comfort of the womb. Swerdlow, Bridenthal, Kelly, and Vine eloquently state this idea:

> Here is where one has the first experience of love, and of hate, of giving, and of denying; and of deep sadness. . . . Here the first hopes are raised and met—or disappointed. Here is where one learns whom to trust and whom to fear. Above all, family is where people get their start in life.[274]

The Functions of the Family

Families, of course, do much more than simply nurture the child. Schneider and Silverman offer you a list of some specific function and duties that face every family:

> Families regulate sexual activities, supervising their members to be sure they conform to sexual norms. Families are in charge of reproduction to keep the society going, and they socialize the children they produce. Also families provide physical care and protection for the members. They also provide emotional support and caring.[275]

We would like to add two additional functions to the list provided by Schneider and Silverman that are relevant to our analysis. First, families are one of the major "carriers" of culture. And, second, they are also instrumental in "teaching" about identity. Let us briefly look at each of these functions.

Transmitting the Culture

Although a culture's core values and world view come from a variety of sources (predominant religious views, cultural history, peers, etc.), the family is the primary caretaker of these views and values and transmits them to new members of the culture. As Gudykunst notes, "Originally, children learn about their cultures from their parents. Parents begin to teach their children the norms and communication rules that guide behavior in their cultures."[276] Not only are norms and communication rules diffused by the family to the child, but they also "give them their initial exposure to questions of faith.[277] In short, we agree with Al-Kaysi when he writes, "The family provides the environment within which human values and morals develop and grow in the new generation; these values and morals cannot exist apart from the family unit."[278]

Transmitting Identity

Families, working in tandem with other institutions, are important because they supply you with a large portion of your identity. Burguiere makes this point in the following way: "Before we become ourselves, we are a son or daughter of X or of Y; we are born into a family, and are identified by a family name before becoming a separate social being."[279] In this sense "family is not only the basic unit of society but also affords the individual the most important social identity."[280] The family does this by giving children knowledge about their historical background, information regarding the permanent nature of their culture, and specific behaviors, customs, traditions, and language associated with their ethnic or cultural group.[281] In short, the family tells you who you are and what groups you are part of.

Types of Families

While all cultures have the family as a major institution, the form and type of the family is, as Haviland notes, "related to particular social, historical, and ecological circumstances."[282] Even with some cultural variation, all people encounter two families during the course of their life: the family they are born into (the family of orientation) and the family that is formed when, and if, they take a spouse (the family of procreation). Kinship bonds link these two families into more complex family systems. In recent years, definitions of family have begun to include a number of different configurations. Berko, Rosenfeld, and Samovar mention three of these:

> Live-in couples, heterosexual or homosexual, with or without child, who are unmarried but have a binding relationship; single-parent family, in which the parent—married, never married, widowed, or divorced—lives with her or his biological or adopted child; and blended family, consisting of two adults and their children, all, some, or none of whom may be the offspring from their union.[283]

For our purposes, we are most concerned with your family of origin—the family in which you grew up. For, regardless of the culture, it is primarily this family that teaches your culture and also "provides you with the foundation of your self-concept and communication competencies."[284]

Communication, Culture, and Family

To this point we have treated the notion of family is somewhat general terms. However, we are now ready to discuss some specific cultural variations regarding the family. As Anderson notes, "The different cultures of our world have bequeathed to us a variety of forms of the family and specific roles that the family plays in society."[285] This subtle and yet powerful link between your culture and how you develop communication patterns and social roles is clearly highlighted by the anthropologist Margaret Mead:

> At birth, babies can grow up to be members of any society. . . . It depends on how they are trained and taught, loved and punished, whether they turn into one kind of person or another. So, if we make a study of this and find out the steps by which these human babies become one kind of grown-up person instead of another, we learn a great deal about them . . . the details of a bath, or the way the baby is fed, the way it's punished or rewarded give us a great many clues about the way character is formed in that society.[286]

What Mead is saying is one of the basic themes of this section. A human being's development can take any number of paths, and culture is one of the major determinants of that path. A child in India who lives with many people in one house learns about extended family. A Mexican child who is raised in a home with many elderly people learns about the treatment of the elderly. A child in Egypt who observes his parents praying five times a day is learning about God. These seemingly insignificant experiences, when combined with thousands of other messages from the family, shape and mold the way children communication and interact with members of their own culture and with strangers. McGoldrick makes much the same point when she writes:

> Families do not develop their rules, beliefs, and rituals in a vacuum. What you think, how you act, even your language, are all transmitted through the family from the wider cultural context. This context includes the culture in which you live, and those from which your ancestors have come.[287]

The family is where children are first introduced to culture.

© Elizabeth Crews/Stock Boston

What McGoldrick is saying is that families, like cultures, vary in everything from "their definition of family" to "their definition of the timing of life cycle phases and the tasks appropriate at each phase."[288] Let us look at some other family differences so that we can appreciate their specific impact on intercultural communication.

We begin this section on the role of family in much the same way we started our analysis of world view—with two disclaimers. First, we remind you that all the major institutions of a culture are tied together. So while we might be treating the concept of family as a single social organization, you should be aware that they work in tandem with other aspects of a culture. As Houseknecht and Pankhurst note, "Family and religion must be viewed in terms of their interactions with other institutions."[289]

Second, because of space considerations, we do not present an in-depth exploration of the family. We simply want to make you more conscious of the cause-and-effect relationship existing between growing up in one's family and the manner in which one perceives and interacts with other people. The basic assumption of this section is simple: The interaction patterns in the family offer clues as to communication patterns found outside the family, or as the Swedish proverb tells us, "Children act in the village as they have learned at home."

Gender Roles

One of the most important of all family patterns, and one that is found in all cultures, is the teaching of appropriate gender roles. Early in life, children learn to differentiate between masculine activities and feminine activities. In fact, studies reveal, "at 24 months children were aware that labels, such as boy, girl, mommy and daddy, applied to certain classes of people."[290] These perceptions are learned and in-

fluence how members of a culture interact with both sexes. Knowing cultural interaction patterns regarding gender roles often offer clues as to how communication is
conducted and should be carried out. For example, with regard to the gender roles in
a health care setting, Purnell and Paulanka note, "An awareness of family dominance patterns is important for determining with whom to speak when health-care
decisions have to be made."[291]

What is intriguing about gender roles is that like all-important aspects of a culture,
specific perceptions can be traced to the deep structure issues we talked about earlier
in the chapter. For example, in cultures such as the Japanese, Vietnamese, Chinese,
and Korean, the history of these roles can be traced to the influence of Confucianism.
Kim says of Korea: "Confucianism made men alone the structurally relevant members
of the society and relegated women to social dependence."[292] In early Confucian families, boys studied the classics and played, while "girls were confined to the inner quar-
ters of the house where they received instruction in womanly behavior and tasks, such
as domestic duties, embroidery and cooking."[293] Jankowiak maintains that at the core
of these gender attitudes, at least for the Chinese, is the belief that both biological and
cultural forces contribute to these differences.[294]

Even today, in Asian families, according to Davis and Proctor, "Males are primarily
responsible for task functions, while females attend to social and cultural tasks."[295]
Children see the father get served first at meals, get the first bath, and receive nods and
deep bows from the rest of the family. What is interesting about gender roles in most
Asian cultures, Hendry says, is that although the family system perceives men as being
superior to women, "the duty of care within the family falls almost automatically to
women, whether it be in times of sickness, injury or senility."[296] This is exemplified in
the Chinese saying, "Strict father, kind mother."

The Mexican culture also places the father in the dominant role and the mother
in the domestic role. As was the case with Confucian philosophy in the shaping of
Asian gender roles, the conception of female roles within Christianity derives, in
part, from the masculine representation of God as "the Father."[297] You see this view
toward gender roles being acted out when Mexican children learn very early in life
that "within the family unit the father is the undisputed authority figure. The father
makes all of the major decisions, and he sets the disciplinary standards. His word is
final and the rest of the family looks to him for guidance and strength."[298] So strong
is the pull of masculinity in the Mexican culture that "when the father is not
present, the oldest son assumes considerable authority."[299] Not being the "leader" in
one's home even carries negative consequences. Think for a moment what is being
implied by the Spanish proverb that states, "Woe to the house where the hen crows
and the rooster is still."

The female role within the Mexican and Spanish family is an important one that is
clearly defined by tradition and religion. As Schneider and Silverman write, "Women,
as mothers, belong to the City of God, set apart in the protected and protecting home.
Motherhood is a sacred value in Mexico."[300] You can observe the same view of women
in Spain. There, "the Spanish husband accords his wife due respect as stronghold of the
family; he thinks of her as if she were a Saint."[301] Female children observe this value
and early in life begin "to play the role of mother and homemaker."[302] Both children
observe yet other female roles within the home. They see a mother who is willing to
sacrifice, is strong, and has great perseverance. As Dana notes, these "behaviors ensure
survival and power through the children."[303]

In India, males are also considered the superior sex. Male children are believed to be entrusted to parents by the gods. Gannon offers the following summary of this view of gender in India:

> The preference for a son when a child is born is as old as Indian society. A son guarantees the continuation of the generations, and he will perform the last rites after his parent's death. This ensures a peaceful departure of the soul to its next existence in the ongoing cycle of life. The word *putra*, or son, literally means 'he who protects from going to hell.' [304]

The Indian perception of gender is reflected in the fact that "Men make most of the important decisions, inheritance is through the male line, and a woman lives in her husband's village after she marries."[305] Very early in life, children begin to see how this belief is acted out: Boys are given much more freedom of expression than are girls; boys are encouraged to take part in the religious festivals and activities as a means of introducing them to the spiritual world; and girls are asked to help with the chores that keep the family functioning.

One of the clearest delineations of gender roles can be found in the Arab culture, which also treats males as the preferred sex. This partiality, as was the case with Confucianism and Christianity, can be traced to religious issues. While the *Qu'ran* has a great deal to say about women, as Anderson notes, "The Koran addresses men only."[306] And the main message is "that wives should obey their husbands."[307] There are countless more specific messages in the *Qu'ran* ranging from not using cosmetics or perfume outside the house to rules about avoiding bathing in public places.[308] Family desire for a male is so strong that, on the wedding day, friends and relatives of the newlyweds wish them many sons.[309] An Arab proverb states, "Your wealth brings you respect, your sons bring you delight." The socialization of the sexes even extends to weaning; as Patai says, "Weaning comes much earlier in the life of a girl than of a boy."[310] Through these and other practices, roles begin to evolve, and women learn to be subservient to men. Patai points out: "The destiny of women in general, and in particular of those within the family circle, is to serve the men and obey them."[311]

It is important to note that gender roles, like all aspects of culture, are subject to change. While change is often slow, you can observe shifts in gender roles throughout the world. In Africa young women are starting to question the notion of female circumcision. And in parts of the Middle East women are asking for the right to vote. The notion of a global economy has also contributed to a reevaluation of females' roles within the family. As Nanda and Warms note, "Women are being increasingly incorporated into the world economy, especially working in multi-national corporations in developing countries."[312] As we have indicated, these new economic roles, of course, influence what happens in the family. For example, studies have shown that as Mexican American women secure employment outside the home, there is, within the family, "joint decision making and greater equality of male and female roles."[313]

Individualism and Collectivism

In the last chapter we discussed the importance of individualism and collectivism to the study of intercultural communication. Favoring one of those values over another is not a matter of chance but rather is part of the enculturation process. Hence, within each family, children begin to learn if they are from a culture that values individualism or one that stresses collectivism. The manifestations of these lessons take a variety of forms. Let us look at some of those forms as a way of understanding how our communication partners, and ourselves, might view other people.

Individualism and the Family.   As we have stressed throughout this chapter, most cultural characteristics have their roots in the deep structure of a culture. For Americans, individualism, as it applies to families, is linked to the history of the United States. From America's western European heritage, to the earliest colonial times, to the industrialization period, the nuclear family has been at the center of American culture. In these first nuclear families, early travelers to the United States would report that parents were proud of their "wildly un-disciplined, self-assertive offspring."[314]

We would suggest that not much has changed during the last two hundred years. As Moghaddam, Taylor, and Wright point out, "In modern North America, 'family' is often described in terms of the isolated nuclear family."[315] As we have already noted, this kind of family tends to "emphasize independence and individual autonomy."[316] This independence and autonomy encourages self-reliance. As Nomura and his colleagues point out, "children in America appear to be encouraged to 'decide for themselves,' 'do their own things,' 'develop their own opinion,' or 'solve their own problems.'"[317] Althen buttresses this view when he writes that "the parents' objective in raising a child is to create a responsible, self-reliant individual who, by the age of 18 or so, is ready to move out of the parents' house and make his or her own way in life."[318] Still speaking about American families, he adds, "Notions about independence, individuality, equality, and informality are all embodied in what takes place in families."[319] You will recall that four of the values mentioned by Althen were discussed in detail in the last chapter when you looked at American cultural patterns. All that is being said now is that those patterns have their origins within the structure of the family.

Collectivism and the Family.   There is an Indian proverb that states "An individual could not more be separated from the family than a finger from the hand." We see the proverb being acted out when Wolpert tells us that in India, people "share property, all material possessions, food, work and love, perform religious rituals together, and often live under the same roof."[320] This collective view of family is very different than the ideas just examined when we looked at the United States. The contrast is very vivid when we turn to the culture of Mexico. In the United States one might say, "I will achieve mainly because of my ability and initiative"; the emphasis in Mexico on the extended family, close attachments, and tight bonds leads the Mexican to say, "I will achieve mainly because of my family, and for my family, rather than myself."[321] We find the same attitude in Costa Rico, where "Kinship ties guide and control individual behavior."[322] According to Asselin and Mastron, France also sees the extended family as a major influence in the individual's life. They note, "The extended family serves as an active support network. Relatives, including godparents, are resources for finding jobs, an apartment, a car, and any number of products and services."[323]

Directly linked to collectivism in the family is the notion of dominance—who controls the child? In the Arab world, children learn that God controls them and must be listened to. In the United States, children learn to answer mainly to themselves or their parents. Among the Maasai of Africa, many people share in raising the child. A Maasai proverb says, "The child has no owner"—all members of the tribe are responsible for the socialization process.

While learning such characteristics as self-reliance and responsibility, the child, through the extended family, is also being taught the parameters of loyalty. In the Bedouin tribes of Saudi Arabia, "Intense feelings of loyalty and dependence are fostered and preserved" by the family.[324] You find much the same attitude toward loyalty in the extended families of Africa. Richmond and Gestrin note, "The African extended family is extended indeed. Among its members are parents and children, grandparents, uncles and aunts, in-laws, cousins of varying degrees, as well as persons not related by blood."[325] There are large networks of loyalty in other cultures. Mexicans are also "intensely loyal to their families and pride themselves on their willingness to put their families first."[326] So important is this value toward family loyalty that even Mexicans living in the United States, as Valenzula tells us, have a "strong sense of loyalty."[327]

The Japanese also "hold loyalty in the highest esteem."[328] This means that children are brought up "to seek fulfillment with others rather than individually."[329] The Chinese family also takes this approach to loyalty. For historical and geographical reasons, most Chinese have always felt detached from their central government. Hence, family loyalty comes first for them, as this Chinese proverb makes clear: "Heaven is high and the Emperor is far away." Chu and Ju make much the same point: "An important Chinese cultural value is filial piety. Traditionally Chinese children felt a lifelong obligation to their parents, ideally exemplified by an unreserved devotion to please them in every possible way."[330] You can also observe the value of collectivism influencing loyalty in the Arab family. As Nydell notes, for Arabs "Family loyalty and obligations take precedence over loyalty to friends or the demands of the job."[331]

Age

The family is the first institution to introduce the child to the notion of age-grading, an important perceptual attribute that greatly influences the way individuals perceive youth as well as old age. It does not take a great deal of documentation to establish the assertion that the dominant American culture prefers youth to old age. From plastic surgery to hair dye, Americans seek to look younger. Even the media extols the values of youth and warns of the consequences of growing old. This condition does not exist in all cultures. In the Arab culture, Lutfiyya says, a very different socialization process exists:

> Children are often instructed to kiss the hands of older people when they are introduced to them, to be polite in the presence of elders, and to stand up and offer them their seats. Young people are encouraged to listen to and to learn from their elders. Only from the older people who have lived in the past can one learn anything of value, they are told.[332]

This respect for the elderly is even reflected in the Arab proverb that states, "A house without an elderly person is like an orchard without a well."

This same respect for the elderly is taught in most Asian cultures where "children read stories of exemplary sons and daughters who care for their parents through good times and bad."[333] In China, Wenzhong and Grove note, "Perhaps the chief determinant of relative power . . . is seniority."[334] You can find a similar attitude toward age in Malaysia, where, according to Gannon, "Malaysians frequently defer to the more senior or elderly member of the organization, who will generally be the first to speak at a meeting."[335] The hierarchy associated with age in this culture is rather clear. After the father, the eldest male has most of the authority. Because of the influence of Confucian principles in Japan, Hendry says, the younger members of the house are taught to be "indebted to the older members for their upbringing."[336] There is even a Chinese proverb that states, "When eating bamboo sprouts, remember who planted them." The Filipino culture is yet another in which the family teaches admiration and respect for the elderly. Says Gochenour, "There is an almost automatic deference of younger to older, both within the family and in day-to-day interaction in school, social life, and work."[337]

The French culture teaches young people that "mature age is preferred to youth."[338] Even the French language has no special word for "youth." As Curtius notes, "The values which French civilization prefer are the values of age."[339]

Within the Mexican American culture you can observe "respect for one's elders is a major organizing principle."[340] Among Native American families, this same attitude is taught early in life. As Still and Hodgins note, "The elderly Navajo are looked on with clear deference."[341] One of the main reasons the elderly are respected in this culture can be found in the idea of oral tradition. Because most tribes do not have a system of writing, the elderly are the "carriers" of much of the knowledge that is deemed important. Commenting as an American Indian, Arnold notes, "Elders are responsible for passing on the collective and personal knowledge that our people have accumulated through thousands of years."[342]

African Americans represent yet another co-culture in the United States that have a view toward the elderly that is different than the one held by the dominant culture. Campinha-Bacote offers an excellent summary of this position: "The elders in an African-American community are valued and treated with respect. The role of grandmother is one of the most central roles in the African-American family."[343]

Social Skills

Earlier in this chapter we discussed how families were important to all cultures for a host of reasons. The reason that is most germane to this book is succinctly stated by Charon: "A family is a primary group living in one household that is expected to socialize children."[344] The key word in Charon's definition is *socialize*. Or put in slightly different terms, he is talking about teaching the child how to interact with other human beings. The specific impact and influence of the family on the development of these interaction skills is seen in the following paragraph offered by Anderson:

> Through socialization the family teaches the child to integrate into the community, to develop his potentials, and to form stable and meaningful relationships. The individual is not born with the ability to participate in-group activities but must learn to take account of others, to share and to cooperate.[345]

Anderson is saying that while children are very young and primarily under the influence of their immediate family, they acquire an understanding of basic social skills. They are learning about politeness, how to communicate and make friends, and even "what subjects can be discussed, and ways of expressing anger or affection."[346] Learning about these social skills comes from children observing and participating in family interactions. As Turner and West note, "We tend to understand and create our sense of family through our perceptions of our family interaction patterns. Thus, we characterize our family as quiet, extroverted, jovial, and so forth, based on how we think we talk to one another."[347]

Although all cultures ask the institution of family to instruct children in the correct use of basic communication skills, the skills that are stressed vary from culture to culture. Studies of Western family life have shown that parents encourage, approve, and reward aggressive behavior.[348] In the traditional Mexican family, which highly values respect, the child is taught to avoid aggressive behavior and to use, says Murillo, "diplomacy and tactfulness when communicating with another individual."[349] One study found that "the Mexican parents were the most punitive for aggression against other children, while the American parents stand out as particularly tolerant of aggression against other children."[350] As we have already indicated, nonaggressive behavior is a part of the Chinese family experience. In Chinese families, children learn the social skills necessary for group harmony, family togetherness, interdependence in relationships, respect for their place in the line of generations, and saving face.[351]

Another vivid example of how each family teaches various social skills can also be seen in the Thai family. Cooper and Cooper offer an excellent summary of the Thai family role in teaching patterns of interaction:

> The child quickly learns that by behaving in a way that openly demonstrates consideration for the feelings of others, obedience, humility, politeness and respect, he can make people like him and be nice to him. This behavior may be summed up in one Thai word, *krengjai*. *Krengjai* is usually translated as consideration.[352]

You can also observe cultural differences in the teaching of communication skills when you look at family patterns regarding how children are taught about the value

What a culture seeks to remember and pass on to the next generation tells us about the character of the culture.

placed on vocal interaction. As Kim notes, "From an early age, Americans are encouraged to talk whenever they wish. American parents tend to respect children's opinions and encourage them to express themselves verbally."[353] As you would suspect, such a view toward value placed on oral expression is not universal. For example, "From childhood Asians quickly learn the importance of reticence, modesty, indirection, and humility: a person should be quiet unless he is absolutely confident about what he has to say."[354] One study even suggested that Chinese infants, compared to children brought up in Caucasian households, are less vocal and active.[355] In the Sioux culture, says McGoldrick, "talking is actually proscribed in certain family relationships."[356] The rationale for this behavior, she continues, is that "the reduced emphasis on verbal expression seems to free up Native American families for other kinds of experience—of each other, of nature, and of the spiritual."[357]

We hope the examples we have provided have demonstrated the prominence of the family in the enculturation process. What is intriguing about this process is that, like most of the deep structure of culture, it is resistant to change. Although, for reasons we have already discussed, this may not apply to the United States, it does apply to most other cultures. In China, for example, in spite of the legal and cultural persecution of the traditional Chinese family, neither Mao's Cultural Revolution nor the Gang of Four could destroy it. As Chu and Ju declared, "They failed to remove the soil in which the Chinese family had been planted."[358] We can find the "deep soil" of the family in the United States among immigrants from different cultures. It appears, say Galvin and Brommel, that the force of the Chinese family is so great that "cultural/ethnic heritages are maintained across generations."[359] In fact, there is abundant evidence that the Chinese family retains ethnic values and identification for many generations after immigration to the United States.[360] The Chinese have a proverb, written long before we had studies to measure human behavior, that expresses both the strength and influence of the family: "To forget one's ancestors is to be a brook without a source, a tree without a root."

HISTORY

The importance of history to the study of culture can be represented by the assertion of English writer Edmund Burke that "history is a pact between the dead, the living, and the yet unborn." Burke's observation takes on added meaning for students of intercultural communication when you realize that you can substitute the word *culture* for the word *history*, for in a very real sense both are the conduits that carry the essential messages that a culture deems important. Smith offers a more intricate and eloquent justification for the study of history:

> For when we immerse ourselves in the flow of time, in the ebb and flow of cultures, in the immense drama of human life on our planet, we acquire a sense of vision of our earth as one small planet among many; so the study of history recognizes that our contemporary culture is but one expression of human life within a vast panorama of different communities and societies.[361]

Before we begin our discussion of how history and culture are interwoven, we remind you that our intention is simply to expose you to some historical examples that will enable you to appreciate the following advice: The study of history needs to be part of the study of intercultural communication. Yu underscores the importance of that recommendation when he writes; "we need to recognize that the history of every society or people deserves to be studied not only as part of world history but also on account of its intrinsic values."[362]

The influence of history is hard to pin down and define. For as we said elsewhere, all the deep structure elements (family, religion, and history) work in combination. In addition, when we talk about history in this section of the book, we are talking about much more than historical events and specific dates. Granted these are important, but when we refer to history as one of the deep structure elements of a culture, we are also talking about a culture's formal and informal government, its sense of community, its political system, its key historical "heroes," and even its geography. All of these, working in combination, provide the members of every culture with their identity, values, goals, and expectations. For example, the history of the United States teaches young people that almost anything is possible—one can even become president. History books are full of stories about Abraham Lincoln's log-cabin background and the simple clothing-store clerk Harry Truman. Such history is deeply rooted in the American psyche.

The penetrating effect of a culture's history on perception and behavior can be seen in countless examples. The deep-seated hatred and killing in Bosnia-Herzegovina did not start in the 1990s. In a newspaper article appropriately titled "How the Seeds of Hate Were Sown," one historian traces the roots of the conflict back to the fourteenth century.[363] You can also see the long arm of history influencing current cultural events in the Middle East. The existing dispute in the area makes much more sense, if mistrust and animosity can make sense, if you realize that for centuries this area has been the site of conflict over land that is sacred to Christians, Muslims, and Jews. Within the United States many of the ill feelings between African Americans and the dominant culture can be traced to a long and agonizing history. An editorial in *Time* magazine, discussing the long-standing tribal conflicts in Africa, reminded all of us that war and killing is seldom surprising "when ethnic enemies use the outbreak of fighting to settle scores that can stretch back for centuries."[364] And even in something as simple as Japan's low murder rate we can see the influence of history. As an article in *U.S. News & World Report* pointed out, "Japan's relatively low murder rate reflects its history and customs, just as America's relatively high numbers do. Since the 17th century, private ownership of most guns has been banned in Japan."[365]

Our interest in the study of history is predicated on two assumptions. First, historical events help explain the character of a culture. As the historian Basile noted, "For all people, history is the source of the collective consciousness."[366] From the earliest westward movement across the plains of the United States to explorations of outer space, Americans have agreed on a history of conquest. Second, what a culture seeks to remember and pass on to the next generation tells us about the character of that culture. American history books and folktales are running over with examples of how one person can make a major difference in the world. We have all learned how Martin Luther King Jr. almost single-handedly shaped the civil rights movement and Bill Gates revolutionized modern technology.

United States History

Any discussion of American history must begin with an analysis of the people who created the United States. It is these *first immigrants* that set the tone for what was to follow from 1607 to the present. The power and influence of these first settlers is clearly pointed out by McElroy when he notes, "Never before in history has a society made up chiefly of self-determining, self-selected immigrants and their descendants come into being in a place that offered so much opportunity for gain for those who would work for it."[367] McElroy also maintains that "primary American cultural beliefs derive from" these initial settlers and that they "began the process of distinguishing American behavior from European behavior, which led during the next eight generations to the formation of a new American culture."[368] What McElroy is suggesting is that much of what we now call American culture can be traced to a distinctive population that arrived at the outset of this country's history—a population that arrived believing in many of the values we discussed in the last chapter such as hard work, improvement, practicality, freedom, responsibility, equality, and individuality.[369]

These first settlers were a very special breed of individuals, who brought with them some English values, the English system of law, and the basic organization of commerce that was prevalent during the sixteenth century. Just as these first settlers were beginning to stake out a culture, they were immediately confronted with a wave of new citizens who arrived through migration. And as we noted in Chapter 1, these "new citizens" continue to arrive even today. This ongoing influx of immigrants, both legal and illegal, has produced what is sometimes referred to as the first multicultural nation in the world.

Cultural integration did not come easily during the early stages of the formation of the United States. The shared, desperate desire of the American people to be separated from what was known as the Crown and Divine Right, as well as from the Church of England, provided the impetus to seek unity. This impetus led, in part, to the binding of Germans, Irish, and English together in a social fabric ample enough to contain Catholics, Congregationalists, and Methodists and to unite North, South, East, and West within a national framework. Americans wanted to separate alienable rights—those that could be voluntarily surrendered to the government—from inalienable rights, those that could not be surrendered or "taken away" even to a government of the people.[370] The fundamental American proposition became "life, liberty, and the pursuit of happiness" for each individual, whose liberties had to be secured against the potentially abusive power of government.

As we have already noted, the people who settled the colonies quickly combined some English values with a new set of beliefs. Chief among them were *individuality, a lack of formality, and efficient use of time*. Centuries later, these values still endure. Historically individualism was perhaps the first value that emerged in the "new country." As McElroy notes, "The self-selecting emigrants who left Europe for America manifested individualism by their emigration. When they got on the ships, they were already individualists."[371]

Distaste for formality and the "wasting of time" was also part of the colonial experience. Settling a new, undeveloped land required a great deal of attention to the daily activities of surviving, a situation that did not lend itself to formality or dependency. There was no time to waste on what was perceived to be the nonsense of rigid European and British rules of formality. Only the independent survived.

These difficult geographical factors also had psychological effects on the settlers: After developing habits of survival based on individualism, a lack of formality, and efficiency, they soon developed thought patterns, beliefs, values, and attitudes attuned to that *environment*. In this way, individualism became even more important for the American culture. They consider anything morally wrong that might violate their right to think for themselves, judge for themselves, and make their own decisions. They developed a pride in individualism that has become fixed in folk history as well as factual history. For instance, there is the story of how Daniel Boone's father knew it was time to move whenever a new neighbor was so close he could see smoke from the neighbor's fireplace.

Another aspect of American history that has shaped the culture is violence. Our history is filled with stories of *violence and war*. Early in the history of the United States we saw the taking of Native American lands by force and fighting the War of Independence and the Civil War. There are, of course, numerous other examples that reflect the American attitude toward military action. McElroy offers an excellent summary of this aspect of American history: "The most remarkable cultural feature of American behavior in the twentieth century is repeatedly deploying huge armies and other military forces on far-distant continents and seas and in transferring colossal quantities of war supplies to distant allies."[372] Your review of history should lead you to recall that we employed force in Europe in 1917 and again in 1942. We went to Korea in the 1950s, Vietnam in the 1960s, and until recently sent troops all over the world to "fight" the cold war. Desert Storm, Kosovo, and Afghanistan followed these encounters. And, in 2002 there was talk of moving into the Middle East. Guns are so much a part of our culture and history that the Constitution guarantees our right to bear arms—a right no other nation grants. It is not our intention here to debate the merit of this heritage but only to point out its impact on the development of our culture.

Americans have historically believed in the principle of *Manifest Destiny*. Although originally applied to Mexicans and Native Americans, this philosophy stressed that we were the people "who would inevitably spread the benefits of democracy and freedom to the lesser peoples inhabiting the region."[373]

Our notions of freedom and independence and the challenge of developing a sparsely populated land have produced a culture with a strong love of *change and progress*. "America," as *U.S News & World Report* said, "incorporates the yearnings of both Daedalus and Icarus, constructing miraculous contraptions of every type with the caution of the industrialist, yet audaciously believing there is no place we cannot reach."[374] In the same commentary, the editors remarked: "Being what we are, it was inevitable that Americans would quickly progress from boats to trains to planes. The constitutionally restless republic that trampled the American road was bound to clutter the American sky, expansionism being in their blood."[375]

A review of American history also offers us clues into the link between history, perception, and the *role of women* in the United States. For example, during the colonial period the legal status of women was influenced by English common law doctrine, under which a woman's legal identity was submerged with her husband's. Even the Constitution of the United States excluded women from equal rights. Women were prohibited from voting, owning land, executing contracts, and conducting business.[376] Even Thomas Jefferson, the great advocate of democracy, was part of the history that subjugated women. The historian Ambrose offers us a synopsis of Jefferson's view of women—a view that in some ways is still part of American history:

> In America, Jefferson rejoiced, women knew their place, which was in the home and, more specifically, in the nursery. Instead of gadding frivolously about town as French women did, chasing fashion or meddling in politics, American women were content with "the tender and tranquil amusements of domestic life" and never troubled their pretty heads with politics.[377]

African American History

The continuous history of African Americans in the United States has it beginning in 1619, when a handful of Africans, who were brought here originally as indentured servants, landed in the English colony of Virginia. From 1619 to around 1860 millions of more *slaves* were brought to the United States against their will. They were, as Campinha-Bacote notes, "involuntary migrants (slaves)."[378] They and their ancestors were captured and enslaved in their own home, brought to the United States, and sold to the colonists as laborers and servants. As Segal notes, "The rule of slavery was forced labor," and the labor was difficult.[379] Life on the plantation was hard. Most slaves worked fifteen to eighteen hours a day and had few rights or privileges. As Esler notes, "They were property, to be bought and sold like farm animals."[380] Slave owners attempted to cut family and tribal links as soon as the slaves arrived in the United States. Yet many important elements of west African cultures survived and have helped shape the African American experience. Bagwell states this idea in the following manner: "Our history of enslavement has defined who we are and what we believe today."[381]

Africans became a group robbed of much of their *cultural identity*. Slaves were forced to adopt a new language and religion and were even assigned new names. Being denied access to the culture of their captors while being told they could not preserve their own culture, they attempted to forge a new one. It was a culture that, in order to survive, stressed companionship and group solidarity. This solidarity was accomplished in part by maintaining historical traditions that had their roots in Africa. As is the case with so many customs, social bonding is still part of the African American experience. Then and now, the bond of the extended families was communicated through the use of names: It became the custom to identify everyone as a member of the same family. As the poet and novelist Maya Angelou notes, "In slave society Mariah became Aunt Mariah and Joe became Uncle Joe. Young girls were called Sister, Sis, or Tutta. Boys became Brother, Bubba, and Bro and Buddy."[382] Angelou adds, "We have used these terms to help us survive slavery, its aftermath, and today's crisis of revived racism."[383] The terms *brother* and *sister* are still heard throughout African American communities.

During the years of enslavement, African men were often removed from their families and required to work in distant locations. Thus, African *women* became a commanding force in the family, and the influence of mothers predominated. This, of course, as Patterson notes, was "an assault on the key roles of fathers and mothers."[384] Even today we see the impact of this phase of history on many African American families.

What is both sad and interesting about African American history is the fact that persecution, prejudice, and treatment as second-class citizens did not end with the Civil War and the passing of the Thirteenth Amendment in 1866, which bans slavery throughout the United States. Most of the freed slaves were largely left on their own with meager resources. As Marable notes, "The promise of '40 acres and a mule' was for most blacks a dream deferred."[385] Patterson confirms the same point when he writes, "The thing that makes African Americans special is the period of Jim Crow which was very much a kind of slave system except without individual masters. In others words, blacks were essentially in bondage into the 1960s."[386]

In the 1960s the civil rights movement became yet another important part of African American history. Mass demonstrations, sit-ins, marches, and even violence, and the formation of groups such as the Black Panthers, got the attention of the government—which in 1964 passed the important Civil Rights Act. So significant was this act that Walker concluded that "The 1964 Civil Rights Act is one of the most important laws every enacted in the United States, declaring that discrimination was illegal as a matter of national policy."[387]

During this same this period the Black Power movement grew in popularity. It helped stimulate a growing pride in issues related to African history and heritage. This pride was manifested in black student programs, black teachers, and even the advent of the slogan "Black is Beautiful." What seemed to happen because of this new black pride and awareness is highlighted by Orbe and Harris when they write, "In the face of historical uses of racial classification systems, many African Americans, for instance, have embraced their Blackness as a source of pride, unity, sense of belonging, and strength."[388]

In spite of many gains in the area of race relations in the United States it seems that the powerful of impact of slavery and other historical markers continue to influences black and white relations in the United States. As Chideya notes, "Although in theory blacks and whites have had every opportunity to live side by side since the sixties, the two races still lead deeply divided lives."[389] Feagin and Sikes add to this analysis when they write, "Sadly, black and white Americans mostly live in separate worlds and often do not speak the same language."[390] We tend to agree with this position and would therefore suggest that you begin to look at the history of all cultures that are different than your own as a way of understanding diverse worlds and languages.

Russian History

Formerly the leading republic in the Union of Soviet Socialist Republics, Russia has been an independent nation since the disbanding of the Soviet Union in 1991. With an area almost twice the size of either China or the United States, Russia is the largest country in the world. In addition, it has the longest border of any country on Earth. As we shall see later in this section, this extensive border has played a major role in shaping both the history and culture of the Russian people.

The Russians, like so many European countries, have been subjected to invasion, persecution, and suffering. For thousands of years Russia has been invaded and occupied time and time again by the Mongols, Germans, Turks, Poles, Swedes, French, and English. Russian cities have been brutally occupied and tightly governed, and entire towns and villages have been slaughtered for failure to pay tribute. Consequently, Russians have developed a perception of the world that incorporates the plundering of "Mother Russia." It is difficult for most Americans to understand this national paranoia toward outsiders. The historian Daniels summarizes these differences in perception and history:

> It is of greatest importance for Americans to appreciate how different was Russia's international environment from the circumstances of the young United States. Russia found itself in a world of hostile neighbors, the United States in secure continental isolation. Living under great threats and equally great temptations, Russia had developed a tradition of militarized absolutism that put the highest priority on committing its meager resources to meet those threats and exploit those temptations.[391]

As is the case with all countries and cultures, historical and political heritage have helped mold the Russian people. Esler depicts those heritages in the following manner: "Russia's political tradition has historically been autocratic, from the legacy of the Byzantine emperors and Tatar khans, through the heavy-handed authoritarianism of Peter the Great, to the totalitarian regime of Joseph Stalin."[392]

The cultural experiences described by Esler created within the Russian people traits that made it easy for them to follow orders and accept the dictums of their leaders. One of the most vivid examples of the Russian people being dominated by harsh and authoritarian rulers can be found in 1917 with the starting of the Bolshevik revolution. This was to be a revolution that freed the people from the hard times and economic inequities they were facing. Instead they saw much of their country destroyed and the entire social culture structure changed in the name of Communism. As we point out later, this harsh rule lasted until 1991, when changes begin to place in what was to be known as the Gorbachev and Yeltsin era.

The link between the Russian *people and their land* is also an essential component in appreciating this culture. As Kohan tells us, "Any understanding of the Russian character must inevitably begin with the land, which covers roughly one-sixth of the globe."[393] The vast sweep of Russia's steppes and forests and the sheer enormousness of their country created a people that "would rather settle down by a warm stove, break out a bottle of vodka and muse about life."[394]

Russian history has been marked with a keep interest in the *performing and cultural arts*. From the first ballet companies beginning in 1732 to the world-famous Bolshoi Ballet in Moscow, Russian ballet has always been viewed with great pride and esteem both in and out of Russia. In the area of classical music, the entire world and the Russian people have, for centuries, admired the work of such masters as Tchaikovsky and Stravinsky.

Today Russia is a country in transition. Over a decade has passed since the old Soviet Union ended its rule over the people of Russia. The transition into the "new world" has been a difficult one for the people of this once great nation. With very little history of democracy or capitalism to draw upon, Russia faces many problems. In the new century President Vladamir Putin is struggling with a social revolution, the privatization of many state enterprises, and widespread corruption. As Montaigne notes, "The Soviet social safety net has been shredded, and articles about the woes and impoverishment of the Russian people could fill volumes."[395] Yet in spite of all these problems, the Russian people and culture seem to be moving forward and attempting to build a new society. "Small businesses are slowly increasing, larger business are becoming more efficient, and students are pouring into colleges and universities."[396]

Chinese History

The Chinese proverb "Consider the past and you will know the present" clearly states how important history is to the study of their culture. Each Chinese derives his or her strongest sense of identity from history. Whatever people's qualities or quirks, whatever their circumstances or political allegiance, and whether they live in China itself or are scattered to distant lands, *pride in China's history* links all members of the culture. So important is history to the Chinese that Mathews writes, "The past obsessed the Chinese in part because there is so much of it. The longest continuing civilization in the annals of mankind, China can document its history back to the *Shang* dynasty."[397] The Chinese assign near-mystical qualities to their history, as Sangren concluded: "For China, history itself is the text through which heaven's order can be known."[398] Fernandez-Armesto summarized this historical pride when he said, "China appears as the home of an uniquely successful imperial experiment, which has endured for over two thousand years without very conspicuous discontinuities."[399]

For the student of intercultural communication, Chinese history is important not only because it is a source of such great pride to the Chinese people, but, as Matocha points out, "Many of the current values and beliefs of the Chinese remain grounded in the tradition of their history."[400] Let us now look at some of those beliefs.

A number of specific aspects of China's history contribute to the shaping of their world view: First and foremost is China's long history of *physical and cultural isolation*.

For centuries, immense natural barriers isolated China. To its north are the desolate Siberian and Mongolian plateaus and the Gobi Desert. To the west, high mountain ranges separate the country from Russia, Afghanistan, and Pakistan. The towering Himalayas form the southwestern border, secluding China from India and Burma. And high mountains and deep valleys separate the country from its southern neighbors. This geographical separation contributed to the formation of a number of familiar Chinese characteristics. Latourette mentions some of them:

> To [isolation] may partly be ascribed their intense national pride. All other civilizations with which the Chinese had close contact were derived from them and, they thought, were inferior to theirs. They were the source of the culture of most of their neighbors, but although they repeatedly profited by contributions from abroad, with the exception of Buddhism they thought themselves as having received but little. Theirs was the Middle Kingdom and all other peoples were barbarous.[401]

Part of China's *self-perception of superiority* was predicated on the their belief that their language, political institutions, and artistic and intellectual creativity were unsurpassed. This idea of Chinese superiority, for thousands of years, was related to the Chinese's preoccupation with remaining aloof from the rest of the world. They believe that any benefits that may come from foreign contact would be outweighed by the idea that this contact would "threaten the integrity of China's own values."[402] So strong was this historical belief that, as Ogden points out, "It is only in the last two centuries that China, however unwillingly, has joined the global community."[403] Even today, China believes that it is the "center of civilization." Esler summarizes the links among geographical separation, feelings of cultural supremacy, and modern-day China:

> This combination of isolation and predominance has fostered distinctive patterns of behavior and attitude among the Chinese. The unique combination, for instance, contributed substantially to the cultural continuity that marks Chinese history. In fact, twentieth-century China is still governed to a striking degree by ideas that first emerged two or three thousand years ago.[404]

Another historical idea that has lasted for thousands of years is the notion of the *Chinese clan and family being more important than the state.* As Stafford notes, "The Chinese dedication to family was among the gravest problems facing any attempt to construct Chinese nationalism."[405] Again and again the Chinese have made great sacrifices for the clans and families, but "for the nation there has never been an instance of the supreme spirit of sacrifice."[406]

The *values of merit and learning,* two traits that mark modern China, have a long historical tradition. As early as 200 B.C. one's merit would be determined by his or her fund of knowledge.[407] And successful candidates for public office and important bureaucratic positions of power and prestige would demonstrate their skills by passing examinations based upon the mastery of the Confucian classics.[408]

Granting that any culture's history is composed of thousands of elements, we offer another historical example that helps explain the bond that exists between a culture's history and its perception of the world. For some five thousand years, Chinese civilization has been built on *agriculture,* as Wenzhong and Grove note: "Generations of peasants were tied to the land on which they lived and worked. Except in times of war and famine, there was little mobility, either socially or geographically."[409] This agrarian lifestyle helps explain a number of Chinese cultural traits and values. For example, say Wenzhong and Grove, "The collective (group-oriented) nature of Chinese values is largely the product of thousands of years of living and working together on the land."[410]

The last eight years has seen China's history undergoing two major cultural events—the Cultural Revolution and the "Modernization" of China. The *Cultural Revolution*, which originally began as a social revolution, was an anti-imperialist, antifeudal revolutionary movement that dramatically changed the politics, economy, and culture of China. Before too long, with leaders such as Mao Zedong, the so-called socialist revolution grew into a rather extreme form of Communism. During this early period, China aligned itself with the old Soviet Union. However, during the 1950s, still holding to the perception that it was the most superior nation in the world, China broke its ties with the Soviet Union and, as Huntington notes, "saw itself as the leader of the Third World against both the superpowers."[411] Mao's major appeal to the people of China was a cultural one. He promised to reclaim the power of China that was usurped by the capitalist world. However, what happened was that during this period China once again become isolated from most of the other nations of the world. In many ways the socialist and communist movements in China, for cultural reasons, was destined to fail from the very start in that both clashed with the cultural values and practices of China.[412]

Starting in the early 1970s, the leaders of the "revolution" started to realize that China's isolation was hurting the culture and economy of their country. Hence, China initiated a series of reforms and also opened itself up to the rest of the world as it attempted to move toward *modernization*. This shift in policy was greatly aided by a trip to China by President Richard Nixon and the restoring of full diplomatic recognition by the United States in 1979. While China's political system has changed very little in the last few decades, its economy has become the fastest growing in the world. Because of this move to a modern economy, and China's new military power, the world has seen a major increase in the amount of intercultural contact they are having with the Chinese people.

Japanese History

As we have pointed out throughout this chapter, there is usually more than one explanation behind most cultural characteristics. This point is clearly illustrated by the *link between Japan's geography and its culture*. In the case of Japan, it was, and in some ways continues to be, the *isolation* imposed by its geography. Japan, as the reading of any map will reveal, is basically a series of islands far removed from most of the other countries of the world. This geographical isolation has influenced both the way the Japanese perceive themselves and how they are viewed by the rest of the world. Regarding self-perception, Reischauer notes that this separation and isolation "has produced in the Japanese a strong sense of self-identity and also an almost painful self-consciousness in the presence of others."[413] So strong is this island nation mentality that schoolchildren learn the following phrase: "Surrounded by seas and enemies, so we must depend on each other."[414] Being isolated from much of the world has generated other traits as well. One of these is the *homogenous* nature of the Japanese people. As Reischauer notes, "One obvious influence of isolation on Japan has been the creation of a highly homogeneous race of people there and, what is more important, a very homogeneous culture."[415] Another expression of the homogeneity found in the Japanese culture can be seen in their view of foreigners. For centuries, very few "outsiders" lived in or traveled to Japan. A *strong allegiance to their country* is yet another by-product of isolation. According to Schneider and Silverman, the Japanese have deep-seated "feelings of loyalty and obligation to their nation."[416]

Another important link between Japan's long history and some of its current values can be seen in its 250-year feudal period. A number of key Japanese cultural traits grew out of this period. First, benevolent lords took care of the people and all of their needs. The Japanese people responded to these perceived acts of caring and kindness by having *great loyalty* toward the warlords. This devotion and dedication to one's "caretaker" has had a major impact on the development of modern industrial Japan. It was easy for the Japanese to transfer loyalty from the feudal lords to large companies and later to the government because these organizations, in a sense, replaced feudalism: Even today companies and the government care for their constituents with a sort of cradle-to-grave social environment. Second, from feudalism the Japanese learned *discipline and sacrifice.* The people were required to walk a certain way, to move their hands a certain way, and even to sleep with their head pointing in a specific direction. Third, this historical period is seen as contemporary by the high degree of *conformity* found in dress, manner, and outlook.[417] Finally, Hays lists three other Japanese values that emerged from this period: the lack of individualism; a sense of one's place in society "so ingrained that all psychic life revolved around it"; and a way of life that generated a long "series of obligations."[418]

As we have said throughout this chapter, a culture's history is just one of many sources that contribute to the character of the people of that culture. This concept is clearly demonstrated with regard to the Japanese view toward *collectivism.* We have already noted that the Japanese family and world view helped create this value, and now we suggest that there are historical antecedents for this value. As far back as the second century A.D., Japanese agriculture depended on many "small dike-surrounded, water-filled plots of land, fed by an intricate man-made system of small waterways."[419] For this system to work, the people of Japan had to learn how to share water. As Reischauer pointed out, "Probably such cooperative efforts over the centuries contributed to the notable Japanese penchant for group identification and group action."[420] This desire to cooperate and conform is vividly expressed in the following Japanese proverb: "When you go to the village, go as the villagers go." We should add that when the Japanese "arrive at the village" they find very few strangers. Throughout Japanese history very few residents have been foreigners. As we noted elsewhere, because of the geographic and cultural isolation that has marked Japanese history, they have not welcomed "outsiders." Even today the term *gaijin* (meaning outer person) is applied to non-Asians living in Japan.

World War II was yet another historical event that greatly influenced the Japanese culture. Prior to 1941 and the start of the war, Japan had become modernized and industrialized. Yet their "progress" quickly ended with the devastation brought about by the war and the dropping of the atomic bomb on Hiroshima and Nagasaki. Most of the factories and major transportation system were destroyed. Shortly after the Japanese surrendered in 1945, aided by the Allied Occupation Forces, the country started to rebuild. Because of a long history of tenacity, hard work, determination, and loyalty to country, Japan was able, in just two short decades, to become a major global economic force. The point we are making is a simple one: The traits we have mentioned in this section of the chapter have endured in Japan for centuries. These are the same qualities that saw Japan rebuild its country even after the devastation caused by World War II.

Mexican History

We agree with Griswold del Castillo when he writes, "Within the last few years Americans have become more aware of the importance of studying Mexico and its relationship to the United States."[421] Part of that study should include Mexican history. As we have noted throughout this chapter, the deep structure of a culture (religion, family, history) offers valuable insights into the makeup of the members of that culture. This is particularly true for Mexicans. As McKiniss and Natella note, "Mexicans tend to be very conscious of their past, to the extent of speaking of historical events as current issues."[422] Schneider and Silverman reiterate the same theme when they write, "Mexicans themselves believe that their history holds the key to their character."[423] Let us now turn to some of that history so that you might better understand the Mexican culture.

The history of Mexico, and how that history has influenced the Mexican people, can be divided into six major periods: (1) the pre-Columbian period, (2) the invasion by Spain, (3) the independence from Spain, (4) the Mexican-American War, (5) the revolution, and (6) modern Mexico.

Although there is now evidence that human existence could be found in Mexico and Central American as far back as 50,000 years ago, most historians begin the story of the Mexican people with what is called the *pre-Columbian period*. This period of Mexican history lasted from around 300 B.D. to A.D. 1519. The great cultures of the Olmec, Maya, Toltec, and Aztec tribes flourished in different parts of Mexico during this period. While each tribe made its own unique contribution to contemporary Mexican culture, collectively they are an important part of Mexico's view of the world and themselves. These groups produced civilizations that were equal to anything in Europe.[425] Even today their legends, artistic heritages, architecture, and their foods "are an integral part of the national identity."[426]

It is important to remember that Mexicans are extremely proud of this period of their history. Not only for achievements in agriculture, creative arts and the establishments of human settlements, but also because tribes such as the Mayas were advanced in astronomy and mathematics. They developed the concept of zero before it was discovered in Europe, and they created one of the world's first calendars.[427] Mexicans are also well aware of the accomplishments of the Aztecs. Aztec art and social and religious structure have survived for thousands of years. The Aztecs were a very proud people and considered themselves the chosen people of the sun and war gods. Feelings of great pride are a trait that is common to Mexicans even today.

The pre-Columbian period of Mexican history ended with the *Spanish Conquest*. On April 22, 1519, with cries of "God, Glory and Gold," Cortes invaded Mexico. As Cockcroft notes, "The European colonization of the original peoples of Mexico and Latin America was a violent affair."[428] The attempt at colonization was, as Foster notes, "a collision of two totally foreign civilizations, each previously unknown to the other."[429] Cortes, because of his use of horses, guns, and interpreters, had very little trouble brutalizing and defeating the indigenous people of Mexico. It is estimated that killings, starvation, disease, and overwork affected about 90 percent of the Indian population by 1650.[430] The Spanish occupation of Mexico, and subsequent subjugation of the Mexican Indians, would change the country and the people for hundreds of years to come. Let us look at three of the major changes brought about by the Spanish military victory. First, was the introduction of Catholicism in Mexico. In the beginning it was left to the Spanish army to demolish Indian idols and replace them with crosses. However, it was the Spanish friars, not the soldiers, who "fanned out across the country" converting the conquered Indians.[431] Actually the conversions were rather easy.

The Indians adapted the new religion to meet their needs. In addition, both cultures "believed in an afterlife and a world created by god(s)."[432]

The second outgrowth of the Spanish domination was the development of a rigid social class that many historians believe had negative consequences on the Indian people. As Foster observed, "The Spanish caste system spread illiteracy, racism, and official corruption through the land, setting one group against the others."[433] Third, Spain's occupation of Mexico resulted in large tracts of land being turned over to Spanish nobles, priests, and soldiers. This created a large gap between the upper and lower classes in much of Mexico—a characteristic that has been part of Mexican history for hundreds of years.

For almost three hundred years Mexico suffered under Spanish rule. Mexico was a feudal and deeply Catholic country where landed aristocrats dominated a population of peasants.[434] In the summer of 1810 Miguel Hildago y Costilla, a creole parish priest, formed a group of his followers and started working and fighting for the *independence of Mexico*. Although Hidalgo was executed in 1811, he is known as the "Father of Mexican Independence," an independence that came on February 24, 1821, in the form of the Plan of Iguala.[435] Final "freedom" did not arrive until 1824 when Mexico became a federal republic under its own constitution. During this period Mexico abolished noble titles and attempted to introduce measures that would produce a more democratic society. However, as Johns points out, "Neither independence from Spain nor the Mexican revolution changed the basic structure of social relations in which a small, largely Hispanic elite presided over the exploitation of the impoverished populace."[436]

The next twenty years was a time of great upheaval in Mexico as the people attempted to adapt to a new form of government. It is during this period that the territory of Texas declared its independence from Mexico. This brought about the *Mexican-American War* in 1846. On May 13, 1846, President Polk declared war on Mexico. In addition to Texas, Polk, with the backing of the American people, wanted to acquire what amounted to half of Mexico's territory. The two countries fought over the land for two years in a war "that Americans hardly remember and that Mexicans can hardly forget."[437] The war ended with the Treaty of Guadalupe Hidalgo. For Mexicans the war was a bitter defeat. But for the United States it was an example of Manifest Destiny—"spreading the benefits of democracy to the lesser peoples of the continent."[438]

What the war between these "neighbors" did had an impact that is felt even today. Historians Samora and Simon speak of that impact when they write, "The Mexican-American War created unparalleled bitterness and hostility toward the United States, not only in Mexico but throughout Latin America."[439] They add, "Even today, Latin American relationships with the United States are often marred by suspicion and distrust"[440] that goes back over a hundred years.

The next important phase of Mexico's history deals with the *Revolution of 1910*. After a long and tiring dictatorship under President Porfirio Diaz, the Mexican people revolted. At the time of the revolution "90 percent of Mexico's mestizos and Indians were still desperately poor on the ranches and haciendas of a handful of wealthy landowners."[441] While the revolution "was an effort to bring about social change and equality for all Mexicans," it was also an attempt to return to local customs and tradition and to break away from European "culture and standards."[442] Under new leadership a constitution was approved in 1917 that was marked by a high degree of social content. The revolution "ended feudalism and peonage and created labor unions and redistributed land."[443]

The last phase of Mexican history that is important to students of intercultural communication is called *"Modern Mexico."* Huge oil and natural gas reserves, manufacturing, agriculture, tourism, and the hundreds of *maquiladora* factories along the Mexican-U.S. border have made Mexico a major economic force in the world. And, of course, with the passage of the North American Free Trade Agreement (NAFTA) Mexico, the United States, and Canada are free-trade partners.

Although economic agreements have improved relations between the governments of Mexico and the United States, there are still historical wounds that influence intercultural interactions. Three recent wounds are worth noting. First, there are different perceptions concerning undocumented immigrants. Many Mexicans resent the physical barriers that some border states have erected to "keep out" illegal immigrants. The events of September 11, 2001, have only increased the calls among many citizens of the United States to become even more resolute in their desire to restrict the flow of Mexican into the United States. Second, hostility toward Americans increased again when "A majority of Californians voted in 1994 to deny education and health services to immigrants who enter the state without proper documentation."[444] Many Mexicans perceived this vote as a sign of racism. Finally, some political leaders in the United States are working to deny medical benefits to illegal immigrants even if they need medical attention. Here again, many Mexicans find this activity to be racist.

As we conclude this chapter, we again remind you that there are thousands of examples of the tandem relationship between history, world view, family, and culture. We have offered but a handful. In each instance, our aim was to demonstrate that the study of intercultural communication must include a study of what Wolfe calls "The sacred trinity"—God, family, and country.[445.]

SUMMARY

- The deep structure of a culture, which includes such elements as religion, family, and history, is important because they carry a culture's most important beliefs, their messages endure, are deeply felt, and help supply much of a culture's identity.
- World view is a culture's orientation toward God, humanity, nature, the universe, life, death, sickness, and other philosophical issues concerning existence. Although world view is communicated in a variety of ways, religion is the predominant element of culture from which your world view is derived.
- The family, because it is the child's first introduction to culture, influences both perception and communication. Family teaches gender roles, views toward individualism and collectivism, perceptions toward aging, and social skills.
- History, by passing on stories of the past, influences perception and teaches group identity, loyalty, and for what you should strive.

INFOTRAC COLLEGE EDITION EXERCISES

1. Want to learn more about changes in the family? Locate and read "Families of the New Millennium: Designer Babies, Cyber Sex and Virtual Communities." This article discusses the influence of new technologies on family structures and family relationships. In what ways do your own experiences compare with the claims of this article? How might those from less technologically dependent cultures view these changes?

2. One of the most popular reality television shows in recent years is MTV's *The Osbournes*. A number of media critics have speculated on the ways in which this show has reflected and/or shaped family values. Locate and read either "Essential lessons from *The Osbournes*" (appearing in *Electronic Media*) or "Ozzy Without Harriet: What The Osbournes tells us about drugs" (appearing in *National Review*). With your classmates, discuss the ways in which television programs such as *Leave it to Beaver*, *I Love Lucy*, *The Jeffersons*, *The Cosby Show*, *All in the Family*, and *The Simpsons* have shaped and reflected our views of families. How has television portrayed families from non-dominant co-cultures?

3. This chapter discusses the ways in which religious views shape our ideas about reality. Religious views often play a significant role in a culture's view towards war. Locate and read one of the following articles: "Religion: A Nation Bound by Faith" (by Dirk Johnson), "Suicide bombers: the 'just war' debate, Islamic style" (by John Kelsay), or "Just war divide: one tradition, two views" (by David P. Gushee). How do your own religious views affect your attitudes towards war? How do your religious views or the views of your culture make it difficult for you to understand others' positions? (Hint: for more on the subject, use the key word search term "just war.")

ACTIVITIES

1. Find out as much as you can about the history of your informant's culture. Try to isolate examples of how your informant's cultural values have been determined by historical events.
2. Ask someone from a different culture specific questions about child-rearing practices. You might inquire about methods of discipline, toys, games, stories, topics discussed at the dinner table, and so forth.

3. Attend a church that is very different from your own, and try to determine the rituals and messages that might influence perceptions of members of that church.
4. In a small group, discuss what aspects of religion are most directly related to perception and communication.

DISCUSSION IDEAS

1. Explain how understanding the religious aspect of a particular culture's lifestyle might help you better communicate with a member of that culture.
2. Determine the link between a culture's historical roots and some current perceptions and behaviors of that culture.

3. How are religion, family, and history linked together?
4. Explain the phrase "a culture's deep structure influences intercultural communication."

part 2
Exchanging Intercultural Messages

chapter 4

Language and Culture: Words and Meaning

The notion that thought can be perfectly or even adequately expressed in verbal symbols is idiotic.

ALFRED NORTH WHITEHEAD

The sum of human wisdom is not contained in any one language and no single language is capable of expressing all forms and degrees of human comprehension.

EZRA POUND

Words should be weighed and not counted.

YIDDISH PROVERB

LANGUAGE AND INTERCULTURAL COMMUNICATION

The Importance of Language

The importance of language to the study of intercultural communication is clearly captured by filmmaker Federico Fellini's simple sentence: "A different language is a different view of life." His observation takes on added significance when you realize that one of the major characteristics identifying you as human is your ability to use language. As Cartmill points out, "People can talk. Other animals can't. These skills make *Homo sapiens* a uniquely successful, powerful, and dangerous animal."[1] Yet language is more than just a skill; it has evolved a rich and expressive versatility that was recognized by Paul Tillich when he observed that "language has created the word 'loneliness' to express the pain of being alone and the word 'solitude' to express the joy of being alone" or by the Athenian poet Aristophanes, who glorified the beauty of words when he remarked "By words the mind winged."

Your ability to use words is indeed a remarkable gift. Over countless thousands of years, *Homo sapiens* has evolved the brain capacity and anatomy necessary to produce and receive sounds; in a much shorter span of time, it has created cultural systems in which those sounds have taken on meaning by representing things, feelings, and ideas. Yet there seems to be some evidence of a genetic basis tied to the use of language. The recently discovered FOXP2 gene, although not believed to have caused speech, seems to enhance the speech process by permitting humans to speak more clearly, contributing to the development of superior language abilities.[2]

This combination of evolution and culture has led to the development of a four-part process that enables you to share your internal states with other human beings. In short, you can receive, store, manipulate, and generate symbols to represent your personalized realities. But, to a large degree, your language behavior is mediated by your culture. That is to say, while how you use language is highly individualistic, many of the forms of language that you use, and the purposes to which you choose to apply language, are subject to your cultural background.

Everything you know and feel is inside your body and can only be shared by language. Most of this internal state is an electrochemical mélange residing in your brain. Your beliefs, values, attitudes, world views, emotions, and myriad other aspects of yourself and personality are locked up inside. You can convey some aspects of yourself nonverbally through facial expressions, gestures, or touching. This nonverbal communication is explored in detail in Chapter 5. Our task in this chapter is to help you understand and appreciate how verbal language functions in intercultural communication.

To state that language is important is merely to acknowledge the obvious, yet the significant influence language has on human behavior is frequently overlooked. The ability to speak and write is often taken for granted. It is through your use of sounds and symbols that you are able to give life to your ideas—as Henry Ward Beecher once wrote, "Thought is the blossom; language the opening bud; action the fruit behind it." Or as Cartmill has observed:

> Language lets us get vast numbers of big, smart fellow primates all working together on a single task—building the Great Wall of China or fighting World War II or flying to the moon. It lets us construct and communicate the gorgeous fantasies of literature and the profound fables of myth. It lets us cheat death by pouring out our knowledge, dreams, and memories into younger people's minds. And it does powerful things for us inside our own minds because we do a lot of thinking by talking silently to ourselves. Without language, we would be only a sort of upright chimpanzee with funny feet and clever hands. With it, we are the self-possessed masters of the planet.[3]

The Functions of Language

We believe that language serves two important cultural functions. First, it is the means of preserving culture; and, second, it is the medium of transmitting culture to new generations. Language also is important to all aspects of human interaction because as Orbe and Harris argue, "in its most basic form, language is a tool humans have utilized, sometimes effectively, sometimes not so effectively, to communicate their ideas, thoughts, and feelings to others."[4] Language is significant because it is capable of performing labeling, interaction, and transmission functions. The labeling function serves to identify or name a person, object, or act, so that he, she, or it may be referred to in communication. The interaction function is concerned with the sharing and communication of ideas and emotions. And transmission is the process by which you pass information to others. Although these functions are generally considered the primary purposes of communication, in many instances of social interaction, the communication of ideas is a marginal or irrelevant consideration. Hence, communication serves a variety of purposes that facilitate and maintain cultural, social, and individual needs.

Let us look at some of these functions as a further means of highlighting the importance of language to the study of intercultural communication.

Conversation

For all cultures, conversation is an overriding concept of language use. It facilitates all of the other uses and functions of language. Basically, conversation reflects the accomplishments of human cultures and what is available for future societies to inherit.[5] Rapport and Overing point out that "Conversation is a meeting of individual voices speaking in different idiom or mode. Science, poetry, practical activity and history are such modes of speech, different universes of discourse."[6] It is this blending of thoughts and ideas without setting out to seek truth or to prove a point that provides the basis for many of the functions and purposes of language that we discuss next.

Emotive Expression

Language permits you to express your internal emotional states. This form of expression may range from a simple statement such as "I feel sad" to the loud cursing of something that is not functioning properly. Whether in the absence of others or in their presence, as Coertze asserts, this use of language serves as a means of getting rid of nervous energy when you are under stress.[7] What is interesting about the emotive expression of language is that while all cultures use language for this purpose, there is a wide range of differences in how these emotional expressions are acted out. That is to say, some cultures, such as the people of Thailand, do not make excessive use of language when expressing most emotions. Yet cultures of the Middle East are extremely expressive in their use of language. Later in this chapter we make some cultural comparisons that will make this point more concretely.

Thinking

People tend to be both visual and verbal thinkers and engage in both forms depending upon their activity. As Crystal indicates, however, verbal thinking plays an extremely important role in human communication where language functions as an instrument of thought when you speak your thoughts out loud as an aid to problem solving or thinking.[8] So important is this function of language that we will develop it in much greater deal later in the chapter.

Control of Reality

Communication also functions to assist in the control of reality. The use of prayers or blessings, which invoke supernatural beliefs, involves the use of language to control the forces that are believed to control one's life. For instance, in the Roman Catholic mass, the speaking of the words "This is my body" is believed to identify the moment when the communion bread becomes the body of Christ.[9]

Keeping of History

The American philosopher Emerson was correct when he wrote, "Language is the archives of history." That is why in Chapter 2 we pointed out how all cultures employ symbols to help pass on the culture from generation to generation. Language functions to record facts, a function represented by all kinds of record keeping ranging from historical records, geographical surveys, and business accounts to scientific reports, legislative acts, and public-record data banks. This arena, Crystal points out, "is an essential domain of language because the material guarantees the knowledge-base of subsequent generations which is a prerequisite of social development and the perpetuation of culture."[10]

Enculturation

Once again with this next function—enculturation—we see the link between language and culture. This link is instrumental in instructing members of a society in acceptable interhuman relations and in the required relations to the physical environment and to the perceived but unseen supernatural. It is, in short, the sharing of a common or similar world view and system of values that not only results in a shared ability for verbal communication but also makes possible other forms of culturally determined ways of communication.[11]

Expression of Identity

In Chapter 2 we talk extensively about the idea that your culture helps supply a great deal of your identity. Much of this definition of your identity is reflected in your language. The verbal expression of identity unites participants in addition to presenting information. Cheering at a football game, reciting the Pledge of Allegiance, or shouting names or slogans at public meetings can reveal a great deal about people and their identity—in particular their culture, regional origins, social background, level of education, occupation, age, sex, and personality.[12]

Beyond shouting slogans or cheers, language functions to express and maintain your social identity. What you are can be very important in the eyes of society. Your sociolinguistic identity derives from the way in which people are organized into hierarchically ordered social groups or classes. The way people talk reveals a great deal about their social position and their level of education.[13]

To this point we have talked about language in general and very little about the specific role language plays in each culture. That is about to change—for in the remaining pages of this chapter we will examine (1) the link between language and culture in both the speaking and thinking process, (2) language diversity among cocultures in the United States, and (3) problems associated with foreign-language translation.

LANGUAGE AND CULTURE

Language has such a commanding influence within a culture that Edwards believes language and culture hold the power to maintain national or cultural identity. For him, language is important in ethnic and nationalist sentiment because of its powerful and visible symbolism; it becomes a core symbol or rallying point.[14] The impact of language as a strong symbol of national identity may be seen in the history of the Basques, an ethnic group in the north of Spain. According to Crystal, the Spanish government from 1937 to the mid-1950s made an active attempt to destroy the Basque culture and forbid the use of the Basque language. Basque could not be taught in the schools or used in the media, church ceremonies, or in public places. Books in the language were publicly burned, and Basque names could not be used in baptism ceremonies. All Basque names in official documents were translated into Spanish, and inscriptions on public buildings and tombstones were removed.[15]

Because of this relationship between language and cultural identity, steps are often taken to limit or prohibit the influence of foreign languages. Costa Rica, for instance, recently enacted a new law that restricts the use of foreign languages and imposes fines on those who break it. Under the law, companies that advertise in a foreign language also must include a Spanish translation in larger letters.[16] Likewise, Iran has banned companies from using Western names. Turkey's government is considering fining anyone who uses foreign names on the airwaves. And France has a list of thirty-five hundred foreign words that cannot be used in schools, bureaucracies, or companies.[17]

Verbal Processes

As we have already indicated, it is impossible to separate language from culture. In its most basic sense, Rubin says, language "is a set of characters or elements and rules for their use in relation to one another."[18] These characters or elements are symbols that are culturally diverse. That is, they differ from one culture to another. You may readily discover this when you study another language. Not only are the (1) words and sounds for those symbols different, but also so are the (2) rules for using those symbols and sounds.

Differences in Words

Word differences are obvious in various languages. In English, you live in a house. In Spanish, you live in a *casa*. In Thai, people live in *bans*. Phonology also varies culturally. While in English there are twenty-one consonant sounds and five vowels that combine to form thirty-eight various sounds, the Filipino language has sixteen consonants and ten vowels forming twenty-six phonemes. The Arabic language has only twenty letters in its alphabet, somewhat limiting the number of available words. Hence, an Arab may need to use a half dozen words to convey the meaning of a single English word. Grammatical structures are unique to each language as well. In English, there are both singular and plural nouns and pronouns, but in Korean, as Honig specifies, "the distinction between singular and plural is made by the context of the sentence."[19] In English, verb tenses express contrast between past, present, and future acts, but in Vietnamese, the same verb reflects all three and the time of the action is inferred from the context.[20] Syntax, or the word order and structure of sentences, also varies depending on the language. In the normal word order of simple sentences for Filipinos the predicate is followed by the subject.[21] For example, the English sentence "The teacher died" would be "*Namatay ang guro*," or "Died the teacher," in the Filipino language. These examples tell you that if you want to communicate in another language, you must know not only the symbols (words) of that language but also the rules for using those symbols.

Pronunciation Differences

In situations where cultures share the same language, there are differences in word meanings and in word pronunciation. Language is much more than just a symbol and rule system that permits communication with another person; it is also the means by which people think and construct reality. As Nanda and Warms point out, "Language does more than just reflect culture: It is the way in which the individual is introduced to the order of the physical and social environment. Therefore, language would seem to have a major impact on the way in which the individual perceives and conceptualizes the world."[22]

Some excellent examples of word and pronunciation differences can be found by comparing American English with British English. Scott believes these differences can be traced to the sixteenth and seventeenth centuries when American settlers found that their homeland English was insufficient for life on a different continent.[23] And, as Cutler has shown, many words used in American English today have their origins in the languages of Native Americans. Such words as *sequoia, caribou, chipmunk, chinook, muigwump,* and *powwow* were borrowed from Native American languages.[24]

Some word differences can at times prove embarrassing: for example, for a British-English-speaking person to ask an American lady for a rubber (an eraser to the British; a condom to Americans) or telling a client that his father, unlike me, was good at sport and was a hooker (UK: rugby player; US: prostitute). [25] Word pronunciations can also cause difficulty to the uninitiated ear. Swain tells of a woman who "wondered why Australians are happy about mothers dying. She said they always smile when they say 'mothers die.'"[26] What she did not understand was that the pronunciation of the word *day* in Australian English sounds like the word "die" in American or British English. Such differences, while sometimes amusing, illustrate just how language diversity can hinder understanding and lead to confusion.

Patterns of Thought

You may easily assume that everyone speaks and thinks in much the same way—just in different languages. But this is not the case; how people think and how they ultimately speak is determined to a large extent by their culture. This process is known as linguistic relativity. As Rogers and Steinfatt suggest:

> The assignment of meaning to a message concerns human perceptions about the relationship between symbols and their referents. Language is used to think as well as to speak. Linguistic relativity is the degree to which language influences human thought and meanings. It proposes that in human thought language intervenes between the symbols and the ideas to which the symbols refer.[27]

Just as verbal behavior differs from one culture to another, thought processes and perceptions of reality also differ. The essence of linguistic relativity is exemplified in the theoretical formulations of Benjamin Lee Whorf, which suggest that language and thought are so intertwined that one's language determines the categories of thought open to him or her. As Whorf has indicated, "We cut up and organize the spread and flow of events as we do largely because through our mother tongue, we are parties to an agreement to do so, not because nature itself is segmented in exactly that way for all to see."[28] What has become known as the Sapir-Whorf hypothesis argues that language is not simply a means of reporting experience but, more important, it is a way of defining experience. Sapir, a student of Whorf, wrote:

> Human beings do not live in the objective world alone, nor alone in the world of social activity as ordinarily understood, but are very much at the mercy of the particular language which has become the medium of expression for their society. . . . The real world is to a large extent unconsciously built up on the language habits of the group. No two languages are ever sufficiently similar to be considered as representing the same social reality. The worlds in which different societies live are distinct worlds, not merely the same world with different labels attached.[29]

Nanda provides an excellent example of the Sapir-Whorf concept in practice:

> If my language has only one term—brother-in-law—that is applied to my sister's husband, my husband's brothers, and my husband's sisters' husbands, I am led by my language to perceive

all of these relatives in a similar way. Vocabulary, through what it groups together under one label and what it differentiates with different labels, is one way in which language shapes our perception of the world.[30]

In a similar sense, in the Hindi language of India, there are no single words that are equivalent to the English words for *uncle* and *aunt*. Instead, as Rogers and Steinfatt relate, Hindi has different words for your father's older brother, father's younger brother, mother's older brother, mother's older brother-in-law, and so forth.[31]

Another instance of how language defines experience can be seen in the Navajo language, which emphasizes the nature and direction of movement. According to Nanda, instead of "One dresses," the Navajo would say, "One moves into clothing." Instead of saying, "One is young," the Navajo would say, "One moves about newly." Language is one aspect of the Navajo culture that coincides with the notion of a universe in motion.[32]

Although complete acceptance of linguistic relativity is controversial, Crystal makes its application to culture and language clear: "There is the closest of relationships between language and thought. . . . Language may not determine the way we think, but it does influence the way we perceive and remember, and it affects the ease with which we perform mental tasks."[33] Thus, you can clearly see that culture influences language by way of its symbols and rules as well as your perceptions of the universe. Equally important is the fact that meaning takes different forms as you move from one culture to another.

Contextualization

Closely allied to patterns of thought is contextualization, which is yet another way in which cultures differ in their internal cognitive processes. Often, it is necessary for you to make sense from fragmentary images of your environment. For instance, as Shea reports, seeing some fur, hind legs, and big ears may lead you to the larger picture of a rabbit.[34] There seem to be cognitive differences between European Americans and East Asians in terms of how they use words to contextualize. According to Shea, "The cognitive differences between Americans and East Asians . . . [show] striking variation in how people brought up in the East and the West view the world."[35] This variation seems to be based in the degree of sensitivity to the social and environmental contexts that affect human decision making.

East Asians appear to be more holistic and make little use of categories and formal logic. Westerners, on the other hand, seem to pay attention primarily to the object and the categories to which it belongs; they use rules, including formal logic, to understand the object.[36] On the other hand, "Asians exhibit greater 'attention to the field' than Americans."[37] Shea provides two examples of these differences in contextualizing. In the first, Asians and Americans were to group together two of three words: *seagull, sky,* and *dog*. Americans chose to group *seagull* and *dog* together. Asians, on the other hand, group *seagull* and *sky*. In the word trio *pen, notebook,* and *magazine*, Asians grouped *pen* and *notebook* together while Americans grouped *notebook* and *magazine*.[38]

This research, while indicating differences between East Asians and Americans, does not reveal why these differences exist. Some argue a genetic difference, holding that the Asian brain is wired differently. Others believe that Asian culture trains the individual to be more sensitive to environmental and social contexts than does American culture.

Culture and Meaning

As children, you most likely asked your parents, "What does that word mean?" This question reflects the way language is viewed. It suggests that people tend to look for meaning in words themselves, but you are incorrect if you believe that words possess meaning. It is far more accurate to say that people possess meaning and that words elicit meanings. The same word can elicit different meanings. For instance, to one person, the word *cool* might mean something related to the weather. To another person, *cool* may mean something that is nice and very trendy or "with it." All people, drawing on their backgrounds, decide what a word means. People have similar meanings only to the extent that they have had or can anticipate similar experiences. If your past experience includes baseball, then a *rope* is a line drive. If your background lies in the world of jazz music, the word *ax* does not indicate something used to chop wood but any horn or woodwind instrument. And it is quite likely that you and a physician will respond very differently to the word *cancer* than does the average layperson.

A word, then, can potentially elicit many meanings. Linguists have estimated that the five hundred most-used words in the English language can produce over fourteen thousand meanings. The word *cat* for example, can refer to a jazz musician, a type of tractor, a type of fish, a kind of sailboat, or even a whip. And the simple word *lap* can stand for the distance around a track, a portion of your anatomy, the drinking method of a cat or dog, or the sound of water washing onto the shore. All of this simply means that there are many more ideas, feelings, and things to represent than there are words to represent them. As the English poet Tennyson said, "Words, like Nature, half reveal and half conceal the Soul within." We add that what is "half concealed" often may be more important than what is revealed.

If culture is included as a variable in the process of abstracting meaning, the problems become all the more acute, for culture teaches us both the symbol (dog) and what the symbol represents (a furry, domesticated animal). When you are communicating with someone from your own culture, the process of using words to represent your experiences is much easier because within a culture people share many similar experiences. But when communication is between people from diverse cultures, different experiences are involved and the process is more troublesome. Objects, events, experiences, and feelings have the labels or names they do because a community of people arbitrarily decided to so name them. If this notion is extended to the intercultural setting, you can see that diverse cultures can have both different symbols and different responses. As an example, consider the word *pain*. In the United States, we try to avoid pain, and most of us would never consider even having a tooth filled without some form of painkiller. In other cultures, however, incisions are made without any anesthesia. *Pain* is a simple word. If you imagine shifting your cultural references for every word and meaning you know, you can begin to visualize the influence of culture on how we send and receive messages. Think for just a moment about the variety of meanings various cultures have for words such as *freedom, sexuality, trespassing, wealth, nature, leadership, assertiveness, security, democracy, outer space,* or *AIDS*.

The Hawaiian and Sami languages offer some additional example of the impact culture has on meaning. The Hawaiian language contains only about twenty thousand words, and only fifteen thousand of those are in dictionaries. The Hawaiian language is very ambiguous to outsiders because some words have up to five different meanings and some of the words can be used in a variety of ways and contexts. As Reineke relates, "Only a knowledge of all the possible meanings of a word and the probable intent of the speaker enables one to arrive at the correct interpretation."[39] Sloane points out, for example, that the Sami language of Kiruna Sweden has five hundred words to explain snow and several thousand more to define *reindeer*, but no word for *computer*.[40] For example, one word describes snow "where reindeer have been digging and eating in one place and then left, so it's no use to go there."[41] Reindeer are a staple of the Sami economy, and snow is a prevalent weather condition in Kiruna. Because these words hold such significance for the Sami culture, their language has hundreds of words to represent them. Computers, however, play no part in the herding of reindeer, so the Sami language has no word to represent such common English terms as *computer, printer, hard drive, gigabytes, Windows XP*, or other software applications.

There are even differences between British and American usage in word meanings. Although some words are spelled and pronounced the same, they have different meanings. For instance, the words *boot, bonnet, lift*, and *biscuit* in British English translate into American English as *car trunk, car hood, elevator*, and *cookie*. In the area of business, there are also some interesting differences. Ruch provides some examples: The British term *annual gunnel meeting* translates in American English as *annual meeting of shareholders*. The British word *billion* translates as *trillion*, and the British term *superannuation scheme* translates as *pension plan*.[42]

From these examples, you can see that culture exerts an enormous influence on language because culture teaches not only the symbols and rules for using those symbols but, more importantly, the meaning associated with the symbols. Further, culture influences the way people use language. In the next section, we examine some of the cultural variations in the use of language.

Culture and the Use of Language

Chaika believes that human language seems to be the only communication system that uses meaningless elements to create meaningful structures.[43] Yet, as Arensberg and Niehoff observe, "nothing more clearly distinguishes one culture from another than its language."[44] A comedic example of this cultural diversity may be seen from the various ways in which a sign announces a broken vending machine. In the United Kingdom, the sign might read "Please Understand This Machine Does Not Take 10p Coins." In the United States, the translation would probably be "NO 10p COINS." The Japanese version would express sorrow at the inability to accept 10p coins and offer apologies to the consumer. Although the rules and uses of a foreign language often appear arbitrary and nonsensical to nonnative speakers, to the native speakers, the rules make perfect sense and seem more logical than those of other languages. For you to understand the wide range of diversity between cultures in how they actually use language, we will examine characteristics of language that include rules for (1) *directness*, (2) the *maintenance of social customs and relationships*, (3) *expression of emotion, and (4) the value of "talk."*

Directness
Language usage reflects many of the deep structure values of a culture by its degree of directness. Most Americans are familiar with language that is direct because it is this style that marks interaction in the United States. Your own experiences will tell you that Americans are rarely reserved. Instead, the language used by most Americans can be characterized as direct bluntness and frank, explicit expressions. Americans try to avoid vagueness and ambiguity and get directly to the point. If that means saying "no," they will say "no" without hesitation. Such direct use of

language is often viewed in other cultures as a disregard for others and can lead to embarrassment and injured feelings. It is also a sign of someone who does not think about what they are saying. There is even an Asian proverb that states, "Once an arrow leaves the bow it cannot be retrieved." And the Buddha advised his disciples to avoid "harsh speech."

As we just noted, many cultures of the world employ less direct language than do Americans in an attempt to preserve the dignity, feelings, and "face" of others. They frequently deem American directness and bluntness as impolite and possibly uncivilized.

Mexicans are very concerned about respecting the individual and preserving dignity. Their values of indirectness and face-saving are evident in their use of language. Direct arguments are considered rude. The Mexican usually attempts to make every interaction harmonious and in so doing may appear to agree with the other person's opinion. In actuality, the Mexican will retain his or her own opinion unless he or she knows the person well or has enough time to explain his or her opinion without causing the other person to lose face. This indirect politeness is often viewed by North Americans as dishonesty and aloof detachment when in actuality it is a sign of individual respect and an opportunity for the other person to save face.

Indirectness, imprecision, and ambiguity are art forms in Africa. Speaking of African languages, Richmond and Gestrin indicate:

> Africans speak naturally, with eloquence, and without hesitation or stumbling over words, but their language is often imprecise and their numbers inexact. Every personal interaction becomes a discussion that establishes a basis for the relationship between the two parties. Westerners should probe gently for specific details until they are reasonably satisfied that they understand what is meant even if not stated.[45]

East Asian people tend toward language and verbalization involving fewer words supported by the aesthetics of vagueness. Cultures with this orientation tend to be concerned more with the overall emotional quality of the interaction than with the meaning of particular words and sentences. Kashima and Kashima explain that Chinese, Japanese, Korean, and Thai cultures, for example, employ language cautiously because they favor moderate or suppressed expression of negative and confrontational messages. Because of the collectivistic nature of their cultures, East Asian speech frequently does not reflect the use of personal pronouns in an effort to emphasize the importance of the group rather than the individual.[46]

As we have mentioned before, in most East Asian cultures, the primary function of speech is the maintenance of social harmony. A Japanese saying states, "The mouth is the cause of calamity." The use of indirect language, therefore, facilitates face-saving, helping to maintain social harmony. Ma states that members of these high-context cultures expect their communication partners to be able to read between the lines or decode messages from a holistic, context-based perspective.[47] Thus, courtesy may often take precedence over truth.

The use of direct and indirect language is a major linguistic difference between North Americans and many East Asian cultures, such as the Chinese. Most North Americans learn to say yes and no as a means of expressing their individual views. But, being a collective culture, the Chinese usually use yes or no to express respect for the feelings of others. "In other words," says Ma, "to say yes for no or no for yes is largely a reflection of the indirect approach to communication, through which undesirable interpersonal communication can be avoided."[48] This contrary-to-face-value aspect of Asian verbal language behavior is often confusing to North Americans.

The use of indirect language is evident in ways other than the use of "yes" and "no." For example, an American host or hostess, when complimented on his or her cooking, is likely to respond, "Oh, I'm so glad you liked it. I cooked it especially for you." In contrast, as Marks stipulates, the Chinese host or hostess will "instead apologize profusely for giving you nothing even slightly edible and for not showing you enough honor by providing proper dishes."[49]

A final example of how the Chinese employ indirect language is evident in their use of offensive language. For many Americans the creation of an "immediate effect" is a major rhetorical goal. When you insult someone, they know its full impact immediately. The Chinese prefer a "corrosive effect" that is deferred and long lasting. Says Ma, for the Chinese, the most powerful insult is to leave the insulted person unable to fall asleep at a later time because the more he or she thinks about the words, the more insulting the words become.[50]

Among Koreans, language behavior is also affected by a consideration of others. Face-saving is crucial, as Park and Moon-soo point out, because Koreans do not want to be responsible for causing someone to feel shame.[51] The Korean philosopher Han Yongun maintained that interpersonal harmony was the key to virtuous "social action."

From an American perspective, the interpersonal communication of Koreans in the presence of family, work associates, and friends may seem strange. As you learned in Chapter 3, Confucian ethics govern most interpersonal relationships, following a basic premise that proper human relationships are the foundation of society. Proper interpersonal communication includes the expression of warm feelings and the placement of interpersonal relationships before personal interests.[52]

Social Customs and Relationships

Language serves to maintain and enhance appropriate social status and relationships between and among members of a culture. Again, this is an instance where language functions to preserve the deep structure values of a culture—be they very formal or informal.

The Spanish language, for instance, expresses formality through separate verb conjugations for formal and informal speech. In Spanish, there are formal and informal pronouns for the English word *you*. In formal speech, the pronoun *usted* is used, whereas in familiar speech, the pronoun *tu* is appropriate.

The use of language to communicate social status is perhaps the most significant difference between Japanese and Western communication styles. In Japan, the very structure of the language requires the speaker to focus primarily on human relationships, whereas Western languages focus on objects or referents and their logical relationships.

Japanese culture and society are bound by rigid rules that govern social relationships and social status in all aspects of life. The Japanese language, therefore, differs substantially in various social situations. Matsumoto and Assar relate that separate vocabularies are used for addressing superiors, peers, and inferiors. When a Japanese is speaking to someone of lower social position, suggest Matsumoto and Assar, he or she must speak in a particular way. If a person is speaking to someone of higher status, however, then he or she must use other appropriate language even though the message content is identical.[53]

In the Japanese language, a number of words take different forms for different situations, sometimes depending on relationships between the speaker and the listener or the person being discussed. For example, there are many words for you: *omae*, *kimi*, *ariata, kisama,* and *anata-sama.* In addition, words that men and women use differ in Japanese. Certain words are used only between a husband and wife to express their delicate conjugal relationship. A man uses the word *omae* in two cases: when calling rudely to another man and when addressing his wife. Thus, only a husband addressing his wife can use *omae,* when the "you" is female. Therefore, only one man in the world can call a woman *omae*: her husband.

The Thai culture places a great deal of importance on the individual's place in the social order. To facilitate this concern, the Thai language contains many forms of address for the various levels of social hierarchy. Different classes use different pronouns, nouns, and verbs to represent rank and intimacy. There are at least forty-seven pronouns, including seventeen forms for *I* and nineteen for *you.* Because the language contains different forms for different classes, it is possible to distinguish four Thai languages: the royal, the ecclesiastic, the common or familiar, and slang.

Language also defines gender roles and relationships within a culture and provides many instances of males and females learning different styles of speech. Pronunciation, grammar, vocabulary, and context of use can all be affected by the gender of the speaker. This is especially evident in the speech of the Japanese. Females use a style known as *joseigno* or *onnakotoba* that evolved among upper-class women as a sign of their position in society. Japanese women have conscious control over their speech styles. Female speech forms are used when women wish to emphasize their femininity; on other occasions, they adopt a sexually neutral style. As Crystal points out, a Japanese woman may, therefore, use the feminine style when talking to other women about children and adopt the neutral style when talking to business colleagues.[54]

Male dominance is a characteristic of Mexican culture, and it is revealed in the Spanish language through the use of gendered nouns and pronouns. A group of men, for instance, would be referred to as *ellos,* and a group of women as *ellas,* the *o* ending being masculine and the *a* ending being feminine. But if a group contains several men and one woman, it is called *ellos,* using the masculine gender; if a group contains several women and one man, the group is still called *ellos.* A group of girls is called *niñas,* but a group of girls that includes a single boy is called *niños.*

Expression of Emotion

The manner in which emotions are expressed is subject to cultural diversity. Koreans, for instance, are far more reserved than Americans; verbally, their feelings are neither freely nor openly expressed. Love is neither expressed as warmly nor as sweetly as in the United States. As Park and Moon-soo point out, a Korean wife will maintain her reserve and not rush to embrace her husband at the airport even though he may have been absent for years.[55]

In Great Britain, the language is interspersed with euphemisms that enable the speaker to avoid expressing strong feelings. For instance, when English persons wish to disagree with someone, they are liable to preface their comments with phrases such as "I may be wrong, but . . ." or "There is just one thing in all that you have been saying that worries me a little." Another example of this subtle form of speech is the frequent use of an expression of gratitude to preface a request, as in "I'd be awfully grateful if . . ." or "Thank you very much indeed." This restraint is also evident in the differences between American and British word choice. Compare the following signs seen in the United States and England:

- United States: "No dogs allowed."
- England: "We regret that in the interest of hygiene, dogs are not allowed on the premises."
- United States: "Video controlled."
- England: "Notice: In the interest of our regular customers, these premises are now equipped with central security closed-circuit television."
- United States: "Please keep hands off door."
- England: "Obstructing the door causes delay and can be dangerous."

The Value of "Talk"

In many cultures people derive a great deal of pleasure from the art of conversation and public speaking. Knowing which cultures delight in verbal play and debate can give you an important insight into how oral interaction differs from culture to culture.

Throughout Africa, the spoken word rather than the written word is generally the main means of communication. Richmond and Gerstin state: "As Tanzania's founding father, Julius Nyerere, has written, 'The very origins of African democracy lay in ordinary oral discussion—the elders sat under a tree and talked until they agreed.'"[56] Whatever language they speak, Africans seem to be natural orators. Visitors are expected to be eqully gifted. As a visitor, you should plan on being called upon to give extemporaneous speeches, and it will pay for you to be prepared with a few appropriate points illustrated with amusing stories.[57]

Drawing from their oral tradition, Africans enjoy debate and exchanges of views. Miller points out that among the Kenyans speaking in public is an unavoidable individual responsibility.[58] Life events are marked by ceremonies involving multiple public speeches. At a wedding, for example, speeches are expected from the best man, the parents of both bride and groom, as well as from grandparents, aunts and uncles, and a host of others.[59]

Like storytellers, according to Richmond and Gerstin, African speakers seek to hold their audiences' attention through the prolific use of proverbs, which enrich their speech and provide insights on how they feel about particular issues.[60] Africans make rich use of the proverb as a means of teaching and perpetuating culture as well as a powerful rhetorical device. As Knappert demonstrates,

> In conversation, as in storytelling, proverbs and parables, which transmit the wisdom of past generations, play an important role. Nothing is closer to the heart of African society and thought than the proverb. More than any other African tradition, it expresses the essence of African wisdom.[61]

Among the Akan, Yankah relates, "Part of the rhetorical power of the proverb derives from its authoritativeness, or rather its ascription to authoritative sources."[62] To the outsider, this can present a problem because knowledge of a tribe's cultural history and traditions is required to make sense of the proverbs.

Proverbs reveal the power and credibility of words when they are ascribed to elderhood and ancestry. They express universal truths that also have parallels in Western wisdom and experience. To facilitate intercultural communication, Westerners should embellish their speech with their own proverbs that the Africans will surely understand, appreciate, and in many cases, find similar to their own.[63]

Arabs share a deep love of language. They believe that Arabic is "God's language" and as such treat language with great respect and admiration. An ancient Arab proverb notes, "A man's tongue is his sword." The Arabic language can exercise an irresistible influence over the minds of its users. It can be persuasive to the point where the words used to describe events become more significant than the events themselves. Words are used more for their own sake than for what they are understood to mean. Whereas an American can adequately express an idea in ten words, the Arabic speaker may use one hundred. Boasting about the superiority of one's abilities, experiences, or friends is expected. Arabs ordinarily do not publicly admit to personal deficiencies. They will, however, spend hours elaborating on the faults and failures of those who are not members of their clique.

Virtually every Saudi speaks Arabic, and those who engage in international activities are usually fluent in English as well. In social discourse, Arabs value what, by American standards, might appear to be an exaggerated speaking style. Because most intercultural communication between Saudis and Westerners is likely to be in English, it is necessary to know about the transference of Arabic communication patterns into English. The most frequently transferred are intonation patterns, a tendency toward overassertion, repetition, exaggeration, and organizational logic. Certain intonation and stress patterns may make it difficult for the English-speaking listener to comprehend what is being said. If the patterns have unwanted affective meanings for the listener, speech can sound aggressive and threatening, or if the flat Arabic intonation pattern has been transferred, this monotonous tone can be interpreted as a lack of interest. Arabs expect overassertion and repetition in almost all types of communication. For example, as Alaney and Always assert, a simple "no" by a guest to the host's request to eat more or drink more will not suffice. To convey the meaning that he (or she) is actually full, the guest must keep repeating "no" several times, coupling it with an oath such as "By God" or "I swear to God."[64]

Greek culture has a long, rich historical tradition that glorifies rhetorical techniques. The Greeks use a variety of key sayings to express much of their culture. In a sense, these sayings are proverbs because they reflect Greek morality and serve as generic forms of expression that convey much meaning in short phrases. For example, Greeks look harshly on lack of gratitude, and a Greek who feels thus slighted might respond, "I taught him how to swim and he tried to drown me." When a Greek is at fault and has no excuse, he or she is liable to say, "I want to become a saint, but the demons won't let me." Greek men have a linguistic tendency toward arrogance and boastfulness. If one succeeds in putting a halt to the bragging of another, he will say, "I cut out his cough." The Greeks' somewhat cavalier attitude toward the truth is expressed in such sayings as "Lies are the salt of life" and "Only from fools and children will you learn the truth."

Insight into the way that the Spanish language is used in Mexico can help you understand the Mexican culture. First, Mexicans love conversation and delight in verbal play. For example, as Condon illustrates, at a party in which Mexican and North American men are introduced to the wives of the guests, the North American man may say, "I am pleased to meet you." In contrast, the Mexican man may say, "I am enchanted to meet you." Mexicans make broad use of double entendres, come up with clever turns of phrases, and insert old quotations at the right moments in an otherwise ordinary conversation.[65] If there are opportunities to engage in talk, the Mexican is ready, even among casual acquaintances. And, as Riding reports, once an emotional bond is established, he or she is open and generous, willing to confide and be very hospitable.[66]

Within the United States, the co-culture of African Americans can also be classified as a culture that highly values talk and conversation. From engaging in verbal games such as playing the dozen, rappin', and runnin' it down, African Americans enjoy verbal interplay. As Weber points out, "Black language and the numerous styles that have been developed are indications of the African-American's respect for the spoken word."[67] It should be pointed out that the respect Weber is referring to should not be defined by dominant culture, but rather by the definitions of language usage that apply in the African American community.

Our goal in this section has been to convey the fact that language is inseparable from culture. Culture influences language symbols and rules for using those symbols. As you have also seen, meaning is culturally determined.

LANGUAGE DIVERSITY IN THE UNITED STATES

Language diversity has become a prominent issue in the United States. Millions of people in the United States speak a language other than English at home. Areas of Florida, California, and the Southwest are heavily Spanish speaking. But, the spread of the Spanish-speaking population is not limited to these areas. Wallace reports, "Even Sioux City, Iowa, now has a Spanish-language newspaper."[68] In addition, there are some 2.4 million Chinese speakers who live in the United States. Of these, some 80 percent prefer to speak Chinese at home.[69] Speakers of Korean and Vietnamese permeate many areas of the United States as well. Wallraff suggests the severity of this problem when she states:

> Small American towns from Huntsville, Alabama, to Meriden, Connecticut, to Wausau, Wisconsin, to El Cenizo, Texas . . . have been alarmed to find that many new arrivals do not speak English well and some may not even see the point of going to the trouble of learning it.[70]

Over 3 million students in the United States speak little or no English. Spanish is the native language of 70 percent of these students, followed by Asian languages at 15 percent.[71] Such language diversity has spurred change and adaptation in linguistic usage. For example, on the U.S.–Mexico border, Spanish is laced with English-sounding words, yielding a dialect known as "Spanglish." In English, we say *to choose*. In Spanish, the equivalent word is *escoger*, and the Spanglish rendition is *chusar*. Even within the English language itself, there are adaptations and variations between British English and American English. For example, Canada has its own distinct usage that combines both U.S. and British English.

Because of its prominence, language diversity has become a controversial issue in the United States. Politicians at all levels of government continue to propose specific legislation to make English the official language of the United States. While we do not endorse such proposals, we do believe, as Brown points out, that knowledge of English and the ability to communicate in English are essential in American society. Brown adds that the "inability to speak the language of the community in which one lives is the first step towards misunderstanding, for prejudice thrives on lack of communication."[72] The obvious solution to this issue is to ensure that all people have access to suitable English-language learning and yet be free to preserve their native cultures and languages, as they desire.

In the upcoming section, we examine the notion that people living within the same geographic boundaries often use language in ways that differ from those of the dominant culture. Specifically, we explore two facets of this idea. First, we will discuss selected co-cultures and their language usage in the United States. Second, we will discuss alternative languages—"private languages" used in the United States.

Co-Cultures and Language Use

When discussing the Sapir-Whorf hypothesis, we indicated that language is a guide to dealing with and understanding social reality. From this notion comes the corollary idea that cultures evolve different languages unique to their own needs. As Nanda and Warms point out:

> All human groups have language and all languages are equally sophisticated and serve the needs of their speakers equally well. A language cannot make its speakers more or less intelligent, sexist, sophisticated, or anything else. Individual knowledge of vocabulary may vary, as may the artfulness with which an individual communicates, but every human speaks with equal grammatical sophistication."[73]

Co-cultures exist within nearly every society, but, as we indicate elsewhere, they function both within and outside the dominant culture. Members of most co-cultures operate in two or more very distinct groups. Hence, their enculturation can be strikingly different from that of the dominant culture. Their process of language evolution tends to be shaped by the dominant culture's attitudes toward them. In many co-cultures, the name given to an experience clearly demonstrates how they perceive and interact with the dominant culture. Through the examination of a co-culture's language, you can learn a great deal about that group's experiences, values, and behaviors. To facilitate this form of understanding, we will examine the unique language behaviors of the Spanish-speaking, African American, and women's co-cultures in the United States.

Spanish-Speaking Americans

The United States is now the third-largest Spanish-speaking country in the world, exceeded only by Mexico and Colombia, and 70 percent of Hispanics in the United States speak Spanish at home.[74] Of these, many have little or no fluency in English. Yet, as Arpan and Arpan tell us, "While not all Hispanics have the same needs, the majority of them need transportation, drivers licenses, and language training."[75] Hispanics have reported communication problems in dealing with such public institutions as hospitals and K-12 schools.[76] Students have reported language barriers and a shortage of suitable programs and materials.[77]

To facilitate integration of the Hispanic community with the dominant culture, there must be reciprocal acts on the part of both Hispanics and the public institutions that serve them. Schools, hospitals, law enforcement agencies, and banks are some of the public institutions that must learn to accommodate the Latino community. Not only will this accommodation help the Hispanic immigrants become fulfilling members of society, but it will also benefit the dominant culture because this large section of the population will contribute to the economic well-being of the country.

It is easy to stand back from the Spanish-speaking population and suggest that all they need to do is learn English. While this is may be a laudable goal, it is not always a practical goal. Parents who are busy earning a living or caring for a household and children do not necessarily have the time or the energy to attend English classes. And some children attending public schools may not have English language training available to them.

African Americans

It is quite obvious that many African Americans and whites speak differently, creating different speech communities. According to Shade,

> These communities employ different varieties of speech, follow different rules for interaction, possess different core cultural elements that influence white and black communication behaviors, and possess different world views which accounts for the differences in communication and the way blacks and whites process and interpret messages.[78]

Many African Americans have evolved a particular language referred to as Ebonics, African American English Vernacular (AAEV), Black English, Pan African Language Systems, and Black Language,[79] which allows them to create, maintain, and express their culture and to deal with the European American prejudices toward their culture.[80] According to Smitherson,

> The Ebonics spoken in the US is rooted in the Black American Oral Tradition, reflecting the combination of African languages (Niger-Congo) and Euro American English. It is a language forged in the crucible of enslavement, US-style apartheid, and the struggle to survive and thrive in the face of domination. Ebonics *is* emphatically *not* "broken" English, nor "sloppy" speech. Nor is it merely "slang." Nor is it some bizarre form of language spoken by baggy-pants-wearing Black youth. Ebonics *is* a set of communication patterns and practices.[81]

Ebonics embraces the African concept of *nommo* that was carried over into African American culture as a belief in the power of the word—"the awareness that the word alone alters the world."[82] In Black America, according to Smitherman, the oral tradition has served as a fundamental vehicle for "gitting ovuh" which has to do with surviving.[83]

Asante suggests that African American English reflects African roots[84] and the adjustment of the African people to American slavery. It has been passed on from generation to generation through socialization.[85] A major difference between Ebonics and the English of the dominant culture lies, as Smitherman suggests

> in the contrasting modes in which Black and White Americans have shaped that language—a written mode for whites, having come from a European, print-oriented culture; a spoken mode for blacks, having come from an African orally-oriented background.[86]

Ebonics involves much more than a vocabulary shift or the rhymed and accented lyrics of a rap artist. It is a distinctive language form with a unique syntax, semantic system, grammar, and rhythm. The grammar rules differ in many ways and form a logical system that is independent of mainstream English. African American English contains a variety of terms denoting different ways of talking that depend on the social context. Its own style and function characterize each manner of speaking. But, you must remember, as Nanda and Warms suggest, that African American English "is in no way linguistically inferior. Like every other language, it is fully systematic, grammatical, symbolic, and certainly no barrier to abstract thought."[87]

Smitherson, as well as Hecht, Collier, and Ribeau, point out that sentence structure and semantics in African American English have been particularly influenced by early African tribal languages.[88, 89] This has led to the development of a language style that has a number of unique identifiable characteristics. Drawing on the work of Rickford, Crystal, and Smitherman, we have provided examples of some of these characteristics as outlined below.

1. Shortening of the third-person present tense by dropping the s: *He walk, She go, He talk*.[90, 91]

2. Use of the verb to be to indicate continuous action: *He be gone* for "He is gone frequently/all the time."[92]
3. Deletion of the verb *to be* in the present indicative: *He tired* for "He is tired."[93]
4. Use of *done* for completed (sometimes used with *been*). *They done been sitting there for a whole hour.*[94]
5. Use of a stressed *been* to emphasize the duration of something: *He been married* for "He has been married for a long time (and still is)."[95]
6. Use of *Uhm* and *ima* for am and am going to. *Uhm really tired* for "I am really tired." *Ima show everybody up* for "I am going to outdo everyone else."[96]
7. Use of double and triple negatives: *Won't nobody do nothing about that. He ain't got no money.*[97, 98]
8. Simplification of consonants at the ends of words: *door* becomes *do*.[99]
9. The final *ng* sound drops the *g*: *talking* becomes *talkin*.[100]
10. The initial voiced *th* realized as *d*: *dem* for "them."[101]
11. The final *th* is sometimes replaced with *f*: *with* becomes *wif*.[102]
12. Substitution of the *x* sound for the *s* sound: *ask* becomes *axe*.

African American street language also uses several different lexical forms. These include syllabic contractions, as in *supoze* for *suppose*; the fore stressing of bisyllabic words, as in *po-lice* for *police*; and hypercorrection, as in *pickted* for *picked*.[103, 104] African American English is also very rhythmic. Weber reports that "It flows like African languages in a consonant-vowel-consonant-vowel pattern."[105] This rhythm is often achieved by holding some syllables longer or giving them a stronger accent than in standard American English.

Ebonics is a vivid and imaginative language that seeks to generate movement and power within its listeners. This is clearly evident in what is referred to as the "call and response." Weber believes this is an interactive play between the speaker and the listener in which the listener's responses are just as important as the speaker's comments. For example, Weber reports, listeners may respond to a message with encouraging remarks such as "all right," "make it plain," and "that all right." These responses make the speaker successful.[106]

African Americans have developed numerous strategies or ways of dealing with the stigma that is often attached to African American English by the dominant culture. Rogers and Steinfatt suggest these include language mobility and code-switching, which is the situational changing between African American English and mainstream American English language groups.[107] Many African Americans prefer style switching and associate the selective adoption of mainstream American English with being educated and professional. According to Hecht, Collier, and Ribeau, in casual settings among other African Americans or with familiar European Americans, African American English and slang may be used to communicate experience and feelings, to create cultural identity and bonds, and even to make a political statement that African Americans have not given up their language.[108] As Garner and Rubin point out, both language systems are important for linguistic competency. Individuals who do not know when and in what context to use mainstream American English rather than slang or street vernacular are held in less regard and viewed as uneducated by both African Americans and European Americans.[109]

Women

In speaking of communication between men and women, Tannen notes, "Different words, different worlds." Communication for women has different purposes and rules than communication for men.[110] Elium and Elium say, "Females put a greater and different emphasis on conversation."[111] In a general sense, it is safe to say that women and men constitute two linguistic groups. Yet, Romaine reports that questions are being raised about language differences between men and women and whether these differences are stereotypical, reflecting not how women and men actually speak but rather how people believe they speak.[112]

We begin our exploration of female communication by identifying the purpose of communication for women. For most women, says Wood, communication is a primary way to establish and maintain relationships with others.[113] Wood identified seven features of women's communication that foster connections, support, closeness, and understanding.[114] First, equality is an important feature of female communication. Women achieve symmetry and equality by matching experiences. For instance, a woman may say, "I've done the same thing many times." This establishes equality in the sense that the speaker is not alone in how he or she feels. This creates an interactive pattern in conversations rather than rigid turn taking.

Second, showing support for others is characteristic of women's speech. Phrases like, "Oh, you must feel terrible" and "I think you did the right thing" demonstrate understanding and sympathy.[115]

Third and closely related to the feature of understanding and sympathy is the presence of questions that probe for greater understanding of feelings. Questions such as, "How did you feel when it occurred?" and "Do you think it was deliberate?" address content while paying serious attention to the feelings involved.[116]

Fourth, women's speech is characterized by conversational maintenance work.[117] That is, women engage in efforts to sustain the conversation by prompting others to speak or elaborate, and by initiating topics for others. Phrases like, "Tell me about your day," or "Was your faculty meeting interesting?" serve to initiate and maintain interaction.

Responsiveness is a fifth feature of women's talk. Females are usually socialized to care about others and to make them feel valued. As such, they usually respond to what others have said. A woman might say, "That's interesting," or she might nod to show she is actively engaged in the conversation.[118]

A sixth characteristic of women's talk is a personal and concrete style. Interpersonal closeness is created by the use of "details, personal disclosures, anecdotes, and concrete reasoning."[119] This personal tone in women's conversation cultivates connection and identification so that communicators' feelings are emphasized and clarified.

Finally, Holmes has identified tentativeness as a feature of women's communication. Tentativeness can take a number of forms. Verbal hedges are phrases like *I think, I believe, I feel, I guess, I mean,* and *I wonder.*[120] Qualifying terms include words like *well, you know, kind of, perhaps,* and *possibly.* An example of a qualifying statement is "I am probably not the best judge of this, but . . ." Intonation also indicates tentativeness. For example, Ivy and Backlund indicate that when a woman is asked, "What is the organizational plan for the new chapter?" she might respond by saying, "An introduction and then the four basic assignments?" The intonation turns the answer into a question, as if to say, "Is that okay with you?"[121] Tag questions also serve to keep the conversation provisional. "That was a pretty good movie, don't you think?" leaves the door open for further conversation.

Much controversy exists about the purpose of tentativeness in women's speech. Prior research claimed that these tentative communication devices were inferior and represented a lack of confidence, uncertainty, and low self-esteem. Others have called this speech powerless, a reflection of women's socialization into subordinate roles.[122] Although there may be some validity to these assertions, more recent research indicates that there may be several different explanations for women's tentative speech.[123]

As evidenced by the seven features identified by Wood, this tentative communication, rather than reflecting powerlessness and inferiority, may instead "express women's desires to keep conversation open and include others."[124] Other researchers have found women's use of tentative communication to be context based. Although some women may use servile, submissive, or polite tentative communication, these traits are often a stereotype of how women talk and not the way they actually do talk. Instead, the way they communicate is heavily influenced by the context. For example, women may use more tentative communication when in the presence of men but less in the presence of women. A board meeting may be conducive to tentative communication in order to establish camaraderie, but the courtroom may not. Holmes reports that one study even found that men were just as likely to use tentative communication as women depending on the context.[125] As a result, it is a good idea to consider the context before stereotypically putting a negative label on women's tentative communication.

These features of female communication stand in sharp contrast to features of male communication. As Tannen suggests, the primary purpose of communication for men is to exert control, preserve independence, and enhance status.[126] Wood identified five tenets of masculine speech. First, it focuses on an instrumental activity and does not acknowledge feelings. This usually involves problem-solving efforts, data collection, and solution suggestions. Content, rather than feelings, is emphasized. "Second, it expresses superiority and maintains control."[127] Despite jokes about women's talkativeness, Aries holds that men usually have conversational dominance. They talk more and for longer periods,[128] and they reroute conversations for their own benefit and interrupt as a controlling or challenging device.[129] Third, Wood says men assert themselves in absolute ways. Their language is usually forceful and direct with infrequent use of tentative communication. Fourth, men tend to speak in abstract terms that are general and removed from personal experiences.[130] Finally, Wood reveals, men's conversation tends not to be very responsive. Sympathy, understanding, and self-disclosure are rarely expressed because the rules of men's speech dictate that these responses are condescending and make one vulnerable.[131]

In summary, it seems that women are primarily concerned with personal relationships when they communicate, but men are concerned only with getting the job done. Women seem to talk more about relationships and feelings than men. But, as Romaine indicates, whether this reflects actual gender differences or reflects the social context of the communication is open to question because "the most frequent venue for all female talk is domestic rather than public."[132]

Women tend to include everyone; men, however, seek to establish their own status. Women's concrete terminology often clashes with the abstract nature of men's verbiage. Whereas women may engage in tentative speech, men's speech is characteristically assertive. Women's communication is decidedly responsive, while men's communication is distinctly unresponsive. It is easy to see how the different rules and features of women and men's speech create the potential for misunderstanding and conflict between women and men.

ALTERNATIVE LANGUAGES

The use of alternative languages reflects a co-culture's need to have a language that permits individuals to share membership, participate in their social and cultural communities, identify themselves and their place in the universe, and communicate with one another about their own social realities. Because alternative languages are usually limited to a particular co-culture, one way to gain insight into that co-culture is to examine its use of language and vocabulary. As Folb states, the rationale is a simple one: Because "vocabulary is a part of language that is most immediately under the conscious manipulation and control of its users, it provides the most accessible place to begin exploration of shared and disparate experiences."[133] To help you better understand the uses and functions of alternative languages, we will (1) examine the types of alternative languages most commonly found in the United States and (2) discuss the functions alternative languages perform within the larger cultural setting.

Types of Alternative Languages

Alternative languages consist of at least two varieties: *argot* and *slang*. These language forms persist and thrive because they serve useful societal functions.

Argot

This is a private vocabulary peculiar to a co-culture or group. One of the characteristics of any culture—or co-culture—is that they possess a language system that is unique to their members. With regard to co-cultures, you would find that groups such as prisoners, African Americans, prostitutes, gays, carnival workers, street gangs, and the like would have this specialized language as part of their cultural identification.

Slang

Slang designates those terms derived from argot that are understood by most people but not often used in normal society or in formal written communication. Slang involves such linguistic terms as *booze* for *alcohol*, *broad* for *woman*, *stud* for *man*, *phat* for *good*, *random* for *completely off the wall*, *hoopty* for a car, *joints* for any popular brand of sneakers, and *byte-bonding* for computer nerds who are discussing things no one else can understand.[134]

A major difference between an alternative language and a foreign language is in the relationship between sounds and meanings. In a foreign language, the sounds are different, but the referents are often the same. In English, the sound of the thing we sit at to eat dinner is *table*; in Spanish, it is *mesa*. In other words, the sounds are different, but the table is still a table. In an alternative language, the sounds remain the same, but the meanings change. Simple words may have multiple meanings unique to the co-cultural reality. The word *pot*, for instance, may refer to the pot you smoke, the pot that hangs over your belt, or the pot in which you cook your dinner. The sound remains the same, but the meanings differ significantly. Another major difference between a sublanguage and a mainstream language is the cultural reference. One can assume specific cultural identifications when referring to dominant languages such as English, Spanish, French, German, Chinese, Tagalog, Japanese, and Arabic. Here, the name of the language suggests its culture. But when we examine an alternative language, we find that it does not refer to a specific dominant culture but to specific co-cultures.

Functions of Alternative Languages

Alternative languages reveal another way in which language and behavior are linked together. They can serve a variety of functions for co-cultures. Although we discuss but two of the most prominent, keep in mind that the alternative language of a specific co-culture may serve only one of these functions, not necessarily all of them.

Empowerment

Alternative languages can function as a form of empowerment. *Nushu* is a three-thousand-year-old language used exclusively by Chinese women. Altman states, "Ancient Chinese women were barred from formal education and were treated as illiterate and unthinking by men. So women of this region empowered themselves by creating their own language which uses a different set of characters."[135] *Nushu* empowered women by giving them a way to detail their private lives on a personal basis. It was used as a powerful source of support between women "who were bound as property to their husbands, bound to Draconian cultural roles, and cripplingly bound about their feet."[136]

Rich believes that this empowerment function also provides the co-culture with a sense of self-defense by providing a code that helps the members culture live in a hostile environment.[137] The use of Yiddish by the European Jews during periods of harsh discrimination is an obvious example of a group that needed to interact with each other, at the same time concealing the content of the interaction. There are, however, even more subtle and contemporary instances of groups using argot for both empowerment and concealment. In the co-culture of carnival workers, for example, a word such as *slum* is used to refer to the cheap prizes that people are scammed into paying high prices for. Prostitutes, because they engage in an illegal profession, also use language to camouflage their conversations. They must not only conceal the sexual acts themselves but camouflage discussion of the acts to avoid arrest. Argot serves this purpose. The following might be a typical conversation between a pimp to a prostitute. "I have a steak if you're interested. I tried for some lobster but couldn't get it." A steak is a client who will pay $50 to be with the prostitute; a $75 client is often called roast beef; someone willing to pay $150 is a lobster; and a $300 client is labeled champagne.[138]

Solidarity and Cohesiveness

A second major function of argot is to establish solidarity and cohesiveness among the members of the co-culture. A sense of identity and pride are associated with knowing the private language the ties the group together. By learning a specialized, and at times secret language code, members feel close to one another. You can see the bonding together in the co-culture of gangs. Gangs have become prominent as co-cultures in the past several years because of the violence associated with their drug dealing and territoriality. They use some of the following argot terms to help isolate themselves from the dominant culture while feeling intimate with other gang members. *Buster* refers to a gang member who does not stand up for his gang, but sells them out. A *claim* is the area that gang members have staked out as their own. If persons are asked what they claim, they are being asked to which gang they belong. A *wannabe* is a person who pretends or wants to be a member of a gang but has not been accepted by it. *Crippin'*, a word that members of the Crips gang use, means to survive any way you can. *Flashing signs* refers to using hand signals to communicate with other gang members. A sign may signify membership in a particular gang or be a signal that some gang activity is in progress. *Gang bangin'* refers to participation in any kind of gang activity, ranging from hanging out to dealing drugs or being involved in drive-bys. A *home girl* is a young woman who hangs out with gang members. *Jump in* is the initiation process whereby a claimer fights members of the gang to which he desires to belong.

Solidarity is found among the gay culture that uses a specialized language. Homosexuals who know *AC/DC* (bisexual), *bill* (a masculine homosexual), *Black Widow* (a person who takes a love mate away from another homosexual), and *chicken* (a homosexual that likes younger men) are privy to an argot that is part of their group.

We conclude our examination of alternative languages by issuing two caveats. First, there is a great deal of overlap between sublanguages. This does not negate the notion that sublanguages are a community's unique language. Instead, it means that an individual may be a member of several co-cultures simultaneously. For instance, a person may be a poor, drug-using, gay prostitute who is in prison. Another person might be a convicted white, drug-using armed robber serving a prison term. Second, we must remember that sublanguges change. As the dominant culture learns words or phrases in the code, the co-culture will usually eliminate the word or phrase. Hence, many of the examples we have cited are no longer used by the co-cultures from which they came. It is not a particular word that is significant but rather the idea that sublanguages offer us valuable insight into the experiences of these groups—experiences to which many of us might not have access.

FOREIGN LANGUAGE AND TRANSLATION

We agree with the Swedish economist Gunner Myrdal when he notes, "Language, as we know, is full of illogicalities." Yet in spite of all the problems associated with language, we need it so we can speak with other cultures. And as we have noted throughout this book, as international contact and interaction continue to increase, the necessity for effective international communication assumes added urgency. In Chapter 7, when we examine cultural differences in the educational setting, we amplified the idea that many cultures insist that their students learn to speak more than just their native language. In fact, it is not uncommon for members of some cultures to speak two or even three languages fluently. In contrast, North Americans have been slower to recognize the importance of acquiring proficiency in more than one language. As Stewart and Bennett indicate, "Most Americans speak only one language, they are usually dependent on finding English speakers or translators."[139] Arrangements such as the North American Free Trade Agreement, involving Canada, the United States, and Mexico, as well as continued immigration to the United States, have been great stimulators for North Americans to expand their language proficiency.

Schools and hospitals print materials in various languages. Employers offer bilingual manuals, and businesses advertise in non-English languages. According to Hernandez, small translation companies have turned into thriving businesses with contracts running in the millions of dollars, and some professional translators make up to 40 cents a word.[140] Schulte concisely portrays the role of the interpreter as we move into a global twenty-first century:

> The person who will have to play a major role in regulating the pendulum between global and local communication is the translator. . . . Translators build bridges not only between languages but also between the differences of two cultures. We have established that each language is a way of seeing and reflecting the delicate nuances of cultural perceptions, and it is the translator who not only reconstructs the equivalencies of words across linguistic boundaries but also reflects and transplants the emotional vibrations of another culture.[141]

Effective translation, as you know if you have attempted to learn another language, is demanding and complex. People tend to assume that text in one language can be accurately translated into another as long as you employ a good bilingual dictionary. Unfortunately, languages are not this simple, and direct translations, in many cases, are difficult if not impossible. A language may be difficult to translate if the structure of the receptor language is different than the source language, for example, translating German, an Indo-European language, into Hungarian, a Finno-Ugrian language. Also, the difficulty in translation multiplies when the cultures are extremely different from each other. As Nida states, "A translation may involve not only differences of linguistic affiliation but also highly diverse cultures, e.g., English into Zulu, or Greek into Javanese."[142]

The slightest cultural difference may affect the way in which a text is understood or interpreted. The feeling of joy is experienced differently in various cultures. In most European languages, the heart is where joy is experienced. But, in the Chadic languages of Africa, joy is related to the liver. In Hebrew, the kidneys are said to experience joy, while in the Mayan language the abdomen is the site of joy.[143]

Even when messages provide adequate interpretations of original text, there is usually no full equivalence through translation. Word-for-word correspondences do not exist, and what may appear to be synonymous messages may not be equivalent. This lack of correspondence may be seen in the translation of biblical references. The Bible idealizes sheep. But, in some cultures, sheep are viewed negatively or do not even exist. Shuttleworth and Cowie relate how the translation of the biblical phrase "Lamb of God" is translated into an Eskimo language using the term "Seal of God." The fact that lambs are unknown in polar regions has led to the substitution of a culturally meaningful item that shares some of the important features of the source language expression.[144] In the following section, we will first briefly explore linguistic equivalence in terms of securing adequate translation.

Problems of Translation and Equivalence

When the American historian Henry Brooks Adams wrote, "Words are slippery," he must have been referring to the fact that language translation is difficult and subject to countless misinterpretations. There is a case of a missionary who was preaching in the West African Bantu language and who, instead of saying, "The children of Israel crossed the Red Sea and followed Moses," mistakenly said, "The children of Israel crossed the red mosquitoes and swallowed Moses." The examples in this section illustrate the difficulties of foreign-language translation and the serious consequences of the inept translation of words with multiple meanings. These difficulties are referred to as linguistic equivalence, including vocabulary, idiomatic, grammatical-syntactical, experiential-cultural, and conceptual equivalence.

Vocabulary or Lexical Equivalence

One of the goals of translation is to convey the meaning and style of the original language, but dictionary translations rarely reflect common language usage in a culture. As Reeves describes, though proficiency in both the source and target languages is important, translators need to translate not only to a target language but to a target culture as well.[145] Translators also need to deal with nuances and with words that have no equivalents in other languages. In English, there is a distinction between the words *taboo* and *sin*. Among the Senoufo people of Africa, there is only one term for both of these concepts: *kapini taboo*. But, the taboos included in the Senoufo term are such things as a man seeing his wife sewing or a man whistling in a field unless he is resting. The Senoufo emotional attitude toward breaking these taboos is akin to the Christian attitude of sin, but the behaviors are quite different. Among the Senoufo, things considered sinful by Christians such as adultery, lying, or stealing are called *silegebafeebi* or "without-shame-people."[146] Additionally, Reeves points out that there are many terms that appear to be universal, but actually are not. Among these are such things as freedom, equality, democracy, independence, free enterprise, equal opportunity, and justice. He argues that in many cases there is no lexical equivalent to the connotative range implied by these terms.[147]

Idiomatic and Slang Equivalence

Seidel and McMordie define idioms as "a number of words which, when taken together, mean something different from the individual words of the idiom when they stand alone."[148] Most idiomatic phrases come from everyday life and are unique to a particular culture. Think for a moment about the single-word translation and the culture-bound definition of some of the following expressions: "He made a clean sweep of his life," "She hit the nail on the head," "They had to eat humble pie," "They went window shopping," "It rained cats and dogs," or "Out of the frying pan and into the fire." As we noted, idiomatic expressions are culture-bound; they do not translate well. Basset-Mcguire provides some examples: The English phrase "The spirit is willing but the flesh is weak," for instance, has been translated into Russian as "The Vodka is good but the meat is rotten." Also, the English slogan "Things come alive with Pepsi" has been translated into German as "Pepsi can pull you back from your grave." Or, consider this example of an Italian idiom translated into English: *Giovanni sta memando il cane per l'aia*. Translated literally, this is "John is leading his dog around the threshing floor." A better translation, with greater correspondence of meaning, is "John is beating around the bush."[149] Coming up with the second translation thus requires that you be familiar with American idioms. As another example, imagine attempting to translate the sports-influenced statement "I don't want to be a Monday-morning quarterback, but . . ." into the language of a culture that does not have or understand the sport of American football. You can see the same problem associated with baseball idioms if someone, engaging in an international negotiation session says "Just give us a ballpark figure so we can get off of first base."

Grammatical-Syntactical Equivalence

Difficulties may also arise when there are no equivalent parts of speech. We discussed many of these earlier in the chapter, but a few more examples will amplify our point. The Urdu language, for instance, has no gerunds, so it is difficult to find an equivalent for one. In the Filipino language, there is no equivalent of the verb *to be*. No relative pronouns in Korean are comparable to the English *who, which, that,* or *what.* "In Japanese, there is no parallel for the distinctions made in English between modifiers of nouns that are "countable" (such as marbles, days, or flavors), and modifiers of nouns that are "uncountable" (such as sugar, advice, or money)."[150] As a result, says Ogawa, Japanese translations may render statements like "much shoes" or "many patience." In addition, the gender of nouns is difficult in translation because the gender may vary by culture or language. *Die Sonne* in German is feminine, but *le soleil* in French is masculine. Both words refer to the same object—the sun—but have different gender attachments. And, in English, nouns have no gender designation.[151]

Experiential-Cultural Equivalence

In dealing with translations, you must grapple not only with structural differences between languages but also with cultural differences, which requires precision and the ability to convey the speaker's or author's approach or attitude. As Tymoczko reminds you, "All meaning is relative to the speaker and the situation in which the words are spoken or written."[152] Also, translators need to consider shared experiences. Peace and war have various meanings for peoples of the world, depending on their conditions, time, and place. The meanings that cultures have for words are based on shared experiences, and the ability of a word to convey or elicit meaning depends on the culturally informed perceptions of both source and receiver.

When we lack cultural equivalents, we lack the words in our vocabulary to represent those experiences. For instance, when the vocabulary of a tribe in a mountainous jungle region has words for rivers and streams but not oceans, how do you translate the notion of an ocean? Or what does a translator do when she or he is faced with the task of translating the biblical verse "Though your sins be as scarlet, they shall be as white as snow" into the language of a tribe that has never experienced snow?

Translations frequently produce misunderstanding or incomprehension because of cultural orientations. For instance, the Quechua language of Peru uses past and future orientations that are the opposite of those used in the English language. Quechua visualizes the past as being in front of or ahead of a person because it can be seen, and it visualizes the future as being behind one because it cannot be seen. Americans instead speak of the past being behind them and the future being ahead. If this difference in cultural orientation were not known or were ignored, translations about time, the past, and the future could be incomprehensible. People could be told to look behind them for what they normally expect to find ahead of them.

Conceptual Equivalence

When two American psychologists ask the Dalai Lama, who speaks perfect English, to discuss the topic of low self-esteem at a conference, the Dalai Lama told them that he would be delighted, but that he did not know what low self-esteem meant. Although the two Americans tried in a variety of ways to explain the concept to the Dalai Lama, he continued to be confused. After countless examples and detailed explanations, the Dalai Lama said he now understood what they were trying to say. He added, however, that the reason he was having trouble with what the Americans were trying to say was that in his culture people did not think poorly of themselves and therefore had no concept of low self-esteem. In this example involving the Dalai Lama you see yet another difficulty in translation—difficulties that deal with a lack of matching concepts. Some concepts are culture-specific (emic) and others culture-general (etic). Triandis believes it is impossible to translate perfectly an emic concept.[153] So different, for instance, are Spanish cultural experiences from the English that many words cannot be translated directly. Strong affection is expressed in English with the verb to love. In Spanish, there are two verbs, *te amo* and *te quiero. Te amo* refers to nurturing love, as between a parent and a child or between two adults. *Te quiero* translates literally as "I want you," which connotes ownership, a concept not present in the English expression "I love you." Commonly used to express love between two adults, *te quiero* falls somewhere between the English statements "I love you" and "I like you."

The Spanish language as spoken in Mexico has at least five terms indicating agreement in varying degrees. These include *me comprometo* (I promise or commit myself), *yo le aseguro* (I assure you), *sí, como no, lo hago* (yes, sure, I will do it), *tal vez lo hago* (maybe I will do it), and *tal vez lo haga* (maybe I might do it). The problem, of course, is to understand the differences between *me comprometo* and *tal vez lo haga* in their cultural sense so that one can render a correct translation. Misunderstandings and confusions may arise if we simply translate each of these phrases of agreement as "okay." Triandis believes that about the only way in which an emic concept can be translated is to attempt to relate it to an etic one and to tie it to the context in which the concept might be used.[154]

What you have seen in this last section of the chapter are some of the difficulties you can encounter when interacting with someone who speaks a language different than your own. What is important to keep in mind is not only that the meanings for specific words need to be considered but that you must also keep in mind the role culture plays in giving meaning to words and phrases. As Reeves points out, you need to also consider such things as (1) the history of the culture, (2) the social and political institutions, (3) the message genre and accompanying vocabulary, and (4) the intentions of the sender. [155]

SUMMARY

- Language is important to human activity because it is how we reach out to make contact with others.
- Language is the primary means of preserving and transmitting culture.
- Language functions to facilitate emotive expression, thought, social interaction, the control of reality, the maintenance of history, and the expression of identity.
- It is impossible to separate our use of language from our culture.
- Symbols (words) and sounds for those symbols vary from culture to culture. The rules (phonology, grammar, syntax, and intonation) for using those symbols and sounds also vary.
- Language serves as a guide to how a culture perceives reality.
- The meanings we have for words are determined by the culture in which we have been raised.
- Cultures "use" language differently when applied to issues of directness, social customs and the value placed on "talk."
- Word usage and meaning are learned, and all cultures and co-cultures have special experiences that frame usage and meaning.
- As the world evolves into a global village, the importance of international communication and language translation takes on added significance.
- African Americans have a distinct language known as Ebonics or African American English Vernacular, which facilitates the creation, maintenance, and expression of their unique culture.
- Women's communication patterns and practices differ in form and substance from those of men.
- Alternative languages are a private vocabulary shared by members of the using co-culture.
- Examining alternative language helps to gain insight into a co-culture and its social realities.
- People tend to assume that text in one language can be accurately translated into another.
- There are difficulties in linguistic equivalence such as vocabulary, idiomatic, grammatical-syntactical, experiential-cultural, and conceptual equivalence.

INFOTRAC COLLEGE EDITION EXERCISES

1. Increasingly in America, state and local governments, as well as business owners have implemented "English-only" policies. Many of these policies have been challenged in court as being discriminatory. Locate and read "Commentary: Are English-only laws wrong?" or use the key word search term "English only" to identify other articles and perspectives on this hotly debated issue. What do you see as the benefits of English-only policies? What do you see as the problems with these policies? Would you support a constitutional amendment making English the official language of the United States? Why or why not? (For more background on this issue, you might wish to also read and locate the following article: "The Varied Voices Of America: Census 2000 Data Tracks an Enormous Increase in the Number of People Who Speak a Language Other than English" by Alison Stein Wellner.)

2. This chapter discusses the difficulties of translating ideas across cultures. Locate and read one of the following articles that describes these challenges: "Here's a Twist: Talk about Translation" (Irina Serebryakova-Collins discusses the differences between American and Russian business letters), "Korean Business Letters: Strategies for Effective Complaints in Cross-Cultural Communication" (Mi Young Park, W. Tracy Dillon, and Kenneth L. Mitchell detail case studies comparing American and Korean complaint letters), and "Dear Friend" (?): Culture and Genre in American and Canadian Direct Marketing Letters" (Roger Graves examines American and Canadian cultural differences). How might language diversity challenges play a role in your future life and career?

3. Want to learn more about differences in the ways in which men and women use language? Locate and read "Why Talk Ain't Cheap: A Conversation with Best-Selling Word Watcher and Author Deborah Tannen." In what ways do your own experiences confirm or dispute Tannen's claims? (Hint: for more on language and gender differences, use the subject search term "Communication" and its subdivision "Sex Differences.")

ACTIVITIES

1. Meet with some of the other students in your class and attempt to invent a new language. Create both the sounds and meanings for the new language.

2. Ask an informant whose native language is not English for examples of expressions from his or her native language that are difficult to translate into English. Idioms are the most likely category in which to find examples. Try to determine why the difficulty exists. What cultural values might these expressions represent?

3. Meet with an informant from a culture for which the native language is not English and discuss the difficulty of trying to make sense out of American English idiomatic statements.

4. Try to think of examples where the alternative language of co-cultures reflects their unique experiences, values, and lifestyles.

5. Visit a class in which English is taught as a second language. Try to distinguish what difficulties the students are experiencing and which, if any, are culturally based.

DISCUSSION IDEAS

1. What problems are associated with language diversity in a country? What are some of the solutions that have been proposed to deal with these problems? Draw examples from the United States and Canada, as well as from any other bilingual or trilingual countries with which you are familiar.

2. What is meant by the phrase "language influences our perceptions and our view of the universe"?

3. Why is foreign language translation so difficult? Try and think of ways in which translation difficulty can be minimized.

4. How can men and women in the United States learn to communicate better with one another?

5. What are some reasons it is difficult to learn a foreign language?

chapter 5

Nonverbal Communication: The Messages of Action, Space, Time, and Silence

Our nature consists in motion.

PASCAL

Do not the most moving moments of our lives find us all without words?

MARCEL MARCEAU

In human intercourse the tragedy begins not when there is misunderstanding about words, but when silence is not understood.

HENRY DAVID THOREAU

In the United States people greet by shaking hands. Arab men often greet by kissing on both checks. In Japan, men greet by bowing, and in Mexico they often embrace. In most Middle Eastern and Asian countries, pointing with the index finger is considered impolite. In Thailand, to signal another person to come near, one moves the fingers back and forth with the palm down. In the United States, you beckon someone to come by holding the palm up and moving the fingers toward your body. In Vietnam that same motion is reserved for someone attempting to summon his or her dog. The Tongans sit down in the presence of superiors; in the West, you stand up. Crossing one's legs in the United States is often a sign of being relaxed; in Korea, it is a social taboo. In Japan, gifts are usually exchanged with both hands. Muslims consider the left hand unclean and do not eat or pass objects with it. Buddha maintained that great insights arrived during moments of silence. In the United States, people talk to arrive at the truth.

The above examples were offered for two reasons. First, we hoped to arouse your interest in nonverbal communication. Second, we wanted to demonstrate that although much of nonverbal communication is universal, many of your nonverbal actions are touched and altered by culture. Hence, this chapter looks at the various ways culture and nonverbal communication work in tandem.

THE IMPORTANCE OF NONVERBAL COMMUNICATION

To appreciate the importance of nonverbal communication to human interaction, re-flect for a moment on the countless times in a single day that you send and receive nonverbal messages. Barnlund highlights some of the reasons why this form of communication is important to the study of intercultural communication:

> Many, and sometimes most, of the critical meanings generated in human encounters are elicited by touch, glance, vocal nuance, gestures, or facial expression with or without the aid of words. From the moment of recognition until the moment of separation, people observe each other with all their senses, hearing pause and intonation, attending to dress and carriage, observing glance and facial tension, as well as noting word choice and syntax. Every harmony or disharmony of signals guides the interpretation of passing mood or enduring attribute. Out of the evaluation of kinetic, vocal and verbal cues, decisions are made to argue or agree, to laugh or blush, to relax or resist, to continue or cut off conversation.[1]

Nonverbal communication can be used to judge internal feelings.

© Robert Fonseca

With just a handful of examples Barnlund makes it extremely clear why nonverbal communication is an indispensable element in human behavior. Let us offer a few additional reasons why we believe any study of intercultural interaction must include information about nonverbal communication.

Judging Internal States

Nonverbal communication is important because people use this message system to express attitudes and emotions. Therefore, it often expresses your internal states. Consciously and unconsciously, intentionally and unintentionally, people make important judgments and decisions concerning the internal states of others—states they often express without words. For example, you evaluate the quality of your relationships according to interpretations of these nonverbal messages. Nonverbal communication is a powerful tool for expressing your emotional and relational feelings toward another person.[2] It is also used to create and manage impressions.[3] From tone of voice, to the distance between you and your partners, to the amount of touching in which you engage, you can gather clues to the closeness of your relationships. Nonverbal communication is so subtle that a shifting of body zones can also send a message. The first time you move from holding hands with your partner to touching his or her face, you are sending a message, and that message takes on added significance if your touch is returned.

If you observe someone with a clenched fist and a grim expression, you do not need words to tell you that this person is not happy. If you hear someone's voice quaver and see his or her hands tremble, you may infer that the person is fearful or anxious, despite what he or she might say. Your emotions are reflected in your posture, face, and eyes—be it fear, joy, anger, or sadness—so you can express them without ever uttering a word. For this reason, most people rely heavily on what they learn through their eyes. In fact, research indicates that you will believe nonverbal messages instead of verbal messages when the two contradict each other.[4] As Heraclitus remarked over two thousand years ago, "Eyes are more accurate witnesses than ears."

Creating Impressions

Nonverbal communication is important in human interaction because it is partially responsible for creating impressions. In fact, in most instances nonverbal messages arrive before the verbal and influence the flow of the interaction. For example, Pauronit conducted a study that clearly demonstrated the effect of first impressions and race on a counseling session involving black and white subjects.[5] What he found is that counselors reacted differently to clients because of their color. Your personal experiences will show you how often your first judgments are based on the color of a person's skin, facial expression, manner of dress, or if he or she is in a wheelchair. Even how you select friends and sexual partners is grounded in first impressions. You often approach certain people because of how attractive you find them, and of course, avoid others because of some rapid decision you made concerning their appearance.

Managing Interaction

A moment of reflection will reveal that managing interaction is one of the most important uses you make of nonverbal communication. That is to say, your nonverbal actions, whether intentional or unintentional, offers your partner clues about the conversation. Among other things, this would include "when to begin a conversation, whose turn it is to speak, how to get a chance to speak, how to signal others to talk more, and how to end a conversation."[6]

From our brief discussion concerning the importance of nonverbal communication and an inventory of your own behavior, it should be obvious that it is omnipresent. You use nonverbal messages to control others, to clarify what you are feeling, and to even mislead others. Guerrero, DeVito, and Hecht are correct when they declare, "Nonverbal communication is all around us."[7]

To better help you understand this important communication component and its role in intercultural communication, we will (1) define nonverbal communication, (2) list its functions, (3) offer some guidelines when studying nonverbal communication, (4) link nonverbal communication to culture, and (5) discuss the major classifications of nonverbal messages. It should be noted that we will begin our discussion of each category of nonverbal communication by noting some of the basic behaviors found in the dominant culture of the United States before relating the classification to other cultures. Knowing what attitudes and behaviors Americans bring to a communication event can help you understand your response to the people you meet.

DEFINING NONVERBAL COMMUNICATION

Because the central concern of this chapter is to examine how and why people communicate nonverbally, and with what consequences in the intercultural setting, we begin with a definition of nonverbal communication. As you discovered in earlier chapters, there is no shortage of definitions for *culture* and *communication*. The same proliferation is characteristic of the term *nonverbal behavior*. We shall, therefore, select a definition that is consistent with current thinking in the field and that reflects the cultural orientation of this book.

We propose that *nonverbal communication involves all those nonverbal stimuli in a communication setting that are generated by both the source and his or her use of the environment and that have potential message value for the source or receiver.* It is not by chance that our definition is somewhat lengthy; we wanted to offer a definition that would not only mark the boundaries of nonverbal communication but would also reflect how the process actually works. Our definition also permits us to include unintentional as well as intentional behavior in the total communication event. This approach is realistic because you send the preponderance of nonverbal messages without ever being aware that they have meaning for other people. In verbal communication, you consciously dip into your vocabulary and decide what words to use. Although you often consciously decide to smile or select a certain piece of jewelry, you also send countless messages that you never intend to be part of the transaction. For example, frowning because of the sun in your eyes may make someone believe you are angry, leaving some shampoo in your hair could make someone think you look silly, and holding someone's hand for an extended period of time could cause that person to think you are flirting when that was not your intent. These are all examples of how your actions, without your blessing, can send a message to someone else.

The sociologist Goffman describes this fusing of intentional and unintentional behavior:

> The expressiveness of the individual (and therefore his capacity to give impressions) appears to involve two radically different kinds of sign activity: the expression that he gives

and the impression that he gives off. The first involves verbal symbols or their substitutes which he uses admittedly and solely to convey the information that he and the other are known to attach to these symbols. This is communication in the traditional and narrow sense. The second involves a wide range of action that others can treat as symptomatic of the actor (communicator), the expectation being that the action was performed for reasons other than the information conveyed in this way.[8]

FUNCTIONS OF NONVERBAL COMMUNICATION

One point should be clear by now: Nonverbal communication is multidimensional. This multidimensional aspect is revealed in the fact that nonverbal communication often interacts with verbal messages. The interfacing of the verbal with the nonverbal carries over to the many uses and functions of nonverbal behavior.[9] Let us examine five of those uses: (1) repeating, (2) complementing, (3) substituting, (4) regulating, and (5) contradicting. Again we remind you that initially we will be describing the dominant culture in the United States before moving on to a discussion of cultural differences in the use of nonverbal communication.

Repeating

In the United States, people often use nonverbal messages to repeat a point they are trying to make. If you were telling someone that what they were proposing was a bad idea, you might move your head from side to side while you were also uttering the word "no." You might hold up a hand in the gesture signifying that a person should stop at the same time you actually use the word *stop*. Or you might point in a certain direction after you have just said, "The new library is south of that building." The gestures and words have a similar meaning and reinforce one another.

Complementing

Closely related to repeating is complementing. Although messages that repeat can stand alone, complementing generally adds more information to messages. For example, you can tell someone that you are pleased with his or her performance, but this message takes on extra meaning if you pat the person on the shoulder at the same time. Physical contact places another layer of meaning on what is being said. Many writers in the area of nonverbal communication refer to this type of message as "accenting" because it accents the idea the speaker is trying to make. You can see how an apology becomes more forceful if your face, as well as your words, is saying, "I'm sorry." You also can accent your anger by speaking in a voice that is much louder than the one you employ in normal conversation.

Substituting

In the United States people substitute nonverbal communication when they perform some action instead of speaking. If you see a very special friend, you are apt to enlarge the size of your smile and throw open your arms to greet him or her, which is a substitute for all the words it would take to convey the same feeling. If a group of people is boisterous, you might place your index finger to your lips as an alternative to saying,

"Please calm down so that I can speak." Or if you object to someone's behavior, you might roll your eyes back as a way of "voicing" your disapproval.

Regulating

You often regulate and manage your communication by using some form of nonverbal behavior: You nod your head in agreement to indicate to your communication partner that you agree and that he or she should continue talking, or you remain silent for a moment and let the silence send the message that you are ready to begin to give the other person a chance to talk. A parent might engage in "stern" and direct eye contact with a child as a way of "telling" him or her to terminate the naughty behavior. In short, your nonverbal behavior helps you control the situation.

Contradicting

On some occasions, your nonverbal actions send signals opposite from the literal meanings contained in your verbal messages. You tell someone you are relaxed and at ease, yet your voice quavers and your hands shake. It also is a contradictory message when you inform your partner that you are glad to see him or her, but at the same time you are sulking and breaking eye contact. Because people rely mostly on nonverbal messages when they receive conflicting data, you need to be aware of the dangers inherent in sending opposing messages. As the German psychiatrist Sigmund Freud noted, "Though we may lie with our lips, betrayal oozes out of us at every pore."

STUDYING NONVERBAL COMMUNICATION: GUIDELINES AND LIMITATIONS

Because the study of nonverbal communication has been popularized in recent years, this complex and multifaceted topic is often misunderstood. Therefore, we need to pause before pursuing the topic any further and mention some potential problems associated with this important area of study.

Nonverbal Communication Is Often Ambiguous

We alluded to the first problem in the study of nonverbal communication earlier when we discussed the intentional and unintentional nature of nonverbal communication. Simply stated, nonverbal communication can be ambiguous. Wood clearly underscores this point when she writes, "We can never be sure that others understand the meanings we intended to express with our nonverbal behavior."[10] Not only are there cultural differences in what a specific action means (in the United States the number one is communicated with the forefinger, in parts of Europe it is the thumb that carries that message), but also nonverbal communication is also contextual. The ambiguity of context is clearly seen if someone brushes your leg on an elevator—was it merely an accident or an aggressive sexual act? Our point should be obvious: When you use nonverbal communication, you need to be aware of the ambiguous nature of this form of interaction. Or as Osborn and Motley tell us, "Meanings and interpretations of nonverbal behaviors often are on very shaky ground."[11]

We Are More Than Our Culture

The next problem relates to individual differences. Simply stated, not all people in a particular culture engage in the same nonverbal actions. As have stated elsewhere, you are all more than your culture. You might, for example, note that many Native American children avoid direct eye contact as a sign of respect; yet because of individual differences, there may well be exceptions to this assertion, and you could encounter a Native American child who looks you directly in the eye. Remember, people are the products of not only their culture but also their regions, occupations, political affiliations, educational backgrounds, and countless other associations that have shaped their perceptions, values, attitudes, beliefs, and nonverbal communication.

Nonverbal Communication Seldom Operates in Isolation

Finally, there is the problem of forgetting that nonverbal behaviors seldom occur in isolation. And although in the remainder of this chapter we examine individual categories and messages, in reality messages are but part of the total communication context. As we noted earlier, you usually send many nonverbal cues simultaneously, and these cues are normally linked to both our verbal messages and the setting in which you find yourself.

NONVERBAL COMMUNICATION AND CULTURE

While much of your nonverbal communication is "part of a universally recognized and understood code,"[12] a great deal of your nonverbal behavior is rooted in your culture. Rosenblatt expressed this important idea in the following manner: "What emotions are felt, how they are expressed, and how they are understood are matters of culture."[13] Rosenblatt is, of course, correct. From your use of eye contact to the amount of volume you employ during an interaction, your culture influences the manner in which you send and receive nonverbal symbols. For example, in many cultures, outward signs of emotion are accepted as natural. People from the Middle East and the Mediterranean are generally expressive and animated. For the Japanese, excessive and public displays of emotion are often considered a mark of rudeness, a lack of control, and even an invasion of another person's privacy.[14]

The key point is that learning about the alliance between culture and nonverbal behavior is useful to students of intercultural communication. Hall underscores the need to learn about nonverbal communication in the following manner:

> I am convinced that much of our difficulty with people in other countries stems from the fact that so little is known about cross-communication. . . . Formal training in the language, history, government, and customs of another nation is only the first step in a comprehensive program. Of equal importance is an introduction to the nonverbal language which exists in every country of the world and among the various groups within each country. Most Americans are only dimly aware of this silent language even though they use it everyday.[15]

By understanding the important cultural differences in nonverbal behavior, you will be able to gather clues about underlying attitudes and values. You have already seen that nonverbal communication often reveals basic cultural traits. Smiling and shaking hands tells us that a culture values amiability. Bowing tells you that another values formality and rank and status. It is not by chance that Hindus greet each other by placing their palms together in front of them while slightly tilting their heads down; this salutation reflects the belief that the deity exists in everyone, not in a single form.

The importance of nonverbal communication, and its significance to the study of intercultural communication, is made even more apparent if you recall from Chapter 2 that culture is invisible, omnipresent, and learned. Nonverbal communication has these same qualities. Hall alerts us to the invisible aspect of culture and nonverbal communication by employing phrases such as "silent language" and "hidden dimension." Andersen makes much the same point by telling you, "Individuals are aware of little of their own nonverbal behavior, which is enacted mindlessly, spontaneously, and unconsciously."[16] Both of these scholars are saying that much of your nonverbal behavior, like culture, tends to be elusive, spontaneous, and frequently beyond your awareness.

We also remind you that culture is all-pervasive, multidimensional, and boundless; it is everywhere and in everything. The same is true of nonverbal behavior.[17] Your clothes and jewelry, the countless expressions you can reflect with your face, the hundreds of movements you can make with your body, where and how you touch people, your gaze and eye contact, vocal behaviors such as laughter, and your use of time, space, and silence are just some of the behaviors in which you engage that serve as messages.

Another parallel between culture and nonverbal behavior is that both need to be learned. Although much of outward behavior is innate (such as smiling, moving, touching, eye contact), you are not born knowing the communication dimensions associated with nonverbal messages. First, we offer a word about some exceptions to this notion before we develop this relationship between learning and nonverbal communication. Research supports the view that because people are all from one species, a general and common genetic inheritance produces universal facial expressions for most of your basic emotions (for example, fear, happiness, anger, surprise, disgust, and sadness).[18] Most scholars would agree, however, that "cultures formulate display rules that dictate when, how, and with what consequences nonverbal expressions will be exhibited."[19] Macionis summarized this important principle in the following manner:

> People the world over experience the same basic emotions. But what sparks a particular emotion, how and where a person expresses it, and how people define emotions in general vary as matters of culture. In global perspective, therefore, everyday life differs not only in terms of how people think and act, but how they infuse their lives with feelings.[20]

CLASSIFICATIONS OF NONVERBAL COMMUNICATION

Most classifications divide nonverbal messages into two comprehensive categories: those that are primarily produced by the body (appearance, movement, facial expressions, eye contact, touch, smell, and paralanguage); and those that the individual combines with the setting (space, time, and silence).

Body Behavior

General Appearance
From hair sprays to hairpieces, from reducing diets to twenty-four-hour fitness centers, from false eyelashes to blue contact lenses, people show their concern for how they look—and we support a multibillion-dollar industry in the process. And how do we

calculate the price you pay in mental anguish over your personal appearance should you not quite measure up to the ideal the culture demands of you? It seems most of you believe the words of philosopher Thomas Fuller: "By the husk you may judge the nut." For most people in the United States, the husk should be flawless. Very early in life most people realize that outward appearances, as revealed in "our sex, clothing style, race, age, ethnicity, stature, body type, and mood all reveal our physical persona."[21] Reflect for a moment on how you make judgments of other people based on personal appearance, dress, and the objects people carry around or place on their bodies. Studies show that being overweight in the United States reduces income, lowers the chances of getting married, and helps decrease the amount of education one receives.[22] When deciding whether or not to strike up a conversation with a total stranger, you are influenced by the way that person looks. One study pointed out that people made decisions about the future success of blind dates based completely on physical appearance.[23] What you are doing by using a person's appearance is summarized by Ruben when he says we make inferences (often faulty) about a person's "intelligence, gender, age, approachability, financial well-being, class, tastes, values, and cultural background" from attractiveness, dress, and personal artifacts.[24] Your culture's obsession with appearance is so deep-seated, and begins so early in life, that, as one study revealed, even very young children select friends based on appearance.[25]

Skin color is perhaps the most obvious example of how general appearance is linked to perception and communication. As Vazquez points out, "skin color is the first racial marker children recognize and can be considered the most salient of phenotypic attributes."[26] Skin color "may also be the basis of the allocation of economic and psychological privileges to individuals relative to the degree those privileges are awarded to valued members of the dominant culture."[27]

Judgments of Beauty. Concern with how one appears is not confined to the United States. It is ancient and universal. As far back as the Upper Paleolithic period (about forty thousand years ago), your ancestors were using bone for necklaces and other bodily ornaments. From that period to the present, historical and archaeological evidence has shown that people are fixated on their bodies. They have painted them, fastened objects to them, dressed them, undressed them, and even deformed and mutilated them in the name of beauty. As the anthropologist Keesing has written, "The use of the body for decoration appears to be a cultural universal."[28] Face painting is still common in parts of Africa, in South America, and among some Native American tribes. In Ethiopia and Eritrea many women still utilize facial tattoos as "beauty marks."[29] And of course, many women in the United States use lipstick and other forms of makeup to alter their features.

In intercultural communication, appearance is important because the standards you apply and the judgments you make are subject to cultural interpretations. In the United States, people tend to value the appearance of tall, slender women, but in many other cultures, the definition of what is attractive calls forth a series of different images.[30] In Japan, diminutive females are deemed the most attractive. In Africa we can see yet another definition of physical attractiveness. Richmond and Gestrin observe:

> Ideas of pulchritude in Africa differ from those of Europe and the Americas. In traditional
> African societies, plumpness is considered a sign of beauty, health and wealth, and slimness
> is evidence of unhappiness or disease or that a woman is being mistreated by her husband.[31]

Buxom and stout people are also valued in parts of Russia. There is a Russian proverb that states, "One need not worry about being fat, just only about being hungry."

Among the Chinese you can see yet another cultural standard for female attractiveness. As Wenzhong and Grove note, "Many women keep their hairstyles simple (often one or two braids) and make little attempt to draw attention to themselves through self-decoration such as colorful scarves, jewelry, or makeup."[32]

As you would suspect, the judgment of beauty across cultures is a perception that is ripe for ethnocentrism. Remland offers an excellent example of this ethnocentrism when he reminds us that "what is seen as beautiful in one culture may look hideous to people from another culture."[33] Remland adds:

> The many exotic rituals we often see in PBS documentaries or in the pages of *National Geographic,* such as neck stretching, lip enlargements, earlobe plugs, teeth filing, and so on represent the beautifying practices common in many parts of the world. Of course, liposuction, hair implants, face-lifts, laser surgery, and the like, while not the least bit extraordinary to many westerners, may seem abhorrent to people from other parts of the world.[34]

Because cultures are dynamic, it might be interesting to observe if perceptions of attractiveness begin to change in Japan, Africa, Russia, and China as these cultures come into greater contact with Western cultures.

Attire. Clothing, as Joseph states, "is very much a social artifact—a form of communication—which can best be understood by sociological concepts."[35] Clothing is also a reflection of a culture's value orientation. Whether it is military attire, clothes as status,

Many of the world's people still dress in their traditional attire.

© Robert Fonseca

uniforms, or costumes, clothing offers clues into a culture's view of the world.[36] For example, modesty is highly valued among Arabs. In most instances, "Girls are not allowed to participate in swimming classes because of the prohibitions against exposing their bodies."[37] Al-Kaysi points out other links between modesty and dress when he discusses the attire of Muslim women: "The main garment must be a 'flowing' one, that is, woman must avoid tight or clinging clothes which exaggerate her figure, or any part of it, such as breasts, legs or arms."[38] Arab women also cover their hair with scarves. The link between cultural values and clothing is also seen among Filipinos. Gochenour tells us, "Values relating to status and authority are the root of the Filipino's need to dress correctly."[39] Of the German culture, Hall and Hall write:

> Correct behavior is symbolized by appropriate and very conservative dress. The male business uniform is a freshly pressed, dark suit and tie with a plain shirt and dark shoes and socks. It is important to emulate this conservative approach to both manners and dress. Personal appearance, like the exterior appearance of their homes, is very important to Germans.[40]

The Spanish also link appearance to one's rank, as Ruch asserts: "Historically, dress has denoted social status."[41] In Spain, it is not uncommon to see people of high status wearing a suit and tie in very hot weather.

Perhaps nowhere in the world is the merger between attire and a culture's value system more evident than in Japan. McDaniel makes the connection when he writes: "The proclivity for conservative dress styles and colors emphasizes the nation's collectivism and, concomitantly, lessens the potential for social disharmony arising from nonconformist attire."[42]

In much of the world, people still dress in their traditional garments. For Arab men, says Ruch, correct business attire would "include a long loose robe called a *dishdasha* or *thobe* and a headpiece, a white cloth *kaffiya* banded by a black egal to secure it."[43] Islamic law also says that men should try to refrain from bright colors.[44]

As we have noted, for Muslims clothing is much more than apparel to cover the body. Torrawa points out this same idea when he writes, "The connection between recompense and garment is an organic in Arabic."[45] What Torrawa is saying is that as is the case with so many aspects of culture, there is often a "below the surface" reason for our actions. This deep structure and its tie to attire in the Arab world are eloquently explained by Torrawa:

> In all its guises, clothing inscribes ideologies of truth and deception, echoing the words of Scripture, and revealing—and unraveling—that honor can only be attained when every robe donned is a robe of honor and every garment a garment of piety.[46]

Whether it is Sikhs in white turbans, Japanese in kimonos, Hasidic Jews in blue yarmulkes, or Africans in white dashikis, or even the black attire of the Amish in the United States, you need to learn to be tolerant of external differences so that you do not let these differences impede communication. What you might consider quite a garish costume or excessive formality in dress may very likely be a reflection of a culture's particular set of values.

Even co-cultures are defined by nonverbal communication nuances. DeFleur, Kearney, and Plax observe that for many African Americans, "Clothing provides not only a functional purpose, but also a 'costume.'"[47] Some writers contend that differences in women's and men's clothing in the United States are due to more than physical differences. They argue that since the Victorian period, the male-dominated culture has encouraged women to wear clothing that restricts their movements, limits their activity, and produces an image of submissiveness and frailty.[48]

Body Movement: Kinesics

People have always known that actions communicate. As Benjamin Franklin said, "None preaches better than the ant, and she says nothing." The study of how movement communicates is called *kinesics*. The basic assumption of this important message system is clearly highlighted by Morreale, Spitzberg, and Barge: "How people hold themselves, stand, sit, and walk communicates strong nonverbal messages. Whether you intend to send a message or not, every move you make potentially communications something about you to others."[49] Specifically, kinesic cues are those visible body shifts and movements that can send messages about (1) your attitude toward the other person (standing face-to-face with a friend, called direct body orientation, or leaning forward may show that you are relaxed), (2) your emotional state (tapping on the table or playing with coins can mean you are nervous), and (3) your desire to control your environment (motioning someone to come closer means you want to talk to him or her).

Because scholars have suggested that people can make as many as 700,000 distinct physical signs, any attempt at cataloging them would be frustrating and fruitless. Our purpose is simply to call your attention to the idea that while all people use movement to communicate, culture teaches you how to use and interpret these movements. In the upcoming sections, we look at a few cultural differences in posture, sitting behavior, and movements of the body that convey specific meanings (gestures). Before we begin, we must once again remind you that in most instances the messages the body generates operate only in combination with other messages. People usually smile and say hello to a friend at the same time. In Mexico, this is illustrated when asking someone to wait for "just a minute" (*un momento, por favor*): The speaker also makes a fist and then extends the thumb and index finger so that they form a sideways *U*.

Posture. Posture and sitting habits offer insight into a culture's deep structure. We can see the bond between culture and values by simply looking at the Japanese, Thai, and Indian cultures. In Japan and other Asian cultures, the bow is much more than a greeting. It signifies that culture's concern with status and rank. In Japan, for example, low posture is an indicator of respect.[50] Although it appears simple to the outsider, the bowing ritual is actually rather complicated. The person who occupies the lower station begins the bow, and his or her bow must be deeper than the other person's. The superior, on the other hand, determines when the bowing is to end. When the participants are of equal rank, they begin the bow in the same manner and end at the same time. The Thai people use a similar movement called the *wai*. The *wai* movement—which is made by pressing both hands close together in front of one's body, with the fingertips reaching to about neck level—is used to show respect. The lower the head comes to the hands, the more respect is shown.[51] You can see yet another greeting pattern in India. Here the posture when greeting someone is directly linked with the idea that Hindus see God in everything—including other people. The *namaskar* (Indian greeting) is carried out by a slight bow with the palms of both hands together, the fingertips at the chin.[52]

In the United States, where being casual and friendly is valued, people, consciously or unconsciously, act out this value by the way they drop into a chair or how they slouch when they stand. In many countries, such as Germany and Sweden, where lifestyles tend to be more formal, slouching is considered a sign of rudeness and poor manners. In fact, according to Nees, "German children are still taught to sit and stand up straight, which is a sign of good character. Slouching is seen as a sign of a poor upbringing."[53] In Belgium, putting one's hands in one's pockets is a sign of disrespect. Cultures also differ in the body orientations they assume during communication. For example, Arabs use a very direct body orientation when communicating. The Chinese, on the other hand, tend to feel uncomfortable with this style and normally will carry out their business in a less direct stance.

The manner in which you sit also can communicate a message. Remland offers an excellent example of this type of message: "An innocent act of ankle-to-knee leg crossing, typical of most American males, could be mistaken for insult (a showing of the sole of the foot gesture) in Saudi Arabia, Egypt, Singapore, or Thailand."[54] And according to Ruch, the same seemingly simple act is extremely offensive when doing business in Ghana and in Turkey.[55] People in Thailand also believe there is something special about the bottoms of the feet. For them the feet are the lowest part of the body and they should never be pointed in the direction of another person.[56] For the Thai, the feet take on so much significance that people avoid stomping with them.

Even within the United States, there are differences in how people move, stand, and sit during interaction. Women often hold their arms closer to their bodies than do men. They usually keep their legs closer together and seldom cross them in mixed company. Their posture is also more restricted and less relaxed than the posture of males. Most research in the area of gender communication concludes that these differences are related to issues such as status, power, and affiliation.[57] Posture and stance also play an important role in the African American co-culture. This is most evident in the walk employed by many young African Americans males. According to Hecht, Collier, and Ribeau, "The general form of the walk is slow and casual with the head elevated and tipped to one side, one arm swinging and the other held limply."[58] The walk, says the *San Diego Union-Tribune*, "shows the dominant culture that you are strong and proud, despite your status in American society."[59]

Gestures. The power of gestures as a form of communication is reflected in the fact that the co-culture of the deaf in the United States has a rich and extensive vocabulary composed of gestures. Another example of the power of gestures can be found in the hand signals used by various urban gangs. The slightest variation in performing a certain gesture can be the catalyst for a violent confrontation.

Andersen offers an excellent introduction to the complex and all-pervasive nature of gestures when he writes, "Gestures are both innate and learned. They are used in all cultures, tend to be tied to speech processes, and are usually automatic."[60] We would also add that many gestures, like all the nonverbal behaviors in this chapter, have a strong connection to culture. For example, an Arabic specialist once cataloged 247 separate gestures that Arabs use while speaking.[61] And, in a large study involving forty different cultures, Morris and his associates isolated twenty common hand gestures that had a different meaning in each culture.[62]

Because there are thousands of gestures found in every culture, we do not intend to offer a taxonomy that is all-inclusive or complete. Such a listing could fill the remaining pages of this book. Instead, it is our purpose to present but a few examples that will assist you in seeing the link between gestures and culture. Rather than presenting a random cataloging of these gestures we will look at *pointing, idiosyncratic gestures, beckoning, acceptance and understanding,* and *variations related to the amount and size of the gestures.*

In the United States *pointing* is a very common gesture. Americans point to objects and at people with the index finger. Directions are even given by pointing in one direction or another with the index finger. Germans point with the little finger, and the Japanese point with the entire hand, palms up. In much of Asia, pointing with the index finger at a person is considered rude.[63]

As we have already indicated, there are a limitless number of *idiosyncratic* gestures found in each culture. These are the gestures whose meaning are the feature and property of a particular culture. For example, in Argentina, one twists an imaginary mustache to signify that everything is "okay." In the United States, "making a circle with one's thumb and index finger while extending the others is emblematic of the word 'OK'; in Japan (and Korea) it signifies 'money' (*okane*); and among Arabs this gesture is usually accompanied by a baring of teeth, and together they signify extreme hostility."[64] This same gesture to a Tunisian means "I'll kill you."

Many sexual connotation gestures are also tied to a certain culture. In the United States someone might use the middle finger to send an insulting obscene gesture. This sexual insult gesture is not universal. For example, the gesture we discussed in the last paragraph (forming an O with the thumb and index finger) is, according to Lynch and Hanson, "an obscene gesture among some Latino cultures."[65] In the Italian culture the gesture referring to someone as a homosexual is moving the finger behind your ear.[66] Because sexual connotation gestures can be misunderstood and offensive, it is important to make sure you identify these gestures before you begin interacting with people for a specific culture.

The taken-for-granted sign we make for *beckoning* is also culturally based. In the United States, when a person wants to signal a friend to come, he or she usually makes the gesture with one hand, palm up, fingers more or less together and moving toward his or her body. Koreans express this same idea by cupping "the hand with the palm down and drawing the fingers toward the palm."[67] When seeing this gesture, many Americans think the other person is waving good-bye. In parts of Burma, the summoning gesture is made palm down, with the fingers moving as though playing the piano. Filipinos often summon someone with a quick downward nod of the head. In Germany and much of Scandinavia, tossing the head back makes a beckoning motion. For many Arabs, holding the right hand out, palm upward, and opening and closing the hand perform nonverbally asking someone to "come here."[68] And in Spain, to beckon someone you stretch your arm out, palm downward, and make a scratching motion toward your body with your fingers.

Head movements denoting *acceptance and understanding* represent another example of how some gestures are rooted in culture. In the United States moving your head up and down is seen as a sign of understanding and agreement. This same movement can have different meanings in different cultures. As Lynch and Hanson point out, "This same gesture is interpreted quite differently in many other cultures. Among Asian, Native American, Middle Eastern, and Pacific Island groups, it often means, 'I hear you speaking.' It does not signal that the listener understands the message nor does it suggest that he or she agrees."[69] Greeks express "yes" with a nod similar to the one used in the United States, but when communicating "no," they jerk their heads back and raise their faces. Lifting one or both hands up to the shoulders strongly emphasizes the "no."

There are also cultural differences regarding the *amount and size of gestures* employed during a communication encounter. Jews, Mexicans, Arabs, Greeks, and South American cultures are quite animated when they interact. This intensity toward gesturing is also found among Italians. As Falassi and Flower note, "Speaking with their hands—or all their bodies in fact—is in tune with the Italian love of theatrics, and their native gusto for social interaction."[70] Members of many Asian cultures perceive such outward activity quite differently, often equating vigorous action with a lack of manners and restraint.[71] And according to Lewis, "Arms are used very little by Nordics during conversation."[72] Germans are also made uncomfortable by gestures that are, by their standards, too flamboyant. Ruch offers the following advice to American executives who work with German corporations: Hands should be used with calculated dignity. They should never serve as lively instruments to emphasize points in conversation. The entire game plan is to appear calm under pressure.[73]

You can also see the significance of gestures by looking at various co-cultures. For example, as compared to males, women tend to use fewer and smaller gestures.[74] African Americans value a lively and expressive form of communication and hence display a greater variety of movements than whites when interacting.[75]

Facial Expressions

At one time or another, most people have been intrigued by how the looks on other people's faces have influenced their reactions to them. The early Greek playwrights and the Kabuki actors of Japan were keenly aware of the shifts in mood and meaning that facial expressions conveyed. Both forms of drama used masks and extensive makeup to demonstrate differences in each actor's character and attitude. Whether it be the Mexican adage that "One's face is the mirror of one's soul," or the Yiddish proverb that states "The face tells the secret," people everywhere have been captivated by the face.

The importance of facial expressions in communication is well established; however, the intercultural implications of these expressions are difficult to assess. At the core of a lingering academic debate lies this question: Is there a nearly universal language of facial expressions? One position holds that anatomically similar expressions may occur in everyone, but the meanings people attach to them differ from culture to culture.[76] The majority opinion, which we introduced earlier in the chapter, is that there are universal facial expressions for which people have similar meanings. Ekman advances this point of view: "The subtle creases of a grimace tell the same story around the world, to preliterate New Guinea tribesmen, to Japanese and American college students alike. Darwin knew it all along, but now here's hard evidence that culture does not control the face."[77] What is being presented is the theory that there is "a basic set of at least six facial expressions that are innate, universal, and carry the same basic meaning throughout the world."[78] These six pancultural and universal facial expressions are happiness, sadness, fear, anger, disgust, and surprise.

Despite the biological-based nature of facial expressions, there seem to be clear cultural expectations as to how cultural norms often dictate when, how, and to whom facial expressions are displayed.[79] As Matsumoto declares, "Different cultures recognize the power of the face and produce many rules to regulate not only what kinds of facial behavior are permitted in social interaction, but also how it may be even to attend to the faces of others during interaction."[80] A few specific examples will illustrate the role of culture in the production and interpretation of facial expressions.

In many Mediterranean cultures, people exaggerate signs of grief or sadness. It is not uncommon in this region of the world to see men crying in public. Yet in the United States, white males suppress the desire to show these emotions. Japanese men even go so far as to hide expressions of anger, sorrow, or disgust by laughing or smiling.[81] In one study, Japanese and American subjects revealed the same facial expressions when viewing a stress-inducing film while they were alone. However, when viewing the film in the presence of others, the Japanese manifested only neutral facial expressions. Min-Sun Kim says that Koreans also withhold emotion and do not engage in animated facial expressions.[82] The Chinese also do not readily show emotion for reasons that are related to a cultural value—that value is the concept of saving face. For the Chinese, displaying too much emotion violates face-saving norms by disrupting harmony and causing conflict.[83]

The smile is yet another emotional display that is linked to one's culture. Everyone is born knowing how to smile. Yet the amount of smiling, the stimulus that produces the smile, and even what the smile is communicating often shifts from culture to culture. As Kraut and Johnson note, culture can "influence smiling both by determining the interpretation of events, which affects the cause of happiness, and by shaping display roles, which determine when it is socially appropriate to smile."[84] In America, a smile can be a sign of happiness or friendly affirmation and is usually used with great regularity. In the German culture, according to Nees, a smile "is used with far more discretion, generally only with those persons one knows and really likes."[85] In the Japanese culture, the smile can also mask an emotion or be used to avoid answering a question.[86] People of lower status in Japan may also use the smile "to denote acceptance of a command or order by a person of higher status when in fact they feel anger or contempt for the order or the person giving the order."[87] In Korean culture, too much smiling is often perceived as the sign of a shallow person. Dresser notes that this "lack of smiling by Koreans has often been misinterpreted as a sign of hostility."[88] Thais, on the other hand, smile much of the time. In fact, Thailand has been called the "Land of Smiles."[89]

There are, of course, countless idiosyncratic facial expressions that are the exclusive domain of a particular culture. Remland presents just a few of these that clearly illustrate the unique character of some facial expressions:

> In Saudi Arabia we can call someone a liar by rapidly moving our tongue in and out of our mouth; in Greece we can say no by raising and lowering our eyebrows once. If we speak out of turn in southern China and Tibet and want to apologize, we can protrude the tip of our tongue and then immediately withdraw it.[90]

Some of these special facial expressions can be troublesome. As Lynch and Hanson note, smiling "is problematic in Indonesia where bared teeth suggest aggression."[91]

Even within a culture, there are groups that use facial expressions differently from the dominant culture. Summarizing the research on gender differences, Pearson, West, and Turner report that, compared to men, women use more facial expressions and are more expressive, smile more, are more apt to return smiles, and are more attracted to others who smile.[92]

Eye Contact and Gaze

In drama, fiction, poetry, and music, eyes have always been a fascinating topic—from Shakespeare's "Thou tell'st me there is murder in mine eye" to Bob Dylan's "Your eyes said more to me that night than your lips would ever say." Even the "evil eye" is more than just an expression. In one study, Roberts examined 186 cultures throughout the world and found that 67 of them had some belief in the evil eye.[93] Zuniga highlights the power of the "evil eye" (*mal ojo*) in Mexico and Puerto Rico with the following observation: "Mal ojo is believed to be the result of excessive admiration and desire on the part of another. Mothers may isolate their children for fear of having one become victim of mal ojo."[94] The Korean culture also has a distinctive approach to eye contact that underscores its significance to human communication. They have the term nunch'i, which means communicating with the eyes. This style of eye contact is so important that Robinson maintains it causes "miscommunication between Westerners and all Asians."[95]

The reason the eyes are such an important communication tool is that the number of messages we can send with our eyes is nearly limitless. We have all heard some of the following words used to describe a person's eyes: direct, sensual, sardonic, expressive, intelligent, penetrating, sad, cheerful, worldly, hard, trusting, and suspicious. The impact of eye contact, gaze, staring and even pupil dilation on human interaction is seen in the fact that people use less eye contact when they are depressed, suffer from low self-esteem, and are uncomfortable in a particular situation.[96] According to Leathers, there is ample evidence to conclude that in the United States, eyes serve six important communication functions: they "(1) indicate degrees of attentiveness, interest, and arousal; (2) influence attitude change and persuasion; (3) regulate interaction; (4) communicate emotions; (5) define power and status relationships; and (6) assume a central role in impression management."[97]

Most studies, as well as your personal observations, tell you that culture modifies the amount of eye contact in which we engage and who is the recipient of the eye contact. For the dominant culture in the United States, eye contact is highly valued.[98] In fact, most people in Western societies expect the person with whom they are interacting to "look them in the eye." There is even a tendency in North America to be suspicious of someone who does not follow the culturally prescribed rules for eye contact. So important is this interpersonal skill that one popular communication textbook offered the following advice to its readers: "You can improve your eye contact by becoming conscious of looking at people when you are talking to them. If you find your eyes straying away from that person, work to regain direct contact."[99] The key word in the above sentence is direct. For direct eye-to-eye contact is not a custom throughout the world. In many cultures direct eye contact is a taboo or an insult. In Japan, for example, prolonged eye contact is considered rude, threatening, and disrespectful.[100] Dresser points out that "people from Latin American and Caribbean cultures also avoid eye contact as a sign of respect."[101] This same orientation toward eye contact is found in Africa. Richmond and Gestrin tell us, "Making eye contact when communicating with a person who is older or of higher status is considered a sign of disrespect or even aggression in many parts of Africa where respect is shown by lowering the eyes."[102] There is even a Zulu saying that states, "The eye is an organ of aggression."

Eye contact often reflects a cultural value. India and Egypt are two good examples of eye contact mirroring a cultural value. According to Luckmann, "In India, the amount of eye contact that is appropriate depends on one's social position (people of different socioeconomic classes avoid eye contact with each other)."[103] In Egypt the issue is not social status but rather gender. "Women and men who are strangers may avoid eye contact out of modesty and respect for religious rules."[104]

Problems can arise when Westerners interact with cultures that practice prolonged eye contact with their communication counterpart. Arabs look directly into the eyes of their communication partner, and do so for long periods. They believe such contact shows interest in the other person and helps them assess the truthfulness of the other person's words.[105] Germans also engage in very direct eye contact. This point and some of the problems that can arise from this behavior are noted by Nees:

> Germans will look you directly in the eye while talking, something which some Americans find vaguely annoying or disconcerting. From the German point of view this is a sign of honesty and true interest in the conversation. For Americans it can seem too intense and direct.[106.]

In America, the prolonged stare is often a part of the nonverbal code that the co-culture of the male homosexual employs. An extended stare, along with other nonverbal messages, at a member of the same sex is often perceived as a signal of interest and sexual suggestion.[107] A few other differences in the use of eye contact in the United States are worthy of our consideration. The Hopi interpret direct eye contact as offensive and usually will avoid any type of staring. The Navajos dislike unbroken eye contact so strongly that they have incorporated it into their creation myth. The myth, which tells the story of a "terrible monster called He-Who-Kills-With-His-Eyes," teaches the Navajo child "a stare is literally an evil eye and implies a sexual and aggressive assault."[108] This same uncomfortable feeling toward direct and prolonged eye contact can be found among Mexican Americans. As Parnell and Paulanka note,

Touch can send messages about what you are thinking and feeling.

© Larry Samovar

"Mexican-Americans consider sustained eye contact when speaking directly to someone rude. Direct eye contact with superiors may be interpreted as insolence. Avoiding direct eye contact with superiors is a sign of respect."[109]

Differences in the use of eye contact also characterize communication between African Americans and white Americans. When speaking, African Americans use much more continuous eye contact than do whites, yet the reverse is true when they are listening. That is, whites make more continuous eye contact when they are listening than do African Americans.[110] This difference, say La France and Mayo, is even more pronounced among African American children, who are "socialized into not looking when being spoken to."[111]

There also are gender variations among members of the dominant culture in how people use their eyes to communicate. For example, "Both sexes signal interest and involvement with others by making eye contact, but men also use it to challenge others or to assert their status and power."[112] In addition, research on the subject indicates that in most instances, women maintain more eye contact than do men; women look at other women more and hold eye contact longer with one another than do men.[113] We should add that gender characteristics regarding eye contact vary from culture to culture. As we noted earlier, in cultures where gender segregation is the norm (India, Saudi Arabia, etc.) direct eye contact between men and women is avoided.[114]

As you might imagine, eye contact is also an important consideration when communicating with a member of the deaf community. Without visual contact, American Sign Language could not be used. Turning your back to someone who is "signing" is essentially the same as ignoring him or her. So delicate is the use of eye contact that you seldom realize the modifications you make. For example, the next time you are talking with a disabled person, perhaps someone in a wheelchair, notice how little eye contact you make with him or her as compared with someone who is not disabled.

Touch

Touch, like your words and movements, are messages about what you are thinking and feeling. The meanings you assign to being touched, and your reasons for touching others, help you gain insight into the communication encounter, as the character Holden Caulfield vividly helps illustrate in the American classic *The Catcher in the Rye*:

> I held hands with her all the time. This doesn't sound like much, but she was terrific to hold hands with. Most girls if you hold hands with them their god damn hand dies, or else they think they have to keep moving their hand all the time, as if they were afraid they'd bore you or something.[115]

Touch is the earliest sense to mature; it manifests itself in the final embryonic stage and comes into its own long before eyes, ears, and the higher brain centers begin to work. Soon after birth, infants begin to employ their other senses to interpret reality. During the same period, they are highly involved with touch: They are being nuzzled, cuddled, cleaned, patted, kissed, and in many cases breast-fed. So important is touch to human communication that researchers now know that people who are denied "caregivers' touch" can have serious biochemical and emotional problems.[116] The American playwright Tennessee Williams eloquently expressed the power of touch when he wrote, "Devils can be driven out of the heart by the touch of a hand on a hand, or a mouth on a mouth."

As you move from infancy into childhood, you learn the rules of touching. You are taught whom to touch and where they may be touched. A set of cultural regulations and an emphasis on other modes of communication replace childhood desires to touch and be touched. By the time you reach adolescence, your culture has taught you how to communicate with touch. Consciously and unconsciously, like culture itself, you use touch out of social politeness, for sex, consolation, support, and control.[117] In the United States, people learn to shake hands with nearly everyone (making sure it is a firm shake), hug certain people (but not everyone with the same intensity), be intimate with still other people (knowing well in advance the zones of the body that you can touch), and make love to one person (being aware of the sexual regions defined by culture and sex manuals).

You need only watch the news on television or stand at an international airport to know that there are major differences in how cultures use touch, even in the simple act of greeting or saying good-bye. In a study involving touch behavior among culturally diverse couples at an international airport, Andersen offers the following narrative of some of their findings:

> A family leaving for Tonga formed a circle, wove their arms around each other's back, and prayed and chanted together. A tearful man returning to Bosnia repeatedly tried to leave his sobbing wife; each time he turned back to her, they would grip each other by the fingertips and exchange a passionate, tearful kiss and a powerful embrace. Two Korean couples departed without any touch, despite the prolonged separation that lay ahead of them.[118]

Let us look at a few other cultural examples so that you see the link between culture and touch. As we have said elsewhere, Muslims, because of religious and social traditions, eat and do other things with the right hand, but to greet with the left can be a social insult. The right hand is used to engage in basic biological functions. Many Asians also see a link between touch and its religious meaning. Dresser offers the following observation regarding touching the head of Asians: "Many Asian people believe the head houses the soul. Therefore, when another person touches their head, it places them in jeopardy. It is prudent for outsiders to avoid touching the heads and upper torsos of Asians."[119] Many African Americans are also annoyed if a white person pats them on the top of their head. They believe it carries the same meaning as being told, in a condescending manner, that they are "a good little boy or girl."

People in much of eastern Europe, Spain, Italy, Portugal, and the Arab world will kiss when they meet their friends. There is also much more same-sex touching in Mexico and Spain. Men will greet each other with an embrace (*abrazo*). As Condon notes, "Hugs, pats on backs, and other physical contact are an important part of communication in Mexico."[120] And in Costa Rica women great each other with a kiss on one cheek and a hand on the shoulder.[121] In much of Southeast Asia people not only avoid touching when meeting, but also have very little physical contact during the course of the conversation. In China men and women seldom "show physical affection in public."[122] When describing business practices in Japan, Rowland asserts, "Touching fellow workers and associates is not common in Japan. Patting someone on the back or putting a friendly arm around them is not done."[123] Even the simple act of kissing has cultural overtones. Although mouth-to-mouth kissing, as a sexual act, is common in most Western cultures, it is not widespread in many parts of Asia. In fact, the Japanese have for centuries rhapsodized about the appeal of the nape of the neck as an erotic zone. The Japanese have no word for kissing, so they have borrowed from the English language for their word *kissu*.

Throughout this chapter we have attempted to demonstrate that touch is a reflection of a culture's attitudes and values. Two more examples will further illustrate this important point. Cultures that believe in emotional restraint and rigid status distinction (German, English, Scandinavian) do very little touching as compared with cultures that encourage outward signs of affection (Latin American, Middle Eastern, Jewish, Greek, eastern European). The connection of cultural values to touch can even be seen in how the Hindus of India believe that you show respect to someone of great importance by touching their feet.[124]

There are also gender and ethnic differences within the United States in how individuals use and react to touch. According to Morreale, Spitzberg, and Barge, "Men use touch to assert power or express sexual desire; and men tend to touch females more than females touch males."[125] There are, of course, other differences in how the two genders employ touch behavior. Bates notes, "Women initiate hugs and embraces far more often than men do, to other women, to men, and to children."[126]

African Americans "give skin" and "get skin" when greeting each other, but they do not normally use "skinning" (touching) when greeting white people unless they are close friends. A limited number of studies reveal that African American males touch each other more often than do white males.[127] And, Leathers says, one study has shown that "black females touch each other almost twice as often as white females."[128]

Smell

When the German philosopher Nietzsche wrote "All credibility, all good conscience, all evidence of truth come only from the senses," we are sure he intended to include the sense of smell in his declaration. Although you receive most of your messages from the outside world through vision and hearing, the sense of smell can also be a conduit for meaning. From the burning of incense in India to the aroma of flowers and herbs used in China for medicinal purposes, cultures have been using odor in a variety of ways. Americans, for example, spend billions of dollars making certain that they, as well as their surroundings, exude the proper fragrance. The reason is obvious: From sexual attraction to the alteration of moods, odor communicates. It communicates not only when you are face-to-face with another person but even when the other person is not present. Victor Hugo said, "Nothing awakens a reminiscence like an odor."

What makes scent part of the communication experience is that smell can alter moods and increase alertness. Summarizing research on a simple smell, Furlow concluded that people agree that lavender contributes to a pleasant mood.[129] A number of elements affect the meaning we give to a smell: (1) *the strength of the smell in relation to competing fragrances and odors* (French perfume versus an inexpensive aftershave lotion), (2) *smell's distance from the other person*, (3) *the perceived relationship between the parties involved*, and (4) *the context of the encounter*.

Although everyone experiences the world of smell through the same sense organ, culture greatly influences your reaction to the odors in your environment.[130] A few examples will help illustrate our point. The traditional Eskimo kiss, what is commonly depicted as rubbing noses, also includes "mutual sniffing."[131] In Bali, when lovers greet one another, they often breathe deeply in a kind of friendly sniffing. Smell plays a big part in "sensory-information gathering among Filipinos."[132] It is not uncommon for young Filipino lovers to trade small pieces of clothing on parting, so that the smell of the other person will evoke their affection for each other. The Filipino culture is so very conscious of the power of smell that after investigating this culture, Gochenour noted, "A not-so-rare complaint against Americans is that they do not bathe enough. . . . Filipinos are scrupulous about personal hygiene and have sensitive noses."[133] In Japan, where smell is an important part of the culture, young girls will often play a game involving the placing of five fragrances in tiny boxes. The girl who identifies the most aromas wins the game. And it is not uncommon in Japan to have various fragrances emitted in the workplace.

Americans represent an example of a culture that tends to be uncomfortable with natural body smells and attempts to cover up innate smells with perfumes and lotions. Many other cultures regard natural odors as normal. In fact, Muslim women are told that "wearing perfume on clothes either outdoors or when meeting strangers indoors should be avoided."[134] The reason is that Arabs actually perceive a person's smell as an extension of the person. Hall describes this cultural value:

> Olfaction occupies a prominent place in the Arab life. Not only is it one of the distance-setting mechanisms, but it is a vital part of the complex system of behavior. Arabs consistently breathe on people when they talk. However, this habit is more than a matter of different manners. To the Arab good smells are pleasing and a way of being involved with each other. To smell one's friends is not only desirable, for to deny him your breath is to act ashamed. Americans, on the other hand, trained as they are not to breathe in people's faces, automatically communicate shame in trying to be polite.[135]

Paralanguage

When the German poet Klopstock wrote, "The tones of human voices are mightier than strings or brass to move the soul," he knew that the sounds we generate, apart from the meaning contained in the word, often communicate more than the words themselves. Most of you have attended the showing of a foreign film with English subtitles. During those intervals when the subtitles were not on the screen, you heard the actors uttering an unfamiliar language but could essentially understand what was happening just from the sound of the voices. Perhaps you inferred that the performers were expressing anger, sorrow, joy, or any of a number of other emotions. Maybe the sound of the voices could even tell you who the hero was and who was cast in the role of the villain. The rise and fall of voices also may have told you when one person was asking a question and another was making a statement or issuing a command. Whatever the case, certain vocal cues provided you with information with which to make judgments about the characters' personalities, emotional states, ethnic background, and rhetorical activity. To be sure, you could only guess at the exact meaning of the words being spoken, but sound variations still told you a great deal about what was happening. Shakespeare said the same thing with great style when he wrote, "I understand the fury in your words, but not the words."

What we have just been considering is often referred to as *paralanguage*, which involves the linguistic elements of speech— how something is said and not the actual meaning of the spoken words. Most classifications divide paralanguage into three kinds of vocalizations, (1) *vocal qualifiers* (volume, pitch, rhythm, tempo, resonance, tone), (2) *vocal characterizers* (laughing, crying, yelling, moaning, whining, belching, yawning), and (3) *vocal segregates* ("un-huh," "shh," "uh," "oooh," "mmmh," "humm").

Vocal Qualities. It is extraordinary how many inferences about content and character can be made just from the sounds people produce. For example, paralanguage cues assist you in drawing conclusions about an individual's emotional state, socioeconomic status, height, ethnicity, weight, age, intelligence, race, regional background, and educational level.[136] Let's pause for a moment and look at some of the paralanguage messages you send and receive that have message value for a particular culture.

You only have to look at differences in the use of volume to see the pull of culture on paralanguage. Arabs speak with a great deal of volume because volume for them connotes strength and sincerity, "while softness communicates weakness and deviousness."[137] For Israelis, increased volume reflects strong beliefs toward the issue under discussion. Ruch says the Germans conduct their business with a "commanding tone that projects authority and self-confidence."[138] On the other end of the continuum, there are cultures that have a very different view toward loud voices. A visitor from Thailand once asked one of the authors if the loud voices she was hearing in America meant Americans were upset or mad at something. Her question made a great deal of sense. For as Cooper and Cooper note, in Thailand "a loud voice is perceived as being impolite."[139] In Japan, raising one's voice often implies a lack of self-control. For them, a gentle and soft voice reflects good manners and helps maintain social harmony—two important values in Japanese culture.

Co-cultures also use vocal qualifiers in subtle and unique ways. For example, as part of their unique communication style, many African Americans use more inflection, are more intense and more dynamic, and have a greater emotional range in their use of voice than most white Americans.[140] Some members of the dominant culture view these characteristics in a negative light.[141] Differences in paralanguage also mark the communication patterns of males and females. In several studies, females evidenced a faster rate of speech than men and also had fewer silent pauses while speaking.[142] After reviewing numerous studies on gender differences in the use of voice, Pearson, West, and Turner concluded that females speak at a higher pitch than men, speak more softly, are more expressive, pronounce the complete "ing" ending to words, and come closer to standard speech norms.[143] Women also have greater variation in their voice when they speak than do men.[144]

Vocal Characteristics. The "noise" people make can also contain cultural meanings. For example the seemingly natural act of sneezing "is considered in Islam a blessing from God."[145] The rationale behind this sound having religious overtones goes to the heart of Islam. Because all actions are "God's will," sneezing is an action triggered by God. In fact, after the sneeze a Muslim would say *Al-hamdu illah* (Praise and thanks to God). The Maasai also use a number of sounds that have special significance, the most common one being the "eh" sound, which the Maasai draw out and which can mean "yes," "I understand," or "continue."[146] In Kenya, the "iya" sound tells the other person that everything is okay; in Jamaica, the "kissing" or "sucking" sound expresses anger, exasperation, or frustration. The Japanese also make ample use of vocalics in their conversations. During interpersonal discussions, say Richmond, McCroskey, and Payne, the "Japanese will often hiss or inhale one's breath while talking to others as a sign of respect."[147] They will also make small utterances (such as *hai* [yes, certainly, all right, very well], *so* [so], or *e* [well. . .; let me see . . .]) to demonstrate their attentiveness.[148]

Laughing also sends different messages, depending on the culture. Lynch and Hanson do an excellent job noting this difference when they write:

> Laughing and giggling are interpreted as expressions of enjoyment among most Americans—signals that people are relaxed and having a good time. . . . Among other cultural groups, such as Southeast Asians, the same behavior may be a sign of extreme embarrassment or discomfort or what Americans might call "nervous laughter" taken to the extreme.[149]

Accents and Dialects. Accents and dialects are additional components of paralanguage that often influence the communication process. In a rather humorous way, this point was made clear to the famous Norwegian anthropologist Thor Heyerdahl during one of his trips to London to appear on British television. The British Broadcasting Company, because he had a very busy schedule, assured Heyerdahl that they would send someone to pick him up and bring him to the television studio. As the minutes ticked by, Heyerdahl became very anxious. Finally, fearing he would miss the broadcast, he approached a man who looked as if he might be a taxi driver. He said to the gentleman, "I'm Thor Heyerdahl. Are you looking for me?" With a very thick British accent, the driver replied, "No sir. I have been sent to pick up four Airedales for the BBC."

Although the above example seems trivial, in many instances accents and dialects can cause serious communication problems. Before we mention some of these problems, let us discuss the subtle difference between accents and dialects. *Accent* refers only to distinctive pronunciation, whereas *dialect* refers to grammar and vocabulary as well.[150] The importance of accents and dialects is obvious to those who have found themselves making a judgment about another person based on the person's accent or dialect. Because most people view "standard English" as proper and correct, anyone not using this standard is perceived to be of lower status and/or not speaking correct English.[151] Andersen summarizes the results of these negative responses to accents when interacting with people from various backgrounds:

> Research has shown that regional, ethnic, and blue-collar accents are preferred by members of one's own group but thought of as signs of low intelligence, low education, low status, and low success by the dominant, or "mainstream" culture.[152]

People who hold the attitudes mentioned by Andersen fail to recognize that anthropologist Haviland is correct when he notes, "Technically, all dialects are languages—there is nothing partial or sub-linguistic about them."[153] It must be remembered that standard English is as much a dialect as any one of the thousands found throughout the world. That is, in one place or another, what one person speaks is a foreign dialect someplace else.

During the first part of the chapter, we focused on nonverbal communication through body behavior. We now examine how people employ space, time, and silence as ways of communicating. Although these variables are external to the communicator, they are nevertheless used and manipulated in ways that send messages. For example, imagine your reaction to someone who stands too close to you, arrives late for an important appointment, or remains silent after you reveal some personal information. In each of these instances, you would find yourself reading meaning into your communication partner's use of (1) *space and distance*, (2) *time*, and (3) *silence*.

Space and Distance

The flow and shift of distance between you and the people with whom you interact are as much a part of communication experiences as the words you exchange. Notice how you might allow one person to stand very close to you and keep another at a distance. The study of this message system, called *proximics*, is concerned with such things as your (1) *personal space*, (2) *seating*, and (3) *furniture arrangement*. All three have an influence on intercultural communication.

Personal Space

Your personal space, that piece of the universe you occupy and call your own, is contained within an invisible boundary surrounding your body. As the owner of this area, you usually decide who may enter and who may not. When your space is invaded, you react in a variety of ways. You may back up and retreat, stand your ground as your hands become moist from nervousness, or sometimes even react violently. Your response is a manifestation not only of your unique personality but also your cultural background. For example, cultures that stress individualism (England, the United States, Germany, Australia) generally demand more space than do collective cultures and "tend to take an active, aggressive stance when their space is violated."[154] In collective cultures, according to Andersen, where people are more interdependent, "the members work, play, live and sleep in close proximity to one another."[155] Mexico and most Arab cultures are good examples of what Andersen is referring to. As Condon tells us, in Mexico the "physical distance between people when engaged in conversation is closer than what is usual north of the border."[156] With regard to Arabs, Ruch writes, "Typical Arab conversations are at close range. Closeness cannot be avoided."[157] According to Richmond and Gestrin "Africans get physically close to complete strangers and stand even closer when conversing."[158]

As you have just seen, a person's use of space is directly linked to the value system of their culture. In some Asian cultures, for example, students do not sit close to their teachers or stand near their bosses; the extended distance demonstrates deference and esteem. Extra interpersonal distance is also part of the cultural experience of the people of Scotland and Sweden, for whom it reflects privacy. In Germany, as Hall and Hall note, private space is sacred.[159] To the Germans, according to Gannon, "This distancing is a protective barrier and psychological symbol that operates in a manner similar to that of the home."[160] You find the opposite view toward space in the Brazilian culture where "closeness and human warmth is apparent," and hence, conversation takes place with less room between participants.[161]

How you respond to space is linked directly to your culture.

© Stone

Seating

Culture also influences seating arrangements. Notice, for example, that Americans, when in groups, tend to talk with those opposite them rather than those seated or standing beside them. This pattern also controls how they select leaders when in groups: in most instances, the person sitting at the head of the table is chosen (or the leader will move directly to the head table position). In America, leaders usually are accustomed to being removed physically from the rest of the group and consequently choose chairs at the end of the table. In China, seating arrangements take on different meanings. The Chinese often experience alienation and uneasiness when they face someone directly or sit on opposite sides of a desk or table from someone. The Chinese "prefer to sit next to others."[162] If you see a news story of American diplomats meeting with government officials from China, you might observe that the meeting is taking place with people sitting side by side on couches. In Korea, seating arrangements reflect status and role distinctions. In a car, office, or home, the seat at the right is considered to be one of honor.

For the Japanese, "Seating arrangements at any formal or semiformal function are also based on hierarchy."[163] The most important person sits at one end of the rectangular table, with those nearest in rank at the right and left of this senior position. The lowest in class is nearest to the door and at the opposite end of the table from the person with the most authority. Seating arrangements are also a way of demonstrating social hierarchy in the culture of Fiji.[164] The seat near the central house post is the seat of honor. Status in this culture is also reflected in the fact that women sit "below" men in the home and seniors sit above junior members of the household. In China, the traditional philosophy of *feng shui* (the relationship of humans to their environment) is often seen in the way some Chinese arrange themselves at a table.[165] In signing business agreements, the Chinese will often want to sit in a seat that they believe allows them to be in consonance with their surroundings.

Furniture Arrangement

Furniture arrangement is yet another "silent dimension" that has communication potential. In the United States furniture arrangement is used for privacy and "can be used to withdraw or avoid interactions."[166] Culture is a major influence on how furniture orientation can communicate. For example, people from France, Italy, and Mexico who visit the United States are often surprised to see that the furniture in the living room is pointed toward the television set. For them, conversation is important, and facing chairs toward a television screen stifles conversation. In their countries, furniture is positioned to encourage interaction.

Even the arrangement of offices gives us a clue to the character of a people. According to Hall and Hall, "French space is a reflection of French culture and French institutions. Everything is centralized, and spatially the entire country is laid out around centers."[167] In Germany, where privacy is stressed, office furniture is spread throughout the office. In Japan, where group participation is encouraged, many desks are arranged hierarchically in the center of a large, common room absent of walls or partitions.[168] The supervisors and managers are positioned nearest the windows. This organization encourages the exchange of information, facilitates multitask accomplishments, and promotes the Confucian concept of learning through silent observation.

Some co-cultures have their own special use of space. Prostitutes, for example, are very possessive of their territory. When they mentally mark an area as their own, even though it may be a public street or hotel lobby, they behave as if it were their private property and attempt to keep other prostitutes away.[169] In prisons, where space is limited, controlled, and at a premium, space and territory are crucial forms of communication. New inmates quickly learn the culture of prison by learning about the use of space. They soon know when to enter another cell, that space reduction is a form of punishment, and that lines form for nearly all activities. Women normally "establish closer proximity to others" than do men.[170] In summarizing other gender differences in the use of space, Leathers has concluded:

> Men use space as a means of asserting their dominance over women, as in the following:
> (a) they claim more personal space than women; (b) they more actively defend violations
> of their territories—which are usually much larger than the territories of women; (c) under
> conditions of high density, they become more aggressive in their attempts to regain a de-
> sired measure of privacy; and (d) men more frequently walk in front of their female partner
> than vice versa.[171]

Spatial distance is also a variable when interacting with members of the deaf culture. For example, when using American Sign Language, it is necessary for the person "signing" to be seen. It would not be uncommon for two signers to sit across from one another at a distance that hearing people might perceive as impersonal.[172]

Time

When Shakespeare wrote "The inaudible and noiseless foot of Time," he was putting into words what we all know but often overlook. Although you cannot hold or see time, you respond to it as if it had command over your life. When three centuries ago the Dutch mathematician Christian Huygens built the first pendulum clock, which allowed people to keep track of hours and minutes, little did he know that his invention would have such an impact on people's lives. You now strap clocks to your wrists, hang them on your walls, see them on your computer screen, and give them power to control everything from your moods to your relationships. Anthropologists Rapport and Overing underscore the importance of time to human behavior when they write, "To cut up life into moments of being, in sum, is for the individual to possess a means by which that life can be filled, shaped and reshaped in significant ways."[173] Self-reflection will reveal how time communicates. If you arrive thirty minutes late for an important appointment and offer no apology, you send a certain message about yourself. Telling someone how guilty you feel about your belated arrival also sends a message. Studies even point out that one of the hallmarks of a successful and intimate relationship is the amount of time people spend together.[174] What is happening is obvious; how the parties are perceiving and using time is sending a message about how much they care for each other. Of course, there is much more to time than "speaking" about your relationships. Gonzales and Zimbardo accentuate this multidimensional aspect of time when they write, "Our temporal perspective influences a wide range of psychological process, from motivation, emotion and spontaneity to risk taking, creativity and problem-solving."[175]

As in the case with all aspects of nonverbal communication, culture plays a substantial role in how you perceive and use time. As Lewis points out, "Fatalism, work ethic, reincarnation, *susu*, Confucianism, *Weltschmerz*, *dusha*, etc., all reveal different notions about time."[176] Ballard and Seibold establish much the same link between culture and time when they note: "The existence and proliferation of objective, independent time-measuring devices is itself a cultural by-product, and the uniform seconds, minutes, and hours that clocks appear to 'measure' also are culturally constructed."[177]

Gannon highlights the bond between time and culture in the United States when he writes:

> Time is also limited in America because there are so many things to do in one's lifetime. The society develops technologically at horrendous speed, and it's difficult to keep up. One has to be continuously on the move. This is America: there is little time for contemplating or meditating.[178]

Your own experience tells you that in North America, most members of the dominant culture adhere to the advice of Benjamin Franklin that tells them that "Time is money." Think of what is being said about the use of time in the common expressions "He who hesitates is lost" and "Just give me the bottom line." The Chinese know the Confucian saying, "Think three times before you act." And a Mexican approach to time is seen in the saying, "Do not today what you can do tomorrow." Consider for a moment how differently each of these cultures perceives time. A culture's conception of time can be examined from three different perspectives: (1) *informal time*; (2) *perceptions of past, present, and future*; and (3) *Hall's monochronic and polychronic classifications*.

Informal Time

In most instances rules for informal time, such as *punctuality and pace*, are not explicitly taught. Like most of culture, these rules usually function below the level of consciousness. Argyle makes much the same point when he compares cultural differences in *punctuality* standards:

> How late is "late"? This varies greatly. In Britain and America one may be 5 minutes late for a business appointment, but not 15 and certainly not 30 minutes late, which is perfectly normal in Arab countries. On the other hand in Britain it is correct to be 5–15 minutes late for an invitation to dinner. An Italian might arrive 2 hours late, an Ethiopian after, and a Javanese not at all—he had accepted only to prevent his host from losing face.[179]

Our reaction to punctuality is rooted in our cultural experiences. In the United States, we have all learned that the boss can arrive late for a meeting without anyone raising an eyebrow; if the secretary is late, he or she may receive a reprimand in the form of a stern glance. A rock star or a doctor can keep people waiting for long periods of time, but the warm-up band and the nurse had better be on time. In Latin America, one is expected to arrive late to appointments as a sign of respect. According to Lewis, in Spain there is even the view that says that "punctuality messes up schedules."[180] And in Africa people often "show up late for appointments, meetings, and social engagements."[181] There is even a Nigerian expression that says, "A watch did not invent man." These two views of tardiness would be perceived as rudeness in Germany. According to Hall and Hall, "Promptness is taken for granted in Germany—in fact, it's almost an obsession."[182]

We can determine a culture's attitude toward time by examining the *pace* at which members of that culture perform specific acts and respond to certain events. Americans, because of the pace of life in the United States, always seem to be in a hurry. As Kim observes, "Life is in constant motion. People consider time to be wasted or lost unless they are doing something."[183] Conveniences—from fast-food restaurants, to one-stop gas stations, to microwave ovens—help Americans get things done quickly. Americans are constantly seeking faster computers and cars. You grow up hearing people say, "Don't waste so much time" and "He who hesitates is lost." Other cultures see time differently and hence live life at a pace different from that of most people in the United States. Asselin and Mastron point out that "the French do not share the American sense of urgency to accomplish tasks."[184] The Japanese and Chinese cultures also treat time in ways that often appear at cross-purposes with American goals. The Chinese have a proverb that states, "He who hurries cannot walk with dignity."

Drawing on the Japanese culture for his example, Brislin illustrates how pace is reflected in the negotiation process:

> When negotiating with the Japanese, Americans like to get right down to business. They were socialized to believe that "time is money." They can accept about 15 minutes of "small talk" about the weather, their trip, and baseball, but more than that becomes unreasonable. The Japanese, on the other hand, want to get to know their business counterparts. They feel that the best way to do this is to have long conversations with Americans about a wide variety of topics. The Japanese are comfortable with hours and hours, and even days and days, of conversation.[185]

Indonesians are yet another group that does not hurry. They perceive time as a limitless pool. According to Harris and Moran, there is even "a phrase in Indonesia describing this concept that translates as 'rubber time,' so that time stretches or shrinks and is therefore very flexible."[186] In Africa, where a slow pace is the rule, "People who rush are suspected of trying to cheat," says Ruch.[187]

As you have seen throughout this chapter, nonverbal behavior is often directly linked to a culture's religious and value orientation. This notion is made manifest when you turn to the Arab culture. As we discussed in Chapter 3 when you looked at Islam, most Arabs believe that their destiny is a matter of fate. The Arab connection to the pace of life and time is clearly pointed out by Abu-Gharbieh:

> Throughout the Arab world, there is a nonchalance about time and deadlines: the pace of life is more leisurely than in the West. Social events and appointments tend not to have a fixed beginning or end.[188]

Manifestations of pace take a host of forms. One study, for example, pointed out that even the speed at which people walk reflects a culture's concept of time. People from England and the United States move much faster than people from Taiwan and Indonesia. [189]

Past, Present, and Future

How a culture perceives and uses the concepts of past, present, and future was discussed in Chapter 2 when looked at cultural values. Let us review some of those findings so that you can see how time is not only tied to cultural values but also to nonverbal communication.

Past-oriented cultures such as the British place much emphasis on tradition and are often perceived as resisting change. A statement often heard in England when people ask about the monarchy is "We have always done it this way." The Chinese and Japanese, with their traditions of ancestor worship and strong pride in their cultures' persistence for thousands of years, are other cultures that use the past as a guide to how to live in the present. As a Chinese proverb advises, "Consider the past and you will know the present." The Irish and Irish Americans also take great pride in their past and hence make them yet another culture that is past oriented. As Wilson notes, "Irish-Americans, with their strong sense of tradition, are typically past oriented.

They have an allegiance to the past, their ancestors, and their history. The past is often the focus of Irish stories."[190]

Native Americans represent another culture that has a past point of reference to help explain life. Still and Hodgins explain this approach in the following manner:

> Most American Indian tribes are not future oriented. Very little planning is done for the future because their view is that many things are outside of the individual's control and may affect or change the future. In fact, the Navajo language does not include a future tense verb. Time is not viewed as a constant or something that one can control, but rather as something that is always with the individual. Thus, to plan for the future is something viewed as foolish.[191]

Cultures and co-cultures that value the past find it normal to take a long-range view of events and are less likely to be rushed when they face decisions. Cultures that value the past are also more likely to respect and venerate the elderly than are cultures that value the future.

Filipinos and Latin Americans are *present oriented* and emphasize enjoying and living in the moment. These cultures tend to be more impulsive and spontaneous than others and often have a casual, relaxed lifestyle. This approach to time frequently misinterprets a concern with the present as a sign of indolence and inefficiency.

The third orientation, which puts great faith in the *future*, is the one most Americans have. As a people, Americans are constantly planning for the future, and their children play with toys (dolls, cars, guns, and so on) that prepare them for adulthood. Many of you can hardly wait to finish what you are doing so that you can move on to something else. As we noted during our discussion of pace, having an eye to the future often produces a very low tolerance for extensions and postponements. What you want, you want now, so you can dispose of this moment and move on to the next. In addition, future-oriented cultures welcome innovation and change and "have less regard for past social or organizational customs and traditions."[192]

Monochronic (M-time) and Polychronic (P-time) Classifications

Anthropologist Hall advanced another classification of time as a form of communication. Hall proposed that cultures organize time in one of two ways: either monochronic (M-time) or polychronic (P-time).[193] Although he did not intend these as either/or categories, they do represent two distinct approaches to time.

M-time. Cultures that can be classified as M-time are people from Germany, Austria, Switzerland, and America. As Hall explains, "People of the Western world, particularly Americans, tend to think of time as something fixed in nature, something around us and from which we cannot escape; an ever-present part of the environment, just like the air we breathe."[194] As the word monochronic implies, this concept explains time as lineal and segmented. More specifically, "A monochronic view of time believes time is a scarce resource which must be rationed and controlled through the use of schedules and appointments, and through aiming to do only one thing at any one time."[195] And above all, time should not be wasted. The English naturalist Charles Darwin echoed this view when he wrote, "A man who dares to waste one hour of time has not discovered the value of life." You behave as if time were tangible; you talk of "saving time," "losing time," or "killing time." The time clock records the hours you must work, the school bell moves you from class to class, and the calendar marks important days and events in your lives. According to Trompenaars and Hampden-Turner, in the business setting cultures that view time in a sequential pattern "schedule in advance and do not run late" and have "a strong preference for following initial plans."[196]

P-time. People from cultures on polychronic time live their lives quite differently than do those who move to the monochronic clock. P-time cultures, which are mostly those we classified in Chapter 2 as collective, deal with time holistically. They can interact with more than one person or do more than one thing at a time. Gannon offers an excellent example of the multidimensional nature of P-time when he talks of the Turkish culture. "'Polychronism' best describes the Turkish ability to concentrate on different things simultaneously at work, at home, or in the coffee house."[197] P-time cultures also stress people over process. As Smith and Bond point out, "A polychronic view of time sees the maintenance of harmonious relationships as the important thing, so that use of time needs to be flexible in order that we do right by the various people to whom we have obligations."[198] Because P-time has this notion of multiple activities and flexibility, Dresser believes it "explains why there is more interrupting in conversations carried on by people from Arabic, Asian, and Latin American cultures."[199] Africans are yet another culture that takes great stock in the activity that is occurring at the moment and emphasize people more than schedules. As Richmond and Gestrin note, "Time for Africans is defined by events rather than the clock or calendar."[200] "For Africans, the person they are with is more important than the one who is out of sight."[201] For P-time cultures, time is less tangible; hence, feelings of wasted time are not as prevalent as in M-time cultures. This leads, of course, to a lifestyle that is more spontaneous and unstructured—characteristics that often confuse and frustrate Americans and other Westerners.

In Table 5-1, Hall and Hall summarize the basic aspects of both approaches. Their condensation takes many of the ideas we have mentioned and translates them into specific behaviors.

Within the United States, there are co-cultures that use time differently from the dominant culture. Mexican Americans frequently speak of "Latino time" when their timing

Table 5-1 *Comparison of Monochronic and Polychronic Cultures*

Monochronic Time People	Polychronic Time People
Do one thing at a time	Do many things at once
Concentrate on the job	Are easily distracted and subject to interruption
Take time commitments (deadlines, schedules) seriously	Consider time commitments an objective to be achieved, if possible
Are low context and need information	Are high context and already have information
Are committed to the job	Are committed to people and human relationships
Adhere to plans	Change plans often and easily
Are concerned about not disturbing others; follow rules of privacy	Are more concerned with people close to them (family, friends, close business associates) than with privacy
Show great respect for private property; seldom borrow or lend	Borrow and lend things often and easily
Emphasize promptness	Base promptness on the relationship
Are accustomed to short-term relationships	Have strong tendency to build lifetime relationships

Source: Adapted from Edward T. Hall and Mildred Reed Hall, *Understanding Cultural Differences: Germans, French, and Americans* (Yarmouth, ME: Intercultural Press, 1990), 15.

varies from that of the dominant culture. Burgoon and Saine have observed that the Polynesian culture of Hawaii has "Hawaiian time,"[202] a concept of time that is very relaxed and reflects the informal lifestyle of the native Hawaiian people. And among Samoans, there is a time perspective referred to as "coconut time," which is derived from the notion that it is not necessary to pick coconuts because they will fall when the time is right. African Americans often use what is referred to as "BPT" (Black People's Time) or "hang-loose time."[203] This concept, which has its roots in the P-time cultures of Africa, maintains that priority belongs to what is happening at that instant. Statements such as "Hey, man, what's happenin'?" reflect the importance of the here and now.

Silence

An African proverb states, "Silence is also speech." We contend that silence sends us nonverbal cues concerning the communication situations in which we participate. Observe the poignant use of silence when the classical composer strategically places intervals of orchestration so that the ensuing silence marks a contrast in expression. Silence can indeed be a powerful message. There is a story of how the American philosopher Ralph Waldo Emerson "talked" in silence for hours to the famous English writer Thomas Carlyle. It seems that Emerson, on a visit to Europe, arranged to meet with Carlyle, who was his idol. Emerson maintains they sat together for hours in perfect silence until it was time for him to go, then parted company cordially, congratulating each other on the fruitful time they had had together.

Silence cues affect interpersonal communication by providing an interval in an ongoing interaction during which the participants have time to think, check or suppress an emotion, encode a lengthy response, or inaugurate another line of thought. Silence also helps provide feedback, informing both sender and receiver about the clarity of an idea or its significance in the overall interpersonal exchange. Silence cues may be interpreted as evidence of agreement, lack of interest, injured feelings, or contempt. Like olfactory and tactile cues, silence cues transcend the verbal channel, often revealing what speech conceals. The intercultural implications of silence are as diverse as those of other nonverbal cues, as Crystal helps to illustrate:

> Cross-cultural differences are common over when to talk and when to remain silent, or what a particular instance of silence means. In response to the question "Will you marry me?", silence in English would be interpreted as uncertainty; in Japanese it would be interpreted as acceptance. In Igbo, it would be considered a denial if the woman were to continue to stand there, and an acceptance if she ran away.[204]

Knowing how various cultures use silence is an essential component for anyone who interacts with a culture different from their own. As Braithwaite points out:

> One of the basic building blocks of competence, both linguistic and cultural, is knowing when not to speak in a particular community. Therefore, to understand where, and when to be silent, and the meaning attached to silence, is to gain a keen insight into the fundamental structure of communication in that world.[205]

Silence is not a meaningful part of the life of most members of the dominant culture in the United States. Talking, watching television, listening to music, and other sound-producing activities keep us from silence. Numerous studies have pointed out that most Americans believe that talking is an important activity and actually enjoy talking.[206] Of course, other cultures have a similar positive view of talking over silence. Within the business context, Lewis notes that "a silent reaction to a business proposal would seem negative to American, German, French, Southern European and Arab executives."[207] It seems that there is a link between cultures that stress social interaction (Jewish, Italian, French, Arab, etc.) and their perception of and use of silence. In fact, talking in these cultures is highly valued. In the Greek culture, there is also a belief that being in the company of other people and engaging in conversation are signs of a good life. There are no references to concepts of solitude and silence; rather, history and literature are replete with allusions to rhetoric and dialogues. A culture that praises Aristotle, Plato, and Socrates is not one that will find silent meditation very appealing. This is in sharp contrast to cultures in which a hushed and still environment is the rule. We now look at a few cultural variations in the use of silence so that you might better understand how a lack of words can influence the outcome of any communication event.

In the Eastern tradition, the view of silence is much different from the Western view. Easterners do not feel uncomfortable with the absence of noise or talk and are not compelled to fill every pause when they are around other people. In fact, there is often a belief in many Eastern traditions that words can contaminate an experience and that inner peace and wisdom come only through silence. Barnlund says of Buddhism, "One of its tenets is that words are deceptive and silent intuition is a truer way to confront the world; mind-to-mind communication through words is less reliable than heart-to-heart communication through an intuitive grasp of things."[208] Further, Buddhism teaches that "what is real is, and when it is spoken it becomes unreal." The Chinese philosopher Confucius had much the same view of silence when he counseled "Believe not others' tales, / Others will lead thee far astray"; "Silence is a friend who will never betray." For many Asian people silence is often used as a means of avoiding conflict. Chan explains this idea when he writes, "A typical practice among many Asian peoples is to refuse to speak any further in conversation if they cannot personally accept the speaker's attitude, opinion, or way of thinking about particular issues or subjects."[209]

Silence is very complex in the Japanese culture in that it can serve a variety of purposes. First, silence is often linked to credibility. That is, someone who is silent is often perceived as having higher credibility than someone who talks too much. Jaworski makes this point when he notes, "Reticent individuals are trusted as honest, sincere, and straightforward. Thus silence is an active state, while speech is an excuse for delaying activity."[210] Second, as is the case with other Asian cultures, the Japanese also use silence to avoid both conflict and embarrassment. [211] The Japanese view of silence is also reflected in the following proverbs: "It is the duck that squawks that gets shot" and "Numerous words show scanty wares," and "A flower does not speak," and "The mouth is to eat with not to speak with." Compare these perceptions of silence with the American saying "The squeaky wheel gets the grease." You can easily imagine how the use of silence might create communication problems when people representing these two divergent styles come together. For example, Adler says that during business negotiations between Japanese and Americans, each has a different rendering of the same silent period. The Japanese use the silence to "consider the Americans' offer, the Americans interpret the silence as rejection."[212]

Silence can also play a dominant role in the Indian culture. The Hindu believes that "self-realization, salvation, truth, wisdom, peace, and bliss are all achieved in a state of meditation and introspection when the individual is communicating with himself or herself in silence."[213]

Some co-cultures living in the United States also differ from the dominant American culture in the use of silence. Many Native Americans believe that silence, not speaking, is a sign of a remarkable person. The famous Indian leader Chief Joseph is quoted as saying, "It does not require many words to speak the truth." Johannesen, in discussing the meaning of silence among Native Americans, noted that for this co-culture "one derives from silence the cornerstone of character, the virtues of self-control, courage, patience and dignity."[214] Native Americans use silence as a gesture of respect to persons of authority, age, and wisdom. Among Navajos, if someone does not use silence and responds too quickly when asked a question, they are considered immature.[215] In social settings, silence is the rule when a Native American is meeting a stranger, in mourning, dealing with someone who is exceptionally angry, or greeting someone who has been gone for a long period of time.[216] Because of the way they have been socialized, women are often silenced intellectually and creatively. In mixed-gender conversations, women are quieter than males.[217]

Two points should be obvious from our discussion. First, you must be careful not to assume that people are communicating only when they talk. As the American composer John Cage declared, "There is no such thing as empty space or an empty time. There is always something to see, something to hear. In fact, try as we may to make silence, we cannot." Second, because of cultural variations in this form of communication, it behooves you to know cultural attitudes toward talk, noise, and silence. This knowledge can save you from both anxiety and ethnocentrism in intercultural communication.

SUMMARY

- We make important judgments and decisions about others based on their nonverbal behavior.
- We use the actions of others to learn about their emotional states.
- Nonverbal communication is culture-bound.
- Nonverbal communication involves all nonverbal stimuli in a communication setting that are generated by both the source and his or her use of the environment and that have potential message value for the source or receiver.
- Nonverbal messages may be both intentional and unintentional.
- Nonverbal communication has five basic functions: to repeat, complement, substitute for a verbal action, regulate, and contradict a communication event.
- It is important to remember that we are all more than our culture.
- In nonverbal communication, we often make differences more important than they should be.
- Nonverbal actions seldom occur in isolation.
- Nonverbal communication and culture are similar in that both are learned, both are passed on from generation to generation, and both involve shared understandings.
- Studying nonverbal behavior can lead to the discovery of a culture's underlying attitudes and values.
- Studying nonverbal behavior can also assist us in isolating our own ethnocentrism.
- Your body is a major source of nonverbal messages. These messages are communicated by means of general appearance and attire, body movements (kinesics), facial expressions, eye contact, touch, smell, and paralanguage.
- Cultures differ in their perception and use of personal space, seating, and furniture arrangement.
- We can understand a culture's sense of time by learning about how members of that culture view informal time, the past, present, and future, and whether or not their orientation toward time is monochronic or polychronic.
- The use of silence varies from culture to culture.

INFOTRAC COLLEGE EDITION EXERCISES

1. Do Americans hate silence? That's the claim of Thomas J. McCarthy in his article "A Culture of Noise: The Commercialization of Public Space Reflects Nothing So Much as Our Aversion to Silence." Locate and read McCarthy's article, then discuss with others your attitudes towards silence. How do age, gender, or membership in a co-culture shape those attitudes?

2. What does your office or your bedroom tell others about you? That's the subject of "Room with a Cue: Personal Space Betrays Personality" by Robin Poultney. Locate and read this article, then discuss with your classmates what you have observed from visiting others' offices and bedrooms. What part does cultural membership play in this kind of communication?

3. Using the subject search term "nonverbal communication," locate the article "Interpersonal Distance, Body Orientation, and Touch: Effects of Culture, Gender, and Age." According to the research reported in this article, what are the differences in nonverbal communication norms between Dutch, English, and French individuals? Conduct your own informal research and observe nonverbal communications occurring in your own culture. How do your own culture's nonverbal communications compare with the nonverbal communications analyzed in this article?

ACTIVITIES

1. Ask your informant (from a culture different from your own) to demonstrate examples of his or her culture's use of communicative body movements (kinesics). What similarities are there between yours and your informant's? What differences are there? What are the potential areas for misunderstandings?

2. In small groups, produce an inventory of common American gestures. An example of one is the "OK" gesture: the thumb and forefinger of one hand form an "O," and the rest of the fingers on that hand arch above the "O." What other gestures can you think of? Compare your findings with those of the rest of the class and make a master list.

3. Watch a foreign film and look for examples of differences in proxemics, touch, and facial expressions. Compare these differences to the dominant culture of North America.

4. In a small group, read the following paragraph and explain what went wrong:

    Jan was in Brazil on business. Ciro, a Brazilian associate, invited her to a dinner party he and his wife were giving. The invitation was for "around 8, this Friday night." Jan arrived at Ciro's house at exactly 8:00. Ciro and his wife were still dressing and had not even begun to prepare the food.

5. Select an airport, supermarket, or shopping mall where people from different cultural backgrounds might be interacting. Observe the interactions in light of some of the items listed below:

    a. What are the average distances between the people you observed? Were there differences related to culture?

    b. What differences did you observe in touching behavior?

DISCUSSION IDEAS

1. In what situations might you need to interpret the nonverbal behavior of someone from another culture? What problems could arise from not understanding differences in nonverbal behavior?

2. Give your culture's interpretation of the following nonverbal actions:
    • Two people are speaking loudly, waving their arms, and using a lot of gestures.
    • A customer in a restaurant waves his hand over his head and snaps his fingers loudly.
    • An elderly woman dresses entirely in black.
    • A young man dresses entirely in black.
    • An adult pats a child's head.
    • Two men kiss in public.

3. How can studying the intercultural aspects of nonverbal behavior assist you in discovering your own ethnocentrism? Give personal examples.

4. How late can you be for the following: a class? work? a job interview? a dinner party? a date with a friend? Now ask these same questions of members of Latin American and Asian cultures.

5. What is meant by "Nonverbal communication is rule governed"?

6. In a small group, discuss the following topic: Are there more nonverbal behaviors across cultures that are alike or more that are different?

part 3

The Role of Context in Intercultural Communication

chapter 6

Cultural Influences on Context: The Business Setting

Live together like brothers and do business like strangers.

ARAB PROVERB

Diversity is a strategic business imperative. A policy of inclusion is essential.

JOHN BRYAN

There is nothing more likely to start disagreement among people or countries than an agreement.

E. B. WHITE

CULTURE AND CONTEXT

There is a well-known saying that everyone has to be someplace. The next three chapters are about those places—the settings in which communication events occur. Communication is not devoid of external influence—it does not take place in a void. All human interaction, therefore, is influenced to some degree by the cultural, social, and physical, settings in which it occurs. These settings are called the *communication context*.

Your culture to a very large degree prescribes your communicative behavior within a variety of social and physical contexts by prescribing rules that dictate appropriate behavior for specific communicative situations. When you communicate with members of your own culture, you and your cohorts rely on internalized cultural rules that prescribe appropriate behavior for the communication situation. You are able to communicate effectively with each other without having to think about those rules. But when you engage in intercultural communication, things can be different. Here you and your communication partners may be operating from sets of very different rules. Consequently, you must be aware of how diverse cultural rules influence the communication context. Otherwise, you may encounter a variety of surprises—some of which could be embarrassing or unpleasant.

COMMUNICATION AND CONTEXT

In order for you to understand how important context is to intercultural communication, we will review three basic assumptions about human communication: (1) communication is rule governed, (2) context prescribes appropriate communication rules, and (3) communication rules are culturally diverse.

Communication Is Rule Governed

Both consciously and unconsciously, people expect that their interactions will follow culturally determined rules or shared forms of behavior. Communication rules prescribe proper behavior by establishing appropriate responses to communication stimuli for the various social contexts found within the larger culture. Social settings usually stipulate which rules govern a particular situation, but it is culture that makes the rules. In Iraq, for instance, a contextual rule prohibits women from having unfamiliar male guests visit them in their homes. In the United States, however, this may not be socially inappropriate. Communication rules cover both verbal and nonverbal behaviors and specify not only what should be said but also how it should be said. Nonverbal rules, as we saw in Chapter 5, apply to touch (who gets touched and where), facial expressions, (where and when to reveal a smile), eye contact (the appropriateness and inappropriateness of staring), and paralanguage (when to whisper, when to shout).

Verbal rules govern such things as turn taking, voice volume, and formality of language. Obviously, the rules differ depending on the context. In an employment interview, you might frequently use such respectful words as "sir" or "ma'am" when responding to your potential employer. At a basketball game, your language would be less formal, incorporating slang phrases and quite possibly negative or derogatory remarks about the opposing

Much of communication in the business setting is rule governed.

team or the officials. For a job interview, you might wear what Americans call a "power suit," whereas at a basketball game, jeans or shorts and a T-shirt could be appropriate. Your nonverbal behavior would also be different. At an interview, you would probably shake hands with your prospective employer, but at the basketball game, you might hug your friends, slap them on the back, or hit a "high-five" (a hand gesture) as a form of greeting.

Context Specifies Communication Rules

Our second assumption about communication is that the context specifies the appropriate rules. Think for a moment about how such diverse contexts as a classroom, bank, church, hospital, courtroom, wedding, or funeral determine which communication rules apply. Also, imagine the responses of others if your behavior departs from accepted norms. Extreme deviations can lead to social sanctions such as being ignored, being asked to leave a theater, or even being cited for contempt of court.

Communication Rules Are Culturally Diverse

A third assumption is that rules are culturally diverse. Although cultures have many of the same social settings or contexts, they frequently abide by different rules. Consequently, concepts of dress, time, language, manners, nonverbal behavior, and control of the communication ebb and flow can differ significantly among cultures. When doing business in Turkey, for example, your Turkish colleagues will insist on paying for all the entertainment. Turkish hospitality is legendary and you will not be allowed to pay for even part of the meal. In the United States, the rules for business entertaining are very different. The cost of the meal or entertainment is often shared. Different cultures, different rules.

To be successful in intercultural communication, it is essential that you know not only your own culture's rules but also the cultural rules of the person with whom you are interacting. If you understand the rules, the other person's behavior will make greater sense to you and you will be able to control and modify your behavior to conform to his or her expectations.

In this chapter we examine the *business setting* and how it effects communication. In the next chapter we will consider the context of the *educational setting*, and in Chapter 8, we will explore the context of *health care setting*. We have selected these three arenas because they are three common contexts in which you are most likely to encounter people from cultures different from your own.

Before we move to a detailed analysis of these specific settings, we need to pause and examine two communication variables that are woven in and out of every communication setting. That is to say, regardless of the communication context (1) *formality and informality*, and (2) *assertiveness and interpersonal harmony* play a major role in how people respond to their interpersonal environments.

ASSESSING THE CONTEXT

Informality and Formality

From the way people dress, to their posture, to the language they use, the manifestations of informality and formality take many forms. Your perceptions of these traits are influenced by culture. Cultures tend to range from very informal views of events and people to perceptions that are quite formal.

Informality

The United States is an *informal* culture, as Javidi and Javidi note: "In North America people tend to treat others with informality and directness. They avoid the use of formal codes of conduct, titles, honorific, and ritualistic manners in their interactions with others."[1]

American informality manifests itself in a host of ways. For example, most Americans will use first names when meeting strangers or beginning a business meeting. Even the simple greeting "Hi" is a badge of informality. Althen offers the following summary of how informality is often reflected in American culture:

> Idiomatic speech (commonly called "slang") is heavily used on most occasions, with formal speech reserved for public events and fairly formal situations. People from almost any station in life can be seen in public wearing jeans, sandals, or other informal attire. People slouch down in chairs or lean on walls or furniture when they talk, rather than maintaining an erect bearing.[2]

Although, Dresser points out, "Americans enjoy their informality, people from Asia and most other places in the world do not see this as a virtue."[3] Steward and Bennett offer some examples to buttress this important point:

> The degree of informality found in American communication patterns is uncommon in other cultures. In most Latin American and European societies, for instance, there are levels of formality attached to status difference. In Asian cultures, formal communication may be demanded by greater age as well as by higher status. In Japan, formality is also extended to strangers with whom a relationship is demanded. This formality is no joking matter, since failure to follow appropriate form may suggest to others a severe flaw in character.[4]

Formality and informality in business shift from culture to culture.

© Gloria Thomas

Formality

There are, of course, many specific examples of cultures that highly value formality. In Egypt, Turkey, and Japan, for instance, the student-teacher relationship is very formal. This may be seen in the Egyptian proverb "Whoever teaches me a letter, I should become a slave to him forever." In these countries, when the teacher enters the room, students are expected to stand. When students meet their teachers on the street, they are expected to bow to them. Contrast this with the relaxed, informal student-teacher relationships found in the United States.

From an American perspective, the degree of formality found in Germany is extreme. Germans address others and conduct themselves in a very formal manner. It is important for Germans to dress well when meeting business associates or going to school. Formality is also evident in how cultures use forms of address. Not knowing these differences can cause problems. Hall and Hall note, "American informality and the habit of calling others by their first names make Germans acutely uncomfortable, particularly when young people or people lower in the hierarchy address their elders or their superiors by their first names."[5] The use of personal titles is yet another way the Germans display formality.[6] They use titles extensively to identify people and their positions in the social structure. If, for instance, a person is both a professor and a physician, he is referred to as Herr Professor Doktor Kaempfer. And because Germany is a male-oriented culture, women are not addressed by their surname, such as Frau (Mrs.) Kaempfer, but always by their husband's title. The wife of Herr Professor Doktor Kaempfer, for example, would be addressed as Frau Professor Doktor Kaempfer. Germany is not the only place where forms of address are directly linked to perception and values. Schneider and Silverman remind us that Mexicans are yet another culture that values formality:

> Mexicans also make heavy use of honorific titles to show respect. New acquaintances met at a party are addressed as *señor, señora,* and *señorita.* In business, people address managers with titles like director, doctor, *ingeniero* (engineer), or *licienciado* (someone who has a higher education degree).[7]

The significance of informality and formality in communication goes well beyond a culture's use of language. The number of friends you have and what you tell those friends are also affected. In a study on intercultural friendships, Gareis noted, "Whereas Americans are easily accessible," Germans tend to be formal and private even when dealing with their friends.[8] This is exemplified by a German proverb that states, "A friend to everyone is a friend to no one." In yet another extensive study conducted on self-disclosure, Barnlund concluded that Americans tend to disclose much more about themselves than do members of cultures such as the Japanese, who value formality.[9] Linking this difference to the deep structure of the Japanese culture, Barnlund concluded:

> Permanently secure within the primary group, supported without qualification at every transition in life, a Japanese has little need to extend himself socially, to seek and cultivate endless series of friends to replenish those who make up his social circle.[10]

You might well imagine how a cross-cultural negotiation session might proceed if Americans were offering personal information about themselves in an informal manner while their Japanese counterparts were more comfortable holding back such information.

Assertiveness and Interpersonal Harmony

The second important dimension of culture that affects communication context is the manner in which people "present" themselves to others. While there are many dimensions to communication styles, *assertiveness* and *interpersonal harmony* influence the intercultural setting—be it a business meeting, classroom, or health care context.

Assertiveness

American culture is known for its assertive and aggressive communication style. It is not uncommon for Americans to actually enroll in assertiveness training classes that encourage them to be frank, open, and direct when they are dealing with other people. This type of behavior is now so commonplace that *U. S. News & World Report* recently presented an essay titled "The American Uncivil Wars." The thrust of the article was to call attention to the variety of ways aggressive behavior is reflected in American culture:

> It is a time when schools use metal detectors to keep out guns and knives, when universities insist on speech and behavior codes to stem the tide of hatred and disrespect, when legal cases become shouting matches, when the Internet is littered with raunch and menace, when political campaigns resemble food fights, when trash talk and head butts are the idiom of sports, and when popular culture tops itself from week to week with displays of violence, sex, foul language and puerile confession.[11]

The many signs of assertive and aggressive behavior in American culture, like all aspects of culture, did not develop by chance. A culture that has a long history of valuing nonconformity, individualism, competition, and freedom of expression is bound to encourage assertive behavior. The reasons Americans value assertive communication, according to Nadler, Nadler, and Broome, are obvious: "North American individuals are expected to stand up for their rights, and this often involves confrontation."[12] Barnlund adds: "The eloquent articulation of conviction is among the most valued virtues of [American] citizens, and the arts of argument and debate encouraged in the home, school, and marketplace."[13] Wenzhong and Grove reinforce this idea:

> In a culture where individualism is as highly valued as it is in the United States, people are expected to take the initiative in advancing their personal interests and well-being and to be direct and assertive in interacting with others. High social and geographic mobility and the comparatively superficial nature of many personal attachments create a climate where interpersonal competition and a modest level of abrasiveness are tolerated and even expected.[14]

Interpersonal Harmony

You can easily visualize the communication problems that can arise when cultures that value assertiveness come in contact with cultures that value accord and harmony. One of the authors recalls that at an international conference, members of the Israeli delegation, who were arguing their position in a dynamic manner, complained that the representatives from Thailand showed no interest in or enthusiasm for the meeting; they were "just sitting there." The Thai delegates, on the other hand, thought the professors from Israel were angry because they were "using loud voices." Both responses were, of course, a product of cultural experiences. As Cooper and Cooper point out, "The Thai learns how to avoid aggression rather than how to defend himself against it."[15] And members of the Jewish culture stress what they believe to be healthy disagreement. There is even a Yiddish saying that pokes fun at this confrontational style: "Wherever there are two Jews there are three arguments."

The Thais are not the only people who seek to avoid confrontation and strive for a communication style that values calmness, equanimity, and interpersonal harmony. We will look at a few of these cultures so that you might be better able to understand their behavior in a business, education, or health care setting.

For members of the Filipino culture, Gochenour says, "The ultimate ideal is one of harmony—between individuals, among the members of a family, among the group divisions of society, and of all life in relationship with God."[16] Filipinos have two words that express their conception of harmony: *amor propio* and *pakikisama*. *Amor propio* translates into English as "harmony" and refers to a very fragile sense of personal worth and self-respect. In interactions with others, it denotes being treated as a person rather an object. This value makes the Filipino especially vulnerable to negative remarks that may affect his or her standing in society. Consequently, Filipinos seldom criticize or verbally confront others, and if they do, it is in the most polite manner.[17] They see bluntness and frankness as uncivilized traits. Instead they value *pakikisama*, or smooth interpersonal relations.[18]

The Japanese also place a high value on interpersonal harmony. In fact, according to Moeran, "Self is subordinated in the interests of harmony."[19] Like so many dimensions of culture, interpersonal harmony can be found in the deep structure of Japanese society. As Hendry notes, "The value attached to harmony in Japan dates back over 1400 years to the Seventeenth Article Constitution of Prince Shotoku which esteemed concord above all things as the subject of the first article and the underlying theme of all the others."[20] It is a cultural pattern that touches all aspects of Japanese life, including child-rearing practices: "The concern of adults to create a secure and an attentive environment for a small child is part of this wider emphasis in Japanese society on harmony in social relationships."[21]

The cultural dynamic that stresses harmony can clearly be seen in the method the Japanese employ when doing business. Perhaps exaggerating slightly, Harris and Moran suggest that harmony is "more important in business dealings for the Japanese, than achieving higher sales and profits."[22] To maintain harmony and avoid interpersonal clashes, Japanese business has evolved an elaborate process called *nemawashii*: "binding the roots of a plant before pulling it out."[23] In this process, any subject that might cause disorder at a meeting is discussed in advance. Anticipating and obviating interpersonal antagonism allow the Japanese to avoid impudent and discourteous behavior.

It is not our intent to imply that the Japanese people do not get insulted or angry just like everyone else, but as Schneider and Silverman point out, "in their society, values and norms forcefully promote self-control and the avoidance of direct personal confrontation."[24]

Like the Thais, Filipinos, and Japanese, Gao and Ting-Toomey point out, the Chinese "tend to regard conflict and confrontation as unpleasant and undesirable."[25] Chen and Xiao underscore this same point when they state: "It is without a doubt that harmony is one of the primordial values of Confucianism and of the Chinese culture."[26] This principle, according to Chen, also has a long and meaningful history in China. Its roots are in Chinese religion: "According to Confucianism, the ultimate goal of human behavior is to achieve 'harmony' which leads Chinese people to pursue a conflict-free and group-oriented system of human relationships."[27] Two Chinese proverbs speak to the issue of outward signs of anger: "The first man to raise his voice loses the argument" and "One hurtful word wounds like a sharp sword." We should add in closing that the

Malaysians are another Asian culture with an aversion to outward signs of interpersonal anger.[28]

For reasons that are very different from those found in Asian cultures, Mexicans also seek smooth interpersonal relationships and try to avoid face-to-face confrontations. They often will say something that is not true or even slightly alter the facts if it makes the other person feel better. From the Mexicans' perspective, this shading of the truth is not a lie but simply part of a long cultural heritage going back to the early marketplaces where people would bargain and negotiate with friends by verbal bartering. These verbal exchanges, as Condon points out, were a kind of game whereby each person demonstrated his or her language skills. Condon further suggests that even today we could learn a great deal about this attribute by visiting a marketplace.[29] This avoidance of discord is seen in a number of different settings. Ruch notes that in the business context, for example, "When a visitor asks for information that a Mexican doesn't have, the Mexican does his best to say something that will please the visitor."[30]

Co-cultures in the United States hold contrary views of assertive and aggressive communication. For example, North American Native Indians, say Moghaddam, Taylor, and Wright, "have developed a distaste for Western assertiveness and tend to avoid those who interact in assertive ways."[31] Cheyenne children, according to Nanda, may be removed from the tribe for short periods if they act aggressively toward other members of the tribe.[32] Parents also find this aggressive behavior highly inappropriate in a classroom environment.

You can also observe in the United States varying aggressive and assertive patterns as they apply to gender. As Wood says, "From childhood on, males learn to be aggressive."[33] This aggression takes the form of assertive and domineering communication patterns, and these patterns get acted out in a variety of situations. As Ivy and Backlund note, "Some men are verbally aggressive on their jobs."[34] They add, "Aggressive behavior might take the form of emphatic sales pitches, interruptions of subordinates, or fevered attempts to persuade colleagues."[35]

Having looked at the potential impact the overarching variables of informality, formality, assertiveness, and interpersonal harmony have on intercultural communication, we are now ready to apply these dynamics, and others, to various intercultural settings. We begin by looking at the international business context and cross-cultural views of management. Next, we examine the conduct of business, including protocol, negotiation, and international marketing. Finally, we survey the domestic business context and give attention to the diversity found in the American workforce in order to see how cultural diversity affects the workplace.

INTERCULTURAL COMMUNICATION AND THE BUSINESS CONTEXT

As you saw in Chapter 1, most countries are tied directly to an international system of economic interdependence, and most countries have at least one asset within their borders that is needed by another country. In 2000, the United States alone exported over $1 trillion in goods and services to its major trading partners.[36] In June 2001, exports to Japan totaled over $5 billion.[37] Trade, however, is reciprocal. During June 2001, for example, the United States imported over $11.5 billion from China and Japan alone.[38]

No country is completely self-sufficient. As Estell notes, "The world today is a swiftly shrinking place."[39] Markets and cultures have continued to converge, and "major businesses have seized the opportunity to go global setting up shop on foreign soil and courting a United Nations–worth collection of customers and suppliers."[40] This has resulted in increased foreign competition, and, as Harris and Moran point out, the need to trade more effectively overseas has forced most corporations to become more culturally sensitive and globally minded.[41] And as Turner asserts, "Businesses today are as likely to have partners on the other side of the globe as on the other side of town."[42]

The increase in globalization in the last few decades has changed the way people view the world and conduct business in that world. Trade agreements like GATT and NAFTA that lower tariffs, tap larger markets, and improve standards of living in the world have become commonplace. Multinational corporations increasingly participate in various international business arrangements involving joint ventures between two or more organizations that share in the ownership of a business undertaking. Turner expresses this impact in the following manner:

> Among key issues facing all countries is the increasing internationalization of the world economy. International competition is faced both at home and abroad as tariffs are reduced, markets are deregulated, and commerce transcends national borders.[43]

Economic globalization requires new approaches to doing business. Business models and practices that once sufficed within a country are usually inadequate for international markets. According to an article in the *Black Enterprise*,

> Global diversity is changing the way we view the world. Whether a global corporation or not, global diversity is here and it impacts us all—directly or indirectly. Cross-cultural teamwork and collaboration are essential for an organization's success. If people are to function productively, they must learn to see their differences as assets, rather than as liabilities. The labels we apply are far less important than what they represent.[44]

Globalization generally results in individuals from one culture working not only with, but also for individuals from another culture. This situation often proves to be difficult because, as Harris and Moran reveal,

> there are many problems when working or living in a foreign environment. Communication across cultural boundaries is difficult. Differences in customs, behavior, and values result in problems that can be managed only through effective cross-cultural communication and interaction.[45]

A major impact of business globalization is the development of diversity in the workforce. Bryan has defined diversity as the inclusion of all groups at all levels in a company.[46] And, as Gilbert and Ivancevich suggest, diversity must become a management priority because it is good in and of itself and because it enhances performance and increases organizational quality.[47]

In the final analysis, as Scott suggests, "Effective international business-communication skills are the backbone that supports the transaction of business around the world."[48] It is therefore essential that managers working in international business develop cultural fluency and acquire cultural-sensitive communication tools.[49]

The development of managerial communicative skills in a diverse workforce is challenging because even a seemingly universal concept like "management" can be viewed differently from culture to culture. We now turn our attention toward the multinational business context and the views various cultures hold regarding management and managers as well as culture-specific business practices.

THE MULTINATIONAL BUSINESS CONTEXT

Cultural Views Toward Management

The development of intercultural management skills is extremely important because, as Gancel and Hills imply, managers need to confront the international realities with which they must deal.[50] Regardless of their culture, managers can find themselves working with culturally diverse project teams. Miller, Fields, Kuman, and Ortiz reflect on the nature of such teams:

> Project teams made up of members with differing cultural, ethnic, and corporate backgrounds and of different genders can be significantly superior to homogenous teams properly managed. They can also be much worse than even a poorly managed homogeneous team if leaders ignore differences between people of different backgrounds. In these situations, leadership characteristics should include an open style of management that increases trust, a good sense of humor to diffuse potential misunderstandings, a sincere interest by the project manager in his or her staff as individuals and good communication style.[51]

Dealing effectively with diversity then becomes the challenge for managers regardless of their culture. Their management orientation, cultural backgrounds, and communication styles, however, can lead to different approaches to achieving these goals.

North American Management Styles

It is imperative that you understand the dynamics of management behavior occurring in other cultures if you are to interact successfully with businesspeople from diverse cultures. But, we believe, you first need to have an appreciation of North American management culture before examining other cultural systems. From a business and management perspective, Harris and Moran describe Americans as being goal and achievement oriented, believing they can accomplish almost anything given sufficient resources. Americans tend to resent governmental or external interference in their affairs and possess a strong work ethic. They tend toward friendliness and informality, yet in greeting behavior they tend to be a noncontact culture in public. In both play and business, Americans tend to be competitive and aggressive because of their drives to achieve and succeed.[52]

Hofstede provides an insightful view of management that is consistent with the American culture:

> [Management] refers not only to the process but also to the managers as a class of people. This class (1) does not own a business but sells its skills to act on behalf of the owners and (2) does not produce personally but is responsible for making others produce, through motivation. Members of this class carry a high status and many American boys and girls aspire to the role. In the United States, the manager is a cultural hero.[53]

This set of values and orientations is not cross-culturally consistent. In fact, the American management culture is quite different from those of much of the rest of the world.

European Management Cultures

While there are similarities between American and European cultures, cultural diversity can produce management styles that differ considerably. Calori and Dufor report that European management culture has a social orientation that is in contrast to the prevailing U.S. management orientation toward profit.[54] This management culture, says Waddock, appears to influence both management practices and management education in the central European nations.[55]

In Germany, for instance, the manager is not recognized as a cultural hero. Like Americans, Germans belong to a data-oriented, low-context culture. As Lewis points out, Germans "like receiving detailed information and instruction to guide them in the performance of tasks at which they wish to excel."[56] Germans believe in a world governed by *Ordnung*—order. Everyone and everything has a place in a grand design calculated to produce maximum efficiency. *Ordnung*, says Lewis, is "inherently a German concept that goes further than even the pragmatic and orderly intent of Americans, British, Dutch, and Scandinavians."[57] The highly skilled and responsible German workers do not necessarily need an American-style manager to motivate them. Hofstede underscores this point when he observes that German workers "expect their boss or *Meister* to assign their tasks and to be the expert in resolving technical problems."[58]

German values include a strong sense of professional calling and pride in work, a tendency toward an authoritarian leadership style, and paternalistic commitment to the country's welfare. From a German perspective, effective managers are self-confident, energetic, open-minded, and particularly competitive. German management style, however, does not necessarily lend itself to working with other management cultures. As Lewis observes, most Latinos and many Anglo-Saxons experience difficulty in working or dealing with Germans because of the seemingly rigid framework within which many German firms operate.[59]

French business practices, while very European, are somewhat different from those of the Germans. The French orientation toward business, in many respects, follows from the philosophy of René Descartes and is based on a tendency toward logic and clarity. The French believe that humans are mainly reasonable beings with a good mind who are able to cope and solve their own problems. According to Lewis, the French believe that people can use their wits to achieve their goals by means of craftiness, cunning, and tricksterism. They employ a set of rules, regulations, and principles that constitute a body of authoritative ideas to govern proper forms of business. In this respect, says Lewis, French management styles are more autocratic than the German.[60] The French language, which, of course, reflects their culture, supports this management style because, as Lewis advises, it is rational, precise, ruthless in clarity, and argues its points with a logical urgency leaving little room for ambiguity or ambivalence.[61]

French culture is high on the power distance scale, which is reflected in their management styles. Hofstede provides this insight into French management practices:

> [The] French do not think in terms of managers versus nonmanagers but in terms of cadres versus non cadres; one becomes a cadre by attending the proper schools and one remains in it forever; regardless of their actual task, cadres have the privileges of a higher social class, and it is very rare for a non-cadre to cross the ranks.[62]

The French obviously value this high power differential. But, there are additional French management values that include individualism and authority based on absolutism. As Peterson explains it, because French managers or cadres are well paid, have attended the best schools (*grand écoles*), and come from well-established families, they tend to have an elitist approach to management.[63]

In a manner similar to the French, the British tend toward elitism in their management practices. Unlike the French, however, their views do not follow from a Cartesian perspective but rather from feudal and imperial origins. Lewis makes this important point clear when he writes: "The class system still persists in the UK and status is still derived, in some degree, from pedigree, title and family name."[64] British managers can be described as diplomatic, tactful, laid back, casual, reasonable, helpful, and willing to seek compromise and to be fair.[65] British English differs significantly from American English because it does not employ the exaggeration and tough talk of the American version. British managers manipulate their subordinates with friendly small talk, reserved statements of objectives, and a casual approach to work.[66]

Asian Management Styles

Asian management cultures differ significantly from those based on European elitism. Asian management styles reflect the values of collectivism and harmony we discussed earlier. As an example, Hofstede summarizes Chinese management styles and their relationship to Confucianism in the following manner:

> Overseas Chinese American enterprises lack almost all characteristics of modern management. They tend to be small, cooperating for essential functions with other small organizations through networks based on personal relations. They are family owned, without the separation between ownership and management typical in the West, or even in Japan and Korea. . . . Decision making is centralized in the hands of one dominant family member, but other family members may be given new ventures to try their skill on. They are low-profile and extremely cost-conscious, applying Confucian virtues of thrift and persistence. Their size is kept small by the assumed lack of loyalty of non-family employees, who, if they are any good, will just wait and save until they can start their own family business.[67]

As Chen explains, harmony is the ultimate goal of human interaction for the Chinese.[68] Additionally, kinship, interpersonal connections, face, and power are major factors dominating Chinese management practices.[69] In Confucian-influenced cultures, seniority is the main source of power. Seniority derives from age and length of service in an organization in China as well as most Asian nations. Seniority, as Chen observes, not only commands respect, it disarms criticism in the Chinese society.[70]

Japanese management styles also place a high value on the harmonious integration of all members of the organization into the corporate structure. Hirokawa points out that Japanese managers typically view their organization as a large extended family.[71] Managers—section chiefs or department heads— according to Peterson, value "groupism, harmony, acceptance of hierarchy in work relationships, sense of obligation, and debt of lower level personnel to superiors, and consensual decision making."[72] Culpan and Kucukemirooglu point out some of the differences between American and Japanese management styles: "While American managers emphasize supervisory style, decision making, and control mechanism, the Japanese are more concerned with communication processes, interdepartmental relations, and a paternalistic approach."[73]

The Japanese language is instrumental in Japanese management culture because it is capable of delicate nuances of states of mind and relationships. Harris and Moran point out that for the Japanese, indirect and vague communication is more acceptable than direct and specific orders. Sentences are frequently left unfinished so that the other person may reach the desired conclusion.[74] Harris and Moran relate that Japanese dress styles and appearance are neat, orderly, and conservative for managers. Workers and students frequently wear a distinctive uniform and frequently a company pin.[75]

Latin American Management Styles

You can observe yet another difference in managerial approaches when you look at Latin America. You should realize that Latin America is not a single culture but, as Marquardt and Engel make clear, a composite that contains a "rich number of cultures"[76] that exist in a widespread area that includes not only Mexico but also the regions of Central and South America. Global managers have discovered that all countries south of the U.S. border are not the same. The languages (Spanish, Portuguese, and Native Indian), food, music, and ethnicity (European, Indian, African, and *mestizo*) vary among countries and even within countries. For the most part, as Marquardt and Engle suggest, the power, politics, economics, and business practices continue to be dominated by people who live in cultures that have evolved from earlier Spanish and Portuguese colonial cultures.[77]

According to Lewis, the Mexican and Latin American managerial styles generally follow that of France, being characterized as autocratic and paternalistic.[78] In middle-sized companies, the CEO is often the owner, and even in very large firms a family name or family connections may dominate the structure.[79] Task orientation is directed from above; strategies and success are dependent largely on social and ministerial connections as well as cooperation between dominant families.[80]

Managerial style in Mexico differs considerably from that in the United States. Mariah de Forest summarizes this notion as it applies to Mexico:

> As in any authoritarian order, Mexicans value status and its observance. Americans regard status as "undemocratic" and try to minimize the differences by dressing casually, calling [someone] by his/her first name (and insisting that we be called by our first name). Americans try to train Mexican supervisors to do the same. But the Mexicans accept the hierarchy and their "stations" in life. To them the issue is honor, not equality. Rather than resent their "rank," workers expect respectful recognition of their roles within the hierarchy. Even the janitor expects respect.[81]

This authoritarian but honorable business system leads to a delicate balance between maintaining formal respect in the hierarchy and portraying informal sensitivity toward workers' dignity. Although Mexican management may appear autocratic and paternalistic, this style no longer functions as in the past. As Stephens and Greer indicate, contemporary managers and professionals, in particular, do not respond well to directives and commands, although they may have done so in the past.[82] Stephens and Greer further note:

> Mexicans are far less tolerant of abrasiveness and insensitivity in managerial styles than are Americans. . . . You can hurt the feelings of Mexican workers very easily. . . . This "soft culture" reflects the informal side of the formal/informal duality of the Mexican management style.[83]

Management style in Mexico is also affected by a company's ownership. Gray and Deane report that Mexican managers who work for large multinational corporations in Mexico, such as Ford and Johnson & Johnson, generally appear more similar to U.S. managers than those who work for Mexican firms.[84] And Stephens and Greer relate that Mexican decision-making authority tends to be centralized, seemingly undemocratic, and retained by a few top-level executives.[85]

This examination of diverse cultural views regarding management styles and managers should let you appreciate how a business procedure, often thought of as universal, can differ from one culture to another. Because of the cultural diversity inherent in the global economy, you may soon find yourself employed by an organization that transacts business with people from many different cultures. You may find yourself managing, being managed by, or co-managing with members of other cultures. Your ability to succeed in these situations will very much depend on your skills as an intercultural business communicator. With this in mind, we now move from broad cultural views of management to cultural-based differences in business protocol and negotiation.

International Business Practices

Business Protocol

A popular bumper sticker in the United States reads "Rules Are for Fools." While this may be expressive of the high value Americans place on individualism and independence, we urge you not to follow that admonition when doing business with people from other cultures. In most parts of the world, culturally correct protocol is both expected and respected. To introduce you to some of the variations in protocol, we start with the elements that help initiate business relationships: (1) *initial contacts*, (2) *greeting behavior*, and (3) *gift giving*.

Initial Contacts. The ways in which you make initial contact and an appointment to conduct business can range from a brief telephone call to writing a formal letter of request or the use of a "go-between" or emissary. The manner in which the initial business contact is made and the amount of advance notice between the contact and appointment are key factors you must consider when doing business in another culture. A few examples should help clarify this point. In El Salvador and much of Latin America, including Mexico, appointments must be made at least a month in advance by mail or telephone and then verified one week before the meeting. In Latin American cultures, you should establish your contacts as high up in the organization as possible. Morrison, Conaway, and Borden suggest you "use a local *persona bien colocada* (well-connected person) to make introductions and contacts for you."[86]

If you want an appointment in Egypt, you must send a letter of introduction to an Egyptian contact who can facilitate obtaining an appointment. Weinbaum points out that a significant majority of Egyptians have ambivalent or negative perceptions of Americans and the Western world.[87] Consequently, the use of an intermediary who is willing to set up appointments with all the right people is essential in the Egyptian business world. Endicott suggests that "Business by 'who you know' has always been an influential force in doing business in Egypt."[88]

In Africa, the use of an intermediary is also essential. There is a Congolese proverb that states: "The friends of our friends are our friends." Richmond and Gestrin relate that intermediaries can open doors, ensure a warm reception for your upcoming visit, and assess the prospects for the proposal you plan to present. An intermediary is an absolute must in Africa when approaching someone of a higher status.[89]

When doing business in China, it is important to establish contacts before you invest in a trip. "The United States Department of Commerce/East Asia and Pacific Office can assist in arranging appointments with local Chinese businesses and government officials, and can identify importers, buyers, agents, distributors, and joint venture partners."[90] To do business in Saudi Arabia, you must have a sponsor act as an intermediary, make appointments, and arrange meetings. In Italy, as well, strong contacts that can represent you and make appropriate introductions are preferred. Even with such a representative, it is important that your initial contact be written and in Italian.

The date you plan your business trip is also of major importance when dealing with another culture. For example, in China, many businesses close the week before and the week after the Chinese New Year. In Saudi Arabia, no business is conducted during *Aid-al-Fitr*—the three-day festival of breaking fast at the end of the month of Ramadan—and *Aid-al-Adha*—the three-day feast of sacrifice.[91]

In Japan, business is not conducted during New Year's holidays, Golden Week, April 29 to May 5, and *Obon*, in mid-August, because many people travel to the graves of their ancestors. In Israel, the Jewish holy day—the Sabbath—begins at sunset on Friday and ends at sunset on Saturday. The business week, therefore, runs from Sunday through Thursday. Attempting to conduct business on the Sabbath would be considered highly inappropriate.

Greeting Behaviors. Once a meeting has been arranged, it is important that the greeting practices of the host culture be observed. Americans tend to be informal and friendly. Both men and women shake hands on meeting and leaving. A small kiss on the cheek or a hug is appropriate between women or between men and women who have known each other for a sufficient time. First names generally are used with the exception of senior persons or formal situations. Business cards are exchanged in business settings but not in social settings. These greeting behaviors, typical to North Americans, are uncommon in many cultures. For instance, in Saudi Arabia, greetings involve numerous handshakes and tend to be expressive and elaborate. Saudi men often embrace and kiss on both cheeks. Saudi women are rarely present for business meetings, but when they are, an introduction is unlikely. Titles are very important for Saudis and are always used. Business cards are routinely exchanged and are printed in both Arabic and English.

China offers a contrasting example. Communicating a good impression to the Chinese businessperson starts with punctuality. The Chinese have a low tolerance for ambiguity, and they do not like surprises. To conduct business successfully, Bucknall believes you should communicate the details of a meeting agenda as well as any other issues to the Chinese prior to a meeting.[92] Also, the Chinese do not like to be touched. You should, therefore, avoid Western touching behaviors such as a slap on the back or an arm around the shoulder. As Harris and Moran indicate, a slight bow and a brief shake of the hands is most appropriate.[93] During introductions you should stand and remain standing for the duration of the introductions. According to Bucknall, social status and rank are highly honored in China. Seating arrangements and order of entrance into the meeting rooms are important because they reflect seniority and status. You should allow others to seat you and walk ahead of you to ensure that you are seated in the right position for the meeting.[94] Business cards are routinely exchanged. They should be translated into standard Chinese and include the name of your company, your position plus titles, for example Ph.D., MBA, vice president, or general manager. It is important to clearly indicate your position in the company so the Chinese can treat you accordingly. When presenting business cards, you should use both hands as a sign of politeness. When receiving a business card do not immediately put it into a pocket or brief case. Instead, as Bucknall advises, spend a few moments looking it over.[95] In China, the family name is always mentioned first.[96] As Bucknall indicates, a name such as Li Chen reflects the family named Li first. Thus, the proper form of address would be Mr. or Mrs. Chen Li.[97]

In Finland, firm handshakes are the normal greeting for men and women. Among the Finns, it is customary for women to be greeted first. So important is a firm handshake to the Finnish that even children are encouraged to shake hands. However, hugs and kisses are reserved for greetings with close friends and family. Introductions include first and last names or a title and a last name.[98] Acuff offers one final example of cultural variations in greeting behavior. In Nepal, he indicates, "The traditional greeting is the *namaste*, formed by pressing the palms together, fingers up, below the chin. A slight bow may be added to show respect."[99]

Gift Giving. An old adage in the United States says "Beware of Greeks bearing gifts." Most Americans view gift giving in the business setting akin to bribery, but in many cultures, gift giving is a standard part of business protocol. As such, it is important to know not only the views concerning gift giving but also what gifts are appropriate for men and women in the culture where you will be doing business. Examples of gift giving in Japan illustrate this point effectively. Gifts are very common among the Japanese. Morrison, Conaway, and Borden underscore the importance of gift giving in Japan: "Business gifts absolutely must be given at midyear (July 15) and at year end (January 1). They are often given at first business meetings."[100] It is also a standard practice to bring flowers, cakes, or candy when invited to a Japanese home. The ceremony of gift giving is more important to the Japanese than the gift itself, although both modest and elaborate gifts are prevalent. It is appropriate to allow your Japanese business colleagues to present gifts first, and then match your gift with the same quality as theirs. Do not expect gifts to be opened directly in front of you because this may be construed as a sign of greed. In the rare instances where gifts are opened in front of you, expect restrained appreciation regardless of what they think of the gift. You should not open gifts in front of your Japanese business colleagues but instead open them when you are alone and thank them later. The paper the gift is wrapped in is also very important to the Japanese. Rice paper is ideal. Although items made by well-known manufacturers are usually good gifts, you should avoid giving knives and scissors, because these items symbolize the severance of the relationship. A clock also is an inappropriate gift because it reminds the recipient that time is running out. As Dresser points out, "To give a clock as a gift is equivalent to saying, 'I wish you were dead.'"[101] Gifts with even numbers of components are also highly inappropriate in Japan, particularly in numbers of four, which could be considered the equivalent of the inauspicious number 13 in the United States.

As the preceding example indicates, the rules for gift giving in Japan are very different from the rules for gift giving in the United States. Instead of gifts, letters of thanks are standard in the United States. If gifts are given at all, they usually conform to the $25 tax-deductible gift allowed by law. Even when visiting a home in the United States, it is not customary to bring a gift, although a small token such as flowers, a plant, or a bottle of wine is appreciated.[102]

We have covered only a few elements of business protocol to make the point that business practices differ from culture to culture. This introduction to variations in protocol should amplify the importance of knowing and utilizing the business practices that are acceptable in the culture in which you will be doing business. As with protocol, there is cultural diversity in negotiation strategies and the communication surrounding negotiation. We now turn our attention to this important matter.

Intercultural Negotiations

In the normal conduct of business, most agreements are achieved through a course of negotiation. Harris and Moran suggest that "negotiation is a process in which two or more entities discuss common and conflicting interests in order to reach an agreement of mutual benefit."[103] Grundling adds, "International negotiation is a dynamic process. Outcomes develop from patterned exchanges between negotiation parties and their constituencies."[104] But, as Druckman points out, "It is important to understand that there are other values and implicit assumptions that influence other international negotiators' perceptions and behaviors in international meetings."[105] Kimmel demonstrates the effect assumption violations can have on the negotiation process:

> Prior to the Geneva meeting between Secretary of State Baker and Iraqi Foreign Minister Aziz both U.S. and Iraqi officials behaved in ways that were not expected by their counter parts in Baghdad and Washington. For example, the U.S. appointed a woman, April Glaspie, as its ambassador. In many Middle Eastern common cultures the American value of gender equality is not well accepted. The ambassador's gender and her status as a "Westerner" made her a very weak representative in Iraq. Even if she had delivered a clearer (from the Western point of view) message, it would not have been treated as seriously as if it had come from a male. The ambiguity of the message, of course, complicated the issue and signaled to Hussein that the U.S. was not concerned with his "retaking of Iraq's territory." To him, what was not said by the U.S. was more important than what was said (high-context communication).[106]

Success in international negotiation then lies in the successful exchange of both verbal and nonverbal messages that can become increasingly complex as both intended and unintended and perceived meanings vary.[107] This holds true whether the goals are business arrangements or international diplomatic processes.

People of many different cultures are busily engaged in negotiations worldwide, and, as Lewis says, the approach taken by each side is strongly affected by their culture.[108] This means that negotiators must heed Kimmel's advice and take a more intercultural approach to negotiation and abandon the type of ethnocentric approach typified by a negotiator who was reported to have said, "I'm representing America. I'll just tell them what to do."[109]

Negotiation involves pacing, negotiating styles, notions of what constitutes evidence and truth, and social trust.[110] All of these aspects of negotiation are subject to cultural diversity. It is important, therefore, to understand the impact culture has on the negotiating styles brought to the bargaining table.

Pacing. The pace at which negotiations occur is culturally diverse. Foster relates the following witticism that clearly illustrates this major difference in cross-cultural negotiation:

> There's a joke about an American and a Japanese sitting on a park bench in Tokyo. Both are businessmen. The American says, "Well, you know I've been in Japan for my company for forty years. Forty years! And now they are sending me back home to the States in just a few days." The Japanese replies, "That's the problem with you Americans: here today and gone tomorrow."[111]

To better understand the negotiation practices of other cultures, it is important for you to first be aware of the standard negotiation practices in the United States. Americans grow up believing in the motto "He who hesitates is lost." Therefore, most Americans conduct business at lightning speed. It is not uncommon for contracts to be signed during the first business meeting. These rapid contracts are facilitated by the fact that middle managers have the authority to make quick decisions without consulting the "boss" or conferring with the group. Sales forces are taught to "close the deal" as rapidly as possible. Brief small talk often precedes the business interaction, but the "bottomline," short-term rewards, and financial arrangements quickly become the focus.

In much of Latin America, business negotiations are conducted at a much slower pace. There is even a proverb that states, "To a hurried demand, a leisurely reply." In Argentina, it may take several trips to accomplish your goal, partly because it takes several people to approve each decision that is made. In some cultures, personal relationships take priority over the product or service, and therefore business does not begin until friendships are established. Personal relationships are so important that if you do not have a contact or intermediary, you may well never get an appointment. For this same reason, Argentines prefer to deal with the same representative for each transaction, or the whole negotiation process must begin again from scratch.[112]

In Mexico, too, relationships are important, and a great deal of time is spent building rapport before business proceeds. Mexicans are verbally expressive, and interactions often involve loud exchanges. These exchanges should not be taken personally, since, as Acuff advises, embarrassing one's counterpart is generally avoided.[113] Brazilians, like Argentines and Mexicans, enjoy bargaining and tend to make concessions slowly. In written agreements, there is the general assumption that unless each item of the contract is approved, it is open to continual renegotiations. Success in much of Latin America is tied to appearances. Business executives dress fashionably and expect their counterparts to embody this same aura of success.

In western Europe, negotiations also follow a different process. The French view the negotiation setting as both a social occasion and a forum for their own expertise. In addition, as Lewis points out, because of France's strong sense of history, the negotiation meeting provides them with the desire to fulfill their traditional role of international mediator.[114] French negotiators are often reserved. But the French team leader will be a highly skilled speaker whose Cartesian logic can reduce less skilled speakers to temporary incoherence.[115]

Negotiation in eastern Europe is also different from that in the United States. In Poland, Hungary, and Russia, for instance, the time it takes to negotiate business usually depends on whether or not the government is involved. When it is, negotiations proceed at an unhurried pace. When you deal with entrepreneurs, however, transactions can progress rapidly. Prior contacts are helpful but not necessary because a person's last successes are deemed more important. Communication is usually indirect, informal, competitive, and at times argumentative.

Cultural Negotiation Styles. Perhaps the most difficult aspect of international negotiation is the style people use in negotiations. Negotiation styles are reflective of the negotiators' culture. When these styles are significantly diverse, confusion, feelings of being pushed around, and misunderstanding easily develop. As Kimmel points out:

> Many misunderstandings and breakdowns in important international meetings and negotiations have resulted from the expectations about negotiation that the representatives brought to these encounters—expectations that were not shared by representatives from other societies. . . . One's own assumptions appear to be normal and realistic, because they are familiar and unquestioned when negotiating domestically. Most people believe that other negotiators should share their "common sense" assumptions, so it is natural for them to assume that those who do or say the unexpected in these international meetings are not as committed to and forthright about the negotiations as they are.[116]

Americans tend to have a negotiation style that emphasizes efficiency and directness. Again, we turn to Kimell:

> For the U.S. negotiator, negotiation is a business, not a social activity. The objective is to get a job done, which usually requires a mixture of problem-solving and bargaining activities. Most negotiations are adversarial with other parties seen as opponents. Negotiation success can be measured in terms of how much each party achieves its bottom-line objectives.[117]

Thus, for American negotiators substantive issues are more important than are social or emotional issues.[118] They want to get directly to the point, reach an agreement, and sign the accords as rapidly as possible. Other cultures, however, use different negotiating styles that frequently are at odds with American experiences and expectations.

In Germany, business is also conducted very formally with great attention to order, planning, and schedules. Because of this slow methodical process, it is virtually impossible to speed up a business transaction. Humor, compliments, and personal questions are not a part of the German negotiating style. Germans may expect business to begin immediately after introductions have been completed.[119] It is important to be well prepared when conducting business in Germany. With regard to the German view toward preparation, Acuff offers the following advice: "Proposals and presentations should be detailed, logical, and filled with appropriate technical data. Be thoroughly knowledgeable in product and contract details."[120] Germans tend to be direct, blunt, and up front. They will ask you difficult questions from the start. Lewis indicates that you must convince them of your efficiency, quality of goods, and promptness of services.[121] It is better to be silent rather than offer an uneducated opinion.

Finns and Swedes expect modernity, efficiency, and new ideas. They believe themselves to be up-to-date and sophisticated. They will expect your company to have the latest in office computers and streamlined factories.[122] Swedes show little emotion during negotiation and expect the same from you. Consensus is important to Swedish negotiators, and they tend to avoid confrontation. They may cut off a discussion abruptly if they think it will lead to an argument over a sensitive topic. In conversations, Swedes do not appreciate exaggeration or superficiality. However, silence is a part of their language pattern, so expect interactions to be filled with long pauses. In Switzerland, "Business is a serious and somber undertaking" as well.[123]

Direct, factual communication is important to Russians. "Russians regard compromise as a sign of weakness; it is morally incorrect."[124] As such, they usually try to "out-sit" the other negotiators for more concessions. Negotiations are often spirited and dramatic, with the Russian negotiator insisting the deal is over and storming out of the room, only to return to the negotiation table a short time later. Formalized contracts take time to construct, but until the process is complete, Russians rely on a signed *protokol* after each meeting to keep track of what occurred. The *protokol* is a "joint statement that delineates what was discussed. It is not a formal agreement."[125] Because business laws in eastern Europe are in a state of flux, it is often a good idea to have a legal representative present when negotiating with the Russians.

In the Middle East, business transactions have a different flavor as well. In Israel, a strong sense of fatalism pervades the business environment. This is probably due to the fact that neighboring countries are hostile to Israel and have frequently attempted to destroy it. Futuristic plans are of little importance if there is no assurance of life in a year. As a result, "Successful business deals in Israel must promise an immediate return. Long-term guarantees and warranties are rarely selling points."[126] Most Israelis, at least by American standards, are confrontational and emotional in their negotiating style. Interactions are conducted at very close distances, and physical contact is common among men, but not with women.

Egyptians, like most Arab businesspeople, love to bargain. In Egypt there are two bargaining styles: "suk" and "Bedouin." Suk bargaining is of the marketplace; it is less formal and usually begins with outrageous first quotes. Based on a process of give and take, suk bargaining eventually leads to a mutually acceptable price. The Bedouin bargaining style revolves around "face" and is based upon uncompromising principles. As Endicott indicates, Bedouin bargaining may involve third-party mediators because the reputation of the individual in the eyes of his or her group is at stake.[127]

Negotiating in Mexico is usually a long and complex procedure. Mexican managers will not engage in business discussions until a working relationship is established between the individuals or organizations involved. The establishment of a warm working relationship with one's counterparts is essential to the process and facilitates negotiation.[128] According to Harris and Moran, courtesy, dignity, tact, and diplomacy dominate Mexican culture. Protocol is important and social competence is as critical as technical competence.[129] Initially, Mexicans are more formal than Americans and are not accustomed to establishing a first-name basis as quickly.[130] They will, however spend time over coffee, meals, or drinks in order to get know a potential associate and his or her intonations. They put as much stock in an individual's character as in their resources and expertise. Contracts may go to a friend rather than to the lowest bidder.[131]

As a final example of cultural diversity in negotiation styles, we examine some cultures found in the Pacific Rim. There are many commonalties in negotiation issues among Pacific Rim countries. You can expect negotiation and decision-making processes to last longer than in the United States. Trust, respect, and long-term relationships are valued above contracts. Face-saving and status are crucial issues; as a result, many Pacific Rim countries prefer to conduct business with an intermediary in order to avoid conflict. Concessions tend to be in an escalating pattern, with minor ones coming first. For many of these cultures, age is equal to status, so the most respect as well as the conversation should be directed to the eldest person present. Communication tends to be very indirect, and silence is prominent in all interactions. As we have already shown, "yes" can really mean "no" as well as a host of other things. Consequently, in China, Japan, and some African nations, negotiators will avoid saying "no." As Richmond and Gestrin indicate, they may use such terms as "inconvenient," "under consideration," or "being discussed" to mean "no."[132] Smiles may hide embarrassment, shyness, bitterness, discord, or loss of face. When a negotiator from one of these countries draws air in through the teeth, there usually is a problem.

Despite many commonalities among Pacific Rim nations, each culture has unique negotiation styles. For example, in South Korea, you may be asked the same question repeatedly because Koreans are trying to make sure they are correct in their decisions. "Consistently repeated answers will help you more than fresh creative ideas."[133] In Japan, big decisions take time. The Japanese dislike making decisions and prefer to let decisions be made for them by gradually building up a weighty consensus. In their case, a decision might involve months of negotiations.[134] Lewis explains:

The Japanese have the most difficult task of all in making the transition from their internal monologue to actual verbal utterance. In their thoughts they agonize over striking a balance between gaining advantage and correctness of behaviour. Their thought (we can also regard this as internalized speech) has to be polite in the extreme in view of the fact that they are to address others. But the speech mechanisms involved in such politeness often lead to incredible vagueness of expression, so that whatever message they seek to convey may well get lost in a fog of impeccable behaviours.[135]

In Indonesia, there is such a great deference to superiors that subordinates will tell them exactly what they want to hear rather than the truth. The purpose of this practice is to shield the superior from bad news in public. The superior will then be told the truth later in private by means of informal channels. In China, says Whigham-Desir, doing business is not about "doing business"; it is about building relationships.[136] Newcomers and new business organizations will have to adapt to the Chinese style of negotiations and contract making.[137] The Chinese, Seligman reports, are genuinely interested in finding common ground and learning from those with whom they do business.[138] They generally give preference to companies with long-standing relationships with state trading companies. Hong Kong negotiators, perhaps because of their Western exposure, tend to be more direct and quick-paced than negotiators from other Pacific Rim cultures. In Hong Kong, negotiations always occur over tea, and the teacups commonly are used as visual aids. "One cup may be used to represent your company, another cup to represent the Hong Kong company, and the position of the cups will be changed to indicate how far apart the companies are on the terms of agreement."[139]

A final word about negotiation style involves the use of humor. As Lewis indicates, humor is culturally diverse: "What is funny for the French may be anathema to an Arab; your most innocent anecdote may seriously offend a Turk."[140] Few Asians are amused by American or European jokes. Lewis believes the Confucian and Buddhist preoccupation with truth, sincerity, politeness, and kindness tend to eliminate humor techniques such as satire, exaggeration, parody, or sarcasm.[141] In some circumstances, it is best to avoid jokes and other forms of humor during business. The Germans and the Japanese especially find it out of place during negotiations. They believe that business is serious and should be treated as such without irrelevant stories or distractions.[142]

Evidence and "Truth." Cultures can differ greatly about what they consider evidence and truth. North American cultures tend to rely on objective observations to establish facts. Truth is that which is verifiable. Statistics and empirical knowledge are of utmost import. In other cultures, however, you will find other approaches to what constitutes acceptable evidence and the truth.

The French have a saying: "Only truth is beautiful." It is also relative, for an important part of the negotiation process is determining what form of truth is acceptable and/or believable. That is, there are many different kinds of truth in the world, and the source of "truth" for a culture can heavily influence business transactions. Whereas many cultures, including the United States, rely on the accumulation of objective facts, other cultures may trust subjective opinions, religious beliefs, and/or mysticism. For successful business negotiations to occur it is important to understand the form of evidence or truth the culture you are doing business with prefers. For example, in much of Latin America, decisions are often based on subjective data that are usually influenced by the Catholic Church or political affiliations. Facts are accepted only if they support subjective feelings.[143] Faith in the Catholic Church as a source of truth often results in a strong sense of fatalism among people in Latin America. This sense of fatalism extends into business transactions. Proverbs such as "If your trouble has some remedy, why worry? And if it has no cure, again why worry?" and "Tomorrow is another day" reflect this outlook. In short, many Latin Americans are far more impressed with affect and emotion than logic.

In eastern Europe, countries are shifting from subjective faith in a communistic ideology to a reliance on more objective facts and reasoning. Western Europe has traditionally relied heavily on analytical, objective facts as the focus of evidence. As early as 43 B.C., Cicero, one of the great Roman orators, said, "Reason is the ruler and queen of all things." The locus of these facts is based in ideologies of democracy in Germany and the social welfare state in Sweden. However, in Switzerland, the segments of the population that are not German or French rely on subjective feelings based on faith in nationalism and utopian ideas.

Middle Eastern countries tend to value their religious faith as the primary source of evidence and truth. For instance, in Israel, subjective faith in Judaism and the success and security of the nation are prominent influences. Objective facts may supplement these feelings, but the strong sense of fatalism pervading Israel is clear in a proverb that states, "Life is too short to keep arguing; let's make a deal and be done with it."[144] In Egypt and Saudi Arabia, faith in Islamic ideas forms the basis of all truth. Objective facts may support Islamic ideologies for many Egyptians, but for most Saudis, objective facts seldom overrule their faith.

Pacific Rim countries generally rely on subjective interpretations as the source of evidence or truth. In South Korea, decisions are often based on nationalistic ideologies, but reliance on some objective facts is becoming common. In Hong Kong, one's feelings are supported by the ideology of the group and wholeness. In China, a faith in the governmental party is the source of truth. Chinese philosophy, which is founded in ideologies of universal order and harmony, has an impact on business. That is, ancient beliefs and religious practices are very much a part of Chinese business dealings today. Two such ritualistic practices are reliance on the lunar calendar and the use of "diviners" or a *feng shui* man to determine auspicious dates and arrangements for meetings, opening new offices, moving, and so forth. For example, "A restaurant column in the *Los Angeles Times* mentions that the chef-owner of an elegant Chinese restaurant was having a piece of property evaluated by a *feng shui* master before purchasing it for a second location."[145] Respecting your counterpart's belief in the *feng shui*'s prophecies is important when conducting business with the Chinese. It should be clear by now that criteria for defining truth are culture bound, and the source of evidence and truth in one culture may not be the source of evidence and truth in another.[146]

Social Trust. Another variable that confounds cross-cultural business negotiation is the issue of trust. Eventually, negotiators have to trust their counterparts. As Foster indicates, trust can be based on written laws of a particular country or it can be based on friendship and mutual respect and esteem.[147] Among the Chinese, for example, Weiss and Stripp note that trust derives from perceptions of personal character, honesty, sincerity, and being true to your word.[148] We have alluded to the fact that establishing trust before conducting business is very important in several cultures, but it is also necessary to consider the trust level of the society as a whole in determining the potential for successful business negotiations. Fukuyama labels this trust variable social capital and defines it in the following manner:

> [Trust is] a capability that arises from the prevalence of trust in a society or in certain parts of it. It can be embodied in the smallest and most basic social group, the family, as well as the largest of all groups, the nation, and in all the other groups in between. Social capital differs from other forms of capital insofar as it is usually created and transmitted through cultural mechanisms like religion, tradition, or historical habit.[149]

Trust or social capital has a profound impact on business from the transaction itself to the entire culture's economic growth. As with the other cultural values and patterns mentioned in Chapter 2, cultures can be placed on a continuum of high trust to low trust. For example, cultures such as Germany, Japan, and the United States are high-trust oriented in their business dealings. They have a marked proclivity toward association with other cultures. Their trust in dealing with other cultures has allowed them to create large, private business organizations. As Fukuyama observes, "It is no accident that the world's best-known brand names—Kodak, Ford, Siemens, AEG, Mitsubishi, Hitachi—come from countries that are also good at creating large organizations."[150] In contrast, in low-trust societies like China, Taiwan, Hong Kong, France, and Italy, the reluctance to trust those who are not kin has resulted in many small family businesses.

As we mentioned earlier, according to Fukuyama the cultures of the world are becoming increasingly dependent on one another. As a result, "The most useful kind of social capital is often not the ability to work under the authority of a traditional community or group, but the capacity to form new associations and to cooperate within the terms of reference they establish."[151] Success in cross-cultural business negotiations requires that you factor social capital or trust intercultural business communication.

International Marketing

Globalization of the world economy and the development of multinational corporations requires businesses to sell their products and services in a variety of culturally diverse markets. To accomplish this goal, products and services must be offered and advertised in a manner that is consistent with the culture in which the commodity is offered. This requires a set of communication strategies that are appropriate to the target market. In the past, this has not been a daunting task. But, as Fletcher and Melewar point out, this approach has its limitations:

> Approaches to international marketing communication for the most part appear to be grounded in ways of communicating with potential customers overseas who are not dissimilar to customers in one's own home market in terms of education levels, access to communications infrastructure, position at the upper end of the socioeconomic scale and who possess a degree of westernization. Although such groups represent the bulk of the world's purchasing power, they do not represent the bulk of the world's population, nor, given their declining birth rates, the possible bulk of purchasing power in the years to come.[152]

The task to be accomplished is to make your product or service brand meaningful to your audience.

Global branding is the process by which a company markets itself in a variety of culturally diverse markets. Tavassoli and Han provide some of the details on the difficulty inherent in this activity when they write:

> Global branding is complicated by the diversity of languages, nationalism, product attributes and culture. Given such complications, how or whether a manager decides to trans-

late brand names is critical to the success of global brand management. The challenge is exacerbated when the manager must decide whether to translate from a Western alphabetic language, such as English, into a language such as Mandarin.[153]

The use of logos is one method or representation. "Logos are the official visual representation of a brand name and are intrinsic to all identity programs. Auditory cues, such as NBC's familiar three-tone chime, and jingles are also used extensively for brand identification.[154]

As world markets continue to increase, there is greater emphasis on successfully entering those markets. For instance, as Tavassoli and Kan suggest,

> With the accession of China to membership in the World Trade Organization, more U.S. companies are marketing goods and services in that country, using the local alphabet and language to brand their offerings. Visual cues are most effective when the marketer is dealing with the logographic Chinese style of writing, whereas auditory cues work better with the English market.[155]

In developing marketing strategies for international markets, it is imperative to understand the cultures for which the product is intended. In China, for instance *Coca-Cola* means "tastes good and makes you happy." The Ford Motor Company has chosen a translation that means "happy and unique or special" while Philip Morris has translated *"Marlboro"* to mean "a road with 10,000 treasures." The choice of a brand name for another culture is more than selecting a simple translation; you must, for instance, consider culture, norms, values, traditions, and history when translating a brand name into Chinese. Waddock points out an important fact to remember: Chinese customers frequently buy products as gifts for holidays and special occasions, and, therefore, the symbolism of the brand name may influence their choice.[156]

We hope that by now you have discovered just how difficult the communicative dynamics of international business can be. This is an arena where well-developed intercultural communication skills are demanded. But, as you will soon see, there also is a great impetuous for the development of intercultural competence at the domestic level.

THE DOMESTIC BUSINESS CONTEXT

As we have noted throughout this book, through birthrates and immigration, the United States is becoming a nation of increasing cultural diversity. With the U.S. minority population exceeding 75 million, about a quarter of the workforce is now composed of minorities.[157] The U.S. Census Bureau's 2000 census revealed that there are 32.8 million Hispanics (12 percent of the total U.S. population) residing in the United States. This makes the United States the third-largest Spanish-speaking country in the world, exceeded only by Mexico and Colombia.[158] Demographers predict that by the year 2015, because of the move toward a multiracial, multiethnic society, minorities will make up more than one-third of the U.S. population.[159] Because the cultural diversity in the United States is so widespread, many of the issues that we discussed under the international context also apply to the domestic business context. By simply using one city in California as a microcosm of diversity, Wood offers a vivid example of domestic diversity. "On Alvarado Street, a paisley-shirted tourist overhears two students speaking in Mandarin Chinese to an Iranian jewelry vendor. In quick succession, pairs of strollers are heard kibitzing in Urdu, Arabic, Farsi, and Korean."[160] In this section, we briefly discuss two areas that are of primary concern for the domestic business context: (1) the importance of diversity in advertising and (2) conflicts in the workplace caused by cultural diversity.

Diversity in Advertising

The driving force behind marketing as we approach the twenty-first century is diversity and culture. Groups of people in the United States can be identified on the basis of ethnicity, gender, nationality, age, class, physical ability, and sexual orientation. Advertisers, say Gray and Deane, must encourage these group alliances as well as individual uniqueness to maintain a business edge.[161] The following look at the purchasing power of several groups illustrates the importance of this marketing balance. The Selig Center for Economic Growth at the University of Georgia estimated the purchasing power of ethnic markets as follows: $400 billion for African Americans, $235 billion for Latino Americans, and $150 billion for Asian Americans.[162] With a combined $785 billion and rising ethnic market, many companies like Procter & Gamble, Colgate-Palmolive, IBM, Avon, Levi-Strauss, Kraft Foods, NYNEX, and Nordstrom are reaching out to these diverse markets.[163] Three specific examples illustrate this point. Nordstrom, which is considered a pacesetter for diversity in advertising, has been presenting persons of color as models for over a decade; today over one-third of the models in their catalogs display diverse characteristics. Nordstrom also routinely features persons with disabilities in their advertisements. According to Deane, they were the first "upscale retailer to advertise in *Ebony*, a magazine that targets African Americans. Now it advertises in several other ethnic magazines including *Essence, Hispanic Magazine,* and *Latina Style Magazine.*"[164] Macy's is yet another retailer that has begun to pay particular attention to its multicultural market. The San Francisco Macy's recognized the large Asian American population that lived in the area, as well as the large percentage of Asian American visitors. In response, they created a "special boutique that stocks a large inventory of women's clothing in petite sizes" to serve the smaller Asian woman.[165] In 2000, the fast-growing Latino population was targeted by a major computer manufacturer. Gateway engaged in a marketing campaign that included Spanish-language ads, bilingual sales and technical staff, and equipping computers with Spanish software and keyboards.

Foreign businesses are also moving into United States markets so that they too can target specific ethnic and racial groups. For instance, the Gigante grocery chain of Mexico, as well as numerous other Mexican retailers, is establishing businesses in Latino enclaves across the southwestern portion of the United States.[166]

Diversity consulting and market analysis firms are appearing throughout the United States. Many of these businesses are owned and operated by ethnic group members. They promise strategy development, cultural assessment, implementation, training and measurement, and, of course, results. One such company is Hispanic Market Connections, Inc., a full-service market and research firm that is bilingual and bicultural. One of its advertisements states, "Understanding Hispanics' lifestyles, values and culture can mean the difference between Hispanic marketing success and failure." Another advertisement from a different advertising agency encourages marketers to tap into the gay market. Part of its advertisement reads, "Why are more companies targeting the GAY market? We'll be STRAIGHT with you. It's a simple fact: gay men and women are a lucrative niche market."

Cultural Conflicts in the Workforce

The United States was in many respects founded on a respect for differences. This respect has been an integral part of the country's history. As Davidhizar, Dowd, and Geiger remind us, it was "a lack of acceptance of differences in their country of origin that brought many immigrants to the United States."[167]

As we have shown throughout this book, cultures differ in their value orientations, and these orientations get acted out in the workforce. It is not hard to imagine how dissimilar values and views regarding gender, age, and ethnic diversity could create clashes in the workplace. There is also a positive side to sharing a business environment with people from diverse backgrounds. "Working with a variety of people with different customs, traditions, communication styles, and beliefs can cause interesting situations in the work setting."[168] Whether the contact is troublesome or "interesting" depends on how you respond to people who you work with. However, one thing is certain: As a wider blend of cultures emerges, such as the non-English speaking and the ethnic and racial co-cultures, business leaders must recruit and educate candidates from these co-cultures in order to create a representative and diverse workforce.

When workplace conflicts occur they usually involve discrimination and sexual harassment. We will examine each of these in turn.

Discrimination

While we will discuss discrimination in great deal in Chapter 9, we touch on the topic at this point to see how it impacts the workplace. We begin with this personal opinion: We strongly believe that discrimination is morally wrong. And when you move discrimination to the workplace it makes the entire working environment a tense and stressful place for everyone. And as such, everyone suffers—from the person who is the target of the discrimination to other workers, and to the businesses itself. The ripple effect discrimination can have on an organization is pointed out by Kunde:

> The more interconnected our world becomes—the closer we get to "one world"—the more each individual human being is empowered. Top companies realize the importance of creating a workforce as broad and diversified as the customer base they serve. Today's migration and globalization of diverse populations demand intercultural dialogue and the commitment from top executives to create and manage diverse and inclusive workforces in all areas of their business.[169]

The creation of competent workforces is going to be complicated by a shortage of qualified workers. As Fletcher and Melewar indicate, employers may face a large talent drain in the twenty-first century because the first of the 76 million baby-boomer generation will have reached the retirement age of fifty-five in 2001.[170] Furthermore, this situation will be exacerbated as the workforce ages and younger workers become scarce.[171] A major recourse to this situation is to seek out and employ a diverse workforce. This, of course, will require that employers stop discrimination at all levels of the business world and that managers acquire competent intercultural communication skills.

Unfortunately, many American businesses do not understand how cultural diversity is reshaping the workplace. As Austin implies, they find it difficult to recognize how building on both similarities and differences can provide the creativity and sense of community requisite to a fully effective workforce.[172] In their absence of vision, they often fail to comply with diversity laws until sued. In 1997, for instance, Texaco was confronted with a major lawsuit that caused the company's market value to drop nearly a billion dollars in a few days. In response to the damage to their pocketbook and reputation, Texaco changed the way it hired, retained, and promoted women and minorities.[173] Even now, workplace discrimination is manifest in many forms including *racial, ethnic, religious,* and *language* discrimination.

Racial/Ethnic Discrimination. Racial and/or ethnic discrimination occurs when an employee is treated differently because of his or her racial or ethnic membership. Blatant discrimination is disappearing, but subtle discrimination is often practiced. Davidhizar, Down, and Geiger report that both African American and Latino professionals are frequently placed in "soft positions" with limited opportunities for mentoring and training and being expected to perform at a lower level.[174] When incidents of open racism in the workplace are discovered, they are often kept below the level of national observation because, as Bernstein and Arndt indicate, all parties have strong urges to keep it quiet. Companies wish to avoid bad publicity and settle many complaints and suits out of court with extra damage award money to buy employees' silence.[175]

Because of real and perceived racial and ethnic discrimination in the workplace, many African Americans report they are steering away from corporate America because they believe they will not fit into the corporate environment. Some believe they are not ready to face the kind of challenge they think corporate America represents. While racial discrimination does persist, diversity is helping change American corporate culture to recognize the strengths and potential contributions people can make regardless of race, gender, age, physical ability, ethnicity, sexual orientation, or any other differences.[177]

Religious Discrimination. Religious practices are another area in which employers frequently discriminate against employees. While only a statistic of one, the case against Doris Karimnadir is an example of what can happen when religious practices become a part of the workplace. Doris, who practices the Islamic tradition of wearing a hijab (a traditional scarf), was sent home from a new assignment as a security guard when she refused to remove her headdress. The company, after realizing its mistake, apologized, reinstated her in a new post, and paid her for lost time at work.[177]

The problem of discrimination against Muslims has taken on added significance since the events of September 11, 2001. When those aircraft struck the buildings in New York City and the Pentagon in Washington, D.C., it greatly altered American attitudes towards Muslims. Muslim employees are finding difficulty reconciling their religious needs with production requirements. The main cause seems to stem from misunderstanding by both employers and employees (both Muslim and non-Muslim) of the religion, particularly with respect to the division between its compulsory, recommended, and optional elements. Additionally, some employers fear that allowing a proportion of the workforce to take time off to follow certain religious practices might jeopardize production. And some employers are concerned that catering to the needs of Muslim employees entails religious favoritism and discriminates against non-Muslims.[178]

Language Discrimination. Language discrimination can be aimed at any group and represent another problem that can plague work environments. For instance, because many workers are new to the United States, they may have an inadequate knowledge and command of the English language. This language deficiency can easily result in misunderstood instructions. Other consequences of multilingualism in the workplace are the suspicion and feelings of uneasiness that frequently develop when some members of the workforce speak a language that is difficult to understand. Unfortunately, employers sometimes display a lack of respect for other people's language and engage in discriminatory practices. In a recent situation, for instance, a Nigerian bank employee of the Rhode Island Hospital Trust National Bank was denied promotion after three years of good evaluations from his supervisors because of his accent. The Rhode Island Commission for Human Rights ruled in the employee's favor and ordered the bank to pay him $50,000 plus back pay.[179]

Gender and Sexual Harassment and Discrimination

Gender harassment and discrimination involve treating employees differently, and often unfairly, because of their gender. Harassment is directed toward individuals, while discrimination usually is directed toward a class of people. In Spokane, Washington, two women alleged that senior male executives of the Tidyman's supermarket chain discriminated against them and did not promote them because of their gender. A federal court jury agreed with the women's claim and awarded them substantial financial damages.[180] But we must recognize the real malevolence is associated with harassment, which is social rather than monetary. The "crime" of harassment, if left unchecked, can ruin lives and destroy an entire business or organization.

Sexual harassment includes unwelcome sexual advances, requests for sexual favors, or other verbal or physical conduct of a sexual nature when it is a term or condition of an individual's employment or when employment is dependent upon submission to requests for sexual favors.[181] Thus, a snide remark, a misperceived look, or an unappreciated touch can lead to concerns about sexual harassment in any workplace.[182] So common are these, and other such behaviors, that cases before the Equal Opportunity Employment Commission have increased dramatically in the past decade.[183] It must be emphasized that the workplace is not an appropriate surrounding in which you should express sexual feelings, desires, or attractions.[184]

Gender and sexual harassment have resulted in numerous legislative actions and court decisions. In one recent harassment case, the U.S. Equal Employment Opportunity Commission filed a civil rights lawsuit against MBNA Corporation, alleging that the company allowed a two-year pattern of harassment against a woman by a male coworker.[185] In another case of harassment, the Ford Motor Company agreed to pay $7.75 million to as many as nine hundred women to settle complaints that they were groped and subjected to crude comments and graffiti at two Chicago-area plants. In addition, the settlement called for sensitivity training at Ford plants across the nation.[186] Even in the realm of education, harassment is frequently present. In St. Tammany Parish, Louisiana, for example, a junior high school teacher believed to be involved with a twelve-year old student and a band teacher accused of fondling and kissing a sixth-grade girl were recently arrested.[187]

Granting there are many areas of conflict in the domestic workforce, we have not intended to create a profile of American business that is deeply embedded with problems that can never be resolved. As we discuss in Chapters 9 and 10, people have the ability to change. An awareness of the important influence culture has on the conduct of business is the first step toward change. As our awareness has increased, there has been progress in the integration of a culturally diverse workforce. For example, many companies appear to be working to promote cultural diversity among their workers. At Silicon Graphics, according to Sandoval, respect for diversity is so much a part of the organizational culture that "in the middle of lunch in the cafeteria, you will see hijabs, Jewish yarmulkes, and Hasidic headwear, and people will not bat an eye."[188] Major companies such as Apple Computer, AT&T, Avon, Coca-Cola, Corning, Gannett, General Motors, Goodyear, IBM, Xerox, Digital Equipment Corporation, Dupont, Hughes, Motorola, and Procter & Gamble have incorporated diversity management programs into their businesses.[189] Kellogg, the world's largest cereal maker, conducts diversity training programs and evaluates its vice presidents in part on their progress in minority hiring and promotion.[190] Prudential Insurance has sent more than seven thousand members of its middle and executive managers to diversity training in the last few years.[191] We conclude this section by urging you to be aware of the important influence culture has on the conduct of business. Part of that awareness is realizing that you may be uninformed of significant aspects of the business context as it relates to culture. Therefore, we implore you to heed the words of former president John F. Kennedy: "The greater our knowledge increases, the greater our ignorance unfolds."

SUMMARY

- The communication context refers to the cultural environment in which communication occurs.
- Culturally diverse rules specify how communication is to take place by prescribing the appropriate behaviors in given contexts.
- Rules concerning informality, formality, assertiveness, and interpersonal harmony can be found in every communication setting.
- In the multinational business area, cultures differ in their approach to management, business protocol, and negotiations.
- International marketing strategies need to adapt to the global marketplace.
- The American workforce is undergoing rapid cultural changes.
- The diversity of American society is changing the manner in which companies advertise their products and services.
- Cultures differ in their value orientations, and these differences sometimes cause conflict in the workplace.
- Issues such as religious practices, human rights, language diversity, sexual harassment, and sexual and racial discrimination present potential areas of conflict in the workplace.

INFOTRAC COLLEGE EDITION EXERCISES

1. To what extent does culture affect business goals? Locate and read "What Goals Do Business Leaders Pursue? A Study in Fifteen Countries" by Geert Hofstede et al. (Hint: To identify the central argument in a long research article like this, focus on the authors' abstract, introduction, discussion, and conclusion.) What is meant by the term "archetypes of business leaders"? In what ways does this article confirm or dispute popular cultural stereotypes?

2. Technology is changing intercultural business communications. Locate and read "Managing Communication within Virtual Intercultural Teams" by Christine Uber Grosse. According to the article, what are the challenges faced by virtual intercultural teams? What strategies are suggested that can help to make intercultural communication more productive?

3. This chapter explains that cultural conflict in the workplace is not limited to international business

experiences. Over the last ten years, the number of religious discrimination charges filed with the Equal Employment Opportunity Commission has nearly doubled. Locate and read Joel Palmer's article, "Religion Becoming Increasingly Interjected into Workplaces" and suggest strategies for responding to these conflicts. (For more on this and related subjects, use the subject search term "workplace multiculturalism.")

ACTIVITIES

1. Locate an ethnic business establishment in your community—grocery store, furniture store, etc. Notice such things as how the business is organized, how people interact verbally and nonverbally, how financial negotiations are dealt with, how long the business transactions take, how members of other ethnic groups are treated, and the like.
2. In a small group, discuss the various negotiation strategies used by negotiators in the United States, Latin America, the Middle East, eastern and western Europe, and the Pacific Rim. How might cultural diversity in these strategies affect intercultural communication?
3. In a small group discuss how the workplace in the United States can adapt to the increasing diversity in this country.
4. List as many words and phrases as you can that might create sexual harassment problems in the workplace.

DISCUSSION IDEAS

1. What is meant by the phrase "communication is rule governed"? What are some of these rules that might impact the business setting?
2. What are some of the elements of business protocol, and how may they differ from culture to culture?
3. What are the typical elements of American negotiation styles, and how might they clash with the negotiation styles of other cultures? Develop a set of recommendations for overcoming these clashes.

chapter 7

Cultural Influences on Context: The Educational Setting

The foundation of every state is the education of its youth.

DIOGENES

There is only one curriculum, no matter what the method of education: what is basic and universal in human experience and practice, the underlying structure of the culture.

WILLIAM HAZLITT

To teach in a manner that respects and cares for the souls of our students is essential if we are to provide the necessary conditions where learning can most deeply and intimately begin.

BELL HOOKS

GLOBALISM, MULTICULTURALISM, AND EDUCATION

We now turn our attention to the topic of education, for we strongly believe that the Chinese philosopher Tehyi Hsieh is correct when he writes, "The schools of the country are its future in miniature." Understanding these "schools," be they in the United States or elsewhere, has never been more important. For as we observed in Chapter 1, globalism and multiculturalism have become guiding international and national developments during the last several decades. These two trends, suggest Keohane and Nye, drive an evolution toward a world linked economically, militarily, environmentally, socially, and culturally at multicontinental distances.[1] These linkages occur through the flow and influence of capital and goods, of information and ideas, and the free movement of people across national borders.

Globalism promotes the ideal of thinking globally and acting locally by bringing forth numerous and profound changes in the economic, cultural, and political life of nations. This implies that when you challenge events at the local level, you need to understand how global forces affect your local reality. Naidoo reminds you that trying to resolve local issues without understanding the influence of global process is insufficient in today's world.[2]

Multiculturalism is concerned with establishing cultural connections that transcend our national experience. For instance, just as economies may be intertwined, cultures also may be intertwined. Multiculturalism, as Malveaux insists, is not only concerned with the mutability of borders and with the ways cultures influence each other but also with people, mobility, and the impacts of immigration.[3] Holland is correct in his assessment that this new multiculturalism requires that appropriate consideration be given to ethnic and racial cultural diversity, native languages, physical and emotional disabilities, and poverty.[4]

Within the democratic perspective, multiculturalism recognizes the personal worth and dignity of each individual. Singh believes that everyone deserves equal respect and equal opportunity for self-realization by virtue of their humanity and human potential as rational beings.[5] There are universal values shared by everyone, and there are particular values that are shared within various co-cultures. Co-cultures, according to Singh, should be seen as a system of values, attitudes, modes of behavior, and lifestyles of a social group that is distinct from, but related to the dominant culture.[6] You must recognize, as does Bruffee, that culturally distinct communities nested together in heterogeneous societies do share solid common ground.[7] Multiculturalism thus serves what Singh refers to as an overarching value that requires the acceptance of cultural diversity as a shared value by both the dominant culture and the various co-cultures of a society in order to establish a multicultural society.[8]

Since these universal and particular values form the core elements of both the dominant culture and co-cultures, Singh holds that education must find a way to combine particular values within the framework of universal values.[9] We, along with educators such as Singh, believe that educational systems should have as a primary goal the preparation of students at all levels to participate fully in the ever-emerging global village. As Stronquist and Monkman suggest, these changes will deeply affect how education is defined, whom it serves, and how it is assessed.[10]

EDUCATION IN A CULTURALLY DIVERSE SOCIETY

The Chinese have a saying, "By nature all men are alike, but by education widely different." This chapter is about the relationship between culture, education, and the changes taking place in the world we discussed in the last few pages. We believe it is important to examine the educational setting for three reasons. First, you can gain valuable insight into a culture by studying its perception of and approach to education. For example, the simple proverb "learning is a treasure which follows its owner everywhere" tells us the importance of education to the Chinese. By contrast, Latinos perceive education and schooling as being closely related yet different. Education, for Latinos, is more than formal schooling; it is seen as an avenue to economic reward. As Tapia points out, "Education also has a moral evaluative connotation such that a well-educated child has respect for elders and authority, has good manners, and is considerate of other people."[11]

Second, education in all of its forms is one of the largest professions in the United States. Consequently, many of you will be encountering members of diverse cultures whether you are a teacher in a traditional classroom, conducting business training seminars, or providing health care guidance to new parents. An awareness of the cultural diversity in education can help your understanding of specific communication behaviors in multicultural classrooms. Finally, as parents, or potential parents, it behooves you to know the dynamics of a culturally diverse classroom.

You should recognize that however large and different in symbolic and operational detail, most cultural communities are nearly identical in many of the most rudimentary elements of social structure, needs, and desires.[12] In essence, then, all cultures teach much the same thing: the perpetuation of the culture passing its history and traditions from generation to generation. Each culture's system of formal and informal education seeks to meet the perceived needs of its society. Thus, in every culture, schools serve a multitude of functions. First, they help fashion the individual. As children grow, what they learn and the ways in which they learn influence their thinking and behavior. From a child's view, education provides a way to certainty. It offers to every child a set of guidelines and values. The English philosopher Herbert Spencer wrote, "Education has for its object the formation of character." Children are also shaped by their schools as they become aware of what they need to know in order to lead productive, successful, and satisfying lives.[13]

Third, schools are a primary means by which a culture's history and traditions are passed from generation to generation. Or as historian Will Durant said, "Education is the transmission of civilization." To transmit civilization, schools teach the formal knowledge a culture deems necessary: language, history, government, science, art, music, and how to survive in society. This is true whether you are considering a country as large and complex as the United States or a small tribal society in the midst of a South American rain forest. For instance, the basis of survival in the United States, as presented in our educational system, is to obtain the knowledge and skills necessary to secure employment that provides income sufficient to live comfortably. In the forest, survival skills may include how to set an animal snare, how to fashion a functional bow and arrow, how to make a fire, or how to recognize which plants are edible and which toxic.

Fourth, the function of an educational system is to teach the informal knowledge of a culture. By the time children attend school, they have already been exposed to and internalized many of the basic values and beliefs of their culture. They have learned the rules of behavior that are considered appropriate for their role in the community

Schools are a primary means by which a culture's history and values are transmitted from generation to generation.

© Stone

and have begun to be socialized into that community.[14] In school, children continue this process and learn the rules of correct conduct, a hierarchy of cultural values, how to treat one another, gender-role expectations, respect, and all of the other informal matters of culture.

CULTURAL DIFFERENCES IN EDUCATION

As you would suspect, most cultures with formal educational systems tend to teach much the same thing—literacy, mathematics, science, history, and so forth. Yet there is still a great deal of diversity in (1) *what cultures teach* and (2) *how it is taught.* We will now look closely at both of these issues.

What Cultures Teach

In order for you to understand how culture influences education, we will begin with an examination of what cultures teach. In earlier chapters we emphasized that cultures impress upon each generation their world view, values, and perceptual filters. This task is in part a function of the formal educational systems within a culture. What is taught, therefore, becomes crucial to the maintenance and perpetuation of a culture.

Although the teaching of history is common to all cultures, a culture will emphasize its own history. Or, as the scholar Abba Eban notes, "A nation writes its history in the image of its ideal." For the United States that "ideal" consists of events such the history of the Industrial Revolution and the many victories America has achieved on the battlefield. In Mexico, the focus could be on the cultural heritage of the early Indians and the Mexican Revolution. The teaching of language is also common to all cultures, but the language emphasized is its own. By teaching a culture's history and language to schoolchildren, a society is reinforcing its values, beliefs, and prejudices. Each culture, whether consciously or unconsciously, tends to glorify its historical, scientific, and artistic accomplishments and frequently to minimize the accomplishments of other cultures. In this way, schools in all cultures, whether they intend to or not, teach ethnocentrism. For instance, the next time you look at a world map, notice that the United States is prominently located in the center—unless, of course, you are looking at a Chinese or Russian map. Many students in the United States, if asked to identify the great books of the world, would likely produce a list of books mainly by Western, white, male authors. This attitude of subtle ethnocentrism, or the reinforcing of the values, beliefs, and prejudices of the culture, is not a uniquely American phenomenon. Studying only the Koran in Iranian schools or only the Old Testament in Israeli classrooms is also a quiet form of ethnocentrism.

What a culture emphasizes in its curriculum can give you some insight into the character of that culture. Spanish students, for instance, are taught the basic skills of reading, writing, and arithmetic. In addition to these basics, Spanish students are also instructed in "formative" skills, "national spirit," and "complementary" skills. Formative skills are taught through religious education. For the Spanish, their culture is a matter of great pride. This pride is partially instilled by the teaching of national spirit as a part of the educational process. Consequently, instruction in history, geography, language, and physical training are an important part of their education process. Complementary skills are those topics the Spanish include because they believe they will be of benefit to their students. English, for instance, has been recently introduced into some Spanish classrooms because the Spanish understand that knowing English can have economic benefits in a global marketplace.

Because Chinese culture is distinctively collectivist, Chinese education emphasizes the goals of the group of society, fosters in-group belonging, demands cooperation and interdependence, and pursues harmony. The Chinese always stress moral education over intellectual and physical education. As Lu points out, Confucian tradition holds that teachers should not only teach knowledge but also cultivate in students a strong sense of moral and righteous conduct. Chinese teachers, consequently, hold a position of moral authority and instruct students in the culture's moral rules of conduct.[15]

The Japanese educational system is characterized by a high degree of uniformity. The *Monbusho,* a centralized ministry of education, science, and culture, controls Japanese education. Curriculum standards are specified in a national course of study. Generally speaking, students throughout Japan in the same grade study essentially the same material in virtually the same kind of classroom at approximately the same time and pace.

The Japanese curriculum, according to Honig, "emphasizes social studies, democratic political processes, and religious tolerance."[16] The Japanese are highly collectivist. This strong collective value is aptly expressed in the Japanese proverb that states "A single arrow is easily broken, but not in a bunch." Like the Chinese, Japanese students are taught cooperation, harmony, and interdependence. The Japanese strongly believe that proper social behavior is absolutely essential to social harmony; it is considered the bedrock of Japanese morality. Proper social behavior, therefore, is something that all students can and must attain and is paramount in the Japanese educational system.[17]

Although reading, writing, and mathematics are emphasized in Japan, unlike the United States, oral language is not. As Honig states:

> Educators in Japanese schools do not overtly concern themselves with "oral language development" in the curriculum. . . . Reticence is valued in the presence of elders and superiors in Japanese culture, and the school complements the home in imbuing this value in youngsters. Furthermore, even when it is one's prerogative to speak, simple and brief remarks are valued over lengthy or pointed statements. . . . Traditional fairy tales concerning "The Monkey and the Crab" show the smooth-talking crab to be quite a disreputable character. Japanese will point out that their nation has never produced a great orator or even a notable historical speech.[18]

This lack of practice in oral skills often causes Japanese students to experience serious problems if they attend school in the United States.

In Korea, all schools follow the same program of study. The Ministry of Education determines the curriculum content. There are few electives in middle schools and high schools, and variations are tailored to the type of school a student attends. Schools take a variety of forms. There are general schools, vocational schools, or specialized schools, and assignment is based on regional examination and lottery.[19] Reading and writing are highly emphasized, and children learn both Korean and Chinese in elementary school. Although children must learn approximately 1,600 Chinese characters to be able to comprehend a daily newspaper, Koreans believe that it is a sign of a well-educated person to be able to use Chinese characters. English, as well as an additional foreign language, is required in middle school and high school. Writing emphasizes penmanship rather than composition, and students are encouraged to imitate classical works rather than initiate their own original creations. In addition to standard subjects, Korean schools also emphasize moral education. Thus, as Honig points out, "Social values, civic awareness and duty, and academic preparation are all integral parts of the educational program."[20]

Mexico presents you with yet another insight of what a culture deems important in the education of its people. Knowledge of Mexican educational practices is also important because so many students from Mexico now attend school in the United States.

Education in Mexico differs in a number of ways from the educational systems found in the United States, China, Japan, Korea, or other countries. Mexico's educational system mandates that students complete the twelfth grade. The severe economic climate in parts of Mexico often precludes students from doing this. Some Mexican classrooms appear similar to those in North America. In rural schools, however, students seldom have the luxury of individual textbooks or the use of videos and computers. According to Grossman, rural schoolteachers frequently may have to read from a single textbook while students recite after them or write down what is said in a notebook.[21]

As is the case with most educational systems, history is emphasized. The arts, trades, vocational skills, and Mexican cultural values also are firmly emphasized. As Mexican children grow up within cooperative environments that emphasize strong family ties, the schools reinforce this primary value. Students are taught the value of cooperation over competition and to obtain rewards for others. So strong is the value of cooperation that "the Mexican student will tend to look down on overt competition because of his or her fear of arousing the envy and destructiveness of peers."[22]

Each year, Mexican students must take a battery of tests and pass every one of them before they are allowed to continue their education. Schools attempt to direct students into fields where they have proven inclinations as indicated from the scores on the tests. At the university level, there are few required classes; instead, a student is encouraged to focus on his or her specialty.

As you can see from the examples we have discussed, cultures tend to teach what is deemed essential for it to continue from generation to generation. In many cases—particularly within industrialized cultures—there are close similarities in the areas of science and mathematics. But, in other areas such as history and philosophy, and social values, there may be extensive differences in what is taught because of diverse cultural perspectives.

How Cultures Teach

As you have seen, being familiar with what a culture teaches can give you knowledge about that culture. But knowing how the culture teaches is just as important because it (1) provides insight into the nature of the culture, (2) helps you understand interpersonal relationships between students and between students and teachers, and (3) gives you a familiarity with the importance a culture places on education.

Inasmuch as cultures vary in what they emphasize, you should not be surprised to learn that there is cultural diversity in how students participate in the learning process. How education proceeds in a culture is tied directly to the values and characteristics of the culture. In some cultures, teachers talk or lecture a great deal of the time, whereas in others students do most of the talking. Silence and minimal vocal participation characterize some classrooms, whereas others tend to be noisy and active. In many cultures, students recite and then write down what their teacher has said rather than using individual textbooks. This is particularly true in countries where the economy does not permit the luxury of textbooks. Also, as we shall see in the next few pages, the authority vested in the teacher varies from culture to culture. Even nonverbal aspects such as space, distance, time, and dress codes are cultural variables in the classroom.

The Spanish classroom is characterized by a lack of competition. Unlike American students, Spanish students do not compete for grades. Ideas and information are shared and not treated as if they were the domain of one person. Classrooms truly reflect the Spanish proverb that states, "Three helping one another will do as much as six men singly." Because Spanish schools do not emphasize extracurricular activities, Spanish students tend to spend about twice as much time studying academic subjects than do American students. Because the Spanish culture has a high level of uncertainty, the classroom tends to be structured so that students feel comfortable. Teachers outline specific objectives for the day, enforce rules of conduct, and explain assignments clearly. Spanish teachers tend toward traditional styles of instruction such as lectures and drills.

Since the Spanish place a high value on loyalty and group consensus, there is very little disagreement in the classroom because it may disrupt the cohesiveness of the learning environment. In the Spanish classroom, teachers are considered to be experts. Students, therefore, are expected to agree with their teachers at all times or be viewed as disloyal. On examinations and written assignments, students are expected to repeat the teacher's ideas rather than provide their own thoughts or creative answers. Students are rewarded for their ability to solve problems accurately rather than for their ability to think creatively.

Reward for student achievement is delayed in the Spanish classroom. Students are expected to complete their homework assignments and other projects on time, but they must wait until their final examination to receive a grade. The evaluation of student work does not emphasize how well the student did but rather what needs to be improved.

In Japan, prestige is determined almost entirely by education. This has led to the development of a teaching system that is intensely competitive yet nourishes group solidarity and collaboration. The Japanese have a school year of 243 days compared to 180 days in the United States.[23] Over the course of nine years of education, this can add up to an extra two full years of schooling. Despite the collective emphasis of the culture, the Japanese educational system makes distinctions in individual ability very early in the academic process. Only the most academically advanced students gain entrance into the most prestigious college-preparatory junior and senior high schools. Many students often attend additional private schools called juku. Classes meet every day after school, on Saturdays, and during school vacations.

Korean educational processes are similar to those of Japan. Teachers assume leadership roles in the areas of social values, civic awareness and duty, and academic preparation. Parents hold teachers responsible for disciplining their children, and children are often told that their teachers will be notified if they misbehave at home.

For most subjects, Korean students remain in their homerooms and teachers rotate among classes. This permits the homeroom teacher to be both the social and academic counselor who can easily deal with discipline problems. As group solidarity and conformity are important goals in the Korean educational system, having students take all of their classes together and wear badges and uniforms leads to the achievement of these goals. These goals are further achieved through rules governing appearance, such as hair length for boys and no makeup for girls, which are strictly enforced even on the way to and from school.

Numerous cultural values get reinforced in the Mexican classroom. For example, Ting-Toomey believes that because Mexico is a collective culture it tends to deal with conflict in a manner that reflects consideration of the feelings of others.[24] Collectivism is also shown by the high level of cooperation in the Mexican classroom. As a result, according to Grossman, Mexican students may allow others to share their homework or answers in order to display group solidarity, generosity, and helpfulness.[25] In the Mexican classroom, group interaction is the primary learning mode, yet there are times when the teacher will talk and students will sit quietly at their desks. Because Mexican culture values conversation, when students are engaged in group interaction, they will participate enthusiastically in classroom discussion. It is not considered impolite for more than one person to speak at the same time. Multiple conversations may be carried out simultaneously. Teachers move about the classroom during these periods, interact at very close distances, and offer pats on the back or touches as a means of praise or reinforcement.

Finally, as we have said elsewhere in this book, Mexicans value the present. As the famous Latino writer Octavio Paz said, "Reality is a staircase going neither up nor down; we don't move, today is today, always is today." This focus on the present pervades the Mexican classroom. As Headden suggests, rather than moving from one subject area to another simply because the clock tells them it is time to change topics, Mexican students work at a relaxed pace even if it means taking longer to finish. Mexican students are more concerned with doing a job well, regardless of the amount of time required.[26]

From our discussion of these representative educational systems, it should be clear that culture dramatically affects the learning process. What the culture teaches exemplifies the culture's unique history and traditions. Cultures also differ in how they teach—lecture versus interaction, cooperation versus competition, silence versus noise, active versus passive, textbook versus recitation, and the like. Even the status of teachers and the esteem in which education is held are reflections of a culture's values, beliefs, and prejudices. We will now turn our attention to the complex issue of multicultural education in the United States and the challenges inherent in meeting the educational needs of many diverse students in the same classroom.

MULTICULTURAL EDUCATION IN THE UNITED STATES

As we indicated in Chapter 1, the world is experiencing a major population explosion. The projected world population in 2025 is 8.3 billion people. The United States is not immune to the effects of this population explosion. The forces of globalization on immigration policies have made it possible for many people of diverse cultures to call the United States "home." "According to the Census Bureau, 8.7 percent of Americans were born in other countries, the highest percentage since before W.W.II."[27] It is also estimated that there are between 8 and 10 million illegal aliens in the United States. What we are suggesting is that the racial and ethnic composition of the American population is changing dramatically. Currently nearly one in three Americans identify themselves as African American, Latino, Asian and Pacific Islander, or American Indian.

The consequences of population growth have produced an American society of unparalleled cultural diversity. And it should not be surprising to discover that this diversity has found its way into American classrooms. As a consequence, multicultural education must take on as an additional central focus the elimination of prejudice and discrimination.[28] In this section, we examine how schools in the United States have attempted to respond to the diversity now found in most classrooms. First, the goals of multicultural education are examined. Second, various approaches to multicultural education are discussed. And third, the impact of language diversity in the classroom is discussed.

Goals of Multicultural Education

Regardless of culture, educational systems must prepare people to become useful, functioning members of society. To help satisfy this need, educational systems must continually adapt to the ever-changing information-age needs of the global marketplace. This, of course, is an evolutionary process. As society changes, so must the educational system. One of the difficulties facing the United States today is the fact that the educational system is not adequately preparing children for today's globalized, multicultural, information-age economy.[29] Recently, a semiconductor company was searching for a manager who understood why computer chips are designed in India, water-etched in Japan, diced and mounted in Korea, assembled in Thailand, encapsulated in Singapore, and distributed everywhere in the world.[30]

Since we live in a multicultural society and world, it is imperative to recognize and affirm our genuine commonality. Buffee insists "schools should be looking for ways to engage culturally dissimilar students in understanding and dealing with one another effectively."[31] Chen and Starosta eloquently point out the value of a multicultural education in preparing students to meet societal needs:

> Academic exposure to the multicultural environment will provide students with the skills to excel in the real world. As the business world adjusts its views to fit a changing society, the academic environment must do the same. Because students ultimately return to the world outside the school, the more fully they learn to recognize and to respect differences in the beliefs, values, and worldviews of people of varying cultural extraction, the more effectively will they promote a multicultural society beyond the classroom.[32]

To this end, schools must provide their students with intellectual awakening and growth. The intellect is exercised through encountering new people, new ideas, and new social constructs. A multicultural student body is important to the experiences of both the dominant culture and co-cultures alike. Diversity, as Hirshon tells you, "prepares students for meaningful participation in our increasingly heterogeneous and multicultural democracy."[33] Such an approach to education requires that attention be given to the characteristics of the students that the system intends to educate.

The problem of educating students in a multicultural nation is not an easy assignment. The challenges and problems facing education in the United States are complicated by two interrelated factors. First, the American educational system, as Althen points out, "is based on the idea that as many people as possible should have access to as much education as possible."[34] This, of course, means that the educational system must be designed to accommodate all levels of student ability and all areas of interest. The second factor is increasing student cultural diversity. Historically, the classroom culture has been an extension of mainstream American culture. Its values were those of independence, individualism, and concern for relevance and application. The problem, as Calloway-Thomas, Cooper, and Blake point out, is that many "students whose backgrounds are different from the dominant culture experience a difficult time adjusting to this classroom culture."[35]

Fortunately, schools are adapting to the increase in student diversity. Teachers, administrators, and parents are coming to recognize that "as classrooms in the

United States become more diverse culturally, it is important for both teachers and students to understand some of the cultural factors that affect learning."[36] Many schools now routinely teach the experiences and values of many ethnic cultures. Current textbooks incorporate a variety of ethnic individuals who have achieved success. Struggles for equality are vividly depicted, and past racism is bluntly acknowledged. Cultural pluralism, according to Ravitch, is now generally recognized as the organizing principle of education, and children in American schools learn that variety and cultural diversity are assets.[37]

Multicultural education, says Holland, "should help students and teachers view the world from different and new diverse frames of reference and take into consideration and give significant and equitable tribute to differing attributes that have had an impact on the development of the modern world."[38] Gay states this goal in the following manner:

> The fundamental aim of culturally responsive pedagogy is to empower ethnically diverse students through academic success, cultural affiliation, and personal efficacy. Knowledge in the form of curriculum content is central to this empowerment. To be effective, this knowledge must be assessible to students and connected to their lives and experiences outside of school.[39]

For young children, who tend to be egocentric, appreciation of diversity is taught most effectively when they study the culture of their peers rather than that of entire groups of people such as "Native Americans." Learning about topics such as their peers' native languages, birth places, families, and ethnicity will help students learn about culture. Cultural awareness may be enhanced when students are taught to find the similarities in cultures among the differences.[40] Elementary school students learn not only about the traditional Thanksgiving celebration in the United States but also about other harvest holidays around the world. They learn that African tribal farmers observe harvest festivals to thank their ancestors for keeping them well and sending rain. The moon's birthday is the start of the Chinese harvest festival called *Chung Ch'ui*, in which the Chinese give thanks and remember a victory over an invading army. In India, Hindu women honor *Gauri*, the goddess of the harvest and the protector of women. In Japan, thanksgiving is a national holiday and a time to give thanks for blessings. Koreans, says Clegg, offer prayers for good harvests on *Tano* day, and in Switzerland and Sweden, children carry lanterns made from vegetables to celebrate their harvest holiday.[41] Middle schools and high schools include literature from around the world offering alternative perspectives on social problems and significant historical events. Ethnic studies departments can be found in high schools and colleges. And, as Letherman points out, many schools further require that students take courses in cultural diversity.[42]

Multicultural education emphasizes that human communication is often dependent on one's knowledge of culture. In this approach, teachers and students gain cultural knowledge and this information can enhance appreciation and sensitivity of students' own as well as others' cultures. This enhanced view of culture can help change misconceptions of culture that at one time may have caused miscommunication between members of diverse cultures. A successful multicultural classroom is one in which students and teachers understand each other in their communicative interactions.

There is some evidence that attempts at multicultural education are working. In the United States, for example, says Schrof, "graduation rates are up. The share of high school students taking a core of academic subjects increased from 13 percent to 47 percent in the past decade. The gap between whites' and minorities' test scores has narrowed."[43] These accomplishments may well be attributed to educators who daily confront diversity in their classrooms and have identified the central issues in educating a culturally diverse population. Those issues deal with (1) learning style differences and (2) language diversity. We will look at these topics so that you can appreciate the link between culture and the educational process.

Approaches to Multicultural Education

Multicultural education, says Holland, seeks to help students develop the knowledge, attitudes, and skills to participate in a free and democratic society.[44] A multicultural education, therefore, must recognize the cultural diversity of students and the effect that diversity has on the learning process. In the classroom setting, both *learning styles* and *language diversity* affect how students learn and participate in the educational process.

Learning Styles

Aristotle once wrote, "To learn is a natural pleasure, not confined to philosophers, but common to all men." Although learning may be natural to humankind, all people do not learn in the same way. There are diverse styles of learning that affect the way in which a learner learns and processes information.[45] Preferred learning styles differ among people and from culture to culture. Or as Calloway-Thomas, Cooper, and Blake point out, "The way students in one culture learn may not be the way students of a different culture learn."[46] The strong link between culture and learning, report Hollins, King, and Haymen, is evidenced by research indicating that culture and ethnicity have a greater influence on cognitive style than does social class.[47] It is important to note at this juncture that no learning style is better or worse than another.[48] As Gay suggests, learning styles should be looked upon as tools to improve the school achievement of diverse students by creating more cultural congruity in the teaching/learning process.[49] Additionally, research has shown that "when students are permitted to learn difficult academic information or skills through their identified learning style preferences, they tend to achieve statistically higher test and aptitude scores than when instruction is dissonant with their preferences."[50] In this section we will examine four dimensions of learning styles subject to cultural variations: (1) *cognitive*, (2) *communication*, (3) *relational*, and (4) *motivational* styles.

Cognitive Styles. In Chapter 4, we discussed the Sapir-Whorf hypothesis and the influence culture has on language and thought. This impact carries over into the education context because people from different cultures may perceive their environments and process information differently. These different ways of perceiving and processing information are known as cognitive styles. Although there are several recognized cognitive styles, culture plays a large role in determining individual preferences. Understanding the different ways people think and process information is essential to developing learning systems appropriate to a multicultural society. Hence, we will look at four common cognitive styles as they apply to the multicultural classroom.

Field independence versus field sensitivity refers to the manner in which people tend to perceive their environment and the emphasis they place on the field (the whole concept) or on the parts of the field. This is sometimes casually referred to as whether one tends to see the forest or the trees. According to Gollnick and Chinn, "Field-sensitive individuals have a more global perspective of their surroundings; they are more sensitive to the social field. Field-independent individuals tend to be more analytical and more comfortably focused on impersonal, abstract aspects of stimuli in the environment."[51] Field-sensitive students prefer to work with others, seek guidance from the teacher, and receive rewards based on group relations. In contrast, field-independent students prefer to work independently, are task oriented, and prefer rewards based on individual competition. Low-context, highly industrialized, individualistic societies such as the United States are predominantly field-independent, whereas high-context, traditional, collectivistic societies like Mexico and Japan are field sensitive. Leung examined a significant amount of research conducted by ethnic minority investigators and found that African Americans, Asian Americans, Hispanic Americans, Native Americans, and Hmong students tend to be field-sensitive, holistic learners.[52] Kush has found growing evidence that children raised in traditional Mexican settings develop a more field-dependent cognitive style than do children raised in Mexican American families that have been assimilated to the Anglo culture.[56] Many educators believe that Gollnick and Chen are correct when they suggest that "teachers should begin to function bicognitively in the classroom and teach students to operate bicognitively" as well.[54]

Cooperation versus competition describes a cognitive style denoting whether learners prefer to work together in a cooperative environment or to work independently in competition with one another. Students from collective cultures expect and accept group work; in fact, they often work harder in a group than they do alone. Students in individualistic cultures expect to be graded more on individual work. Latino cultures, says Grossman, teach their children cooperation and to work collectively in groups. North Americans, on the other hand, teach their young to work individually and to compete with each other.[55] Cultures vary in the degree to which they stress cooperation or competition. In addition to the Latino culture, African Americans, Asian and Pacific Rim Americans, Filipino Americans, and Hawaiian Americans tend to raise their children cooperatively. Students working together on class assignments manifest this emphasis in the classroom. For example, in Hawaiian families, multiple caretakers, particularly older siblings, bring up children. According to Hollins, King, and Haymen, this behavior extends to the classroom and is evidenced by "high rates of peer interaction, frequently offering help to peers or requesting assistance from them."[56] Cleary and Peacock indicate that Native Americans also tend to thrive in cooperative rather than competitive learning environments.[57] Teachers who understand which of their students respond to cooperative learning and which students prefer more competitive situations can provide classroom opportunities to accommodate both.

Trial and error versus "watch then do" refers to people's preference to learn by engaging themselves in a task and learning to do it by trial and error or whether they prefer to observe first and then attempt the task. Mainstream American students like to solve problems and reach conclusions by trial and error. This is not the rule in all cultures. As Grossman notes, "In other cultures, individuals are expected to continue to watch how something is done as many times and for as long as necessary until they feel they can do it."[58] Cleary and Peacock suggest that many Native American students, for example, prefer to watch until they feel competent to engage in an educational activity.[59]

Tolerance versus intolerance for ambiguity indicates how well people deal with ambiguous situations. Some cultures are open-minded about contradictions, differences, and uncertainty. Other cultures prefer a structured, predictable environment with little change. American culture has a low tolerance for ambiguity in the classroom. As such, the school day is highly structured and students move from subject to subject based on the clock. The level of tolerance or intolerance for ambiguity also affects what is taught in the classroom. For example, American culture emphasizes right/wrong, correct/incorrect, yes/no answers. Native American cultures, on the other hand, have a high tolerance for ambiguity and give little regard to truth in absolute terms.

Communication Styles. In the classroom, communication is probably the most vital activity because it is the mechanism by which learning occurs. Communication involves speaking, listening, and critical thinking. There are, however, various manners in which people engage in these activities. The preferred way in which people interact with one another is called communication style. In this section we will look at four styles of communication most relevant to the multicultural classroom.

Direct versus indirect communication reflects the degree to which culture influences whether people prefer to engage in direct or indirect communication. The communication style of Americans, according to Shade, Kelly, and Oberg, tends to be frank and blunt.[60] This level of openness, however, is often shunned by Asian Americans, particularly first-generation immigrants, because such behavior often causes a loss of face. These cultures also view directness as a lack of intelligence. As a Chinese proverb addressing this issue states, "Loud thunder brings little rain." Also, Native American children do not like to speak in front of the class; they feel put on the spot and become uncomfortable. Cleary and Peacock make it clear that teachers who are not familiar with cultural preferences for direct or indirect forms of communication may perceive students who prefer indirect communication as stupid, unmotivated, or learning disabled.[61]

Formal versus informal communication reflects the degree of formality expected in communication situations. Cultural differences regarding formality and informality can cause serious communication problems in a classroom. According to Althen, many foreign students are accustomed to quite formal relationships and sometimes have difficulty bringing themselves to speak to their teachers at all, let alone address them by their given names.[62] In Egypt, Turkey, and Iran, for example, teacher-student relationships are extremely formal and respectful. An Egyptian proverb exemplifies this formal respect: "Whoever teaches me a letter, I should become a slave to him forever." In cultures that value formal communication, students are expected to rise when the teacher enters the room, and teachers are addressed with their appropriate titles and last names, or referred to honorably as "teacher." For example, Dresser notes that in Taiwan,

> Students rise when the teacher enters the room, and in chorus they say, "Good morning, teacher." They remain standing until the teacher gives them permission to be seated. When students hand papers to teachers, they use both hands, avoid looking them in the eye and bow.[63]

Contrast the formality we have been discussing with the relaxed, informal student-teacher relationships in American colleges. Althen offers a clear picture of the informal and formal approach to education in the following two examples: "'My advisor wants me to call him by his first name,' many foreign students have said. 'I just can't do it! It doesn't seem right. I have to show my respect.'"[64] On the other hand, professors have said of foreign students, "They keep bowing and saying 'yes sir, yes sir.' I can hardly stand it! I wish they'd stop being so polite and just say what they have on their minds."[65]

Nonverbal communication is too varied to categorize into either/or styles. As we pointed in Chapter 5, however, this subtle form of communication is heavily influenced by culture and is often misinterpreted in the classroom. A few examples will amplify the notion that teachers need to become familiar with the nonverbal behaviors associated with their students' cultures. Puerto Rican students use a nonverbal wrinkling of the nose to indicate "What do you mean?" or "I don't understand." "In Alaskan Native cultures . . . raised eyebrows are often used to signify yes and a wrinkled nose means no."[66] In Jamaica, students snap their fingers when they know the answer to a question, but in the United States, students raise their hands. In most Asian and Latin American cultures, direct eye contact with the teacher is perceived as rude, whereas in the United States a lack of direct eye contact is considered rude and disrespectful. Even the color of ink used by the teacher can have nonverbal communicative effects. Teachers in the United States often use red ink to grade papers. However, in many cultures, such as Korea and parts of Mexico and China, red ink is a sign of death, and a person's name is written in red only at the time of death or the anniversary of a death. According to Dresser, to see the names of their children written in red ink may be horrifying to parents from these cultures.[67] A familiarity with the nonverbal behaviors of each student's culture will help to reduce miscommunication and improve learning.

Topic-centered communication versus topic-associating communication addresses the manner in which students examine and study a topic. European American students tend to be topic centered in their approach. As Au notes, their "accounts [are] focused on a single topic or closely related topics, [are] ordered in a linear fashion, and [lead] to a resolution."[68] For example, a topic-centered approach might include a rendition of a day at camp when candles were made. It would begin with the selection of different colored wax and progress to heating the wax, dipping the string in the wax, and finally cooling the wax in water to set the candle. In contrast, African American students often use a topic-associating approach. As Au indicates, their accounts, often "present a series of episodes linked to some person or theme. These links are implicit in the account and are generally left unstated."[69] For instance, a topic-associating approach might include a rendition of the purchase of a new coat. The story might include the following information: It was summer when the coat was purchased, the plastic bag had to be kept away from baby sister, a cousin began to cry because he wanted to wear the new coat outside to play, and mother was not at home that day. When instructors are not familiar with the topic-associating approach, they may not permit a student to finish his or her thought.

Relational Styles. The manner in which people relate to each other is called their relational style. As with other aspects of human behavior, relational style is yet another activity that is learned and subject to cultural preferences. Individual response styles carry over into the classroom context and can affect the way in which interaction occurs within the culturally diverse classroom. Of the various relational styles, we will examine five that have the greatest impact on multicultural education.

Dependent versus independent learning reflects the degree to which students rely on the support, help, and opinions of their teachers. Grossman highlights some cultural differences regarding this learning style when he notes that "compared to European American students, many but not all non-European American students, especially Hispanic Americans, Native Americans, Filipino Americans, and Southeast Asian Americans, tend to be more interested in obtaining their teachers' direction and feedback."[70] When teachers are aware of this issue, they can develop an effective support strategy in the classroom for students who show little initiative or independence.

Participatory versus passive learning describes how students prefer to participate in the learning process. In some cultures, students are taught to participate actively in the learning process by asking questions and engaging in discussion. In other cultures, the teacher holds all the information and disseminates it to the students, who passively listen and take notes. Many Hispanic, Asian, and Pacific Rim cultures expect their students to learn by listening, watching (observing), and imitating. In the American school system, however, critical thinking, judgmental questioning, and active initiation of discussion are expected of students. Here, again, there is an opportunity for teachers who are not familiar with cultural differences in how students participate in the learning process to make inappropriate judgments about a student's interest, motivation, and intelligence if they do not participate actively in the classroom.

Reflectivity versus impulsivity is indicative of how long students think about a question or problem before arriving at a conclusion. In the United States, students are taught to make quick responses to questions. As Gollnick and Chinn observe, "Impulsive students respond rapidly to tasks; they are the first ones to raise their hands to answer the teacher's question and the first ones to complete a test."[71] In other cultures, such as the Japanese, students are reflective and seek answers slowly. There are two Japanese proverbs that underscore the idea of being reflective: "Add caution to caution" and "He who rushes after two hares will catch neither." In cultures that emphasize this view toward being reflective, if a student guesses or errs, it is an admission of not having taken enough time to find the correct answer. This can result in a painful loss of face. Asian and Native Americans, indicates Grossman, are examples of students who are taught to examine all sides of an issue and all possible implications before answering.[72] In the reflectivity and impulsivity dimension, Mexican and North American cultures are the most similar. Both cultures teach their children to think on their feet and make quick responses or guesses to questions. The major difference between the two cultures is in their motivation to respond. According to Grossman, Latino students respond quickly because they wish to please their teachers and make the moment pleasant. North American students respond rapidly because individual success and achievement motivate them.[73]

Aural, visual, and verbal learning is concerned with the degree to which students are primarily aural, visual, or verbal learners. For example, say Cleary and Peacock, Native Americans tend to be both visual and oral learners and tend to use a combination of visual and oral learning styles, although they lean toward visual learning.[74] This means that they learn better through observation and images. Yet, because of the strong oral tradition of Native American cultures, Indians are also oral learners. As Cleary and Peacock point out:

> The strong oral tradition of American Indian tribal groups remains a potent influence on the ways many of the students learn, despite the fact that many of these students are first language English speakers or the fact that many have not been directly influenced by traditional storytellers.[75]

As a result of their cultural tradition, listening is highly valued in Native American cultures. This may seem like an advantage for Indian students, but because they listen with little feedback, teachers may perceive them as not paying attention or not being involved in learning. In contrast, says Grossman, "Many students, including African Americans, Hispanic Americans, Haitian Americans and Hmong Americans tend to be aural learners."[76] "Haitians usually have a highly developed auditory ability as evidenced by the oral traditions and rote learning methods."[77] Also, the Hmong, who do not have a written language, have highly developed aural skills.[78] When the classroom contains aural, visual, and verbal learners, a multisensory approach to teaching is often effective.

Energetic learning versus calm learning describes whether students function better in highly active and animated classrooms or calm and placid environments. African American students are used to more stimulation than is found in many schools. Franklyn makes this point in the following paragraph:

> Many African American children are exposed to high-energy, fast-paced home environments, where there is simultaneous variable stimulation (e.g., televisions and music playing simultaneously and people talking and moving in and about the home freely). Hence, low-energy, monolithic environments (as seen in many traditional school environments) are less stimulating. . . . Variety in instruction provides the spirit and enthusiasm for learning.[79]

Motivation Styles. Cultures provide diverse reasons why it is important and desirable to learn. These reasons are the motivational bases that prompt students to participate and excel in the educational process. Here, we will discuss two types of motivational style that impact the multicultural classroom.

Intrinsic versus extrinsic motivation is concerned with the source of motivation. Motivation is a primary concern for the multicultural teacher who must employ a variety of motivational techniques that coincide with the students' cultural backgrounds. Intrinsic motivation implies that the locus of motivation is found within. Extrinsic motivation reflects outside forces that impact upon the learner. Some students are motivated intrinsically to succeed, whereas others are motivated extrinsically. European American students generally are motivated to learn for intrinsic reasons. For example, many European American students desire to succeed academically so that they can secure a good position and earn a great deal of money. In contrast, Asian students are often motivated extrinsically. As Yao observes, "Asian children are often found to be motivated extrinsically by their parents and relatives. They study hard because they want to please their parents and impress their relatives."[80] Native American students are often motivated to learn so that they can please others rather than offend or hurt them.[81]

Learning on demand versus learning what is relevant or interesting describes whether learning proceeds best based on a set curriculum or whether students should be permitted to learn about what is of interest and immediately relevant to them. Says Grossman, "All cultures require children to learn many things whether they want to or not."[82] Some cultures, however, emphasize learning what is useful and interesting rather than learning information for the sake of learning. The Japanese culture, for example, requires that all students memorize information such as dates, complex sequences, and lengthy formulas in mathematics, science, and social studies. Each student is also required to learn how to play a musical instrument, regardless of his or her musical ability, and instruction often begins in first grade.[83] In contrast, the Hispanic and Native American cultures stress the importance of learning what is relevant and useful. For example, as Walker, Dodd, and Bigelow point out:

> Native American students prefer to learn information that is personally interesting to them; therefore, interest is a key factor in their learning. When these students are not interested in a subject, they do not control their attention and orient themselves to learning an uninteresting task. Rather, they allocate their attention to other ideas that are more personally interesting, thus appearing detached from the learning situation.[84]

There is a great deal of language diversity in the classrooms of the United States.

© Ariel Skelley/Corbis

In light of the numerous examples we have examined, it should be clear that multicultural educators have a complex matrix of learning styles to attend to in the classroom. It may be impossible to accommodate all of these learning styles simultaneously. When teachers are aware of these various learning styles, however, they can better choose which styles are most appropriate for their particular classroom.

Language Diversity in the United States

Language holds particular significance both in and out of the classroom. As we noted in Chapter 4, language is a system of symbolic substitution that enables us to share our experiences and internal states with others. A common language assumes mutual understanding. It facilitates shared meaning and allows you to communicate on a similar level.

Language and Identity. Language, as it applies to the educational setting, performs the vital function of providing the individual with his or her ethnic identity. As Dicker notes, "It is not surprising that our native language is often referred to as our 'mother tongue,' a term which recalls our earliest memories and influences."[85] A person's native language has a deep significance because it is the seed of identity that blossoms as children grow.[86] This language passes on the cultural tradition of the group and thereby gives the individual an identity that ties him or her to the in-group and at the same time sets him or her apart from other possible groups of reference.[87] When non- or limited-English-speaking students enter the American school system, they are encouraged to assimilate into the English-speaking culture. This very activity acts as a wedge between their existing identity and the social system into which they are entering.

Degree of Diversity. Language diversity in the American classroom has confounded the educational process. Not only is it a difficult problem to deal with, but the lack of a common language is a major statistical reality in many urban American schools. The

U.S. Census has determined that of the estimated 45 million school-aged students in the nation's public schools, about 9.9 million, or approximately 22 percent, lived in households in which languages other than English are spoken.[88] According to Leppert, if existing trends continue, by 2040 one-half of the U.S. population will speak Spanish as a first language.[89] In many urban schools, diversity has already eliminated the concept of an ethnic majority. Nationally, one-third of all students attending urban public schools speak a foreign language first.[90] In New York City public schools, children are taught in ten different languages; in Dade County, Florida, students speak no fewer than fifty-six tongues; and in California, one in three students speaks a language other than English at home.[91] As a result, some children come to school barely speaking English, some students are limited in their English usage, and other students are fully bilingual.

It is imperative that teachers respect students for whom English is a second language. King suggests this requires the demonstration of patience and the valuing of students' contribution to the class. To this end, teachers need to model respectful yet challenging communication and questioning skills that show respect for the diverse modes of student learning.[92]

Limited English Proficiency Students. Limited English Proficiency, or LEP, students are the fastest growing student population in the United States. These limited English students have a difficult time in school because of both cognitive and linguistic problems. McKeon identified four such problems. First, LEP students must be concerned with both the cognitive aspects of learning and with the linguistic problems of learning English. LEP students "must decipher the many structures and functions of the language before any content will make sense."[93] They must not only grasp the content but also make the new language express what they have learned. This requires LEP students to perform at a much higher cognitive and linguistic level than their English-speaking peers who need only to deal with the cognitive aspects of learning.

Higher cognitive and linguistic levels are often difficult to attain because of a second problem that plagues LEP students—academic delays. Many students who enter American schools are academically delayed in their first language. As a result, it is virtually impossible for them to function at the prescribed grade levels, much less higher cognitive and linguistic levels.[94]

Another problem for LEP students is that they enroll in U.S. schools at various points in their academic career—kindergarten, second grade, eleventh grade, and so on. The problem this creates, according to McKeon, is that "the higher the grade level, the more limited-English-proficiency is likely to weigh on students because at higher levels of schooling, the cognitive and linguistic loads are heavier."[95]

A final complication for LEP students is that they arrive from countries that may emphasize special curricular sequences, content objectives, and instructional methodologies. For example, Asian students use different rules and formulas for algebra. A deductive instructional approach generally is used in the United States, but Asian cultures use an inductive approach. American schools emphasize written education, whereas African and Middle Eastern schools emphasize oral education. As we noted many times, the North American culture values argumentation, debate, directness, assertiveness and the like. We also told you that many other cultures emphasize accord, harmony, and cooperation. Hence, students from these cultures may not possess the argumentative skills that are often found in North American classrooms.

IMPROVING COMMUNICATION IN THE MULTICULTURAL CLASSROOM

One important point should have emerged by now—it is imperative that classroom teachers acquire a comprehensive understanding of the ethnic, cultural, and social-class diversity present in today's schools. Ramsey makes that same point when noting that it is axiomatic to realize that "multicultural teaching cannot be taught in a mono-culture way."[96] Thus, "a western monoculture educational focus is inappropriate for students who regard this country as home but whose cultural values are different from the White population."[97] Ramsey clearly denotes this problem by indicating that

> Students experience courses differently based on their race, ethnicity, gender, sexual orientation, and other group identities. Consequently, students from different cultural groups will frame a course, conceptualize ideas, respond to ideas, relate to discussions and class exercises, and expect different things from a course.[98]

Teachers, therefore, must discover that culture creates expectations about appropriate behaviors for teachers and students and describes the "best" way to learn. Culture, suggests Cardenas, also determines how classroom activities are structured, dictates how classroom behavior is regulated and controlled, prescribes how teachers should teach, and affects perceptions about the importance of education.[99] Ramsey believes that in order "for a course to be truly multicultural in its perspective, that course must offer ways of learning, goals and assignments, and forms of grading and evaluation that reflect culturally diverse learning styles."[100] Without this perspective, Menchaca believes, teachers will face the difficulty of instructing effectively in classrooms made up of 51 percent minority students.[101] Additionally, teachers must obtain a more coherent view of knowledge that will provide not only personal empowerment but a social perspective truly reflective of the social reality in the larger world.[102]

We have highlighted several key issues in multicultural education. By so doing, it has not been our intent to generate an image of an educational system that is helplessly mired in problems. Instead, by identifying the impact of culture in educating a diverse society, illuminating the problematic issues, and considering the concerns of all those involved, we hope to extend the dialogue of multicultural education. Because the schools contain such diversity, educators, students, and parents must learn to communicate with one another and work together to find workable solutions to the problems. With this optimistic outlook in mind, we will consider some perspectives and some competencies teachers should acquire to improve learning within their diverse classrooms. Perspectives refer to a philosophical orientation toward multicultural education. Competencies refer to demonstrable characteristic behaviors of a competent multicultural teacher. Although there is an overlap between perspectives and competencies, we have chosen to discuss them separately because they represent different aspects of the same goal: improving communication in the multicultural educational environment.

Multicultural Teaching Perspective

Although teachers may neither be of the same culture nor speak the native languages of their students, they should adopt the concept of creating a socially sensitive multicultural classroom setting that will assist the learning of their students. As Ramsey points out:

Multicultural teaching requires incorporation of a new educational paradigm if it is to be truly responsible to cultural diverse students. This new paradigm requires greater knowledge of multicultural process skills as well as content. This incorporates students' experience, attention to the learning process, recognition of how culture is reproduced in the classroom and creative use of conflict as a basis for change.[103]

Teachers, suggests King, should attempt to build nonthreatening learning environments where diverse students are encouraged to contribute to discussions without requiring them to speak for their communities or races. In a nonthreatening learning environment, the teacher sets the tone by example.[104]

There are a number of perspectives teachers can employ to assist them in the creation of a socially sensitive classroom. These include perceiving the classroom as a community and structuring the classroom for optimal learning.

Classroom as Community

Teachers can begin this approach by creating a sense of community in the classroom. Palmer holds that "real learning does not happen until students are brought into a relationship with the teacher, with each other, and with the subject."[105] To achieve classroom community, Ramsey suggests that teachers must move away from teaching practices that exclude and ignore diversity and move toward teaching approaches that recognize and incorporate these differences in all aspects of their instructional approach.[106] To this end, Orbe offers six characteristics of a "true community" that may be applied to the multicultural classroom.[107]

First, *a community must be inclusive*. It must generate a general acceptance and appreciation of differences. A community must stress that differences are necessarily neither positive nor negative, but just different.

Second, the *members of a community must have a strong sense of commitment*. Such a commitment will allow them to "persevere through both positive and negative experiences."[108]

Third, *a community must recognize the necessity of consensus*. A true classroom community must possess the ability to acknowledge and process cultural differences until a consensus is reached.

Fourth, *members of a community must have an awareness of both themselves and others*. This recognition will lead them to develop knowledge of how "these two entities interact with the larger external surroundings."[109]

Fifth, *members of the community must feel secure enough to be vulnerable to one another*. This is accomplished through the creation of a safe classroom "where students are accepted for whom they are."[110]

And, sixth, *the community must be able to resolve differences*. In such a community the members must address problems using productive conflict-reduction strategies instead of avoiding or minimizing or disregarding differences.

Structure in the Multicultural Classroom

Another approach to the development of a socially sensitive pedagogy is the maintenance of structure in the classroom. Structure may consist of commonalties in day-to-day routines that help integrate meaning even with minimal linguistic forms. For example, elementary students learn that the roll is called at the start of every day, followed by mathematics and then a break. Students in higher grades may learn that class begins with a discussion of a recent current event, then proceeds to a lecture, and culminates with an activity. These standard classroom scripts, assert Saville-Troike and Kleifgen, help students to learn the intended information and respond appropriately.[111]

Structure also consists of coherent and uniform manners in which teachers approach classroom learning. Ofori-Dankwa and Lane, for example, suggest that instructors employ what they call a *diversimilarity* paradigm that stresses equal and in appropriate measure both cultural differences and cultural similarities.[112] In this application, teachers examine similarities and differences in trying to reach a fuller understanding of the contextual complexities of the diverse classroom. To the benefit of the students, this paradigm more accurately reflects the complexities of the real world. It gives students a better and more comprehensive understanding of communities and societies that are increasingly characterized by cultural diversity.[113]

Social psychologist Elliot Aronson offers yet another structural concept known as the jigsaw classroom.[114] The jigsaw classroom is a type of group learning that requires everyone's cooperative effort to produce the final product. Analogous to a jigsaw puzzle, each piece—each student's part—is essential for the production and full understanding of the final product. If each student's part is essential, then each student is essential.[115] Aronson notes:

> The major benefit of the jigsaw classroom is its remarkable efficient way to learn the material. But even more important, the jigsaw process encourages listening, engagement, and empathy by giving each members of the group an essential part to play in the academic activity. . . . Jigsaw students have expressed significantly less prejudice and negative stereotyping, showed more self-confidence, and reported that they liked school better.[116]

It is important to remember that children have the capacity to make rapid adaptations across vastly different cultural and linguistic systems.[117] When teachers and students work together, learning is facilitated. As Malcolm points out, "We are underestimating teachers when we consider them to be captives to the invisible culture of the classroom and we are underestimating pupils when we consider them to be captives to their own cultural patterns which contradict it."[118]

Multicultural Teaching Competencies

In addition to the adoption of the teaching perspectives discussed above, multicultural classroom teachers must develop several important competencies appropriate for the multicultural education process. These competencies include (1) *understanding diversity*, (2) *understanding the self*, (3) *assessing acculturation*, (4) *multicultural communication skills*, and (5) *empathy*.

Understanding Diversity

As an educator, it is important for you to be unbiased and to know as much as possible about the cultural backgrounds of your students. This includes a familiarity with the educational structure of the students' cultural heritages, as well as their particular learning-style preferences, linguistic rules, nonverbal behaviors, and gender-role expectations. As Wan says, "When people experience a new cultural environment, they are likely to experience conflict between their own cultural predispositions and the values, beliefs, and opinions of the host culture."[119] Although this knowledge acquisition places an initial burden on the instructor, such knowledge will facilitate understanding and learning in the classroom. Acknowledging diversity is consistent with the traditional educational goals that are to explore alternatives that change students' lives.[120] As Belatti points out, "If we do not stereotype students and consider their skills and experiences, you keep the door open to more talent and more potential."[121]

Understanding Self

The American writer Thoreau once wrote, "Explore thyself." This is excellent advice for anyone who is going to teach in a multicultural classroom. Put into practical terms, teachers should be aware of what they "bring" to the classroom. Teachers in a multicultural classroom must be aware of how their own cultural identities affect classroom dynamics.[122] An honest, straightforward evaluation can be very helpful in promoting the learning of all students. Rhine suggests several questions teachers might ask themselves such as, "What are my strengths?" "What are my weaknesses?" "How can I enhance my strengths and compensate for my weaknesses?" "Do I have any ethnic or gender biases?" "How do these biases manifest themselves in the classroom?" "Does my own ethnic or gender identification affect the classroom?" "Am I prepared to handle attacks on my racial background or those of my students?" "What new knowledge or experiences can I seek to assist in these issues?"[123]

Assessing Acculturation

The ability to assess students' acculturation levels will help teachers determine how much their students are involved in their own culture as well as the Anglo-American culture. Educators can choose from a wide selection of formal assessment procedures for evaluating students' acculturation levels. There are numerous scales and other assessment tools for Mexican Americans and Asian students. Teachers also can determine acculturation levels by observing students' behavior—which students they socialize with, the language they prefer, how they identify themselves, how they dress, their reaction to ethnic holidays, and the like. Grossman offers yet another assessment technique when he suggests that teachers can interview students or consult with colleagues who are familiar with students' backgrounds.[124]

Communication Competence

Teachers must maintain an open dialogue with their students. This is not to imply that the students should be in charge of the learning environment. Instead, it means that teachers and students need to discuss and negotiate learning styles, communication patterns, and expectations. This requires students to make connections between course content and their preferred method of learning. Students' voices should be routinely honored in the classroom through open discussion or teacher/ student dialogues.[125] In this way, teachers and students can achieve shared understanding and common communication codes.

Communication can serve to help students like and respect their teachers. Teachers may employ immediacy behaviors of approach and avoidance to develop their relationships with students and enhance their credibility. According to Johnson and Miller, students are attracted to persons and things they like, evaluate highly, and prefer. They avoid or move away from things they dislike, evaluate negatively, or do not prefer.[126] Teacher immediacy, therefore, has to do with how well teachers are liked by their students.

Research has shown a positive relationship between immediacy and cognitive learning and between immediacy and credibility across numerous cultures. Even in high-power-distance cultures such as Kenyan, say Johnson and Miller, students seem to benefit from seeing their teachers as approachable.[127] Additionally, Jazayeri reports that immediacy is also related to students' perceptions of teacher effectiveness in Mexico, Norway, China, Japan, and Australia, as well as the United States.[128]

Empathy

Finally, a key characteristic of the competent teacher is empathy. The empathic teacher must be able to infer the feelings and needs of his or her students. He or she must be able to imagine what it might be like to try and adapt to a classroom where surroundings, language, and behavior are often different and unfamiliar. Additionally, teachers must use cultural knowledge and acculturation assessment information to determine appropriate cultural responses to their students' needs. From observing the teacher's empathy and actions, students too will learn empathy and tolerance. As the American author Helen Keller wrote, "The highest result of education is tolerance."

It is our hope at this point that you understand and appreciate the impact cultural diversity has on the American classroom. And we want you to acknowledge that an educational system that fails to understand cultural diversity will lose the richness of values, world views, lifestyles, and perspectives of the diverse American co-cultures.

SUMMARY

- Globalism and mutticulturalism influence education.
- Systems of formal and informal education seek to meet the perceived needs of societies.
- Schools help to fashion the individual.
- Schools are a primary means by which a culture's history and traditions are passed from generation to generation.
- Schools teach the informal knowledge of a culture.
- Schools are a primary vehicle for teaching cultural values.
- Schools in the United States are becoming increasingly more diverse.
- Schools no longer teach only Eurocentric cultural values; instead, today schools routinely teach the experiences and values of many cultures.
- Despite improvements in multicultural education, there is still much controversy about approaches to teaching multiculturally.
- Learning styles are particular ways that individuals receive or process information.
- Cognitive, communication, relational, and motivational learning styles have a profound impact on classroom learning.
- Language diversity is an important issue in the multicultural classroom.
- Students who are limited in their English proficiency face various obstacles in the classroom.
- Teachers should know as much about students' cultural backgrounds as possible.
- Teachers should be aware of what they bring to the classroom.
- Assessing the acculturation levels of the students in the classroom will help teachers determine how much their students are involved in their own culture as well as the Anglo American culture.
- Teachers need to develop communication competencies.

℘ INFOTRAC COLLEGE EDITION EXERCISES

1. What is your opinion of using affirmative action to en-sure diversity in college admissions? In what ways does your membership in a co-culture shape or influence that opinion? Locate and read Jonathan Alter's article "What Merit Really Means," or use the subject search term "Universities and Colleges" and its subdivision "Admission" to locate others' perspectives. As you see it, how important is cultural diversity in higher educa-tion? How should diversity be achieved? Compare your viewpoints with those of your classmates.

2. Using the subject search term "Bilingual Education," locate one of the following articles: "Teaching and Learning in Bilingual Countries: the Examples of Bel-gium and Canada" by William Ross McEachern, or "English-Language Assistance Programs, English-Skill Acquisition, and the Academic Progress of High School Language Minority Students" by Marie T. Mora. What do these articles suggest about the viability of a "one-size-fits-all" answer to the challenges of bilingual education? What are your views on bilingual education and how are they shaped by your language experiences?

3. Want to learn more about the debated relationship between religion and education? Locate and read Cathy Young's article "One Nation, Many Gods: Vouchers, the Pledge of Allegiance, and the Separa-tion of Church and State." Summarize Young's views, and then respond with a paragraph in which you ex-plain your own perspectives on school vouchers and the Pledge of Allegiance.

ACTIVITIES

1. List some classroom curriculum topics that might help overcome ethnocentrism.

2. Drawing upon your school experiences, develop a list that indicates the impact of culture on the classroom.

3. Develop a plan for how you would approach a sixth-grade classroom with the following student clientele: six Latinos, eight European Americans, five African Americans, four Japanese, and one Iranian.

4. Given the classroom described above, what kinds of communication problems would you anticipate at the beginning of the school year?

DISCUSSION IDEAS

1. A college professor has a new student from Mexico with limited English language proficiency in her class. What factors might influence classroom interaction?

2. In what ways does your current classroom setting embody American cultural values?

3. What problems might students from various cultural backgrounds encounter in a classroom setting that does not foster a variety of approaches to learning?

4. How can multicultural education be effective if it must deal with a large variety of learning styles and language differences?

chapter 8

Cultural Influences on Context: The Health Care Setting

If you are not in tune with the universe,

There is sickness in the heart and mind.

NAVAJO SAYING

He who has health, has hope; and he who has hope has everything.

ARABIAN SAYING

CULTURE, HEALTH CARE, AND COMMUNICATION

The cultural context of the health care setting is important for many reasons. First, the promotion of health and the prevention of disease constitute an urgent need for studying this context. Graeff, Elder, and Booth report that thousands of people die daily from lack of immunization and from diseases and viruses such as AIDS, tuberculosis, cholera, and dysentery.[1] In addition, many of these diseases are highly contagious, and if immigrants with these disorders are not brought into the health care system, they can transmit these diseases to other people.

Exposure to global and multicultural populations has major implications for health care providers.[2] The goal of any health-care system must be to provide optimal care for all of its clients. This goal, however, can be difficult in multicultural societies because diverse cultural experiences yield different expectations and forms of communication. As Purnell and Paulanka note, "Health-care providers must be culturally sensitive and aware if they are to communicate culturally congruent health and treatment information."[3] They also believe that effective health care communication requires individuals to share freely their thoughts and feelings.[4] As you will discover later in this chapter, cultural diversity affects this ability and can result in ineffective communication between caregivers and patients.

Haffner notes that misunderstandings from ineffective communication cause many people to suffer needlessly. Misdiagnosis, risky procedures, and unnecessary treatments can be the result of miscommunication.[5] Finally, one way or another, you may be part of an intercultural health care interaction. The health care industry is one of the fastest-growing industries in the United States, and as such, you could someday become associated with the health care profession.

Communication between health care professionals and clients is complex even when the two are from the same culture. But, the influx of immigrants from different ethnic and racial origins can make it difficult for care providers to provide safe, effective, and culturally congruent care. This requires that providers have knowledge and understanding of a patient's cultural orientation, language, interaction patterns, and attitudes toward health and illness. According to Donnelly, when people are unaware of a person's cultural values as well as their family's expectations about roles and relationships, a communication disconnect can occur that may result in serious if not fatal outcomes.[6]

The factor of language diversity alone can create a seemingly impossible situation. How, for instance, does a young woman from Mexico who speaks no English explain to a medical team in an emergency ward in Los Angeles that the liquid drops she put into her baby's mouth (which the doctors intended for the baby's ears) have made her child worse? Why does a young Japanese woman on her way to surgery begin to cry when she notices that she is being wheeled into operating room number four? Why might an East Indian Hindu woman refuse to answer personal questions about her health in the presence of her husband? Or why might some hospitalized Chinese Americans politely decline offers of food or water?

To help alleviate some of these problems, and to underscore the importance of culture in the health care setting, the American Medical Association developed a policy of training physicians to be culturally sensitive. This training may be part of the medical school curricula, residency program rotations, or continuing medical education.[7] But, as Lipson suggests, cross-cultural health care requires more than just knowledge about various ethnic/cultural groups. It is a complex and interacting combination of knowledge, attitudes, and skills.[8]

As the nexus of thought and relationships, communication is the means by which people connect. When people do not share the same language or the same culture, their attempts to communicate may fail to establish the necessary connection that facilitates healing. Kerps and Thornton indicate that "human communication is the singularly most important tool health professionals have to provide health care to their clients."[9] But, as Spector indicates, "When there is a conflict between the provider's and the client's belief system, the provider is typically unable to understand the conflict, and hence, usually finds ways of minimizing it."[10] Health care providers, therefore, must learn ways of caring for their clients that match the clients' perceptions of particular health problems and their treatment.[11] Communication becomes the tool by which health care providers can understand the folk beliefs and cultural pressures that are common to various cultures and co-cultures. Understanding the belief systems, however, may not mean the health professional can change them. It is important to remember Koenig and Gates-Williams's suggestion that "calls for 'culturally competent care' ignore the dynamic nature of culture."[12]

As children grow up, they learn about culturally appropriate health care behaviors from their parents, families, and schools. They learn from medical workers and from many others with whom they interact. Culture teaches children what makes people sick or causes injury. And, as Fitzgerald indicates, it also teaches them the language or words they should use to describe body parts and illness sensations, how they should behave when they are ill or injured, and what they need to say or do to feel better.[13] People who have grown up in diverse cultures have acquired very different sets of knowledge, beliefs, values, and attitudes about health.

It should be obvious to you that effective intercultural communication is necessary in the resolution of health care issues. This chapter explores six dimensions of cultural diversity that impact the health care system. First, we begin by looking at the relationship between worldview and health care. Second, we consider health care belief systems. Third, we turn to cultural diversity in causes of illness, how illness is treated, and how it can be prevented. Fourth, we explore some specific issues concerning religion, spirituality, and health care. Fifth, we examine communication patterns in the multicultural health care setting of the United States. And, finally, we offer some suggestions for improving cross-cultural health care.

WORLDVIEW AND HEALTH CARE

Based upon our discussion in Chapter 3, you should recognize that religious elements of culture account for many of the differences in how people view the world—including views of health. However, religion is not the only worldview that influences health and illness. *Dualistict or holistic worldviews* and *mechanistic or nonmechanistic worldviews* also help determine how cultures perceive everything from the causes of illness to how illness is treated. We will discuss these two views briefly before we proceed into the specifics of cultural diversity and the health care context. From this discussion you should be able to identify the role worldview plays in determining patterns of communication and behavior in the health care setting.

Dualistic and Holistic Worldviews

Dualism distinguishes people from nature. Because it holds that people and nature are separate and distinct entities, it places a great deal of stock in medical intervention that is carried out by doctors, nurses, and other heath practitioners. This dualistic relationship between humans and nature is found, according to Smart, among members of Western religions such as Judaism, Christianity, and Islam "because they see two separate parts to reality—God and creation."[14]

While dualism posits a distinct separation of mind and body widely accepted in Western cultures, you need to be aware of the fact that other cultures hold a view different view. For example, Elgin points out that "the Eastern view is profoundly nondualistic."[15] In fact, most Eastern cultures tend toward a holistic vision of the world. This philosophy sees the world as a unit—a world continuously creating and intimately infusing every aspect of the cosmos from its smallest detail to its grandest feature. Human beings in this orientation are a unified body, mind, and spirit existing in a world that is profoundly holistic. This view would suggest that the person's entire body must be part of the healing process. In these cultures many remedies and techniques are employed when a person becomes ill. In short, it is necessary to take care of the whole person, not just part of the person.

Mechanistic and Nonmechanistic Worldviews

A mechanistic worldview is common in the United States and goes by many different names. Some refer to it as *reason versus intuition, objectivity versus subjectivity,* or *science versus religion*. Regardless of the label, this aspect of the American worldview deals with ways of knowing. Hoebel and Frost summarize this view:

> American thought patterns are rational rather than mystic; the operative conception of the universe is mechanistic. The bedrock proposition upon which the whole worldview stands is the belief that the universe is a physical system operating in a determinate manner according to discoverable scientific laws. . . . Because they view the universe as a mechanism, Americans implicitly believe that individuals can manipulate it. Human beings need not accept it as it is; they may work on it, and as they gain in knowledge and improve their techniques, they even redesign it so that it will be more to their liking.[16]

Paden holds that many Westerners believe that reasoning is humankind's "highest faculty and achievement."[17] For most Americans, facts are more reliable and dependable than subjective evaluations based on "feelings" and "intuition." In short, mechanism is orthodoxy and remains a pervasive view in Western culture.[18]

When this view is moved into the health care setting you find that Westerners have a strong faith in science and technology. They use modern scientific tools such as X rays, full body scans, blood tests, and the like to discover why they are ill and how they can get well.

The Eastern views of reality and truth, however, are very different from those found in the West. Elgin, for instance, notes that the nonmechanistic worldview is "a perspective that historically has emerged in countries such as India, Tibet, Japan, China, and Southeast Asia and is exemplified by spiritual traditions such as Buddhism, Hinduism, Taoism and Zen."[19] Whereas the Western view tends to place intellect and rationality above other traits, the Eastern view often maintains, say Fisher and Luyster, that "intuition transcends the data of the senses and the manipulation of the mind to

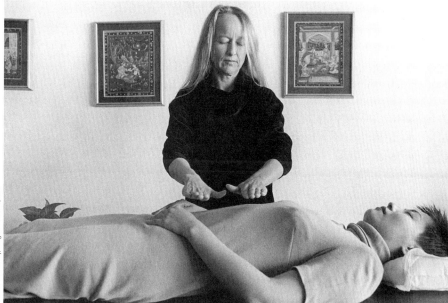

Cultures differ in their understanding of the causes, treatment, and prevention of illness.

perceive truths that seem to lie beyond reason." When dealing with illness, people who value the Eastern nonmechanistic worldview often believe that faith, magic, and supernatural forces can be employed as a means to good health.

In the next section, we are going to consider diversity in health belief systems. As you encounter these differing beliefs, we urge you consider how the dualistic/holistic and mechanistic/non-mechanistic dimensions cause individuals from different cultures to differ significantly in their perception of health care.

HEALTH CARE BELIEF SYSTEMS

Cultures differ in their understanding of the causes, treatment, and prevention of illness. The Chinese, for instance, tend to hold an ideal of a happy, long, and healthy old age. As a consequence, Hunter and Sexton suggest, the Chinese tend to be interested in health care that helps them attain this ideal.[21] Many Africans and African Americans employ folk medicine. From a cultural perspective, African Americans often perceive pain as a sign of illness or disease.[22] Despite this diversity, Angelucci provides a means by which all health belief systems may be divided into three categories: *biomedical, personalistic,* and *naturalistic.*[23]

Biomedical System

The biomedical system follows from dualistic and mechanistic views and is the dominant belief system in the United States, focusing on the objective diagnosis and scientific explanation of disease.[24] In this approach to medical issues, illness is the result of abnormalities in the body's functioning or structure. Agents such as bacteria and viruses or a physical condition such as an injury or aging generally cause these. Treatment destroys or removes the causative agent, repairs the affected body part, or controls the affected body system. Angellucci adds, "Prevention of disease involves avoiding pathogens, agents, or activities known to cause abnormalities."[25]

Personalistic System

In the personalistic system, according to Angelucci, disease is the result of active intervention by a supernatural being (deity or god), a nonhuman being (ghost or evil spirit), or a human (witch or sorcerer). The person is a victim of punishment and is rendered ill by the agent. Treatment involves assuring positive association with spirits, deities, and so forth.[26] Hmong culture provides a vivid illustration of the personalistic system. In Fresno, California, the courts were asked to decide if a young immigrant boy from Laos should be forced to have surgery on his clubfoot against the wishes of his parents. The parents believed that the surgery would arouse angry spirits who have punished the boy for a wrong deed committed by an ancestor. In this orientation the family believed that the evil spirit could be appeased only if the boy suffered for the entire family.

Naturalistic System

Naturalistic approaches to medicine tend to be nonmechanistic and explain sickness as a result of impersonal forces or conditions including cold, heat, winds, dampness, and an upset in the balance of the basic body elements. In this system, disease may result from disequilibria between the hot and cold elements of the body. "All foods, medicines, conditions and emotions are ascribed hot and cold qualities."[27] The Vietnamese, claims Nowak, explain poor health as resulting from eating spoiled food and exposure to inclement weather.[28] Treatment involves restoring the balance by prescribing hot remedies for cold illnesses and cold remedies for hot illnesses. As Angelucci explains, "Prevention of illness involves maintaining balance of the hot and cold forces within the mind, body, and environment."[29]

Now that you have a basic understanding of the three major categories of health belief systems, we will consider some cultural manifestations of those beliefs.

CULTURAL DIVERSITY IN THE CAUSES OF ILLNESS

Most health care practitioners in Western cultures subscribe to the biomedical model of health and illness that we just described. This approach emphasizes biological concerns and is primarily interested in abnormalities in the structure and function of body systems and in the treatment of disease. Adherents of this approach view this model as "more 'real' and significant in contrast to psychological and sociological explanations of illness."[30] Disease is diagnosed when a person's condition is seen as a deviation from clearly established norms based on biomedical science. Treatment through surgery, medicine, or therapy is designed to return the person to the scientifically established "norm."

The Hmong, say Geiger and Davidhizar, "believe an individual's spirit is the guardian of the person's well being. If the spirit is happy, then the person is happy—and well. A severe shock or scare may cause the individual's spirit to leave, resulting in unhappiness and ill health."[31] As Dresser demonstrates, the Laotian has a belief similar to the Hmong, believing that "Phi (the spirits of nature) control people's lives and can cause illness."[32] Illness also may be caused by losing one of the body's thirty-two souls or by a sorcerer who can cast a spell by projecting foreign objects into a person's body. Often, examining the yolk of a freshly broken egg will tell the Laotian the exact cause of illness. In a similar manner, many Vietnamese subscribe to personalistic causes of illness.[33] And, according to Nowak, for many Vietnamese, the natural element called *cao gio* is associated with bad weather and cold drafts, which cause problems such as the common cold, mild fever, and headache.[34]

In reviewing beliefs about naturalistic causes among Asian cultures, Giger and Davidhizar suggest that many people of Asian origin (Chinese, Filipinos, Koreans, Japanese, and Southeast Asians) do not believe they have control over nature. They possess a fatalistic perspective in which people adjust to the physical world rather than controlling or changing the environment.[35] Traditional Asian teaching stresses a harmonious relationship with nature in which the forces of yin and yang are kept in balance. Yin represents a negative, inactive, feminine principle, while yang represents a positive, active, masculine force.[36] Yin and yang combine to produce every occurrence in life. Consequently, many Asians believe that an imbalance in this combination causes illness.[37]

Traditional Mexican and Puerto Rican medical beliefs are based on the Hippocratic humeral theory that specifies four humors of the body.[38] Dresser reveals that these body humors are "blood—hot and wet; yellow bile—hot and dry; phlegm—cold and wet; and black bile—cold and dry."[39] An imbalance of one of the four body humors is seen as a cause of illness.

Spector suggest that people of African, Haitian, Jamaican, or Native American origin often view illness as a result of disharmony with nature.[40] Haitians, for instance, believe that both natural and unnatural events such as spells, curses, magic, and evil people can cause others to become ill.[41] In Native American cultures, where people hold strong beliefs about fate, reasons for becoming ill often are not even questioned. For them, ill health and even death itself are accepted as part of the process of birth and rebirth. An Indian proverb summarizes this view: "That which blossoms must also decay."

CULTURAL DIVERSITY IN THE TREATMENT OF ILLNESS

The English satirist Jonathan Swift once wrote, "We are so fond of one another, because our ailments are the same." Notice he did not say that the treatments for ailments were the same. Just as cultures differ in their beliefs of what causes illness, so too do they differ in views of what constitutes proper treatment of illness. As with health belief systems and causes of illness, cultural diversity in the treatment of illness may be approached from the *biomedical, personalistic,* and *naturalistic* perspectives.

Biomedical Treatments

As the cause of illness from a biomedical perspective is an abnormality in the body's function or structure, the treatment is to return the body to normal through medical intervention where treatment destroys or removes the cause of illness. In this sense, antibiotics are used to destroy illness-causing bacteria. Surgery, chemotherapy, and radiation are employed to destroy cancers. And nutritional supplements such as vitamins and minerals are used to return the body to its normal state.

Biomedical treatments are the dominant form of treatment in the United States and in many Western countries. In the United States, however, members of co-cultures may subscribe to a combination of beliefs about treatment and seek biomedical treatment for some illnesses and personalistic or naturalistic treatments for others. As Giger and Davidhizar point out, many Chinese Americans use both Western and Chinese medical services.[42] Many Filipinos are familiar with and accept Western medicine, although some Filipinos accept the efficacy of folk medicine and may consult with both Western-trained and indigenous healers.[43] Although Jewish-Americans usually follow biomedical treatment protocols, their treatment may require adjustment to religious requirements. For instance, the Sabbath, as Selekman relates, is one of the holiest days for Jews. Consequently, if an Orthodox patient's condition is not life threatening, medical and surgical procedures should not occur on the Sabbath or holy days such as Yom Kippur.[44] Vietnamese may not seek biomedical treatment until they have exhausted their own resources. But, as Nowak points out, once a physician or nurse has been consulted, the Vietnamese are usually quite cooperative and respect the wisdom and experience of biomedical practitioners.[45]

Personalistic Treatments

For many Asians—including Laotians, Hmong, and Vietnamese, as well as many people from Cuba, Puerto Rico, and Brazil—the belief that illness is in part caused by evil winds or spirits leads to treatments that are meant to induce the evil influence to leave the afflicted person.

In this vein, many Asian groups use "cupping" to cure illness. "Cupping" involves placing a heated glass upside down on the chest or back of the sick person and pulling it off after it has cooled. Another common practice among Asian cultures is "spooning" or "coining." In the spooning treatment, a spoon is rubbed vigorously back and forth across the patient's body, most often on the back and the back of the neck. Coining involves the use of a coin about the size of a quarter, which one rubs on the back of the neck, the stomach, the chest, the upper arms, and even along the forehead and temples. These practices are believed to "rub out" evil winds and spirits, but often leave marks that the unaware Western practitioner may interpret as a form of physical abuse. The Hmong use folk healers to cure illness. These shamans enter the spiritual world by chanting, which summons good spirits who then diagnose illness and prescribe treatment through the shamans. And, for the Mein, healing treatment involves elaborate ceremonies that require the offering of an animal, which the family cooks and eats.[46]

Filipinos hold personalistic or magic religious beliefs about illness that fit a general conceptualization of balance among traditional Filipinos. Miranda, McBride, and Spangler note that some Filipinos believe some disease is caused by a sorcerer who causes a poison or noxious substance to be introduced into the body disturbing the normal equilibrium.[47] Filipinos also view pain as a part of living an honorable life. Some view pain as an opportunity to attain a fuller spiritual life and to atone for past transgressions. They may appear stoic and be tolerant of a high degree of pain. Miranda, McBride, and Spangler maintain that because of this, health care providers must recognize this stoic toleration and offer and encourage pain-relief medication for the Filipino who does not complain of pain.[48]

Naturalistic Treatments

In Chinese medicine, the restoration of balance between the yin and yang forces is of primary importance. As Matocha notes:

> The Chinese believe that health and a happy life can be maintained if the two forces of the *yang* and the *yin* are balanced. The hollow organs (bladder, intestines, stomach, gallbladder), head, face, back, and lateral parts of the body are the *yang*. The solid viscera (heart, lung, liver, spleen, kidney, and pericardium), abdomen, chest, and the inner parts of the body are the *yin*. The *yin* is cold and the *yang* is hot. Health care providers need to be aware that the functions of life and the interplay of these functions, rather than the structures, are important to Chinese.[49]

The Chinese are apt to self-medicate if they believe they know what is wrong or have been successfully treated by medicine or herbs in the past.[50] They may also rely on fortune-tellers to determine auspicious times to perform scheduled surgeries or other medical procedures.

Laotian women, say Warren and Munoz,

> are expected to rest after having a baby. In their country, they often lay on a bed that has hot coal under it for heat. This practice is based on the Asian belief that heat is good for some ailments and cold is good for others. However, in Western medicine, this can be a problem because the hygiene of postpartum patients is an important part of discharge instructions, and women are encouraged to shower. This active intervention associated with water that at times can be cold is not always acceptable to women from Laos who embrace their traditions.[51]

In Mexico, folk medicine is a common form of treating illness. Mexican folk medicine can be traced back to sixteenth-century Spain. It looks beyond illness symptoms and seeks an imbalance in an individual's relationship with the environment, emotional states, and social, spiritual, and physical factors. When one becomes ill, folk healers use foods and herbs to restore the desired balance. A hot disease is treated with cold or cool foods. A cold disease is treated by hot foods. Hot and cold do not refer to the temperature of the foods but to their intrinsic nature. Hot foods include chocolate, garlic, cinnamon, mint, and cheese. Cold foods include avocados, bananas, fruit juice, lima beans, and sugarcane.[52]

According to Burke, Wieser, and Keegan, the common folk healers in Mexico are *Curanderos, Yerberos,* and *Sobadors:*

> *Curanderos* (healers), believed to be chosen and empowered by God, are the most respected folk healers. . . . *Yerberos* (herbalists) specialize in the use of herbs and spices to treat and prevent illness. . . . *Sobadors* (masseuses) attempt to correct musculoskeletal imbalances through massage or manipulation.[53]

Many people from Cuba, Puerto Rico, and Brazil believe in *Santeria* (a type of religion). Dresser holds that when someone becomes sick, a *santero* is contacted, who consults an *Orisha* (saintlike deity) to assist in the cure.[54] Also, according to Galanti, it is not uncommon for Haitians to consult voodoo priests and priestesses for treatment that can involve candles, baths, charms, and spirit visits. Within the United States, some groups, particularly African Americans, rely on pica—a craving for nonfood substances—to treat illness. For example, an individual may eat laundry starch to "build up the blood" after an auto accident.[55] And, as Grossman relates, "Cubans may use traditional medicinal plants in the form of teas, potions, salves, or poultices. In the Little Havana community of Miami, *botanicas* sell a variety of herbs, ointments, oils, powders, incenses, and religious figurines to relieve maladies, bring good luck, drive away evil sprits, or break curses."[56]

Not everyone subscribes to a specific approach in the treatment of illness. In Africa, for instance, there is no typical approach to seeking medical treatment. The effects of colonialism, spirituality, and ancestral traditions affect the varying perceptions toward health care. Many Africans differentiate health care into modern and traditional. Modern medicine follows the active biomedical model of Western medicine. Traditional medicine follows the folk healer tradition. Depending on the type of illness, patients will choose what they believe the most effective treatment.[57] Finally, as Campinha-Bacote relates, many African Americans draw upon their roots and employ folk practitioners who can be spiritual leaders, grandparents, elders of the community, or voodoo doctors or priests.[58]

Although some of these treatments may seem unusual or even bizarre from a Western perspective, medical practitioners in other cultures have employed these methods for centuries.

CULTURAL DIVERSITY IN THE PREVENTION OF ILLNESS

Cultures reflect various degrees of diversity in their beliefs and practices about what can be done to prevent illness. Unlike the causes and treatment of illness, where the approaches are rather systematic, in the prevention of illness, people from many cultures employ a combination of biomedical, personalistic, and naturalistic approaches. In the United States and other highly technological cultures, for instance, good health is based on annual physicals, immunizations at specified times, exercise, and good nutrition. Yet, many people also follow health regimens that may include stress-reducing meditation and the ingestion of a variety of "natural" herbs to stimulate sexual performance, prevent or reduce memory loss, and promote energy. In addition, they may seek treatment from chiropractors, acupuncturists, or colon irrigationists as preventive measures.

In sharp contrast, many Muslim Afghanis rely on the Koran to protect them from illness. In a practice called *ta' wiz,* Koran verses are written on paper, wrapped in cloth, and worn by babies and the sickly. Dressler reports that

> Shuist are Koran verses written on paper, and then soaked in water that is drunk. Dudi are Koran verses written on paper and burned with rue close to the patient so the smoke will kill germs and ward off evil spirits.[59]

Many members of Mexican and Puerto Rican cultures, as Giger and Davidhizar report, "believe that health may be the result of good luck or a reward from God for good behavior."[60] Consequently, they frequently depend on a variety of items for protection. Amulets or charms, often inscribed with magic symbols or sayings, are common to protect the wearer from disease or evil. Candles, herbs, crystals, statues of saints, shells, and teas also provide protection.

In many Asian cultures, a *Baci* ceremony is a common practice. During pregnancy, birth, marriage, a change of location, illness, or surgery, the family hosts a ceremony. According to Galanti, family members, including a community elder, gather around an altar of "candles, incense, rice, holy water, flowers, and strings."[61] Because some Asians believe that the spirit might depart from the body on these occasions, the body spirits are contacted by the chanting of the elder, and then strings are tied around the patient's wrist to bind the spirits to the body. These strings are usually worn for three days.

Many other cultures shun violating cultural taboos for protection from illness or in an attempt to avoid exacerbating the illness. For example, several Native American cultures believe it is taboo to cut a child's hair because the child will become sicker and die. This belief can even extend to procedures on the child's head, such as stitches that require removal of the hair. The only way to avoid the death of the child is to counteract the violation of the taboo by attaching a medicine bundle to the child's chest.[62] In a similar manner, Galanti explains, Hmong women who become pregnant ensure the health of their children by paying close attention to food cravings. It is their belief, for example, that if a woman "craved ginger and failed to eat it, her child will be born with an extra finger or toe."[63]

Although many cultures practice preventive measures, for others prevention is a totally new concept. Many Haitians, for example, do not believe in preventive strategies and rarely engage in immunization. They may bring their ailing to the hospital only when death is imminent. Some cultures believe that the cure for our illnesses can often be found within us. A Yugoslavian proverb says, "Good thoughts are half of health."

Our examination of explanations, treatments, and prevention of illness clearly indicates that what a patient believes can profoundly affect the treatment process. We must also point out that Western medicine, like the Western media, is reaching more people worldwide. As a consequence, many of the cultures we have discussed, while still adhering to their traditional medical practices, are becoming aware of and adapting Western biomedical approaches either alone or in conjunction with traditional cultural practices in the treatment of some illnesses.

Throughout this discussion, we have alluded to the impact of religion and spirituality. Because these deep structural issues have such a profound effect on health care, they warrant further consideration.

RELIGION, SPIRITUALITY, AND HEALTH CARE

Hufford has indicated that "the linguistic, religious, and other cultural patterns of American society are more diverse than ever, and medicine, like other institutions, must work to develop methods for a pluralistic society."[64] Spirituality involves more than formal religious beliefs related to faith and affiliation and the use of prayer. For some, religion has a strong influence over and shapes nutrition practices, health care practices, and other cultural domains. Spirituality includes all behaviors that give meaning to life and provide strength to the individual.[65]

In Western biomedicine, religion and magic have limited explanatory power. Curers require no supernatural abilities. For the most part, health tends to be segmented from religion and social relationships. Loustaunau and Sobo state that "biomedicine even divorces the mind from the body with different branches specializing in physical and mental health."[66]

What has long been believed in multiple cultures around the world is now becoming recognized in Western society—a person's mental attitude and spirituality can help in the prevention and healing of illness. In many cultures religion, spirituality, and health care are intertwined, and religion provides solutions and solace when one is in ill health. As Spector specifies, "It [religion] dictates social, moral, and dietary practices that are designed to keep a person in balance and healthy and plays a vital role in a person's perception of the prevention of illness."[67]

A person's religious beliefs can have a profound effect on health care practices. For Hindus, Jews, Catholic, and Islamics, religion may be the primary focus underlying the manner in which certain health services and practices such as seeking or limiting methods of birth control are practiced. Dietary rules in the Jewish faith include specific methods for slaughtering animals and strict proscriptions against mixing meat and milk at the same meal.[68] And, as we mentioned earlier, Jews seek to avoid nonemergency medical procedures on the Sabbath or other holy days.

The Navajo believe wellness is related to their view of being in harmony with one's surroundings. When people are ill, a medicine man will tell them what they have done to disrupt their harmony. Harmony is restored through the use of a healing ceremony. If a patient is being treated by a Western biomedical approach, according to Still and Hodgins, the healer may be summoned to conduct a healing ceremony before biomedical procedures are employed.[69]

For many members of the African American community, religion and religious behavior are an integral part of life. African American churches often play a major role in the development and survival of African Americans.[70]

In predominantly Catholic Mexico, fatalism saturates many Mexicans' existence. Many Mexicans believe that good health is primarily a matter of God's will, and that it can be maintained by dietary practices.[71] Mexicans have two sayings that illustrate this view perfectly: "We submit to pain because it is inevitable, to bereavement because it is irreparable, and to death because it is our destiny," and "Man proposes and God disposes."

In many Eastern religions, says Miller, people are portrayed as spiritual, and a sense of wellness or good health influences a person's spiritual journey.[72] In these cases, health and spirituality are reciprocal. Bhayana highlights this balance:

> Quiet acceptance of one's fate, also pervasive in some Eastern philosophies, is difficult to reconcile with a commitment to preventive methods. Symptoms may be ignored because the fear of dying is lessened. Extraordinary efforts to preserve life may be hard to accept when a deep-rooted belief in reincarnation exists.[73]

Although many traditional Chinese consider religion to be a form of superstition, in some parts of China and among Chinese Americans, religion is becoming more popular.[74]

Buddhism and Hinduism both offer examples of how religion influences health care practices. Although it is not a common practice, some Buddhists do not accept responsibility for illness because they believe that illness is caused by spirits.[75] There are also some Hindu sects that are not concerned about ill health because they believe that it is a result of misdeeds committed in a past life. They also believe that praying for health is the lowest form of prayer because medical treatment, although useful, is transitory.[76]

For many Arabs, illness is often regarded as punishment for one's sins. Yet, according to Abu Gharbieh, by providing cures, Allah manifests mercy and compassion and supplies a vehicle for repentance and gratitude.[77]

Most Western religions are accepting of modern medicine, although there is a great deal of diversity in religious practice. Christian beliefs, for the most part, are very much in line with modern medical practices, and good health is valued highly. One exception that can pose difficulty to physicians is the Jehovah's Witnesses' refusal to accept blood transfusions.[78] Jehovah's Witnesses base their philosophy of refusal to accept blood transfusions on biblical injunctions against "eating blood." They believe that the blood of individuals contains both the moral and physical characteristics of that person and accepting a transfusion would result in pollution and the loss of holiness.[79] In a similar vein, because of their religious orientation, Christian Scientists, Orthodox Jews, Greeks, and some Spanish-speaking cultures may not participate in organ donation because they believe the body will not be whole on resurrection.[80]

By now, it should be obvious that religion and spirituality have a strong influence on the way people define illness and choose to prevent it. In the United States, modern medicine and technology have often outweighed spiritual faith and alternative-healing methods. As medical practices in other cultures become better known, some health care personnel are becoming more open to the influence of spiritual healing and acknowledging it as an effective form of recovery and prevention. The Harvard Medical School, for instance, recently conducted a course entitled "Spirituality and Healing Medicine" attended by eight hundred scholars, doctors, clinicians, chaplains, and nurses from around the United States. The course consisted of presentations about the healing traditions of various faiths, including Islam, Roman Catholicism, Christian Science, Seventh Day Adventist, and Hinduism.[81]

Western medical practitioners, quite naturally, are requiring research data and experience before wholeheartedly advocating these positions. Evidence supporting the health–spirituality connection is fairly straightforward. Marquand, for example, reports that "in 212 clinical studies conducted since the mid-1980's, 160 showed positive effects of religious commitment on health, while only 15 showed negative effects."[82] Consequently, many medical institutions are incorporating mind–body components into their programs.

HEALTH CARE FOR A DIVERSE POPULATION

The delivery of health care in the United States presents a unique challenge. Part of this challenge is, of course, cultural. As Marquand indicates, "With the rising cultural diversity of individuals entering the United States comes increasing diversity in the health care beliefs and practices of those seeking health care."[83] In dealing with this diversity, satisfying ways of caring for all members of society must be discovered and practiced. As Spector suggests:

> In many situations, this is not difficult; in other situations, it seems impossible. . . . [T]he needs most difficult to meet are those of people whose belief systems are most different from the "mainstream" health-care provider culture.[84]

Transcultural medicine thus becomes a major aspect of American society. In health care, culture intervenes at every step of the way.[85] As should be evident by now, the opportunities for miscommunication constitute a major problem in the health care setting. If optimal health care is to be a goal in the multicultural United States, then health care providers must be aware of potential problems related to cultural differences. As Qureshi points out:

> Ignorance of culture can lead to false diagnosis. Only by taking a full history and being sensitive to a patient's culture can a doctor make an accurate diagnosis, understand the patterns of illness in various ethnic groups, and isolate diseases which may or may not be specific to a particular ethnic group.[86]

In this next section, we focus on the cultural and communication problems related to (1) family roles, (2) self-disclosure, (3) language, (4) nonverbal messages, and (5) formality.

Family Roles

As you saw in Chapters 2 and 3, cultures assign specific roles to various members of a family. As you would suspect, these roles contribute guidelines that tell family members how to perceive and communicate regarding health care issues. In this section, we examine some of those guidelines as they affect communication in the health care setting. To this end we will consider how family roles governing dominance patterns, modesty and female purity, and cultural differences in pregnancy and childbirth affect health care communication.

Dominance Patterns

In much of the world male and female roles are not as fluid as they are in the United States; many cultures make sharp distinctions between what is appropriate behavior for men and for women. An awareness of family dominance patterns is important for determining with whom to speak. "In the African-American family, the traditional head of the household is the mother."[87] Yet, this pattern is the exception. Among many Mexican Americans and newer Italian immigrants, the male may consider it rude to direct questions about a child's illness to the mother.[88] In the Middle East, Asia, Latin America, Mexico, and Africa, for instance, men are in positions of authority both in and out of the home. This cultural characteristic can become a source of misunderstanding and conflict in the health care setting.

Earlier in this chapter, we posed the question: "Why might an East Indian Hindu woman refuse to answer personal questions about her health in the presence of her husband?" Reddy suggests the answer lies in the assignment of family roles within this culture. Traditionally, the role of East Indian Hindu women is faithfulness and servility to the husband.[89] The husband is regarded as the head of the family and is the primary spokesperson regarding family matters, including the health care of the individual members.[90] As with the East Indian Hindu culture, in the Saudi Arabian culture, men believe it is their duty to act as an intermediary between the world and their wives. When men from this country and others like it bring in their wives for emergency room or doctor visits, they usually answer all the questions directed to their wives. Abu Gharbieh says that even if the wife can speak English, the Saudi male will speak for her, usually relating the client's complaints with greater vehemence than the patient might.[91]

The traditional Vietnamese family is strictly patriarchal and is almost always an extended family with the male having the duty of carrying on the family name through his progeny. Some families, say Still and Hodgins, are not accustomed to female authority figures and may have difficulty relating to women as professional health care providers.[92]

When dealing with patients from these and similar cultures, health care practitioners should expect the wife to be deferring all questions to her husband. He may consult with his wife about her health status before he answers the question. The practitioner who ignores the husband and seeks information directly from the wife runs the risk of raising feelings of personal humiliation and disrespect of the husband in the eyes of the family.[93]

Such misunderstanding may have severe consequences. At one extreme, routine procedures may be delayed, and at the other extreme, the life of the patient may be endangered. As Galanti reports, the case of Rosa Gutierrez and her two-month-old son demonstrates this. Rosa had brought her son to the emergency room because he was having diarrhea and had not been nursing.

> The staff discovered that he was also suffering from sepsis, dehydration, and high fever. The physician wanted to perform a routine spinal tap, but Rosa refused to allow it. When asked why, she said she needed her husband's permission before anything could be done to the baby. The staff tried to convince her that this was a routine procedure, but Rosa was adamant. Nothing could be done until her husband arrived.[94]

In most traditional Mexican households, the man makes all the major decisions. Rosa could have legally signed the spinal tap consent form, but from her cultural perspective, she did not hold the authority to do so.

An additional issue of male dominance of concern for health care practitioners is that men from cultures with strong masculine values often give little credibility to female physicians and nurses. In the extreme, they may refuse to be treated or have their family treated by women.

Modesty and Female Purity

The English essayist Joseph Addison wrote, "Modesty is not only an ornament, but also a guard to virtue." Modesty and female purity are also issues that can affect the health care setting. Because of the cultural emphasis placed on modesty, Abu Gharbieh believes that many Arab women are reluctant to seek health care.[95] They often are shy about disrobing for examinations. In addition, men must be treated by males and women by females. In an instance where flu shots were being administered to immigrant Somalis, the shots had to be given to males and females in separate rooms. Male nurses had to give shots to men and female nurses had to give shots to women.[96]

In many male-dominated cultures, modesty and female purity are of paramount importance. Marriage eligibility is an important dimension of Arabic culture. As Abu Gharbieh relates, "Fear that a diagnosed illness such as cancer or psychiatric illness may influence marriageability of a woman and her female relatives and can contribute to delays in seeking medical care."[97] Males are charged with protecting female honor. Females are expected to be virgins until they are married. Only their husbands are allowed to see them naked. If these rules are broken, it brings dishonor to the family. The only way honor can be restored to a family in which a female's purity and modesty have been compromised is to punish the girl.

A female from such a culture may be reluctant to seek medical attention, follow medical advice, or undress for a medical examination because of these values. Western practitioners often do not understand the possible consequences of violating one of these cultural norms, particularly if the woman is from an extremely traditional background.

Galanti, a medical anthropologist, reported a story that clearly illustrates the importance of female purity and family honor. Fatima was an eighteen-year-old Saudi Arabian who had been brought to an Air Force hospital with a gunshot wound in her pelvis. Her cousin to whom she was betrothed had shot her. As was customary, her parents had arranged the marriage. Fatima, however, was in love with someone else and did not wish to marry her cousin. An argument followed in which her drunken cousin shot her, paralyzing her from the waist down. At the hospital, X rays to examine the bullet revealed that Fatima was pregnant. One of the doctors in the case had lived in the Middle East for ten years and realized the potentially explosive situation facing him—and the girl. Girls with out-of-wedlock pregnancies typically were stoned to death. The doctor swore the X-ray technician to secrecy and arranged to have Fatima flown to London for a secret abortion and to remove the bullet. The internist involved was reluctant to go along with the plan, but finally agreed. Unfortunately, as Fatima was being wheeled to the waiting plane, the internist could not live with his conscience and told Fatima's father about the pregnancy. Galanti continues the story:

> The father did not say a word. He simply grabbed his daughter off the gurney, threw her into the car, and drove away. Two weeks later, the obstetrician saw one of Fatima's brothers. He asked him how Fatima was. The boy looked down at the ground and mumbled, "She died."[98] Family honor had been restored.[98]

Pregnancy and Childbirth

Much of the world embraces the Irish saying "Bricks and mortar make a house, but children make a home." We can say with some degree of accuracy that in every culture, childbearing and the gift of life are treated with celebration. All cultures have specific attitudes, practices, gender-related roles, and normative behaviors with regard to pregnancy and childbirth.[99] For these reasons, childbearing is another crucial issue in the health care setting. Although childbearing is a deeply felt emotional experience, the meaning and significance of the experience are often dictated by culture. Childbearing is valued for distinct reasons in different cultures. In the Mexican culture, a woman's status is often derived from the number of children she has borne. In Asian cultures, children, especially males, are valued because they carry on the family name and care for their parents in old age. For Orthodox Jews, childbirth is valued because it is in obedience to biblical law to multiply and replenish the earth. In some cultures, children are valued because of the labor and support they can contribute to the family.

Whereas birth might be a private experience in one culture, it can be a societal event in another. For North Americans, the birth experience is normally a private affair involving only the nuclear family. In many non-Anglo cultures, the birth experience is anticipated and shared by a large extended family. Often, Asian, Mexican, and Gypsy families crowd outside delivery rooms awaiting the event. Attendance of the actual birth itself varies from culture to culture as well. In North America, it is not unusual for the woman's husband to assist her in the labor and delivery of their child, but for many cultures this is not the case. Orthodox Jewish men rarely participate in childbirth because a man is forbidden to touch a woman during "unclean" times—when blood is present during menstruation or childbirth. Many Arab men feel that birthing is a female's job. Many Mexicans feel this way as well, so the woman's mother usually accompanies her during birth, and the husband does not see his wife or child until delivery is over and they have both been cleaned and dressed. In Asian families, because couples generally reside with the husband's parents, the mother-in-law is often the birth attendant.[100]

In some cultures, the pain of childbirth is responded to with self-restraint and silence; yet in other cultures, pain is openly and freely expressed. As we noted earlier in this book, culture dictates the expression of emotion. In many Asian cultures, pain and discomfort are expected to be a part of labor and delivery, but to express the pain brings shame. As a result, many Asian women are stoic, and only white knuckles and looks of intense concentration evidence pain.[101] In Middle Eastern and Mexican cultures, women are not expected to be inhibited in their expression of pain. In the Iranian culture, women are compensated for their suffering during childbirth with gifts. Larger, more expensive gifts are given for greater suffering.[102]

As this discussion shows, family roles relationships can have a profound impact on communication in the health care setting. Communication, assessment, and identification of the various family role beliefs, values, attitudes, and behaviors held by patients are essential to providing efficient, optimal health care.

Self-Disclosure

Closely related to cultural diversity in family roles are the cultural norms that govern self-disclosure. Proper health care demands that the patient trust the health care professional so that both parties can exchange essential medical information. Cultural norms about openness and self-disclosure, however, can often impede the communication process. Although Americans tend to have few qualms about disclosing personal information, in other cultures information of a personal nature may be less forthcoming.

Cultural rules can have a strong influence on patient self-disclosure and communication. Additionally, culture often dictates who can discuss what with whom. Some women from Mexico and Latin America, for instance, may feel embarrassed or shy when talking about "female problems." Frequently, they will refrain from talking about birth control or childbirth with American physicians. When a Latina who spoke no English had to sign an informed consent form for a hysterectomy, she relied upon her son to act as a translator. When the son explained the procedure to his mother, he seemed to be translating accurately and indicating the proper body parts. The next day, however, his mother was very angry when she learned that her uterus had been removed and she could no longer bear children. Because of the cultural prohibition against the son discussing his mother's private parts, the embarrassed son had explained that a tumor would be removed from her abdomen and pointed to the general area where the surgery would be performed. Even speaking the same language may be insufficient. It is best to use same-sex interpreters when translating matters of a sexual or private nature.

As you learned in Chapter 2, Asian cultures are generally classified as high-context. Therefore, for Asian Americans, the problems associated with self-disclosure are directly linked to this value. Among the Chinese, for instance, too much talk about personal matters is often considered in poor taste. The Japanese are expected to be shy, withdrawn, and diffident—at least in public.[103] Asian women, as a consequence, tend not to talk about or discuss female problems. In this collective culture, self-importance is a violation of a cultural norm.

The Germans, because they value proper decorum, are also reluctant to disclose highly personal information in most settings. The German proverb "A friend to everyone is a friend to no one" clearly underscores their view of superficial relationships. This reticent and reserved attitude often transfers to the health care context.

Communication characteristics among Russian immigrants have been fashioned by traditions and experiences over centuries of historical context. The culture remains unique from that of other Europeans as well as Americans. Many Russians fear nurses and physicians for treatment. Elliott indicates that Russians tend not to trust doctors. This leads to a lower reliance on health care professionals and a reluctance to talk about or disclose personal information.[104]

The above examples demonstrate that not all patients are willing to talk to health care providers with the same degree of openness. Being familiar with these cultural variations regarding communication styles and self-disclosure can help the professional extract important and valuable information concerning the patient's health.

Language Barriers

Many of the problems we discussed in Chapter 4 concerning language diversity apply to the health care context as well. Obvious problems such as language differences and the use of interpreters complicate medical interactions. As noted earlier, literal translations often do not convey the true meaning of a communicated message. Think for a moment about the potential for confusion if a Western doctor speaks of a woman's "period" to someone whose culture does not use this euphemism. Also, a literal translation of the phrase "have your tubes tied" may render an understanding that they can just as easily be "untied." Medical implications resulting from such miscommunication can be detrimental to the patient.

Subtle forms of communication behavior can have just as great an impact. Galanti provides the following example from which you can see how the use of idioms can cause misunderstandings.

> A Chinese-born physician called the night nurse one evening to check on a patient scheduled for surgery the next day. The nurse advised the physician that she noticed a new hesitancy in the patient's attitude. "To tell you the truth, doctor, I think Mrs. Colby is getting cold feet." The physician was not familiar with this idiom, suspected circulation problems, and ordered vascular tests.[105]

The use of medical jargon may also complicate health care interaction. For example, the use of words like *rhinitis* rather than *hay fever*, *anosmia* instead of *loss of taste*, and *dementia* rather than *memory loss* can be confusing to native-language speakers and even more so for individuals who speak a different language. In addition, Witte and Morrison suggest that "it is sometimes difficult for members of diverse cultures to articulate their symptoms and feelings in the nonnative language."[106] As a result, vague symptoms and generalized descriptions of health may be conveyed. Finally, members of some cultures may be reluctant to reveal personal or private problems, particularly if their children are used as interpreters. For instance, Haftner tells of a Mexican woman whose son usually interpreted for her. She suffered a great deal before the doctor discovered her actual problem—a fistula in her rectum. She was so embarrassed about her condition that she was reluctant to reveal her symptoms through her son. Only when a cultural interpreter was called did she reveal her true symptoms.[107]

Latinos are one of the most medically underserved co-cultures in the United States. Variation in language performance is a crucial determinant of health service utilization where not speaking English will deter Latinos from using health care services.[108] The seriousness of this problem is spelled out by Alcaley: "Compared with non-Hispanic whites in the United States, Hispanics, especially Mexican-Americans, underutilize preventive health services. They tend to forgo such routine procedures as physical checkups, dental and eye examinations, and prenatal care."[109] Within the Mexican American community, the most obvious barrier to health care is language. In spite of the fact that Spanish-speaking people constitute one of the largest minority groups in this country, very few health care deliverers speak Spanish.[110]

Nonverbal Messages

Cultural diversity in nonverbal behavior can affect health care communication. Both health care practitioners and recipients frequently express beliefs, feelings, and attitudes about illness and treatment nonverbally. While it would be ideal if health care providers were knowledgeable about the nonverbal behavior of all cultures, it does not seem unreasonable to ask that they do learn more about the meaning and use of nonverbal behavior across cultures.[111] There are four areas of nonverbal communication that are especially salient in health care communication: eye contact, facial expressions, touch, and time. Although these were discussed extensively in Chapter 5, we will look at these again briefly in the specific context of health care.

Eye Contact
Eye contact can be a nonverbal source of confusion. Eye contact is valued in the dominant American culture, and lack of eye contact may be interpreted as a sign of rudeness or an indication of a lack of attention.[112] Many other cultures and co-cultures, however, avoid direct eye contact because they believe it is a sign of disrespect, especially when conversing with authority figures such as physicians and other medical professionals. According to Gleave and Manes, Central Americans, for instance, feel uncomfortable making immediate eye contact with strangers.[113] Chan reports that for the Japanese, avoidance of eye contact traditionally denotes respect, and direct or sustained eye contact with relative strangers may be interpreted as a sign of hostility.[114] Native Americans often stare at the floor during conversations to indicate that they are paying close attention to the speaker.[115] And Vietnamese people are sometimes uncomfortable with steady or direct eye contact and prefer fleeting glances.[116]

Facial Expressions
Facial expressions are commonly perceived as being a guide to a person's feelings. Many cultures and co-cultures such as Italians, Jews, African Americans, and Spanish-speaking people smile readily and use a wide variety of facial expressions. In other cultures, such as in England and Ireland, as well as in many northern European countries, fewer facial expressions are used.[117]

Smiling and laughing are indicative of happiness in the dominant American culture. In other cultures, however, smiles may reflect a variety of other emotions, including confusion, embarrassment, or politeness. Facial expressions can be used to express feelings that are opposite those being felt. In many Asian cultures, negative emotions are often concealed with a smile. As Dinh and his associates report, the Vietnamese have a tendency toward impassive facial expressions that make it difficult to understand what the individual is communicating or thinking.[118] In some cases, members of cultural groups such as Native Americans may not use facial expressions to display emotion unless the observer has a deep understanding of the person and the cultural norms.[119]

Touch

Tactile behavior is yet another form of nonverbal behavior that can affect health care. Although members of the dominant American culture are usually accustomed to being touched by their physicians and nurses, individuals from many other cultures are not. Vietnamese patients, for instance, prefer touching of the body be kept to a minimum.[120]

Cultural modesty can affect feelings toward touching in the health care context. Members of Latino cultures seem to engage in high levels of touching behavior. Yet, Brownke believes that Mexican females are reluctant to expose their bodies to men or other women and can become especially embarrassed during pelvic examinations.[121] Many Latino men may also feel threatened during physical examinations because of strong feelings about modesty.[122]

In some cultures, touch has overtones of magic. Among some Latinos and Native Americans, touch is a symbol for undoing an evil spell; it is seen as a means of preventing harm and of healing.[123] Some Vietnamese, on the other hand, believe their spirits may leave the body through physical contact, which can result in health problems.[124] Additionally, as Muencke point out, the Vietnamese perceive the human head to be the seat of life, and any procedure that invades the surface or orifice of the head may cause strong feelings of fear.[125]

Time

A patient's orientation to time may affect when or whether he or she shows up for appointments. Time orientation may also affect how consistently a patient will take medicine according to a particular schedule or whether he or she will return for follow-up visits.

Differences in time orientations can also influence the amount of time health care professionals spend with patients. Members of the dominant American culture tend to follow a monochronic time orientation, and they do not expect to spend much time with physicians establishing rapport or discussing the causes and cures of illness. Members of other cultures with a polychronic time orientation may have different expectations. They expect a physician or nurse to spend sufficient time to build an appropriate interpersonal relationship and to explain all of the details of their illness and its cure.

Formality

Although we discussed formality or informality in detail in Chapter 6, the impact of these behaviors on the health care setting warrant a second examination of each of these concepts. Members of Asian, Mexican, and European cultures, as well as others who value formality in language use, may be disturbed by the North American practice of addressing each other by first names. A physician who addresses an Asian by his or her first name rather than by title and first and last name may inadvertently diminish his or her credibility.

Formality is also reflected in varying degrees of politeness. Marks relates, for example, that "Chinese politeness calls for three refusals before one accepts an offer."[126] In North America, however, "no" means "no" the first time. Imagine the confusion and misunderstanding experienced by a Chinese patient politely declining the first offer of pain medication from a North American nurse and then politely suffering while waiting for the second and third offer, which were not forthcoming.

Formal politeness is also reflected in face-saving communication. In many cultures, authority figures are not to be disagreed with or challenged. Even if the patient does not concur or understand the physician's advice, he or she may agree to comply because of politeness norms. Many Mexican Americans, for example, believe that directly contradicting a physician is rude and disrespectful. They may indicate compliance in order not to embarrass the physician, but in actuality, they have no intention of following the instructions. Klessig warns that the physician who then perceives agreement can erroneously believe that a plan of action has been agreed upon.[127]

As these examples suggest, many misunderstandings in the health care setting can be traced to miscommunications in language or nonverbal patterns. Although being sensitive to cultural differences is important, health care professionals also need to have excellent intercultural communication skills to be able to handle cultural issues. This need for sensitivity and effective communication skills is clearly evident, for instance, when a folk illness represents a real medical emergency. In the Mexican culture, *caida de mollera* is a folk illness in which a baby has a fever, irritability, vomiting, and diarrhea. This illness is often treated with folk remedies. But these symptoms can also indicate a far more serious illness in an infant for which prompt medical attention is needed.[128] In situations like this, the health care provider must be sensitive to a pa-

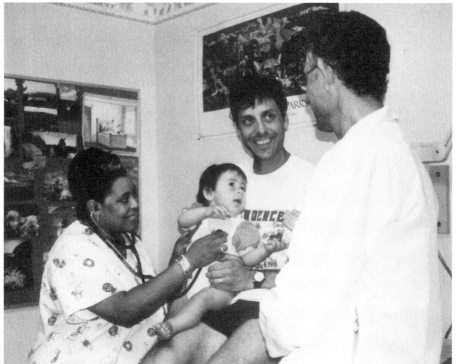

Health care professionals need excellent intercultural communication skills.

© Robert Fonseca

tient's beliefs while educating him or her (or the parents in this case) about the negative consequences of relying on folk remedies. Conveying this information in a respectful manner requires excellent communication skills so that the patient is not humiliated or insulted, which would prevent compliance with the medical advice. This often is not as easy as it might sound. Many health care professionals as well as researchers have sought strategies to facilitate the unique interactions necessary in the medical environment. In the final section of this chapter, we share some tactics for improving the multicultural health care interaction.

IMPROVING MULTICULTURAL HEALTH CARE

When you think of multicultural issues, the reference is usually to racial and ethnic differences among people. Yet, as Gillmor aptly indicates, there is a distinct medical and hospital culture that can be extremely disorienting and frightening to those on the outside.[129] This medical culture is often overwhelming to people who do understand Western medical practices. For example, as Gillmor points out, there is a specialized language within this culture that makes many communications from medical staff unintelligible and perhaps even frightening to those not initiated.[130] When awareness, acknowledgment, and action characterize the multicultural health care context, greater empathy is achieved. Health care professionals can better understand the problem from the patient's perspective, and solutions that are satisfactory to all can be the result. In this way, optimal health care for all patients can be accomplished.

It is important that you do not presume that the suggestions offered here are mutually exclusive or exhaustive. We likewise recommend that you do not assume that the information contained in this chapter applies to all people associated with a particular culture. If you do so, you fail to acknowledge individuality. Additionally, acculturation and assimilation levels will affect a patient's response to illness and treatment. Despite these caveats, the three suggestions we provide should be helpful in facilitating communication in the cross-cultural health care encounter.

Recognizing Diverse Medical Systems

As we have said throughout this chapter, it is important to recognize that many cultures may have several medical systems on which they rely. Even in the United States, many alternative medical systems exist, including the mind-body and spiritual connections discussed earlier. Chiropractic, naturopathy, herbalism, and the laying on of hands can also be considered alternative medical systems.[131] In many instances, Western biomedicine is combined with an alternative method with great success. You can now, on occasion, find the same multiple approach to medical treatment in other parts of the world. For example, in Mozambique, in addition to Western approaches to medicine, the government is embracing traditional healers as vital bearers of the safe-sex message. It is not unusual, because of the AIDS epidemic in the region, for a healer to begin an interaction by using such traditional behaviors as drum beating, rattle shaking, and making an appeal to a local god. Following this, the healer may approach the audience and ask, "Have you ever heard of condoms?"[132]

Successful treatment of patients requires that their beliefs concerning the causes of illness, how illness should be treated, and how it can be prevented in the future must be acknowledged. Galanti makes much the same point when he writes, "Even in cases where Western scientific medicine is superior, if the patient believes it is insufficient for treating the problem, it probably will be."[133] This concept is clearly illustrated in the following story. An eighty-three-year-old Cherokee Indian woman was brought to a hospital emergency room after she passed out at home. X rays revealed a bowel obstruction that required surgery. The woman refused to sign the consent form because she first wanted to see the medicine man on the reservation. At the request of the social worker, the woman's grandson drove to the reservation and returned with the medicine man in full traditional dress. He conducted a healing ceremony complete with bells, rattles, chanting, and singing for forty-five minutes. At the end of the ceremony, the medicine man indicated that the woman was ready to sign the consent form. She did, and her immediate surgery was uneventful and without complications.[134] What is being said should be obvious—from folk-healing to modern medical advances, health care beliefs shift from culture to culture and all must be respected.

Recognizing being sensitive to patients' beliefs require a great deal of information. In addition to cultural knowledge and an awareness of communication patterns, particular knowledge of the individual is necessary. McDonagh recommends that when first treating a new patient, it can be helpful if you determine how "westernized" the patient might be. Some of the following questions will help this process:

1. Is the medical problem typical of recent immigrants from a given area?
2. What language(s) is spoken by the patient?
3. What religious beliefs are held by the patient?
4. What cultural traits does the patient possess?
5. What are the traditional concepts of disease and health held by the patient?
6. What types of medicine is practiced by the patient's culture?
7. What is the patient's attitude toward health care?[135]

Recognize Ethnocentrism

Finally, imbedded in all that we have said in this entire chapter is the fact that you must recognize that there is no one answer to all health care questions. When you behave as if you believe that your culture possesses that single answer, you are engaging in ethnocentrism. While we have discussed ethnocentrism elsewhere and will look at the concept again in later chapters, our point now is that ethnocentrism, if not kept in check, can influence issues related to health care. The first step in avoiding ethnocentrism is to identify any feeling you have about other cultures that might influence the health care setting. This same idea about starting with yourself is clearly articulated by Geist-Martin and her colleagues when they write, "The call to expand our understanding and appreciation of cultural communities implies that we need to acknowledge our own ethnocentrism."[136] Once you have acknowledged that you might possess ethnocentric notions, ask yourself if you are guilty of imposing your own views about illness and treatment on other people without ever considering their needs. In short, avoiding ethnocentrism demands that you take into consideration the cultural background of both patients and practitioners.[137] In so doing you become culturally sensitive to the health care expectations held by people whose cultural background is different from your own.

SUMMARY

- Cultures differ in the way they explain, treat, and prevent illness.
- Health belief systems can be divided into three categories: biomedical, personalistic, and naturalistic.
- There is cultural diversity in beliefs about the causes of illness.
- There is cultural diversity in beliefs about the appropriate treatment of illness.
- There is cultural diversity in the approaches to the prevention of illness.
- Religion, spirituality, and health care are often intertwined.
- Health care practices must accommodate a culturally diverse population.
- Culturally determined family roles could affect communication in the health care setting. These roles deal with dominance patterns, modesty and female purity, and pregnancy and childbirth.
- Issues related to self-disclosure, language, nonverbal communication, and formality can influence the heath care setting.
- If optimal health care is to be provided in a multiethnic society such as the United States, you must recognize diverse medical systems, diverse approaches to treatment, and personal ethnocentrism.

INFOTRAC COLLEGE EDITION EXERCISES

1. Want to learn more about the ways in which cultural values and practices affect health care? Locate and read "Why Your Patient Won't Let You Touch Her" by Elizabeth A. Pector and Gil L. Solomon. According to Pector and Solomon, what cultural differences do health care providers need to be aware of if they are to provide quality care to everyone? Would you ever choose to receive health care from someone from a co-culture different from yours? What challenges might you expect to confront? What might be the benefits?

(For more on this subject, use the subject search terms "Transcultural Medical Care" and "Communication in Medicine" and its subdivision "Social Aspects.")

2. How does culture affect our views of death? Locate and read "Mortality Around the World" by Lawrence E. Sullivan. How does it explain differences between Dutch, Muslim, and Japanese views of death and dying? Compare your own views on dying, euthanasia, organ transplant, and funeral services with those of your classmates and discuss the cultural roots of these perspectives.

ACTIVITIES

1. Approach someone who is a member of a culture different from yours, and determine what differences exist between your beliefs and your informant's beliefs about the causes, treatment, and prevention of illness.
2. In a small group, discuss the impact of spirituality on the health care setting.

3. Interview members of your local health care community in order to determine the challenges of providing optimal health care to all patients in a multicultural society.
4. Interview people from other cultures and ask them about any "special forms of treatments" that are practiced in their culture.

DISCUSSION IDEAS

1. What is necessary to achieve effective intercultural communication in the health care setting?
2. How might cultural diversity in language usage complicate the multicultural health care setting?
3. How might diversity in gender roles affect the giving and receiving of health care treatment?

4. Why might it be important to incorporate more than one medical belief system into the treatment of patients in a multicultural health care setting?
5. Why would high levels of ethnocentrism affect the intercultural health care setting?

part 4

Knowledge into Action

chapter 9

Intercultural Challenges: Recognizing and Dealing With Difference

In some ways, Sept. 11 was a harrowing reminder of how truly we all live in the same neighborhood now, even if the differences and distances between us remain as great as ever.

PICO IYER

Learning, the destroyer of arrogance begets arrogance in fools, even as light, that illumines the eye, makes owls blind.

PANCHATANTRA

The unsolved problems pile up and inevitably produce catastrophes at regular intervals.

LUIGI BARZINI

In 1963, President John F. Kennedy offered a fitting introduction to this chapter when he noted, "No problem of human destiny is beyond human beings." The appropriateness of his observation is germane because this is a chapter about many of the problems that you face when you engage in intercultural communication. It is also a chapter about the faith we have that you can triumph over those problems. In short, in this chapter and the next, we seek to improve your intercultural behavior. While this entire book has been about your becoming a more effective intercultural communicator, in these two remaining chapters we explicitly focus on the actual act of engaging in communication.

Before we begin our discussion of potential communication problem, we must remind you of two interrelated manifestos regarding intercultural communication. First, shifting demographics and changes in transportation, information systems, political dynamics, economics, and global conflicts have brought people from diverse cultures and religions into contact with each other with a regularity and urgency that is unique to this period of history. As Smith noted, "Lands around the planet have become our neighbors—China across the street, the Middle East at our back door."[1] This new century has demonstrated that the person next door may speak a different language, that a boss or office mate may be from another culture, and that your Internet "chat-room" partner is thousands of miles away. In short, by chance and design, cultural contact is unavoidable.

Second, the manner in which you face and respond to these intercultural contacts, be they personal or professional, influences your life in subtle and profound ways. As Schneider and Silverman point out, "In today's global world, condemning other societies leads to misunderstanding and violence. The world's peoples need to learn about each other."[2] In an even more dramatic fashion, Hofstede echoes the same idea when he writes, "The survival of mankind will depend to a large extent on the ability of people who think differently to act together."

In this chapter we submit two interrelated goals as we seek to improve how you "think" and "act." First, we will offer a personal philosophy that reflects our optimism about your ability to improve the manner in which you communicate. Second, we will examine some potential problems in attempting to communicate with someone from a cultural background different from your own.

A PHILOSOPHY OF CHANGE

When the Greek philosopher Heraclitus wrote, "Everything flows, nothing stays still," he was not only talking about nature and the universe changing, but he was also referring to how people change. This acceptance of the change, and the companion belief that we can shape that change, is at the heart of our approach to intercultural communication—an approach that maintains that improving intercultural communication is not only expedient, but also possible. This optimistic view is based on three interrelated assumptions about human communication: (1) *the brain is an open system*, (2) *we have free choice*, and (3) *our communication behavior influences other people*. If these three axioms seem familiar, it is because we introduced them in Chapter 1.

The Brain Is an Open System

Our opening characteristic relates to your ability to learn and never stop learning. That is to say, there is not a "top end" to how much new information a person can acquire. We present the following two examples to make our point. The first word in our dictionary is *aal*, and it is an East Indian shrub; the root of which yields a red dye. We also want to tell you that Buddha was the son of a rich king born into the Shakyan clan. If these two facts were new information for you, your brain would be adding to your fund of knowledge. These two specific examples are not what is important but rather the idea that you are capable of acquiring new knowledge for your entire life. This is why we describe the brain as an open system. Being able to take in new data as long as you live has implications for anyone interested in improving their intercultural communication skills.

First, your capacity to learn new information throughout life and your response at any event are products of your genes and what your nervous system has experienced. Because many of your experiences are linked directly to culture, it is obvious that not all brains have gathered the same information. Put rather simply, at the moment of birth, depending where that birth takes place, you can turn out to be one kind of individual or another. A Maasai child born in Africa will receive information that might be very different from the experiences that confront a baby born in Tokyo or Beverly Hills. This idea about learning, although elementary, is often overlooked by people who fail to understand why cultures often have different ways of perceiving the world and interacting in that world.

Second, the notion of the brain as an open system reminds you that you can learn from each other. One culture's special skill for treating heart disease can be transmitted

*We are able to learn
new ideas throughout
our lives.*

© Gloria Thomas

to a culture lacking that information. A culture that uses acupuncture to cure ailments can teach this art to groups of people who lack it in their culture. Yet another culture may transmit the rewards of patience to a culture whose members are always dashing from place to place. In short, the best that we have as a people can be shared.

Third, because you can continue to learn, you are capable of learning new information about other people and other cultures. For example, if we tell you that most Native American languages do not even have a word for *second*, *minute*, or *hour* you can use this new information to change your perception of how Native Americans might use "time." A strong belief in change is at the very core of this book. We hope that by learning new information about intercultural communication, you will be able to make alterations to your own communication behavior.

We Have Free Choice

Having just developed the idea that learning and change are inescapable, we now offer another truism about human behavior that adds support to our belief that improvement is possible. This supposition, although intricate in how it is acted out, is uncomplicated in its wording: *You have free choice.* Although you might face biological limitations (you may not run as fast as you might like), in most instances what you do in life, from selecting a single word when you speak to deciding if you should drive over the posted speed limit, you do of your own free will. Although many cultures have a strong belief in fate ("It is God's will"), and others limit the choices available to their members (having woman cover their faces when they go out in public), in most instances people choose what to do and what not to do. Reflect on the two examples we just used: selecting words and driving fast. We said that each word we choose is under our jurisdiction. We could, for example, have used the word *control* instead of *jurisdiction* in the last line, but we selected the word we wanted—it was our choice. The same idea applies to the influence you have over your nonverbal actions. Even though many actions are habitual, when you greet a stranger, you can still decide to smile, frown, look the person in the eye, or glance down.

Our example of driving fast, also underscores the degree of freedom you enjoy in conducting your life. When you decide how to spend your time, or whom to select as a friend or a mate, you are reflecting free choice. Although selecting a lover might be harder than selecting what words to use, the principle is the same—you have free will. The key, of course, is how we use those choices. As the Irish novelist George Moore wrote, "The difficulty in life is the choice."

Communication Has a Consequence

Our final introductory edict concerning our positive view toward improvement is yet another one of those ideas that first appeared in Chapter 1. In that chapter we discussed how each of our actions produces a response in another human being. Some of the responses are obvious and others are subtle. But they all produce a result. Much like the Arab proverb that notes, "If you strike mud against the wall, even though it does not stick, it will leave a mark," when you communicate your actions you "leave a mark." Part of improving your communication behavior demands that you take control of your actions.

We are now ready to begin talking about improving intercultural communication by asking you to see the interconnective nature of the three points we developed in the last few pages: The brain is an open system (you can learn), you have choices (you can communicate one way or another), and your actions produce a response (you do something to other people). Remembering these ideas should convince you that you have a great deal of power over whether or not you improve your communication behavior.

POTENTIAL PROBLEMS IN INTERCULTURAL COMMUNICATION

Before we begin our analysis of potential communication problems, we need to remind you of three important points. First, in most instances, communication problems occur for an assortment of reasons. If you lose your temper while talking to a friend, a little introspection will often reveal that it was not solely your friend that prompted the anger but rather an accumulation of events and that your friend was merely a handy target. So while we will discuss potential problems one at time, they often occur in combination. Second, common sense tells you that the complex nature of human behavior produces many more communication problems than the list we have created in this section of the book. We have trimmed our list based on space constraints and a careful review of the existing literature. Third, although our discussion of potential problems and solutions has a strong theory base, it nevertheless is colored by our personal and cultural backgrounds. We are two white university professors born and raised in America, and although we have visited many countries and studied countless cultures, we have done so from our culture's perspective. Therefore, the "hidden grip" of culture has undoubtedly influenced the way we perceive and interact with the world. Although we have tried to assume a global orientation, we need to alert you to the Western bias that may occasionally, and we hope only accidentally, creep into our commentary.

Seeking Similarities

Think for a moment about the meaning of the following proverb, which, in one form or another, is found in nearly every culture: "Birds of a feather flock together." The meaning is clear—most people seek to be near others with whom they share common outlooks, habits, and traits. Now ask yourself the following two questions: What group of people do you choose to be around, and how do you select those people? If you are consistent with the research in interpersonal communication, you gravitate toward people who are similar to you. Although this observation is not profound, it is nevertheless true. For decades, the research in initial attraction and the development of friendships has revealed an overwhelming tendency among everyone to seek out people whom they perceive to be much like themselves.[4] It is a very natural inclination when meeting someone to talk about a topic that both parties might enjoy; and should those talks prove interesting, it is equally natural for friendships to form and evolve. The more points of contact you can establish, the more comfortable you feel.[5]

A corollary to our observing people we know in a friendly light is the idea that we often feel uncomfortable when confronted with strangers. As early as 1961 Herman and Schield summarized these often disquieting feelings when they wrote, "The immediate psychological results of being in a new situation is lack of security. Ignorance of the potentialities inherent in the situation, of the means to reach a goal, and of the probable outcomes of an intended action leads to insecurity."[6]

The connection between intercultural communication and your inclination to solicit friends and acquaintances that mirror your personality should be obvious. As we have said throughout this book, a culture offers its members specialized patterns of communication—patterns that are often dissimilar to those of people from other cultures. The seriousness of this problem is seen globally as well as interpersonally. As the world gets more complex, and people feel overwhelmed by events, we find that "many millions of people believe that their best haven of certainty and security is a group based on ethnic similarity, common faith, economic interest or political like-mindedness."[7] We are not suggesting that there is anything basically wrong with seeking ethnic or cultural similarity; in fact, we already mentioned how common it is to seek out the familiar. The problem arises when the pull of similarities is at the exclusion or even the elimination of those who are different. You can see extreme examples of this tendency in all parts of the world. Cleveland offers us two vivid instances of valuing likenesses at the expense of those you deem ethnically or culturally different:

> In Africa ethnicity took over as an exclusive value, resulting in mass murder by machete. In ex-Yugoslavia (and too many other places), gunpowder and rape accomplished the same purpose, trampling on human rights and erasing human futures.[8]

What we have been suggesting in this first problem is that culture often separates you from people with a history different from your own. The poet Emily Dickinson vividly described this separation when she wrote, "The Soul selects her own Society— / Then shuts the Door— / To her divine Majority— / Present no more." Her message is crystalline: Most people prefer their "own kind" and "shut the door" on the unfamiliar. This tendency is the very reason the bias of similarity can be a potential communication problem.

Uncertainty Reduction

Our second potential problem is directly related to our first and stems from the theory of uncertainty reduction.[9] Some of the communication axioms this theory has generated are directly related to intercultural communication. Berger and Calabrese summarize this theory: "Central to the present theory is the assumption that when strangers meet, their primary concern is one of uncertainty reduction or increasing predictability about the behavior of both themselves and others in the interaction."[10] According to the theory, people have a desire to reduce the uncertainty built into every new meeting. As your ability "to predict which alternative or alternatives are likely to occur next decreases, uncertainty increases."[11] In addition, as Gudykunst notes, "There is greater uncertainty in our initial interactions with strangers than with people from our ingroup."[12] What is being suggested is that uncertainty is magnified when you meet people from cultures different from your own. As Luckmann notes, "Fear, dislike and distrust are emotions that all too often erupt when people from diverse cultures first meet."[13] Gudykunst also links this problem to intercultural communication when he adds, "If the amount of uncertainty present in initial interactions is not reduced, further communication between the people will, in all likelihood, not take place."[14]

Withdrawal

Your next problem is an extension of the first two, for if you can not find similarities and/or fail to reduce uncertainty in a satisfactory manner, you are apt to withdraw from the communication event. When we speak of withdrawal, we are referring to withdrawal on both an interpersonal, intercultural, and international level. In short, problems occur when you withdraw from face-to-face interactions or when entire countries withdraw from the world community. Although it is a rather somber commentary of our times, it appears that "modern life," with its rapid pace, urbanization, massive institutions, and mediated contacts, has created a sense of bewilderment, alienation, and detachment. A common response to disaffection is to retreat rather than confront the cause of the separation. When this happens, the consequences are obvious. Communication, as we have discussed it throughout this book, is impossible.

Withdrawal, at both the international and domestic levels, has often been the rule rather than the exception. History is full of examples of how one nation or group of people has refused to be part of an international dialogue. For decades the governments of China and the former Soviet Union rebuffed each other, only to discover that "talking" to each other was beneficial to all parties. The relationship between East and West Germany and Israel and Egypt represents two other vivid examples of choosing interaction over withdrawal. In those cases, it produced peaceful coexistence instead of carnage. Perhaps if you examine your own behavior, you might discover, like governments, instances when you withdraw from communication. In many of these cases the other person might have had a different skin color, sexual orientation, or cultural heritage. In an age when what happens in one part of the world happens throughout the world, retreat and withdrawal can have devastating effects. As the philosopher Flewelling once wrote, "Neither province, parish, nor nation; family, nor individual, can live profitably in exclusion from the rest of the world."

Stereotyping

Stereotyping represents yet another problem that is often easier to talk about than to arrest, for it, like culture, often lies below the level of awareness. Stereotyping is rooted in your compulsion to make in-group and out-group distinctions.

Defining Stereotypes

Stereotyping is a complex form of categorization that mentally organizes your experiences and guides your behavior toward a particular group of people. Lippmann, who called attention to this concept as early as 1922, indicated that stereotypes were a means of organizing your images into fixed and simple categories that you use to stand for an entire collection of people.[15] Stereotyping has the potential to be found in nearly every intercultural situation. The reason for the pervasive nature of stereotypes is that human beings have a psychological need to categorize and classify. The world you confront is too big, too complex, and too transitory for you to know it in all its detail. Hence, you want to classify and pigeonhole. Stereotypes, because they tend to be convenient and expeditious, help you with your classifications. Rapport and Overing underscore this point when they note that "stereotypes allow simplistic and fantastic claims to be made about a group's manifold memberships, claims which are all more ambiguous and gross the higher the societal level to which the collective label is applied."[16]

Developing Stereotypes

How do you acquire stereotypes? You are not born with them. Stereotypes, like culture, are learned in a variety of ways. First, people learn stereotypes from their parents, relatives, and friends. Individuals who hear their parents say "It is too bad that all those Jews are in control of the film industry" are learning stereotypes. Second, stereotypes develop through limited personal contact. If you meet a person from Brazil who is very wealthy, and from this meeting you conclude that all people from Brazil are wealthy, you are acquiring a stereotype from limited data. Third, many stereotypes are provided by the mass media. Television has been guilty of providing distorted images of many ethnic groups, the elderly, and gays. Think for a moment of the stereotype embedded in the advertisement seen on television for e-mail that heralds the idea the product is so simple that "Even granny can use it." The problem is that for many people, these false facsimiles often become their private realities. Finally, stereotypes may evolve out of fear of persons from groups that differ from your own. For example, many people have the view of a person with mental illness as someone who is violence prone. This conflicts with statistical data, which indicates that persons with mental illness tend to be no more prone to violence than the general population. Yet because of isolated examples of well-publicized isolated cases of mentally ill persons killing other people, the stereotype is the rule instead of the exception. We should add that this is how many stereotypes develop in the first place: a series of isolated behaviors by a member of a group that unfairly become the generalized stereotype that represents all members of the group.

Variations in Stereotyping

Because stereotypes are often a conglomerate of perceptions, emotions, and feelings, they vary in scope and magnitude. Let us pause for a moment and examine some of the variations and configurations that stereotypes can take.

Stereotypes, as Smith and Bond observe, "may be widely shared by others, even by the stereotyped persons themselves, or they may be idiosyncratic to the individual holding them."[17] What is being suggested is that one person or a large collection of individuals may hold stereotypes. This notion of how people may share the stereotype is often referred to as the "consensus variance" of stereotyping. In most instances group stereotypes that cause the greatest damage in intercultural communication are those that have a wide consensus. These stereotypes become institutionalized and are much harder to overcome.

Stereotypes can be positive or negative. Stereotypes that refer to a large group of people as lazy, coarse, vicious, and moronic are obviously negative. There are, of course, positive stereotypes. You can say that the same group mentioned above is hardworking, well mannered, kind, and intelligent. However, because stereotypes, as the word is currently defined, narrow our perceptions, they usually jeopardize intercultural communication.

A final variation in stereotyping deals with the intensity of the stereotype. Simply stated, is the particular stereotype resolutely held, or is it temperate in its intensity? Examine your own catalogue of stereotypes and you will likely discover that some of them are strongly held while others are tentative and loosely held.

Problems in Stereotyping

As we have pointed out, in most instances, stereotypes are the products of limited, lazy, and misguided perceptions. Adler reminds you of the harmful effect stereotypes have on intercultural communication when she notes:

> Stereotypes become counterproductive when we place people in the wrong groups, when we incorrectly describe the group norm, when we inappropriately evaluate the group or category, when we confuse the stereotype with the description of a particular individual, and when we fail to modify the stereotype based on our actual observations and experience.[18]

Let us look at a few additional reasons why stereotypes hamper intercultural communication. First, it is not the act of classifying that creates intercultural problems; rather, it is assuming that all culture-specific information applies to all individuals from the cultural group.[19] That is to say; stereotypes assume that all members of a group have exactly the same traits. As Atkinson, Morten, and Sue note, "They are rigid preconceptions which are applied to all members of a group or to an individual over a period of time, regardless of individual variations."[20] This problem of assuming similarities at the expense of exceptions is the main reason we have, throughout this book, reminded you that culture is one of the characteristics that determine attitudes, values, beliefs, and ways of behaving.

Second, stereotypes also keep us from being successful as communicators because they are oversimplified, overgeneralized, and/or exaggerated. They are based on half-truths, distortions, and often-untrue premises and assumptions. As Guirdham posits, stereotypes distort intergroup communication because they lead people to base their messages, their way of transmitting them, and their reception of them on false assumptions."[21] In short, stereotypes create inaccurate pictures of the people with whom we are interacting.

Third, stereotypes tend to impede intercultural communication in that they repeat and reinforce beliefs until they often become taken for "truth." For years, women were stereotyped as a rather one-dimensional group. The stereotype of women as "homemakers" often keeps women from advancing in the workplace.

Finally, stereotypes can serve as a "self-fulfilling prophecies." Once the stereotype is in place, there is a tendency to perceive the stereotyped person engaging in behavior that corroborates your stereotype—even when the behavior is not present. That is to say, negative stereotypes confirm your expectations even if they are invalid. Gudykunst reiterates this idea when he notes, "Stereotypes can create self-fulfilling prophecies. Individuals tend to see behavior that confirms their expectations, even when it is absent."[22]

It should be obvious from our brief discussion of stereotyping that it can prevent successful intercultural communication by keeping you from making fair and honest judgments about other people. As you shall see in the next few sections of this chapter, once created and perpetuated, stereotypes often lead to unfair discrimination and persecution.

Prejudice

The French essayist Voltaire knew of the dangers associated with prejudice when he wrote that "prejudices are what fools use for reason." His rationale for this observation was simple—deeply felt prejudices cause serious problems. Let us examine the problems associated with prejudice as they apply to intercultural communication. Specifically, we will define *prejudice*, look at its functions and how it is expressed, and conclude with a few suggestions on how to escape the destructive results built into prejudicial behavior.

Defining Prejudice

Macionis offers a detailed definition of prejudice while explaining its damaging effect on intercultural communication:

> Prejudice amounts to a rigid and irrational generalization about a category of people. Prejudice is irrational to the extent that people hold inflexible attitudes supported by little or no direct evidence. Prejudice may target people of a particular social class, sex, sexual orientation, age, political affiliation, race or ethnicity.[23]

In yet a related definition, Brislin adds the emotional element of prejudice when he notes:

> Prejudice refers to the emotional component of people's reactions to other groups. It involves not only a set of beliefs about others, which are captured in stereotypes, but it is also a deeply felt set of feelings about what is good and bad, right and wrong, moral and immoral, and so forth.[24]

Both of these definitions, when applied to the interpersonal and intercultural setting, often include levels of hostility. This hostility dimension is explained by Levin, who believes that prejudice deals with "negative feelings, beliefs, and action-tendencies, or discriminatory acts, that arise against human beings by virtue of the status they occupy or are perceived to occupy as members of a minority group."[25]

Functions of Prejudice

As was the case with stereotypes, prejudices also serve various functions for the people who hold them. An understanding of these functions is a useful first step in identifying and overcoming prejudices—both your own and of the people with whom you interact. Levin underscores the importance of examining the functions of prejudice when he writes, "It follows that we can only reduce prejudice and attendant majority-minority inequities to the extent that we actually come to grips with the important functions that prejudice serves."[26] Let us spend a moment looking at four of the most common functions prejudices provide for the individual who holds the prejudice.[27]

Ego-Defensive Function. The ego-defensive function of prejudice allows people to hold a prejudice without having to admit they possess these beliefs about a member of the out-group. In this way they can protect themselves be denying they are prejudiced. An example of this type of prejudice might be found in someone who says, "My grades are low this semester because most professors feel sorry for those minority students and are giving them the higher grades." These types of remarks permit the person who utters them to articulate prejudiced statements while maintaining a sense of self instead of truly examining why their grades were low.

Utilitarian Function. The utilitarian function of prejudice allows people to believe that they are receiving rewards by holding on to their prejudiced beliefs. The most vivid examples of this function are found in attitudes related to the economic arena. People often find it very useful, and to their economic advantage, to say, "Those poor people have so little education they are lucky to have the jobs we offer them." This sort of sentence reflects utilitarian prejudice because the holder of the prejudice can use the belief as a justification for offering minimal pay to the workers in question.

Value-Expressive Function. We see people maintaining the value-expressive function of prejudice when they believe their attitudes are expressing the highest and most moral values of the culture. These usually revolve around values related to religion, government and politics. If you believe, for instance, that your God is the only one true God, it is to be prejudiced against people who hold differing views.

Knowledge Function. When carrying out the knowledge function of prejudice a person is able to categorize, organize, and construct their perceptions of other people in a manner that make sense to them—even if the sense making is not accurate. In this way the world is easy to deal with in that individuals are perceived not person by person but rather as member of a group. It is the knowledge level that produces an abundance of labels. People are seen not as persons with a variety of characteristics but rather as "Jews," "Mexicans, "gays," and "feminists."

Expressions of Prejudice

Prejudices, like stereotypes, are learned. For some people, prejudices offer rewards ranging from feelings of superiority to feelings of power. Prejudice is expressed in a variety of ways—at times subtle and on other occasions overt. Allport discussed five of those expressions.[28] Although Allport's analyses were presented over forty years ago, they are still relevant today. In fact, many contemporary social scientists base their current theories on the work of Allport.[29] Knowing how prejudice is manifested will help you identify your own prejudices and in so doing will greatly improve the manner in which you perceive, approach, and interact with other people.

First, prejudice can be expressed through what Allport refers to as antilocution. This level of prejudice involves talking about a member of the target group in negative and stereotypic terms. Someone would be engaging in this form of prejudice if he or she told a friend, "Those Germans did it once, so we can never trust any of them ever again." Another example of antilocution prejudice is the statement "Don't pay the Mexicans very much. They don't have any education and will work for almost nothing."

Second, people act out prejudice when they avoid and/or withdraw from contact with the disliked group. The problems associated with this form of prejudice are obvious. How do you interact, solve problems, and resolve serious conflicts when you are separated from other people? On both the international and domestic levels, avoidance and withdrawal often have marked the intercultural exchange. History is full of examples of how one nation or group of people refused to attend (withdrew from) an important peace conference. For decades, the political leaders from East and West Germany and from Israel and Egypt rebuffed each other, only to discover decades later that talking benefited both parties. What is true with regard to governments is also characteristic of individual behavior. Have there been occasions when you, like governments, withdrew from communication because a person was a different color or spoke a different language? In an age when each cultural group has some sway over another, prejudice that produces retreat can harm everyone.

Third, when discrimination is the expression of prejudice, the prejudiced person undertakes to exclude all members of the group in question from certain types of employment, residential housing, political rights, educational and recreational opportunities, churches, hospitals, or some other type of social institution. Often in cases of discrimination, we observe ethnocentrism, stereotyping, and prejudice coming together in a type of fanaticism that completely obstructs any form of successful intercultural communication. When discrimination replaces communication, you see overt and covert expressions of anger and hate that restrict one group's opportunity or access to opportunities that rightly belong to everyone. When a real-estate agent will not show certain homes to African Americans, there is discrimination. When businesses promote less qualified males instead of competent women, you have discrimination.

Fourth, when prejudice moves to the next level of expression, you often see physical attacks. This form of prejudice often accelerates in hostility and intensity if it is left unchecked. From the burning of churches to the writing of anti-Semitic slogans in Jewish cemeteries, physical acts occur when minorities are the targets of prejudiced activity.

The fifth, and most alarming, form of prejudice is extermination. This expression of prejudice leads to acts of physical violence against the out-group. History is replete with examples of lynching, massacres, and programs of genocide. In cases such as Hitler's "master plan," the former Serbian "ethnic cleansing," and the religious and tribal warfare in Afghanistan, we saw attempts to destroy an entire racial or ethnic group.

To this point, we have talked only about the problems associated with stereotyping, prejudice, and discrimination. In the next chapter we will provide some practical guidelines for dealing with these three serious impediments to intercultural communication.

Racism

Early in this new century it appears that for most people of color Martin Luther King's "dream" that children "will be judged not by the color of their skin but by the content of their character" is still only a dream. For as Dana points out, "Both subtle and overt racism still permeates mainstream American society."[30] Racism is damaging to those who are the recipients of this destructive behavior as well as those who are racist. It devalues the target person by denying their identity. It destroys the culture by creating divisions and making it less cohesive.

What is sad but true about racism is that it has existed for centuries throughout the world. In the past we saw African American being forced to ride in the back of busses, Jews being required to wear a yellow "Star of David," Japanese Americans being isolated in camps during World War II, and Native Americans having their land confiscated simply because of their race. And today we see racism in the form of racial graffiti, property damage, intimidation, or physical violence. There are also more subtle forms of racism such as uttering racial slurs or telling ethnic jokes. Let us examine this harmful and insidious characteristic of racism so that you can work to eliminate it in your professional and private lives.

Defining Racism

Racism, in many ways, is an extension of prejudice in that "racism refers to the belief that one racial category is innately superior to another."[31] Built into this idea of superiority is the belief that a group of people can be mistreated on the basis of race, color, religion, national origin, or ancestry. A more detailed explanation of racism, and some of the false suppositions behind it, is offered by Nanda and Warms:

> There are biological fixed races; different races have different moral, intellectual, and physical characteristics; an individual's aptitudes are determined primarily by his or her race; races can be ranked on a single hierarchy; and political action should be taken to order society so that it reflects this hierarchy.[32]

The folly of the racist thinking described above is that it is not only unethical and cruel, but it is also constructed on false premises. It is now common knowledge, for those who are willing to be receptive to the knowledge, that "the big differences among human groups are the result of culture, not biological inheritance or race. All human beings belong to the same species and the biological features essential to human life are common to us all."[33] Yet in spite of the truth and wisdom contained in the last paragraph, racism remains a major hindrance to successful intercultural communication.

Forms of Racism

As we alluded to earlier, racism ranges from forms that are almost impossible to detect to signs that are blatant and transparent. Four of the most common forms are identified by Brislin and are worthy of our consideration.

Intense Racism. In this form of racism, "Some people believe that virtually all members of certain out groups are inferior in various ways and are not able to benefit fully from society's offerings such as education, good jobs, and participation in community affairs."[34] This form of racism begins with the belief that certain people (those of a race different from the person making and drawing the conclusion) are inferior, and hence are perceived as being of low worth.

Symbolic Racism. Some people hold racist views because "they feel that the outgroup is interfering with important aspects of the culture."[35] This "interference," reflected in racism, can be in the form of "causing trouble" to "getting more economically than they deserve."[36]

Tokenism. Tokenism, whether it be in the form of prejudice or racism, is difficult to detect. In this case the person does not want to admit that he or she harbors negative or racist views. People will even engage in "token" activities to "prove" they are even-handed in the treatment of other races.

Arm's-Length. Brislin describes this negative behavior in the following manner: Some people engage in friendly, positive behaviors toward out-group members in some social settings but treat those same out-group members with noticeably less warmth and friendliness in other settings.[37] We see this kind of subtle racism when the "friendly" real-estate agent will not show certain homes that are for sale to African Americans.

Avoiding Racism

While lifelong views about race are difficult to overcome, there are two simple activities in which you can engage that can help you combat racism in your personal life. First, try to be honest with yourself when deciding if you hold some racist views. It is a simple point to state, and a difficult one to accomplish. Yet, confronting your racist views, if you hold any, is an important first step in conquering any racist beliefs you might hold. Second, object to racist jokes and insults when you hear them being uttered by other people. This daring, and at times courageous, act will send a message to other people that you denounce racism in whatever form it may take.

We conclude by reminding you that racism, stereotyping, and prejudice are pervasive because they are often learned early in life, and like much of culture, become part of our worldview without our realization. In a somewhat poetic manner the African American author Maya Angelou makes the same point when she writes, "The plague of racism is insidious, entering into our minds as smoothly and quietly and invisibly as floating airborne microbes enter into our bodies to find lifelong purchase in our bloodstreams."

Power

Much of what we have been talking about, whether it is prejudice or racism, has its roots in issues related to power. Power has been a consideration among people and cultures for a long time. Groups have employed guns, bombs, language, space, money, and even history as devices for gaining and keeping power over others. The reason is apparent, if not wholly justifiable—people who hold power achieve their will regardless of the type of relationship. Power, in one form or another, seems to be built into all human liaisons. The famous British philosopher Bertrand Russell made the same observation when he wrote, "The fundamental concept in social science is Power, in the same sense in which Energy is the fundamental concept in Physics."[38] Granting that there are many kinds of power (interpersonal, corporate, organizational, governmental, etc.), we will concentrate on power in the intercultural context.

Defining Power

Why do humans seek out power whenever they can? The answer to this question can be found in the very definition of power: Power is the ability to control what happens, to cause things you want to happen and to block things you don't want to happen.[39] What makes power an important dimension in intercultural communication, and a potential problem, is that power usually means controlling not only your own life but also the lives of others. As Nanda and Warms tell you, "Power is thus the ability to make and carry out decisions affecting one's own life, control the behavior of other human beings, and transform objects and resources."[40] In many cultures this often means that the people in power can "follow their own interests at the expense of the goals of others."[41]

What is interesting about power is that the methods of power are as diverse as they are widespread. That is to say, power is present in nearly every human experience, from global politics to face-to-face interactions between the dominant culture and co-cultures. Therefore, the dynamics of power greatly influence all phases of intercultural communication. Martin and Nakayama offer an excellent summary of this point when they note, "We are not equal in intercultural encounters, nor can we ever be equal. Long histories of imperialism, colonialism, exploitation, wars, genocide campaigns, and more leave cultural groups out of balance when they communicate."[42]

Degrees of Power

It should be clear that power, both in definition and in practice is complex. For example, not all power, either perceived or implemented, is the same. Charon points out that it is best to view power on a continuum.[43] At one end of the spectrum, both parties hold some degree of control over the interaction and the outcome of the interaction. As you move along the continuum, one person would have a little influence over the other. At the opposite end of the scale, one person would have complete control. Here is were you find the idea of the "powerlessness." Again we turn to Charon for an explanation of what it means to be powerless:

> To be powerless means to be helpless in relation to others, to be determined by the will of others. Powerless means that one lacks control over one's own life, is unable effectively to resist the exertion of power by others, and lacks the ability to influence the direction of social organization, including society. Powerless brings dependence of others and exploitation (self use) by others, if they choose.[44]

Power and Intercultural Communication

The reason power is such an important consideration in the study of intercultural communication is that it can show itself in a variety of ways. In interpersonal communication the amount of power you have, or do not have, influences who you talk to, what you talk about, and how much control you have when you talk. Folb adds to the list when she tells us that the people in power have a major impact on what people "believe and do," and also influence the "rules of appropriate and inappropriate behavior, thought, speech, and action."[45] Carried to an extreme, and it often is, we find in many cultures that the following expression is true: "All men (perhaps even women) are created equal—some are just more equal than others."[46]

Your degree of power is contingent on the person(s) with whom you are interacting and the resources that you control. In intercultural communication, these two factors take on added significance, for the sources of power are culturally based. What one culture deems as a source of power, another culture may not consider a power variable. For example, in England, one's language is often a sign of potential power because it signals one's class and station. There also are instances when one culture believes that power is derived from simply being a member of that particular culture. African Americans have long expressed feelings of being controlled and manipulated by white males.[47] Many women in the United

States have expressed this same view. It is easy to see how this use, or misuse, of power, when employed to control and determine another's behavior, can restrict openness and communication. As Smith notes, "To allow customary subservience or power a place in human interaction is to introduce an inevitable obstruction."[48]

We again remind you that there are vast cultural differences in both the perception and use of power. In North America, there is a strong cultural message that one should not be powerless. People grow up hearing that they should be "captains of their ships" and "masters of their own fate." Not only do they want power, and think they deserve it, they do not want other people to have power over them. They often leave home at an early age so their parents will not have power over them, and they make teachers, police, and bosses the brunt of jokes because they often are annoyed over the amount of power these people have over them. In America there are cries of black power, gray power, and gay power. Women and minority groups ask for power so that they can have freedom from internal and external restraints. In short, people are taught in North America not to be powerless.

Although all cultures abhor the abuse of power, much of the world is composed of cultures that do not seek individual power. They believe that power resides outside of them and that fate, nature, or God has all the power. Power is not something they want, need, or have. Muslims use the phrase "It is God's will." For the Hindu, power is the acting out of individual karma, and in much of Mexico and Latin America, a strong belief in fatalism often replaces power. These cultures hold the view that, in most instances, the legitimacy of power is irrelevant.[49]

As an intercultural communicator, it is important that you become aware of each culture's approach to power. However, regardless of the culture you are interacting with, an adherence to the following philosophy advanced by Blubaugh and Pennington could greatly improve most intercultural transactions: "The ideal power relationship . . . is not concerned with the idea of control. . . . Rather, the desire is to attribute to all groups the credibility that allows them positive influence in communication."[50]

Culture Shock

An old English saying states, "That song is best esteemed with which our ears are most acquainted." Everyone likes the familiar. As we noted in Chapter 2, culture, by repeating experiences, makes them known to the members of the culture. This familiarity helps you reduce stress, for in most instances you know what you can expect from your environment and from those around you. However, you are now, by either chance or design, leaving these comfortable surroundings and journeying into new areas and confronting people who are often unlike yourself. Leaving the known and moving to the unknown can create a number of secondary communication problems. Smith and Bond offer an excellent summary of some of these problems:

> Separation from previous support networks, climate differences, increased health problems, changes in material and technical resources, lack of information about daily routines (e.g. how to travel from A to B), and so forth all exact their price.[51]

It should not be surprising that dealing with a new culture can create problems. Nolan mentions two serious problems when he writes, "Your new environment makes demands for which you have no ready-made responses; and your responses, in turn do not seem to produce the desired results."[52]

Difference in food can create culture shock.

© Gloria Thomas

The problems associated with confronting a new culture are, of course, compounded by the fact they "serve to distract the new arrival from the culture-learning task, and deplete the energy and motivation necessary to master the communication process."[53]

As we have pointed out throughout this book, contact with other cultures is not only increasing in number and intensity, but they are taking a variety of forms. Millions of Americans are now overseas attending school, conducting business, or performing government service.[54] When you are thrust into another culture and experience psychological and physical discomfort from this contact, you have become a victim of culture shock.[55]

Defining Culture Shock

The term *culture shock* was first introduced by the anthropologist Oberg. In the following paragraph, he offers a detailed definition and account of this phenomenon:

> Culture shock is precipitated by the anxiety that results from losing all our familiar signs and symbols of social intercourse. These signs or cues include the thousand and one ways in which we orient ourselves to the situation of daily life: how to give orders, how to make purchases, when and where not to respond. Now these cues which may be words, gestures, facial expressions, customs, or norms are acquired by all of us in the course of growing up and are as much a part of our culture as the language we speak or the beliefs we accept. All of us depend for our peace of mind and efficiency on hundreds of these cues, most of which we are not consciously aware.[56]

The feelings associated with culture shock not only apply to businesspersons, students, and government employees, but, as Brislin notes, can "be experienced by individuals who have face-to-face contact with out-group members within their own culture."[57]

Understanding Culture Shock

The reactions associated with culture shock vary from individual to individual. For the person who is constantly encountering other cultures, the anxiety period might be mild and brief. However, for many people culture shock can be characterized by depression, serious physical reactions (such as headaches or body pains), anger, irritability, aggression toward the new culture, and even total withdrawal. Therefore, we agree with Lynch and Hanson when they say, "Understanding the concept of culture shock and its characteristics and stages provides a framework that enable individuals to recognize their feelings, analyze the cause, alter their approach, consciously manage their own behavior, and regain emotional equilibrium."[58] Having already mentioned the characteristics of culture shock, let us now turn to a discussion of the most common stages of culture shock.

The Stages of Culture Shock (The U-Curve)

Although there might be great variations in how people respond to culture shock, and the amount of time needed for that adjustment, most of the literature in the area of culture shock suggests that people normally go through four stages. We should first mention that the seam separating the stages is almost impossible to see. That is to say, the transition from stage to stage is not as clear cut as our description might imply. It might be helpful if you were to view the stages as a U-shaped curve.[59]

"Honeymoon Phase." The initial phase, visualized as the top of one side of the U, is often called the "honeymoon phase." It usually is filled with excitement, optimism, and a sense of euphoria as the individual anticipates being exposed to a new culture. Marx offers an excellent review of how this first phase might be perceived by someone undertaking an international management assignment:

> The new life is viewed as providing endless opportunities and the manager is usually in a state of exhilaration. There is openness and curiosity, combined with a readiness to accept whatever comes. Most importantly, at this stage judgment is reserved and even minor irritations are suppressed in favor of concentrating on the nice things about the job, the country, the colleagues, the food, etc.[60]

Culture Shock Phase. This initial phase is followed by feelings of disappointment and discontent. It is the crisis period of culture shock. The person becomes confused and baffled by his or her new surroundings. This frustration can make them easily irritated, hostile, impatient, angry, and even incompetent. In extreme cases these uncomfortable feelings "can border on hating everything foreign."[61]

Recovery Phase. The third stage is characterized by gaining some understanding of the new culture. Here the person is gradually making some adjustments and modifications in how he or she is coping with the new culture. Events and people now seem much more predictable and less stressful.

Adjustment Phase. In the final phase, the top of the U, the person now understands the key elements of the new culture (values, special customs, beliefs, communication patterns, etc.), and can now function with some degree of success. This ability to "live within two" cultures is often accompanied by feelings of enjoyment and satisfaction.

Some researchers suggest that there is also a kind of reverse culture shock that takes place when people return "home." As Harris and Moran note, "Having objectively perceived his or her culture from abroad, one can have a severe and sustained jolt through reentry shock."[62] These expatriates often arrive home missing the new friends they made while overseas. Some bemoan the loss of prestige associated with foreign assignments. One common sign of reentry shock is being highly critical of one's own culture. Regardless of the manifestations of reentry shock, it is yet another hindrance to effective human interaction.

Learning from Culture Shock

Although we have placed the topic of culture shock under the category of "problems," we would be remiss if we did not emphasize the idea that culture shock can be an explicit learning experience. For example, as Adler notes, "Severe culture shock is often a positive sign indicating that the expatriate is becoming deeply involved in the new culture instead of remaining isolated in an expatriate ghetto."[63] This involvement helps people learn about themselves and, at the same time, other cultures. In a study examining culture shock, Kawano concluded that culture shock "gives the sojourners a chance to learn about themselves. In this sense experiencing culture shock has a strong potential to make people be multicultural or bicultural."[64]

Ethnocentrism

Defining Ethnocentrism

One culture views the eating of animals as barbarous and abnormal; the people with such habits are apt to consider the custom of confining the elderly to convalescent homes just as cruel and unnatural—this is ethnocentrism. Ethnocentrism might well be the problem that most directly relates to intercultural communication. Sumner, generally credited with introducing the term to the study of culture, defined *ethnocentrism* as "the technical name for the view of things in which one's own group is the center of everything, and all others are scaled and rated with reference to it."[65] Nanda and Warms offer a more contemporary explanation:

> Ethnocentrism is the notion that one's own culture is superior to any other. It is the idea that other cultures should be measured by the degree to which they live up to our cultural standards. We are ethnocentric when we view other cultures through the narrow lens of our own culture or social position.[66]

Understanding Ethnocentrism

A few important points need to be made as part of our introduction to ethnocentrism. First, anthropologists generally agree that ethnocentrism, with varying degrees, is found in every culture in that "most peoples in the world regard their own culture as superior."[67] And like culture, ethnocentrism is usually learned at the unconscious level. For example, schools that teach mainly the history, geography, literature, and government of only their country are also, without realizing it, encouraging ethnocentrism. When you study only the accomplishments of white males, you

Ethnocentrism is learned early in life and is continuously reinforced.

© Robert Fonseca

are quietly learning ethnocentrism. Students exposed to limited orientations develop the belief that America is the center of the world, and they learn to judge the world by American standards. What is true about American ethnocentrism is true about other cultures. As children in Iran only learn about the wisdom of Allah, they are learning to judge all religious truths by this singular standard. And when the Chinese, for thousands of years, "place themselves in the center of the world, referring to their nation using a Chinese character that literally means central state," they are teaching ethnocentrism.[68] Even the stories and folktales that each culture tells their young people contribute to ethnocentrism. Keesing described this subtle learning when he writes, "Nearly always the folklore of a people includes myths of origin which give priority to themselves, and place the stamp of supernatural approval upon their particular customs."[69]

Second, another reason ethnocentrism is so pervasive is that it serves to help the members of the culture associate and identify with the culture. Haviland clearly summaries this function when he writes:

> To function effectively, a society must embrace the idea that its ways are the only proper ones, irrespective of how other cultures do things. This provides individuals with a sense of ethnic pride in and loyalty to their cultural traditions, from which they derive psychological support, and which binds them firmly to their group. In societies where one's self-identification derives from the group, ethnocentrism is essential to a sense of personal worth.[70]

Advancing this same thought concerning the link between ethnocentrism and devotion to one's culture, Brislin helps us understand America's response to the events surrounding September 11, 2001. He notes, "If people view their own group as central to their lives and as possessing proper behavioral standards, they are likely to aid their group members when troubles arise. In times of war the rallying of ethnocentric feelings makes a country's military forces more dedicated to the defeat of the (inferior) enemy."[71]

Consequences of Ethnocentrism

Although we have just mentioned some of the reasons cultures engage in ethnocentric behavior, we must once again remind you that "the problem with ethnocentrism is that it all too often can be taken as a charter for condemning other cultures as inferior, and as such exploiting them for the benefit of one's own."[72] What we are suggesting is that ethnocentrism takes on a negative condition and becomes "destructive when it is used to shut others out, provide the bases for derogatory evaluations, and rebuff change."[73] These feelings that you are right and they are wrong pervade every aspect of a culture's existence. Examples range from the insignificant ("Earrings should be placed on the ears, not on the nose") to the significant ("We need to build up our defenses to protect ourselves from those foreign fanatics"). Ethnocentrism is strongest in moral and religious contexts, where emotionalism may overshadow rationality and cause the type of hostility the world witnessed September 11, 2001. In more subtle ways, ethnocentrism can cause the alienation of co-cultures from the dominant culture, or one group from another. For example, we often find white-collar workers isolated from blue-collar workers, African Americans living apart from whites, and those with disabilities removed from our sight.

The negative impact of ethnocentrism on intercultural communication is clearly highlighted by Stewart and Bennett:

> First, ethnocentric beliefs about one's own culture shape a social sense of identity which is narrow and defensive. Second, ethnocentrism normally involves the perception of members of other cultures in terms of stereotypes. Third, the dynamic of ethnocentrism is such that comparative judgments are made between one's own culture and other cultures under the assumption that one's own is normal and natural. As a consequence, ethnocentric judgments usually involve invidious comparisons that ennoble one's culture while degrading those of others.[74]

To fully appreciate the significance of ethnocentrism as a potential problem, you need only recall one of the major themes of this book: Culture, by selecting and evaluating certain experiences, helps determine your perspective on reality. For example, if males in the dominant culture value women who are thin, young, and blonde, then they will perceive women who are stout, older, and dark-haired in a less favorable light. If you perceive openness as a positive trait while another culture values privacy, we again have perceptual differences. If you value directness in speech and another culture values vagueness, we might misinterpret what is being said. These three cases—and there are countless others—are examples of how perception influences communication.

When your perceptions are narrow and your subsequent behaviors rigid, you are easily susceptible to ethnocentrism. When that ethnocentrism is excessive, serious communication problems can arise. As Jandt points out:

> Extreme ethnocentrism leads to a rejection of the richness and knowledge of other cultures. It impedes communication and blocks the exchange of ideas and skills among peoples. Because it excludes other points of view, an ethnocentrism orientation is restrictive and limiting.[75]

Although in the next chapter we discuss methods to overcome ethnocentrism, we conclude our analysis of some of the problems associated with intercultural communication by asking you to think about the following questions. Jews cover their heads when they pray, but Protestants do not—Is one more correct than the other? The Catholic speaks to God, the Buddhist has no god, and the Hindu has many gods—Is one more correct than the others? In parts of Turkey and Saudi Arabia, women cover their faces with veils, whereas women in the United States do not—Is one more correct than the other? These sorts of rhetorical questions are never-ending. We urge you to remember, however, that it is not the questions that are important but rather the dogmatic manner in which people often answer them. We must be attentive to the ease with which we judge the actions of others. The danger of ethnocentrism is that it is strongest in political, moral, and religious settings. In these contexts, it is easy to let culturally restricted views overshadow rationality. Hence, we again urge you to be alert to narrowness and intolerance in any form. St. Thomas Aquinas said much the same thing hundreds of years ago: "Beware of the man of one book."

SUMMARY

- The belief that improvement in intercultural communication is possible is based on three assumptions: (1) the brain is an open system, (2) we have free choice, and (3) communication has a consequence.
- Avoidance of the unfamiliar, the desire to reduce uncertainty, withdrawal, stereotyping, prejudice, racism, misuse of power, culture shock, and ethnocentrism are major barriers to successful intercultural communication.

INFOTRAC COLLEGE EDITION EXERCISES

1. To what extent is stereotyping a useful practice? What are your views on racial profiling? Locate and read the following two articles: "Fear and Ignorance Fueling Racial Profiling after September 11" by Acel Moore, and "Profiling's Place on September 11" by Thomas Ambrose. What are the competing issues underlying this debate? How does cultural membership affect views of racial profiling? How have the events of September 11 affected American cultural views with regard to this issue?

2. Want to learn more about culture shock? Locate and read the following two articles: "Coping with Culture Clash" appearing in *African Business* and "Wal-Mart Runs into Culture Shock in Germany." In these articles, what cultural differences are likely to cause conflicts? What can be learned from these articles and other similar case studies? (Hint: for related articles, use the subject search terms "Ethnocentrism" and "Culture Shock.")

DISCUSSION IDEAS

1. With some members of your class, try to list some examples of what you believe to be examples of American ethnocentrism.
2. What is the relationship between stereotypes, prejudice, racism, and ethnocentrism?
3. Can you think of some intercultural communication problems that were not discussed in this chapter?

4. Discuss the following statement: "Prejudice can never be eliminated because it is so deeply rooted in human nature."
5. Do you believe there is still discrimination in the United States? If so, discrimination against which groups?

chapter 10

Becoming Competent: A Point of View

The greatest danger to our future is apathy.

JANE GOODALL

Mankind has become so much one family that we cannot insure our own prosperity except by insuring that of everyone else.

BERTRAND RUSSELL

If one finger is sore, the whole hand will hurt.

CHINESE PROVERB

In the last chapter we looked at some potential problems facing you as you engage in intercultural communication. Here in Chapter 10, we will attempt to offer some advice on how you may solve some of those problems. Shakespeare expressed poetically the rationale for the sequence of the chapters (moving from problems to solutions) in his play *Much Ado About Nothing*, where he writes, "Happy are they that hear their detractions and can put them to mending." Having noted "detractions" in Chapter 9, we now move to "mending."

In addition to exploring the resolutions to the problems we examined in the last chapter, we will also recommend some ethical guidelines when you are part of an intercultural communication event. At the end of the chapter, we will look at four issues that influence the future of intercultural communication.

BECOMING COMPETENT

Being able to understand another culture is at the heart of becoming a competent communicator. However, that understanding is often impeded by the fact that you have grown so accustomed to your own culture that it is difficult to understand or operate outside of it. Hence, let us pause at this time and look at some of the reasons for the difficulties you might have when to trying to improve your intercultural skills while trying to understand another culture.[1]

First, as we pointed out in Chapter 2, much of what we call culture occurs early in life—often before four years of age. What this means is that "lessons learned at such an early age become an integral part of thinking and behavior."[2] In this sense culture produces perceptions and actions that are often automatic and second nature by the time you become an adult. Hence, when attempting to develop new communication skills, you bring a lifetime of ingrained habits and unconscious responses.

Second, a result of the early leaning associated with culture is the notion that your values and your worldview come from that culture. For example, if you are from the North American culture, where informality is valued and good manners are not highly esteemed, you might have a difficult time when interacting with Germans. In that culture, "Good manners are part of a child's upbringing" and stressed in everything from family relationships to the business environment.[3]

Finally, as Lynch reminds us, "Long-standing behavior patterns are typically used to express one's deepest values."[4] What this means is that cultural habits, responses, perceptions, behaviors, and so forth are hard to change. That they are difficult to change does not mean they are impossible to change. As we observed in Chapter 9, because of free choice change is possible.

Before we submit specific techniques for improving your intercultural skills, we need to offer a few definitions related to the issue of intercultural communication competence.

Defining Intercultural Competence

In its most unadorned form we would agree with Spitzberg when he suggests that intercultural communication competence is simply "behavior that is appropriate and effective in a given context."[5] Kim offers a more detailed definition when she notes that

All people value the traditions and history of their culture.

© Gloria Thomas

intercultural communication competence is "the overall internal capability of an individual to manage key challenging features of intercultural communication: namely, cultural differences and unfamiliarity, inter-group posture, and the accompanying experience of stress."[6] What these two definitions, one general and one specific, are telling you is that being a competent communicator means analyzing the situation and selecting the correct mode of behavior.

Basic Components of Communication Competence[7]

Most of the research in the area of communication competence maintains that in selecting the most appropriate course of action (exercising free choice), effective communicators are those who are (1) *motivated*, (2) *have a fund of knowledge to draw upon*, and (3) *possess certain communication skills*.[8] Let us look at these three components as a general prologue to a detailed analysis of intercultural competence.

Motivation

Motivation as it relates to competence means that as a communicator you want to do a good job. Simply put, you have a positive attitude toward the communication event and put forth the effort to bring about constructive results. Because the topic of motivation is such an important one, we will return to it later in the chapter when we discuss intercultural communication competence. For now the message is basic—be motivated to improve your communication behavior and you will increase the chances that you will be successful in your efforts.

Knowledge

Knowledge as it applies to competence means being able to do and say the right thing at the right time. Acquiring the necessary fund of knowledge to be competent is an important task. Luckmann points out the need for knowledge as it applies to the health care profession: "Nurses who are not knowledgeable about cultural differences risk misinterpreting patients' attempts to communicate. As a result, patients may not receive the proper care."[9]

According to Morreale, Spitzberg, and Barge you need two kinds of knowledge to be competent—content knowledge and procedural knowledge. "Content knowledge involves knowing what topics, words, meanings and so forth, are required in a situation. Procedural knowledge is knowing how to assemble, plan and perform content knowledge in a particular situation."[10] While we would agree with this position, we would add that you should also learn to find information to add to your fund of knowledge. The English essayist Samuel Johnson held to the same idea when he wrote, "Knowledge is of two kinds: we know a subject ourselves, or we know where we can find information on it." This entire book has been about your finding that information.

Skills

Skills are the specific behaviors you engage in to accomplish your goals. This point is further explained by Morreale, Spitzberg, and Barge when they observe, "Skills are goal directed because they must be designed to accomplish something."[11] You have learned those skills all of your life. As we shall note later in this chapter, as a competent intercultural communicator you may have to adjust those skills as you face people from cultures different from your own.

Approaches to the Study of Intercultural Competence

Having briefly discussed communication competence in general, we are now ready to shift the emphasis to intercultural competence. When scholars and professional intercultural communication trainers examine the topic of competence, they normally speak of three methods of improving intercultural competence: (1) *culture-specific*, (2) *context-specific*, and (3) *culture-general*. Let us look briefly at these methods of learning so that you might appreciate some of the alternatives available to anyone who is interested in improving intercultural communication. We add before we begin that in many instances some scholars in the area of intercultural competence suggest combining some of the three methods we will be discussing.

Culture-Specific

The culture-specific method assumes that the most effective way to improve intercultural communication is to study one culture at a time and learn all the distinct and specific communication features of that culture. This approach assumes that the person is preparing to work or visit a specific culture for a period of time, and hence necessitates an in-depth culture-specific orientation. For example, to interact with an Arab, you should know his or her values regarding gender, hospitality, pride, honor, and rivalry. You should also know that Islam is a regulator of behavior as well as a religion and that Arab males engage in very direct eye contact. You should even learn about the Arabic language because your communication with Arabs will improve if you know that

> Arab language abounds with forms of assertion. Metaphors, similes, long arrays of adjectives, and repetition of words are frequently used by the Arabs in communicating their ideas. Repetition of words is especially common in extending, or rejecting, invitations for coffee, dinner, and the like.[12]

If you were going to Japan, you might benefit from advice about gift giving, the use of first names, greeting behavior, indirect speech, politeness, the use of business cards, the importance of group harmony, social stability, the use of "yes" and "no," and the like.[13]

Context-Specific

In recent years scholars have begun to talk about not only specific cultures but also specific contexts or settings of the intercultural encounter. In Chapters 6, 7, and 8, for example, we explored the business, educational, and health care settings as a way of assessing the link between culture and the context of the communication encounter. There are now numerous books, journals, training manuals, and the like that look at improving intercultural competence when working with very young children in an early education environment.[14] Scholars have also offered specific suggestions to psychological service providers so they can more effectively deal with their culturally diverse clients.[15]

The health care environment is yet another setting where developing intercultural communication competence is useful. Purnell and Paulanka, for example, believe it is important for anyone involved in intercultural health care to know the connection between the individual's culture and such issues as "communication, family roles, biocultural ecology, high risk health behaviors, nutrition, pregnancy and childbearing practices, death rituals, spirituality, heath-care practices and health-care practitioners."[16]

Culture-General

Brislin offers an excellent explanation of cultural-general as a learning and training approach when he writes, "Cultural-general training deals with aspects of people's movement across cultures that are common to virtually all intercultural experiences."[17] The two key words in Brislin's definition are *across* and *common*. What is being said is that the skills learned in cultural-general training, classes, and textbooks are common enough that they can be transferred from culture to culture. You can see how such training allows you to interact with a variety of cultures. It is also "practical when individuals or group members are about to go to many different countries."[18]

As you have learned by now, the approach of this book is culture-general. Although we have offered many specific examples, we primarily have looked at cultural traits and behaviors that are shared, to one extent or another, by all cultures. In this chapter, we treat the subject of improvement in the same manner; we look at a series of skills that can be in most intercultural situations. Although there might be slight variations in how each culture manifests the skills we will discuss, the attributes we have selected tend to cut across cultures. For example, in one study Zhong looked at intercultural communication competence as found in the Chinese and American cultures. She concluded that there were no significant differences between the groups in their perceptions of what constituted competent intercultural communication.[19] What we are suggesting is that regardless of the culture you are encountering, it is important to have knowledge of the person's culture and try to adapt whenever possible. These are but two traits we shall be discussing that are not culture-specific but rather are found in most intercultural experiences. As was the case when we discussed potential problems, the discussion that follows combines our personal advice and the research of others in the area of intercultural communication.

IMPROVING INTERCULTURAL COMMUNICATION

Although this book is aimed at improving intercultural communication, our suggestions, admonitions, counsel, and proposals in previous chapters have been only tangentially related to improvement. Our recommendations in this chapter are very direct. And more importantly, all of the suggestions for improvement enable you to exercise your ability to make choices. Our propositions place you in the center of the activity. Whether we are asking you to learn more about a culture's view toward the elderly or appealing to you to develop some new skills, the power is all yours. What is being said here should be quite clear—you must act on your knowledge. The Persian poet Sa'di said much the same thing over seven thousand years ago: "Whoever acquires knowledge and does not practice it resembles him who ploughs his land and leaves it unsown."

Before we offer our first bit of advice, we want to acknowledge a major danger in offering anyone personal advice. Whenever you tell another individual how to think or act, you run the risk, particularly if he or she listens to you, of making matters worse. The person may have been better off without your advice. For example, we believe that many of you already know a great deal about intercultural communication and, in fact, are very good practitioners of the art. In these cases, we run the risk of spoiling what it took you years to develop. What we are saying is somewhat analogous to the following Chinese fable. In this fable, a monkey and a fish were very good friends. One day, however, a dreadful flood separated them. Because the monkey could climb trees, he was able to scramble up a limb and escape the rising waters. As he glanced into the raging river, he saw his friend the fish swimming past. With the best of intentions, he scooped his paw into the water, snatched his friend from the river, and lifted him into the tree. The result was obvious. From this modest story, you can see the dilemma we face; so please remember as we offer advice that, like the monkey, we have the best of intentions.

Know Yourself

It seems only fitting that we ask you to begin with yourself, for as simplistic as it sounds, what you bring to the communication event greatly influences the success or failure of that event—and what you bring is *you*. Although the idea of knowing yourself seems obvious, it is nevertheless a crucial element in becoming a competent intercultural communicator. The novelist James Baldwin said it best when he wrote, "The questions which one asks oneself begin, at last, to illuminate the world, and become one's key to the experience of others." Baldwin's remarks serve as an ideal introduction for the portion of this book that urges you to begin your path to improvement with some self-analysis. As with many of the suggestions we offer in this section, it is easier to state the advice than to practice it. We can write the words "know yourself" with just a few strokes on our keyboard, but it will take a great deal of effort for you to translate this assignment into practice. We believe that the application of introspection should take four directions: first, *know your culture*; second, *know your perceptions*; third, *know how you act out those perceptions*; and finally, *monitor yourself*. Although these four concepts work in tandem, it might be useful to examine them separately.

Know Your Culture

Your first step toward introspection should begin with your own culture. Remember, one of the major themes of this book has been that everyone sees the world through the lens of their culture. As Kim points out:

> Each of us is a product of our cultural background, including gender, ethnicity, family, age, religion, profession, and other life experiences. Our cultural inventory provides us with valuable insights for understanding our beliefs and attitudes, our values and assumptions. Thus, it is critical that we reflect on the various aspects of our own cultural identity and examine their positive and negative impacts on our personal and professional development.[20]

Stewart and Bennett, while speaking about the American culture, made a similar observation when they wrote: "An awareness of American culture along with examples of contrasting cultures contribute to the individual's understanding of her- or himself as a cultural being."[21] In short, you are a "cultural being" and therefore must be ever vigilant as to the impact of your cultural "membership" on perception and communication.

Know Your Personal Attitudes

By exhorting you to examine your attitudes and perceptions, we are not referring to any mystical notions involving another reality, nor are we suggesting you engage in any deep psychological soul searching. Rather, we are asking you to identify those attitudes, prejudices, and opinions that you carry around and that bias the way the world appears to you. If you hold a certain attitude toward gay men, and a man who is gay talks to you, your precommunication attitude will color your response to what he says. Knowing your likes, dislikes, and degrees of personal ethnocentrism enables you to place them out in the open so that you can detect the ways in which these attitudes influence communication. Hidden personal premises, be they directed at ideas, people, or entire cultures, are often the cause of many of your difficulties.

Know Your Communication Style

The third step in knowing yourself is somewhat more difficult than simply identifying your prejudices and predispositions. It involves discovering the kind of image you portray to the rest of the world. Ask yourself, "How do I communicate and how do others perceive me?" If you perceive yourself in one way, and the people with whom you interact perceive you in another way, serious problems can arise. To improve the way you communicate, you must have some idea of how you present yourself. If, for instance, you see yourself as patient and calm, but you appear rushed and anxious, you will have a hard time understanding why people respond to you as they do. As we have noted elsewhere, your most taken-for-granted behaviors often are hidden from your consciousness.

As a starting point, we suggest that you learn to recognize your communication style—the manner in which you present yourself to others. Many communication scholars have attempted to isolate the characteristics that compose a communication personality. One such inventory, which Norton has proposed, has nine characteristics.[22] In Table 10-1, we offer a summary of each of these so that you can begin to evaluate your own communication style. Remember, awareness is the first step to meaningful action.

Barnlund offers yet another insightful interpretation of what our individual styles often include:

> By communication style is meant the topics people prefer to discuss, their favorite forms of interaction—ritual, repartee, argument, self-disclosure—and the depth of involvement they demand of each other. It includes the extent to which communicants rely upon the same channels—vocal, verbal, physical—for conveying information, and the extent to which they are tuned to the same level of meaning, that is, to the factual or emotional content of messages.[23]

Here again, asking yourself how you manifest Barnlund's characteristics can help you understand the manner in which you present yourself to your communication partner.

Table 10-1 *Communication Characteristics*

Trait	Communication Characteristics
Dominant	Speaks frequently; interrupts and controls conversations
Dramatic	Very expressive language; often exaggerates and embellishes
Contentious	Argumentative and often hostile
Animated	Energetic and expressive gestures and facial expressions
Impression–leaving	States ideas and feelings in an indelible fashion
Relaxed	Calm, comfortable, and seldom nervous around others
Attentive	Good listener; offers verbal and nonverbal encouragement to the speaker
Open	Discloses personal information; shows emotions and feelings
Friendly	Offers positive feedback and encouragement

In addition to the challenges inherent in Norton's and Barnlund's descriptions, we also urge you to ask yourself some of the following questions:

- Do I seem at ease or tense?
- Do I often change the subject without taking the other person into consideration?
- Do I deprecate the statements of others?
- Do I smile often?
- Do I interrupt repeatedly?
- Do I show sympathy when someone has a problem?
- Do my actions tend to lower the other person's self-esteem?
- Do I employ a pleasant tone of voice when I talk to people?
- Do I tend to pick the topics for discussion or do I share topic selection?
- What does my tone of voice suggest?
- How do I react to being touched by a stranger?

Monitor Yourself

What should emerge from the last few paragraphs is that all of you have unique ways of interacting. Discovering how you communicate is not always an easy task. It is awkward and highly irregular for you to walk around asking people if they think you are relaxed, argumentative, friendly, animated, and the like. You must, therefore, be sensitive to the feedback you receive and candid in the reading of that feedback. The process of self-observation and analysis is often called "self-monitoring."[24] Some of the advantages associated with self-monitoring are discovering what is appropriate behavior in each situation, having control of your emotional reactions, creating good impressions, and modifying your behavior as you move from situation to situation.[25]

We conclude this section on self-awareness by once again reminding you that there is a vast difference between being self-aware and self-absorbed. Being self-aware is not watching actions so that you can be the center of attraction; rather, it is for the purpose of gaining honest and candid insight into your cultural and individual patterns of communication so that you can improve your intercultural skills. Such frankness with your own behavior is not easy, but the benefits are rewarding. Shakespeare said it far more eloquently when he penned the often quoted line from *Hamlet*, "This above all: to thine own self be true, / And it must follow, as the night the day, / Thou canst not then be false to any man." And we would add, "thou canst not then be false to yourself."

Consider the Physical and Human Settings

As we stressed in Chapters 6, 7, and 8, even setting carries meaning. Three attributes of the setting that can influence the encounter are timing, physical setting, and customs.

Timing

The effective communicator knows the importance of timing and has developed the skill to determine the appropriate time to talk about a subject. You know from your own experiences that there are right and wrong times to ask your parents for a loan or to ask an acquaintance for a date. Few professors will sympathize with the student who waits until the last week of the semester to announce, "I would like to come to your office and talk about the midterm examination I missed a few months ago." *This is poor timing!*

Your use of timing is also influenced by culture. For example, as we noted in Chapter 7, students use different views of timing when they are asked to respond to questions from the teacher. And in Chapter 6 we pointed out that considering the "correct time" is a crucial aspect of doing business with other cultures. In the United States, people learn to "get down to business" quickly. Even the overused phrase "just give me the bottom line" is a reflection of North Americans' desire to get things done quickly. However, in Japan, other Asian countries, and Mexico, the most fitting time to talk about business matters is not at the start of a business session. Ruch, discussing Mexico, highlights cultural differences in timing: "Business contacts are often made during the two- or three-hour lunch break. These are social meetings for the most part, with business being conducted in the last few minutes."[26] Notice the words "the last few minutes." This is a vivid example of what we mean by the phrase "consider the timing."

Physical Setting

As you have observed, the topic of social and physical context is important enough to justify three chapters in this book. The basic assumptions behind Chapters 6, 7, and 8 are that communication is rule governed and different cultures have different rules as they move from setting to setting. In the United States, during business negotiations, the two negotiation teams usually sit facing each other. However, for much of the world, this arrangement maximizes competition, not cooperation.[27] In many Arab countries, people often conduct business while sitting on the floor. And in Finland, there are major corporations that use the sauna bath as a setting for meetings. Clutterbuck describes that setting: "In the warm, informal atmosphere both sides are more open to frank discussion. The trappings of rank tend to disappear when no one has any clothes on."[28] In America, one would not, of course, find himself or herself sitting on the floor or conducting business in a sauna.

As we noted in Chapter 7, teachers facing culturally diverse students must also be aware of the role culture plays in the education setting. For example, "The U.S. educational system tends to favor a more interactive classroom."[29] In this setting students will often move about the classroom and interact with the teacher and fellow students. This is not a physical setting that is found throughout the world. In Japan and China, there is far less student activity in the classroom.[30] In short, the setting reflects culture. Being aware of the physical setting, and adapting to it, is often the hallmark of a successful intercultural communicator.

Customs

Your ability to adapt to the customs of each culture will, to a large extent, determine the success of your intercultural encounters. Your experience will not be fruitful if custom calls for you to remain standing when you enter a room but you take a seat. When, if at all, do you bow? And what is the appropriate bow? When, if at all, do you touch members of the opposite sex? And where do you touch them? What are the customs that prevail with regard to age? These and other questions need to be asked and answered so that you can fashion your behavior to meet the needs of each culture. While there are hundreds of customs and "rules" in each culture that must be considered, let us mention but five "rules" that will help us illustrate our point.

First, we begin with Germany, a culture that is "structured by a large number of explicit rules and regulations."[31] These rules, written and unwritten, cover both the professional and private life of Germans. Many are obvious (all residents must register with a local office) and some are subtle (when you bring flowers as a gift, the bouquet should consist of an odd number of flowers).[32]

Knowing the customs of a culture can offer insight into that culture.

© Gloria Thomas

Second, we turn to an important business custom in Japan—the exchanging of business cards. Adler tells us, "The Japanese must know the other person's company and position before being able to select the grammatically correct form of address. For this reason, the Japanese always exchange business cards—*meishe*—before a conversation begins."[33]

Third, there are also subtle yet important cultural customs in the perception and manifestation of rank and status. Protocol in Germany has the junior executive walking on the left side of the senior manager. The customs of class are even more elaborate in the Middle East, as Ruch notes:

> Both class and rank are quite important to Arabs despite the Muslim concept of all being equal before God. This becomes rather clear at doorways as they sort themselves out by status, the senior man going through first, being followed by the next and then the next in hierarchy.[34]

Fourth, there are social customs in each culture concerning the importance of family and friends in the workplace. People in the United States, because they do not want to be accused of nepotism, seldom show preferential treatment to family members. However, in much of the Arab world and Latin America, custom and tradition produce a very different response to the same issue. For example, "In Mexico, family and friends are often favored as employees because they are seen as being trustworthy."[35]

Finally, as insignificant as it may sound, you can avoid serious communication problems if you know that the number three and sequences that contain three items have connotations in the Thai culture that they take very seriously.[36] In religious practices you hear repeatedly Buddha (the man), the Dharma (the teachings of Buddha), and Sangha (the monastic order)—a set of three. In many ceremonies, from childbirth to birthdays, the number three is very evident. Knowing about this custom can enable you to adapt your behavior (giving three small gifts before a business meeting) to Thai culture.

As we conclude this section on physical and human settings, we again urge you to be aware of your surroundings and the cultural customs that influence communication. Because you all have free choice, you can make the necessary concessions to custom, but first you must know the custom.

Seek to Understand Diverse Message Systems

The American poet Ezra Pound offers you an excellent introduction to this section when he reminds you, "The sum of human knowledge is not contained in any one language." This is yet another way of saying that while all cultures have verbal and non-verbal codes, these codes evoke meanings that reflect the experiences and ideas of each particular culture. Therefore, as you would suspect, it is difficult to arrive at a common code if you and your communication partner speak different languages. To overcome this problem, let us offer some advice regarding the use of both verbal and nonverbal codes.

Try to Learn the Languages of Other Cultures

Our first piece of advice is rather obvious. With over 6,000 different languages in the world, we are not suggesting you learn all of them. What we are recommending is that if you plan to spend time with one particular culture, you learn all you can about their specific language. You would be far more effective if you could speak Spanish when doing business in Mexico. Because much of the world speaks English, many Americans have a tendency to assume they need not learn a foreign language. The very fact that others have made an attempt to learn your language should motivate you to reciprocate. Even within the United States there is a need to develop second-language skills. As Luckmann reminds us, "Large communities of people who speak languages other than English are flourishing in Southern California, Texas, New Mexico, and Arizona. In Los Angeles alone, over 100 languages other than English are spoken."[37] With over 20 million people in the United States being foreign-born, you can see why we urge you to try to expend the time and energy to learn a language different from your own.

Understand Cultural Variations in the Use of Language

If you do not speak the foreign language of your communication partner, there still are things you can do to facilitate understanding. Try to keep in mind that language is more than a vehicle of communication; it teaches one a culture's lifestyle, ways of thinking and perceiving the world, and different patterns of interacting. A few examples demonstrating some variations in how cultures use language might help you appreciate the variety of language patterns you might encounter as you seek to become a more competent communicator.

Much of Jewish culture is reflected in the wide use of stories, parables, and allegories. People, events, and circumstances are talked about in vivid narratives. For many Jews, the story is as important as the point being made by the story. And if you are interacting with Arabs, it would be useful to understand some unique characteristics of their language code. As Nydell points out:

There are many situations in which verbal statements are required by etiquette. Meeting someone's small child calls for praise, carefully mixed with blessings; the most common are "May God keep him" or "This is what God wills." Such statements reassure the parents that there is no envy (you certainly would not add, "I wish I had a child like this!").[38]

The Chinese are yet another culture that perceives and uses language in a manner different from most Americans. As Geo and Ting-Toomey note, "Speech in Chinese culture is constantly exercised with caution and, consequently, perceived as less important."[39] This lack of emphasis on the spoken word means that the Chinese "believe that talk has limitations and that meanings reside beyond mere words."[40] Knowing this simple fact about Chinese language usage could help you in two ways. First, you could understand why "the ability to surmise and decipher hidden meanings is highly desirable in the Chinese culture."[41] Second, knowing the Chinese view of language could influence the manner in which you send and receive messages from members of the Chinese culture and also how you deal with silence.

The Germans embody another example of a culture the uses language in a manner that is somewhat different from what you would find among North Americans. Germans value objectivity when they speak and even have a special word (*Sachlichkeit*) for this trait. As Nees points out, *Sachlichkeit* "is a mode or style of speaking and means sticking to the matter at hand, leaving out any personal references, and being as unemotional and matter-of-fact as possible."[42]

We turn to France for our final example of how cultures might use language in ways that are distinctive to their culture. Asselin and Mastron note one of these distinctions when they write, "In conversation French people prefer to make their points quite directly but in well-phrased, articulate arguments. The linguistic subtleties may be lost on Americans, who hear only the brutally frank (for them) opinions."[43]

Remember That Words Are "Culture Bound"

In much of the world English is taught as a second language, and therefore you will face countless situations when you will be in a country where you are speaking English to someone who might not be as fluent in the language as you are. And, of course, in the United States the Census Bureau points out that English is the second language for the over 31 million immigrants who now live in this country.[44] As we noted in Chapter 4, some special problems arise when you speak to someone whose second language is English. In this next section we will look at some ways to improve the manner in which you speak to someone who is not a native speaker. We will look at *idioms*, *ambiguity*, and *culturally based words and phrases*.

Idioms. Remembering that most words are culture-bound, you might be extremely careful when using idioms. It is estimated that the English language has over fifteen thousand idioms that native English speakers use on a regular basis. By definition, idioms are a group of words that when used together have a particular meaning different from the sum of the meanings of the individual words in isolation. Hence, idioms are not capable of literal translations. Try to imagine having English as a second language and defining each word on its own because you do not know the cultural meaning of the idiom.

"Now just hold your horses, you are acting like a bull in a china shop."
"Of course it is true, I have had my eyes and ears peeled and got it from the grapevine."
"Let's put this plan to the acid test by looking at the nuts and bolts of the deal."

"If we stop beating our heads against a brick wall, we would not appear to be such wimps."

"We need to be careful that the tail doesn't wag the dog."

"Do not listen to John—he's got an ax to grind and often makes waves."

"She's not the least bit funny—in fact, she's laid an egg."

"John dropped the ball on this one, and he's sure ticked off."

"If you think we're on the same wavelength, just give me a buzz, or we can play it by ear."

"We need to stop dilly-dallying and get off the dime."

Ambiguity. Ambiguous words and phrases represent yet another problem you face when speaking to someone who speaks English as their second language. Ambiguity, when used in either speaking or writing, is confusing because what is being spoken or written can be interpreted in more than one way. This multiple-meaning dimension of the discourse can cause a great deal of confusion. Again we ask you to put yourself in the place of someone who is not a native speaker and hears or reads some of the following sentences:

"At our school we have cut dropouts in half."

"It appears that red tape is holding up the new bridge."

"The new vaccine may contain rabies."

"At our school kids make nutritious snacks."

"The new study of obesity is looking for larger test groups."

Culturally Based Expressions. We remind you once again to keep in mind that the words you use and meaning you give them are part of your cultural experiences. And people with different experiences will have different words and meanings. Confusion is the rule if you employ common American expressions that are not part of another culture's frame of reference. We have had numerous international students tell us they did not have a clear meaning for the word or phrase when Americans talked about "dialoguing," "being stressed out," "affirmative action," "interfacing," "pro-life," "networking," "uptight," or "sexual harassment." As a competent communicator you must be ever vigilant in your selection of words and phrases.

Be Aware of Subcodes

In Chapter 4, we pointed out that the English language contains countless subcodes. Although it might be highly improper for you to use these codes if you are not a member of the co-culture, understanding them can offer you insight into both the word and the experiences behind the word. In addition, you also learn some of the differences between various speech styles. For African Americans, Black English is a highly rule-governed speech style that is shared by and reflects the norms of their co-culture.[45] Communication can be impeded when, according to Walters, someone who is speaking mainstream American English feels uncomfortable with the linguistic dissimilarity.[46] We recommend that you realize there are different styles of "talk." One is not right and the others wrong—*they are only different.*

Be Aware of Nonverbal Codes

As you learned in Chapter 5, nonverbal behaviors also shift from culture to culture. For example, in Japan, a female may cover her mouth out of shyness, but in America, we often associate this same action with fear. In China, blinking eyes at someone is impolite.[47]

And in many Buddhist traditions, it is highly improper to sit with the soles of one's feet pointed at the image of the Buddha.

Even within the United States we find instances of differences in the display and interpretation of nonverbal codes. Orbe and Harris indicate how these differences, if not understood, can create problems. They point out that for many African Americans public displays of intense emotion "is valued and regarded as appropriate in most settings."[48] Yet, as Orbe and Harris further note, these displays violate "U. S. societal expectations for self-controlled public behaviors" and are "inappropriate for most public settings."[49]

These few examples should remind you of the two points we made with regard to verbal codes. First, the initial step in discovering a common code is learning how to read existing codes. Second, cultural differences should not keep us from looking for a common code. For example, although there are cultural variations in what makes people smile, and even in to whom they smile, one does not have to speak a foreign language to know that a smile carries nearly the same meaning throughout the world. Those of you who have visited other countries know the power of pointing and laughing as ways of talking.

Be Sensitive to Diverse Coding Systems

Being sensitive to your surroundings and to other people is one of the hallmarks of a competent intercultural communicator. According to Chen and Starosta, intercultural sensitivity is "an individual's ability to develop a positive emotion towards understanding and appreciating cultural differences in order to promote appropriate and effective behavior in intercultural communication."[50] We would suggest that part of the sensitivity means learning about diverse coding systems and developing code sensitivity toward the message systems used by other cultures. We have already alluded to the inappropriateness of using African American argot if you are white. If you interact with disabled people, you need to learn a list of what are called the "no-no words." *Crippled, gimp, deaf and dumb, deaf mute, victim, abnormal, unfortunate,* or *victim* are examples of words that exhibit a lack of cultural awareness.[51]

It is also employing an improper verbal code and displaying insensitivity when you use words to refer to a co-culture that are not the ones preferred by it. It would reflect respect if you used *Asian* for *Oriental, gays* for *homosexual, Latino* for *Mexican, Native American* for *Indian,* and *African Americans* for *Negroes.* What is important is not the name, for those often change over time, but rather remembering what Lynth and Hanson tell you: "Defining and describing individuals from any culture, ethnic, linguistic, or racial group is similar to defining and describing families, that is, the words that are used should be those that the members prefer."[52]

Achieving Clarity

The section is concerned with your understanding diverse message systems. Guirgham offers you a useful checklist to use as a guide when your message system is different from that of people you are communicating with.[43]

- State points clearly and precisely.
- Adjust to the other person's level of understanding without being demeaning.
- Explain jargon.
- Be careful in your use of idioms.
- Slow your speaking down without being insulting.

- Speak in smaller units.
- Repeat key points.
- Encourage others to ask questions.
- Check for understanding.

Develop Empathy

A well-known Native American saying tells us "We should not judge another person until we have walked two moons in his moccasins." Our next suggestion for improvement is about "wearing those moccasins." Actually, what we should say is that it is about your trying to imagine wearing those moccasins. We used the word *imagine* because it is physically and psychologically impossible to ever really know what another person is actually experiencing. As we noted in Chapter 1, the envelope of our skin separates us from every other individual. Hence, this is why we said your goal might best be described as trying to imagine things from the point of view of others. Ting-Toomey makes the same point about imagining when she describes the process of empathy in the following manner: "Through empathy we are willing to imaginatively place ourselves in the dissimilar other's cultural world and to experience what she or he is experiencing."[54]

The importance of empathy to the study of interpersonal and intercultural competence cannot be overstated. After reviewing the literature on the topic of empathy, Broome concluded, "Empathy has been recognized as important to both general communication competence and as a central characteristic of competent and effective intercultural communication."[55] Calloway-Thomas, Cooper, and Blake echo Broome's commentary when they write, "Empathy is the bedrock of intercultural communication."[56]

Understanding Empathy

Before we begin our discussion of empathy, we need to mention three ideas that will aid you in understanding the role of empathy in intercultural communication. First, as with so much of our counsel, you are again faced with a skill that is easier to talk about than to put into practice. The fact remains that while people are similar in a host of ways, there is something distinctive and unique about each of us. As the English poet John Lyly wrote over five hundred years ago, "Though all men be made of one metal, yet they be not cast all in one mold." Not only are you different one from another, but also your internal thoughts are elusive and fleeting, and you know yourself only as a distorted shadow. When you add trying to know the other person to the mix, you can see why predicting his or her reactions and needs is a difficult and troublesome activity. And now when you add culture to the formula, you compound the difficulty of the assignment.

Second, although we have focused primarily on culture, we also are concerned with the "interpersonal aspects" of intercultural communication. Perhaps the interpersonal dimension of communication is most evident in the area of empathy. As Miller and Steinberg note, "To communicate interpersonally, one must leave the cultural and sociological levels of predications and psychically travel to the psychological level."[57] Simply put, empathy, while using knowledge about another's culture to make predications, also demands that the point of analysis be the individual personality.

Finally, it is best to view empathy as a complex activity composed of many variables. It involves a cognitive component (thinking), an affective (emotional identification) dimension, and a communication element (activity). Bell explains these three variables, and how they interact with each other:

> Cognitively, the empathic person takes the perspective of another person, and in so doing strives to see the world from the other's point of view. Affectively, the empathic person experiences the emotions of another; he or she feels the other's experiences. Communicatively, the empathic individual signals understanding and concern through verbal and nonverbal cues.[58]

Before we look at some of the ways to improve our role-taking skills, it might be helpful to examine a few characteristics that can impede empathy.

Hindrances to Empathy

Constant Self-focus. Perhaps the most common of all barriers to empathy is a constant self-focus. It is difficult to gather information about the other person, and to reflect on that information, if you are consumed with thoughts of yourself. Attending to your own thoughts, as if they were the only ones that mattered, uses much of the energy that you should direct toward your communication partner. At times everyone is guilty of behaving according to the German proverb, "Everyone thinks that all the bells echo his own thoughts."

The Tendency to Note Only Some Features to the Exclusion of Others. Focusing on only a small portion of the individual often causes you to misuse the data you gather about another person. If, for example, you notice only a person's skin color or that his or her surname is Lopez, and from this limited information assume you know all there is to know about the person, you are apt to do a poor job of empathizing. Admittedly, color and names offer you some information about the other person, but you must add to this type of data. Although it is an overused analogy, you should remember that most outward features represent only the tip of the iceberg.

Stereotyped Notions Concerning Gender, Race, and Culture. We have already talked about the destructive nature of stereotypes, so now we only need to add that they also serve as potential stumbling blocks to empathy. If you believe that "all English people dislike the Irish," you might allow this stereotype to influence your view of an English person. Stereotyped notions are so much a part of your personality that you must be careful not to allow these unsupported generalizations to serve as your models of other people.

Defensive Behavior. People often engage in defensive behavior that keeps others from wanting to reveal information about themselves—information you need if you are going to engage in empathetic behavior. If people feel rebuffed by your actions, they are not likely to disclose very much to you. Because defensive behaviors are so common, it would be useful for you to examine how some of these actions inhibit your ability to empathize.

When you appear to be *evaluating other people*, whether by what you say or what you do, you are likely to make them feel defensive toward you. If you believe others are judging and evaluating you, you will hesitate to offer information that will foster empathy. Think about how awkward you feel when, after sharing some personal information, the other person quickly lectures you on the foolhardiness of your act. After a few minutes of criticism and ridicule, you probably would decide not to disclose any other information to that person. In the intercultural situation, you would discourage communication if you referred to a person's cultural habit of meditating as "a complete waste of time."

Manifesting a lack of interest often makes people feel defensive. Empathy is best when it is reciprocal; hence, most of you have an aversion to revealing very much to a person who seems uninterested in you and your ideas. Empathy cannot take place when one of the individuals becomes defensive over the other person's lack of interest. Again, you must answer this question: How much do I enjoy talking to a person who shows no interest in me or in what I am saying?

An attitude of superiority, which produces defensive behavior, seldom elicits the kind of information you need for empathizing. Imagine how defensive you would become if someone from France told you that Americans used language in a very dull and unimaginative manner.

Dogmatism is yet another attitude that keeps you from developing empathy. If someone behaved as if he or she had doubted everything you said and had all the answers, even to questions you had not even asked, you probably would become defensive. With a dogmatic person, your defensiveness may take the form of silence or of dogmatism of your own. In either case, this defensive behavior will not be conducive to empathy. Be cautious of dogmatism on your part and on the part of others.

A Lack of Motivation. Many of the hindrances to empathy can be traced to a lack of motivation. This problem might well be the most difficult to conquer. You are most motivated to respond to people who are close to you both physically and emotionally. You are primarily concerned about your family. As your personal circle widens, it includes relatives and friends. Interest in other people then moves to neighbors and other members of the community. As you get farther and farther away from people in your immediate circle, you will find it difficult to empathize with them. Think for a moment about your reaction to the news that someone you know had been seriously injured in an automobile accident versus your response to reading that 700,000 people were suffering from severe famine in the Sudan. In most instances you would be more motivated to learn about your friend than about the people thousands of miles away in Africa. Although this is a normal reaction, it often keeps you from trying to understand the experiences of people far removed from our personal sphere. For intercultural communication to be successful, you must all learn to go beyond personal boundaries and try to learn about the experiences of people who are not part of your daily lives. You must avoid following the Russian proverb that states, "When you live next to the cemetery you cannot weep for everyone." Instead, you must realize that you live in an interconnected world, and you must therefore be motivated to understand everyone—regardless of how much you seem separated from them by either distance or culture.

Improving Empathy

Up to this point, we have painted a rather dark picture of empathy and the problems related to it. Although it is nearly impossible to know another person completely and accurately, you can, with practice, develop the skills necessary to overcome the problems we have mentioned.

Pay Attention. Our first bit of advice grows out of a problem we mentioned earlier in this section; however, this time we will put a positive face on the topic of "paying attention." Or as Trenholm and Jensen tell us: "The single most important thing you do is remind yourself to pay attention to the spontaneous emotional expressions of others."[59] As you know from personal experience, concentrating on one idea or one person is difficult. This high level of attention is even more strenuous when applied to empathy, for it, like our attention span, is dynamic. Barnlund underscored this idea when he writes, "Empathy tends to be a fleeting phenomenon, fluctuating from moment to moment and from situation to situation."[60] Thus, problems associated with concentration can be overcome if you work on staying focused on both the other person and the situation.

Communicate Empathy. Because empathy is a reciprocal act, you and your communication partner must be expressive (unless you are interacting with someone from a culture that values interpersonal restraint). You cannot expect individuals from other cultures to offer you verbal and nonverbal messages about their internal states if your behavior is not reciprocal with their efforts. Trenholm and Jensen say much the same thing: "If your own expressive behavior promotes others to be more expressive and we pay attention to the wider range of nonverbal cues they display, we should be more accurate in reading others' emotional state."[61]

Use Culturally Accepted Behaviors. Empathy can be enhanced through awareness of specific behaviors that members of a particular culture or co-culture might find impertinent or insulting. For example, according to Rich, many African Americans find it offensive when they hear stereotypic statements ("All African Americans have good voices"), when they are called "boy" or "son," or when they are referred to as being "a culturally deprived minority."[62] And you would not receive vital information to use for empathy if you refused the hospitality offered by an Arab. In both these examples, we have made the same point: To be successful as an intercultural communicator, you must develop empathy, and that can be cultivated only if you become sensitive to the values and customs of the culture with which you are interacting.

Avoid Ethnocentric Responses. Our final proposal is perhaps the one that most closely parallels the main mission of this book. Again we remind you that empathy can be increased if you resist the tendency to interpret the other's verbal and nonverbal actions from your culture's orientation. Learn to suspend, or at least keep in check, the cultural perspective that is unique to your experiences. Knowing how the frame of reference of other cultures differs from your own will assist you in more accurately reading what meaning lies behind words and actions. For example, in the Chinese culture, as a means of "saving face," people will often say one thing when they mean something else; knowing this can help you understand what is actually being expressed.[63]

Be Aware of Cultural Differences in Listening

One of the major themes of this book has been that the ways in which we communicate, what we communicate, and our response to communication are greatly influenced by our culture. Listening is one of those ingredients embedded in all three of those important communication components. Simple put, listening and culture are linked. Morreale, Spitzberg, and Barge speak to the importance of that connection when they write, "Cultural differences in how people engage in listening are a reality, so you need to recognize and respect such culturally based differences in listening style."[64] To help you better understand the role of culture in listening, let us look a few ways culture and listening work together.

First, as we have noted elsewhere, in many cultures in the Far East, the amount of time spent talking and the value placed on talking are very different from what happens in cultures that value conversation (Middle East, Latin America, United States). Japan is a very homogeneous culture, and therefore most people have a pool of common experiences. This commonality often allows them to know what the other is thinking and feeling without using words. In fact, at times they believe words can get in the way of understanding. Hence, silence is valued over talk. Think about the connection between speaking, listening, and silence in the Buddhist expression, "There is a truth the words cannot reach." Place that against the Arab proverb that notes, "Your mouth is your sword." Two orientations—one favoring talk and one preferring silence.

Second, when listening to different cultures, you must also be aware of cultural variations in how speakers present themselves and their ideas. As you learned in Chapter 5 when we discussed nonverbal communication, some cultures value a dynamic presentation of ideas while others are almost passive. For example, in Japan, Thailand, and Korea, people tend to speak in soft voices, while in the Mediterranean area the appropriate volume is much more intense. Both of these communication styles put different demands on the listening process.

Even the nonverbal responses to what you hear are often influenced by culture. In the United States it is often a sign of paying attention when you make the sound "um-humm" or "uh-huh" when someone is talking. Many other cultures often find such interruptions by a listener to be impolite.

Eye contact is another nonverbal action that influences the listening process. In the United States and other Western cultures, a good listener is seen paying attention if he or she is having direct eye contact with the person talking. But you will recall that direct eye-to-eye contact is not the correct custom in many Asian cultures or in the Native American co-culture. In short, to be a good listener you need to know what nonverbal actions are appropriate and which might hamper the communication encounter.

Finally, as you listen you will experience the sway of culture as it affects accents. Accents by people trying to speak English as a second language often make it more difficult for you to listen and comprehend what is being discussed. In these instances our advice is simple and straightforward—be tolerant, pay attention, and practice being patient. You might also put yourself in the place of someone trying to speak a second language that is new and complex. This attempt at role reversal usually will increase your concentration and your compassion.

Encourage Feedback

The interactive nature of communication brings us to our next suggestion: Encourage feedback. Feedback is the information generated by the person who receives the message—information that is "fed back" to the person who sent the original message. This information may be a smile, the words "No thank you," or even complete silence void of any outward expression. As Wood points out, "Feedback may be verbal, nonverbal, or both, and it may be intentional or unintentional."[65] Regardless of the form of the feedback, it allows you the opportunity to make qualitative judgments about the communication event while it is taking place. These judgments offer useful data that enable you to correct and adjust your next message. Being able to invite feedback, even from members of those cultures that are reluctant to offer such data, is an effective communication skill. In this sense, a competent communicator uses feedback both to monitor the communication process and to exercise some control over it. Feedback clearly manifests the three axioms we discussed in Chapter 9—*you can learn*, *you can make choices*, and *act differently*. Put another way, with feedback you see or hear what is happening (learn), decide to change (exercise free will), and alter your actions (behave differently).

Granting that feedback is critical, you must learn to create an atmosphere that encourages other people to offer you feedback—feedback you need in order to adjust your own behavior. Therefore, we will review a number of communication skills that encourage other people to send you messages about the current situation—messages that might be useful as you continue the communication event.

Nonverbal Feedback

The first step in improving nonverbal feedback is recognizing that it takes many forms. Think for a moment of all the positive attitudes and images you associate with smiling, head nodding, leaning forward, and laughing. Although these behaviors seem very Western, they often produce positive reactions in other cultures. Each of these actions, separately or in combination with verbal messages, creates an atmosphere that tells other people you are interested in them and want to hear what they have to say.

Verbal Feedback

Positive verbal behavior can also encourage feedback. Like your nonverbal messages, your use of words also takes a variety of forms. In cultures that value conversation and openness, asking questions is an excellent method of encouraging feedback about the quality of your messages. You can ask questions such as, "Perhaps we should start the meeting by introducing ourselves. Is that agreeable?" Or "How do you think we should start the meeting?" Further, questions can be used to seek additional clarification. If asked in a nonthreatening manner, even the question "Do you understand?" assists in monitoring the level of comprehension. We should remind you before we leave this point that in some Asian cultures, the word *no* is seldom used. In Japan, for example, instead of responding negatively to your question, "they may simply apologize, keep quiet, become vague, or answer with a euphemism for no."[66] Your use of words also encourages feedback if you relate them directly to what the other person has just said. You know from your own experience that it is very disconcerting if you tell a friend that you do not feel well, and your friend responds that she or he just received an "A" on an examination.

Silence as Feedback

There are times when silence instead of words will inspire feedback. You have repeatedly seen that every culture has a unique communication style. Some cultural styles call for periods of silence and/or long pauses, and you must learn to respect these phases in the encounter. Giving the person this quiet period creates an atmosphere that promotes feedback once the silence is broken. There are even occasions when the silence itself is a form of feedback. As we noted elsewhere in the book, many Asian cultures do not enjoy being hurried when they are negotiating and/or solving problems. If you learn to remain silent, you will be sending them some positive feedback about the transaction. As we noted, in some cultures there is no positive compensation for a quick decision, particularly if you made that decision without sufficient feedback. Remember the French proverb: "Patience is bitter but its fruit is sweet."

Avoid Negative Feedback

Although the items mentioned thus far tend to help you solicit accurate information about what is going on and also put your communication partner at ease, some behaviors have the opposite effect. We will now list a few of these so that you might avoid them. We should mention that while some of them might have a Western point of reference, your experiences should tell you they are common enough that they have a negative outcome regardless of the culture. Hence we suggest (a) you avoid frequent shifting of your body as if you are bored with what the other person is saying, (b) a slouching posture, (c) engaging in other activities (talking to someone else, writing) while the other person is talking, (d) having your arms folded in front of your chest, and (e) frowning and scowling.

Develop Communication Flexibility

Our next bit of advice asks you to be flexible when deciding on how to present yourself to another person—particularly if that person is from a culture different from your own. Many experts in communication competence actually believe that one definition of competence is having the ability to adjust and fashion your communication behavior to fit the setting, the other person, and yourself.[67] What is being said is that a competent intercultural communicator "must . . . develop a repertoire of interpersonal tactics."[68] When speaking to the issue of how communication flexibility applies to international negotiations, Foster used an analogy:

> The better [international] negotiators are ultimately pragmatic. They are not oaks; rather, they are more like willows. Unable to predict every situation, every twist and turn, even in a domestic situation, they know that it is nearly impossible to do so in a cross-cultural one.[69]

All of you have learned a host of communication tactics as part of the socialization process. You know what communication strategies to employ when you buy a new automobile or when you want to make a good impression. Shakespeare wrote, "One man in his time plays many parts." And, of course, we would add the same applies to women.

Regardless of the parts you play or the techniques you employ, you need to acquire the skills that will allow you to respond to various conditions, people, and situations. Having the skills to play these multiple roles means being able to be reflective instead of impulsive when interacting with a culture that moves at a slower pace. It means behaving in a formal manner when encountering a culture that employs a formal style. It means speaking softly instead of loudly when talking with people who use a subdued communication pattern. It means remembering the Spanish proverb "I dance to the tune that is played."

Learn to Tolerate Ambiguity

A close companion of flexibility is developing a tolerance for ambiguity. Because many intercultural encounters are unpredictable and often involve dealing with a new set of values and customs, confusion and ambiguity can often proliferate. For example, if your culture values competition and aggressive action, and you are around someone from a culture that values cooperation and interpersonal harmony, you might find his or her behavior ambiguous and confusing; yet coping with ambiguity is a key element in intercultural competence. As Ruben and Kealey note, "The ability to react to new and ambiguous situations with minimal discomfort has long been thought to be an important asset when adjusting to a new culture."[70] If you are self-conscious, tense, and anxious when confronted with the unknown, you are apt to use your energy to alleviate your frustration instead of trying to decide how best to communicate to the person and situation.

There are some selective behaviors that the competent intercultural communicator can employ to increase tolerance for ambiguity. For example, Guirdham suggests some specific actions that might be helpful. First, "delaying the decision on how to approach a new person or situation until as much information as possible has been gained by observation."[71] Second, "using trial and error rather than the same formula until what works becomes clear."[72] Perhaps the best advice on how to develop a tolerance for ambiguity is to except the unexpected, be nonjudgmental, and practice patience.

Learn to Manage Conflict

It is not an exaggeration to say that as long as people have been coming into contact with one another there has been conflict. In an intercultural setting, Ting-Toomey defines conflict "as the perceived and/or actual incompatibility of values, expectations, processes, or outcomes between two or more parties from different cultures over substantive and/or relational issues."[73] To improve the manner in which you deal with conflict we will (1) *identify some common causes of conflict,* (2) *discuss some Western approaches for dealing with conflict,* (3) *look at how other cultures cope with conflict,* and (4) offer *some specific conflict skills that apply directly to intercultural communication.*

Causes of Conflict

Conflicts usually occur because one or more of the participants perceive incompatible goals or threats to their ego. Hence, it is easy to see how personality traits, be they introvert, argumentative, extrovert, aggressive, passive, and so on, can cause conflict. Most people, without much forethought, gravitate to their basic personality whenever they communicate. Often that personality creates behaviors that, rightly or wrongly, are seen by others in a negative light.

Conflicts also arise when someone else's meaning for a word or phrase is not fully understood. When you add the layer of culture to the use of language, as we noted in Chapter 4, you can obtain disagreement and discord. Words such as "gay," "liberal," "sexual harassment," "abortion," or "affirmative action" may cause an emotional reaction and even conflict when you are talking to someone who has a different value system. When you are dealing with other cultures, these emotionally laden words and phrases can become even more complicated. We saw a vivid example of conflict over words in September 2001 when Americans misunderstood the meaning of the Islamic notion of *Jihad*. For Muslims it means an internal struggle to follow their faith. Yet most Americans interpreted the word to only mean a holy war against all non-Muslims.

Conflict: An American Perspective

We started this section by noting that there are as numerous causes of conflict. We can begin our discussion of how people deal with conflict with the same observation. However, a substantial body of literature indicates that Americans usually employ five approaches to dealing with conflict.[74] Knowing these approaches will help you appreciate how you might deal with conflict. Later we will offer a cross-cultural comparison of these approaches so that you might be able to adapt to intercultural discord when it arises.

Withdrawal. Dealing with conflict by withdrawal is very common—at least in the United States. In some ways this is the easiest way to cope with conflict. Avoiding conflict can be either mental (being silent and not taking part in the interaction) or physical (removing yourself from the conflict). In either case the person is saying, "I do not want to get involved." Often when avoidance is the method used, the situation that created the conflict seems to intensify and worsen as the parties mull over what happened.

Accommodating. Accommodating is a form of dealing with conflict that is closely related to withdrawal, except this time you satisfy the other person's desires to the point that you are willing to give up your own needs and goals. As you would suspect, saying "I do not care what you do" has some built in weaknesses. First, it often leads to poor conclusions because only one point of view is being discussed. Second, accommodating can also create a situation where one person can take advantage of another.

Competing. The competing approach to conflict simply means winning at all costs. Forcing your wishes on another person as a means of resolving conflict can take a variety of forms. It can involve threats, verbal aggression, intimidation, or exploitation.

Compromise. As Morreale, Spitzberg, and Barge note, "Compromise is about finding the middle course with each party agreeing to make concessions to the others."[75] In this approach people usually have to give something up or make a "trade" in order to resolve the conflict.

Collaborating. At the core of collaboration is the idea that all parties resolve conflict. By employing creative devices, everyone's goals and needs can be satisfied. Because the conflict is viewed in a positive manner, collaboration is the most sought-after method of settling conflicts.

Conflict: An Intercultural Perspective

Although interpersonal conflict is part of every culture, each culture's way of perceiving and dealing with conflict is part of that culture's value system. For example, in the United States there is often a belief that conflict is part of competition and "self-awareness" and therefore can be useful. For example, Roloff claims that conflict in and of itself is not pejorative and, if handled properly, may actually lead to human growth and development.[76] This positive view of conflict is also seen in other cultures. In the Middle East people perceive conflict as a natural way of life. People are expected to have intense feelings on many issues and to express those feelings in an animated and confrontational manner. Think for a moment of what is being said in the humorous Jewish proverb that venerates disputes and conflict by noting "Where there are two Jews there are three opinions." Greeks also have an expressive approach to conflict and are proud of their long tradition of argumentation and debate. As Broome points out, for Greeks "challenges, insults and attacks are, within appropriate limits, almost synonymous with conversing."[77] As we have indicated, viewing conflict as something this natural and acceptable is not the rule for all cultures. Let us offer a few examples that underscore the point the culture and conflict are linked.

We begin with the Japanese and their perception of conflict. For the Japanese, conflict is seen as interpersonally embarrassing and distressing since it potentially disrupts social harmony.[78] For them, an indirect and passive approach to conflict would be the preferred method for dealing with social discord.[79] A similar view toward conflict can be found in the Chinese culture where social harmony is important.[80] Some European cultures also deal with conflict in ways that are dissimilar to the conflict style found in the United States. While interpersonal harmony is not the driving force, Germans do not engage in direct face-to-face conflict. Nees summarizes the German approach in the following manner: "Conflict is generally avoided, not by emphasizing harmony in personal relationships or by smoothing over differences of opinion, but rather by maintaining formality and social distance."[81] And for the French to lose control and to outwardly engage in social conflict is "a sign of weakness."[82] Regardless of the motivation used to justify or avoid conflict, one thing should be clear by now—not all cultures display or deal with conflict in the same manner.

Dealing with Conflict

As we have just noted, perceiving and dealing with conflict is rooted in your culture. However, some skills for responding to conflict can be employed regardless of the culture you are interacting with. Let us now examine some of these skills.

If you are from a culture that values individualism, such the United States, you must begin, according Ting-Toomey, to "discard the Western-based model of effective communication skills in dealing with conflict situations in the collective cultures."[83] Ting-Toomey illustrates her point by offering some very specific skills that you can follow:

> Individualists should learn to use qualifiers, disclaimers, tag questions, [and] tentative statements to convey their point of view. In refusing a request, learn to avoid using a blunt "no" as a response because the word "no" is typically perceived as carrying high face-threat value in collective cultures. Use situational or self-effacing accounts ("Perhaps someone else is more qualified than I am in working on this project,") counter questions ("Don't you feel someone else is more competent to work on this project…") or conditional statements ("Yes, but…") to convey the implicit sense of the refusal.[84]

Learning to use collective pronouns can also help defuse conflict. Although at times you may have to refer to people by name, you should, when with a group of people, try to develop the practice of using group pronouns as a way of centering on content instead of people. Notice how words such as *we* and *our* focus the conversation on everyone instead of simply one person as is the case with *I, me,* or *you.*

Do not rush to resolve that conflict when interacting with cultures that are collective in nature. As Ting-Toomey notes, "Be sensitive to the importance of quiet, mindful observation."[85] Even more specifically, she offers the following non-Western advice for responding to conflict: "Use deep-level silence, deliberate pauses, and patient conversational turn taking in the conflict interaction process with collectivists."[86]

Although we have just talked about the importance of taking time, it is just as crucial to realize that you cannot manage the conflict if you fail to clearly identify the issues. Whether the conflict be over personalities or content, you must discover what is the core of the disagreement. Once you have clarified the issues, all parties can begin to focus on solutions to the controversy.

Seek a position of compromise whenever possible. In America there is often a notion that compromise is associated with defeat—avoid this idea when dealing with other cultures. Winning at all costs and placing that conflict in an either/or frame usually does not resolve the core of the conflict and with time the conflict resurfaces. In short, you need to suspend the belief that compromise is a form of appeasement. A healthier view is the one expressed by the late British statesman Edmund Burke: "Every human benefit and enjoyment, every virtue and every prudent act, is founded on compromise and barter."

Finally, we would suggest that because of cultural differences regarding conflict, there might be times when the best method is to simply ignore the conflict. Remember when we discussed Buddhism in Chapter 3, we indicated that Buddha taught that all things in life are transitory and will eventually "fall away." In fact, there is even a Buddhist expression that relates directly to conflict. It is simply the phrase "Let it go." Ting-Toomey makes the same point in contemporary terms when she writes, "A cooling period sometimes may help mend a broken relationship and the substantive issue may be diluted over a period of time."[87]

Learn About Cultural Adaptation

The issue of cultural adaptation is somewhat related to our early discussion of communication flexibility. Except now we are talking about people who must adapt to all aspects of a new culture—and for a long period of time, perhaps permanently. Before we begin a more detailed analysis of the adaptation process, we should point out that the word *adaptation* is but one of a number of words the field of intercultural communication has used to represent this concept. Kim further develops this idea when she writes, "Cross-cultural adaptation embraces other similar but narrow terms, from assimilation . . . and acculturation . . . to coping and adjustment . . . as well as integration."[88] Because adaptation does "embrace" all the other concepts, and because in the final analysis the people involved have to learn to "adapt," we shall use the term "adaptation" in our discussion.

We begin with these two questions: What problems hamper the adaptation process? What is the best way to adapt to a new culture if your exposure to that culture will take place for an extended period of time? The answers to these questions are at the heart of the adaptation process. In this section we discuss cultural contacts that are not transitory but rather are sustained and ongoing. Immigrants, refugees, international businesspeople with overseas assignments, military personnel, government workers, and exchange students are just a few of the people who need to adapt to a new culture for a long period of time. These people need to cope with the cultural changes brought about by continuous firsthand contact with another culture. The problem is that on many occasions, these "newcomers" have a difficult time adapting to the host culture. As Mak, Westwood, Ishiyama, and Barker point out, "Newcomers may not be ready to learn and practice social behaviors appropriate to the new culture in the initial period of settlement. It is not unusual for recent arrivals to be overwhelmed by the immediate demands and challenges in the orienting to living in a new place."[89] To better deal with these challenges, let us examine some challenges that face anyone who is attempting to adapt to a new culture and than conclude by offering a number of behaviors that can make the adaptation process a successful and rewarding experience.

Challenges of Adaptation

As you would suspect, the problems and challenges facing anyone trying to adapt to new and often strange culture are numerous. During the adjustment period the sojourner experiences fear, feelings of being disliked, and even distrust.[90] A review of some of the reasons behind these feelings is an excellent first step in developing the skills needed to adapt to a new culture.

Ethnocentrism. What is interesting about the role of ethnocentrism in adapting to a new culture is the fact that ethnocentrism is often found in both cultures. That is to say, ethnocentrism moves in both directions. As we pointed out earlier, ethnocentrism is that cultural bias that leads people to judge another culture by the standards and practices that they are most familiar with—their own. This means that members of the host culture pass judgment on the sojourner while the person trying to adapt cannot, or does not want to, expunge their "home" culture. Hence, they bring some ethnocentrism to the host culture. Anderson makes this point very clear when he notes that "one of the chief characteristics of the adaptation process is that elements of the original culture can never be completely erased."[91] The key to effective adaptation is, of course, for both parties to recognize the strong pull of ethnocentrism and attempt to keep it in check.

Language. It is obvious that someone living in a new culture will usually face problems associated with having to learn and use a second language. Long-term sojourners and immigrants who have not mastered English experience social isolation and are, as Leong and Chou note, forced "into fields that require less mastery of English language and less interpersonal interaction."[92]

When we talk of problems associated with being exposed to a new language, we are talking about two ideas—language acquisition and the ways of speaking unique to the new culture. As we just indicated, both of these can delay the adaptation process. Harper summarizes this view when she notes, "Lack of language skills is a strong barrier to effective cultural adjustment and communication whereas lack of knowledge concerning the ways of speaking of a particular group will reduce the level of understanding that we can achieve with our counterparts."[93] The person trying to adapt to a new culture and who wants to interact with that culture must face challenges associated not only with learning a second language but also the special and unique patterns found within every language. As we mentioned in Chapter 4, cultural variations in the use of language can mean everything from the use of idioms to different rules for turn taking, to linguistic ways of showing respect.

Disequilibrium. Successful adaptation demands a certain level of knowledge about the host country and making correct choices regarding that knowledge. Those choices can include everything from learning proper greeting behaviors (bowing, shaking hands, hugging, etc.) to deciding about eating utensils (chopsticks, knife and forks, hands, etc.). As you would suspect, indecision creates problems. As Kim points out, sojourners are "at least temporarily, in a state of disequilibrium, which is manifested in many emotional 'lows' of uncertainty, confusion, and anxiety."[94] The condition of disequilibrium complicates the adaptation process as the sojourner experiences a high level of apprehension as he or she attempts to decide what is appropriate behavior.

Improving the Adaptation Process

Now let us turn our attention to a few strategies that will expedite and facilitate the adaptation process.

Acquire Knowledge About the Host Culture. Adaptation is less troublesome if you are aware of the characteristics of the culture with which you will be interacting. For someone coming to the United States, this means much more than learning how to order a Big Mac and working a VCR. It means learning about the values, beliefs, and modes of behavior unique to each culture. Chen and Starosta note: "Culture awareness refers to an understanding of one's own and others' cultures that affect how people think and behave. This includes understanding commonalties of human behavior and differences in cultural patterns."[95]

As you have learned throughout this book, gathering a fund of knowledge about another culture takes a variety of forms, ranging from the apparent to the subtle. For example, as we just indicated, it is rather clear that learning the language of the host culture produces positive results. If you cannot learn the language of the host culture, you can at least try to master some of the basics of language such as greeting behaviors, proper polite responses, and words that deal with public transportation and shopping.

Increase Contact with the Host Culture. Direct contact with the host culture promotes successful adaptation to a new culture. Begley accentuates the importance of direct contact when she notes, "Although insight and knowledge can be gained through prior intercultural study, additional practical wisdom is attained through everyday conversations with people from other cultures."[96] Hence, you should try to take the advice of Harris and Moran when they say, "Immerse yourself in the host culture. Join in, whenever feasible, the artistic and community functions, the carnivals, the rites, the international and fraternal or professional organizations."[97]

Although there are no substitutes for face-to-face interactions with host nationals, mediated communication such as radio, film, television, and the Internet can still moderately influence cross-cultural adaptation. Kim has pointed out that a host culture's mass communication "serves as an important source of cultural language learning, particularly during the early phases of the adaptation."[98] In addition to assisting in language learning, exposure to a culture's mass media can also aid in discovering some cultural values—at least those that are portrayed on television.

When listening, watching, and interacting with people from the host culture, it is important to learn about what Althen calls "ritual social actions."[99] Althen offers a list of some of the "rituals" that contribute to understanding interaction in the host culture:

> Notice what people say (and how they say it) and what they do (and how they do it) when they greet an acquaintance, take leave of an acquaintance, are introduced to a new person, and take leave of a person they have just met. Watch for variations according to the age, sex, and apparent social status of the people involved.[100]

We end this section on improvement by reminding you that successful intercultural communication should always begin with gaining a fund of knowledge about another culture. Once you acquire this knowledge, you can then decide what is appropriate and inappropriate behavior. Confucius said it far more eloquently: "The essence of knowledge is, having it, to apply it." We suggest you do both: have accurate knowledge and apply it.

ETHICAL CONSIDERATIONS

One basic theme in this book has been the idea that communication is an instrumental act; and whether it is used to sell cars, secure a mate, get elected to public office, teach children a foreign language, or secure directions, it will always have an impact, either good or bad, desirable or undesirable, significant or insignificant. Put in slightly different terms, communication creates effects—something happens when you send someone a message. Your words or actions can change behavior, attitudes, beliefs, a person's self-concept, their perceptions, and even their mood. While the change might be short term or long term, immediate or delayed, public or private, you are producing change in another individual. This very fact speaks of the ethical component associated with communication.

Most cultures recognize the ethical dimensions of communication on both a legal and interpersonal level. Legally, in the United States, ethical communication is manifested in our libel, slander, truth-in-advertising, and campaign-practice laws. But just because most of our communication does not involve mass media or attorneys does not relieve us of considering the effects of our actions in the interpersonal setting. Whether the consequences of our messages be simple or profound, we cannot hide from the fact that our actions affect other people. As Shakespeare told us in *The Comedy of Errors*, "Every why hath a wherefore." We now ask you to think about "why" and "wherefore"—to think about your actions and the results they produce. In this section, we suggest an interpersonal ethic that will have beneficial consequences for you, for your interpersonal partners, and, because of the symbiotic relationship now existing in the world, for all humanity.

A Definition of Ethics

Ethics refers to judgments that focus "on degrees of rightness and wrongness, virtue and vice, and obligation in human behavior."[101] What ethics attempts to do is "provide the tools for making difficult moral choices, in both our personal and our professional lives."[102] These choices are made difficult when ethical practices collide—as they often do. Day identifies this problem when he writes: "The most difficult ethical dilemmas arrive when conflicts arise between two 'right' moral obligations. Thus, ethics often involves the balancing of competing rights when there is no 'correct' answer."[103]

Religious thinkers, philosophers, and ordinary people have been struggling with the issues surrounding the consequences of our acts for thousands of years. From the Ten Commandments, to Buddha's Eightfold Path, to the writings in the Koran, to Epicurus's justification of egotistical behavior, to Martin Buber's "ethics with a heart," people have been trying to decide what their ethical obligations are to others and how they should treat them. As we have indicated, answers range from simplistic and selfish observations ("It is a dog-eat-dog world") to philosophical mandates that focus on our moral obligation to other people. This view is eloquently articulated by the great humanitarian Albert Schweitzer: "Just as the wave cannot exist for itself, but is ever a part of the heaving surface of the ocean, so must I never live my life for itself, but always in the experience which is going on around me."

You can see by the last paragraph that ethics is an elusive topic. As Griffin reminds us, "Ethics has to do with the gray areas of our lives. When moral decisions are black and white, knowing what we should do is easy."[104] But what about those countless occasions when the decision is not easy? Where do you turn when you need ethical guidance? To God, to family, to friends, to philosophers, to yourselves? What you find in many instances when seeking ethical advice is a multitude of approaches representing a variety of orientations. Let's briefly pause and look at two of these approaches—relativism and universalism—and discuss their application to intercultural communication.

Relativism

Cultural relativism is predicated on the notion that all cultures are equally worthy of respect and that in studying other cultures you need to suspend judgment, empathize, and try to understand the way each particular culture sees the world. Ting-Toomey makes the same point when she notes, "Under the ethical-relativism approach, right and wrong are determined predominantly by the culture of the individual. Ethical relativists try to understand each cultural group 'in its own terms, with a minimum of contamination' by outside influence."[105] As indicated, this ethical philosophy holds to the view that there is no one correct moral code for all times and people, that each group has its own morality relative to its wants and values, and that all moral ideas are necessarily relative to a particular group of people. Wilson underscored this issue of multiple perspectives:

> Anthropologists believe that morality has no meaning outside the culture that defines it, philosophers argue that morality depends on a person's motives or the results he achieves, and ordinary people claim that personal freedom is supreme and that its exercise should be uninhibited unless it harms others.[106]

As you can see, by adding the issue of culture to the topic of ethics, we append yet another dimension to this already troublesome subject. Howell clearly summarizes some of the problems associated with a relativism (culture-specific) orientation to ethics when he writes:

> The fundamental connection between culture and ethics is this: Ethical standards are products of particular cultures. So it is not surprising that basic appropriate and inappropriate behavior important to a group varies from place to place. Consequently, we should not be surprised that one way of behaving has a high moral value—rightness—in one culture, has no ethical significance in a second culture, and in a third culture may be negatively moral, that is, considered by the majority of the population to be ethically wrong.[107]

Universalism

Cultural universalism takes the stance that regardless of the context or the culture, there are fixed and universal ethical precepts that apply to all cultures. This view maintains that there is a set of values, standards, morals, and the like that weave their way in and out of every culture. The underpinnings of the generalist approach to ethics can be found in the writings of the German philosopher Immanuel Kant. It was Kant's conviction that for action to be ethically correct, one must be able to will one's words or actions to be a universal law, that is, be willing to have everyone act in the same way.[108] This approach toward ethics is perhaps best summarized by Kant's single sentence: "Act only on that maxim whereby you can at the same time will that should become a universal law."

The problems related to the universalism approach seem rather obvious, and like relativism, underscore the difficulty of deciding on a standard of intercultural ethics that is applicable to all cultures in all situations. Think for a moment how problematic it would be even to somehow suggest that there is only one correct way for people to act.

It should be clear by now that the study of ethics is complex and complicated. We cannot, however, let the difficulty of the issues keep us from searching for possible answers. Let us spend the remainder of the chapter considering some ethical guidelines that you should consider when interacting with people from different cultures. We will maintain that although there are cultural differences regarding specific ethical behaviors that cannot be condoned (cannibalism, slavery, the abusing of women, and the like), there are nevertheless universal codes of conduct that we believe apply to all people and all cultures. In short, it is our contention that you can develop a universal ethic that also grants the relativistic nature of cultures. Let us now look at those common codes.

GUIDELINES FOR AN INTERCULTURAL ETHIC

Be Mindful That Communication Produces a Response

From Chapter 1 to these final few pages we have continued to stress the notion that the messages you send produce a response. In the intercultural environment, because of the diversity of backgrounds, it is much more difficult to assess and predict the type of response your messages will produce. For example, people in the United States have learned, as part of their cultural endowment, how to thank someone for a compliment or a gift. They can predict, with some degree of accuracy, what others expect from them and how they will respond to their signs of veneration and appreciation. As we indicated earlier in the chapter, forecasting the responses of other cultures is a far more difficult task. Let us stay with our simple example of thanking someone. In Arab cultures, one is expected to be profuse in offering thanks, whereas in England, one is expected to offer restrained thanks because too much exuberance is considered offensive.

Because of the potential power of messages, you must always be aware of *the effects of those message on other people*. This focus on your actions and the results of those actions is called, in the Buddhist tradition, *being mindful*. "Mindfulness is the aware, balanced acceptance of the present experience. It isn't more complicated than that. It is opening to and receiving the present moment."[109] When practicing mindfulness during communication, you are giving your full attention to what is transpiring right now. This is somewhat like the self-monitoring we discussed earlier in the chapter. This awareness of the here and now enables you to avoid letting habit instead of insight dictate your actions. By being mindful, you can adjust your messages to both the context and the person. You can, in short, be aware of what you are doing to another person. Tead links the need for mindfulness with the power of communication when he writes:

> Without indulging in too great refinements, let us remind ourselves that communication also has at bottom a moral aspect. It does, when all is said, anticipate a change in the conduct of the recipient. If the change has any large significance it means an interposing or interference with the autonomy of the other person or persons. And the tampering with personal drives and desires is a moral act even if its upshot is not a far-reaching one, or is a beneficial result. To seek to persuade behavior into a new direction may be wholly justifiable and the result in terms of behavior consequences may be salutary. But the judgment of benefit or detriment is not for the communicator safely to reach by himself. He is assuming a moral responsibility. And he had better be aware of the area with which he concerns himself and the responsibility he assumes. He should be willing to assert as to any given policy, "I stand behind this as having good personal consequences for the individuals whom it will affect." That judgment speaks a moral concern and desired moral outcome.[110]

Again, we remind you to reflect on your requests and your messages when you interact with another person or another culture.

Respect the Worth of the Individual

We begin this next ethical precept with this simple question: How do you feel when someone "puts you down" or acts like you are insignificant? The answer is obvious. You do not like being diminished. Everyone wants some level of respect, dignity, and a feeling of worth. It is our contention that an ethical stance gives this respect to every human being. We, of course, are not alone in this conviction. Johannesen, in his book on ethics, uses words such as "devalues," "ridicule," and "excluding" when he speaks of ethical guidelines.[111] On a more universal scale we can turn to the United Nations Universal Declaration of Human Rights. While there are a total of thirty articles, three of them directly relate to intercultural communication.

ARTICLE 1. All human beings are born free and equal in dignity and rights. They are endowed with reason and conscience and should act toward one another in a spirit of brotherhood.

ARTICLE 18. Everyone has a right to freedom of thought, conscience and religion.

ARTICLE 19. Everyone has the right to freedom of opinion and expression.

What these proclamations are saying is that the ethical person respects people both physically and emotionally. Confucius said much the same thing when he told us, "Without feelings of respect, what is there to distinguish men from beasts?"

Although there are cultural variations in what makes people smile, it is nevertheless true that a smile is common to all cultures—and carries the same meaning.

© Gloria Thomas

Seek Commonalties Among People and Cultures

We have spent much time in this book talking about differences that make a difference in the intercultural setting. However, we are going to argue that our similarities, not our differences, often can serve as part of an intercultural ethic. The photographer Edward Steichen had some guidance that we might be able to use as a starting point for this suggestion: "I believe that in all things that are important, in all of these we are alike." This credo of similarity is important to the study of ethics in that it helps you look for common ground as a way of deciding how to treat other people regardless of their culture. It might be intriguing to know that "an American child sticks out his tongue to show defiance, a Tibetan to show courtesy to a stranger, and a Chinese to express wonderment,"[112] but it is more important to know that they share a series of more crucial characteristics that link them together. The similarities that unite people, and in a very real sense make everyone part of a single "community," range from the obvious to the subtle. For example, it is apparent that all six-plus billion people inhabit the same planet for a rather short period. And that all people share the same emotion and desire to be free from external restraint: The craving for freedom is basic. There is also a universal link between children and family: People all share the same thrill and excitement at a new birth. Mating and wanting good friends tie everyone together. All people must eventually face old age and the potential suffering that often goes with it; and, of course, all people are joined in knowing that death, like birth, is part of life's process. All cultures love music and art, play and have sports, tell jokes, believe in being civil to one another, and search for ways to be happy. And there is nothing religious or metaphysical in the fact that all people seek to avoid physiological and psychological pain while searching for some degree of tranquility in life.

As a species, not only do you have similarities in feelings and experiences, but there are values that are common to all cultures. Even something as simple as the children's television program *Sesame Street* highlights your matching value system. As was pointed out in *U.S. News & World Report*, children in 130 countries view and respond to "universal values, such as racial harmony, peaceful dispute resolution, respect for the environment."[113]

There are also countless religious and philosophical values that bind people together. All religious traditions offer the same instructions to their members with regard to killing, stealing, bearing false witness, adultery, and the like. Variations of the "Golden Rule" you learned about growing up in the United States are found in all cultures. Although the words are different, the wisdom contained within the words is universal.[114]

Buddhism: "Hurt not others in ways that you yourself would find hurtful." *Udana-Virga*, 5:8

Christianity: "All things whatsoever ye would that men should do to you, do ye even so to them." Matthew, 7:12

Confucianism: "Do not do unto others what you would not have them do unto you." *Analect*, 15:23

Hinduism: "This is the sum of duty: do naught unto others which would cause you pain if done to you." Mahabharata, 5:1517

Islam: "No one of you is a believer until he desires for his brother that which he desires for himself." Sunnah

Jainism: "In happiness and suffering, in joy and grief, we should regard all creatures as we regard our own self." Lord Mahavira, 24th Tirthankara

Judaism: "What is hateful to you, do not to your fellow man. That is the law: all the rest is commentary." Talmud, Shabbat, 31 a

Native American: "Respect for all life is the foundation." The Great Law of Peace

If it were not for space constraints, we could have included an even longer list of those cultures that exhort their members to the "oneness of the human family." On an interpersonal level Kale counsels us regarding the "Rule" in the following fashion: "Ethical communicators address people of other cultures with the same respect that they would like to receive themselves."[115]

We believe, however, that from this brief sample you can begin to see that Steichen, whom we quoted earlier, was correct—in all those things that are important, we are all alike. What is important is that in a multicivilization world you begin to see their commonalities. Huntington expressed the same idea when he wrote, "People in all civilizations should search for and attempt to expand the values, institutions, and practices they have in a common with people of other civilizations."[116]

Recognize the Validity of Differences

Former Israeli Prime Minister Shimon Peres offers us a wonderful introduction to our next ethical canon when he tells us, "All people have the right to be equal and the equal right to be different." Therefore, in this guideline we recommend that you become aware of and tolerant of cultural differences as a way of establishing an intercultural ethic. Put in slightly different terms, keep in mind one of our themes from Chapter 1—people are both alike and different. Barnlund wrote of this double-sided nature:

> Outwardly there is little to distinguish what one sees on the streets of Osaka and Chicago—hurrying people, trolleys and buses, huge department stores, blatant billboards, skyscraper hotels, public monuments—beneath the surface there remains great distinctiveness. There is a different organization of industry, a different approach to education, a different role for labor unions, a contrasting pattern of family life, unique law enforcement and penal practices, contrasting forms of political activity, different sex and age roles. Indeed, most of what is thought of as culture shows as many differences as similarities.[117]

Thus, a complete and honest intercultural ethic grants similarities and recognizes differences. By accepting and appreciating both, you can better assess the potential consequences of your acts and be more tolerant of those of others. Wood discusses the need to recognize differences in male and female communication styles:

> In cross-gender communication, we need to remind ourselves there is logic and validity to both feminine and masculine communication styles. Feminine emphases on relationships, feelings, and responsiveness don't reflect inability to adhere to masculine rules for competing any more than masculine stress on instrumental outcomes is a failure to follow feminine rules for sensitivity to others. It is inappropriate to apply a single criterion—either masculine or feminine—to both genders' communication. Instead we need to realize different goals, priorities, and standards pertain to each.[118]

Thomas Jefferson said much the same thing about accepting differences when he wrote, "It does me no injury for my neighbor to say there are twenty gods, or no God."

Take Individual Responsibility for Your Actions

In the last chapter we made reference to an axiom regarding free choice. We also mentioned that you should be aware (mindful) of what those choices do to other people. Our final ethical consideration places those two ideas into an intercultural context. We advocate a three-point declaration that grants individual uniqueness, the ability to exercise free choice, and the interdependent nature of the world. All your decisions, actions, and even your failures to act have consequences for yourself and countless other people. The obvious ethical consequence of this fact leads us to what the Dalai Lama called "our universal responsibility." Gomez-Ibanez spoke to that responsibility when he wrote:

> If I am linked in some way to all this is, however tenuous the links may seem, then, I am in some respect responsible for the welfare of all this is, also, I am responsible for the common good. That realization, it seemed to me, might be the foundation for all ethics.[119]

The central message is that if you are going to live in this crowded, interconnected world, and if that planet and you, its "temporary residents" are to survive, you must accept your individual roles within that world. Remember, as we have shown throughout this book, people and cultures are inextricably linked. As the English anthropologist Gregory Batson noted, "What pattern connects the crab to the lobster and the orchid to the primrose and all four of them to me? And me to you?"

THE FUTURE OF INTERCULTURAL COMMUNICATION

Future Contacts

Attempting to chart the implications and the course of future events is a very tricky and perplexing assignment because no one knows with any degree of certainty what tomorrow will be like—let alone the next five minutes. As Shakespeare wrote in *Hamlet*, "We know what we are, but know not what we may be." The same, of course, can be said for intercultural communication. You know what you have been, but what of the future? You can, however, use the past and present as a predictor and speculate about the future of intercultural communication. If you use the past as a guide, the most apparent notion of the future is that your intercultural relationships and interactions will grow in both number and intensity. That growth will impact the future of intercultural communication in four dimensions: (1) *cultural diversity*, (2) *international problems*, (3) *global culture*, and (4) *ethnic and cultural identity*. We will begin by looking at these four trends and then conclude with our personal recommendation for the future.

Cultural Diversity

We start with a statement that is at the heart of this book—and one that we developed in detail in detail in Chapter 1—*cultural diversity has become a fact of life*. We have used statistics and demographic studies to document the fact that on a variety of levels and in a multitude of settings, people from different cultures will come together. Whether or not the people of the world accept this reality is not the issue. In one way or another people must recognize that for the first time in history, cultural groups throughout the world are increasingly in contact with one another. In the United States diversity will pick up the pace because of increasing immigration. Even now nearly one in ten "Americans" were born outside of the country.[120] In addition, the immigrant population is growing six and one-half times faster than the native-born population. Increasing diversity is forcing Americans to think about intercultural communication in new terms. As Booth points out, "Today, the United

States is experiencing its second great wave of immigration, a movement of people that has profound implications for a society."[121] Booth's "implications" will see future demands for employment, education, health care, and civil rights. You must work to ensure these increased contacts are not plagued with racism and prejudice but with tolerance and understanding.

While this book has focused primarily on the diversity and challenges Americans face at home and abroad, it safe to say that most other countries are also experiencing a coming together of ethnic and cultural groups. Fueled both by a worldwide flood of refugees (some 16 million now seeking asylum), and a need to be part of the "global marketplace," no nation may remain immune to diversity.

International Problems

We have just mentioned the issue of cultural diversity will be a major concern in the future. If you peruse the daily newspaper, or switch from news channel to news channel, you will encounter a long list of problems requiring your attention in the next decade. These problems will require that people learn to "talk" to each other.

Population increases, coupled with clashes related to diversity, will continue to create numerous stress points that cannot be ignored. Three of these are worth examining— *increased violence, world hunger,* and *population.*

Increased Violence

Once again you can use the past and present as a partial guide to the future. Long before the tragic events of September 11, 2001, conflicts between ideologies and neighbors were going on in places such as Israel, India, and Africa. But when those three planes struck the Twin Towers and the Pentagon, people were jolted into the realization that cultural or religious discord can lead to violence anywhere in the world. While the September 11 attack is a most striking example of the dangers of cultural ethnocentrism, it may only be a prelude to what the future might bring. For example, the National Defense Council Foundation noted that at the start of 2002 fifty-nine countries were experiencing serious violence that was related to ethnic, religious, and cultural conflicts.[122] These clashes are, of course, only part of the problems that face the world as cultures collide. Huntington speaks of this potential "collision" when he noted, "The world is indeed anarchical, rife with tribal and nationality conflicts, but the conflicts that pose the greatest dangers for stability are those between states or groups from different civilizations."[123] There is little doubt that the future will require you to deal with these conflicts by communicating with people who are from cultures different than our own.

World Hunger

As we noted in Chapter 1, world hunger is a major problem facing humankind. Yet, despite massive efforts by the food-producing nations, world hunger continues to accelerate. "Millions of people at the start of the 21st century continue to face malnutrition and starvation."[124] This problem reveals that people from different cultures must interact with each other in the next decide. The reason is simple, and clearly stated by Haviland: "The immediate cause of world hunger has less to do with food production than with warfare and food distribution."[125] In short, both these causes have their roots in a lack of communication.

Pollution

Worldwide pollution is yet another reason that makes it necessary for cultures to interact. Global warming, deforestation, soil erosion, chemicals poisoning water and soil, acid rain, water scarcity, and the like know no boundaries. Pollution is indeed one of those topics that reflect the truism that notes, "What happens in one part of the world happens in all parts of world." While people know the causes of pollution and dangers of pollution, most have refused to make any significant advances in dealing with this crisis. Haviland suggests part of the reason lies in the cultural, philosophical, and theological traditions found in much of the world.[126] More specifically, he notes, "Western industrialized societies accept the biblical assertion (found in the *Qu'ran* as well) they have dominion over the earth with all that grows and lives on it, which is their duty to subdue."[127] Whether or not you agree with Haviland's interpretation, you cannot reject the notion that in the future global pollution must be part of an international dialogue.

Global Culture

Since Marshall McLuhan first proposed his notion of a "Global Village," there has been a belief that the world would evolve into one massive homogeneous culture. The voices behind such a hypothesis were abundant. You can find surface examples such as people from Australia to Zambia eating a Big Mac and holding a Coca-Cola, to the wide spread of people wearing jeans. On a less superficial level, those who advance the single-culture argument make note of the rapid demise of many of the world's languages and the replacement of these languages with English. They also point to some other Western symbols and icons such as people "reading the same kinds of newspapers, watching the same kind of television programs, communicating directly with one another via the Internet, satellites, and World Wide Web, and so on."[128] There were even predictions that the world would see a single political system by the 23rd century.[129] Regardless of the merit of such arguments it is nevertheless true that the future of intercultural interaction will have to confront the issues associated with the idea of a homogeneous, single, unified culture.

Ethnic and Cultural Identity

There is a second trend moving throughout the world that would seem to contradict those who predict a single global culture. This counterhypothesis has its roots in the belief that people and cultures, for a host of reasons, are refusing to accept globalization and a universal ideology. In fact, scholars who give voice to this position see a world where nations, cultures, and individuals are turning inward. This "turning inward" movement seems to be gaining strength as the world becomes more unpredictable, complex, and stressful. Cleveland makes the same point when he writes, "Many millions of people believe that their best haven of certainty and security is a group based on ethnic similarity, common faith, economic interests, or political like-mindedness."[130] Many Americans believe everyone wants to be just like them and often have a difficult time accepting the view that other people are retreating to the sanctuary of their own ethnic and cultural identity. The real dilemma we will face in the future is how the world balances ethnic and cultural identity with the interconnective nature of the world and its cultures. Often the cost of cultural isolationism, comfort, and security is conflict. As the philosopher Krishnamurti points out, "For safety and comfort we are willing to kill others who have the same kind of desire to be safe, to feel protected, to belong to something."[131] Cleveland voices the same fear when he says, "Ethnic and religious diversity is creating painful conflicts around the world."[132] Ethnic discords are not confined to distant locations. As Ling-Ling tells us, there are "disturbing signs of rising racial and ethnic tension at home."[133] This, of course, makes the need for cultural understanding even more demanding. Cleveland notes, "Finding ways to become unified despite diversity may be the world's most urgent problems in the years ahead."[134] Perhaps the first step in seeking Cleveland's idea of marrying unification with diversity can be found in the words of the anthropologist Laura Nader when she says, "Diversity is rich."[135] We must all begin to realize that diversity can be rich without being threatening, for in the end, people of all cultures long for the same things: a place to raise their children, ply their trades, and express themselves aesthetically and socially. When those forms of expression differ from our own, we must respect the rights of people from other cultures. John Comenius articulated this same idea over three hundred years ago:

> To hate a man because he was born in another country, because he speaks a different language, or because he takes a different view of this subject or that, is a great folly. Desist, I implore you, for we are all equally human. . . . Let us have but one end in view, the welfare of humanity.

We would ask those who claim that such a view is simplistic and fanciful to provide alternatives. In a world that can now destroy itself with powerful bombs, toxic gases, or global pollution, we do not consider it romantic or idealistic to issue an appeal that we strive to develop a greater understanding of people who may not be like us. The task is not simple, for Cleveland reminds us, "We do not yet quite know how to create 'wholeness incorporating diversity,' but we owe it to the world, as well as ourselves, to keep trying."[136] Because we agree with Cleveland, we add our voice to the call for you "to keep trying."

SUMMARY

- The basic components of communication competence are motivation, knowledge, and skills.
- The intercultural study of communication competence can focus on culture specific, context specific, and culture general.
- Following some basic guidelines such as knowing yourself and you culture, considering the physical and human setting, seeking to understand diverse message systems, developing empathy, encouraging feedback, developing communication flexibility, learning to tolerate ambiguity, managing conflict, and learning about cultural adaptation can help improve intercultural communication.
- Because communication is an activity that has a consequence, we must develop a communication ethic.
- An intercultural ethic asks you to be mindful of the power of communication, respect the worth of all individuals, seek commonalties among people and cultures, recognize the validity of differences, and take individual responsibility for your actions.
- The future of intercultural communication will face four interrelated issues: (1) an ever increasing amount of contact between people from different cultures, (2) international problems related to violence, world hunger, and pollution, (3) calls for a global culture, and (4) an increase in ethnic and cultural identity.

INFOTRAC COLLEGE EDITION EXERCISES

1. Want to learn specific ways to become a more effective intercultural communicator? Locate and read "Cultural Diversity and Your Future: Cultural Diversity Is All Around Us—at School and in The Workplace. Here's How To Boost Your Cultural Competence" by Janice Arenofsky. Identify at least two specific things you can do to boost your cultural competence.

2. The concept of human rights seems natural to most Westerners, but as this text argues, assumptions that seem natural to some may seem strange and offensive to others. To what extent is the concept of human rights culturally bound? Locate and read Matt Granato's article "Is Culture a Barrier to Human Rights?" Summarize Granato's discussion, then discuss with your classmates ways of constructively addressing the complexities raised by Granato's article.

3. One of the most discussed findings of the 2000 U.S. Census Report was the significant increase in America's Hispanic population. Locate and read "The House that Roared" by Linda Jacobsen. What does Jacobsen's article suggest about the future of intercultural communications in the United States? This article presumes that the primary reason for understanding Hispanic Americans is to more effectively market consumer goods to this population. What other reasons has this class suggested for learning about cultural differences? For related articles on this subject, use the subject search term "Hispanic Americans" and its subdivisions "Demographic Aspects" and "Statistics."

ACTIVITIES

1. Locate someone from a culture different from your own, and interview him or her regarding the characteristics of a successful communicator. Include some of the following questions in your interview:
   a. What are the characteristics of a highly credible person?
   b. What communication skills are associated with a person who has low credibility?
   c. What communication skills are less desirable in your culture?
   d. What communication skills are most valued in your culture?

2. Define your communication style to the best of your ability by answering these questions:
   Do I give my full attention to people?
   Do I seem at ease or tense?
   Do I often change the subject without taking the other person into consideration?
   Do I deprecate the statements of others?
   Do I smile often?
   Do I interrupt repeatedly?
   Do I show sympathy when someone has a problem?
   Do my actions tend to lower the other person's self-esteem?
   You may find it helpful to record yourself in conversation with another person or, if you have the means, to videotape yourself.

3. Discuss the pros and cons of the following proposition: There should be a constitutional amendment that English be declared the official language of the United States.

4. Do you see a future where people of different cultures become closer together or a future where they become increasingly isolated from each other?

5. Because individual and cultural differences exist, can we ever truly empathize with another person? How do cultural differences compound the problem?

6. Can you think of some ways to improve intercultural communication that were not discussed in this chapter?

7. Find a newspaper or magazine article or story that you believe demonstrates a clash in cultural definitions of ethics. What are those differences? How can they be resolved?

DISCUSSION IDEAS

1. In small groups discuss the following topic: Why is it difficult to know yourself and your culture?

2. In small groups discuss the following topic: Granting the notion of individual and cultural differences, can we ever truly empathize with another person?

3. Do you see a future where people from different cultures become closer together or a future where they become increasingly isolated from each other?

4. In small groups discuss the following question: What should an intercultural ethic be?

Notes

Notes for Chapter 1

1. *U.S News & World Report*, March 12, 2001, 12.
2. J. M. Swomley, "When Blue Becomes Gold," *The Humanist*, September/October 2000, 5.
3. Ibid., 6.
4. R. E. Schmid, "African Dust Could Be Killing Coral Reefs," *Las Vegas Review-Journal*, September 23, 2000, 16A.
5. L. Morrow, "Killing with Kindness?" *Time*, October 21, 2002.
6. D. Mattern, "Humanity's Juncture: Abandoning the Road of War for the Road to Peace," *The Humanist*, March/April, 2000, 9.
7. A. Specter and C. Robbins, *Passion for Truth* (New York: HarperCollins, 2000), 531.
8. A. Schlesinger, Jr. *The Disuniting of America: Reflections on a Multicultural Society* (New York: Norton, 1992).
9. Ibid., 10.
10. G. Cowin, "Multiculturalism: Simply a Matter of Respect," *Australian Nursing Journal*, 10 (1), July 2002, 40.
11. M. Goldsmith, C. Walt, and K. Doucet, "New Competencies for Tomorrow's Global Leader," *CMA Management*, 73 (10), December 1999/January 2000, 20.
12. Ibid., 20.
13. T. Anthony, "China Embraces Socialist Market Economy," *Las Vegas Review-Journal*, November 17, 2001, 36A.
14. N. Gibbs, "A Whole New World," *Time*, June 11, 2001, 38.
15. S. Victor, "Election 2000 and the Culture War," *The Humanist*, January/February, 2001, 5.
16. S. D. McLemore, *Racial and Ethnic Relations in America* (Boston: Allyn and Bacon, 1994), 60.
17. E. A. Folb, "Who's Got Room at the Top? Issues of Dominance and Nondominance in Intracultural Communication," in *Intercultural Communication: A Reader*, 8th ed., L. A. Samovar and R. E. Porter, eds. (Belmont, CA: Wadsworth, 1997), 140.
18. Ibid., 140.
19. S. Lane, "Deafness Shouldn't Be Called Handicap," *Dallas Morning News*, March 5, 1995, 6-J.
20. J. Goodwin, "Sexuality as Culture," in *Handbook of Intercultural Training*, 2nd ed., D. Lanis and R. S. Bhagat, eds. (Thousand Oaks, CA: Sage Publications, 1996), 417.
21. J. T. Wood, "Gender, Communication, and Culture," in *Intercultural Communication: A Reader*, 7th ed., L. A. Samovar and R. E. Porter, eds. (Belmont, CA: Wadsworth, 1994), 57.
22. M. L. Hecht, S. Ribeau, and M. Sedano, "A Mexican American Perspective on Interethnic Communication," *International Journal of Intercultural Relations*, 14, 1990, 33.
23. J. T. Wood, *Communication Mosaics: A New Introduction to the Field of Communication* (Belmont, CA: Wadsworth, 1998), 205.
24. B. Bate, *Communication and the Sexes* (New York: Harper and Row, 1988), 35.
25. J. T. Wood, *Gendered Lives: Communication, Gender, and Culture* (Belmont, CA: Wadsworth, 1994), 27.
26. Wood, 1998, 205.
27. Wood, "Gender, Communication and Culture," 158–159.
28. D. Guerrière, "Multiculturalism: American Success, Liberal Education, or Political Correctness?" *Modern Age*, Spring 2001, 175.
29. R. Grant, "The Social Contract and Human Rights," *The Humanist*, January/February, 2000, 18.

30. E. Wax, "Immigration Researchers See a World of Struggles," *Washington Post*, May 28, 2001, A9.
31. *San Diego Union-Tribune*, March 13, 2001, A12.
32. P. Osio, Jr., "New Urgency for Immigration Reform," *San Diego Union-Tribune*, October 23, 2001, B9.
33. A. Acuña, "Changes in State's Ethnic Balance are Accelerating," *Los Angeles Times*, October 20, 1999, A20.
34. Guerrière, 2001, 175.
35. M. Therrien and R. R. Ramirez, "The Hispanic Population in the United States: March 2000," *Current Population Reports*, P20-535 (Washington, D.C.: U.S. Census Bureau, 1000), 1.
36. I. R. Carlo-Casellas, "Marketing to U. S. Hispanic Population Requires Analysis of Cultures," *National Underwriter*, 14, January 2002, 9.
37. S. Gamboa, "Spanish-Language Political TV Ads Air Increasingly," *Las Vegas Review-Journal*, November 22, 2002, 14A.
38. http://www.lenzine.com/census/.
39. R. Estrin, "Study Sees America Far from Color-blind," *The Sacramento Bee*, October 2, 1999, A10.
40. http://www.census.gov/prod 2002 pubs/c2kbr01-16.pdf.
41. R. N. Ostling, "First Detailed Survey of U. S. Muslims Find a Growing Faith," *Las Vegas Review-Journal*, April 27, 2001, 11A.
42. Ibid.
43. Ibid.
44. F. E. X. Dance and C. E. Larson, *Speech Communication: Concepts and Behavior* (New York: Holt, Rinehart, and Winston, 1972).
45. D. Rubin and L. P. Stewart, *Communication and Human Behavior*, 4th ed. (Boston: Allyn and Bacon, 1998), 16.
46. J. Mascara, *Dhammapada* (New York: Penguin, 1973), 40.
47. W. B. Gudykunst and Y. Y. Kim, *Communicating with Strangers: An Approach to Intercultural Communication*, 3rd ed. (New York: McGraw-Hill, 1997), 6.
48. S. Trenholm and A. Jensen, *Interpersonal Communication*, 2nd ed. (Belmont, CA: Wadsworth, 1992), 152.
49. S. W. Littlejohn, *Theories of Human Communication*, 3rd ed. (Belmont, CA: Wadsworth, 1989), 152.
50. S. Shimanoff, *Communication Rules: Theory and Research* (Beverly Hills, CA: Sage, 1980), 57.
51. E. T. Hall and M. R. Hall, *Understanding Cultural Differences: Germans, French and Americans* (Yarmouth, ME: Intercultural Press, 1990), 18.
52. Wood, *Gendered Lives*, 29.
53. J. T. Wood, *Communication in Our Lives* (Belmont, CA: Wadsworth, 2000), 132.
54. A. G. Smith, ed., *Communication and Culture: Readings in the Codes of Human Interaction* (New York: Holt, Rinehart, and Winston, 1966), v.
55. P. Recer, "DNA Study Traces Ancient Ancestry of Europeans to Common Ancestor," *Las Vegas Review-Journal*, October 10, 2000, 29A.
56. K. S. Sitaram and R. T. Cogdell, *Foundations of Intercultural Communication* (Columbus, OH: Charles E. Merrill, 1976), 50.
57. "America's New Ambassador to South Africa," *Ebony*, August 1996, 82.

58. M. Weinberg, "Defining Multicultural Education," *Multicultural Newsletter* (California State University, Long Beach), December 1992, 2.

Notes for Chapter 2

1. E. T. Hall, *Beyond Culture* (Garden City, NY: Anchor Doubleday, 1977), 14.

2. E. T. Hall, *The Silent Language* (New York: Doubleday, 1959), 169.

3. G. Hofstede, *Culture's Consequence: Comparing Values, Behaviors, Institutions, and Organizations Across Nations*, 2nd ed. (Thousand Oaks, CA: Sage Publications, 2001), 10.

4. R. W. Nolan, *Communicating and Adapting Across Cultures: Living and Working in the Global Village* (Westport, CN: Bergin and Barvey, 1999), 3.

5. G. Smith, Ed., *Communication and Culture: Readings in the Codes of Human Interaction* (New York: Holt, Rinehart, and Winston, 1966), 1.

6. M. J. Hanson, "Ethnic, Cultural, and Language Diversity in Intervention Settings," in *Developing Cross-Cultural Competence: A Guide for Working with Young Children and Their Families*, E. W. Lynch and M. J. Hanson, eds. (Baltimore: Paul H. Brookes, 1992), 3.

7. W. A. Haviland, *Cultural Anthropology*, 7th ed. (Fort Worth, TX: Harcourt Brace Jovanovich, 1993), 29.

8. H. C. Triandis, "Culture and Conflict," *International Journal of Psychology*, 35 (2000), 146.

9. W. A. Haviland, *Cultural Anthropology*, 10th ed. (Belmont, CA: Wadsworth, 2002), 34.

10. H. L. Shapiro, *Aspect of Culture* (New Brunswick, NJ: Rutgers University Press, 1956), 21.

11. M. Harris, *Cows, Pigs, Wars, and Witches: The Riddles of Culture* (New York: Random House, 1974), 84.

12. S. Nanda, *Cultural Anthropology*, 5th ed. (Belmont, CA: Wadsworth, 1994), 50.

13. See J. J. Macionis, *Society: The Basics*, 4th ed. (Upper Saddle River, NJ: Prentice Hall, 1997), 33–37; and C. M. Parkes, P. Laungani, and B. Young, eds., *Death and Bereavement Across Cultures* (New York: Routledge, 1997), 14–15.

14. Parkes, Laungani, and Young, 1997, 14.

15. Macionis, 1997, 34.

16. Parkes, Laungani, and Young, 1997, 15.

17. Nolan, 1999, 3.

18. L. E. Harrison and S. P. Huntington, eds., *Culture Matters: How Values Shape Human Progress* (New York: Basic Books, 2000), xv.

19. A. L. Kroeber and C. Kluckhohn, "Culture: A Critical Review of Concepts and Definitions," *Harvard University Peabody Museum of American Archaeology and Ethnology Papers*, 47 (1952), 181.

20. A. J. Marsella, "The Measurement of Emotional Reactions to Work: Methodological and Research Issues," *Work and Stress*, 8 (1994), 166–167.

21. Harrison and Huntington, 2000, xv.

22. S. P. Huntington, "The West Unique, Not Universal," *Foreign Affairs*, November/December 1996, 28.

23. R. Brislin, *Understanding Culture's Consequence on Behavior*, 2nd ed. (Fort Worth, TX: Harcourt College Publishers, 2000), 10.

24. Shapiro, 1956, 54.

25. C. Kluckhohn, *Mirror for Men* (New York: McGraw-Hill, 1944), 24–25.

26. D. G. Bates and F. Plog, *Cultural Anthropology*, 3rd ed. (New York: McGraw-Hill, 1990), 19.

27. E. A. Hoebel and E. L. Frost, *Culture and Social Anthropology* (New York: McGraw-Hill, 1976), 58.

28. F. M. Keesing, *Cultural Anthropology: The Science of Custom* (New York: Holt, Rinehart, and Winston, 1965), 18.

29. B. Rubin, *Communication and Human Behavior*, 3rd ed. (New York: Macmillan, 1988), 384.

30. J. M. Sellers, *Folk Wisdom of Mexico* (San Francisco: Chronicle Books, 1994), 7.

31. E. G. Seidensticker, in *Even Monkeys Fall from Trees, and Other Japanese Proverbs*, David Galef, ed. (Rutland, VT: Charles E. Tuttle, 1987), 8.

32. Ibid., 8.

33. W. Wolfgang Mieder, *Encyclopedia of World Proverbs: A Treasury of Wit and Wisdom Through the Ages* (New Jersey: Prentice-Hall, 1986), xi.

34. Ibid., 1986, x.

35. Ibid., 1986, vii.

36. S. Nanda and R. L. Warms, *Cultural Anthropology*, 6th ed. (Belmont, CA: Wadsworth, 1998), 92.

37. Haviland, 2002, 294.

38. C. Tomlinson, "Myth of Invincibility Draws Children to Battles in Zaire," *San Diego Union-Tribune*, December 17, 1996, A-21.

39. R. Erdoes and A. Ortiz, eds. *American Indian Myths and Legends* (New York: Pantheon, 1984), xv.

40. Ibid., 1984, xv.

41. Joseph Campbell, *The Power of Myth* (New York: Doubleday, 1988), 5.

42. Ibid., 1988, 6.

43. E. H. Gombrich, *The Story of Art* (New York: Phaidon, 1955), 102.

44. Nanda, 1994, 403.

45. A. Hunter and J. Sexton, *Contemporary China* (New York: St. Martin's Press, 1999), 158.

46. J. Campbell, *Myths to Live By* (New York: Penguin, 1972), 106.

47. Ibid., 106.

48. Keesing, 1965, 279.

49. Haviland, 1993, 392.

50. J. Thompson, "Mass Communication and Modern Culture: Contribution to a Critical Theory of Ideology," *Sociology*, 22 (1988), 359.

51. F. Williams, *The New Communications*, 2nd ed. (Belmont, CA: Wadsworth, 1989), 269.

52. F. P. Delgado, "The Nature of Power Across Communicative and Cultural Borders" (paper presented at the Annual Convention of the Speech Communication Association, Miami Beach, FL, November 1993), 12.

53. L. S. Gross, *The International World of Electronic Media* (New York: McGraw-Hill, 1995), 1.

54. E. Y. Kim, *The Yin and Yang of American Culture: A Paradox* (Yarmouth, ME: Intercultural Press, Inc., 2001), 2.

55. L. P. Stewart, A. D. Stewart, S. A. Friedly, and P. J. Cooper, *Communication Between the Sexes: Sex Differences and Sex-Role Stereotypes* (Scottsdale, AZ: Gorsuch Scarisbrick, 1990), 84–85.

56. E. Smith, *The Religion of Man* (New York: Harper and Row, 1986), 1–2.

57. Nanda and Warms, 1998, 47.

58. See M. J. Gannon, *Understanding Globe Culture: Metaphorical Journeys Through 23 Nations*, 2nd ed. (Thousand Oaks, Ca: Sage Publications, 2001).

59. Ibid., vi.

60. R. Brislin, *Understanding Culture's Influence on Behavior* (Fort Worth, TX: Harcourt Brace Jovanovich, 1993), 6.

61. J. M. Charon, *The Meaning of Sociology*, 6th ed. (Upper Saddle River, N. J.: Prentice Hall, 1999), 4.

62. Ibid., 1999, 94.

63. Keesing, 1965, 28.

64. J. J. Macionis, *Society: The Basics*, 4th ed. (Saddle River, NJ: Prentice-Hall, 1998), 33.

65. Kluchhohn, 1944, 26.

66. H. L. Weinberg, *Levels of Knowing and Existence* (New York: Harper and Row, 1959), 157.

67. W. H. Goodenough, "Evolution of the Human Capacity for Beliefs," *American Anthropologist*, 92 (1990), 605.

68. Bates and Plog, 1990, 20.

69. P. Ethington, "Toward Some Borderlands Schools for American Urban Ethnic Studies?" *American Quarterly*, 48 (1996), 348.

70. J. Luckmann, *Transcultural Communication in Nursing* (Albany, NY: Delmar Publishers, 1999), 22.

71. Nanda, 1994, 62.

72. Macionis, 1998, 47.

73. Haviland, 2002, 427.

74. Hoelbel and Frost, 1976, 48.

75. W. B. Gudykunst and Y. Y. Kim, *Communicating with Strangers: An Approach to Intercultural Communication*, 2nd ed. (New York: McGraw-Hill, 1992), 215.

76. D. C. Barnlund, *Communicative Styles of Japanese and Americans: Images and Realities* (Belmont, CA: Wadsworth, 1989), 192.

77. Nanda and Warms, 1998, 57.

78. Haviland, 2002, 41.

79. E. T. Hall, *Beyond Culture* (New York: Doubleday, 1976), 13–14.

80. R. Benedict, *Patterns of Culture*, 2nd ed. (New York: Mentor, 1948), 2.

81. R. Benedict, *Patterns of Culture* (Boston: Houghton Mifflin, 1934), 21–22.

82. N. Dresser, *Multicultural Manners* (New York: Wiley, 1996), 89–90.

83. M. Singer, *Intercultural Communication: A Perceptual Approach* (Englewood Cliffs, NJ: Prentice-Hall, 1987), 9.

84. T. K. Gamble and M. Gamble, *Communication Works*, 5th ed. (New York: McGraw-Hill, 1996), 77.

85. Singer, 1987, 9.

86. J. W. Bagby, "A Cross-Cultural Study of Perceptual Predominance in Binocular Rivalry," *Journal of Abnormal and Social Psychology*, 54 (1957), 331–334.

87. G. Guilmet, "Maternal Perceptions of Urban Navajo and Caucasian Children's Classroom Behavior," *Human Organization*, 38 (1979), 87–91.

88. S. W. King, Y. Minami, and L. A. Samovar, "A Comparison of Japanese and American Perceptions of Source Credibility," *Communication Research Reports*, 2 (1985), 76–79.

89. R. B. Adler and G. Rodman, *Understanding Human Communication*, 5th ed. (Fort Worth, TX: Harcourt Brace Jovanovich, 1994), 37.

90. W. B. Gudykunst, *Bridging Differences: Effective Intergroup Communication*, 2nd ed. (Thousand Oaks, CA: Sage, 1994), 67.

91. P. R. Harris and R. T. Moran, *Managing Cultural Differences: Leadership Strategies for a New World of Business* (Houston, TX: Gulf, 1996), 274.

92. H. C. Triandis, "Cultural Influences upon Perception," in *Intercultural Communication: A Reader*, 2nd ed., L. A. Samovar and R. E. Porter, eds. (Belmont, CA: Wadsworth, 1976), 119.

93. N. J. Adler, *International Dimensions of Organizational Behavior*, 3rd ed. (Cincinnati, OH: South-Western College Publishing, 1997), 71.

94. Adler, 1997.

95. E. M. Rogers and T. M. Steinfatt, *Intercultural Communication* (Prospect Heights, IL: Waveland Press, 1999), 81.

96. L. D. Purnell and B. J. Paulanka, "Transcultural Diversity and Health Care," in *Transcultural Health Care: A Culturally Competent Approach*, L. D. Purnell and B. J. Paulanka, eds. (Philadelphia, PA: F. A. Davis, 1998), 3.

97. M. Rokeach, *The Nature of Human Values* (New York: Free Press, 1973), 161.

98. S. Nanda and R. L. Warms, *Cultural Anthropology*, 6th ed. (Belmont, CA: Wadsworth, 1998), 49.

99. Hofstede, 2001, 5.

100. E. Albert, "Value System," in *The International Encyclopedia of the Social Sciences*, vol. 16 (New York: Macmillan, 1968), 32.

101. Hofstede, 2001, 6.

102. Rokeach, 1973, 5.

103. Hofstede, 2001, 6.

104. G. Gao and S. Ting-Toomey, *Communicating Effectively with the Chinese* (Thousand Oaks, CA: Sage Publications, 1998), 39.

105. A. Oppenheimer, "Geography, Culture and Prosperity," *San Diego Union-Tribune*, 1 August, 2000, B11.

106. L. Damen, *Culture-Learning: The Fifth Dimension in the Language Classroom* (Reading, MA: Addison-Wesley, 1987), 110.

107. E. W. Lynch, "Conceptual Framework: From Culture Shock to Cultural Learning," in *Developing Cross-Cultural Competence: A Guide for Working with Young Children and Their Families*, 2nd ed., E. W. Lynch and M. J. Hanson, eds. (Baltimore: Paul H. Brookes, 1998), 27.

108. Lynch and Hanson, 1998, 24.

109. Ibid., 1998, 25.

110. L. P. Goodson, *Afghanistan's Endless War: State Failure, Regional Politics and the Rise of the Taliban* (Seattle, WA: University of Washington Press, 2001), 12–13.

111. "Women Are Degrees Ahead," *San Diego Union-Tribune*, May 10, 1999, C-2.

112. Gannon, 2001, 13–17.

113. Ibid., 13.

114. Ibid., 16.

115. Ibid., 16.

116. F. Trompenaars and C. Hampden-Turner, *Riding The Waves of Culture: Understanding Diversity in Global Business*, 2nd ed. (New York: McGraw-Hill, 1998), 8–11.

117. M. Grondona, "A Cultural Typology of Economic Development," in *Culture Matters: How Values Shape Human Progress*, L. E. Harrison and S. P. Huntington, eds. (New York: Basic Books, 2000), 44–55.

118. G. R. Weaver, "Contrasting and Comparing Cultures," in *Culture, Communication and Conflict*, 2nd ed., R. G. Weaver, ed. (Boston: Pearson, 2000), 72–77.

119. Charon, 1999, 99.

120. Ibid.

121. Kim, 2001, xv.

122. For a more detailed discussion of American values see Adler and Rodman, 1994, 388–389; J. J. Berman, ed., *Cross-Cultural Perspectives* (Lincoln: University of Nebraska Press, 1990), 112–113; Kim, 2001; J. L. Nelson, *Values and Society* (Rochelle, NJ: Hayden, 1975), 90–95; E. C. Stewart and M. J. Bennett, *American Cultural Patterns: A Cross-Cultural Perspective* (Yarmouth, ME: Intercultural Press, 1991); Trenholm and Jensen, 1992, 156–158; R. M. Williams, *American Society: A Sociological Interpretation*, 3rd ed. (New York: Knopf, 1970).

123. Stewart and Bennett, 1991, 133.

124. Gannon, 2001, 213.

125. S. P. Huntington, "The West Unique, Not Universal," *Foreign Affairs*, November/December 1996, 33.

126. Kim, 2001, 35.

127. M. J. Hanson, "Families with Anglo-European Roots," in *Developing Cross-Cultural Competence: A Guide for Working with Children and Their Families*, 2nd ed., E. W. Lynch and M. J. Hanson, eds. (Baltimore: Paul H. Brookes, 1998), 103.

128. J. J. Macionis, *Society: The Basics*, 4th ed. (Saddle River, NJ: Prentice Hall, 1998), 37.

129. Macionis, 1998, 37.

130. Hanson, 1998, 104–105.

131. Stewart and Bennett, 1992, 119.

132. G. Althen, *American Ways* (Yarmouth, ME: Intercultural Press, 1988), 16.

133. M. E. Clark, "Changes in Euro-American Values Needed for Sustainability," *Journal of Social Issues*, 51 (1995), 72.

134. Clark, 1995, 72.

135. Macionis, 1998, 36.

135. Hanson, 1998, 105.

137. Althen, 1988, 11.

138. Hanson, 1998, 105.

139. Althen, 1988, 11.

140. J. H. McElroy, *American Beliefs* (Chicago: Ivan R. Dee, 1999), 37.

141. Kim, 2001, 40.

142. Ibid.

143. Ibid., 42.

144. Harris and Moran, 1996, 316.

145. G. Hofstede, *Culture's Consequences: International Differences in Work-Related Values*, 2nd ed., (Beverly Hills, CA: Sage, 2001). See also G. Hofstede, *Cultures and Organizations: Software of the Mind* (London: McGraw-Hill, 1991).

146. Hofstede, 2001, xix.

147. J. O. Yum, "The Impact of Confucianism on Interpersonal Relationships and Communication Patterns," in *Intercultural Communication: A Reader*, 8th ed., L. A. Samovar and R. E. Porter, eds. (Belmont, CA: Wadsworth, 1997), 78.

148. S. Ting-Toomey, *Communicating Across Cultures* (New York: Guilford Press, 1999), 67.

149. H. C. Triandis, *Individualism and Collectivism* (Boulder, CO: Westview Press, 1995). See also H. C. Triandis, "Cross-Cultural Studies of Individualism and Collectivism," in *Cross-Cultural Perspectives*, J. J. Berman, ed. (Lincoln: University of Nebraska Press, 1990), 41–133.

150. Brislin, 2000, 53.

151. Triandis, 1995.

152. D. Goleman, "The Group and Self: New Focus on a Cultural Rift," *New York Times*, December 22, 1990, 40.

153. D. A. Foster, *Bargaining Across Borders* (New York: McGraw-Hill, 1992), 267.

154. S. P. Morreale, B. H. Spitzberg, and J. K. Barge, *Human Communication: Motivation, Knowledge and Skills* (Belmont, CA: Wadsworth, 2001), 311.

155. P. Andersen, "In Different Dimensions: Nonverbal Communication and Culture," in *Intercultural Communication: A Reader*, 10th ed., L. A. Samovar and R. E. Porter, eds. (Belmont, CA: Wadsworth, 2003).

156. Hanson, 1998, 105.

157. R. D. Lewis, *When Cultures Collide: Managing Successfully Across Cultures* (London: Nicholas Brealey, 2000), 167.

158. Hofstede, 2001, 236.

159. Triandis, 1990, 52.

160. H. C. Triandis, "Collectivism and Individualism as Cultural Syndromes," *Cross-Cultural Research*, 27 (1993), 160.

161. D. Etoung-Manguelle, "Does Africa Need a Cultural Adjustment Program," in *Culture Matters: How Values Shape Human Progress*, in L. E. Harrison, ed. (New York: Basic Books, 2000), 71.

162. M. Meyer, *China* (Totowa, NJ: Rowman and Littlefield, 1994), 54.

163. Y. Richmond and P. Gestrin, *Into Africa* (Yarmouth, ME: Intercultural Press, 1998), 2.

164. M. L. Hecht, M. J. Collier, and S. A. Ribeau, *African American Communication: Ethnic Identity and Interpretation* (Newbury Park, CA: Sage, 1993), 97.

165. Luckman, 1999, 29.

166. M. Kim, W. F. Sharkey, and T. Singelis, "Explaining Individualist and Collective Communication—Focusing on the Perceived Importance of Interactive Constraints" (paper presented at the Annual Convention of the Speech Communication Association, Chicago, October 1992).

167. G. Hofstede, "Cultural Differences in Teaching and Learning," *International Journal of Intercultural Relations*, 10 (1986), 301–319.

168. L. Schneider and A. Silverman, Global Sociology: *Introducing Five Contemporary Societies* (New York: McGraw-Hill, 1997), 48.

169. E. Marx, *Breaking Through Culture Shock* (London: Nicholas Brealey, 1999), 51.

170. Hofstede, 1986, 308.

171. Ibid., 301–319.

172. Hofstede, 2000, 169.

173. Lewis, 2000, 65.

174. Harris and Moran, 1996, 217.

175. G. Hofstede, "The Cultural Relativity of the Quality of Life Concept," in *Cultural Communication and Conflict: Readings in Intercultural Relations*, 2nd ed., G. R. Weaver, ed. (Boston: Pearson, 2000), 139.

176. Foster, 1992, 265.

177. W. B. Gudykunst, *Asian American Ethnicity and Communication* (Thousand Oaks, CA: Sage, 2001), 41.

178. D. Etounaga-Manguelle, 2000, 68.

179. Adler, 1997, 51.

180. Brislin, 2000, 288.

181. C. Calloway-Thomas, P. J. Cooper, and C. Blake, *Intercultural Communication: Roots and Routes* (Boston: Allyn and Bacon, 1999), 196.

182. Hofstede, 2001, 107–108.

183. Ibid., 280.

184. H. Meguro, Address to the World Affairs Council, San Diego, CA, June 16, 1988.

185. Hofstede, 2000, 139.

186. "Women in the House," *Time*, June 16, 1997, 20.

187. Kim, 2001, 50.

188. Gudykunst, 2001, 47.

189. Hofstede 2001, 251.

190. Chinese Culture Connection, "Chinese Values and the Search for Culture-Free Dimensions of Culture," *Journal of Cross-Cultural Psychology*, 18 (1987), 143–164. See also G. Hofstede and M. H. Bond, "Confucius and Economic Growth: New Trends in Culture's Consequence," *Organizational Dynamics*, 16 (1988), 4–21.

191. Hofstede, 2001, 351.

192. Ibid., 360, 366–367.

193. F. R. Kluckhohn and F. L. Strodtbeck, *Variations in Value Orientations* (New York: Row and Peterson), 1960.

194. Stewart and Bennett, 1991.

195. R. L. Kohls, *Survival Kit for Overseas Living* (Chicago: Intercultural Network/SYSTRAN, 1979), 22.

196. M. L. Borrowman, "Traditional Values and the Shaping of American Education," in J. H. Chilcott, N. C. Greenberg, and

H. B. Wilson, eds., *Readings in the Socio-Cultural Foundations of Education* (Belmont, CA: Wadsworth, 1968), 175.

197. L. Stevenson and D. L. Haberman, *Ten Theories of Human Nature*, 3rd ed. (New York: Oxford University Press, 1998), 4.

198. Ibid., 1998, 74–75.

199. Ibid., 1998, 28.

200. N. C. Jain and E. D. Kussman, "Dominant Cultural Patterns of Hindus in India," in *Intercultural Communication: A Reader*, 9th ed., L. A. Samovar and R. E. Porter, eds. (Belmont, CA: Wadsworth, 2000), 89.

201. L. D. Purnell, "Mexican Americans," in *Transcultural Health Care: A Culturally Competent Approach*, L. D. Purnell and B. J. Paulanka, eds. (Philadelphia, PA: F. A. Davis, 1998), 411.

202. J. R. Joe and R. S. Malach, "Families With Native American Roots," in *Developing Cross-Cultural Competence*, 2nd ed., E. W. Lynch and M. J. Hanson, eds. (Baltimore: Paul H. Brookes, 1998), 137.

203. *Newsweek*, 5 June 1989, 71.

204. Haviland, 2002, 479.

205. N. J. Adler, *International Dimensions of Organizational Behavior* (Boston: PWS-Kent, 1991), 24–25.

206. Ibid., 32.

207. E. R. Curtius, *The Civilization of France* (New York: Random House, 1962), 221.

208. Ibid., 222.

209. A. C. Wilson, "American Indian History or Non-Indian Perceptions of American History?" in *Natives and Academics: Researching and Writing About American Indians*, D. A. Mihesuah, ed. (Lincoln, NE: University of Nebraska Press, 1998), 24.

210. Trompenaars and Hampden-Turner, 1998, 142.

211. Lewis, 2000, 65.

212. Ting-Toomey, 1999, 62.

213. Luckmann, 1999, 31.

214. N. J. Adler and M. Jelinek, "Is 'Organization Culture' Culture Bound?" in *Culture, Communication and Conflict: Readings in Intercultural Relations*, 2nd ed., G. R. Weaver, ed. (Boston: Pearson, 2000), 130.

215. Gannon, 2001, 89.

216. Kim, 2001, 115.

217. Gannon, 2001, 301.

218. R. Newman, "The Virtues of Silence," *Time*, June 2, 1997, 15.

219. Hecht, Collier, and Ribeau, 1993, 102–103.

220. L. Skow and L. A. Samovar, "Cultural Patterns of the Maasai," in *Intercultural Communication: A Reader*, 8th ed., L. A. Samovar and R. E. Porter, eds. (Belmont, CA: Wadsworth, 1997), 110.

221. E. T. Hall, *Beyond Culture* (Garden City, NY: Doubleday, 1976), 7.

222. Ibid., 74.

223. E. T. Hall and M. R. Hall, *Understanding Cultural Differences: Germans, French and Americans* (Yarmouth, ME: Intercultural Press, 1990), 6.

224. Ibid., 1990.

225. Hofstede, 2001, 30.

226. Hall and Hall, 1990.

227. Gannon, 2001, 9.

228. P. Andersen, "Cues of Culture: The Basis of Intercultural Differences in Nonverbal Communication," in *Intercultural Communication: A Reader*, 8th ed., L. A. Samovar and R. E. Porter, eds. (Belmont, CA: Wadsworth, 1997), 253.

229. Foster, 1992, 280.

230. Gudykunst, 2001, 32; Hall and Hall, 1990.

231. Hall and Hall, 1990.

232. Lynch, 1998, 69.

233. Althen, 1988, 27.

234. S. Ting-Toomey, "Managing Intercultural Conflicts Effectively," in *Intercultural Communication: A Reader*, 8th ed., L. A. Samovar and R. E. Porter, eds. (Belmont, CA: Wadsworth, 1997), 394.

235. Harris and Moran, 1996, 25.

Notes For Chapter 3

1. "Racist Sect, Activists Square Off at Rally," *San Diego Union-Tribune*, July 5, 1999, A-8.

2. Y. Ling-Ling, "Ethnic Strife Is Not a Geographically Distant Phenomenon," *San Diego Union-Tribune*, June 10, 1999, B-11.

3. J. Leo, "War Against Warriors," *U.S. News & World Report*, March 8, 1999, 16.

4. G. McKenzie, "Ethnic Rioting Calmed in Nigeria," *San Diego Union-Tribune*, February 5, 2002, A-14.

5. C. W. Dugger, "Toll Rises As Rampaging Hindus Burn Muslims Alive in India," *San Diego Union-Tribune*, March 1, 2002, A-3.

6. P. Marshall and L. Gilbert, *Their Blood Cries Out: The Untold Story of Persecution Against Christians in the Modern World* (Word Publishing, 1997).

7. S. P. Huntington, "The Clash of Civilizations," *Foreign Affairs*, 72 (1993), 22.

8. Ibid., 25.

9. F. P. Delgado, "The Nature of Power Across Communicative and Cultural Borders" (paper delivered at the Annual Convention of the Speech Communication Association, Miami Beach, FL, November 1993), 11.

10. J. G. Pankhurst and S. K. Houseknecht, "Introduction," in *Family, Religion and Social Change*, S. K. Houseknecht and J. G. Pankhurst, eds. (New York: Oxford University Press, 2000), 27.

11. F. Ajami, "The Ancient Roots of Grievance," *U.S. News & World Report*, April 12, 1999, 20.

12. J. M. Charon, *The Meaning of Sociology*, 6th ed. (Upper Saddle River, New Jersey: Prentice Hall, 1999), 27.

13. S. P. Huntington, *The Clash of Civilizations and the Remaking of World Order* (New York: Simon and Schuster, 1996), 128.

14. S. Kakar, *The Colors of Violence: Cultural Identities, Religion, and Conflict* (Chicago: The University of Chicago Press, 1996), 189.

15. S. P. Huntington, 1996, 21.

16. M. Guirdham, *Communicating Across Cultures* (West Lafayette, IN: Ichor Business Books, 1999), 63.

17. E. L. Lynch and M. J. Hanson, *Developing Cross-Cultural Competence: A Guide for Working with Young Children and Their Families* (Baltimore: Paul H. Brookes, 1992), 358.

18. N. Rapport and J. Overing, *Social and Cultural Anthropology: The Key Concepts* (New York: Routledge, 2000), 394.

19. Ibid., 404.

20. E. A. Hoebel and E. L. Frost, *Cultural and Social Anthropology* (New York: McGraw-Hill, 1976), 324.

21. B. J. Hall, *Among Cultures: The Challenge of Communication* (Orlando, FL: Harcourt College Publishers, 2002), 29.

22. R. H. Dana, *Multicultural Assessment Perspectives for Professional Psychology* (Boston: Allyn and Bacon, 1993), 9.

23. E. A. Hoebel, *Man in the Primitive World* (New York: McGraw-Hill, 1958), 159.

24. R. O. Olayiwola, "The Impact of Islam on the Conduct of Nigerian Foreign Relations," *Islamic Quarterly*, 33 (1989), 19–26.

25. For a summary of the elements associated with world view see: S. Ishii, P. Cooke, and D. Klopf, "Our Locus in the Universe:

Worldview and Intercultural Misunderstandings/Conflicts, *Dokkyo International Review*, 12 (1999), 301–317.

26. D. L. Pennington, "Intercultural Communication," in *Intercultural Communication: A Reader*, 4th ed., L. A. Samovar and R. E. Porter, eds. (Belmont, CA: Wadsworth, 1985), 32.

27. T. Bianquis, *A History of the Family*, Vol. 4, A. Burguiere, gen. ed. (Cambridge, MA: Harvard University Press, 1996), 618.

28. R. Bartels, "National Culture-Business Relations: United States and Japan Contrasted," *Management International Review*, 2 (1982), 5.

29. W. S. Howell, *The Empathic Communicator* (Belmont, CA: Wadsworth, 1982), 223.

30. P. Gold, *Navajo and Tibetan Sacred Wisdom: The Circle of the Spirit* (Rochester, VT: Inner Traditions, 1994), 60.

31. S. Nanda and R. L. Warms, *Cultural Anthropology*, 6th ed. (Belmont, CA: Wadsworth, 1998), 275.

32. W. A. Haviland, *Cultural Anthropology* (Fort Worth, TX: Harcourt Brace Jovanovich, 1993), 346.

33. M. D. Coogan, "Introduction, " in *The Illustrated Guide to World Religion*, M. D. Coogan, ed. (New York: Oxford University Press, 1998), 6.

34. W. A. Haviland, *Cultural Anthropology* (Belmont, CA: Wadsworth, 2002), 361.

35. S. Nanda, *Cultural Anthropology*, 5th ed. (Belmont, CA: Wadsworth, 1994), 349.

36. H. Smith, *The World's Religions* (New York: HarperCollins, 1991), 9.

37. M. Grondona "A Cultural Typology of Economic Development," in *Culture Matters: How Values Shape Human Progress*, L. E. Harrison and S. P. Huntington, eds. (New York: Basic Books, 2000), 47.

38. Haviland, 1993.

39. C. Lamb, "The Claim to Be Unique," in *Eerdmans' Handbook to the World's Religions*, R. PierceBeaver et al., eds. (Grand Rapids, MI: Eerdmans, 1982), 358.

40. A. W. P. Guruge, "Survival of Religion: The Role of Pragmatism and Flexibility" (paper presented at the Religious Studies Department, George Washington University, Washington, DC, November 1, 1995), 30.

41. R. L. Monroe and R. H. Monroe, "Perspectives Suggested by Anthropological Data," in *Handbook of Cross-Cultural Psychology: Vol. 1 Perspectives*, H. C. Triandis and W. W. Lambert, eds. (Boston: Allyn and Bacon, 1980), 259.

42. W. E. Paden, *Religious Worlds: The Comparative Study of Religion* (Boston: Beacon, 1994), 170.

43. "One Nation Under Gods," *Time*, Fall 1993, 62.

44. D. L. Carmody and J. T. Carmody, *In the Path of the Masters: Understanding the Spirituality of Buddha, Confucius, Jesus, and Muhammad* (New York: Paragon House, 1994), Preface.

45. Smith, 1991, 3.

46. K. Crim, *The Perennial Dictionary of World Religions* (New York: HarperCollins, 1989), 665.

47. Coogan, 1998, 9.

48. D. Crystal, *The Cambridge Encyclopedia of Language* (New York: Cambridge University Press, 1987), 384.

49. Ibid.

50. Crim, 1989, 624.

51. Haviland, 2002, 274.

52. Crim, 1989.

53. Paden, 1994, 96.

54. H. Smith, *The Illustrated World's Religions: A Guide to Our Wisdom Traditions* (New York: HarperCollins, 1994), 210.

55. Ibid., 387.

56. Ibid.

57. Ibid.

58. Coogan, 1998, 10.

59. J. J. Macionis, *Society: The Basics*, 4th ed. (Upper Saddle River, NJ: Prentice Hall, 1998), 319.

60. Coogan, 1998, 11.

61. F. Ridenour, *So What's the Difference* (Ventura, CA: Regal Books. 2001), 7.

62. J. Hendry, *Understanding Japanese Society* (New York: Routledge, 1987), 103.

63. Coogan, 1998, 13.

64. W. C. Smith, *Modern Culture From a Comparative Perspective* (New York: State University of New York Press, 1997), 32.

65. *Newsweek*, April 16, 2001, 49.

66. R. D. Hale, "Christianity," in *The Illustrated Guide to World Religions*, M. D. Coogan, ed. (New York: Oxford University Press, 1998, 54.

67. K. L. Woodward, "2000 Year of Jesus," *Newsweek*, March 29, 1999, 55.

68. D. S. Noss and J. B. Noss, *Man's Religions*, 7th ed. (New York: Macmillan, 1984), 412.

69. Hale, 1998, 77.

70. *Prime Time School Television: The Long Search* (Chicago, 1978).

71. Carmody and Carmody, 1994, 116.

72. Ibid.

73. M. P. Fisher and R. Luyster, *Living Religions* (Englewood Cliffs, NJ: Prentice-Hall, 1991), 228.

74. Smith, 1994, 212.

75. Woodward, 1999, 56.

76. H. T. Blanche and C. M. Parkes, "Christianity," in *Death and Bereavement Across Cultures*, C. M. Parkes, P. Laungani, and B. Young, eds. (New York: Routlege, 1997), 145.

77. Woodward, 1999.

78. Ibid.

79. B. Storm, *More Than Talk: Communication Studies and the Christian Faith* (Dubuque, IA: Kendall/Hunt, 1996).

80. Smith, 1994, 210.

81. Woodward, 1999, 55.

82. T. C. Muck, *Those Other Religions in Your Neighborhood: Loving Your Neighbor When You Don't Know How* (Grand Rapids, MI: Zondervan, 1992), 165.

83. Blanche and Parkes, 1997, 145.

84. Storm, 1996, 19.

85. Crim, 1989, 171.

86. C. Murphy, "The Bible According to Eve," *U.S. News & World Report*, August 10, 1998, 49.

87. Woodward, 1999, 58.

88. Ibid., 57.

89. Murphy, 1998, 50. 90. Ibid., 49.

91. Carmody and Carmody, 1994, 104.

92. D. Crystal, ed. *The Cambridge Factfinder* (New York: Cambridge University Press, 1994), 343.

93. Smith, 1991, 271.

94. C. S. Ehrlich, "Judaism," in *The Illustrated Guide to World Religion*, M. D. Coogan, ed. (New York: Oxford University Press, 1998), 16.

95. Fisher and Luyster, 1991, 175.

96. R. Banks, "The Covenant," *Eerdmans' Handbook to the World's Religions*, 278.

97. D. J. Boorstin, *The Creators* (New York: Random House, 1992), 43.

98. D. Prager and J. Telushkin, *The Nine Questions People Ask About Judaism* (New York: Simon and Schuster, 1981), 112.

99. Smith, 1991, 287.

100. *Prime Time School Television*, 1978.

101. Ehrich, 1998, 39.

102. C. Van Doren, *A History of Knowledge* (New York: Ballantine Books, 1991), 16. Smith, 1994, 193.

103. Prager and Telushkin, 1981, 29.

104. Ibid.

105. Boorstin, 1992, 39.

106. Van Doren, 1991, 16.

107. F. E. Peters, *Judaism, Christianity and Islam: The Classical Texts and Their Interpretation* (Princeton, NJ: Princeton University Press, 1990).

108. Crim, 1989, 732.

109. L. Rosten, *Religions of America* (New York: Simon and Schuster, 1975), 143.

110. Rosten, 1975.

111. P. Novak, *The World's Wisdom: Sacred Tests of the World's Religions* (New York: HarperCollins, 1994), 179.

112. Prager and Telushkin, 1981, 46.

113. Smith, 1994, 189.

114. Rosten, 1975, 575.

115. Smith, 1991, 267.

116. D. Belt, "The World of Islam," *National Geographic*, January 2002, 77.

117. J. Blank, "The Muslim Mainstream," *U.S. News and World Report*, July 20, 1998, 22.

118. J. L. Sheler, "Muslim in America," *U.S. News and World Report*, October 29, 2001, 51.

119. Belt, 2002, 76.

120. Noss and Noss, 496.

121. K. L. Woodward, "In the Beginning, There Were the Holy Books," *Newsweek*, February 11, 2001, 52.

122. C. Van Doren, 1991, 20.

123. M. S. Gordon, "Islam," in *The Illustrated Guide to World Religion*, M. D. Coogan, ed. (New York: Oxford University Press, 1998), 92.

124. Ibid., 91.

125. J. J. Elias, *Islam* (Upper Saddle River, NJ: Prentice Hall, 1999), 61.

126. Ibid.

127. Gordon, 1998, 100.

128. Fisher and Luyster, 1991, 278.

129. Crim, 1989, 346.

130. Elias, 1999, 62.

131. Ibid., 63.

132. Ibid.

133. Ridenour, 2001, 80.

134. Fisher and Luyster, 1991, 281.

135. Elias, 1999, 64.

136. Fisher and Luyster, 1991, 282.

137. Elias, 1999, 64.

138. Ibid., 65.

139. Fisher and Luyster, 1991, 282.

140. Ibid., 289.

141. Gordon, 1998, 115.

142. Nydell, 1987, 91.

143. L. Schneider and A. Silverman, *Global Sociology: Introducing Five Contemporary Societies* (New York: McGraw-Hill, 1997), 165.

144. Gordon, 1998, 116.

145. Ibid., 1998.

146. Nydell, 1987, 91.

147. Gordon, 1998, 116.

148. Elias, 1999, 71.

149. Ibid., 73.

150. Gordon, 1998, 114.

151. Novak, 1994, 300.

152. J. L. Sheler, "Alive in the Presence of Their Lord," *U.S. News & World Report*, October 1, 2001, 38.

153. Gordon, 1998, 114.

154. Elias, 1999, 73.

155. Ibid.

156. K. Armstrong, *A History of God: The 4000-year Quest of Judaism, Christianity and Islam* (New York: Knopf, 1994), 344.

157. Sheler, 2001, 38.

158. Gordon, 1998, 114.

159. Sheler, 2001, 38.

160. Elias, 1999, 73.

161. Belt, 2002, 82–83.

162. Novak, 1994, 282.

163. Elias, 1999, 21.

164. C. Wilson, "The Quran," in *Eerdmans' Handbook to the World's Religions*, 315.

165. M. K. Nydell, *Understanding Arabs: A Guide for Westerners* (Yarmouth, ME: Intercultural Press, 1987).

166. Novak, 1994, 282.

167. M. I. Al-Kaysi, *Morals and Manners In Islam: A Guide to Islamic Abab* (United Kingdom: The Islamic Foundation, 1986).

168. Smith, 1991, 189.

169. A. M. Lutfiyya, "Islam in Village Culture," in *Readings in Arab Middle Eastern Societies and Cultures*, A. M. Lutfiyya and C. W. Churchill, eds. (Paris: Mouton, 1970), 49.

170. A. Esler, *The Human Venture*, 2nd ed. (Englewood Cliffs, NJ: Prentice-Hall, 1992), 257–258.

171. Ibid., 250.

172. Gordon, 1998, 122.

173. Elias, 1999, 105. See also Smith, 1994, 166–167.

174. Elias, 1999, 105–106.

175. Novak, 1994, 306.

176. Elias, 1999, 107.

177. Esler, 1992, 250.

178. Crim, 1989, 57.

179. L. Schmalfuss, "Science, Art and Culture in Islam," in *Eerdmans' Handbook to the World's Religions*, 328.

180. Esler, 1992, 80.

181. V. Narauaman, "Hinduism," in *The Illustrated Guide to World Religion*, M. D. Coogan, Ed. (New York: Oxford University Press, 1998), 126.

182. Boorstin, 1992, 5.

183. Ridenour, 2001, 89.

184. Narayanan, 1998, 130.

185. Boorstin, 1992, 4–5.

186. Crim, 1998, 785.

187. B. Usha, *A Ramakrishna-Vedanta Handbook* (Hollywood, CA: Vedanta Press, 1971) 79–80.

188. S. Prabhavanda and F. Manchester, *The Upanishads: The Breath of the Eternal* (Hollywood, CA: Vedanta Press, 1978), xvii.

189. Usha, 1971, 17–18.

190. R. Hammer, "The Eternal Teaching: Hinduism," in *Eerdmans' Handbook to the World's Religions*, 170.

191. R. S. Hegde, "Passages from Tradition: Communication Competence and Gender in India" (paper presented at the Annual Convention of the Speech Communication Association, Miami Beach, FL, November 1993), 5.

192. T. K. Venkateswaran, "Hinduism: A Portrait," in *A Source Book for Earth's Community of Religions*, J. D. Beversluis, ed. (Grand Rapids, MI: Co Nexus Press, 1995), 40.

193. Narayanan, 1998, 128–129.

194. G. Kolanad, *Culture Shock: India* (Portland, OR: Graphic Arts Center, 1994), 56.

195. Usha, 1971, 52.

196. Ibid., 1971.

197. R. Smart, "Religious-Caused Complications in Intercultural Communication," in *Intercultural Communication: A Reader*, 5th ed., L. A. Samovar and R. E. Porter, eds. (Belmont, CA: Wadsworth, 1988), 70.

198. Usha, 1991, 21–22.

199. N. Jain and E. D. Kussman, "Dominant Cultural Patterns of Hindus in India," in *Intercultural Communication: A Reader*, 9th ed., L. A. Samovar and R. E. Porter, eds. (Belmont, CA: Wadsworth, 2000), 83.

200. Hammer, 1982.

201. Jain and Kussman, 2000, 84.

202. Ibid., 2000, 85.

203. Smith, 1994, 21.

204. Jain and Kussman, 2000, 86.

205. N. Thera, *An Outline of Buddhism* (Singapore: Palelai Buddhist Temple Press, n.d.), 19.

206. R. Brabant-Smith, "Two Kinds of Language," *The Middle Way: Journal of the Buddhist Society*, 68 (1993), 123.

207. Smith, 1994, 68.

208. Thich-Thien-An, *Zen Philosophy, Zen Practice* (Emeryville, CA: Dharma, 1975), 17.

209. Van Doren, 1991, 21.

210. Crim, 1989, 124.

211. M. D. Echel, "Buddhism," in *The Illustrated Guide to World Religion*, M. D. Coogan, ed. (New York: Oxford University Press, 1998), 166.

212. Ibid., 1998, 165–166.

213. W. Rahula, *What The Buddha Taught* (New York: Grove, 1974), 1.

214. Rahula, 1974.

215. Fisher and Luyster, 1991, 103.

216. Crim, 1989, 264–265.

217. Rahula, 1974.

218. Smith, 1991, 99.

219. W. Metz, "The Enlightened One: Buddhism," in *Eerdmans' Handbook of the World's Religions*, 231–232.

220. A. Sole'-Leris, *Tranquility and Insight: An Introduction to the Oldest Form of Buddhist Meditation* (Boston: Shambhala, 1986), 14.

221. Rahula, 1974, 17.

222. Ridenour, 2001, 101.

223. Crim, 1998, 264.

224. Ibid., 1998, 540.

225. Ibid., 1998, 540–541.

226. Smith, 1994, 71.

227. Sole'-Leris, 1986, 17.

228. Eckel, 1998, 171.

229. Rahula, 1974, 45.

230. Sole'-Leris, 1986, 19.

231. Fisher and Luyster, 1991, 110.

232. Rahula, 1974, 47.

233. Crim, 1998, 236.

234. Sole'-Leris, 1986, 19.

235. Ibid., 1986.

236. Fisher and Luyster, 1991.

237. Thich-Thien-An, 1975, 38.

238. Novak, 1994, 67.

239. B. Bodhi, *Nourishing The Roots and Other Essays on Buddhist Ethics* (Sri Lanka: Buddhist Publication Society, 1978), 7.

240. Smith, 1994, 68.

241. Oldstone-Moore, "Chinese Traditions," in *The Illustrated Guide to World Religion*, M. D. Coogan, ed. (New York: Oxford University Press, 1998), 200.

242. L. E. Harrison, "Promoting Progressive Cultural Change, in *Culture Matters: How Values Shape Human Progress*, L. E. Harrison and S. P. Huntington, eds. (New York: Basic Books, 2000), 296.

243. Crim, 1989, 188–189.

244. W. T. Barry, W. T. Chen, and B. Watson, *Sources of Chinese Tradition* (New York: Columbia University Press, 1960), 17.

245. Z. Lin, "How China Will Modernize," *American Enterprise*, 2 (1991).

246. Schneider and Silverman, 1997, 15.

247. Ibid., 1997.

248. J. O. Yum, "Confucianism and Interpersonal Relationships and Communication Patterns in East Asia," in *Intercultural Communication: A Reader*, 9th ed., L. A. Samovar and R. E. Porter, eds. (Belmont, CA: Wadsworth, 2000), 64.

249. I. P. McGreal, *Great Thinkers of the Eastern World* (New York: HarperCollins, 1995), 3.

250. Crim, 1989, 192.

251. J. Oldstone-Moore, 1998, 205.

252. Ibid., 212.

253. Smith, 1994, 110.

254. McGreal, 1995, 4.

255. M. J. Gannon, *Understanding Global Cultures: Metaphorical Journeys Through 23 Nations* (Thousand Oaks, CA: Sage Publications, 2001), 423.

256. Smith, 1994, 111.

257. Gannon, 2001, 424.

258. Smith, 1994.

259. Ibid., 110.

260. Yum, 2000, 70.

261. G. Chen and J. Chung, "The Impact of Confucianism on Organizational Communication," *Communication Quarterly*, 42 (1994), 97.

262. Novak, 1994, 120.

263. Gannon, 2001, 147.

264. G. Gao and Ting-Toomey, *Communicating Effectively with the Chinese* (Thousand Oaks: CA, Sage Publications, 1998), 75.

265. Yum, 2000, 70.

266. T. L. Friedman, "A War We Can't Win with Guns Only," *San Diego Union-Tribune*, November 28, 2001, B-8.

267. Ibid., 2001.

268. D. E. Brown, *Human Universals* (New York: McGraw-Hill, 1991).

269. E. Y. Kim, *The Yin and Yang of American Culture* (Yarmouth, MA: Intercultural Press, 2001), 159.

270. Kim, 2001.

271. B. G. Farrell, *Family: The Making of an Idea, an Institution, and a Controversy in American Culture* (Boulder, CO: Westview Press, 1999), 5.

272. F. I. Nye and F. M. Berardo, *The Family: Its Structures and Interaction* (New York: Macmillan, 1973), 3.

273. K. M. Galvin and B. J. Brommel, *Family Communication: Cohesion and Change*, 3rd ed. (New York: HarperCollins, 1991), 1.

274. A. Swerdlow, R. Bridenthal, J. Kelly, and P. Vine, *Families in Flux* (New York: Feminist Press, 1989), 64.

275. Schneider and Silverman, 1997, 77.

276. W. B. Gudykunst, *Asian American Ethnicity and Communication* (Thousand Oaks, CA: Sage Publications, 2001), 6.

277. K. J. Christiano, "Religion and the Family in Modern American Culture," in *Family, Religion and Social Change in Diverse Societies*, S. K. Houseknecht and J. G. Pankhurst, eds. (New York: Oxford University Press, 2000) 43.

278. Al-Kaysi, 1986, 36.

279. A. Burguiere et al., *A History of the Family* (Cambridge, MA: Harvard University Press, 1996), 9.

280. K. K. Lee, "Family and Religion in Traditional and Contemporary Korea," *Religion and The Family in East Asia*, G. A. De Vos and T. Sofue, eds. (Berkeley, CA: University of California Press, 1986), 185.

281. K. A. Ocampo, M. Bernal, and G. P. Knight, "Gender, Race, and Ethnicity: The Sequencing of Social Constancies," in *Ethnic Identity: The Formation and Transmission Among Hispanic and Other Minorities*, M. E. Bernal and G. P. Knight, eds. (New York: State University of New York Press, 1993), 106.

282. Haviland, 2002, 243.

283. R. M. Berko, L. B. Rosenfeld, and L. A. Samovar, *Connecting: A Culture-Sensitive Approach to Interpersonal Communication Competency* (Fort Worth, TX: Harcourt Brace Jovanovich, 1997), 331.

284. Berko, Rosenfeld, and Samovar, 1997, 331.

285. G. L. Anderson, "The Family in Transition," in *The Family in Global Transition*, G. L. Anderson, ed. (St. Paul, MN: Paragon House, 1997), ix.

286. *Comparisons: Four Families* (Part I), film, I. MacNeill, writer and producer, National Film Board Production: McGraw-Hill Films, 1965.

287. M. McGoldrick, "Ethnicity, Cultural Diversity, and Normality," in *Normal Family Processes*, F. Walalish, ed. (New York: Guilford Press, 1973), 331.

288. M. McGoldrick, "Ethnicity and the Family Life Cycle," in *The Changing Family Life Cycle: A Framework for Family Therapy*, 2nd ed., B. Carter and M. McGoldrick, eds. (Boston: Allyn and Bacon, 1989), 69.

289. J. G. Pankurst and S. K. Houseknecht, 2000, 28.

290. Ocampo, Bernal, and Knight, 1993, 14.

291. L. D. Purnell and B. J. Paulanka, "Purnell's Model for Cultural Competence," in *Transcultural Health Care: A Culturally Competent Approach*, L. D. Purnell and B. J. Paulanka, eds. (Philadelphia, PA: F. A. Davis, 1998), 20.

292. M. Kim, "Transformation of Family Ideology in Upper-Middle-Class Families in Urban South Korea," *International Journal of Cultural and Social Anthropology*, 32 (1993), 70.

293. Ibid., 70.

294. W. R. Jankowiak, *Sex, Death, and Hierarchy in a Chinese City: An Anthroplogical Account* (New York: Columbia University Press, 1993), 166.

295. L. E. Davis and E. K. Proctor, *Race, Gender and Class: Guidelines with Individuals, Families, and Groups* (Englewood Cliffs, NJ: Prentice-Hall, 1989), 67.

296. Hendry, 1987, 5.

297. M. Ferguson, *Feminism and Postmodernism* (Durham, NC: Duke University Press, 1994).

298. E. S. Kras, *Management in Two Cultures* (Yarmouth, ME: Intercultural Press, 1995), 64.

299. C. H. Mindel and R. W. Habenstein, *Ethnic Families in America: Patterns and Variations*, 2nd ed. (New York: Elsevier Science Publishing, 1981), 275.

300. Schneider and Silverman, 1997, 71.

301. Gannon, 2001, 394.

302. Mindel and Habenstein, 1981, 276–277.

303. Dana, 1993, 70.

304. Gannon, 2001, 67.

305. Nanda, 1994, 137.

306. Anderson, 1997, 47.

307. S. K. Houseknecht, "Social Change in Egypt: The Roles of Religion and the Family," in *Family, Religion and Social Change in Diverse Societies*, S. K. Houseknecht and J. G. Pankhurst, eds. (New York: Oxford University Press, 2000), 79.

308. Al-Kaysi, 1986, 41.

309. R. Patai, *The Arab Mind* (New York: Scribner's, 1973), 28.

310. Patai, 1994, 31.

311. Ibid., 1994, 32.

312. Nanda and Warms, 1998, 221.

313. Lynch and Hanson, 1992, 161–162.

314. L. Veysey, "Growing Up in America, " in *American Issues: Understanding Who We Are*, W. T. Alderson, ed. (Nashville, TN: American Association for State and Local History, 1976), 118.

315. F. M. Moghaddam, D. M. Taylor, and S. C. Wright, *Social Psychology in Cross-Cultural Perspective* (New York: W. H. Freeman, 1993), 73, 98.

316. K. McDade, "How We Parent: Race and Ethnic Differences," in *American Families: Issues in Race and Ethnicity*, C. K. Jacobson, ed. (New York: Garland Publishing, 1995), 283.

317. N. Nomura, Y. Noguchi, S. Saito, and I. Tezuka, "Family Characteristics and Dynamics in Japan and the United States: A Preliminary Report from the Family Environment Scale," *International Journal of Intercultural Relations*, 19 (1995), 63.

318. Althen, 1988, 5.

319. Ibid., 50.

320. S. Wolpert, *India* (Berkeley, CA: University of California Press, 1991), 134.

321. J. W. Santrock, *Life-Span Development*, 4th ed. (Dubuque, IA: Wm. C. Brown, 1992), 261.

322. R. Beisanz et al., *The Costa Ricans* (Englewood Cliffs, NJ: Prentice-Hall, 1982), 88.

323. G. Asselin and Mastron, *Au Contraire! Figuring Out The French* (Yarmouth, MA: Intercultural Press, 2001), 62.

324. Gannon, 2001, 84.

325. Y. Richmond and P. Gestrin, *Into Africa: Intercultural Insights* (Yarmouth, ME: Intercultural Press, 1998), 3.

326. Schneider and Silverman, 1997, 73.

327. A. Valenzula, "Liberal Gender Role Attitudes and Academic Achievement Among Mexican-Origin Adolescents in Two Houston Inner-City Catholic Schools," *Hispanic Journal of Behavior Sciences*, August 15, 1993, 294.

328. R. Shorto, "Made-In-Japan Parenting," *Health*, 23 (1991), 54.

329. Shorto, 1991.

300. G. C. Chu and Y. Ju, *The Great Wall in Ruins: Communication and Culture Change in China* (Albany, NY: State University of New York Press, 1993), 9–10.

331. Nydell, 1989, 75.

332. Lutfiyya, 1970, 55.

333. Kim, 2001, 163.

334. H. Wenzhong and C. L. Grove, *Encountering the Chinese: A Guide for Americans* (Yarmouth, ME: Intercultural Press, 1991), 6.

335. Gannon, 2001, 259.

336. Hendry, 1987, 24.

337. T. Gochenour, *Considering Filipinos* (Yarmouth, ME: Intercultural Press, 1990), 19.

338. E. R. Curtius, *The Civilization of France* (New York: Vintage Books, 1962), 225.

339. Curtius, 1962, 226.

340. A. J. Rubel, "The Family," in *Mexican-Americans in the United States: A Reader*, J. H. Burma, ed. (New York: Canfield Press, 1970), 212.

341. O. Still and D. Hodgins, "Navajo Indians," *Transcultural Health Care: A Culturally Competent Approach*, L. D. Purnell and B. J. Paulanka, eds. (Philadelphia, PA: F. A. Davis, 1998), 430.

342. G. Arnold, "Living in Harmony: Makah," in *Stories of the People: Native American Voices*, National Museum of the American Indian, ed. (New York: Universe Publishing, 1997).

343. J. Campinha-Bacaote, "African-Americans," in *Transcultural Health Care: A Culturally Competent Approach*, L. D.

Purnell and B. J. Paulanka, eds. (Philadelphia, PA: F. A. Davis, 1998), 57.

344. J. M. Charon, *The Meaning of Sociology* (Upper Saddle River, NJ: Prentice-Hall, 1999), 202.

345. Anderson, 1997, 265.

346. J. Yerby, N. Buerkel-Rothfuss, and A. P. Bochner, *Understanding Family Communication*, 2nd ed. (Scottsdale, AZ: Gorsuch Scarisbrick, 1995), 63.

347. L. H. Turner and R. West, *Perspectives on Family Communication* (Mountain View, CA: Mayfield, 1998), 10.

348. Moghaddam, Taylor, and Wright, 1993, 125.

349. N. Murillo, "The Mexican Family," *Chicanos: Social and Psychological Perspective*, C. A. Hernandez, M. J. Hang, and N. N. Wagner, eds. (Saint Louis, MO: C. V. Mosby, 1976), 19.

350. Moghaddam, Taylor, and Wright, 1993, 124.

351. McGoldrick, 1973, 341.

352. R. Cooper and N. Cooper, *Thailand: A Guide to Customs and Etiquette* (Portland, OR: Graphic Arts Center, 1982), 83.

353. Kim, 2001, 181.

354. Ibid., 182.

355. A. Hunter and J. Sexton, *Contemporary China* (New York: St. Martin's Press, 1999), 150.

356. McGoldrick, 1973, 336.

357. Ibid., 1973.

358. Chu and Ju, 1993, 79.

359. Galvin and Brommel, 1991, 9.

360. Ibid., 9.

361. Smith, 1997, vii.

362. Y. Yu, "Clio's New Cultural Turn and the Rediscovery of Tradition in Asia" (keynote address presented to the 12th Conference of the International Association of Historians of Asia, June 1991), 26.

363. "How the Seeds of Hate Were Sown," *San Diego Union-Tribune*, May 9, 1993, G5.

364. *Time*, May 16, 1994, 63.

365. "Beautiful Dreamers Killed in California," *U.S. News & World Report*, March 25, 1996, 59.

366. B. Kerblay, Modern Soviet Society (New York: Pantheon, 1983), 271.

367. J. H. McElroy, *American Beliefs: What Keeps a Big Country and Diverse People United* (Chicago, IL: Ivan R. Dee, 1999), 51.

368. Ibid., 37.

369. Ibid., 1999, 220.

370. Van Doren, 1991, 224.

371. J. H. McElroy, *Finding Freedom: America's Distinctive Cultural Formation* (Carbondale, IL: Southern Illinois University Press, 1987), 65.

372. McElroy, 1987, 143.

373. R. G. Del Castillo, *The Treaty of Guadalupe Hidalgo: A Legacy of Conflict* (Norman, OK: University of Oklahoma Press, 1990), 4.

374. *U.S. News and World Report*, March 20, 1989, 9.

375. Ibid.

376. L. Bem, *The Lenses of Gender* (New Haven: Yale University Press, 1993).

377. S. E. Ambrose, *Undaunted Courage: Meriwether Lewis, Thomas Jefferson and the Opening of the American West* (New York: Simon and Schuster, 1996), 36.

378. Campinha-Bacote, 1998, 54.

379. R. Segal, *The Black Diaspora: Five Centuries of the Black Experience Outside Africa* (New York: Farrar, Straus, and Giroux, 1995), 56.

380. A. Esler, *The Human Venture*, 3rd. ed. (Upper Saddle River, NJ: Prentice Hall, 1996), 526.

381. E. Cose, "Slavery's Real Roots," *Newsweek*, October 26, 1998, 75.

382. M. Angelou, *Wouldn't Take Nothing for My Journey Now* (New York: Random House, 1993), 102.

383. Ibid., 102.

384. *Newsweek*, December 8, 1997, 63.

385. M. Marable, "An Idea Whose Time Has Come," *Newsweek*, August 27, 2001, 22.

386. *Newsweek*, December 8, 1997, 63.

387. S. Walker, *The Rights Revolution: Rights and Community in Modern America* (New York: Oxford University Press, 1998), 32.

388. M. P. Orbe and T. M. Harris, *Interracial Communication: Theory Into Practice* (Belmont, CA: Wadsworth, 2001), 42.

389. Chideya, *Don't Believe the Hype: Fighting Cultural Misinformation About African-Americans* (New York: Penguin, 1995), 47.

390. J. R. Feagin and M. P. Sikes, *Living Racism: The Black Middle Class Experience* (Boston: Beacon Press, 1994), 320.

391. R. V. Daniels, *Russia: The Roots of Confrontation* (Cambridge, MA: Harvard University Press, 1985), 55.

392. Esler, 1996, 668.

393. J. Kohan, "A Mind of Their Own," *Time*, December 7, 1992, 66.

394. Ibid.

395. F. Montaigne, "Russia Rising," *National Geographic*, November 2001, 8.

396. Ibid., 2001, 9.

397. J. Mathews and L. Mathews, *One Billion: A China Chronicle* (New York: Random House, 1983), 11.

398. S. Sangren, *History and Magical Power in a Chinese Community* (Stanford, CA: Stanford University Press, 1987), 3.

399. F. Fernandez-Armesto, *Millennium: A History of the Last Thousand Years* (New York: Scribner's, 1995), 44.

400. L. K. Matocha, "Chinese Americans," in *Transcultural Health Care: A Culturally Competent Approach*, L. D. Purnell and B. J. Paulanka, eds. (Philadelphia, PA: F. A. Davis, 1998), 164.

401. K. Scott Latourette, *The Chinese: Their History and Culture*, 4th ed. (New York: Macmillan, 1964), 22.

402. S. Ogden, *China's Unresolved Issues: Politics, Development, and Culture*, 2nd ed. (Englewood Cliffs, NJ: 1992), 19.

403. Ogden, 1992, 13.

404. Esler, 1992, 86.

405. C. Stafford, "Good Sons and Virtuous Mothers: Kinship and Chinese Nationalism in Taiwan," *Journal of the Royal Anthropological Institute*, June 27, 1992, 368.

406. Ibid.

407. Van Doren, 1991, 9.

408. F. Kaplan, J. Sobin, and A. Keijer, *The China Handbook*, 6th ed. (New York: Eurasia Press, 1985), 37.

409. Wenzhong and Grove, 1991, 1.

410. Ibid.

411. Huntington, 1996, 168.

412. Ogden, 1992, 5.

413. E. D. Reischauer, *The Japanese Today: Change and Continuity* (Cambridge, MA: Harvard University Press, 1988), 32.

414. Schneider and Silverman, 1997, 2.

415. E. D. Reishauer, *The United States and Japan*, 3rd ed. (New York: Viking Press, 1962), 101.

416. Scheider and Silverman, 1997, 2.

417. P. Tasker, *Inside Japan: Wealth, Work and Power in the New Japanese Empire* (London: Sidgwick and Jackson, 1987).

418. H. R. Hays, *From Ape to Angel: An Informal History of Social Anthropology* (New York: Knopf, 1965), 413–414.

419. Reischauer, 1988, 15.

420. Ibid., 1988, 15–16.

421. Del Castillo, 1990, xi.

422. C. McKiniss and A. Natella, *Business Mexico* (New York: Haworth Press, 1994), 70.

423. Schneider and Silverman, 1997, 60.

424. J. D. Cockcroft, *Mexico's Hope: An Encounter with Politics and History* (New York: Monthly Review Press, 1998), 13.

425. Schneider and Silverman, 1997, 60.

426. L. V. Foster, *A Brief History of Mexico* (New York: Facts On File, 1997), 2.

427. J. Norman, *Guide to Mexico* (Garden City: Doubleday, 1972) 53.

428. Cockcroft, 1998, 11.

429. Foster, 1997, 43.

430. Cockcroft, 1998, 19.

431. Foster, 1997, 65.

432. Ibid., 66.

433. Ibid., 96.

434. H. B. Parkes, *A History of Mexico*, 3rd ed. (Boston: Houghton Mifflin, 1969).

435. Foster, 1997, 111.

436. C. J. Johns, *The Origins of Violence in Mexican Society* (Westport, CT: Praeger, 1995), 202.

437. J. Eisenhower, "The War Nobody Knows," *On Air,* September 1998, 17.

438. Del Castillo, 1990, xii.

439. J. Samora and P. V. Simon, *A History of Mexican American People* (London: University of Notre Dame Press, 1977), 98.

440. Samora and Simon, 1977, 98.

441. Esler, 1996, 613.

442. O. Najera-Ramirez, "Engendering Nationalism: Identity, Discourse, and the Mexican Charro," *Anthropological Quarterly, 67* (1944), 9.

443. Foster, 1997, 156.

444. D. J. Weber, "Conflicts and Accommodations: Hispanic and Anglo-American Borders in Historical Perspective," *Journal of the Southwest,* 39 (1997), 1.

445. Gergen, D. "One Nation, After All," *U.S. News & World Report,* March 16, 1998, 84.

Notes for Chapter 4

1. M. Cartmill, "The Gift of Gab," *Discover,* November 1998, 56.

2. A. Dominguez, "Research: Gene Tied to Use of Language," *Las Vegas Review Journal,* August 15, 2002, 7A.

3. Cartmill, 1998, 56.

4. M. P. Orbe and T. M. Harris, *Interracial Communication: Theory into Practice* (Belmont, CA: Wadsworth, 2001), 50.

5. N. Rapport and J. Overing, *Social and Cultural Anthropology: The Key Concepts* (New York: Routledge, 2000), 88.

6. Rapport and Overing, 89.

7. R. D. Coertze, "Intercultural Communication and Anthropology," *South African Journal of Ethnology,* 23, nos. 2/3 (2000), 117.

8. Crystal, *The Cambridge Encyclopedia of Language,* 2nd ed. (Cambridge, NJ: Cambridge University Press, 1997), 10.

9. Ibid., 13.

10. Ibid., 12.

11. Ibid.

12. Ibid., 13.

13. Ibid., 38.

14. J. Edwards, *Language, Society, and Identity* (Oxford, UK: Blackwell, 1985), 15.

15. Crystal, 1997, 34.

16. *San Diego Union-Tribune,* February 13, 1997, A-20.

17. *Newsweek,* February 3, 1997, 4.

18. B. D. Rubin, *Communication and Human Behavior,* 3rd ed. (Englewood Cliffs, NJ: Prentice-Hall, 1992), 92.

19. B. Honig, *Handbook for Teaching Korean-American Students* (California Department of Education, 1992), 66.

20. California Department of Education, *Handbook for Teaching Vietnamese-Speaking Students* (California Department of Education, 1994), 29.

21. B. Honig, *Handbook for Teaching Filipino-Speaking Students* (California Department of Education, 1986), 27.

22. S. Nanda and R. L. Warms, *Cultural Anthropology,* 6th ed. (Belmont, CA: Wadsworth, 1998), 69.

23. I. C. Scott, "Differences in American and British Vocabulary: Implications for International Business Communication," *Business Communication Quarterly,* December 2000, 28.

24. C. L. Cutler, *Tracks That Speak: The Legacy of Native American Words in North American Culture* (Boston: Houghton Mifflin, 2002).

25. P. Watson, "Lost in Translation," *Strategic Direct Investor,* September/October 2001, 84.

26. G. Swain, "How to Communicate with People Who Speak English as a Second Language (ESL)," *Et Cetera,* Summer 2000, 140.12.

27. E. M. Rogers and T. M. Steinfatt, *Intercultural/Communication* (Prospect Heights, IL: Waveland Press, 1998), 135.

28. B. L. Whorf, *Language, Thought, and Reality: Selected Writings of Benjamin Lee Whorf,* I. B. Carrroll, ed. (Cambridge, MA: MIT Press, 1940/1956), 239.

29. D. G. Mandelbaum, ed., *Selected Writings of Edward Sapir* (Berkeley and Los Angeles: University of California Press, 1949), 162.

30. S. Nanda, *Cultural Anthropology,* 4th ed. (Belmont, CA: Wadsworth, 1991), 120.

31. Rogers and Steinfatt, 1998, 138.

32. Nanda, 1991, 121.

33. Crystal, 1997, 15.

34. C. Shea, "White Men Can't Contextualize," *Linguafranca* 11, no. 6 (2001), 44.

35. Ibid.

36. Ibid., 46.

37. Ibid., 47.

38. Ibid., 49.

39. I. Reineke, *Language and Dialect in Hawaii* (Honolulu: University of Hawaii Press, 1969), 28–30.

40. W. Sloane, "Lapps' Ski-Doos Put Rudolph in Back Seat," *Christian Science Monitor,* December 7, 1995, 7.

41. Ibid.

42. W. V. Ruch, *International/ Handbook of Corporate Communication* (Jefferson, NC: McFarland, 1989), 174.

43. E. Chaika, *Language: The Social Mirror,* 2nd ed. (New York: Newbury House, 1989).

44. C. Arensberg and A. Nichoff, *Introducing Social Change: A Manual for Americans Overseas* (Chicago: Aldine, 1964), 30.

45. Y. Richmond and P. Gestrin, *Into Africa: Intercultural Insights* (Yarmouth, ME: Intercultural Press, 1998), 85.

46. E. S. Kashima and Y. Kashima, "Culture and Language," *Journal of Cross-Cultural Psychology,* 29 (1998), 461–487.

47. R. Ma, "Saying 'Yes' for 'No' and 'No' for 'Yes': A Chinese Rule," *Journal of Pragmatics,* 25 (1996a), 257–266.

48. Ibid., 260.

49. M. B. Marks, "Straddling Cultural Divides with Grace," *Christian Science Monitor,* November 15, 1995, 16.

50. R. Ma, "Language of Offense in the Chinese Culture: The Creation of Corrosive Effects" (paper presented at the 92nd Annual Convention of the Speech Communication Association, November 23–26, 1996b, San Diego, California).

51. M. Park and K. Moon-soo, "Communication Practices in Korea," *Communication Quarterly,* 40 (1992), 299.

52. Ibid., 398.

53. P. Matsumoto and M. Assar, "The Effects of Language on Judgments of Universal Facial Expressions of Emotion," *Journal of Nonverbal Behavior* 16 (1992), 87.

54. *Crystal,* 1997, 21.

55. Park and Moon-soo, 1992, 399.

56. Richmond and Gerstin, 1998, 75.

57. Ibid., 77.

58. A. N. Miller, "An Exploration of Kenyan Public Speaking Patterns with Implications for the American Introduction Public Speaking Course," *Communication Education* 51, no. 2 (2002), 58.

59. Ibid., 59.

60. Richmond and Gerstin, 1998, 77.

61. J. Knappert, *The A-Z of African Proverbs* (London, UK: Karnak House, 1989), 3.

62. K. Yankah, *The Proverb in the Context of Akan Rhetoric: A Theory of Proverb Praxis* (New York: Peter Lang, 1982), 71.

63. Richmond and Gerstin, 1998, 77.

64. A. Almaney and A. Alwan, *Communicating with Arabs* (Prospect Heights, IL: Waveland Press, 1982), 84.

65. J. C. Condon, *Interact: Guidelines for Mexicans and North Americans* (Chicago: Intercultural Press, 1980), 37.

66. A. Riding, *Distinct Neighbors: A Portrait of Mexico* (New York: Knopf, 1985), 8.

67. S. N. Weber, "The Need to Be: The Socio-Cultural Significance of Black Language," in *Intercultural Communication: A Reader,* 7th ed., L. A. Samovar and R. E. Porter, eds. (Belmont, CA: Wadsworth, 1994), 224.

68. B. Wallraff, "What Global Language?" *The Atlantic Monthly,* November 2000, 54.

69. Ibid., 54.

70. Ibid., 54.

71. *Newsweek,* October 23, 1995, 89.

72. D. M. Brown, *Other Tongue to English: The Young Child in the Multicultural School* (London: Cambridge University Press, 1979), 37.

73. Nanda and Warms, 1998, 78.

74. I. R. Carlo-Casellas, "Marketing to U.S. Hispanic Population Requires Analysis of Cultures," *National Underwriter,* January 14, 2002, 9.

75. L. R. Arpan and L. S. Arpan, "Hispanic Connections," *Business and Economic Review,* October–December, 2001, 3.

76. Ibid., 5.

77. Ibid., 6.

78. B. L. Shade, "Afro-American Cognitive Style: A Variable in School Success," *Review Educational Research,* 52 (1982), 219–244.

79. G. Smitherman, *Talkin That Talk: Language, Culture and Education in African America* (New York: Routledge, 2001), xii.

80. M. L. Hecht, M. L. Collier, and S. A. Ribeau, *African American Communication: Ethnic Identity and Cultural Interpretation* (Newbury Park: Sage, 1993), 5.

81. Smitherman, 2001, 19.

82. L. Iahn, *Muntu* (London: Faber and Faber, 1961), 125.

83. Smitherman, 2001, 199.

84. M. K. Asante, *Language, Communication, and Rhetoric in Black America* (New York: Harper and Row, 1972), x.

85. Hecht, Collier, and Ribeau, 1993, 86.

86. Smitherman, 2001, 204.

87. Nanda and Warms, 1998, 78.

88. Smitherman, 2001.

89. Hecht, Collier, and Ribeau, 1993, 85.

90. J. R. Rickford, "A Suite for Ebony and Phonics," *Discover,* 18 (1997), 3.

91. Crystal, 1997, 35.

92. Rickford, 1997, 3.

93. Ibid.

94. Smitherman, 2001, 23.

95. Rickford, 1997, 3.

96. Smitherman, 2001, 23.

97. Crystal, 1997, 35.

98. Rickford, 1997, 3.

99. Ibid.

100. Crystal, 1997, 35.

101. Smitherman, 2001, 24.

102. Crystal, 1997, 35.

103. Smitherman, 2001, 25.

104. Hecht, Collier, and Ribeau, 1993, 86.

105. Weber, 1994, 222.

106. Ibid.

107. Rogers and Steinfatt, 1998, 148.

108. Hecht, Collier, and Ribeau, 1993, 91; Weber, 1994, 224.

109. T. E. Garner and D. L. Rubin, "Middle Class Blacks' Perceptions of Dialect and Style Shifting: The Case of Southern Attorneys," *Journal of Language and Social Psychology* 5 (1986), 33–48.

110. D. Tannen, *You Just Don't Understand: Women and Men in Conversation* (New York: William Morrow, 1990).

111. L. Elium and D. Elium, *Raising a Daughter* (Berkeley, CA: Celestial Arts, 1994), 21.

112. S. Romaine, *Communicating Gender* (Mahwah, NJ: Lawrence Earlbaum, 1999), 153.

113. Tannen, 1990.

114. J. T. Wood, *Gendered Lives: Communication, Gender, and Culture* (Belmont, CA: Wadsworth, 1994).

115. Ibid., 142.

116. Ibid.

117. Ibid.

118. Ibid.

119. Ibid.

120. J. Holmes, "Hedges and Boosters in Women's and Men's Speech," *Language and Communication* 10 (1990), 185–202.

121. D. K. Ivy and P. Backlund, *Exploring Gender Speak* (New York: McGraw-Hill, 1994).

122. R. Lakoff, *Language and Woman's Place* (New York: Harper and Row, 1975).

123. B. Bate, *Communication Between the Sexes* (New York: Harper and Row, 1988); Holmes, 1990; J. T. Wood and L. F. Lenze, "Gender and the Development of Self: Inclusive Pedagogy in Interpersonal Communication," *Women's Studies in Communication* 14 (1991), 1–23.

124. Wood, 1994, 143.

125. Holmes, 1990.

126. Tannen, 1990; Wood, 1994.

127. Wood, 1994, 144.

128. E. Aries, "Gender and Communication," in *Sex and Gender,* P. Shaver and C. Hendricks, eds. (Newbury Park, CA: Sage, 1987), 149–176.

129. A. T. Beck, *Love Is Never Enough* (New York: Harper and Row, 1988); L. P. Steward, A. D. Steward, S. A. Friedley, and P. I. Cooper, *Communication Between the Sexes: Sex Differences and Sex Role Stereotypes,* 2nd ed. (Scottsdale, AZ: Gorsuch Scarisbrick, 1990).

130. Wood, 1994, 144.

131. Ibid., 145.

132. Romaine, 1999, 165.

133. E. Folb, "Vernacular Vocabulary: A View of Interracial Perceptions and Experiences," in *Intercultural Communication: A*

Reader, 2nd ed., L. A. Samovar and R. E. Porter, Ed., (Belmont, CA: Wadsworth, 1976), 194.

134. "Learning American Lingo," *Christian Science Monitor*, October 24, 1995, 2.

135. D. Altman, "For Chinese Women's Ears Only: A Secret Language of Sisterhood Nears Extinction," *The Christian Science Monitor*, October 11, 1995, 14.

136. Ibid.

137. A. Rich, *Interracial Communication* (New York: Harper and Row, 1974), 142.

138. L. A. Samovar and F. Sanders, "Language Patterns of the Prostitute: Some Insights into a Deviant Subculture," *ETC: A Review of General Semantics*, 34 (1978), 34.

139. E. C. Stewart and M. I. Bennett, *American Cultural Patterns: A Cross-Cultural Perspective* (Yarmouth, ME: Intercultural Press, 1991), 45.

140. I. Hernandez, "Computers and Translation: Translation Software," *Translation Review* 47 (1995), 55.

141. R. Schulte, "Editorial: The Reviewing of Translations: A Growing Crisis," *Translation Review* 48–49 (1995), 1.

142. E. A. Nida, *Toward a Science of Translating* (Leiden: E.I. Brill, 1964), 160.

143. I. deWard and E. A. Nida, *From One Language to Another: Functional Equivalnce in Bible Translating* (Nashville: Thomas Nelson, 1986).

144. M. Shuttleworth and M. Cowie, *Dictionary of Translation Studies* (Manchester: St. Jerome Publishing, 1997).

145. N. B. R. Reeves, "Translating and Interpreting as Cultural Intermediation: Some Theoretical Issues Reconsidered," in *Translation and Interpreting: Bridging East and West*, R. K. Seymour and C. C. Liu, eds. (Honolulu: University of Hawaii Press, 1994), 33–50.

146. T. Givron, *Mind, Code and Context: Essays in Pragmatics* (Hillsdale, NJ: Lawrence Earlbaum, 1989), 350–351.

147. Reeves, 1994.

148. J. Seidel and W. McMordie, *English Idioms and How to Use Them* (Oxford: Oxford University Press, 1978), 4.

149. S. Basset-McGuire, *Translation Studies* (New York: Methuen, 1980), 28.

150. Honig, 1992, 32.

151. T. Ogawa, "Translation as a Cultural-Philosophical Problem: Toward a Phenomenology of Culture," *Monist* 78 (1995), 18–29.

152. T. Tymoczko, "Translation and Meaning," in *Meaning and Translation: Philosophical and Linguistic Approaches*, F. Guenthner and M. Guenthner-Reutter, eds. (New York: New York University Press, 1978), 20–43.

153. H. C. Triandis, " Approaches Toward Minimizing Translation," in *Translation Applications and Research*, R. Brislin, ed. (New York: Gardner, 1976), 229–243.

154. Ibid.

155. Reeves, 1994, 41.

Notes for Chapter 5

1. D. C. Barnlund, *Interpersonal Communication: Survey and Studies* (Boston: Houghton Mifflin, 1968), 536–537.

2. M. P. Keeley and A. J. Hart, "Nonverbal Behavior in Dyadic Interaction," in *Understanding Relationship Processes, 4: Dynamics of Relationships*, S. W. Duck, ed. (Thousand Oaks, CA: Sage, 1994), 135–161.

3. L. K. Guerrero, J. A. DeVito and M. L. Hecht, *The Nonverbal Communication Reader: Classic and Contemporary Readings*, 2nd ed. (Prospect, IL: Waveland Press, 1999), 1.

4. J. K. Burgoon, D. B. Buller, and W. G. Woodall, *Nonverbal Communication: The Unspoken Dialogue* (New York: Harper and Row, 1989), 9–10.

5. N. Pauronit, "The Role of Verbal/Nonverbal Cues in the Formation of First Impressions of Black and White Counselors," *Journal of Counseling Psychology*, 29 (1982), 371–378.

6. Guerro, DeVito, and Hecht, 1999, 9.

7. Ibid., 1999, 1.

8. E. Goffman, *The Presentation of Self in Everyday Life* (New York: Doubleday, 1957), 2.

9. L. A. Malandro and L. L. Barker, *Nonverbal Communication* (Reading, MA: Addison-Wesley, 1983), 13–15; see also P. Ekman and W. Friesen, "The Repertoire of Nonverbal Behavior: Categories, Origins, Usage and Coding," *Simiotica*, 1 (1969), 49–98.

10. J. T. Wood, *Communication Mosaics: A New Introduction to the Field of Communication* (Belmont, CA: Wadsworth, 1998), 105.

11. S. Osborn and M. T. Motley, *Improving Communication* (Boston: Houghton Mifflin, 1999), 50.

12. J. K. Burgoon, D. B. Buller, and W. G. Woodall, *Nonverbal Communication: The Unspoken Dialogue*, 2nd ed. (New York: McGraw-Hill, 1996), 5.

13. P. C. Rosenblatt, "Grief In Small-Scale Societies," in *Death and Bereavement Across Cultures*, C. M. Parks, P. Laungani, and B. Young, eds., (New York: Routledge, 1997) 36.

14. D. G. Leathers, *Successful Nonverbal Communication: Principles and Applications*, 2nd ed. (New York: Macmillan, 1992), 355–356.

15. E. T. Hall, *The Silent Language* (New York: Fawcett, 1959), 10.

16. P. Andersen, "Cues of Culture: The Basis of Intercultural Differences in Nonverbal Communication," in *Intercultural Communication: A Reader*, 9th ed., L. A. Samovar and R. E. Porter, eds. (Belmont, CA: Wadsworth, 2000), 258.

17. Andersen, 2000.

18. P. Ekman and W. Friesen, *Unmasking the Face: A Guide to Recognizing Emotions from Facial Expressions* (Englewood Cliffs, NJ: Prentice-Hall, 1975). Also see P. Ekman, R. Sorenson, and W. V. Friesen, "Pan-Cultural Elements in Facial Displays of Emotion," *Science*, 64 (1969), 86–88.

19. Burgoon, Buller, and Woodall, 1996, 23.

20. J. J. Macionis, *Society: The Basics*, 4th ed. (Upper Saddle River, NJ: Prentice Hall, 1998), 92.

21. P. A. Andersen, *Nonverbal Communication: Forms and Functions* (Mountain View, CA: Mayfield, 1999), 31.

22. "Obesity: A Heavy Burden Socially," *San Diego Union-Tribune*, September 30, 1993, A14.

23. J. Berg and K. Piner, "Social Relationship and the Lack of Social Relationships," in *Personal Relationship and Support*, S. W. Duck and R. C. Silver, eds. (London: Sage, 1990), 104–221.

24. B. D. Ruben, *Communication and Human Behavior*, 3rd ed. (Englewood Cliffs, NJ: Prentice-Hall, 1992), 213.

25. E. Berscheid and E. Walster, "Beauty and the Best," *Psychology Today*, March 1972, 42–46.

26. L. A. Vazquez, E. Garcia-Vazquez, S. A. Bauman, and A. S. Sierra, "Skin Color, Acculturation, and Community Interest Among Mexican American Students: A Research Note," *Hispanic Journal of Behavioral Sciences*, 19 (1997), 337.

27. G. E. Codina and F. F. Montalvo, "Chicano Phenotype and Depression," *Hispanic Journal of Behavioral Sciences*, 16 (1994), 296–306.

28. F. Keesing, *Cultural Anthropology: The Science of Custom* (New York: Holt, Rinehart, and Winston, 1965), 203.

29. G. Griffen, "Laser Treatments Remove Immigrants Tattoos, Stigma, " *San Diego Union-Tribune*, June 26, 2001, E-7.

30. Malandro and Barker, 1989, 28–29.

31. Y. Richmond and P. Gestrin, *Into Africa: Intercultural Insights* (Yarmouth, ME: 1998), 45.

32. H. Wenzhong and C. L. Grove, *Encountering the Chinese* (Yarmouth, ME: Intercultural Press, 1991), 135.

33. M. S. Remland, *Nonverbal Communication In Everyday Life* (New York: Houghton Mifflin, 2000), 113.

34. Remland, 2000, 113–114.

35. N. Joseph, *Uniforms and Nonuniforms: Communication Through Clothing* (New York: Greenwood Press, 1986), 1.

36. Joseph, 1986, 211–212.

37. N. Dresser, *Multicultural Manners* (New York: Wiley, 1996), 58.

38. M. I. Al-Kaysi, *Morals and Manners in Islam: A Guide to Islamic Adab* (London, United Kingdom: The Islamic Press, 1986), 84.

39. T. Gochenour, *Considering Filipinos* (Yarmouth, ME: Intercultural Press, 1990), 59.

40. E. T. Hall and M. R. Hall, *Understanding Cultural Differences: Germans, French and Americans* (Yarmouth, ME: Intercultural Press, 1990), 53.

41. W. V. Ruch, *International Handbook of Corporate Communication* (Jefferson, NC: McFarland, 1989), 166–167.

42. E. McDaniel, "Nonverbal Communication: A Reflection of Cultural Themes," in *Intercultural Communication: A Reader*, 9th ed., L. A. Samovar and R. E. Porter, eds. (Belmont, CA: Wadsworth, 2000), 274.

43. Ruch, 1989, 242.

44. Al-Kaysi, 1986, 82.

45. S. M. Torrawa, "Every Robe He Dons Becomes Him," *Parabola* (Fall, 1994), 21.

46. Torrawa, 1994, 25.

47. M. L. De Fleur, P. Kearney, and T. G. Plax, *Fundamentals of Human Communication* (Mountain View, CA: Mayfield, 1993), 384.

48. H. Roberts, "The Exquisite Slave: The Role of Clothes in the Making of the Victorian Woman," *Signs*, 2 (1977), 554–569.

49. S. P. Morreale, B. H. Spitzberg, and J. K. Barge, *Human Communication: Motivation, Knowledge and Skills* (Belmont, CA: Wadsworth/Thomson Learning, 2001), 125.

50. S. Ishii, "Characteristics of Japanese Nonverbal Communication Behavior," *Communication*, 2 (1973), 163–180.

51. R. Cooper and N. Cooper, *Culture Shock: Thailand* (Portland, OR: Graphic Arts Center, 1994), 14.

52. G. Kolanad, *Culture Shock: India* (Portland, OR: Graphic Arts Center, 1997), 114.

53. G. Ness, *Germany: Unraveling An Enigma* (Yarmouth, ME: Intercultural Press, 2000), 93.

54. Remland, 2000, 229.

55. Ruch, 1989, 279.

56. Cooper and Cooper, 1994, 22–23.

57. For a more detailed account of posture and other nonverbal differences between males and females, see P. A. Andersen, 1999, 106–129; L. P. Arliss, *Gender and Communication* (Englewood Cliffs, NJ: Prentice Hall, 1991), 87; J. A. Doyle and M. A. Paludi, *Sex and Gender: The Human Experience*, 2nd ed. (Dubuque, IA: Wm. C. Brown, 1991), 235; J. C. Pearson, R. L. West, and L. H. Turner, *Gender and Communication*, 3rd ed. (Dubuque, IA: Wm. C. Brown, 1995), 126; L. P. Steward, P. J. Cooper, and S. A. Friedley, *Communication Between the Sexes: Sex Differences and Sex Role Stereotypes* (Scottsdale, AZ: Gorsuch Scarisbrick, 1986), 75.

58. M. L. Hecht, M. J. Collier, and S. A. Ribeau, *African American Communication: Ethnic Identity and Cultural Interpretation* (Newbury Park, CA: Sage, 1993), 102.

59. *San Diego Union-Tribune*, May 20, 1992, D4.

60. Andersen, 1999, 38.

61. "Arabic: The Medium Clouds the Message," *Los Angeles Times*, February 12, 1977.

62. D. Morris, P. Collett, P. Marsh, and M. O'Shaughnessy, *Gestures: Their Origins and Distribution* (New York: Stein and Day, 1979).

63. Dresser, 1996, 19.

64. R. G. Harper, A. N. Wiens, and J. D. Matarazzo, *Nonverbal Communication: The State of the Art* (New York: Wiley, 1978), 164.

65. E. W. Lynch, and M. J. Hanson, *Developing Cross-Cultural Competence*, 2nd ed., (Baltimore, MD: Paul H. Brookes, 1998), 74.

66. A. Falassi, and R. Flower, *Culture Shock: Italy* (Portland, OR: Graphic Arts Center, 2000), 42.

67. *Handbook for Teaching Korean-American Students* (Sacramento, CA: California Department of Education, 1992), 95.

68. M. K. Nydell, *Understanding Arabs* (Yarmouth, ME: Intercultural Press, 1987), 46.

69. Lynch and Hanson, 1998, 74.

70. Falassi and Flower, 2000, 42.

71. M. Kim, "A Comparative Analysis of Nonverbal Expression as Portrayed by Korean and American Print-Media Advertising," *Howard Journal of Communications*, 3 (1992), 321.

72. R. D. Lewis, *When Cultures Collide: Managing Successfully Across Cultures* (London: Niccholas, 2000), 138.

73. Ruch, 1989, 191.

74. See P. A. Andersen, 1999, 118; Pearson, West, and Turner, 1995, 127.

75. Hecht, Collier, and Ribeau, 1993, 112.

76. F. Davis, *Inside Intuition* (New York: Signet, 1975), 47. See also Ray L. Birdwhistell, *Kinesics and Context* (Philadelphia: University of Pennsylvania Press, 1970).

77. Ekman, "Face Muscles Talk Every Language," *Psychology Today*, September 1975, 35–39. Also see P. Ekman, W. Friesen, and P. Ellsworth, *Emotion in the Human Face: Guidelines for Research and an Integration of the Findings* (New York: Pergamon Press, 1972).

78. Andersen, 1999, 35.

79. R. E. Porter and L. A. Samovar, "Cultural Influences on Emotional Expression: Implications for Intercultural Communication," in *Handbook of Communication and Emotion: Research, Theory, Applications, and Contexts*, P. A. Andersen and L. K. Guerrero, eds. (San Diego, CA: Academic Press, 1998) 454.

80. D. Matsumoto, *Unmasking Japan: Myths and Realities About the Emotions of the Japanese* (Stanford, CA: Stanford University Press, 1996) 54.

81. Matsumoto, 1996, 18–19.

82. Kim, 1992, 321.

83. Wenzhong and Grove, 1991, 116.

84. R. E. Kruat and R. E. Johnson, "Social and Emotional Messages of Smiling," in *The Nonverbal Communication: Classic and Contemporary Reading*, 2nd ed., L. K. Guerro, J. A. De Vito, and H. L. Hecht, eds. (Prospect Heights, IL: Waveland Press, 1999), 75.

85. Nees, 2000, 93.

86. E. R. McDaniel, "Japanese Nonverbal Communication: A Review and Critique of Literature" (paper presented at the Annual Convention of the Speech Communication Association, Miami Beach, FL, November 1993).

87. Matsumoto, 1996, 54.

88. Dresser, 1996, 21.

89. Cooper and Cooper, 1994, 18.

90. Remland, 2000, 193.

91. Lynch and Hanson, 1998, 71.

92. Pearson, West, and Turner, 1995, 123.

93. "The Evil Eye: A Stare of Envy," *Psychology Today*, December 1977, 154.

94. M. E. Zuniga, "Families with Latino Roots," E. W. Lynch, and M. J. Hanson, *Developing Cross-Cultural Competence*, 2nd ed. (Baltimore, MD: Paul H. Brookes, 1998), 231.

95. J. H. Robinson, "Communication in Korea: Playing Things by Ear," in *Intercultural Communication: A Reader*, 9th ed., L. A. Samovar and R. E. Porter, eds. (Belmont, CA: Wadsworth, 2000), 74.

96. C. Segrin, "Interpersonal Communication Problems Associated with Depression and Loneliness," in *Handbook of Communication and Emotion: Research, Theory, Applications, and Contexts*, P. A. Andersen and L. K. Guerrero, eds. (San Diego, CA: Academic Press, 1998), 213.

97. D. Leathers, *Successful Nonverbal Communication: Principles and Applications* (New York: Macmillan, 1986), 42.

98. E. W. Lynch, "From Culture Shock to Cultural Learning," in *Developing Cross-Cultural Competence: A Guide for Working with Young Children and Their Families*, E. W. Lynch and M. J. Hanson, eds. (Baltimore, MD: Paul H. Brookes, 1992), 19–33.

99. K. S. Verderber and R. F. Verderber, *Inter-Act: Interpersonal Communication Concepts, Skills, and Context*, 9th ed. (Belmont, CA: Wadsworth, 2001), 140.

100. H. Morsbach, "Aspects of Nonverbal Communication in Japan," in *Intercultural Communication: A Reader*, 3rd ed., L. A. Samovar and R. E. Porter, eds. (Belmont, CA: Wadsworth, 1982), 308.

101. Dresser, 1996, 22.

102. Richmond and Gestrin, 1998, 88.

103. J. Luckmann, *Transcultural Communication In Nursing* (Albany, NY: Delmar, 1999), 57.

104. A. F. Meleis and M. Meleis, "Egyptian-Americans," in *Transcultural Health Care: A Culturally Competent Approach*, L. D. Purnell and B. J. Paulanka, eds. (Philadelphia, PA: F. A. Davis, 1998) 221.

105. Nydell, 1987, 45.

106. Nees, 2000, 93.

107. For a discussion of homosexual nonverbal communication see J. P. Goodwin, *More Man Than You'll Ever Be* (Indianapolis, IN: Indiana University Press, 1989).

108. "Understanding Culture: Don't Stare at a Navajo," *Psychology Today*, June 1974, 107.

109. L. D. Purnell, "Mexican-Americans," in *Transcultural Health Care: A Culturally Competent Approach*, L. D. Parnell and B. J. Paulanka, eds. (Philadelphia, PA: F. A. Davis, 1998) 400.

110. M. L. Knapp and J. A. Hall, *Nonverbal Communication in Human Interaction*, 3rd ed. (Fort Worth, TX: Harcourt Brace Jovanovich, 1992), 310.

111. M. LaFrance and C. Mayo, *Moving Bodies: Nonverbal Communication in Social Relationships* (Monterey, CA: Brooks/Cole, 1978), 188.

112. Morreale, Spitzberg, and Barge, 2001, 127.

113. For a more detailed account of gender differences in the use of eye contact and gaze see P. A. Andersen, 1998, 106–128; M. L. Hickson and D. W. Stacks, *Nonverbal Communication: Studies and Applications*, 3rd ed. (Dubuque, IA: Brown and Benchmark, 1993), 20; D. K. Ivy and P. Backlund, *Exploring Gender Speak: Personal Effectiveness in Gender Communication* (New York: McGraw-Hill, 1994), 226; Remland, 2000, 158–159; J. T. Wood, *Gendered Lives: Communication, Gender, and Culture* (Belmont, CA: Wadsworth, 1994), 164.

114. D. C. Herberg, *Frameworks for Cultural and Racial Diversity* (Toronto, Canada: Canadian Scholars' Press, 1993), 48.

115. J. D. Salinger, *The Catcher in the Rye* (New York: Grosset and Dunlap, 1945), 103.

116. Knapp and Hall, 1992, 230.

117. P. A. Andersen, 1999, 46–47.

118. Ibid., 78.

119. Dresser, 1996, 16.

120. J. Condon, *Good Neighbors: Communicating with the Mexicans* (Yarmouth, ME: Intercultural Press, 1985), 60.

121. C. Helmuth, *Culture and Customs of Costa Rica* (Westport: Greenwood Press, 2000), 61.

122. L. K. Matocha "Chinese-Americans," in *Transcultural Health Care: A Culturally Competent Approach*, L. D. Parnell and B. J. Paulanka, eds. (Philadelphia, PA: F. A. Davis, 1998) 184.

123. D. Rowland, *Japanese Business Etiquette* (New York: Warner, 1985), 53.

124. G. Kolanad, 1997, 118.

125. Morreale, Spitzberg, and Barge, 2001, 128.

126. B. Bates, *Communication and the Sexes* (New York: Harper and Row, 1988), 62. See also Pearson, West, and Turner, 1995, 129; Wood, 1994, 162–163.

127. Hecht, Collier, and Ribeau, 1993, 97. See also Burgoon, Buller, and Woodall, 1996, 230.

128. Leathers, 1986, 138–139. 129. F. B. Furlow, "The Smell of Love," in *The Nonverbal Communication: Classic and Contemporary Reading*, 2nd ed., L. K. Guerro, J. A. De Vito, and H. L. Hecht, eds. (Prospect Heights, IL: Waveland Press, 1999), 118–125.

130. C. Classen, "Foundations For An Anthropology of The Senses: Transgressing Old Boundries," *International Social Science Journal*, September 1997), 401–411.

131. Furlow, 1999, 119.

132. Dresser, 1996, 29.

133. Gochenour, 1990, 61.

134. Al-Kaysi, 1986, 84.

135. E. T. Hall, *The Hidden Dimension* (New York: Doubleday, 1966), 149.

136. V. P. Richmond, J. C. McCroskey, and S. K. Payne, *Nonverbal Communication in Interpersonal Relations*, 2nd ed. (Englewood Cliffs, NJ: Prentice Hall, 1991), 94–109. Also see M. L. Knapp and J. A. Hall, 1992, 331–352.

137. Burgoon, Buller, and Woodall, 1996, 226.

138. Ruch, 1989, 191.

139. Cooper and Cooper, 1994, 31–32.

140. Hecht, Collier, and Ribeau, 1993, 113.

141. M. Houston, "When Black Women Talk With white Women: Why Dialogues Are Difficult," in *Our Voices: Essays in Culture, Ethnicity, and Communication*, 2nd ed., A. Gonzalez, M. Houston, and Victoria Chen (Los Angeles, CA: Roxbury, 1997), 187–194.

142. A. W. Siegman and S. Feldstein, *Nonverbal Communication and Behavior*, 2nd ed., (Hillsdale, NJ: Laurence Erlbaum, 1987), 355.

143. Pearson, West, and Turner, 1995, 131. Also see Wood, 1994, 164–165; Ivy and Backlund, 1994, 162–163.

144. M. Argye, "Nonverbal Vocalizations," in *The Nonverbal Communication: Classic and Contemporary Reading*, 2nd ed., L. K. Guerro, J. A. De Vito, and H. L. Hecht, eds. (Prospect Heights, IL: Waveland Press, 1999), 144.

145. Al-Kaysi, 1996, 55.

146. L. Skow and L. Samovar, "Cultural Patterns of the Maasai," in *Intercultural Communication: A Reader*, 9th ed., L. A. Samovar and R. E. Porter, eds. (Belmont, CA: Wadsworth, 2000), 97.

147. Richmond, McCroskey, and Payne, 1991, 302.

148. McDaniel, 1993, 18.

149. Lynch and Hanson, 1998, 26.

150. D. Crystal, *The Cambridge Encyclopedia of Language* (New York: Cambridge University Press, 1987), 24.

151. Crystal, 1987. See also the literature review on accents and dialects by Argle, 1999, 143–144: H. Giles and A. Franklyn-Stokes, "Communication Characteristics," in *Handbook of International and Intercultural Communication*, M. Asante and W. B. Gudykunst, eds. (Newbury Park, CA: Sage, 1989), 117–144. Also see M. J. Collier, "A Comparison of Conversations Among and Between Domestic Culture Groups: How Intra- and Intercultural Competencies Vary," *Communication Quarterly*, 36 (1988), 122–124.

152. Andersen, 1999, 81.

153. W. A. Haviland, *Cultural Anthropology* 10th ed., (Belmont, CA: Wadsworth, 2002), 109.

154. W. B. Gudykunst, S. Ting-Toomey, S. Sudweeks, and L. P. Steward, *Building Bridges: Interpersonal Skills for a Changing World* (Boston: Houghton Mifflin, 1995), 325.

155. P. Andersen, "In Different Dimensions: Nonverbal Communication and Culture," in *Intercultural Communication: A Reader,* 10th ed., L. A. Samovar and R. E. Porter, eds. (Belmont, CA: Wadsworth, 2003), 239.

156. Condon, 1985, 60.

157. Ruch, 1989, 239.

158. Richmond and Gestrin, 1998, 95.

159. Hall and Hall, 1990, 38.

160. M. J. Gannon, *Understanding Global Culture,* 2nd ed., (Thousand Oaks: CA: Sage, 2001), 165.

161. Ibid., 122.

162. L. K. Matocha, 1998, 167.

163. McDaniel, 2000, 274.

164. D. N. Berkow, R. Richmond, and R. C. Page, "A Cross-cultural Comparison of Worldviews: Americans and Fijian Counseling Students," *Counseling and Values,* 38 (1994), 121–135.

165. Chen and Starosta, 1998, 96.

166. A. L. S. Buslig "Stop Signs: Regulating Privacy with Environmental Features," in *The Nonverbal Communication: Classic and Contemporary Reading,* 2nd ed., L. K. Guerro, J. A. De Vito, and H. L. Hecht, eds. (Prospect Heights, IL: Waveland Press, 1999), 243.

167. Hall and Hall, 1990, 91.

168. McDaniel, 2000.

169. L. A. Samovar, "Prostitution as a Co-Culture: Speaking Well for Safety and Solidarity, Part II" (paper presented at the Western States Communication Association Convention, Vancouver, 1999).

170. M. S. Remland, T. S. Jones, and H. Brinkman, "Interpersonal Distance, Body Orientation, and Touch: Effects of Culture, Gender and Age," *Journal of Social Psychology,* 135 (1995), 282.

171. Leathers, 1986, 236. Also see Andersen, 1998, 115; Remland, 2000, 157–160; Wood, 1994, 160–162; Pearson, West, and Turner, 1995, 121.

172. L. A. Siple, "Cultural Patterns of Deaf People," *International Journal of Intercultural Relations,* 18 (1994), 345–367.

173. N. Rapport and J. Overing, *Social and Cultural Anthropology: The Key Concepts* (New York: Routledge, 2000), 261.

174. K. L. Egland, M. A. Stelzner, P. A. Andersen, and B. H. Spitzberg, "Perceived Understanding, Nonverbal Communication and Relational Satisfaction," in *Intrapersonal Communication Proccess,* J. Aitken and L. Shedletsky, eds. (Annandale, VA: Speech Communication Association, 1997), 386–395.

175. A. Gonzalez and P. G. Zimbardo "Time in Perspective," in *The Nonverbal Communication: Classic and Contemporary Reading,* 2nd ed., L. K. Guerro, J. A. De Vito, and H. L. Hecht, eds. (Prospect Heights, IL: Waveland Press, 1999), 227.

176. Lewis, 2000, 53.

177. D. I. Ballard and D. R. Seibold, "Time Orientation and Temporal Variation Across Work Groups: Implications for Group and Organizational Communication," *Western Journal of Communication,* 64 (2000), 219.

178. Gannon, 2001, 222.

179. M. Argyle, "Inter-cultural Communication," in *Cultures in Contact: Studies in Cross-Cultural Interaction,* Stephen Bochner, ed. (New York: Pergamon Press, 1982), 68.

180. Lewis, 2000, 56.

181. Richmond and Gestin, 1998, 108.

182. Hall and Hall, 1990, 35.

183. E. Y. Kim, *The Yin and Yang of American Culture: A Paradox* (Yarmouth, ME: Intercultural Press, 2001), 115.

184. G. Asselin and R. Maston, *Au Contraire! Figuring Out The French* (Yarmouth, ME: Intercultural Press, 2001), 233.

185. R. Brislin, *Understanding Culture's Influence on Behavior* (Fort Worth, TX: Harcourt Brace Jovanovich, 1993), 211.

186. P. R. Harris and R. T. Moran, *Managing Cultural Differences,* 4th ed. (Houston TX: Gulf, 1996), 266.

187. Ruch, 1989, 278.

188. P. AbuGharbeih, "Arab-American," in *Transcultural Health Care: A Culturally Competent Approach,* L.D. Purnell and B. J. Paulanka, eds. (Philadelphia, PA: F. A. Harris, 1998), 140.

189. R. Levine, "Social Time: The Heartbeat of Culture," *Psychology Today,* March 1985, 35.

190. S. A. Wilson, "Irish -American," in *Transcultural Health Care: A Culturally Competent Approach,* L.D. Purnell and B. J. Paulanka, eds. (Philadelphia, PA: F. A. Harris, 1998), 357.

191. O. Still and D. Hodgins "Navajo Indians," in *Transcultural Health Care: A Culturally Competent Approach,* L.D. Purnell and B. J. Paulanka, eds. (Philadelphia, PA: F. A. Harris, 1998), 427–428.

192. N. J. Adler, *International Dimensions of Organizational Behavior,* 2nd ed. (Boston: PWS-KENT, 1991), 30.

193. E. T. Hall, *The Dance of Life: Other Dimensions of Time* (New York: Anchor Press/Doubleday, 1983), 42.

194. E. T. Hall, *The Silent Language* (New York: Fawcett, 1959), 19.

195. P. B. Smith and M. H. Bond, *Social Psychology Across Cultures: Analysis and Perspective* (Boston: Allyn and Bacon, 1994), 149.

196. F. Trompenaars and C. Hampden-Turner, *Riding the Waves of Culture: Understanding Diversity in Global Business,* 2nd ed. (New York: McGraw-Hill, 1998), 143.

197. Gannon, 2001, 101.

198. Smith and Bond, 1994, 149.

199. Dresser, 1996, 26.

200. Richmond and Gestrin, 1998, 109.

201. Ibid., 110.

202. K. Burgoon and T. Saine, *The Unspoken Dialogue: An Introduction to Nonverbal Communication* (Boston: Houghton Mifflin, 1978), 131.

203. J. Horton, "Time and the Cool People," in *Intercultural Communication: A Reader,* 2nd ed., L. A. Samovar and R. E. Porter, eds. (Belmont, CA: Wadsworth, 1976), 274–284. Also see A. L. Smith, D. Hernandez, and A. Allen, *How to Talk with People of Other Races, Ethnic Groups, and Cultures* (Los Angeles: Trans-Ethnic Education, 1971), 17–19.

204. D. Crystal, *The Cambridge Encyclopedia of Language,* 2nd ed. (New York: Cambridge University Press, 1997), 174.

205. C. Braithwaite, "Cultural Uses and Interpretations of Time," in *The Nonverbal Communication: Classic and Contemporary Reading,* 2nd ed., L. K. Guerro, J. A. De Vito, and H. L. Hecht, eds. (Prospect Heights, IL: Waveland Press, 1999), 164.

206. J. Wiemann, V. Chen, and H. Giles, "Beliefs About Talk and Silence in a Cultural Context" (paper presented at the Annual Convention of the Speech Communication Association, Chicago, 1986).

207. Lewis, 1999, 13.

208. D. C. Barnlund, *Communicative Styles of Japanese and Americans: Images and Realities* (Belmont, CA: Wadsworth, 1989), 142.

209. S. Chan, "Families with Asian Roots," in *Developing Cross-Cultural Competence* 2nd ed., E. W. Lynch, and M. J. Hanson, eds. (Baltimore, MD: Paul H. Brookes, 1998), 321–322.

210. A. Jaworski, "The Power of Silence in Communication," in *The Nonverbal Communication: Classic and Contemporary Reading,* 2nd ed., L. K. Guerro, J. A. De Vito, and H. L. Hecht, eds. (Prospect Heights, IL: Waveland Press, 1999), 161.

211. Ibid.

212. N. J. Adler, *International Dimension of Organizational Behavior* (Cincinnati, OH: South-Western, 1997), 217.

213. N. Jain and A. Matukumalli, "The Functions of Silence in India: Implications for Intercultural Communication Research" (paper presented at the Second International East Meets West Conference in Cross-Cultural Communication, Comparative Philosophy, and Comparative Religion, Long Beach, CA, 1993), 7).

214. R. L. Johannesen, "The Functions of Silence: A Plea for Communication Research," *Western Speech*, 38 (1974), 27.

215. Still and Hodgins, 1998, 427.

216. K. Basso, "'To Give Up Words:' Silence in Western Apache Culture," *Southwestern Journal of Anthropology*, 26 (1970), 213–230.

217. Pearson, West, and Turner, 1995, 134. Also see Doyle and Paludi, 1991, 226–228.

Notes for Chapter 6

1. A. Javidi and M. Javidi, "Cross-Cultural Analysis of Interpersonal Bonding: A Look at East and West," in *Intercultural Communication: A Reader*, 8th ed., L. A. Samovar and R. E. Porter, eds. (Belmont, CA: Wadsworth, 1997), 89.

2. G. Althen, *American Ways* (Yarmouth, ME: Intercultural Press, 1988), 10.

3. N. Dresser, *Multicultural Manners* (New York: Wiley, 1996), 151.

4. E. C. Stewart and M. J. Bennett, *American Cultural Patterns: A Cross-Cultural Perspective* (Yarmouth, ME: Intercultural Press, 1991), 160.

5. E. T. Hall and M. R. Hall, *Understanding Cultural Differences: Germans, French, and Americans* (Yarmouth, ME: Intercultural Press, 1990), 48.

6. Hall and Hall, 1990, 49.

7. L. Schneider and A. Silverman, *Global Sociology: Introducing Five Contemporary Societies* (New York: McGraw-Hill, 1997), 70.

8. E. Gareis, *Intercultural Friendships: A Qualitative Study* (New York: University Press of America, 1995), 27.

9. D. C. Barnlund, *Communication Styles of Japanese and Americans* (Belmont, CA: Wadsworth, 1989), 101–108.

10. Ibid., 117.

11. *U.S. News & World Report*, April 22, 1996, 66–67.

12. L. B. Nadler, M. K. Nadler, and B. Broome, "Culture and the Management of Conflict Situations," in *Communication, Culture and Organizational Processes*, W. B. Gudykunst, L. P. Stewart, and S. Ting-Toomey, eds. (Beverly Hills: Sage, 1985), 109.

13. Barnlund, 1989, 157.

14. H. Wenzhong and C. L. Grove, *Encountering the Chinese: A Guide to Americans* (Yarmouth, ME: Intercultural Press, 1990), 23.

15. R. Cooper and N. Cooper, *Culture Shock: Thailand* (Portland, OR: Graphic Arts Center, 1994), 86.

16. T. Gochenour, *Considering Filipinos* (Yarmouth, ME: Intercultural Press, 1990), 23.

17. Ibid., 25.

18. Ibid., 24.

19. B. Moeran, "Individual, Group and Seishin: Japan's Internal Cultural Debate, " in *Japanese Culture and Behavior*, rev. ed., T. S. Lebra and W. P. Lebra, eds. (Honolulu: University of Hawaii Press, 1968), 75.

20. J. Hendry, *Understanding Japanese Society* (New York: Routledge, 1987), 194.

21. Ibid., 43.

22. P. R. Harris and R. T. Moran, *Managing Cultural Differences* (Houston, TX: Gulf, 1979), 296.

23. W. V. Ruch, *International Handbook of Corporate Communication* (Jefferson, NC: McFarland, 1989), 273.

24. Schneider and Silverman, 1997, 9.

25. Gao and Ting-Toomey, 1998, 61.

26. G. Chen and X. Xiao, "The Impact of Harmony on Chinese Negotiations" (paper presented at the Annual Convention of the Speech Communication Association, Miami Beach, FL, November 1993), 4.

27. G. Chen, "A Chinese Perspective of Communication Competence" (paper presented at the Annual Convention of the Speech Communication Association, Miami Beach, FL, November 1993), 6.

28. A. Abdullah, "Understanding the Asian Workforce: The Malaysian Experience" (paper presented at the Twentieth Annual Conference of the Asian Regional Training and Development Organization, Jakarta, Indonesia, November 1993), 7.

29. J. Condon, *Good Neighbors: Communicating with the Mexicans* (Yarmouth, ME: Intercultural Press, 1986), 46.

30. Ruch, 1989, 75.

31. F. M. Moghaddam, D. M. Taylor, and S. C. Wright, *Social Psychology in Cross-Cultural Perspective* (New York: W. H. Freeman, 1993), 124.

32. S. Nanda, *Cultural Anthropology*, 5th ed. (Belmont, CA: Wadsworth, 1994), 142.

33. J. T. Wood, *Gendered Lives: Communication, Gender, and Culture* (Belmont, CA: Wadsworth, 1994), 80. See also J. C. Pearson, R. L. West, and L. H. Turner, *Gender and Communication*, 3rd ed. (Dubuque, IA: Brown and Benchmark, 1995), 168–171.

34. D. K. Ivy and P. Backlund, *Exploring Gender Speak: Personal Effectiveness in Gender Communication* (New York: McGraw-Hill, 1994), 48.

35. Ivy and Backlund, 1994, 48.

36. U.S. Department of Commerce (usembassy.state.gov/japan/wwwhec0184.html).

37. Ibid.

38. Ibid.

39. L. Estell, "I see London, I see France . . . ," *Incentive*, 175 (1), August 2001, 59.

40. Ibid., 59.

41. P. R. Harris and R. T. Moran, *Managing Cultural Differences: Leadership Strategies for a New World of Business*, 4th ed. (Houston: Gulf Publishing, 1996), 6.

42. J. E. Turner, "You're Not in Kansas Anymore," *Security Management*, 45 (11), November 2001, 91.

43. Ibid., 91.

44. "Managing a Multicultural Workforce," *Black Enterprise*, July 2001, Special Advertising Section, 121.

45. Harris and Moran, 1996, 19.

46. J. H. Bryan, "The Diversity Imperative," *Executive Excellence*, 16 (6), 1999.

47. J. A. Gilbert and J. M. Ivancevich, "Valuing Diversity: A Tale of Two Organizations," *Academy of Management Executive*, 14 (1), 2000, 94.

48. J. C. Scott, *Facilitating International Business Communication: A Global Perspective* (Little Rock, AR: Delta Pi Epsilon, 1996), 1.

49. J. C. Scott, "Developing Cultural Fluency: The Goal of International Communication Instruction in the 21st Century," *Journal of Education for Business*, January/February 1999, 140–141.

50. C. Gancel and C. Hills, "Managing the Pitfalls and Challenges of Intercultural Communication," *Communication World*, 15 (1) (1998), 24.

51. D. M. Miller, R. Fields, A. Kuman, and R. Ortiz, "Leadership and Organizational Vision in Managing a Multiethnic and Multicultural Project Team," *Journal of Management in Engineering*, November/December 2000, 18.

52. Harris and Moran, 1966, 210.

53. G. Hofstede, "Cultural Constraints in Management Theories," *Executive*, 7 (1993), 81–94.

54. R. Calori and D. Dufour, "Management European Style," *Academy of Management Executive*, 9 (3), 1995, 61–73.

55. S. Waddock, "The Emergence of Management Education in Central Europe," *Journal of Education for Business*, 72 (6), July/August 1997.

56. R. D. Lewis, *When Cultures Collide: Managing Successfully Across Cultures* (London: Nicholas Brealey, 1996), 108.

57. Ibid., 70.

58. Hofstede, 1993, 83.

59. Lewis, 1996, 71.

60. Ibid., 73.

61. Ibid., 111–112.

62. Hofstede, 1993, 84.

63. R. B. Peterson, *Managers and National Character: A Global Perspective* (Westport, CT: Quorum Books, 1993), 418.

64. Lewis, 1996, 75.

65. Ibid., 1996, 75.

66. Ibid., 1996, 109.

67. Hofstede, 1993, 86.

68. G. M. Chen, "An Examination of PRC Business Negotiating Behaviors" (paper presented at the annual meeting of the National Communication Association, Chicago, IL, November 1997, 6).

69. G. M. Chen and W. J. Starosta, "Chinese Conflict Management and Resolution: Overview and Implications," *Intercultural Communication Studies*, 7 (1996), 1–11.

70. Chen, 1996, 6.

71. R. Y. Hirokawa, "Improving Intra-organizational Communication: A Lesson from Japanese Management," *Communication Quarterly*, 30, Winter 1981, 35–40.

72. Peterson, 1993, 410.

73. R. Culpan and O. Kucukemiroglu, "A Comparison of U.S. and Japanese Management Styles and Unit Effectiveness," *Management International Review*, 33 (1993), 27–42.

74. Harris and Moran, 1996, 268.

75. Ibid., 1996, 269.

76. M. J. Marquardt and D. W. Engel, *Global Human Resource Development* (Englewood Cliffs, NJ: Prentice Hall, 1993), 232.

77. Ibid., 1993, 232.

78. Lewis, 1996, 80.

79. Ibid., 80.

80. Ibid., 1996, 81.

81. *San Diego Union-Tribune*, July 4, 1999, B-1.

82. G. K. Stephens and C. R. Greer, "Doing Business in Mexico: Understanding Cultural Differences," *Organizational Dynamics*, 24 (1995), 39–55.

83. Ibid.

84. T. Gray and B. Deane, "Launching a Diversity Market Effort," *Diversity Marketing Outlook*, Spring 1996, 3.

85. Stephens and Greer, 1995, 42–43.

86. T. Morrison, W. A. Conaway, and G. A. Borden, *Kiss, Bow, or Shake Hands: How to Do Business in Sixty Countries* (Holbrook, MA: Bob Adams, 1994), 232.

87. M. G. Weinbaum, *Egypt and the Politics of U.S. Economic Aid* (Boulder, CO: Westview, 1986).

88. D. Endicott, "Doing Business in Egypt," *Bridge*, Winter 1981, 34.

89. Y. Richmond and P. Gestrin, *Into Africa: Intercultural Insights* (Yarmouth, ME: Intercultural Press, 1998), 128–129.

90. Morrison et al., 1994, 58.

91. Ibid., 326.

92. K. B. Bucknall, *Kevin Bucknall's Cultural Guide to Doing Business in China* (Oxford, UK: Butterworth-Heinemann, 1994).

93. Harris and Moran, 1996, 256.

94. Bucknall, 1994.

95. Ibid.

96. Harris and Moran, 1996, 256.

97. Bucknall, 1994.

98. Morrison et al., 1994.

99. Acuff, 1993, 308.

100. Morrison et al., 1994, 208.

101. N. Dresser, *Multicultural Manners* (New York: Wiley, 1996), 94.

102. Morrison et al., 1994, 411.

103. Harris and Moran, 1966, 40.

104. E. Grundling, "How to Communicate Globally," *Training and Development*, 53 (6), June 1999.

105. D. Druckman, "Turning Points in International Negotiation," *Journal of Conflict Resolution*, 45 (4), August 2001, 519.

106. P. R. Kimmel, "Cultural Perspectives on International Negotiations," *Journal of Social Issues*, 550 (1), 1994, 401.

107. Ibid., 402.

108. Lewis, 1966, 116.

109. Kimmel, 1994, 406.

110. Ibid., 1994, 402–403.

111. D. A. Foster, *Bargaining Across Borders: How to Negotiate Business Successfully Anywhere in the World* (New York: McGraw-Hill, 1992), 35.

112. Morrison et al., 1994, 4.

113. Acuff, 1993, 219.

114. Lewis, 1966, 122.

115. Acuff, 1993, 52.

116. Kimmel, 1994, 395, 396.

117. Ibid., 396.

118. Ibid., 397.

119. Morrison et al., 1994, 131.

120. Acuff, 1993, 156.

121. Lewis, 1966, 116.

122. Ibid., 117.

123. Morrison et al., 1994, 370.

124. Ibid., 317.

125. Ibid., 131.

126. Ibid., 191.

127. Endicott, 1981.

128. Harris and Moran, 1996, 232.

129. Ibid.

130. Winsor, 1994, 20.

131. Malat, 1996, 44.

132. Richmond and Gestrin, 1998.

133. Acuff, 1993, 294.

134. Lewis, 1966, 124.

135. R. D. Lewis, *When Cultures Collide: Managing Successfully Across Cultures* (London: Nicholas Brealey, 1999), 21, 20.

136. M. Whigham-Desir, "Business Etiquette Overseas: The Finer Points of Doing Business Abroad," *Black Enterprise*, 26, 142–143.

137. Harris and Moran, 1966, 256.

138. S. D. Seligman, *Dealing with the Chinese: A Practical Guide to Business Etiquette in the People's Republic Today* (New York: Warner Books, 1989).

139. Morrison et al., 1994, 157.

140. Lewis, 1999, 20–21.

141. Ibid.

142. Ibid., 23.

143. Morrison et al., 1994.

144. Ibid.

145. Ibid.

146. Dresser, 1996, 104–105.

147. Foster, 1992, 210.

148. S. Weiss and W. Stripp, *Negotiation with Foreign Business Persons: An Introduction for Americans with Propositions of Six Cultures* (New York University/Faculty of Business Adminisration, February, 1985).

149. F. Fukuyama, *Trust: The Social Virtues and the Creation of Prosperity* (New York: Free Press, 1995), 26.

150. Ibid., 31.

151. Ibid.

152. Fletcher and Melewar, 2001, 10.

152. N. T. Tavassoli and J. K. Han, "Saying with Pictures: Branding in China," *Marketing News*, 36 (10), May 13, 2002, 30.

153. Ibid., 29.

154. Ibid.

156. Waddock, 1997.

157. *San Diego Union-Tribune*, July 4, 1999, B-1.

158. J. R. Carlo-Casellas, "Marketing to U.S. Hispanic Population Requires Analysis of Cultures," *National Underwriter*, 106 (20), 8–11.

159. *Sacramento Bee*, September 15, 1999, A-4.

160. D. B. Wood, "Monterey Spins Itself as Cultural Kaleidoscope," *Christian Science Monitor*, October 6, 1995, 11.

161. T. Gray and B. Deane, "Launching a Diversity Market Effort," *Diversity Marketing Outlook*, Spring 1996, 3.

162. Ibid.

163. Ibid.

164. B. R. Deane, "Nordstrom Sets the Pace," *Diversity Marketing Outlook*, Spring 1996, 8.

165. *Sacramento Bee*, October 1, 1999, F1.

166. L. Gornstein, "Mexican Retailers Take Stores North of Border," *Las Vegas Review-Journal*, June 15, 2001, 10B.

167. Davidhizar, Down, and Geiger, 1999.

168. "Managing a Multicultural Workforce," *Black Enterprise*, July 2001, 121.

169. D. Kunde, "Who Will Work as Boomers Retire?" *Sacramento Bee*, January 3, 2000, C1.

170. Fletcher and Melewar, 2001.

171. A. Austin, "How Cultural Diversity Will Shape Your Career," *Career World*, 28 (6), April/May 2000, 16–17.

172. Ibid.

173. Ibid.

174. Davidhizar, Down, and Geiger, 1999.

175. A. Bernstein and M. Arndt, "Racism in the Workplace," *Business Week*, 248 (17), 65.

176. D. R. Francis, "Bosses Kill Loyalty: What Happens Now?" *Christian Science Monitor*, November 24, 1995, 8.

177. R. Sandoval, "When Cultures Collide," *San Diego Union-Tribune*, December 18, 1995, E1–E2.

178. *San Diego Union-Tribune*, November 23, 1998, A-8.

179. *Providence Sunday Journal*, January 24, 1999, A-01.

180. D. A. Ondeck, "Sexual Harassment in the Workplace," *Home Health Care Management and Practice*, 12 (1), December 1999, 54.

182. Ibid.

183. Ibid.

184. L. A. Wertin and P. A. Andersen, "Cognitive Schemata and Perceptions of Sexual Harassment: A Test of Cognitive Valence Theory" (paper presented at the annual meeting of the Western Speech Communication Association, Pasadena, California, February, 1996).

185. *Columbian*, August 21, 1999, C-2.

186. *Times-Picayune*, September 8, 1999, C-6.

187. *Times-Picayune*, April 23, 1999, A-1.

188. Sandoval, 1995, E-2.

189. D. D'Souza, *The End of Racism* (New York: Free Press, 1995). ·

190. M. Land, "Where Diversity Survives Hard Times," *USA Today*, January 8, 1992, B-8.

191. S. Evans, "The Prudential," *Cultural Diversity at Work*, March 1992.

Notes for Chapter 7

1. Keohane and J. S. Nye, Jr., "Globalization: What's New? What's Not? (And So What?)," *Foreign Policy*, 118, Spring 2000.

2. K. Naidoo, "The New Civic Globalism," *Nation*, 270 (18), May 8, 2000.

3. J. Malveaux, "A Multicultural Globalism," *Black Issues in Higher Education*, 18 (24), January 17, 2002.

4. J. Holland, "Enhancing Multicultural Sensitivity through Teaching Multiclturally in Recreation," *Parks and Recreation*, 32 (5), May 1997.

5. B. R. Singh, "Multicultural Education: Education—Social Aspects," *Educational Review*, 4 (1), 1995, 11–25.

6. Ibid.

7. K. A. Bruffee, "Taking the Common Ground: Beyond Cultural Identity," *Change*, February 2002, 15.

8. B. R. Singh, 1995.

9. Ibid.

10. N. P. Stromquist and K. Monkman, *Globalization and Education: Integration and Contestation Across Cultures* (New York: Rowman and Littlefield, 2000), 21.

11. J. Tapia, "Living the Dream: The Cultural Model of Schooling in Latino Communities," *Latino Studies Journal*, 9 (1) Winter 1998, 9.

12. K. A. Bruffee, 2002, 14.

13. J. Henry, "A Cross-Cultural Outline of Education," in *Educational Patterns and Cultural Configurations*, J. Roberts and S. Akinsanya, eds. (New York: David McKay, 1976).

14. M. Saville-Troike, *A Guide to Culture in the Classroom* (Rosslyn, VA: National Clearinghouse for Bilingual Education, 1978).

15. S. Lu, "Culture and Compliance Gaining in the Classroom: A Preliminary Investigation of Chinese College Teachers' Use of Behavior Alteration Techniques," *Communication Education*, 46, January 1997, 13–14.

16. B. Honig, *Handbook for Teaching Japanese Speaking Students* (Sacramento, CA: California State Department of Education, 1987), 10.

17. M. J. White, *The Japanese Educational Challenge: A Commitment to Children* (New York: Free Press, 1987), 150.

18. Honig, 1987, 17.

19. B. Honig, *Handbook for Teaching Korean-American Students* (Sacramento, CA: California Department of Education, 1992), 25.

20. Ibid., 23.

21. H. Grossman, *Educating Hispanic Students: Cultural Implications for Instruction, Classroom Management, Counseling, and Assessment* (Springfield, IL: Charles C. Thomas, 1984).

22. Ibid., 85.

23. *U.S. News & World Report*, September 9, 1997.

24. S. Ting-Toomey, *Communicating Across Cultures* (New York: Guilford Press, 1999), 216–217.

25. Grossman, 1984.

26. S. Headden, "One Nation, One Language," *U.S. News & World Report*, September 25, 1995, 38–42.

27. U.S. Census Bureau (http://www.census.gov/population/estimation/nation/intfile3-1.txt), August 27, 1999.

28. B. R. Singh, 1995.

29. *Sacramento Bee*, April 28, 1999, E-2.

30. *Newsweek*, December 2, 1996, 55.

31. K. A. Burfee, 2002, 12.

32. G. M. Chen and W. J. Starosta, *Foundations of Intercultural Communication* (Needham Heights, MA: Allyn and Bacon, 1998), 226.

33. R. E. Hirshon, "Excellence and Diversity," *ABA Journal*, 88 (6), June 2002.

34. G. Althen, *American Ways: A Guide for Foreigners in the United States* (Yarmouth, ME: Intercultural Press, 1988), 54.

35. C. Calloway-Thomas, P. J. Cooper, and C. Blake, *Intercultural Communication: Roots and Routes* (Boston: Allyn and Bacon, 1999), 193.

36. Ibid., 194.

37. D. Ravitch, "Multiculural: E Pluribus Plures," *American Scholar*, 59 (1990), 163–174.

38. J. Holland, 1997.

39. G. Gay, *Culturally Responsive Teaching: Theory, Research, and Practice* (New York: Teachers College Press, 2000), 111.

40. Bilingual Education Office, *Individual Learning Programs for Limited-English Proficient Students: A Handbook for School Personnel* (Sacramento, CA: California Department of Education, 1984), 5.

41. L. B. Clegg, E. Miller, and W. Vanderhoff, Jr., *Celebrating Diversity: A Multicultural Resource* (New York: Delmar, 1995).

42. C. Letherman, "The Minefield of Diversity," *Chronicle of Higher Education*, April 1, 1996, 57–60.

43. J. M. Schrof, "What Kids Have to Know," *U.S. News & World Report*, April 1, 1996, 57–60.

44. J. Holland, 1997.

45. Calloway-Thomas et al., 1999, 199.

46. Ibid., 198.

47. E. R. Hollins, J. E. King, and W. C. Haymen, *Teaching Diverse Populations: Formulating a Knowledge Base* (New York: State University of New York Press, 1994).

48. Calloway-Thomas et al., 1999, 199.

49. G. Gay, 2000, 147.

50. Calloway-Thomas et al., 1999, 199.

51. D. M. Gollnick and P. C. Chinn, *Multicultural Education in a Pluralistic Society* (New York: Macmillan, 1994), 306.

52. B. P. Leung, "Culture as a Study of Differential Minority Student Achievement," *Journal of Educational Issues of Language Majority Students*, 13 (1994).

53. J. C. Kush, "Field-Dependence, Cognitive Ability, and Academic Achievement in Anglo American and Mexican American Students," *Journal of Cross-Cultural Psychology*, 27 (5), September 1996, 563.

54. Gollnick and Chinn, 1994, 307.

55. Grossman, 1984.

56. Hollins, King, and Haymen, 1994, 19.

57. L. M. Cleary and T. D. Peacock, *Collected Wisdom: American Indian Education* (Boston: Allyn and Bacon, 1998).

58. H. Grossman, *Teaching in a Diverse Society* (Boston: Allyn and Bacon, 1995), 270.

59. Cleary and Peacock, 1998.

60. B. J. Shade, C. Kelly, and M. Oberg, *Creating Culturally Responsive Classrooms* (Washington, D.C: American Psychological Association, 1997), 23.

61. Cleary and Peacock, 1998.

62. Althen, 1988, 129.

63. N. Dresser, *Multicultural Manners: New Rules of Etiquette for a Changing Society* (New York: Wiley and Sons, 1996), 42.

64. Althen, 1988, 128.

65. Ibid.

66. S. Nieto, *Affirming Diversity: The Sociopolitical Context of Multicultural Education* (New York: Longman, 1992), 115.

67. Dresser, 1996, 39.

68. K. H. Au, *Literacy Instruction in Multicultural Settings* (New York: Harcourt Brace Jovanovich, 1993), 96.

69. Ibid.

70. Grossman, 1995, 265.

71. Gollnick and Chinn, 1994, 306.

72. Grossman, 1995.

73. Grossman, 1984.

74. Cleary and Peacock, 1998.

75. Ibid., 160.

76. Grossman, 1995, 269.

77. C. L. Hallman, M. R. Etienne, and S. Fradd, "Haitian Value Orientations," Monograph Number 2, August 1992, ERIC ED 269–532.

78. Grossman, 1995.

79. M. E. Franklin, "Culturally Sensitive Instructional Practices for African-American Learners with Disabilities," *Exceptional Children*, 59 (1992), 115–122.

80. E. L. Yao, "Asian-Immigrant Students—Unique Problems That Hamper Learning," *NASSP Bulletin*, 71 (1987), 82–88.

81. Grossman, 1995.

82. Ibid., 273.

83. White, 1987.

84. B. J. Walker, J. Dodd, and R. Bigelow, "Learning Preferences of Capable American Indians of Two Tribes," *Journal of American Indian Education* (1989 Special Issue), 63–71.

85. S. J. Dicker, *Languages in America: A Pluralist View* (Philadelphia: Multilingual Matters, Ltd., 1996), 2.

86. Ibid., 4.

87. Ibid.

88. V. D. Menchaca, "Multicultural Education: The Missing Link in Teacher Education Programs," *Journal of Educational Issues of Language Minority Students*, Special Issue, 17, Fall 1996, 1–9.

89. P. Leppert, *Doing Business with Mexico* (Freemont, CA: Jain, 1996), 13.

90. Headden, 1995, 25.

91. Headden, 1995.

92. D. King, "Experience in the Multicultural Classroom," *Community College Week*, 13 (4), October 2000.

93. D. McKeon, "When Meeting Common Standards Is Uncommonly Difficult," *Educational Leadership*, 51 (1994), 45–49.

94. Ibid.

95. Ibid.

96. M. Ramsey, "Monocultural versus Multicultural Teaching: How to Practice What We Preach," *Journal of Humanistic Counseling, Education, and Development*, 38 (3), March 2000.

97. Ibid.

98. Ibid.

99. J. A. Cardenas, *Multicultural Education: a Generation of Advocacy* (Needham Heights, MD: Simon and Schuster, 1995).

100. M. Ramsey, 2000.

101. Menchaca, 1996, 1.

102. Ibid., 2.

103. M. Ramsey, 2000.

104. D. King, 2000.

105. P. J. Palmer, *To Know as We Are Known: Education as a Spiritual Journey* (San Francisco: Harper, 1993), 5.

106. M. Ramsey, 2000.

107. M. P. Orbe, "Building Community in the Diverse Classroom: Strategies for Communication Professors" (paper presented at the annual meeting of the Central States Communication Association, Indianapolis, Indiana, April, 1995).

108. Ibid., 4.

109. Ibid., 5.

110. Ibid.

111. M. Saville-Troike and J. A. Kleifgen, "Culture and Language in Classroom Communication," in *English Across Cultures, Cultures Across English: A Reader in Cross-Cultural Communication*, O. Garcia and R. Otheguy, eds. (New York: Mouton de Gruyter, 1989), 84–102.

112. J. Ofori-Dankawa and R. W. Lane, "Four Approaches to Cultural Diversity: Implications for Teaching at Institutions of Higher Education," *Teaching in Higher Education*, 5 (4), 2000, 494.

113. Ibid., 497, 495.

114. E. Aronson, *Nobody Left to Hate: Teaching Compassion After Columbine* (New York: W. H. Freeman, 2000a).

115. E. Aronson, "Nobody Left to Hate," *The Humanist*, May/June, 2000b, 18.

116. Ibid., 19.

117. I. G. Malcolm, "Invisible Culture in the Classroom: Minority Pupils and the Principle of Adaptation," in *English Across Cultures, Cultures Across English: A Reader in Cross-Cultural Communication*, O. Garcia and R. Otheguy, eds. (New York: Mouton de Gruyter, 1989), 117–135.

118. Ibid., 134.

119. G. Wan, "The Learning Experience of Chinese Students in American Universities: A Cross-cultural Perspective," *College Student Journal*, 35 (1), March 2001.

120. A. S. Jazayeri, "Immediacy and its Relationship to Teacher Effectiveness: A Cross-Cultural Examination of Six Cultures" (paper presented at the National Communication Association Convention, Chicago, 1999).

121. F. J. Belatti, "Diversity, America's Treasure Chest," *Vital Speeches of the Day*, 68 (20), August 1, 2002.

122. M. Ramsey, 2000.

123. R. D. Rhine, "Pedagogical Choices in the Teaching of Communication and Multicultural Diversity" (paper presented at the annual meeting of the Speech Communication Association, San Antonio, Texas, November 1995).

124. Grossman, 1995.

125. L. Murry and J. Williams, "Diversity and Critical Pedagogy in the Communication Classroom" (paper presented at the annual meeting of the Western States Communication Association, Pasadena, California, February, 1996).

126. S. D. Johnson and A. N. Miller, "A Cross-cultural Study of Immediacy, Credibility, and Learning in the U. S. and Kenya," *Communication Education*, 51 (3), July 2002, 281.

127. Ibid., 289.

128. Jazayeri, 1999.

Notes for Chapter 8

1. J. A. Graeff, J. P. Elder, and E. M. Booth, *Communication for Health and Behavioral Change: A Developing Country Perspective* (San Francisco: Jossey-Bass, 1993).

2. L. D. Purnell and B. J. Paulanka, eds., *Transcultural Health Care: A Culturally Competent Approach* (Philadelphia: F. A. Davis, 1998), xiii.

3. Purnell and Paulanka, 1998, xiii.

4. Purnell and B. J. Paulanka, "Purnell's Model for Cultural Competence," in L. D. Purnell and B. J. Paulanka, eds., *Transcultural Health Care: A Culturally Competent Approach* (Philadelphia: F. A. Davis, 1998), 16–17.

5. L. Haffner, "Translation Is Not Enough: Interpreting in a Medical Setting, *Western Journal of Medicine*, 157 (1992), 225–260.

6. P. J. Donnelly, "Ethics and Cross-cultural Nursing," *Journal of Cross Cultural Nursing*, 11 (2), April 2000, 19.

7. J. Greene, "More Med Students Bone Up on Diversity Issues," *The San Diego Union-Tribune*, November 22, 1999, E-3.

8. J. G. Lipson, "Cross-cultural Nursing: The Cultural Perspective," *Journal of Transcultural Nursing*, 10 (1), 6.

9. G. L. Kreps and B. C. Thornton, *Health Communication: Theory and Practice* (Prospect Heights, IL: Waveland Press, 1992), 2.

10. R. E. Spector, *Cultural Diversity in Health and Illness*, 4th ed. (Stamford, CT: Appleton and Lange, 1996), 4.

11. Spector, 1996, 4.

12. B. Koenig and J. Gates-Williams, "Understanding Cultural Differences in Dying for Dying Patients," *Western Journal of Medicine*, 163 (1995), 246.

13. M. H. Fitzgerald, "Multicultural Clinical Interactions," *Journal of Rehabilitation*, April/May/June 1992, 39.

14. R. Smart, "Religious-Caused Complications in Intercultural Communication," in *Intercultural Communication: A Reader*, 5th ed., L. A. Samovar and R. E. Porter, eds. (Belmont, CA: Wadsworth, 1988), 65.

15. D. Elgin, *Voluntary Simplicity* (New York: William Morrow, 1981), 225.

16. E. A. Hobel and E. L. Frost, *Cultural and Social Anthropology* (New York, McGraw-Hill, 1976), 331.

17. W. E. Paden, *Religious Worlds: The Comparative Study of Religion* (Boston: Beacon, 1994), 26.

18. W. W. Cobern, "College Students' Conceptualization of Nature: An Interpretive World View Analysis," *Journal of Research in Science Teaching*, 30 (1993), 937.

19. Elgin, 1981, 225.

20. M. P. Fisher and R. Luyster, *Living Religions* (Englewood Cliffs, NJ: Prentice-Hall, 1991), 22.

21. A. Hunter and J. Sexton, *Contemporary China* (New York: St. Martin's Press, 1999), 155.

22. J. Campinha-Bacote, "African Americans," in J. D Purnell and B. J. Paulanka (eds), *Transcultural Health Care: A Culturally Competent Approach* (Philadelphia: F. A. Davis, 1988), 68.

23. P. Angelucci, "Notes from the Field: Cultural Diversity: Health Belief Systems," *Nursing Management*, 26 August 1995, 8.

24. J. N. Giger and R. E. Davidhizar, *Transcultural Nursing: Assessment and Intervention*, 2nd ed. (St. Louis, MO: Mosby, 1995), 121.

25. Angelucci, 1995, 8.

26. Ibid.

27. Ibid.

28. T. T. Nowak, "Vietnamese Americans," in L. D. Purnell and B. J. Paulnaka, eds., *Transcultural Health Care: A Culturally Competent Approach* (Philadelphia: F. A. Davis, 1998), 468.

29. Angelucci, 1995, 8.

30. A. Kleinman, L. Eisenberg, and B. Good, "Culture, Illness, and Care," *Annals in Internal Medicine*, 88, 1978, 251–258.

31. Giger and Davidhizar, 1995, 456.

32. N. Dresser, *Multicultural Manners: New Rules of Etiquette for a Changing Society* (New York: John Wiley and Sons, 1996), 236.

33. Giger and Davidhizar, 1995, 465.

34. Nowak, 1998, 468.

35. Giger and Davidhizar, 1995, 404.

36. Ibid., 405.

37. Ibid.

38. I. Murillo-Rhode, "Hispanic American Patient Care," in *Transcultural Health Care*, G. Henderson and M Primeaux, eds. (Menlo Park, CA: Addison-Wesley, 1981), 59–77.

39. Dresser, 1996, 236.

40. R. E. Spector, "Cultural Concepts of Women's Health and Health-Promoting Behavior," *JOGNN*, March/April 1995, 243.

41. Giger and Davidhizar, 1995, 510–511.

42. Ibid., 404.

43. B. F. Miranda, M. R. McBride and Z. Spagler, "Filipino-Americans," in L. D. Purnell and B. J. Paulanka, eds., *Transcultural Health Care: A Culturally Competent Approach* (Philadelphia: F. A. Davis, 1998), 267.

44. J. Selekman, "Jewish-Americans," in L. D. Purnell and B. J. Paulanka, eds., *Transcultural Health Care: A Culturally Competent Approach* (Philadelphia: F. A. Davis, 1998), 389.

45. Nowak, 1998, 462.

46. Dresser, 1996.

47. Miranda, McBride and Spagler, 1998, 265.

48. Ibid.

49. L. K. Matocha, "Chinese Americans," in L. D. Purcell and B. J. Paulanka, eds., *Transcultural Health Care: A Culturally Competent Approach* (Philadelphia, F. A. Davis, 1998), 181.

50. Ibid., 180.

51. B. J. Warren and C. Munoz, "Understanding Differences Can Improve Education," *Patient Education Management,* 8 (5), May 2001, 58.

52. Murillo-Rhode, 1981.

53. M. E. Burk, P. C. Wieser, and L. Keegan, "Cultural Beliefs and Health Behaviors of Pregnant Mexican-American Women: Implications for Primary Care," *Advances in Nursing Science,* June 1995, 27–52.

54. Dresser, 1996, 238.

55. G. A. Galanti, *Caring for Patients from Different Cultures: Case Studies from American Hospitals* (Philadelphia: University of Pennsylvania Press, 1991), 101.

56. D. Grossman, "Cuban-Americans," in L. D. Purnell and B. J. Paulanka, eds., *Transcultural Health Care: A Culturally Competent Approach* (Philadelphia. F. A Davis, 1998), 208.

57. P. A. Twumasi, "Improvement of Health Care in Ghana: Present Perspectives" in *African Health and Healing Systems: Proceedings of a Symposium,* P. S. Yoder, ed. (Los Angeles: Crossroads Press, 1982).

58. Campinha-Bacote, 1998, 69.

59. Dresser, 1996, 249.

60. Giger and Davidhizar, 1995, 216.

61. Dresser, 1996, 230.

62. Galanti, 1996, 106.

63. A. Fadiman, *The Spirit Catches You and You Fall Down* (New York: Farrar, Strauss and Giroux, 1997), 4.

64. D. J. Hufford, "Ethics: Cultural Diversity, Folk Medicine and Alternative Medicine," *Alternative Therapies in Health and Medicine,* 3 (4), 1997, 78–80.

65. Purnell and Paulanka, 1998, 39.

66. M. O. Loustaunau and E. J. Sobo, *The Cultural Context of Health, Illness and Medicine* (Westport, CT: Bergin and Garvey, 1997), 93.

67. Spector, 1995, 244.

68. Purnell and Paulanka, 1998, 39.

69. O. Still and D. Hodgins, "Navajo Indians," in *Transcultural Health Care: A Culturally Competent Approach* (Philadelphia, F. A. Davis, 1998), 442.

70. Campinha-Bacote, 1998, 66.

71. L. D. Purnell, "Mexican-Americans," in L. D. Purcell and B. J. Paulanka, eds., *Transcultural Health Care: A Culturally Competent Approach* (Philadelphia: F. A. Davis, 1998), 119.

72. M. A. Miller, "Culture, Spirituality, and Women's Health," *JOGMN,* March/April 1995, 256–263.

73. B. Bhayana, "Healthshock," *Healthsharing,* 12 (3), 1991, 28–31.

74. Matocha, 1998, 178.

75. Miller, 1995.

76. C. G. Helman, *Culture, Health, and Illness,* 2nd ed. (London: Wright, 1990).

77. P. Abu Gharbieh, "Arab-Americans," in L. D Purnell and B. J. Paulanka, eds., *Transcultural Health Care: A Culturally Competent Approach* (Philadelphia: F. A. Davis, 1998), 154.

78. B. S. Nelson, L. E. Heiskell, S. Cemaj, A. O'Callaghan, and C. E. Koller, "Traumatically Injured Jehovah's Witnesses: A Sixteen-Year Experience of Treatment and Transfusion Dilemmas at a Level I Trauma Center," *Journal of Trauma, Injury, Infection, and Critical Care,* 39 (4), October 1995, 683.

79. Ibid., 681.

80. Purnell and Paulanka, 45.

81. M. C. Gonzalez, "An Invitation to Leap from a Trinitarian Ontology in Health Communication Research to a Spiritually Inclusive Quatrain," in *Communication Yearbook 17,* S. A. Deetz, ed. (Thousand Oaks, CA: Sage, 1994), 378–387.

82. R. Marquand, "Healing Role of Spirituality Gains Ground," *Christian Science Monitor,* December 6, 1995, 18.

83. Ibid.

84. Spector, 1996, 4.

85. L. Payer, *Medicine and Culture: Varieties of Treatment in the United States, England, West Germany, and France* (New York: Henry Holt, 1988), 26.

86. B. Qureshi, *Transcultural Medicine: Dealing with Patients from Different Cultures,* 2nd ed. (Lancaster, UK: Kluwer Academic Publishers, 1994), vii.

87. Campinha-Bacote, 1998, 56.

88. Purnell and Paulanka, 1998, 20.

89. G. Reddy, "Women's Movement: The Indian Scene," *Indian Journal of Social Work,* 46 (4), 1986, 507–514.

90. Giger and Davidhizar, 1995, 487.

91. Abu Gharbieh, 1998, 144.

92. Still and Hodgins, 1998, 454.

93. Giger and Davidhizar, 1995, 487.

94. Galanti, 1991, 63.

95. Abu Gharbieh, 1998, 154.

96. *San Diego Union-Tribune,* October 23, 1998, B-6.

97. Abu Gharbieh, 1998, 154.

98. Galanti, 1991, 76.

99. L. C. Callister, "Cultural Meaning in Childbirth," *JOGNN,* May 1995, 327–331.

100. Galanti, 1991.

101. Ibid.

102. Ibid.

103. Purnell and Paulanka, 1998, 18.

104. R. L. Elliott, "Cultural Patterns in Rural Russia," *Journal of Multicultural Nursing and Health,* 3 (1), Winter 1997, 22–28.

105. Galanti, 1991, 17.

106. K. Witte and K. Morrison, "Intercultural and Cross-Cultural Health Communication," in *Intercultural Communication Theory,* R. L. Wiseman, ed. (London: Sage, 1995).

107. Haftner, 1992, 256.

108. R. Alcalay, "Perceptions About Prenatal Care Among Health Providers and Mexican-American Community Women," *International Quarterly of Communication Health Education,* 13 (2), 1992, 107–118.

109. Alcalay, 1992.

110. Spector, 1996.

111. E. W. Lynch, "From Culture Shock to Culture Learning," in *Developing Cross-Cultural Competence: A Guide for Working with Young Children and Their Families,* E. W. Lynch and M. J. Hanson, eds. (Baltimore, MD: Paul H. Brookes, 1992), 19–33.

112. Giger and Davidhizar, 1995.

113. D. Gleave and A. S. Manes, "The Central Americans," in *Cross-Cultural Caring: A Handbook for Health Professionals in Western Canada,* N. Waxler-Morrison, J. Anderson, and E. Richardson, eds. (Vancouver, BC: The University of British Columbia Press, 1990), 36–67.

114. S. Chan, "Families with Asian Roots," in *Developing Cross-Cultural Competence: A Guide for Working with Young Children and Their Families*, E. W. Lynch and M. J. Hanson, eds. (Baltimore, MD: Paul H. Brookes, 1992), 181–258.

115. M. M. Andrews, "Transcultural Nursing Care," in *Transcultural Concepts in Nursing Care*, M. M. Andrews and J. S. Boyle, eds. (Philadelphia: J. B. Lippincott, 1995), 49–96.

116. E. Dihn, S. Ganesan, and N. Waxler-Morrison, "The Vietnamese," in *Cross-Cultural Caring: A Handbook for Health Professionals in Western Canada*, N. Waxler-Morrison, J. Anderson, and E. Richardson, eds. (Vancouver, BC: The University of British Columbia Press, 1990), 181–213.

117. Giger and Davidhizar, 1995.

118. Dihn et al., 1990.

119. G. Althen, *American Ways: A Guide for Foreigners in the United States* (Yarmouth, ME: Intercultural Press, 1988).

120. Dihn et al., 1990.

121. A. T. Brownlee, *Community, Culture, and Care* (St. Louis, MO: C. V. Mosby, 1978).

122. N. Murillo, "The Mexican American Family," in *Chicanos: Social and Psychological Perspectives*, C. A. Hernandez, M. J. Haug, and N. N. Wagner, eds. (St. Louis, MO: C. V. Mosby, 1978), 15–25.

123. A. Montagu, *Touching: The Significance of the Human Skin* (New York: Columbia University Press, 1971).

124. L. Rocereto, "Selected Health Beliefs of Vietnamese Refugees," *Journal of School Health*, 15 (1981), 63–64.

125. M. Muencke, "Caring for Southeast Asian Refugee Parents in the USA," *American Journal of Public Health*, 74 (1983), 431–438.

126. M. B. Marks, "Straddling Cultural Divides with Grace," *Christian Science Monitor*, November 15, 1995, 16.

127. J. Klessig, "The Effect of Values and Culture of Life Support Decisions," *Western Journal of Medicine*, 157 (1992), 316–322.

128. Burke, Weiser, and Keegan, 1995.

129. M. Gillmor, "The Hospital: A Foreign Culture," *International Journal of Childbirth Education*, 16 (1), March 2001, 18; Gillmor, 1998, 18.

130. Gilmor, 1998, 18.

131. Fitzgerald, 1992.

132. R. L. Swarms,"Mozambique Enlists Traditional Healers in War on AIDS," *San Diego Union-Tribune*, December 11, 1999, A-25.

133. Galanti, 1991, 109.

134. Ibid., 102.

135. M. S. McDonagh, "Cross-cultural Communication and Pharmaceutical Care," *Drug Topics*, 144 (18), 2000, 108.

136. P. Geist-Martin, E. B. Ray, and B. F. Sharf, *Communicating Health: Personal, Cultural and Political Complexities* (Belmont, CA: Wadsworth Publishing, 2003), 69.

137. Ibid.

Notes for Chapter 9

1. H. Smith, *The Illustrated World's Religions* (New York: Harper San Francisco, 1994), 13.

2. L. Schneider and A. Silverman, *Global Sociology: Introducing Five Contemporary Societies* (New York: McGraw-Hill, 1997), xxi.

3. G. Hofstede, *Culture's Consequences: Comparing Values, Behavior, Institutions, and Organizations Across Cultures*, 2nd ed. (Thousand Oaks, CA: Sage Publishers, 2001), xv.

4. E. Griffin, *A First Look at Communication Theory*, 2nd ed. (New York: McGraw-Hill, 1994), 173.

5. Ibid.

6. S. Herman and E. Schield, "The Stranger Group in a Cross-cultural Situation," *Sociometry*, 24 (1961), 165.

7. H. Cleveland, "The Limits of Cultural Diversity," in *Intercultural Communication: A Reader*, 9th ed., L. A. Samovar and R. E. Porter, eds. (Belmont, CA: Wadsworth, 2000), 427.

8. Ibid., 431.

9. C. M. Berger and R. J. Calabrese, "Some Explorations in Initial Interaction and Beyond," *Human Communication Research*, 1 (1975), 99–112.

10. Ibid., 100.

11. C. Berger and W. Gudykunst, "Uncertainty and Communication," in *Progress in Communication Sciences*, vol. 10, B. Dervin and M. Voigt, eds. (Norwood, NJ: Ablex, 1991), 23.

12. W. Gudykunst, *Bridging Differences: Effective Intergroup Communication*, 3rd ed. (Thousand Oaks, CA: Sage Publications, 1998), 19.

13. J. Luckmann, *Transcultural Communication in Nursing* (New York: Delmar Publishers, 1999), 66.

14. Gudykunst, 1998, 272.

15. W. Lippman, *Public Opinion* (New York: Macmillan, 1957), 79–103.

16. N. Rapport and J. Overing, *Social and Cultural Anthropology: The Key Concepts* (New York: Routledge, 2000), 343.

17. P. B. Smith and M. H. Bond, *Social Psychology Across Cultures: Analysis and Perspectives* (Boston: Allyn and Bacon, 1994), 169.

18. N. J. Adler, *International Dimensions of Organizational Behavior*, 2nd ed. (Boston: PWS-KENT, 1991), 74.

19. E. W. Lynch and M. J. Hanson, *Developing Cross-Cultural Competence: A Guide for Working with Young Children and Their Families* (Baltimore, MD: Paul H. Brookes, 1992) 44.

20. D. R. Atkinson, G. Morten, and D. Wing Sue, "Minority Group Counseling: An Overview," in *Intercultural Communication: A Reader*, 4th ed., L. A. Samovar and R. E. Porter, eds. (Belmont, CA: Wadsworth, 1982), 172.

21. M. Guirdham, *Communicating Across Cultures* (West Lafayette: Purdue University Press, 1999), 163.

22. W. B. Gudykunst, *Asian American Ethnicity and Communication* (Thousand Oaks: Sage Publications, 2001), 140.

23. J. J. Macionis, *Society: The Basics*, 4th ed. (Upper Saddle River: NJ: Prentice Hall, 1998), 217.

24. R. Richard Brislin, *Understanding Culture's Influence on Behavior*, 2nd ed. (New York: Harcourt College Publishers, 2000), 209.

25. J. Levin, *The Functions of Prejudice* (New York: Harper and Row, 1975), 13.

26. Levin, 1975, 10.

27. For a more detailed account of the functions of prejudice, see Brislin, 2000, 208–213; D. Katz, "The Functional Approach to the Study of Attitudes," *Public Opinion Quarterly* 24 (1960), 164–204; B. Hall, *Among Cultures: The Challenge of Communication* (New York: Harcourt College Publishers, 2002), 224–227.

28. A. G. Allport, *The Nature of Prejudice* (Cambridge, MA: Addison-Wesley, 1954).

29. J. Feagin, *Racial and Ethnic Relations*, 3rd ed. (Englewood Cliffs, NJ: Prentice Hall, 1989).

30. R. H. Dana, *Multicultural Assessment Perspectives for Professional Psychology* (Boston: Allyn and Bacon, 1993), 23.

31. Macionis, 1998, 217.

32. S. Nanda and R. L. Warms, *Cultural Anthropology*, 6th ed. (Belmont: CA: Wadsworth, 1998), 9.

33. Ibid., 10.

34. R. Brislin, *Understanding Culture's Influence on Behavior* (Fort Worth, TX: Harcourt Brace Jovanovich, 2000), 214.

35. Ibid., 215.

36. R. W. Brislin, "Prejudice in Intercultural Communication," in *Intercultural Communication: A Reader,* 6th ed., L. A. Samovar and R. E. Porter, eds. (Belmont, CA: Wadsworth, 1991), 386.

37. Brislin, 2000, 220.

38. B. Russell, *Power* (New York: W.W. Norton, 1938), 10.

39. R. A. Barraclough and R. A. Stewart, "Power and Control: Social Science Perspectives," in *Power in the Classroom,* V. P. Richmond and J. McCroskey, eds. (Hillsdale, NJ: Prentice Hall, 1991), 1–4.

40. Nanda and Warms, 1998, 226.

41. Ibid.

42. J. N. Martin and T. K. Nakayama, *Intercultural Communication in Context* (Mountain View, CA: Mayfield, 1997), 103.

43. J. M. Charon, *The Meaning of Sociology,* 6th ed. (Englewood Cliffs, NJ: Prentice Hall, 1999), 152–153.

44. Ibid., 153.

45. E. Folb, "Who's Got the Room at the Top?" in *Intercultural Communication: A Reader,* 9th ed., L. A. Samovar and R. E. Porter, eds. (Belmont, CA: Wadsworth, 2000), 122.

46. E. Folb, 2000, 122.

47. M. L. Hecht, M. J. Collier, and S. A. Ribeau, *African American Communication: Ethnic Identity and Cultural Interpretation* (Newbury Park, CA: Sage, 1993), 135–137, 144. Also see A. Smith, *Transracial Communication* (Englewood Cliffs, NJ: Prentice Hall, 1973), 118–119.

48. Smith, 1973, 71.

49. G. A. Borden, *Cultural Orientation: An Approach to Understanding Intercultural Communication* (Englewood Cliffs, NJ: Prentice Hall, 1991), 116.

50. J. A. Blubaugh and D. L. Pennington, *Crossing Differences: Interracial Communication* (Columbus, OH: Charles E. Merrill, 1976), 39.

51. Smith and Bond, 1994, 192.

52. R. W. Nolan, *Communicating and Adapting Across Cultures* (Westport, Conn: Beergin and Garvey, 1999), 19.

53. Smith and Bond, 1994, 192.

54. C. Storti, *The Art of Coming Home* (Yarmouth, ME: Intercultural Press, 1997), 2.

55. A. Furnham and L. Bochner, *Culture Shock—Psychological Reactions to an Unfamiliar Environment* (New York: Methuen, 1986).

56. K. Oberg, "Culture Shock: Adjustments to New Cultural Environments," *Practical Anthropology,* 7 (1960), 176. Also see P. K. Bock, *Culture Shock* (New York: Knopf, 1970).

57. R. W. Brislin, *Cross-Cultural Encounters: Face-to-Face Interactions* (New York: Pergamon Press, 1981), 155.

58. Lynch and Hanson, 1992, 23.

59. J. T. Gullahorn and J. E. Gullahorn, "An Extension of the U-Curve Hypothesis," *Journal of Social Science,* 17 (1963), 33–47.

60. E. Marx, *Breaking Through Culture Shock* (London: Nicholas Brealey, 1999), 7.

61. Ibid., 7.

62. P. R. Harris and R. T. Moran, *Managing Cultural Differences: Leadership Strategies for a New World of Business,* 4th ed. (Houston, TX: Gulf, 1996), 142.

63. N. J. Adler, *International Dimensions of Organizational Behavior,* 3rd. ed. (Cincinnati, OH: South-Western College Publishing, 1997), 238.

64. I. Kawano, "Overcoming Culture Shock: Living and Learning in Japan Through the JET Program" (paper presented at the Annual Convention of the Western States Communication Association, Monterey, CA, February, 1997), 25.

65. W. G. Sumner, *Folkways* (Boston: Ginnand, 1940), 13.

66. Nanda and Warms, 1998, 6.

67. Nanda and Warms, 1996, 7. Also see D. G. Bates and F. Plog, *Cultural Anthropology,* 3rd ed. (New York: McGraw-Hill,

1990), 17; W. A. Haviland, *Cultural Anthropology,* 7th ed. (Fort Worth, TX: Harcourt Brace Jovanovich, 1993), 48.

68. Macionis, 1998, 48.

69. F. M. Keesing, *Cultural Anthropology: The Science of Custom* (New York: Holt, Rinehart, and Winston, 1965), 45.

70. W. A. Haviland, *Cultural Anthropology* (Belmont, CA: Wadsworth, 2002), 470.

71. R. Brislin, 2000, 45.

72. W. Haviland, 2002, 470–471.

73. L. Damen, *Cultural Learning: The Fifth Dimension in the Language Classroom* (Reading, MA: Addison-Wesley, 1987), 45.

74. E. C. Stewart and M. J. Bennett, *American Cultural Patterns: A Cross-Cultural Perspective* (Yarmouth, ME: Intercultural Press, 1991), 161.

75. F. E. Jandt, *Intercultural Communication: An Introduction* (Thousand Oaks, CA: Sage, 1995), 43.

Notes for Chapter 10

1. See, G. M. Guthrie, "A Behavioral Analysis of Culture Learning, " in *Cross-Cultural Perspectives on Learning,* R. W. Brislin and W. J. Lonner, eds. (New York: John Wiley and Sons, 1975), 95–115.

2. W. Lynch, "Conceptual Framework: From Culture Shock to Culture Learning, " in *Developing Cross-Cultural Competence,* 2nd ed., E. W. Lynch and M. J. Hanson, eds. (Baltimore, MD: Paul H. Brookes, 1998), 24.

3. G. Ness, Germany: *Unraveling the Enigma* (Yarmouth, ME: Intercultural Press, 2000), 137.

4. W. Lynch, 1998, 26.

5. B. H. Spitzberg, "A Model of Intercultural Communication Competence," in *Intercultural Communication: A Reader,* 9th ed., L. A. Samovar and R. E. Porter, eds. (Belmont, CA: Wadsworth, 2000), 375.

6. Y. Y. Kim, "Intercultural Communication Competence: A Systems-Theoretic View," in *Cross-Cultural Interpersonal Communication,* S. Ting-Toomey and R. Korzenny, eds. (Newbury Park, CA: Sage, 1991), 259.

7. S.P. Morreale, B. S. Spitzberg, and J. K. Barge, *Human Communication: Motivation, Knowledge and Skills* (Belmont, CA: Wadsworth/Thomson Learning, 201), 37–40.

8. B. Spitzberg and W. Cupach, *Interpersonal Communication Competence* (Beverly Hills, CA: Sage, 1984).

9. J. Luckmann, *Transcultural Communication in Nursing* (Albany, NY: Delmar, 1999), 64.

10. Morreale, Spitzberg, and Barge, 2001, 39–40.

11. Ibid., 2001, 40.

12. A. J. Almaney and A. J. Alwan, *Communicating with Arabs* (Prospect Hills, IL: Waveland Press, 1982), 87.

13. E. R. McDaniel and S. Quasha, "The Communicative Aspects of Doing Business in Japan," in *Intercultural Communication: A Reader,* 9th ed., L. A. Samovar and R. E. Porter, eds. (Belmont, CA: Wadsworth, 2000), 312–324.

14. E. W. Lynch and M. J. Hanson, *Developing Cross-Cultural Competence: A Guide for Working with Young Children and Their Families* (Baltimore, MD: Paul H. Brookes, 1992), 44.

15. R. H. Dana, *Multicultural Assessment Perspectives for Professional Psychology* (Boston: Allyn and Bacon, 1993).

16. L. D. Purnell and B. J. Paulanka, *Transcultural Health Care: A Culturally Competent Approach* (Philadelphia, PA: F. A. Davis, 1998), 10.

17. R. Brislin, *Understanding Culture's Influence on Behavior,* 2nd ed. (Fort Worth, TX: Harcourt, 2000), 263.

18. Ibid., 264.

19. M. Zhong, "Perceived Intercultural Communication Competence in Cross-Cultural Interactions Between Chinese and Americans," *Critical Studies*, 12 (1998), 161–179.

20. E. Y. Kim, *The Yin and Yang of American Culture* (Yarmouth, ME: Intercultural Press, 2001), 207.

21. E. C. Stewart and M. J. Bennett, *American Cultural Patterns: A Cross-Cultural Perspective* (Yarmouth, ME: Intercultural Press, 1991), 175.

22. R. Norton, *Communication Style: Theory, Application and Measures* (Beverly Hills: Sage, 1982).

23. D. C. Barnlund, *Public and Private Self in Japan and the United States: Communication Styles of Two Cultures* (Tokyo: Simul Press, 1975), 14–15.

24. See M. Snyder, *Public Appearance, Private Realities: The Psychology of Self-Monitoring* (New York: Freeman), 1987.

25. M. Guirdham, *Communication Across Cultures* (West Lafayette, IN: Purdue University Press, 1999), 243.

26. W. V. Ruch, *International Handbook of Corporate Communication* (Jefferson, NC: McFarland, 1989), 76.

27. N. J. Adler, *International Dimensions of Organizational Behavior*, 2nd ed. (Boston: PWS-KENT, 1991), 190.

28. D. Clutterbuck, "Spanning the Communication Gap," *International Management*, October 1975, 18–22.

29. L. M. Skow and L. Stephan, "Intercultural Communication in the University Classroom," in *Intercultural Communication: A Reader*, 9th ed., L. A. Samovar and R. E. Porter, eds. (Belmont, CA: Wadsworth, 2000), 361.

30. Ibid., 359.

31. Ness, 2000, 38.

32. Ibid., 39.

33. Adler, 1991, 192.

34. Ruch, 264.

35. P. Kenna and L. Sondra, *Business Mexico: A Practical Guide to Understanding Mexican Business Culture* (Lincolnwood, IL: Passport Books, 1996), 25.

36. R. Cooper and N. Cooper, *Culture Shock: Thailand* (Portland, OR: Graphic Arts Center, 1990), 152.

37. Luckmann, 1999, 72.

38. M. K. Nydell, *Understanding Arabs: A Guide for Westerners* (Yarmouth, ME: Intercultural Press, 1987), 121.

39. G. Geo and Stella Ting-Toomey, *Communicating Effectively with the Chinese* (Thousand Oaks, CA: Sage, 1998), 36.

40. Ibid.

41. Ibid., 36.

42. Nees, 2000, 83.

43. G. Asselin and R. Mastron, *Au Contraire: Figuring Out The French* (Yarmouth, ME: Intercultural Press, 2001), 37.

44. G. C. Armas, "8 Million Illegal Immigrants Call U.S. Home," *San Diego Union Tribune*, October 25, 2001, B-4.

45. H. Walters, Jr., "Race, Culture and Interpersonal Conflict," *International Journal of Intercultural Relations*, 16 (1992), 447.

46. Ibid., 448.

47. Ruch, 1989, 361.

48. M. P. Orbe and T. M. Harris, *Interracial Communication: Theory Into Practice* (Belmont, CA: Wadsworth, 2001), 65.

49. Orbe and Harris, 2001, 65.

50. G. Chen and W. J. Starosta, "Intercultural Communication in the University Classroom," in *Intercultural Communication: A Reader*, 9th ed., L. A. Samovar and R. E. Porter, eds. (Belmont, CA: Wadsworth, 2000), 408.

51. J. Johnson, "The Press Should Show More Sensitivity to Disabled People," *Editor and Publisher*, February 22, 1986, 64.

52. Lynch and Hanson, 1998, 77.

53. Guirdham, 1999, 346.

54. S. Ting-Toomey, *Communicating Across Cultures* (New York: Guilford Press, 1999), 160.

55. B. J. Broome, "Building Shared Meaning: Implications of a Relational Approach to Empathy for Teaching Intercultural Communication," *Communication Education*, 40 (1991), 235.

56. C. Calloway-Thomas, P. J. Cooper, and C. Blake, *Intercultural Communication: Roots and Routes* (Boston: Allyn and Bacon, 1999), 106.

57. G. R. Miller and M. Steinberg, *Between People: A New Analysis of Interpersonal Communication* (Chicago: Science Research Associates, 1975), 167.

58. R. Bell, "Social Involvement," in *Personality and Interpersonal Communication*, J. McCroskey and J. Daly, eds. (Newbury Park, CA: Sage, 1987), 205.

59. S. Trenholm and A. Jensen, *Interpersonal Communication*, 2nd ed. (Belmont, CA: Wadsworth, 1992), 254.

60. D. C. Barnlund, *Communication Styles of Japanese and Americans* (Belmont, CA: Wadsworth, 1989), 162.

61. Trenholm and Jensen, 1992, 255.

62. A. L. Rich, *Interracial Communication* (New York: Harper and Row, 1974), 35–36.

63. H. Wenzhong and C. Grove, *Encountering the Chinese: A Guide for Americans* (Yarmouth, ME: Intercultural Press, 1991, 114.

64. Morreale, Spitzberg, and Barge, 2001, 160.

65. J. T. Wood, *Communication Mosaics: A New Introduction to the Field of Communication* (Belmont, CA: Wadsworth, 1998), 25.

66. D. Rowland, *Japanese Business Etiquette* (New York: Warner, 1985), 47.

67. R. Hart, R. E. Carlson, and W. F. Eadie, "Attitudes Toward Communication and the Assessment of Rhetorical Sensitivity," *Communication Monographs*, 47 (1980), 1–22.

68. S. Trenholm, *Human Communication Theory* (Englewood Cliffs, NJ: Prentice Hall, 1986), 112.

69. D. A. Foster, *Bargaining Across Borders: How to Negotiate Successfully Anywhere in the World* (New York: McGraw-Hill, 1992), 253.

70. B. D. Ruben and D. J. Kealey, "Behavioral Assessment of Communication Competency and the Prediction of Cross-Cultural Adaptation," *International Journal of Intercultural Relations*, 3 (1979), 19.

71. Guirdham, 1999, 242.

72. Ibid.

73. S. Ting-Toomey, "Managing Intercultural Conflicts Effectively," in *Intercultural Communication: A Reader*, 9th ed., L. A. Samovar and R. E. Porter, eds. (Belmont, CA: Wadsworth, 2000), 388.

74. See R. H. Kilman and K. W. Thomas, "Developing a Forced-Choice Measure of Conflict Handling Behavior: MODE Instrument," *Educational and Psychological Measurement*, 37, 1977, 309–325; R. S. Lulofs and D. D. Cahn, *Conflict: From Theory to Action*, 2nd ed., (Boston: Allyn and Bacon, 2000); Morreale, Spitzberg, and Barge, 2001, 364–366; W. W. Wilmont and J. L. Hocker, *Interpersonal Conflict*, 5th ed. (Boston: McGraw-Hill, 1998).

75. Morreale, Spitzberg, and Barge, 2001, 365.

76. M. Roloff, "Communication and Conflict," in *Handbook of Communication Science*, C. Berger and S. H. Chaffee, eds. (Beverly Hills, CA: Sage, 1990), 484–534.

77. B. J. Broome, "Palevome: Foundations of Struggle and Conflict," in *Intercultural Communication: A Reader*, 9th ed., L. A. Samovar and R. E. Porter, eds. (Belmont, CA: Wadsworth, 2000), 110.

78. S. Miyagi, B. Spitzberg, and L. Samovar, "Dealing With Conflict: A Study of Japanese and American Strategies" (paper presented at the Annual Convention of the Western States Communication Association Convention, Vancouver, Canada, 1999).

79. D. Barnland, *Public and Private Self in Japan and the United States* (Tokyo, Japan: The Simul Press, 1975), 35.

80. Geo and Ting-Toomey, 1998, 60.

81. Ness, 2000, 63.

82. Asselin and Mastron, 2001, 186.

83. Ting-Toomey, 2000, 397.

84. Ibid.

85. Ibid., 396.

86. Ibid.

87. Ibid., 397.

88. Y. Y. Kim, "Cross-Cultural Adaptation: An Integrative Theory," in *Theories in Intercultural Communication*, R. L. Wiseman, ed. (Thousand Oaks, CA: Sage, 1995), 171.

89. A. S. Mak, M. J. Westwood, F. I. Ishiyama, "Optimising Conditions for Learning Sociocultural Competencies for Success," *International Journal of Intercultural Relations*, 23 (1999), 80.

90. R. L. Rothenburger, "Transcultural Nursing: Overcoming Obstacles to Effective Communication," *AORN Journal*, 51, (1990) 1349–1363.

91. E. Anderson, "A New Look at an Old Construct: Cross-Cultural Adaptation," *International Journal of Intercultural Relations*, 18 (1994), 293–328.

92. F. T. Leong and E. L. Chou, "The Role of Ethnic Identity and Acculturation in the Vocational Behavior of Asian Americans: An Integrative Review," *Journal of Vocational Behavior*, 44 (1994), 165.

93. A. M. Harper, "Cultural Adaptation and Intercultural Communication: Some Barriers and Bridges" (paper presented at the Annual Convention of the Western Speech Communication Association, Monterey, CA, February 1997), 13.

94. Kim, 1995, 177.

95. G. M. Chen and W. J. Starosta, "Intercultural Communication Competence: A Synthesis," in *Communication Yearbook*, vol. 19, B. R. Burleson and A. W. Kunkel, eds. (Thousand Oaks, CA: Sage, 1996), 365.

96. P. A. Begley, "Sojourner Adaptation," in *Intercultural Communication: A Reader*, 9th ed., L. A. Samovar and R. E. Porter, eds. (Belmont, CA: Wadsworth, 2000), 404.

97. P. R. Harris and R. T. Moran, *Managing Cultural Differences: Leadership Strategies for a New World of Business*, 4th ed. (Houston, TX: Gulf, 1996), 143.

98. Kim, 1995, 172.

99. G. Althen, *American Ways* (Yarmouth, ME: Intercultural Press, 1988), 165.

100. Ibid.

101. R. K. Johannesen, *Ethics in Human Communication*, 4th ed. (Prospect Heights, IL: Waveland Press, 1996), 1.

102. L. A. Day, *Ethics In Media Communications: Cases and Controversies*, 3rd ed. (Belmont, CA: Wadsworth, 2000), 3.

103. Ibid., 2.

104. E. Griffin, *A First Look at Communication Theory*, 2nd ed. (New York: McGraw-Hill, 1994), 458.

105. Ting-Toomey, 1999, 273.

106. J. Q. Wilson, *San Diego Union-Tribune*, November 29, 1993, B5.

107. W. S. Howell, *The Empathic Communicator* (Belmont, CA: Wadsworth, 1982), 179.

108. Johannesen, 1996, 244.

109. S. Boorestein, *It's Easier Than You Think: The Buddhist Way to Happiness* (New York: HarperCollins, 1995), 60.

110. O. Tead, *Administration: Its Purpose and Performance* (New York: Harper and Row, 1959), 52.

111. Johannesen, 1996, 257.

112. Y. Chu, "Six Suggestions for Learning About People and Cultures," in *Learning About Peoples and Cultures*, S. Fersh, ed. (Evanston, IL: McDougal and Littell, 1974), 52.

113. "Bert and Ernie Go to Moscow," *U.S. News & World Report*, February 12, 1996, 4.

114. J. Beversluis, *A Source Book for Earth's Community of Religions* (New York: Global Education Associates, 1995), 138.

115. D. W. Kale, "Peace as an Ethic for Intercultural Communication," in *Intercultural Communication: A Reader*, 9th ed., L. A. Samovar and R. E. Porter, eds. (Belmont, CA: Wadsworth, 2000), 452.

116. S. Huntington, *The Conflict of Civilizations and the Remaking of World Order* (New York: Simon and Schuster, 1996), 320.

117. Barnlund, 1989, 92–93.

118. J. Wood, "Gender, Communication, and Culture," in *Intercultural Communication: A Reader*, 8th ed., L. A. Samovar and R. E. Porter, eds. (Belmont, CA: Wadsworth, 1997), 171–172.

119. D. Gomez-Ibanes, "Moving Toward a Global Ethic," in *A Source Book for Earth's Community of Religions*, J. Beversluis, ed. (New York: Global Education Associates, 1995), 128.

120. W. Booth, "Diversity and Division," *Washington Post*, March 2, 1998, 6.

121. Ibid.

122. "Attacking Terrorism," *San Diego Union-Tribune*, December 24, 2001, A-5.

123. Huntington, 1996, 36

124. W. A. Haviland, *Cultural Anthropology*, 10th ed. (Belmont, CA: Wadsworth, 2002), 476.

125. Ibid.

126. Ibid., 479.

127. Ibid., 455.

128. C. R. Ember and M. Ember, *Cultural Anthropology*, 4th ed., (Englewood Cliffs, NJ: 1985), 230.

129. H. Cleveland, "The Limits to Cultural Diversity," *Futurist*, March–April 1995, 23.

130. Ibid.

131. J. Krishnamurti, *Krishnamurti to Himself* (San Francisco, CA: HarperCollins, 1987), 60.

132. Cleveland, 1995, 23.

133. Y. Ling-Ling, "Ethnic Strife Is Not a Geographically Distant Phenomenon," *San Diego Union-Tribune*, June 10, 1999, 11.

134. Cleveland, 1995, 23.

135. V. Lynch Lee, ed., *Faces of Culture* (Huntington Beach, CA: KOCE-TV Foundation, 1983), 69.

136. Cleveland, 1995, 26.

Index